The Essayist

THE ESSAYIST

Fifth Edition

SHERIDAN BAKER
The University of Michigan
C. JERIEL HOWARD
Northeastern Illinois University

1817

HARPER & ROW, PUBLISHERS, New York
Cambridge, Philadelphia, San Francisco,
London, Mexico City, São Paulo, Singapore, Sydney

Sponsoring Editor: Phillip Leininger
Project Editor: Dorothy H. Cappel / Susan Goldfarb
Cover Design: Jack Ribik
Production: Marion Palen / Delia Tedoff
Compositor: ComCom Division of Haddon Craftsmen,
          Inc.
Printer and Binder: R. R. Donnelley & Sons Company

THE ESSAYIST, Fifth Edition

Acknowledgments begin on facing page.

Library of Congress Cataloging in Publication Data

Baker, Sheridan Warner, 1918–
    The essayist.

    1. College readers. 2. English language—Rhetoric.
I. Howard, C. Jeriel, 1939–   II. Title.
PE1417.B28   1985   808.4   84–19217
ISBN 0-06-040441-8

84 85 86 87 9 8 7 6 5 4 3 2 1

Acknowledgments

———————— ● ————————

Albert Einstein, "Johannes Kepler," from his book *Ideas and Opinions* (New York: Crown Publishers, 1954). Copyright © 1954 by Crown Publishers, Inc. Used by permission of Crown Publishers, Inc.

Loren Eiseley, "Thoreau's Unfinished Business," from his book *The Star Thrower.* Copyright © 1978 by the Estate of Loren Eiseley. Reprinted by permission of Times Books/The New York Times Book Company, Inc. from *The Star Thrower.*

T. S. Eliot: Excerpts from "Burnt Norton" and "East Coker" in *Four Quartets* by T.S. Eliot are reprinted by permission of Harcourt Brace Jovanovich, Inc.; copyright 1943 by T. S. Eliot, renewed 1971 by Esme Valerie Eliot.

Newton Garver, "Four Kinds of Violence," *The Nation,* June 24, 1968. Copyright 1968 Nation magazine, The Nation Associates, Inc.

Stephen Jay Gould, "Caring Groups and Selfish Genes," *Natural History,* vol. 86, no. 10. Reprinted with permission. Copyright the American Museum of Natural History, 1977.

Bob Greene, "Permanent Record—A Big Paper Tiger." Reprinted by permission: Tribune Company Syndicate, Inc.

Robert L. Heilbroner, "The Eye of the Needle," from his book *Between Capitalism and Socialism* (New York: Random House, 1970). Copyright © 1970 by Robert L. Heilbroner. Reprinted by permission of Random House, Inc.

Richard Hofstadter, "What Is an Intellectual?" Reprinted from *Michigan Alumnus Quarterly Review (Michigan Quarterly Review),* The University of Michigan, Summer 1953.

Martin Luther King, Jr., "The Answer to a Perplexing Question." Reprinted by permission of Joan Daves. Copyright © 1963 by Martin Luther King, Jr. All rights reserved.

Charles Krauthammer, "Reflections on a Farce: Grenada and the End of Revolution." Reprinted from *The New Republic,* January 20, 1984.

Margaret Loeb, "If the Moon Controls the Tide, Just Think What It Does to You." Reprinted by permission of *The Wall Street Journal,* © Dow Jones & Company, Inc. 1983. All Rights Reserved.

Archibald MacLeish, "Why Do We Teach Poetry?" from his book *A Continuing Journey.* Copyright © 1967 by Archibald MacLeish. Reprinted by permission of Houghton Mifflin Company.

Margaret Mead, "One Vote for This Age of Anxiety," © 1956 by The New York Times Company. Reprinted by permission.

Aubrey Menen, "My Grandmother and the Dirty English," from his book *Dead Men in the Silver Market* (New York: Charles Scribner's Sons, 1953). Originally published in *The New Yorker,* July 4, 1953.

Farley Mowat, "Snow," from his book *The Snow Walker.* Copyright © 1975 by McClelland and Stewart Limited. Reprinted by permission of Little, Brown and Company and McClelland and Stewart, the Canadian publisher.

New Yorker, "Changing Horses in Mid-Dream." Reprinted by permission; © 1980 The New Yorker Magazine, Inc.

George Orwell, "Politics and the English Language," from his book *Shooting an Elephant and Other Essays.* Copyright 1946 by Sonia Brownell Orwell; renewed 1974 by Sonia Orwell. Reprinted from *Shooting an Elephant and Other Essays* by permission of Harcourt Brace Jovanovich, Inc.

———, "Shooting an Elephant." From *Shooting an Elephant and Other Essays* by George Orwell, copyright 1950 by Sonia Brownell Orwell; renewed 1978 by Sonia Pitt-Rivers. Reprinted by permissions of Harcourt Brace Jovanovich, Inc.

Alan Paton, "The Challenge of Fear," *Saturday Review,* September 9, 1967. Copyright 1967 Saturday Review Magazine Co. Reprinted by permission.

Alexander Petrunkevitch, "The Spider and the Wasp." Reprinted with permission from *Scientific American,* August 1956. Copyright © 1956 by Scientific American, Inc. All rights reserved.

Richard Reeves, "Vulnerable," from his book *Jet Lag.* Copyright 1981, Richard Reeves. Reprinted with permission of Andrews and McMeel, Inc. All rights reserved.

Murray Ross, "Football Red and Baseball Green," *Chicago Review,* vol. 22, nos. 2 and 3 (January and February 1971). Copyright 1971 by *Chicago Review.*

Susan Schiefelbein, "Return of the Native," *Saturday Review,* 1977. Copyright © 1977 Saturday Review Magazine Co. Reprinted by permission.

Arthur Schlesinger, Jr., "Politics and the American Language," *The American Scholar,* Autumn 1974. Copyright © 1974 by Arthur Schlesinger, Jr. Reprinted by permission of the author.

Acknowledgments

W. T. Stace, "Man Against Darkness," *The Atlantic Monthly,* September 1948. Copyright © 1948 renewed 1976 by The Atlantic Monthly Company, Boston, Mass. Reprinted with permission.

Gay Talese, "New York," *Esquire,* July 1960. Copyright 1960 by Gay Talese. Reprinted by permission of Candida Donadio & Associates.

Lewis Thomas, "The Hazards of Science," from his book *The Medusa and the Snail.* Copyright © 1977 by Lewis Thomas. Originally published in *The New England Journal of Medicine.* Reprinted by permission of Viking Penguin Inc.

Arthur Waley, "Li Fu-Jen" by Wu-ti and "A beautiful place is the town of Lo-yang" by Ch'ien Wen-ti, from *Translations from the Chinese* by Arthur Waley. Copyright 1919 and renewed 1947 by Arthur Waley. Reprinted by permission of Alfred A. Knopf, Inc.

Andrew Ward, "They Also Wait Who Stand and Serve Themselves," *The Atlantic Monthly,* May 1979. Copyright © 1979 by the Atlantic Monthly Company, Boston, Massachusetts. Reprinted with permission.

E. B. White, "A Slight Sound at Evening—Allen Cove, Summer 1954" from *The Essays of E. B. White.* Copyright 1954, 1982 by E. B. White. Originally appeared in *The Yale Review* under the title "Walden—1954." Reprinted by permission of Harper & Row, Publishers, Inc.

Charles V. Willie, "Black Colleges Redefined." Reprinted by permission of Heldref Publications.

James A. Winn, "The Beatles as Artists: A Meditation for December Ninth," *Michigan Quarterly Review* 23 (1984): 1–20. Reprinted by permission of the author.

Thomas Wolfe, "Circus at Dawn," in *From Death to Morning.* Copyright 1935 Charles Scribner's Sons; copyright renewed 1963 Paul Gitlin. Reprinted with the permission of Charles Scribner's Sons.

Virginia Woolf, "How Should One Read a Book?" From *The Second Common Reader* by Virginia Woolf, copyright 1932 by Harcourt Brace Jovanovich, Inc.; renewed 1960 by Leonard Woolf. Reprinted by permission of the publisher.

Contents

————————— ● —————————

ix

Contents

3. PARAGRAPHS: BEGINNING, MIDDLE, END

4. TACTICS OF DEVELOPMENT   155

PREFACE

Of the forty-five essays in this fifth edition, twenty are new, several of them never anthologized before. In selecting new essays and retaining former ones, we had two major objectives. We were, of course, interested in selections as models for composition. But we were also interested in variety—in topics, in attitudes, in styles, and in techniques—because we know that not all students are interested in the same things, have the same values, or even learn most effectively from the same materials.

We think these essays meet both of our objectives. They are well written, each ably demonstrating organizational and stylistic traits peculiar to its own rhetorical type. And they offer variety. Women and minority writers speak out in this new edition. Topics range from the moral state of the human race to self-service gas stations, from liberal to conservative, from formal, perhaps even formulaic, to colloquial and humorous.

This new edition begins with two essays on reading, one a pragmatic approach, the other on values, both offering advice and material for discussion during those first few days of a term.

As before, the book is focused toward one end: how to write an essay. Each section concentrates on a part of the process. We first discuss the *thesis,* or inner idea; then we move on to *structure,* or outer form. With a sense of this larger unity, students can more easily manage paragraphs, sentences, and words—the woods, streams, and pebbles of our verbal world—than if they were to pick up the small things first and wonder how they fit. Each section begins by describing a rhetorical focus and suggesting what to look for, what to query—where to assay the author's faults and virtues.

An apparatus after each essay suggests three categories: "Ideas," "Organization and Style," and "Writing." "Ideas" encourages students to read for details and suggests questions for discussion. "Organization and Style" focuses on those matters students can easily comprehend and imitate. "Writing" suggests topics, organizational patterns, and considerations of audience.

These essays collectively illustrate how a thesis may organize an essay at a stroke, and also how even a seasoned writer may miss the clearest opportunity to do so. They show how structure works; how the paragraph, the sentence, and the word may work their various wiles. They illustrate the problems of writing, encouraging students to discover their own ideas by questioning the ideas of others and to make their ideas persuasive in the process as they find their own voices and styles. Readers of *The Practical Stylist, The Complete Stylist and Handbook,* and the earlier editions of *The Essayist* will recognize this basically argumentative approach.

SHERIDAN BAKER
C. JERIEL HOWARD

The Essayist

INTRODUCTION: ON READING

Good reading makes for good writing. Reading strengthens and expands our interests. We experience other minds, other concepts, other lives, other cultures, thus awakening our sole selves to the possibilities around us. The writer who reads is seldom at a loss for something to say. The reader always has an idea brewing somewhere.

Good reading also improves one's style. As we read, the murmured written voice becomes our own, tracing something of its enchantment of pattern, rhythm, and word into our own verbal resources. Dull writing, of course, leaves us nothing. But the dullness may be our own. Enchanted or not, we must stay wide awake, approving, questioning, arguing, pausing to digest the impact of language and thought. This is the good reading that makes for good writing.

The two essays that follow are both classics. Adler explains how to let your pencil work along with your eyes for effective reading. Woolf helps us to get beyond the printed page, the obvious, to synthesize our reading, to test it, and, finally, to evaluate it.

How to Mark a Book

MORTIMER J. ADLER

—————————— ● ——————————

Adler tells us how to read actively. The mere act of underlining and making brief marginal notes keeps us alert and etches much more in the memory—in our possession—than does an inert and placid scanning. Frequently anthologized as an example of process analysis, this essay, first published in 1940, is a precious guide to the green pastures of reading. You might try Adler's suggestions as you read the essays in this text.

You know you have to read "between the lines" to get the most out of anything. I want to persuade you to do something equally important in the course of your reading. I want to persuade you to "write between the lines." Unless you do, you are not likely to do the most efficient kind of reading.

I contend, quite bluntly, that marking up a book is not an act of mutilation but of love.

You shouldn't mark up a book which isn't yours. Librarians (or your friends) who lend you books expect you to keep them clean, and you should. If you decide that I am right about the usefulness of marking books, you will have to buy them. Most of the world's great books are available today, in reprint editions, at less than a dollar.

There are two ways in which one can own a book. The first is the property right you establish by paying for it, just as you pay for clothes and furniture. But this act of purchase is only the prelude to possession. Full ownership comes only when you have made it a part of yourself, and the best way to make yourself a part of it is by writing in it. An illustration may make the point clear. You buy a beefsteak and transfer it from the butcher's icebox to your own. But you do not own the beefsteak in the most important sense until you consume it and get it into your bloodstream. I am arguing that books, too, must be absorbed in your bloodstream to do you any good.

Confusion about what it means to own a book leads people to a false reverence for paper, binding, and type—a respect for the physical thing—the craft of the printer rather than the genius of the author. They forget that it is possible for a man to acquire the idea, to possess the beauty, which a great book contains, without staking his claim by pasting his bookplate inside the cover. Having a fine library doesn't prove that its owner has a mind enriched by books; it proves nothing more than that he, his father, or his wife, was rich enough to buy them.

There are three kinds of book owners. The first has all the standard sets and best-sellers—unread, untouched. (This deluded individual owns woodpulp and ink, not books.) The second has a great many books—a few of them read through, most of them dipped into, but all of them as clean and shiny as the day they were bought. (This person would probably like to make books his own, but is restrained by a false respect for their physical appearance.) The third has a few books or many—every one of them dogeared and dilapidated, shaken and loosened by continual use, marked and scribbled in from front to back. (This man owns books.)

Is it false respect, you may ask, to preserve intact and unblemished a beautifully printed book, an elegantly bound edition? Of course not. I'd no more scribble all over a first edition of "Paradise Lost" than I'd give my baby a set of crayons and an original Rembrandt! I wouldn't mark up a painting or a statue. Its soul, so to speak, is inseparable from its body. And the beauty of a rare edition or of a richly manufactured volume is like that of a painting or a statue.

But the soul of a book *can* be separated from its body. A book is more like the score of a piece of music than it is like a painting. No great musician confuses a symphony with the printed sheets of music. Arturo Toscanini reveres Brahms, but Toscanini's score of the C-minor Symphony is so thoroughly marked up that no one but the maestro himself can read it. The reason why a great conductor makes notations on his musical scores—marks them up again and again each time he returns to study them—is the reason why you should mark your books. If your respect for magnificent binding or typography gets in the way, buy yourself a cheap edition and pay your respects to the author.

Why is marking up a book indispensable to reading? First, it keeps you awake. (And I don't mean merely conscious; I mean wide awake.) In the second place, reading, if it is active, is thinking, and thinking tends to express itself in words, spoken or written. The marked book is usually the thought-through book. Finally, writing helps you remember the thoughts you had, or the thoughts the author expressed. Let me develop these three points.

If reading is to accomplish anything more than passing time, it must be active. You can't let your eyes glide across the lines of a book and come up with an understanding of what you have read. Now an ordinary piece of light fiction, like, say, "Gone with the Wind," doesn't require the most active kind of reading. The books you read for pleasure can be read in a state of relaxation, and nothing is lost. But a great book, rich in ideas and beauty, a book that raises and tries to answer great fundamental questions, demands the most active reading of which you are capable. You don't absorb the ideas of John Dewey the way you absorb the crooning of Mr. Vallee. You have to reach for them. That you cannot do while you're asleep.

If, when you've finished reading a book, the pages are filled with your notes, you know that you read actively. The most famous *active* reader of great books I know is President Hutchins, of the University of Chicago. He also has the hardest schedule of business activities of any man I know. He invariably reads with a pencil, and sometimes, when he picks up a book and pencil in the evening, he finds himself, instead of making intelligent notes, drawing what he calls "caviar factories" on the margins. When that happens, he puts the book down. He knows he's too tired to read, and he's just wasting time.

But, you may ask, why is writing necessary? Well, the physical act of writing, with your own hand, brings words and sentences more sharply before your mind and preserves them better in your memory. To set down your reaction to important words and sentences you have read, and the questions they have raised in your mind, is to preserve those reactions and sharpen those questions.

Even if you wrote on a scratch pad, and threw the paper away when you had finished writing, your grasp of the book would be surer. But you don't have to throw the paper away. The margins (top and bottom, as well as side), the end-papers, the very space between the lines, are all available. They aren't sacred. And, best of all, your marks and notes become an integral part of the book and stay there forever. You can pick up the book the following week or year, and there are all your points of agreement, disagreement, doubt, and inquiry. It's like resuming an interrupted conversation with the advantage of being able to pick up where you left off.

And that is exactly what reading a book should be: a conversation between you and the author. Presumably he knows more about the subject than you do; naturally, you'll have the proper humility as you approach him. But don't let anybody tell you that a reader is supposed to be solely on the receiving end. Understanding is a two-way operation; learning doesn't consist in being an empty receptacle. The learner has to question himself and question the teacher. He even has to argue with the teacher, once he understands what the teacher is saying. And marking a book is literally an expression of your differences, or agreements of opinion, with the author.

There are all kinds of devices for marking a book intelligently and fruitfully. Here's the way I do it:

1. *Underlining:* of major points, of important or forceful statements.

2. *Vertical lines at the margin:* to emphasize a statement already underlined.
3. *Star, asterisk, or other doo-dad at the margin:* to be used sparingly, to emphasize the ten or twenty most important statements in the book. (You may want to fold the bottom corner of each page on which you use such marks. It won't hurt the sturdy paper on which most modern books are printed, and you will be able to take the book off the shelf at any time and, by opening it at the folded-corner page, refresh your recollection of the book.)
4. *Numbers in the margin:* to indicate the sequence of points the author makes in developing a single argument.
5. *Numbers of other pages in the margin:* to indicate where else in the book the author made points relevant to the point marked; to tie up the ideas in a book, which, though they may be separated by many pages, belong together.
6. *Circling of key words or phrases.*
7. *Writing in the margin, or at the top or bottom of the page, for the sake of:* recording questions (and perhaps answers) which a passage raised in your mind; reducing a complicated discussion to a simple statement; recording the sequence of major points right through the book. I use the end-papers at the back of the book to make a personal index of the author's points in the order of their appearance.

The front end-papers are, to me, the most important. Some people reserve them for a fancy bookplate. I reserve them for fancy thinking. After I have finished reading the book and making my personal index on the back end-papers, I turn to the front and try to outline the book, not page by page, or point by point (I've already done that at the back), but as an integrated structure, with a basic unity and an order of parts. This outline is, to me, the measure of my understanding of the work.

If you're a die-hard anti-book-marker, you may object

that the margins, the space between the lines, and the end-papers don't give you room enough. All right. How about using a scratch pad slightly smaller than the page-size of the book—so that the edges of the sheets won't protrude? Make your index, outlines, and even your notes on the pad, and then insert these sheets permanently inside the front and back covers of the book.

Or, you may say that this business of marking books is going to slow up your reading. It probably will. That's one of the reasons for doing it. Most of us have been taken in by the notion that speed of reading is a measure of our intelligence. There is no such thing as the right speed for intelligent reading. Some things should be read quickly and effortlessly, and some should be read slowly and even laboriously. The sign of intelligence in reading is the ability to read different things differently according to their worth. In the case of good books, the point is not to see how many of them you can get through, but rather how many can get through you—how many you can make your own. A few friends are better than a thousand acquaintances. If this be your aim, as it should be, you will not be impatient if it takes more time and effort to read a great book than it does a newspaper.

You may have one final objection to marking books. You can't lend them to your friends because nobody else can read them without being distracted by your notes. Furthermore, you won't want to lend them because a marked copy is a kind of intellectual diary, and lending it is almost like giving your mind away.

If your friend wishes to read your "Plutarch's Lives," "Shakespeare," or "The Federalist Papers," tell him, gently but firmly, to buy a copy. You will lend him your car or your coat—but your books are as much a part of you as your head or your heart.

How Should One Read a Book?

VIRGINIA WOOLF

———————— ● ————————

First published in 1932, this essay has never been superseded, probably because no one since Virginia Woolf has been such an omnivorous and joyous reader, with a writer's gift to match. She poses the essential question of evaluating anything, whether books or ballplayers or family tiffs: how personal perceptions can become generally valid judgments. Note what she says about Lear *at beginning and end. How do you explain this contradiciton? Note, too, how she contrasts the present reality outside the window with all those seen through the differing windows of books. As you read, underline those words that seem unusually effective or striking.*

This essay is a masterpiece of inductive argument (see pp. 319–362), the "leading into" one's thesis. Virginia Woolf begins with a question, and insists on the personal view and infinite differences. But as she swings her questions and answers pro and con, she eventually conveys her thesis, which might be fully stated something like this: You should read for yourself, sympathetically, joyfully, and then you will experience the ultimate pleasure of judging perceptively. *She would have been clearer for stating this thesis and arguing deductively, since she begins by saying that nobody can judge and ends by saying that everyone must judge, and by standards that cannot be merely personal. But she probably would have been less engaging, as she leads us to follow the wonders and play of her fine mind in its inductive teasing. Her paragraphs are full and nicely proportioned, and well pegged on topic sentences. Though one may not know more than a few of Woolf's allusions, one can still absorb Woolf's enthusiasm for reading; the idea is curiosity and discovery: the joy of reading.*

In the first place, I want to emphasize the note of interrogation at the end of my title. Even if I could answer the question for myself, the answer would apply only to me and not to you. The only advice, indeed, that one person can give another about reading is to take no advice, to follow your own instincts, to use your own reason, to come to your own conclusions. If this is agreed between us, then I feel at liberty to put forward a few ideas and suggestions because you will not allow them to fetter that independence which is the most important quality that a reader can possess. After all, what laws can be laid down about books? The battle of Waterloo was certainly fought on a certain day; but is *Hamlet* a better play than *Lear?* Nobody can say. Each must decide that question for himself. To admit authorities, however heavily furred and gowned, into our libraries and let them tell us how to read, what to read, what value to place upon what we read, is to destroy the spirit of freedom which is the breath of those sanctuaries. Everywhere else we may be bound by laws and conventions—there we have none.

But to enjoy freedom, if the platitude is pardonable, we have of course to control ourselves. We must not squander our powers, helplessly and ignorantly, squirting half the house in order to water a single rose-bush; we must train them, exactly and powerfully, here on the very spot. This, it may be, is one of the first difficulties that faces us in a library. What is "the very spot"? There may well seem to be nothing but a conglomeration and huddle of confusion. Poems and novels, histories and memoirs, dictionaries and bluebooks; books written in all languages by men and women of all tempers, races, and ages jostle each other on the shelf. And outside the donkey brays, the women gossip at the pump, the colts gallop across the fields. Where are we to begin? How are we to bring order into this multitudinous chaos and so get the deepest and widest pleasure from what we read?

It is simple enough to say that since books have classes—fiction, biography, poetry—we should separate them and take from each what it is right that each should give us. Yet few people ask from books what books can give us. Most commonly we come to books with blurred and divided minds, asking of fiction that it shall be true, of poetry that it shall be false, of biography that it shall be flattering, of history that it shall enforce our own prejudices. If we could banish all such preconceptions when we read, that would be an admirable beginning. Do not dictate to your author; try to become him. Be his fellow-worker and accomplice. If you hang back, and reserve and criticise at first, you are preventing yourself from getting the fullest possible value from what you read. But if you open your mind as widely as possible, then signs and hints of almost imperceptible fineness, from the twist and turn of the first sentences, will bring you into the presence of a human being unlike any other. Steep yourself in this, acquaint yourself with this, and soon you will find that your author is giving you, or attempting to give you, something far more definite. The thirty-two chapters of a novel—if we consider how to read a novel first—are an attempt to make something as formed and controlled as a building: but words are more impalpable than bricks; reading is a longer and more complicated process than seeing. Perhaps the quickest way to understand the elements of what a novelist is doing is not to read, but to write; to make your own experiment with the dangers and difficulties of words. Recall, then, some event that has left a distinct impression on you—how at the corner of the street, perhaps, you passed two people talking. A tree shook; an electric light danced; the tone of the talk was comic, but also tragic; a whole vision, an entire conception, seemed contained in that moment.

But when you attempt to reconstruct it in words, you will find that it breaks into a thousand conflicting impressions. Some must be subdued; others emphasized; in the process you will lose, probably, all grasp upon the emotion itself. Then turn from your blurred and littered pages to the opening pages of some great novelist—[Daniel] Defoe, Jane Austen, Hardy. Now you will be better able to appreciate their mastery. It is not merely that we are in the presence of a different person—Defoe, Jane Austen, or Thomas Hardy—but that we are living in a different world. Here, in [Defoe's] *Robinson Crusoe,* we are trudging a plain high road; one thing happens after another; the fact and the order of the fact is enough. But if the open air and adventure mean everything to Defoe they mean nothing to Jane Austen. Hers is the drawing-room, and people talking, and by the many mirrors of their talk revealing their characters. And if, when we have accustomed ourselves to the drawing-room and its reflections, we turn to Hardy, we are once more spun round. The moors are round us and the stars are above our heads. The other side of the mind is now exposed—the dark side that comes uppermost in solitude, not the light side that shows in company. Our relations are not toward people, but toward Nature and destiny. Yet different as these worlds are, each is consistent with itself. The maker of each is careful to observe the laws of his own perspective, and however great a strain they may put upon us they will never confuse us, as lesser writers so frequently do, by introducing two different kinds of reality into the same book. Thus to go from one great novelist to another—from Jane Austen to Hardy, from Peacock to Trollope, from Scott to Meredith—is to be wrenched and uprooted; to be thrown this way and then that. To read a novel is a difficult and complex art. You must be capable not only of great fineness of perception, but of great boldness of imagination if you are going to make use of all that the novelist—the great artist—gives you.

But a glance at the heterogeneous company on the shelf will show you that writers are very seldom "great artists"; far more often a book makes no claim to be a work of art at all. These biographies and autobiographies, for example, lives of great men, of men long dead and forgotten, that stand cheek by jowl with the novels and poems, are we to refuse to read them because they are not "art"? Or shall we read them, but read them in a different way, with a different aim? Shall we read them in the first place to satisfy that curiosity which possesses us sometimes when in the evening we linger in front of a house where the lights are lit and the blinds are not yet drawn, and each floor of the house shows us a different section of human life in being? Then we are consumed with curiosity about the lives of these people—the servants gossiping, the gentlemen dining, the girl dressing for a party, the old woman at the window with her knitting. Who are they, what are they, what are their names, their occupations, their thoughts, and adventures?

Biographies and memoirs answer such questions, light up innumerable such houses; they show us people going about their daily affairs, toiling, failing, succeeding, eating, hating, loving, until they die. And sometimes as we watch, the house fades and the iron railings vanish and we are out at sea; we are hunting, sailing, fighting; we are among savages and soldiers; we are taking part in great campaigns. Or if we like to stay here in England, in London, still the scene changes; the street narrows; the house becomes small, cramped, diamond-paned, and malodorous. We see a poet, [John] Donne, driven from such a house because the walls were so thin that when the children cried their voices cut through them. We can follow him, through the paths that lie in the pages of books, to Twickenham; to Lady Bedford's Park, a famous meeting-ground for nobles and poets; and then turn our steps to Wilton, the great house under the downs, and hear [Philip] Sidney read the *Arcadia* to his sister; and ramble among the very marshes and see the very herons that figure in that famous romance; and then again travel north with that other Lady Pembroke, Anne Clifford, to her wild moors, or plunge into the city and control our merriment at the sight of Gabriel Harvey in his black velvet suit arguing about poetry with [Edmund] Spenser. Nothing is more fascinating than to grope and stumble in the alternate darkness and splendour of Elizabethan London. But there is no staying there. The Temples and the Swifts, the Harleys and the St. Johns beckon us on; hour upon hour can be spent disentangling their quarrels and deciphering their characters; and when we tire of them we can stroll on, past a lady in black wearing diamonds, to Samuel Johnson and [Oliver] Goldsmith and [David] Garrick; or cross the channel, if we like, and meet Voltaire and Diderot, Madame du Deffand; and so back to England and Twickenham—how certain places repeat themselves and certain names!— where Lady Bedford had her Park once and [Alexander] Pope lived later, to [Horace] Walpole's home at Strawberry Hill. But Walpole introduces us to such a swarm of new acquaintances, there are so many houses to visit and bells to ring that we may well hesitate for a moment, on the Miss Berrys' doorstep, for example, when behold, up comes [William Makepeace] Thackeray; he is the friend of the woman whom Walpole loved;* so that merely by going from friend to friend, from garden to garden, from house to house, we have passed from one end of English literature to another and wake to find ourselves here again in the present, if we can so differentiate this moment from all that have gone before. This, then, is one of the ways in which we can read these lives and letters; we can make them light up the many windows of the past;

*Horace Walpole (1717–1797) left all of his books and manuscripts to Robert Berry and his two daughters, Mary (1763–1852) and Agnes (1764– 1852), along with £4000 a year each for the two girls, and the house (formerly that of the actress Kitty Clive) adjoining his estate of Strawberry Hill at Twickenham, on the Thames southwest of London. Mary Berry was Walpole's literary executor, bringing out the first edition of his *Works,* five volumes, in 1798, the year after his death. Rumor whispers that Walpole wanted to marry Mary, almost fifty years his junior. Thackeray, fascinated with the eighteenth century, became acquainted with the Berry sisters, when both were nearing ninety, and called on them frequently in their house in Curzon Street, London. Thackeray's younger daughter, Harriet Marian (1840–1875), was the first wife of Sir Leslie Stephen (1832–1904), Virginia Woolf's father. Virginia Woolf was born in 1882 by his second wife, seven years after the death of Harriet Thackeray Stephen.

we can watch the famous dead in their familiar habits and fancy sometimes that we are very close and can surprise their secrets, and sometimes we may pull out a play or a poem that they have written and see whether it reads differently in the presence of the author. But this again rouses other questions. How far, we must ask ourselves, is a book influenced by its writer's life—how far is it safe to let the man interpret the writer? How far shall we resist or give way to the sympathies and antipathies that the man himself rouses in us—so sensitive are words, so receptive of the character of the author? These are questions that press upon us when we read lives and letters, and we must answer them for ourselves, for nothing can be more fatal than to be guided by the preferences of others in a matter so personal.

But also we can read such books with another aim, not to throw light on literature, not to become familiar with famous people, but to refresh and exercise our own creative powers. Is there not an open window on the right hand of the bookcase? How delightful to stop reading and look out! How stimulating the scene is, in its unconsciousness, its irrelevance, its perpetual movement—the colts galloping round the field, the woman filling her pail at the well, the donkey throwing back his head and emitting his long, acrid moan. The greater part of any library is nothing but the record of such fleeting moments in the lives of men, women, and donkeys. Every literature, as it grows old, has its rubbish-heap, its record of vanished moments and forgotten lives told in faltering and feeble accents that have perished. But if you give yourself up to the delight of rubbish-reading you will be surprised, indeed you will be overcome, by the relics of human life that have been cast out to moulder. It may be one letter—but what a vision it gives! It may be a few sentences—but what vistas they suggest! Sometimes a whole story will come together with such beautiful humour and pathos and completeness that it seems as if a great novelist had been at work, yet it is only an old actor, Tate Wilkinson, remembering the strange

story of Captain Jones;* it is only a young subaltern serving
under Arthur Wellesley [the Duke of Wellington] and falling in love with a pretty girl at Lisbon;† it is only Maria
Allen letting fall her sewing in the empty drawingroom
and sighing how she wishes she had taken Dr. Burney's
good advice and had never eloped with her Rishy.‡ None of

*Tate Wilkinson (1739–1803), long-time actor in London and eventually
manager of several theaters in Yorkshire, tells of a Captain James Jones in
his *Memoirs of His Own Life* (York: Wilson, Spence, & Mawman, 1790),
four volumes. Captain Jones, of His Majesty's Third Regiment of Guards,
was the father of the future Lady Cornwallis, wife of General Charles
Cornwallis, whom Washington defeated at Yorktown to culminate the
American Revolution. Wilkinson's mother was a neighbor of Lady Cornwallis's mother in London, years later, whence Wilkinson had the story.
    Jones, an officer on half-pay and heavily in debt from gambling, used to
sit on a bench in St. James's park on Sundays, within the verge of court and
out of reach of his creditors. Here he would chat with a sour old General
Skelton. Later, much to his surprise, he learned that Skelton had made
him his sole heir if he would take the name of Skelton, who had no
offspring. When inspecting one of his new estates, Jones (who evidently
had not gotten around to changing his name) had himself lowered into a
lead mine, and died in agony a few days later. But his fortune enabled his
widow (who, in fact, remarried) to educate their daughter and catch the
eminent thirty-year-old Lord Cornwallis for her husband (in 1768). When
war with America broke out (in 1775), Cornwallis immediately volun-
teered, but his young wife persuaded King George III not to send him.
When he learned why his orders were changed, he persuaded the king to
send him in any case, and his distraught wife, according to Wilkinson,
died of grief (*Memoirs,* I.57–70). Actually, Cornwallis, over his wife's
protests, sailed for America 10 February 1776. Late in 1778, Cornwallis
returned to England on news of his wife's desperate illness. She died 16
February 1779. Cornwallis, returning to his command in America, landed
in New York in August 1779.
    †This anecdote evidently comes from somewhere in the papers or
writings of Sir Henry Edward Bunbury (1778–1860), whose name Virginia
Woolf mentions in the next paragraph. He was an able officer and diplomat, who served in Egypt and the Mediterranean, and later became an
envoy to Arthur Wellesley, the future Duke of Wellington, in his campaign against Napoleon in Spain, 1808–1814. We have been unable to
locate Virginia Woolf's source.
    ‡Maria Allen (1751–1820) is the stepsister of Fanny Burney, the novel-
ist (1752–1840). Dr. Charles Burney (1726–1814), music historian, is her
stepfather. "Rishy" is Martin Folkes Rishton (c. 1747–1820), whom Maria
ran away to meet in Geneva on his Grand Tour in November 1771, and to
marry at Ypres, France, in May 1772. He was a young country squire
whom she soon found "austere, haughty, irascible & impracticable" (*The
Journals and Letters of Fanny Burney,* ed. Joyce Hemlow [Oxford: Claren-
don Press, 1973], IV.75). She eventually ran away from him and obtained a
settled separation. We have been unable to find Virginia Woolf's incident
in any of the seven published selections from the voluminous diaries and
letters of Fanny Burney still in manuscript.

this has any value; it is negligible in the extreme; yet how absorbing it is now and again to go through the rubbish-heaps and find rings and scissors and broken noses buried in the huge past and try to piece them together while the colt gallops round the field, the woman fills her pail at the well, and the donkey brays.

But we tire of rubbish-reading in the long run. We tire of searching for what is needed to complete the half-truth which is all that the Wilkinsons, the Bunburys, and the Maria Allens are able to offer us. They had not the artist's power of mastering and eliminating; they could not tell the whole truth even about their own lives; they have disfigured the story that might have been so shapely. Facts are all that they can offer us, and facts are a very inferior form of fiction. Thus the desire grows upon us to have done with half-statements and approximations; to cease from searching out the minute shades of human character, to enjoy the greater abstractness, the purer truth of fiction. Thus we create the mood, intense and generalised, unaware of detail, but stressed by some regular, recurrent beat, whose natural expression is poetry; and that is the time to read poetry, when we are most able to write it.

> *Western wind, when wilt thou blow?*
> *The small rain down can rain.*
> *Christ, if my love were in my arms,*
> *And I in my bed again!**

The impact of poetry is so hard and direct that for the moment there is no other sensation except that of the poem itself. What profound depths we visit then—how sudden and complete is our immersion! There is nothing here to catch hold of; nothing to stay us in our flight. The illusion of fiction is gradual; its effects are prepared; but who when they read these four lines stops to ask who wrote them, or conjures up the thought of Donne's house

*An anonymous fragment, dated about A.D. 1300, but the spelling that has come down to us, which Virginia Woolf quotes, dates from the sixteenth century, reflecting its long popularity.

or Sidney's secretary; or enmeshes them in the intricacy of the past and the succession of generations? The poet is always our contemporary. Our being for the moment is centered and constricted, as in any violent shock of personal emotion. Afterwards, it is true, the sensation begins to spread in wider rings through our minds; remoter senses are reached; these begin to sound and to comment and we are aware of echoes and reflections. The intensity of poetry covers an immense range of emotion. We have only to compare the force and directness of

> *I shall fall like a tree, and find my grave,*
> *Only remembering that I grieve,*

with the wavering modulation of

> *Minutes are numbered by the fall of sands,*
> *As by an hour glass; the span of time*
> *Doth waste us to our graves, and we look on it;*
> *An age of pleasure, revelled out, comes home*
> *At last, and ends in sorrow; but the life,*
> *Weary of riot, numbers every sand,*
> *Wailing in sighs, until the last drop down,*
> *So to conclude calamity in rest,*

or place the meditative calm of

> *whether we be young or old,*
> *Our destiny, our being's heart and home,*
> *Is with infinitude, and only there;*
> *With hope it is, hope that can never die,*
> *Effort, and expectation, and desire,*
> *And something evermore about to be,*

beside the complete and inexhaustible loveliness of

> *The moving Moon went up the sky,*
> *And nowhere did abide:*
> *Softly she was going up,*
> *And a star or two beside—*

or the splendid fantasy of

> *And the woodland haunter*
> *Shall not cease to saunter*
> *When, far down some glade,*
> *Of the great world's burning,*
> *One soft flame upturning,*
> *Seems, to his discerning,*
> *Crocus in the shade,*

to bethink us of the varied art of the poet;* his power to make us at once actors and spectators; his power to run his hand into character as if it were a glove, and be Falstaff or Lear; his power to condense, to widen, to state, once and for ever.

"We have only to compare"—with those words the cat is out of the bag, and the true complexity of reading is admitted. The first process, to receive impressions with the utmost understanding, is only half the process of reading; it must be completed, if we are to get the whole pleasure from a book, by another. We must pass judgment upon these multitudinous impressions; we must make of these fleeting shapes one that is hard and lasting. But not directly. Wait for the dust of reading to settle; for the conflict and the questioning to die down; walk, talk, pull the dead petals from a rose, or fall asleep. Then suddenly without our willing it, for it is thus that Nature undertakes these transitions, the book will return, but differently. It will float to the top of the mind as a whole. And the book as a whole is different from the book received currently in separate phrases. Details now fit themselves into their places. We see the shape from start to finish; it is a barn, a pig-sty,

---

*These five quotations are from (1) Beaumont and Fletcher, *The Maid's Tragedy* (1619), IV.i.214–215; (2) John Ford, *The Lover's Melancholy* (1629), IV.iii.57–64; (3) William Wordsworth, *The Prelude* (1805), VI.603–608; (4) Samuel Taylor Coleridge, *The Rime of the Ancient Mariner* (1798), ll. 263–266; (5) Ebenezer Jones, "When the World Is Burning" (1860), ll. 21–27. We are grateful to Anthony W. Shipps, Librarian for English, University of Indiana, for identifying the quotations from Beaumont and Fletcher, Ford, and Jones.

or a cathedral. Now then we can compare book with book as we compare building with building. But this act of comparison means that our attitude has changed; we are no longer the friends of the writer, but his judges; and just as we cannot be too sympathetic as friends, so as judges we cannot be too severe. Are they not criminals, books that have wasted our time and sympathy; are they not the most insidious enemies of society, corrupters, defilers, the writers of false books, faked books, books that fill the air with decay and disease? Let us then be severe in our judgments; let us compare each book with the greatest of its kind. There they hang in the mind, the shapes of the books we have read solidified by the judgments we have passed on them—*Robinson Crusoe,* [Austen's] *Emma,* [Hardy's] *The Return of the Native.* Compare the novels with these— even the latest and least of novels has a right to be judged with the best. And so with poetry—when the intoxication or rhythm has died down and the splendour of words has faded, a visionary shape will return to us and this must be compared with [Shakespeare's] *Lear,* with [Racine's] *Phèdre,* with [Wordsworth's] *The Prelude;* or if not with these, with whatever is the best or seems to us to be the best in its own kind. And we may be sure that the newness of new poetry and fiction is its most superficial quality and that we have only to alter slightly, not to recast, the standards by which we have judged the old.

It would be foolish, then, to pretend that the second part of reading, to judge, to compare, is as simple as the first— to open the mind wide to the fast flocking of innumerable impressions. To continue reading without the book before you, to hold one shadow-shape against another, to have read widely enough and with enough understanding to make such comparisons alive and illuminating—that is difficult; it is still more difficult to press further and to say, "Not only is the book of this sort, but it is of this value; here it fails; here it succeeds; this is bad; that is good." To carry out this part of a reader's duty needs such imagination, insight, and learning that it is hard to conceive any one mind sufficiently endowed; impossible for the most self-confident to find more than the seeds of such powers in himself. Would it not be wiser, then, to remit this part of reading and to allow the critics, the gowned and furred authorities of the library, to decide the question of the book's absolute value for us? Yet how impossible! We may stress the value of sympathy; we may try to sink our own identity as we read. But we know that we cannot sympathise wholly or immerse ourselves wholly; there is always a demon in us who whispers, "I hate, I love," and we cannot silence him. Indeed, it is precisely because we hate and we love that our relation with the poets and novelists is so intimate that we find the presence of another person intolerable. And even if the results are abhorrent and our judgments are wrong, still our taste, the nerve of sensation that sends shocks through us, is our chief illuminant; we learn through feelings; we cannot suppress our own idiosyncrasy without impoverishing it. But as time goes on perhaps we can train our taste; perhaps we can make it submit to some control. When it has fed greedily and lavishly upon books of all sorts—poetry, fiction, history, biography—and has stopped reading and looked for long spaces upon the variety, the incongruity of the living word, we shall find that it is changing a little; it is not so greedy, it is more reflective. It will begin to bring us not merely judgments on particular books, but it will tell us that there is a quality common to certain books. Listen, it will say, what shall we call *this*? And it will read us perhaps *Lear* and then perhaps the [Aeschylus's] *Agamemnon* in order to bring out the common quality. Thus, with our taste to guide us, we shall venture beyond the particular book in search of qualities that group books together; we shall give them names and thus frame a rule that brings order into our perceptions. We shall gain a further and a rarer pleasure from that discrimination. But as a rule only lives when it is perpetually broken by contact with the books themselves—nothing is easier and more stultifying than to make rules which exist out of touch with facts, in a vacuum—now at last, in order to steady ourselves in this difficult attempt, it may be well to turn to the very rare writers who are able to enlighten us upon literature as an art. Coleridge and Dryden and Johnson, in their considered criticism, the poets and novelists themselves in their unconsidered sayings, are often surprisingly relevant; they light up and solidify the vague ideas that have been tumbling in the misty depths of our minds. But they are only able to help us if we come to them laden with questions and suggestions won honestly in the course of our own reading. They can do nothing for us if we herd ourselves under their authority and lie down like sheep in the shade of a hedge. We can only understand their ruling when it comes in conflict with our own and vanquishes it.

If this is so, if to read a book as it should be read calls for the rarest qualities of imagination, insight, and judgment, you may perhaps conclude that literature is a very complex art and that it is unlikely that we shall be able, even after a lifetime of reading, to make any valuable contribution to its criticism. We must remain readers; we shall not put on the further glory that belongs to those rare beings who are also critics. But still we have our responsibilities as readers and even our importance. The standards we raise and the judgment we pass steal into the air and become part of the atmosphere which writers breathe as they work. An influence is created which tells upon them even if it never finds its way into print. And that influence, if it were well instructed, vigorous and individual and sincere, might be of great value now when criticism is necessarily in abeyance; when books pass in review like the procession of animals in a shooting gallery, and the critic has only one second in which to load and aim and shoot and may well be pardoned if he mistakes rabbits for tigers, eagles for barndoor fowls, or misses altogether and wastes his shot upon some peaceful cow grazing in a further field. If behind the erratic gunfire of the press the author felt that there was another kind of criticism, the opinion of people reading for the love of reading, slowly and unprofessionally, and judging with great sympathy and yet with great severity, might this not improve the quality of his work? And if by our means books were to become stronger, richer, and more varied, that would be an end worth reaching.

Yet who reads to bring about an end, however desirable? Are there not some pursuits that we practise because they are good in themselves, and some pleasures that are final? And is not this among them? I have sometimes dreamt, at least, that when the Day of Judgment dawns and the great conquerors and lawyers and statesmen come to receive their rewards—their crowns, their laurels, their names carved indelibly upon imperishable marble—the Almighty will turn to Peter and will say, not without a certain envy when He sees us coming with our books under our arms, "Look, these need no reward. We have nothing to give them here. They have loved reading."

1

THE ARGUMENTATIVE EDGE

Argumentation is our surest way to knowledge. It rubs ideas together to see what can stand the wear and tear. It discovers what is valid, what insubstantial. So, as an essayist, you set out to persuade your readers that what you believe true is in fact demonstrably true, not merely a private fancy. You do this by taking your subject and sharpening it into a thesis, putting an argumentative edge on it, then demonstrating the trueness of that edge in the rest of your essay.

The essayist's whetstone is an *aboutness,* asserting something ABOUT your subject. You take fishing, Harlem, tyranny, whatever, and assert something *about* it. This *aboutness* makes your thesis. This assertion whets your subject to its argumentative edge.

This edge is no mere gimmick. It is basic to thinking. It

concerns purpose. It concerns beliefs about why we are here and what we should do about it. Writing an essay, or understanding one, is a partial answer to our most fundamental question: "Why?" Why life? Why DNA? We cannot answer that basic *why* conclusively, of course. But we can and do—indeed, we must—answer it in its particular manifestations. Should we conserve and shiver, or spend and dance? The anxious ant, or the ebullient grasshopper? On any issue, we instinctively make our choice. Your thesis formulates your choice. Your essay makes your choice persuasive, and, with luck, shows that it is right.

Each of the five essayists in this section believed something deeply, and personally. Each has taken his general subject and dignified it with the edge of his belief. Each feels he has persuaded us that his belief is true. We may have our doubts, of course. Here our own essays will begin, cutting across the subject with our own argumentative edges. We all begin in a personal perception. But we do not argue an eccentric case. Personal experience and thought have shown each of these five essayists something deeply valid for all. Even Thomas Jefferson, speaking of "the course of human events" for a whole "people," speaks as one who has personally thought these things through from what he has seen and read. The individual thinker finds in his or her private thoughts, with their argumentative edge, something true for all of us.

Thus the argumentative edge—the thesis—has a great advantage for us readers, too. From it, we can grasp the main idea, and also judge the writer's skill. We can use this edgy idea for both knowledge and judgment. At the end of every essay you read—or story, play, or poem, too—write down, *in one sentence,* your own statement of the point, its thesis. You have grasped the main idea, even if, as in stories or poems, it is only implied and never stated. Now go back to the essay itself, and see *where* the author has stated this most explicitly, or implied it most strongly. Then see how he carries it through, or leads up to it, or contradicts it, or forgets it. Thus you will see the writer's structure, play, and display of thought and evidence.

Each of these essayists has instinctively put his thesis in its most effective place—early, after some remarks to orient the reader. He introduces his subject, then states his *aboutness.* Then he brings in the evidence and the persuasion. To study and enjoy these essays, read each one through. Then, at the end, in your own words, write out your statement of its thesis. Now go back and test the essay. You may find your own formulation more explicit (as we suggest with Baldwin). You may wish it a little earlier (as we suggest with Jefferson). You may be wrong, of course. They may be right. But formulating your own thesis and judging the essay from it will teach you more about the essayist's craft than a month of theory.

Fifth Avenue Uptown: A Letter from Harlem

JAMES BALDWIN

———————— ● ————————

Baldwin's argumentative edge cuts into his subject, "Fifth Avenue," with images of entrapment. Fishhooks catch the poor fish. Barbed wire surrounds the animal and the prisoner, and entangles the running soldier. Baldwin might have spelled out his thesis more fully: "Although Fifth Avenue means elegance and freedom to many, uptown in Harlem it means entrapment in the fishhooks and barbed wire of white power." With his novelist's gift for detail, he sketches his subject and emerging thesis—rehabilitation with snarling trees, alleged progress with no progress, noses against a windowpane. He even dramatizes his thesis novelistically as the shared idea of the shoemaker and the storekeeper. He places his thesis, with his writer's instinct, at the sharpest strategical point: at the end of those introductory remarks that put his subject before us, ready for the cut: its "fishhooks and barbed wire."

There is a housing project standing now where the house in which we grew up once stood, and one of those stunted city trees is snarling where our doorway used to be. This is on the rehabilitated side of the avenue. The other side of the avenue—for progress takes time—has not been rehabilitated yet and it looks exactly as it looked in the days when we sat with our noses pressed against the windowpane, longing to be allowed to go "across the street." The grocery store which gave us credit is still there, and there can be no doubt that it is still giving credit. The people in the project certainly need it—far more, indeed, than they ever needed the project. The last time I passed by, the Jewish proprietor was still standing among his shelves, looking sadder and heavier but scarcely any older. Farther down the block stands the shoe-repair store in which our shoes were repaired until reparation became impossible and in which, then, we bought all our "new" ones. The Negro proprietor is still in the window, head down, working at the leather.

These two, I imagine, could tell a long tale if they would (perhaps they would be glad to if they could), having watched so many, for so long, struggling in the fishhooks, the barbed wire, of this avenue.

The avenue is elsewhere the renowned and elegant Fifth. The area I am describing, which, in today's gang parlance, would be called "the turf," is bounded by Lenox Avenue on the west, the Harlem River on the east, 135th Street on the north, and 130th Street on the south. We never lived beyond these boundaries; this is where we grew up. Walking along 145th Street—for example—familiar as it is, and similar, does not have the same impact because I do not know any of the people on the block. But when I turn east on 131st Street and Lenox Avenue, there is first a soda-pop joint, then a shoeshine "parlor," then a grocery store, then a dry cleaners', then the houses. All along the street there are people who watched me grow up, people who grew up with me, people I watched grow up along with my brothers and sisters; and sometimes in my arms, sometimes underfoot, sometimes at my shoulder— or on it—their children, a riot, a forest of children, who include my nieces and nephews.

When we reach the end of this long block, we find ourselves on wide, filthy, hostile Fifth Avenue, facing that project which hangs over the avenue like a monument to the folly, and the cowardice, of good intentions. All along the block, for anyone who knows it, are immense human gaps, like craters. These gaps are not created merely by those who have moved away, inevitably into some other ghetto; or by those who have risen, almost always into a greater capacity for self-loathing and self-delusion; or yet by those who, by whatever means—World War II, the Korean war, a policeman's gun or billy, a gang war, a brawl, madness, an overdose of heroin, or, simply, unnatural exhaustion—are dead. I am talking about those who are left, and I am talking principally about the young. What are they doing? Well, some, a minority, are fanatical churchgoers, members of the more extreme of the Holy Roller sects. Many, many more are "moslems," by affiliation or sympathy, that is to say that they are united by nothing more—and nothing less—than a hatred of the white world and all its works. They are present, for example, at every Buy Black street-corner meeting—meetings in which the speaker urges his hearers to cease trading with white men and establish a separate economy. Neither the speaker nor his hearers can possibly do this, of course, since Negroes do not own General Motors or RCA or the A & P, nor, indeed, do they own more than a wholly insufficient fraction of anything else in Harlem (those who *do* own anything are more interested in their profits than in their fellows). But these meetings nevertheless keep alive in the participators a certain pride of bitterness without which, however futile this bitterness may be, they could scarcely remain alive at all. Many have given up. They stay home and watch the TV screen, living on the earnings of their parents, cousins, brothers, or uncles, and only leave the house to go to the movies or to the nearest bar. "How're you making it?" one may ask, running into them along the block, or in the bar. "Oh, I'm TV-ing it"; with the saddest, sweetest, most shamefaced of smiles, and from a great distance. This distance one is compelled to respect; anyone who has traveled so far will not easily be dragged again into the world. There are further retreats, of course, than the TV screen or the bar. There are those who are simply sitting on their stoops, "stoned," animated for a moment only, and hideously, by the approach of someone who may lend them the money for a "fix." Or by the approach of someone from whom they can purchase it, one of the shrewd ones, on the way to prison or just coming out.

And the others, who have avoided all of these deaths, get up in the morning and go downtown to meet "the man."

They work in the white man's world all day and come home in the evening to this fetid block. They struggle to instill in their children some private sense of honor or dignity which will help the child to survive. This means, of course, that they must struggle, stolidly, incessantly, to keep this sense alive in themselves, in spite of the insults, the indifference, and the cruelty they are certain to encounter in their working day. They patiently browbeat the landlord into fixing the heat, the plaster, the plumbing; this demands prodigious patience; nor is patience usually enough. In trying to make their hovels habitable, they are perpetually throwing good money after bad. Such frustration, so long endured, is driving many strong, admirable men and women whose only crime is color to the very gates of paranoia.

One remembers them from another time—playing handball in the playground, going to church, wondering if they were going to be promoted at school. One remembers them going off to war—gladly, to escape this block. One remembers their return. Perhaps one remembers their wedding day. And one sees where the girl is now—vainly looking for salvation from some other embittered, trussed, and struggling boy—and sees the all-but-abandoned children in the streets.

Now I am perfectly aware that there are other slums in which white men are fighting for their lives, and mainly losing. I know that blood is also flowing through those streets and that the human damage there is incalculable. People are continually pointing out to me the wretchedness of white people in order to console me for the wretchedness of blacks. But an itemized account of the American failure does not console me and it should not console anyone else. That hundreds of thousands of white people are living, in effect, no better than the "niggers" is not a fact to be regarded with complacency. The social and moral bankruptcy suggested by this fact is of the bitterest, most terrifying kind.

The people, however, who believe that this democratic anguish has some consoling value are always pointing out that So-and-So, white, and So-and-So, black, rose from the slums into the big time. The existence—the public existence—of, say, Frank Sinatra and Sammy Davis, Jr., proves to them that America is still the land of opportunity and that inequalities vanish before the determined will. It proves nothing of the sort. The determined will is rare— at the moment, in this country, it is unspeakably rare—and the inequalities suffered by the many are in no way justified by the rise of a few. A few have always risen—in every country, every era, and in the teeth of regimes which can by no stretch of the imagination be thought of as free. Not all of these people, it is worth remembering, left the world better than they found it. The determined will is rare, but it is not invariably benevolent. Furthermore, the American equation of success with the big time reveals an awful disrespect for human life and human achievement. This equation has placed our cities among the most dangerous in the world and has placed our youth among the most empty and most bewildered. The situation of our youth is not mysterious. Children have never been very good at listening to their elders, but they have never failed to imitate them. They must, they have no other models. That is exactly what our children are doing. They are imitating our immorality, our disrespect for the pain of others.

All other slum dwellers, when the bank account permits it, can move out of the slum and vanish altogether from the eye of persecution. No Negro in this country has ever made that much money and it will be a long time before any Negro does. The Negroes in Harlem, who have no money, spend what they have on such gimcracks as they are sold. These include "wider" TV screens, more "faithful" hi-fi sets, more "powerful" cars, all of which, of course, are obsolete long before they are paid for. Anyone who has ever struggled with poverty knows how extremely expensive it is to be poor; and if one is a member of a captive population, economically speaking, one's feet have simply been placed on the treadmill forever. One is victimized, economically, in a thousand ways—rent, for example, or car insurance. Go shopping one day in Harlem—for anything—and compare Harlem prices and quality with those downtown.

The people who have managed to get off this block have only got as far as a more respectable ghetto. This respectable ghetto does not even have the advantages of the disreputable one—friends, neighbors, a familiar church, and friendly tradesmen; and it is not, moreover, in the nature of any ghetto to remain respectable long. Every Sunday, people who have left the block take the lonely ride back, dragging their increasingly discontented children with them. They spend the day talking, not always with words, about the trouble they've seen and the trouble—one must watch their eyes as they watch their children—they are only too likely to see. For children do not like ghettos. It takes them nearly no time to discover exactly why they are there.

The projects in Harlem are hated. They are hated almost as much as policemen, and this is saying a great deal. And they are hated for the same reason: both reveal, unbearably, the real attitude of the white world, no matter how many liberal speeches are made, no matter how many lofty editorials are written, no matter how many civil-rights commissions are set up.

The projects are hideous, of course, there being a law, apparently respected throughout the world, that popular housing shall be as cheerless as a prison. They are lumped all over Harlem, colorless, bleak, high, and revolting. The wide windows look out on Harlem's invincible and indescribable squalor: the Park Avenue railroad tracks, around which, about forty years ago, the present dark community began; the unrehabilitated houses, bowed down, it would seem, under the great weight of frustration and bitterness they contain; the dark, the ominous schoolhouses from which the child may emerge maimed, blinded, hooked, or enraged for life; and the churches, churches, block upon block of churches, niched in the walls like cannon in the walls of a fortress. Even if the administration of the projects were not so insanely humiliating (for example: one must report raises in salary to the management, which will then eat up the profit by raising one's rent; the management has the right to know who is staying in your apartment; the management can ask you to leave, at their discretion), the projects would still be hated because they are an insult to the meanest intelligence.

Harlem got its first private project, Riverton[1]—which is now, naturally, a slum—about twelve years ago because at that time Negroes were not allowed to live in Stuyvesant Town. Harlem watched Riverton go up, therefore, in the most violent bitterness of spirit, and hated it long before the builders arrived. They began hating it at about the time people began moving out of their condemned houses to make room for this additional proof of how thoroughly the white world despised them. And they had scarcely moved in, naturally, before they began smashing windows, defacing walls, urinating in the elevators, and fornicating in the playgrounds. Liberals, both white and black, were appalled at the spectacle. I was appalled by the liberal innocence—or cynicism, which comes out in practice as much the same thing. Other people were delighted to be able to point to proof positive that nothing could be done to better the lot of the colored people. They were, and are, right in one respect: that nothing can be done as long as they are treated like colored people. The people in Harlem know they are living there because white people do not think they are good enough to live anywhere else. No amount of "improvement" can sweeten this fact. Whatever money is now being earmarked to improve this, or any other

[1]The inhabitants of Riverton were much embittered by this description; they have, apparently, forgotten how their project came into being; and have repeatedly informed me that I cannot possibly be referring to Riverton, but to another housing project which is directly across the street. It is quite clear, I think, that I have no interest in accusing any individuals or families of the depredations herein described: but neither can I deny the evidence of my own eyes. Nor do I blame anyone in Harlem for making the best of a dreadful bargain. But anyone who lives in Harlem and imagines that he has not struck this bargain, or that what he takes to be his status (in whose eyes?) protects him against the common pain, demoralization, and danger, is simply self-deluded. [Baldwin's footnote]

ghetto, might as well be burnt. A ghetto can be improved in one way only: out of existence.

Similarly, the only way to police a ghetto is to be oppressive. None of the Police Commissioner's men, even with the best will in the world, have any way of understanding the lives led by the people they swagger about in twos and threes controlling. Their very presence is an insult, and it would be, even if they spent their entire day feeding gumdrops to children. They represent the force of the white world, and that world's real intentions are, simply, for that world's criminal profit and ease, to keep the black man corraled up here, in his place. The badge, the gun in the holster, and the swinging club make vivid what will happen should his rebellion become overt. Rare, indeed, is the Harlem citizen, from the most circumspect church member to the most shiftless adolescent, who does not have a long tale to tell of police incompetence, injustice, or brutality. I myself have witnessed and endured it more than once. The businessmen and racketeers also have a story. And so do the prostitutes. (And this is not, perhaps, the place to discuss Harlem's very complex attitude toward black policemen, nor the reasons, according to Harlem, that they are nearly all downtown.)

It is hard, on the other hand, to blame the policeman, blank, good-natured, thoughtless, and insuperably innocent, for being such a perfect representative of the people he serves. He, too, believes in good intentions and is astounded and offended when they are not taken for the deed. He has never, himself, done anything for which to be hated—which of us has?—and yet he is facing, daily and nightly, people who would gladly see him dead, and he knows it. There is no way for him not to know it: there are few things under heaven more unnerving than the silent, accumulating contempt and hatred of a people. He moves through Harlem, therefore, like an occupying soldier in a bitterly hostile country; which is precisely what, and where, he is, and is the reason he walks in twos and threes. And he is not the only one who knows why he is always in company: the people who are watching him know why, too. Any street meeting, sacred or secular, which he and his colleagues uneasily cover has as its explicit or implicit burden the cruelty and injustice of the white domination. And these days, of course, in terms increasingly vivid and jubilant, it speaks of the end of that domination. The white policeman standing on a Harlem street corner finds himself at the very center of the revolution now occurring in the world. He is not prepared for it—naturally, nobody is—and, what is possibly much more to the point, he is exposed, as few white people are, to the anguish of the black people around him. Even if he is gifted with the merest mustard grain of imagination, something must seep in. He cannot avoid observing that some of the children, in spite of their color, remind him of children he has known and loved, perhaps even of his own children. He knows that he certainly does not want *his* children living this way. He can retreat from his uneasiness in only one direction: into a callousness which very shortly becomes second nature. He becomes more callous, the population becomes more hostile, the situation grows more tense, and the police force is increased. One day, to everyone's astonishment, someone drops a match in the powder keg and everything blows up. Before the dust has settled or the blood congealed, editorials, speeches, and civil-rights commissions are loud in the land demanding to know what happened. What happened is that Negroes want to be treated like men.

Negroes want to be treated like men: a perfectly straightforward statement, containing only seven words. People who have mastered Kant, Hegel, Shakespeare, Marx, Freud, and the Bible find this statement utterly impenetrable. The idea seems to threaten profound, barely conscious assumptions. A kind of panic paralyzes their features, as though they found themselves trapped on the edge of a steep place. I once tried to describe to a very well-known American intellectual the conditions among Negroes in the South. My recital disturbed him and made him indignant; and he asked me in perfect innocence, "Why don't all the Negroes in the South move North?" I tried to explain what *has* happened, unfailingly, whenever a significant body of Negroes move North. They do not escape Jim Crow: they merely encounter another, not-less-deadly variety. They do not move to Chicago, they move to the South Side; they do not move to New York, they move to Harlem. The pressure within the ghetto causes the ghetto walls to expand, and this expansion is always violent. White people hold the line as long as they can, and in as many ways as they can, from verbal intimidation to physical violence. But inevitably the border which has divided the ghetto from the rest of the world falls into the hands of the ghetto. The white people fall back bitterly before the black horde; the landlords make a tidy profit by raising the rent, chopping up the rooms, and all but dispensing with the upkeep; and what has once been a neighborhood turns into a "turf." This is precisely what happened when the Puerto Ricans arrived in their thousands—and the bitterness thus caused is, as I write, being fought out all up and down those streets.

Northerners indulge in an extremely dangerous luxury. They seem to feel that because they fought on the right side during the Civil War, and won, they have earned the right merely to deplore what is going on in the South, without taking any responsibility for it; and that they can ignore what is happening in Northern cities because what is happening in Little Rock or Birmingham is worse. Well, in the first place, it is not possible for anyone who has not endured both to know which is "worse." I know Negroes who prefer the South and white Southerners, because "At least there, you haven't got to play any guessing games!" The guessing games referred to have driven more than one Negro into the narcotics ward, the madhouse, or the river. I know another Negro, a man very dear to me, who says, with conviction and with truth, "The spirit of the South is the spirit of America." He was born in the North and did his military training in the South. He did not, as far as I can gather, find the South "worse"; he found it, if anything, all too familiar. In the second place, though, even if Birmingham is worse, no doubt Johannesburg,

South Africa, beats it by several miles, and Buchenwald was one of the worst things that ever happened in the entire history of the world. The world has never lacked for horrifying examples; but I do not believe that these examples are meant to be used as justification for our own crimes. This perpetual justification empties the heart of all human feeling. The emptier our hearts become, the greater will be our crimes. Thirdly, the South is not merely an embarrassingly backward region, but a part of this country, and what happens there concerns every one of us.

As far as the color problem is concerned, there is but one great difference between the Southern white and the Northerner: the Southerner remembers, historically and in his own psyche, a kind of Eden in which he loved black people and they loved him. Historically, the flaming sword laid across this Eden is the Civil War. Personally, it is the Southerner's sexual coming of age, when, without any warning, unbreakable taboos are set up between himself and his past. Everything, thereafter, is permitted him except the love he remembers and has never ceased to need. The resulting, indescribable torment affects every Southern mind and is the basis of the Southern hysteria.

None of this is true for the Northerner. Negroes represent nothing to him personally, except, perhaps, the dangers of carnality. He never sees Negroes. Southerners see them all the time. Northerners never think about them whereas Southerners are never really thinking of anything else. Negroes are, therefore, ignored in the North and are under surveillance in the South, and suffer hideously in both places. Neither the Southerner nor the Northerner is able to look on the Negro simply as a man. It seems to be indispensable to the national self-esteem that the Negro be considered either as a kind of ward (in which case we are told how many Negroes, comparatively, bought Cadillacs last year and how few, comparatively, were lynched), or as a victim (in which case we are promised that he will never vote in our assemblies or go to school with our kids). They are two sides of the same coin and the South will not change—*cannot* change—until the

North changes. The country will not change until it reexamines itself and discovers what it really means by freedom. In the meantime, generations keep being born, bitterness is increased by incompetence, pride, and folly, and the world shrinks around us.

It is a terrible, an inexorable, law that one cannot deny the humanity of another without diminishing one's own: in the face of one's victim, one sees oneself. Walk through the streets of Harlem and see what we, this nation, have become.

IDEAS

1. In what way does the description of the housing project with which Baldwin begins imply everything that follows?

2. What is Baldwin's concept of morality? His view of success?

3. Explain Baldwin's distinction between Southern and Northern whites. Is that distinction still valid?

4. What is the thesis that you have made to summarize this essay? Compare it with those of your classmates. See if your class as a group can come up with a single thesis statement.

ORGANIZATION AND STYLE

1. How do Baldwin's references to the past and the present unify his essay and provide transition from one idea to another?

2. How does the second paragraph function? Would it have worked as well as part of the first paragraph? Why or why not?

3. The final sentence of the third paragraph accumulates details about different groups of people. What effect would have been lost by presenting these in two or

three separate sentences? Are there any similar sentences elsewhere in the essay?

4. If you had to describe the tone (mood) of this selection, what one word would you use? Bitter? Hostile? Pity? Anger? What words in the essay reinforce the tone?

5. How effective is the final paragraph as a conclusion to Baldwin's argument?

WRITING

1. Develop your own essay by using as thesis Baldwin's sentence "It is a terrible, an inexorable, law that one cannot deny the humanity of another without diminishing one's own."

2. Assume that you are a housing director of a large city with slums similar to those described by Baldwin. Present an essay in which you offer specific solutions to the problems Baldwin describes. Remember that you are going to have to argue with some of your opponents to get your ideas accepted.

The Declaration of Independence

THOMAS JEFFERSON

———————————●———————————

*Jefferson sharpens his thesis in three steps: the first
asserting God-given rights; the second, consequent obligations to overthrow any tyranny; the third, the
obligation to overthrow George III's tyranny. A modern essayist might have put it in one sentence (and
one introductory paragraph): "Since God has created
us free from all political tyranny, we have a right and
duty to overthrow such impending tyrannies as that
of George III."*

*Jefferson's essay is a model of deductive argumen-
tation (see pp. 9, 319–362); his three-step thesis follows
the basic deductive rhythm: "This, This also, Then
therefore this." His final this is his thesis: George is a
tyrant ordained for overthrow by God-given freedom.
Then Jefferson lays out his evidence, beginning with
his smallest piece—George's refusing assent to good
laws—and building up to his biggest—George's incit-
ing savages to implement his savagery. Now, Jefferson
faces the opposition's "What have you done to miti-
gate these evils?" We have tried repeatedly, he says.
Then he sweeps on to his magnificent concluding paragraph—"therefore"—which drives his whole argument home.*

When in the course of human events, it becomes necessary
for one people to dissolve the political bands which have
connected them with another, and to assume among the
Powers of the earth, the separate and equal station to
which the Laws of Nature and of Nature's God entitle
them, a decent respect to the opinions of mankind requires
that they should declare the causes which impel them to
the separation.

We hold these truths to be self-evident, that all men are created equal, that they are endowed by their Creator with certain unalienable Rights, that among these are Life, Liberty and the pursuit of Happiness. That to secure these rights, Governments are instituted among Men, deriving their just powers from the consent of the governed. That whenever any Form of Government becomes destructive of these ends, it is the Right of the People to alter or to abolish it, and to institute new Government, laying its foundation on such principles and organizing its powers in such form, as to them shall seem most likely to effect their Safety and Happiness. Prudence, indeed, will dictate that Governments long established should not be changed for light and transient causes; and accordingly all experience hath shown, that mankind are more disposed to suffer, while evils are sufferable, than to right themselves by abolishing the forms to which they are accustomed. But when a long train of abuses and usurpations pursuing invariably the same Object evinces a design to reduce them under absolute Despotism, it is their right, it is their duty, to throw off such government, and to provide new Guards for their future security. Such has been the patient sufferance of these Colonies; and such is now the necessity which constrains them to alter their former Systems of Government. The history of the present King of Great Britain* is a history of repeated injuries and usurpations, all having in direct object the establishment of absolute Tyranny over these States. To prove this, let Facts be submitted to a candid world.

He has refused his Assent to Laws, the most wholesome and necessary for the public good.

He has forbidden his Governors to pass Laws of immediate and pressing importance, unless suspended in their operation till his Assent should be obtained; and when so suspended, he has utterly neglected to attend to them.

He has refused to pass other Laws for the accommoda-

---

*George III, reigned 1760–1820.

tion of large districts of people, unless those people would relinquish the right of Representation in the Legislature, a right inestimable to them and formidable to tyrants only.

He has called together legislative bodies at places unusual, uncomfortable, and distant from the depository of their Public Records, for the sole purpose of fatiguing them into compliance with his measures.

He has dissolved Representative Houses repeatedly, for opposing with manly firmness his invasions on the rights of the people.

He has refused for a long time, after such dissolutions, to cause others to be elected; whereby the Legislative Powers, incapable of Annihilation, have returned to the People at large for their exercise; the State remaining in the mean time exposed to all the dangers of invasion from without, and convulsions within.

He has endeavoured to prevent the population of these States; for that purpose obstructing the Laws of Naturalization of Foreigners; refusing to pass others to encourage their migration hither, and raising the conditions of new Appropriations of Lands.

He has obstructed the Administration of Justice, by refusing his Assent to Laws for establishing Judiciary Powers.

He has made Judges dependent on his Will alone, for the tenure of their offices, and the amount and payment of their salaries.

He has erected a multitude of New Offices, and sent hither swarms of Officers to harass our People, and eat out their substance.

He has kept among us, in time of peace, Standing Armies without the Consent of our Legislature.

He has affected to render the Military independent of and superior to the Civil Power.

He has combined with others to subject us to jurisdictions foreign to our constitution, and unacknowledged by our laws; giving us Assent to their acts of pretended Legislation:

For quartering large bodies of armed troops among us:

For protecting them, by a mock Trial, from Punishment for any Murders which they should commit on the Inhabitants of these States:

For cutting off our Trade with all parts of the world:

For imposing Taxes on us without our Consent:

For depriving us in many cases, of the benefits of Trial by Jury:

For transporting us beyond Seas to be tried for pretended offenses:

For abolishing the free System of English Laws in a Neighbouring Province,* establishing therein an Arbitrary government, and enlarging its boundaries so as to render it at once an example and fit instrument for introducing the same absolute rule into these Colonies:

For taking away our Charters, abolishing our most valuable Laws, and altering fundamentally the Forms of our Governments:

For suspending our own Legislatures, and declaring themselves invested with Power to legislate for us in all cases whatsoever.

He has abdicated Government here, by declaring us out of his Protection and waging War against us.

He has plundered our seas, ravaged our Coasts, burnt our towns and destroyed the Lives of our people.

He is at this time transporting large Armies of foreign Mercenaries to complete the works of death, desolation and tyranny, already begun with circumstances of Cruelty & perfidy scarcely paralleled in the most barbarous ages, and totally unworthy the Head of a civilized nation.

He has constrained our fellow Citizens taken Captive on the high Seas to bear Arms against their Colony, to become the executioners of their friends and Brethren, or to fall themselves by their Hands.

He has excited domestic insurrections amongst us, and has endeavoured to bring on the inhabitants of our frontiers, the merciless Indian Savages, whose known rule of

*Quebec, in Canada.

warfare, is an undistinguished destruction of all ages, sexes and conditions.

In every stage of these Oppressions We have Petitioned for Redress in the most humble terms: Our repeated petitions have been answered only by repeated injury. A Prince, whose character is thus marked by every act which may define a Tyrant, is unfit to be the ruler of a free People.

Nor have We been wanting in attention to our British brethren. We have warned them from time to time of attempts by their legislature to extend an unwarrantable jurisdiction over us. We have reminded them of the circumstances of our emigration and settlement here. We have appealed to their native justice and magnanimity and we have conjured them by the ties of our common kindred to disavow these usurpations, which would inevitably interrupt our connections and correspondence. They too have been deaf to the voice of justice and of consanguinity. We must, therefore, acquiesce in the necessity, which denounces our Separation, and hold them, as we hold the rest of mankind, Enemies in War, in Peace Friends.

We, therefore, the Representatives of the United States of America, in General Congress, Assembled, appealing to the Supreme Judge of the world for the rectitude of our intentions, do, in the Name, and by Authority of the good People of these Colonies, solemnly publish and declare, That these United Colonies are, and of Right ought to be Free and Independent States; that they are Absolved from all Allegiance to the British Crown, and that all political connection between them and the State of Great Britain, is and ought to be totally dissolved; and that as Free and Independent States, they have full power to levy War, conclude Peace, contract Alliances, establish Commerce, and to do all other Acts and Things which Independent States may of right do. And for the support of this Declaration, with a firm reliance on the protection of Divine Providence, we mutually pledge to each other our lives, our Fortunes and our sacred Honor.

IDEAS

1. What does Jefferson mean by "all men are created equal"?

2. How do Jefferson's ideas of "the consent of the governed" operate in his argument?

3. Explain Jefferson's accusation in the paragraph beginning "He has dissolved Representative Houses" and in the paragraph that follows.

4. Where, and how effectively, does Jefferson face the opposition?

5. What parts of this Declaration, if any, do you feel would be changed were they created today instead of in the eighteenth century?

ORGANIZATION AND STYLE

1. The second paragraph contains a rather long list of truths, each introduced by a *that* clause. This paragraph is then followed by another list of facts, each written as a separate paragraph. What reasons can you see for the different methods of handling the two lists?

2. In the sentence "He has plundered our seas, ravaged our Coasts, burnt our towns and destroyed the Lives of our people," Jefferson arranges his parallel items in an increasing order of importance. What governing principle orders parallel elements in other sentences?

3. What language in the Declaration seems dated in the twentieth century? What substitutions would you make?

WRITING

1. Write an essay of three or four paragraphs using the following thesis: Judging from his Declaration, Jefferson's "pursuit of happiness" means _____.

2. Some people feel that the self-evident truths listed in the second paragraph are no longer valid. Select one such truth and develop an essay in which you argue that it is now flagrantly abused or disregarded.

3. Write a declaration of independence as Thomas Jefferson of Harlem, using Baldwin's essay for your bill of complaints and Jefferson's format for your statement. Follow Jefferson's scheme of phrasing as closely as you can, but in twentieth-century language.

The Responsive Men

NORMAN COUSINS

———————— ● ————————

Cousins writes about wholeness. His essay (an excerpt from his introduction to his book, In God We Trust [1958]*) is a definition of the "whole man," illustrated by Jefferson and his colleagues, and consequently explains their greatness. His opening paragraph narrows to his thesis, "They saw no walls separating science, philosophy, religion, and art." He then goes on to fill out his definition with brief summaries of how these men acted and thought, since examples have a certain "power to settle argument," describing first what "wholeness" is, then what it is not, then what it is in further detail.*

The young men who designed the government of the United States—many of them were in their thirties—were a talented and influential group of joiners. They were joiners not in the sense that they belonged to any band or group that presented itself. They were the kind of working joiners who, like the philosopher-statesmen of early Greece, sought perfection through an integrated wholeness. The young American giants knew how to put men and ideas together. They connected their spiritual beliefs to political action. They saw no walls separating science, philosophy, religion, and art.

The term "whole man" has become somewhat frayed in our times through endless argument over its essential meaning: exactly what is a "whole man"; what is he like; how did he become one? To the extent that example has the power to settle an argument, it may be rewarding to scrutinize the human display case of the Revolutionary period of our history. The youthful Founding Fathers were, many of them, dramatic examples of whole men. What was most remarkable about this was that they themselves saw nothing remarkable about it. They believed it entirely natural that a human being should seek and achieve the broadest possible personal development. Indeed, it was unnatural for a man to be shut off from anything inside him capable of growth. For man's natural rights were not limited to the political. His natural rights had something to do with his place in the world and the stretching power of his spirit and talent. The end of government, therefore, was to translate freedom into creative growth. The government that understood this was a wise one, for the whole men it helped to produce were best fitted to understand the difficult business of operating a complex society.

I must not make it seem that we are dealing here with men who were so preoccupied with grand designs and abstractions that they knew little about the enjoyment of living. Far from it. They had a zest for life. It grew out of the conviction that life must be lived at its fullest, whether for the individual or the society itself. An exciting life was more than high adventure or fancy diversions. It depended not at all on the standardized situations that were supposed to stimulate or satisfy. A truly exciting life was connected to high sensitivity. For awareness came with the gift of life. In order to mean anything, awareness had to be sharpened and put to work. It was not enough that awareness should enable the human being to respond to beauty. He had to respond to people. Thus, awareness meant compassion.

The letters the Founding Fathers wrote to each other reflected the rounded view of life and a sensitivity to the needs and potentialities of human beings. There is a concern here for the growing universe of knowledge and the possibilities of progress. But these letters also tell us a great deal about the kind of men who wrote them. They make it clear that these men helped to educate one another. They shared in an adventure of mutual growth, pooling their observations about life, their insights into behavior, and their convictions about government. . . .

It has often been asked how it was that within a short span of time on the east coast of the North American continent there should have sprung up such a rare array of genius—men who seemed in virtual command of historical experience and who combined moral imagination with a flair for leadership. Part of the answer, at least, is that these men knew how to invest their combined strength in a great idea. A young man like James Madison had urgent thoughts about what people had to do to become free and remain free; but he did not feel he had relieved himself of his obligation to serve those ideas when he set them down in the public prints. It was necessary for him to join his concerns to those of other men who were also in a position to exert leadership. Madison wanted to prove his ideas in direct contact with minds he respected.

Most of the men generally regarded as the Founding Fathers carried on a vast correspondence—much of it with one another—long after the Revolution was won and the United States of America had become an established government. They considered letter-writing an essential part of the intellectual diet of a rounded man. The exchange between Thomas Jefferson and John Adams, for example, knows few equals for depth, range of subject matter, literary style, and general intellectual achievement in recorded correspondence. Philosophy, religion, science, literature, economics, history, anthropology, music, politics—nothing in human experience or attainment was alien to them. And all the strands of their multiple interests were woven together into a single smooth texture. Adams and Jefferson were dealing with the nature of man and the needs of man. Any great area of human achievement was therefore a logical and important part of their total concern.

None of this is to minimize the importance of direct contact. In particular, George Washington and Benjamin

Franklin registered their main impact on their contemporaries through the force of their personalities rather than through any detailed exposition of their political ideas and philosophy. They had declared their allegiance to certain fundamental principles. Others might analyze and refine those principles and project them against the historical background, or become their inspired advocates before the public. Washington and Franklin were concerned with the larger design and the need to keep it intact. Washington's sense of timing was excellent. He permitted just enough play of debate to bring out the full color of an issue; but he generally stepped in when the momentum of argument threatened a costly showdown. Franklin, too, was the architect of consent, more interested in helping to create an atmosphere in which meaningful agreement was possible than in advancing fixed ideas of his own. Both Franklin and Washington maintained a substantial correspondence, but it never reached the volume or philosophical dimensions of the exchanges between Jefferson and Madison and Adams. In any case, all these men were part of the total process of mutual education that figured so largely in the intellectual achievements of the group as a whole.

IDEAS

1. What, exactly, is Cousins's definition of "wholeness"?

2. Explain the idea of perfection as Cousins describes it. How does it work for the individual? For the group? Which, among the men whom he mentions, would be higher and lower in his estimate?

3. From what you know about history, do you feel Cousins has made a fair assessment of the individuals he discusses?

4. How do present-day leaders or politicians measure up to what Cousins describes as "the intellectual achievements of the group as a whole"?

5. What is the thesis that you have made to summarize this essay? Compare it with those of your classmates. See if your class as a group can come up with a single thesis statement.

ORGANIZATION AND STYLE

1. The headnote to this essay suggests that Cousins organizes his ideas around what " 'wholeness' is, then what it is not, then what it is in further detail." Where do those divisions occur in the selection? How does Cousins introduce them?

2. The second sentence of the third paragraph is in fact a stylistic fragment, containing neither a subject nor a verb. Cousins uses it to balance, like a fulcrum, two rather long sentences. How effective is this technique?

3. In several sentences in the essay, Cousins separates certain material with dashes. What kind of material does he set off in this way?

WRITING

1. Using Cousins's concept of "wholeness," develop an essay with the following thesis sentence: Modern education does (or does not) aim to develop an "integrated wholeness."

2. Select a political action group with which you are familiar (perhaps your own student association, an antinuke or pro-abortion organization, a citizens' action committee). Evaluate the leaders of that group by comparing them against the standards of "wholeness" that Cousins sets forth.

Grenada and the End of Revolution

CHARLES KRAUTHAMMER

———————— ● ————————

Krauthammer's first paragraph is a beauty. His open-ing sentence engages us in his subject: revolution, in-congruously displayed on tiny Grenada. He then moves more explicitly to his view that this teapot revolution sprang from the universal tragicomedy of idealogues fighting over their agreed concepts. Then, having funneled down to its strongest position—a first paragraph's final sentence—he gives us his the-sis: "Revolution eats its children." As you read, see how his evidence supports his thesis.

Revolution is a large idea, and Grenada a small island. Of such incongruities comedy is made. In Grenada, of course, it turned out not to be all comedy. As the bloody fratricidal denouement showed, even comedy staged on small islands can end in tragedy when the actors are jealous ideologues. ("The most terrible fight is not when there is one opinion against another," says Kierkegaard. "The most terrible is when two men say the same thing—and fight about the interpretation.") And when they use live ammunition. We now have the memory of Maurice Bishop to remind us that even in parody the revolution eats its children.

That the Grenadian revolution was a parody is evident from its only remaining legacy, its documents. These have been largely ignored because they are not portentous enough. True, there are secret treaties with North Korea, Cuba, and the Soviet Union; close ties with East Germany and Libya; and the airport, whose military uses were amply demonstrated by the U.S. Army. But Grenada was not exactly an active threat to world peace. Geopolitically, its documents are as uninteresting as the island itself. But as historical artifacts, as the unselfconscious autobiography of a revolution, they are fascinating. Their interest lies principally in their texture, in the tone of high seriousness with which they render the story of what happened when revolution came to Grenada. They tell us something about what happened to Grenada, and much about what has happened to revolution.

First, and always, there is the problem of scale. The memos addressed to Yuri Andropov, then chief of the K.G.B., and Defense Minister Dimitri Ustinov are from "Hudson Austin, General of the Army." The Soviets did not take kindly to such strutting. When Soviet Chief of Staff Marshal Ogarkov was pressed by his Grenadian counterpart, Chief of Staff Major Einstein Louison (in Moscow for military training), for slightly more aid than the Soviets had agreed to in writing, the somewhat nervous Grenadian report of the meeting records that "Marshal Ogarkov replied rather jokingly that students should be concerned with their studies."

Then there was Cde. (Comrade) Ian Jacobs's one month, eight-city tour of the United States to raise American consciousness and American money. His report on the trip judges both goals to have been accomplished. Media coverage was good, and the fundraising a success. What exactly does that mean? Usually when third world officials come to the United States to raise money, they have in mind, say, a new air defense system or an ambitious industrial project. Jacobs came for a word processor. He didn't quite get it. He reports with satisfaction, "We should be able to raise between three to five thousand U.S. dollars—a figure that should allow us to purchase a word processor within the next three to six months." Inflated figures, it turns out. By his own account, though he shilled for the "word processor project" at every stop from Sacramento to Philadelphia, it was not until he got to Miami that he found a contributor willing to donate "between $1,000 and $2,000"—but only on the condition that it be laundered to get him a tax exemption. ("In this context," adds Jacobs, "I spoke to a contact at the American Friends Service Committee in Philadelphia and I intend to follow up with them so that he can send the money to them and then they will send it here.")

And it is not hard to see why historians won't linger long over the secret agreement between the Communist Party of Cuba and the ruling party of Grenada, the New Jewel Movement. The protocol begins with the invocation, "Brotherly united by the same ideals of struggle in their respective countries, as well as of active solidarity in favor of the peoples that struggle for national liberation, and likewise, sharing the same convictions against imperialism, colonialism, neocolonialism, Zionism and racism," etc., etc. Accordingly, Cuba agrees to send Grenada, among other things, "two technicians in billboards and posters," "two technicians in sound equipment for public meetings," a "specialist in the work of the religious people," and a press cartoonist. (In another document, Bishop urges that someone be sent to Cuba or Nicaragua to learn how to keep a phony set of books for the I.M.F.)

Armed with a chief of staff, a word processor, and a press cartoonist (no record about whether it found a crooked accountant), Grenada was ready to do battle with imperialism.

What the revolution lacked in scale, it made up for in volume. The American invasion force turned up tons of documents, boxes upon boxes of reports, minutes, diaries— a sort of gigantic *Reflections on the Revolution.* The report of a meeting of the Party's Central Committee in mid-September 1983 runs to more than twenty thousand words. It begins by calling to the attention of the Central Committee sixteen previous and available reports from "1. Minutes of the last emergency Central Committee [meeting]" to "16. Workers' Committee analysis of the Working Class for the Month of August." Things move quickly in a month.

Before his death Lenin said, "We have become a bureaucratic utopia." Grenada aspired to that—the number of meetings, reports, reports on meetings, and meetings on reports, is staggering—but, unfortunately, the bureaucratic revolution appears to have occurred very early in the literacy campaign. One example: Cde. Hazel-Ann (no last name given), in Moscow for ideological training, reports that one of her fellow Grenadian students is ill. "The doctor's report is that he has high pertension and is sick with his heart."

Back home high pertension was epidemic. Heart sickness followed. For there is poignancy in the idealism shown by ordinary people caught up in the enthusiasm of revolution, committed to its promise, utterly and sincerely devoted to making it work—whatever it is. Hazel-Ann, for example, had apparently heard of the party strife of mid-September 1983 that was ultimately to lead to the final massacre and collapse of the revolution. Her fourteen-page, painfully neat, handwritten report from Moscow detailing the progress she and the other Grenadian comrades in her cell had made ends thus:

> We take this opportunity to express our deep concern about the situation as analyzed by the C.C. [Central Committee]; and our confidence in the Party's leadership and our collective ability to avert the situation through hard, organised, systematic, self-critical Leninist-type work. The C.P.S.U. [Communist Party of the Soviet Union] International Leninist Party School N.J.M. [New Jewel Movement] Party Cell repledges our commitment to the Party; to building a strong Party on Marxist-Leninist principles and to the defence and building of the Revolution, along the lines that would bring us to achieving SOCIALISM. Long Live Our Party!

The several features of this citation characterize much of the party's internal communication: (1) an earnestness born of an intense will to believe; (2) an ambiguity bordering on confusion as to what exactly one is believing in; all expressed in (3) the most rigid Marxist-Leninist language, a jargon so jarring that it lends a touch of irony to

Grenada's boast to having been the first Marxist revolution in the English-speaking world. Interestingly, this Marxist-Leninist mumbo jumbo appears less in the Party's public discourse—after all, Bishop's speeches had to be understood by ordinary people—than in the private communications of the leadership. Unlike Orwell's cynical O'Brian, in Grenada the big brothers and sisters were not too worldly to believe what they made others believe.

At its crucial final meeting, the Central Committee recognizes that the country, the "material base" as Bishop puts it, is falling apart. Major Louison (Einstein, back from Moscow) observes that the roads are the worst he's ever seen, and the Central Committee falls into a fierce debate over defects in party structure and ideology that can account for this state of affairs. (With the island's productive energies being poured into meetings, reports, and note-taking, it isn't surprising that there was little left to devote to the material base. Louison did observe that "while we are losing links with the masses, the middle-class types have been coming to the revolution for jobs." That clue is quickly ignored.) The minutes are full of criticism and self-criticism of "right opportunism," "petit bourgeois deviationism," "economism." They all agree on the antidote, "firm Leninism," but they're stuck on exactly what that means. A comrade called on to explain his vote against a two-man leadership for the party replies that "He is not clear how the dialectics will unfold. He said that he has not seen it anywhere in the science." People who talk like that in the Kremlin surely are referred (to the K.G.B. perhaps) for psychiatric evaluation.

In Grenada they rise to the Central Committee. At its penultimate meeting of August 26, 1983, the consensus is that the party is in deep crisis and the revolution in danger of collapsing. Bishop speaks last. His summary remarks include the recommendation to "research the history of the Party during the last five or six years, minutes and conclusions will be useful to look at," "study the history of the Communist Party of the Soviet Union," and "reread *Standards of Party Life* by Pronin [sic]." At a 1981 rally Bishop had called on the masses to "Unionise! Mobilise! Educate! Democratise!" In the privacy of the Central Committee, his final advice is plagiarize.

In the end, plagiarism, jargon, and ideological study are not enough. Even Bishop admits that the mood of the "masses" is very low and the revolution falling apart; the consensus estimate is that it has no more than three to six months left. What could save it? What is missing? For that the Central Committee, by all accounts, had no answer. But the revolution did.

"General Rule: no social revolution without terror," said Napoleon. Bishop may have been grandiose, but he was not cruel. He may have been a dictator (hundreds, perhaps thousands, passed through his prisons), but he was not a terrorist.

> Bulletin From The Main Political Department, October 19, 1983. Revolutionary soldiers and men of the People's Revolutionary Armed Forces: Today our People's Revolutionary Army has gain [sic] victory over the right opportunist and reactionary forces which attacked the Headquarters of our Ministry of Defense. These anti-worker elements using the working people as a shield entered Fort Rupert. . . . [T]he counter-revolutionary elements, headed by Maurice Bishop . . . [and comprised of] only businessmen, nuns, nurses and lumpen elements. . . .

Bishop and many lumpen were killed in the final massacre. But even the last tragic act could not escape the revolution's parodic destiny. The final communiqué of the new junta concludes with a stirring invocation of the memory of those who had just died fighting against Bishop and for the newest revolution:

> Comrades, the death of OC Conrad Mayers, WO2 Raphael Mason, Sgt Dorset Peters, and L/Cpl Martin Simon have not gone in vain, but have further manured the struggle of our Grenadian people. Long live the Memory of our fallen comrades. Long live the Grenada Revolution. Forward Ever, Backward Never. Death to Imperialism.

The hero as fertilizer.
Then the curtain falls.

I started by suggesting that revolution is a large idea. Perhaps one should say *was* a large idea. Decades of trying to shoehorn it into the Grenadas of this world has diminished it greatly. It still has legitimacy: the first act of any gang of thugs that can seize a radio station and an airport is to proclaim itself a revolutionary junta, usually of national salvation. But it is precisely because every gang of thugs, or posturers, or dreamers, claims its honor that it has become so debased. Like other newly internationalized Western concepts ("rights" as defined by the U.N., for example), it has been emptied of meaning. And empty of meaning it acquires power.

Michael X, the Trinidadian hanged in his native country for (simple) murder after a career in London as a salon revolutionist, declared that "the only politics I ever understood is the politics of revolution." To which V. S. Naipaul, also a Trinidadian, answers, "London words, London abstractions, capable of supporting any meaning . . . [he] chose to give them." Maurice Bishop, who like Michael X had been through both London and the West Indian Black Power Movement of the early 1970s, was adept at the political use of empty abstractions. In 1981 he gave a speech on "freedom of the press" to explain why he shut down the last remaining independent newspaper in Grenada: "[The] most important reason of all: This is revolution, we live in revolutionary Grenada, this is a revolutionary condition, and there is a revolutionary legality, and they will have to abide by the law of the revolution. When the revolution speaks, it must be heard, listened to. Whatever the revolution decrees, it must be obeyed; when the revolution commands, it must be carried out; when the revolution talks, no parasite must bark in their corner."

Any word that grants automatic legitimacy and at the same time is capable of supporting any meaning becomes a source of great power. The circle is vicious: as "revolution" becomes more ubiquitous, it becomes more empty of meaning, more powerful a tool, and thus more attractive to the next gang of thugs, posturers, and dreamers, who further empty it of meaning.

The idea of revolution is debased first by its ubiquity. There is, though, an exception, which paradoxically makes the situation worse. Revolution is not a serious idea everywhere. In the Eastern bloc it evokes only cynicism; in the West, where it is considered a safe form of play for the young, nostalgia. (Or else it is used trivially to denote any change of habits: it seems we are now in the midst of a telephone revolution.) People who want to believe in revolution have now to believe in third world revolution. The idea of revolution has devolved of necessity upon that part of the world to which it is least suited. For what, in a post-colonial world, with the wars of independence won, can revolution mean? Almost invariably—from Tanzania to Cambodia to Grenada—it is said to mean socialism. That makes for problems of scale, or to state it more broadly, of culture and development, as the Grenada documents show. After all, what can socialism mean in a place where there is no working class? What can working class mean where there is no industry? To speak of revolution in such circumstances is either an act of deception or a form of false consciousness.

But there is a deeper, older reason for the fallen state of the revolutionary idea. It is not cultural, but ideological; not a function of revolution's current entrapment in the developing world, but a function of its entrapment in nineteenth-century Marxism. For it was not just London-talk that Maurice Bishop spoke, but Marx-talk; not just an alien idea he brought to his island, but a socialist one—and of a particular kind: "scientific" socialism. (Remember the baffled Grenadian central committee member: "I have not seen it in the science"?) By "scientific" Marx intended to distinguish his historicist socialism from the "utopian" variety, on which he could not heap enough ridicule. The folly of the utopian socialists, like Proudhon, was to betray an interest in what post-revolutionary society would look like. Marx denounced as infantile the idea of detailing the society of the future. The working class has "no ideals to realize," he said, "but to set free the elements of the new society with which old collapsing bourgeois society itself is pregnant." The purpose of revolution is to allow "the solution to the riddle of history" (communism) to unfold; to guess at the answer in advance is to misunderstand the entire revolutionary process.

"In Marx you will find no trace of utopianism in the sense of inventing the 'new' society and constructing it out of fantasies," said Lenin. The end of Marxist revolution—i.e., what socialism is to be—is explicitly, inherently, purposely left open and undefined. In a word, empty. As Melvin Lasky points out, this indeterminateness of the revolutionary idea, this sundering of utopia from revolution, of ends from means is the great legacy of Marx's overthrow a century ago of the utopian socialists.

Since the preferred form even of national revolutions today is Marxist, the modern revolutionary idea necessarily is capable of supporting any meaning. (It is no accident that the only authentically transforming revolution of our time was the Iranian revolution, a decidedly non-, indeed, anti-Marxist affair.) The triumph of anti-utopian revolutionism has bequeathed to us a generation of revolutionaries with no idea of the kind of society they wish to construct (again, the Ayatollah knows precisely what he wants the world to look like—Qum) and, most importantly, with no hesitation about pursuing revolution in the absence of such an idea. A century ago an Irish Chartist leader denounced such negative revolutionaries as "mere speculators in anarchy." Today they are not only a majority at the U.N., they are custodians of the revolutionary idea itself.

"What socialism will look like when it takes on its final forms we do not know and cannot say," said Lenin. Little wonder that neither could the Central Committeemen in Grenada, so desperate to build socialism, so bereft of any idea what that meant. They not only suffered from the problem of the size of their island; they suffered from the nihilism of their guiding ideology. It is a cardinal feature of this age—indeed it is what makes this the age of revolution—that they should have decided to carry on regardless. The result is instructive.

IDEAS

1. How much of the meaning of this essay is embedded in the very first sentence: "Revolution is a large idea, and Grenada is a small island"?

2. What, exactly, is a parody? What elements of a parody does Krauthammer find in the Grenada revolution?

3. Do you agree with Napoleon's statement that there can be no "social revolution without terror"? What does this suggest for the future social and political climate of this country? If you think Napoleon's statement false, how might future social revolutions be brought about?

4. Near the end of his essay, Krauthammer suggests that the idea of revolutions is a form of "entrapment in nineteenth-century Marxism" and that it may not fit into the social movements of the twentieth century. Does this seem a valid argument against revolutions or, perhaps, an argument for maintaining the status quo?

5. How does Krauthammer support his thesis with ideas from Marxist speakers and writers?

ORGANIZATION AND STYLE

1. What is the stylistic effect of the fragment—"And when they use live ammunition"—in the first paragraph?

2. Krauthammer ends his ninth paragraph with an excerpt from Hazel-Ann's report followed by his three-point analysis. What evidence in the report supports Krauthammer's analysis.

3. What shift in focus does the essay take with the paragraph beginning "I started by suggesting. . . ."?

4. How effective is Krauthammer's final, four-word sentence? How is the Grenadian result instructive?

WRITING

1. Use the quotation from Kierkegaard (first paragraph) as a springboard to discuss how politicians, students, or any two people of your acquaintance say the same thing but argue about the interpretation. You might wish to work some of Krauthammer's ideas about parody into your analysis.

2. Krauthammer writes, "Any word that grants automatic legitimacy and at the same time is capable of supporting any meaning becomes a source of great power." Select a word or phrase currently favored by politicians that fits this description. Analyze what you think gives the word or phrase legitimacy and how you feel it develops power; finally, evaluate the potential danger of that power to society as a whole.

The Answer to a Perplexing Question

MARTIN LUTHER KING, JR.

———————— ● ————————

*From the beginning of time, writers have pondered
the problem of evil. After carefully explaining why
human beings acting alone cannot cast evil out of the
world and after examining the blind expectation
that God should eliminate all evil, King devotes the
last of his essay to explaining his answer: an alliance
between God and humankind. By asking questions
and then answering them, a trademark of black sermon rhetoric, King moves steadily through the complexities of his problem.*

Human life through the centuries has been characterized
by man's persistent efforts to remove evil from the earth.
Seldom has man thoroughly adjusted himself to evil, for
in spite of his rationalizations, compromises, and alibis,
he knows the "is" is not the "ought" and the actual is not
the possible. Though the evils of sensuality, selfishness,
and cruelty often rise aggressively in his soul, something
within him tells him that they are intruders and reminds
him of his higher destiny and more noble allegiance.
Man's hankering after the demonic is always disturbed by
his longing for the divine. As he seeks to adjust to the
demands of time, he knows that eternity is his ultimate
habitat. When man comes to himself, he knows that evil
is a foreign invader that must be driven from the native
soils of his soul before he can achieve moral and spiritual
dignity. . . .

How can evil be cast out? Men have usually pursued two
paths to eliminate evil and thereby save the world. The

first calls upon man to remove evil through his own power and ingenuity in the strange conviction that by thinking, inventing, he will at last conquer the nagging forces of evil. Give people a fair chance and a decent education, and they will save themselves. This idea, sweeping across the modern world like a plague, has ushered God out and escorted man in, and has substituted human ingenuity for divine guidance. Some people suggest that this concept was introduced during the Renaissance when reason dethroned religion, or later when Darwin's *Origin of Species* replaced belief in creation by the theory of evolution, or when the industrial revolution turned the hearts of men to material comforts and physical conveniences. At any rate, the idea of adequacy of man to solve the evils of history captured the minds of people, giving rise to the easy optimism of the nineteenth century, the doctrine of inevitable progress, Rousseau's maxim of "the original goodness of human nature," and Condorcet's conviction that by reason alone the whole world would soon be cleansed of crime, poverty, and war.

Armed with this growing faith in the capability of reason and science, modern man set out to change the world. He turned his attention from God and the human soul to the outer world and its possibilities. He observed, analyzed, and explored. The laboratory became man's sanctuary and scientists his priests and prophets. A modern humanist confidently affirmed:

> The future is not with the churches but with the laboratories, not with prophets but with scientists, not with piety but with efficiency. Man is at last becoming aware that he alone is responsible for the realization of the world of his dreams, that he has within himself the power for its achievement.

Man has subpoenaed nature to appear before the judgment seat of scientific investigation. None doubt that man's work in the scientific laboratories has brought unbelievable advances in power and comfort, producing machines that think and gadgets that soar majestically through the skies, stand impressively on the land and move with stately dignity on the seas.

But in spite of these astounding new scientific developments, the old evils continue and the age of reason has been transformed into an age of terror. Selfishness and hatred have not vanished with an enlargement of our educational system and an extension of our legislative policies. A once optimistic generation now asks in utter bewilderment, "Why could not we cast it out?"

The answer is rather simple: Man by his own power can never cast evil from the world. The humanist's hope is an illusion, based on too great an optimism concerning the inherent goodness of human nature.

I would be the last to condemn the thousands of sincere and dedicated people outside the churches who have labored unselfishly through various humanitarian movements to cure the world of social evils, for I would rather a man be a committed humanist than an uncommitted Christian. But so many of these dedicated persons, seeking salvation within the human context, have become understandably pessimistic and disillusioned, because their efforts are based on a kind of self-delusion which ignores fundamental facts about our mortal nature.

Nor would I minimize the importance of science and the great contributions which have come in the wake of the Renaissance. These have lifted us from the stagnating valleys of superstition and half-truths to the sunlit mountains of creative analysis and objective appraisal. The unquestioned authority of the church in scientific matters needed to be freed from paralyzing obscurantism, antiquated notions, and shameful inquisitions. But the exalted Renaissance optimism, while attempting to free the mind of man, forgot about man's capacity for sin.

The second idea for removing evil from the world stipulates that if man waits submissively upon the Lord, in his own good time God alone will redeem the world. Rooted in a pessimistic doctrine of human nature, the idea, which eliminates completely the capability of sinful man to do anything, was prominent in the Reformation, that great spiritual movement which gave birth to the protestant concern for moral and spiritual freedom and served as a necessary corrective for a corrupt and stagnant medieval church. The doctrines of justification by faith and the priesthood of all believers are towering principles which we as Protestants must forever affirm, but the Reformation doctrine of human nature overstressed the corruption of man. The Renaissance was too optimistic, and the Reformation too pessimistic. The former so concentrated on the goodness of man that it overlooked his capacity for goodness. While rightly affirming the sinfulness of human nature and man's incapacity to save himself, the Reformation wrongly affirmed that the image of God has been completely erased from man.

This led to the Calvinistic concept of the total depravity of man and to a resurrection of the terrible idea of infant damnation. So depraved is human nature, said the doctrinaire Calvinist, that if a baby dies without baptism he will burn forever in hell. Certainly this carries the idea of man's sinfulness too far.

This lopsided Reformation theology has often emphasized a purely other-worldly religion, which stresses the utter hopelessness of this world and calls upon the individual to concentrate on preparing his soul for the world to come. By ignoring the need for social reform, religion is divorced from the mainstream of human life. A pulpit committee listed as the first essential qualification for a new minister: "He must preach the true gospel and not talk about social issues." This is a blueprint for a dangerously irrelevant church where people assemble to hear only pious platitudes.

By disregarding the fact that the gospel deals with man's body as well as with his soul, such a one-sided emphasis creates a tragic dichotomy between the sacred and the secular. To be worthy of its New Testament origin, the church must seek to transform both individual lives and the social situation that brings to many people anguish of spirit and cruel bondage.

The idea that man expects God to do everything leads inevitably to a callous misuse of prayer. For if God does everything, man then asks for anything, and God becomes little more than a "cosmic bellhop" who is summoned for every trivial need. Or God is considered so omnipotent and man so powerless that prayer is a substitute for work and intelligence. A man said to me, "I believe in integration, but I know it will not come until God wants it to come. You Negroes should stop protesting and start praying." I am certain we need to pray for God's help and guidance in this integration struggle, but we are gravely misled if we think the struggle will be won only with prayer. God, who gave us minds for thinking and bodies for working, would defeat his own purpose if he permitted us to obtain through prayer what may come through work and intelligence. Prayer is a marvelous and necessary supplement of our feeble efforts, but it is a dangerous substitute. When Moses strove to lead the Israelites to the Promised Land, God made it clear that he would not do for them what they could do for themselves. "And the Lord said unto Moses, Wherefore criest thou unto me? speak unto the children of Israel, that they go forward."

We must pray earnestly for peace, but we must also work vigorously for disarmament and the suspension of weapon testing. We must use our minds as rigorously to plan for peace as we have used them to plan for war. We must pray with unceasing passion for racial justice, but we must also use our minds to develop a program, organize ourselves into mass nonviolent action, and employ every resource of our bodies and souls to bring into being those social changes that make for a better distribution of wealth within our nation and in the underdeveloped countries of the world.

Does not all of this reveal the fallacy of thinking that God will cast evil from the earth, even if man does nothing except sit complacently by the wayside? No prodigious thunderbolt from heaven will blast away evil. No mighty army of angels will descend to force men to do what their wills resist. The Bible portrays God, not as an omnipotent czar who makes all decisions for his subjects nor as a cosmic tyrant who with gestapolike methods invades the inner lives of men, but rather as a loving Father who gives to his children such abundant blessings as they may be willing to receive. Always man must do something. "Stand upon thy feet," says God to Ezekiel, "and I will speak unto you." Man is no helpless invalid left in a valley of total depravity until God pulls him out. Man is rather an upstanding human being whose vision has been impaired by the cataracts of sin and whose soul has been weakened by the virus of pride, but there is sufficient vision left for him to turn his weak and sin-battered life toward the Great Physician, the curer of the ravages of sin.

The real weakness of the idea that God will do everything is its false conception of both God and man. It makes God so absolutely sovereign that man is absolutely helpless. It makes man so absolutely depraved that he can do nothing but wait on God. It sees the world as so contaminated with sin that God totally transcends it and touches it only here and there through a mighty invasion. This view ends up with a God who is a despot and not a Father. It ends up with such a pessimism concerning human nature that it leaves man little more than a helpless worm crawling through the morass of an evil world. But man is neither totally depraved, nor is God an almighty dictator. We must surely affirm the majesty and sovereignty of God, but this should not lead us to believe that God is an Almighty Monarch who will impose his will upon us and deprive us of the freedom to choose what is good or what is not good. He will not thrust himself upon us nor force us to stay home when our minds are bent on journeying to some far country. But he follows us in love, and when we come to ourselves and turn our tired feet back to the Father's house, he stands waiting with outstretched arms of forgiveness.

Therefore we must never feel that God will, through some breathtaking miracle or a wave of the hand, cast evil out of the world. As long as we believe this we will pray unanswerable prayers and ask God to do things that he will never do. The belief that God will do everything for man is as untenable as the belief that man can do everything for himself. It, too, is based on a lack of faith. We must learn that to expect God to do everything while we do nothing is not faith, but superstition.

What, then, is the answer to life's perplexing question: "How can evil be cast out of our individual and collective lives?" If the world is not to be purified by God alone nor by man alone, who will do it?

The answer is found in an idea which is distinctly different from the two we have discussed, for neither God nor man will individually bring the world's salvation. Rather, *both* man and God, made one in a marvelous unity of purpose through an overflowing love as the free gift of himself on the part of God and by perfect obedience and receptivity on the part of man, can transform the old into the new and drive out the deadly cancer of sin.

The principle which opens the door for God to work through man is faith. This is what the disciples lacked when they desperately tried to remove the nagging evil from the body of the sick child. Jesus reminded them that they had been attempting to do themselves what could be done only when their lives were open receptacles, as it were, into which God's strength could be freely poured.

Two types of faith in God are clearly set forth in the Scriptures. One may be called the mind's faith, wherein the intellect assents to a belief that God exists. The other may be referred to as the heart's faith, whereby the whole man is involved in a trusting act of self-surrender. To know God, a man must possess this latter type of faith, for the mind's faith is directed toward a theory, but the heart's faith is centered in a Person. Gabriel Marcel claims that faith is *believing in, not believing that.* It is "opening a credit; which puts me at the disposal of the one in whom I believe." When I believe, he says "I rally to with that sort of interior gathering of oneself which the act of rallying implies." Faith is the opening of all sides and at every level of one's life to the divine inflow.

This is what the Apostle Paul emphasized in his doctrine of salvation by faith. For him, faith is man's capacity to accept God's willingness through Christ to rescue us from the bondage of sin. In his magnanimous love, God freely offers to do for us what we cannot do for ourselves. Our humble and openhearted acceptance is faith. So by faith we are saved. Man filled with God and God operating through man bring unbelievable changes in our individual and social lives.

Social evils have trapped multitudes of men in a dark and murky corridor where there is no exit sign and plunged others into a dark abyss of psychological fatalism. These deadly, paralyzing evils can be removed by a humanity perfectly united through obedience with God. Moral victory will come as God fills man and man opens his life by faith to God, even as the gulf opens to the overflowing waters of the river. Racial justice, a genuine possibility in our nation and in the world, will come neither by our frail and often misguided efforts nor by God imposing his will on wayward men, but when enough people open their lives to God and allow him to pour his triumphant, divine energy into their souls. Our age-old and noble dream of a world of peace may yet become a reality, but it will come neither by man working alone nor by God destroying the wicked schemes of men, but when men so open their lives to God that he may fill them with love, mutual respect, understanding, and goodwill. Social salvation will come only through man's willing acceptance of God's mighty gift.

Let me apply what I have been saying to our personal lives. Many of you know what it means to struggle with sin. Year by year you were aware that a terrible sin—slavery to drink, perhaps, or untruthfulness, impurity, selfishness—was taking possession of your life. As the years unfolded and the vice widened its landmarks on your soul, you knew that it was an unnatural intruder. You may have thought, "One day I shall drive this evil out. I know it is destroying my character and embarrassing my family." At last you determined to purge yourself of the evil by making a New Year's resolution. Do you remember your surprise and disappointment when you discovered, three hundred and sixty-five days later, that your most sincere efforts had not banished the old habit from your life? In complete amazement you asked, "Why could not I cast it out?"

In despair you decided to take your problem to God, but instead of asking him to work through you, you said, "God, you must solve this problem for me. I can't do anything about it." But days and months later the evil was still with you. God would not cast it out, for he never removes sin without the cordial co-operation of the sinner. No problem is solved when we idly wait for God to undertake full responsibility.

One cannot remove an evil habit by mere resolution nor by simply calling on God to do the job, but only as he surrenders himself and becomes an instrument of God. We shall be delivered from the accumulated weight of evil only when we permit the energy of God to come into our souls.

IDEAS

1. What do you think would be King's definition of *religion*? Of *evil*?

2. King writes, "Men have usually pursued two paths to eliminate evil and thereby save the world." What are those two paths? Does this division seem valid to you, or can you think of other strategies for eliminating evil not discussed by King?

3. King attacks Calvinistic thinking, especially the concept of predestination. How, then, does he get back to the idea that there is still a God who does exercise control over the universe?

4. What does King mean when he suggests "the mind's faith is directed toward a theory, but the heart's faith is centered in a Person." Do you agree or disagree?

5. How can one be certain that what he or she identifies as a social evil is really that and not simply a product of ego or selfishness?

6. This essay was first published in a book entitled *Strength in Love.* Does this title suggest anything important to King's meaning in the essay?

ORGANIZATION AND STYLE

1. King, himself a minister, uses a large number of biblical allusions. For instance, in paragraph three he speaks about appearing "before the judgment seat of scientific investigation." What other biblical references can you find? How do they help reinforce King's ideas?

2. Other than the biblical allusions, what elements of the essay make it sound somewhat like a sermon? Look specifically at the organization of the entire essay, the language used, and the manner in which King addresses or recognizes his audience.

3. King frequently asks a question and immediately answers it. How does this technique contribute to his style? How does he sometimes use it to provide transition from one idea to another?

4. The essay takes a decided change in direction about two-thirds of the way through, beginning with the paragraph "What, then, is the answer to life's perplexing question . . .?" What is the purpose of this final section of the essay? Why does it appear at this location in King's development?

5. Throughout most of the essay, King writes in the third person. The final three paragraphs, however, shift to both the first person and the second person. Why? What, especially, is the effect of using *we* twice in the last sentence?

WRITING

1. Do you think the church of today should concern itself with social evils, or should it primarily attend to pre-

paring people for life after death? Develop an essay arguing your position. Try to follow King's organizational format. Present the opposing views first and show what is wrong with them; then present and defend your own position.

2. Write your own "answer to a perplexing question," especially if you do not believe in a god, or if you believe in a god but do not think that god at all responsible for evil in the universe. Just why is there evil and what, if anything, is the solution?

2

---●---

STRUCTURE: FRONTING
THE OPPOSITION

---●---

You have already considered structure by considering where, and how well, an essayist places his or her thesis. You probably will have sensed the basic three-part structure of all temporal things—beginning, middle, end—in an essay, a story, a concerto, or a human life. You will have noticed Baldwin's and Cousins's firm beginning paragraphs, and Jefferson's and King's resounding end paragraphs. Now we need to consider the middle, and a basic tactical point: fronting the opposition.

As you have probably also noticed, argumentation depends on and assumes an opposition. As we assert something about Harlem, natural rights, duty, or even old age, we instinctively assume that someone will assert the opposite. Indeed, we cannot think without these contrasts. We cannot think of an uptown without a downtown, of tyranny without freedom, of wholeness without fragmentation. Every assertion arouses its opposite, every *for* its *against,* every *pro* its *contra.* Indeed, our word *conversation* literally means a turning back and forth, just as *reply* means "bending back again." This is the way we discuss. This is how our minds work, turning questions and answers pro and con until we find something to stand on.

This pattern is called *dialectics* ("two-telling"), as we assert our argumentative pro and test it against the cons. As you have seen, Jefferson concedes that people will endure evils rather than risk change, that rebelling is unjustified until all pleas have failed. Baldwin concedes that whites have their slums, that some blacks are successful and contented, that the South has some virtues over the North. Krauthammer establishes the magnitude of a revolution and then balances that concept against the smallness of the Grenada invasion. King best illustrates the classic tactic: facing the opposition immediately after setting one's thesis, getting the opposition out of the way: "Men have usually pursued two paths to eliminate evil. . . ."

The following selections illustrate the dialectic process, and will also give you something to discuss, pro and con. Mead admits that certain types of anxiety or worry can be negative, but she then moves on to define her view of anxiety in a very limited way, a definition that lets her argue that anxiety can, indeed, be positive. Bond presents accepted concepts about the role of a college education; then he shows how those concepts do not work for many black students. Willie presents arguments for integrated colleges from both blacks and whites, but he counters each of these with opposing arguments of his own. Stace examines the existential view of the world by countering arguments made by the various opposition voices.

One Vote for This Age of Anxiety

MARGARET MEAD

————————●————————

Anthropologist Mead argues that some anxiety can be good; that it, indeed, is what "binds men to life with an intense concern." Her thesis, however, depends upon the careful definition of anxiety she works out as the essay moves along. Her dialectic pattern for fronting the opposition begins with her first sentence. She never forgets that opposition, continuing, even in the last paragraph, to refute some of its positions.

When critics wish to repudiate the world in which we live today, one of their familiar ways of doing it is to castigate modern man because anxiety is his chief problem. This, they say, in W. H. Auden's phrase, is the age of anxiety. This is what we have arrived at with all our vaunted progress, our great technological advances, our great wealth—everyone goes about with a burden of anxiety so enormous that, in the end, our stomachs and our arteries and our skins express the tension under which we live. Americans who have lived in Europe come back to comment on our favorite farewell which, instead of the old goodbye (God be with you), is now "Take it easy," each American admonishing the other not to break down from the tension and strain of modern life.

Whenever an age is characterized by a phrase, it is presumably in contrast to other ages. If we are the age of anxiety, what were other ages? And here the critics and carpers do a very amusing thing. First, they give us lists of the opposites of anxiety: security, trust, self-confidence, self-direction. Then, without much further discussion, they let us assume that other ages, other periods of history, were somehow the ages of trust or confident direction.

The savage who, on his South Sea island, simply sat and let breadfruit fall into his lap, the simple peasant, at one with the fields he ploughed and the beasts he tended, the craftsman busy with his tools and lost in the fulfillment of the instinct of workmanship—these are the counter-images conjured up by descriptions of the strain under which men live today. But no one who lived in those days has returned to testify how paradisiacal they really were.

Certainly if we observe and question the savages or simple peasants in the world today, we find something quite different. The untouched savage in the middle of New Guinea isn't anxious; he is seriously and continually *frightened*—of black magic, of enemies with spears who may kill him or his wives and children at any moment, while they stoop to drink from a spring, or climb a palm tree for a coconut. He goes warily, day and night, taut and fearful.

As for the peasant populations of a great part of the world, they aren't so much anxious as hungry. They aren't anxious about whether they will get a salary raise, or which of the three colleges of their choice they will be admitted to, or whether to buy a Ford or Cadillac, or whether the kind of TV set they want is too expensive. They are hungry, cold and, in many parts of the world, they dread that local warfare, bandits, political coups may endanger their homes, their meager livelihoods, and their lives. But surely they are not anxious.

For anxiety, as we have come to use it to describe our characteristic state of mind, can be contrasted with the active fear of hunger, loss, violence, and death. Anxiety is the appropriate emotion when the immediate personal terror—of a volcano, an arrow, the sorcerer's spell, a stab in the back and other calamities, all directed against one's self—disappears.

This is not to say that there isn't plenty to worry about in our world of today. The explosion of a bomb in the streets of a city whose name no one had ever heard before may set in motion forces which end up by ruining one's carefully planned education in law school, half a world away. But there is still not the personal, immediate, active sense of impending disaster that the savage knows. There is rather the vague anxiety, the sense that the future is unmanageable.

The kind of world that produces anxiety is actually a world of relative safety, a world in which no one feels that he himself is facing sudden death. Possibly sudden death may strike a certain number of unidentified other people— but not him. The anxiety exists as an uneasy state of mind, in which one has a feeling that something unspecified and undeterminable may go wrong. If the world seems to be going well, this produces anxiety—for good times may end. If the world is going badly—it may get worse. Anxiety tends to be without focus; the anxious person doesn't know whether to blame himself or other people. He isn't sure whether it is the current year or the Administration or a change in climate or the atom bomb that is to blame for this undefined sense of unease.

It is clear that we have developed a society which depends on having the *right* amount of anxiety to make it work. Psychiatrists have been heard to say, "He didn't have enough anxiety to get well," indicating that, while we agree that too much anxiety is inimical to mental health, we have come to rely on anxiety to push and prod us into seeing a doctor about a symptom which may indicate cancer, into checking up on that old life-insurance policy which may have out-of-date clauses in it, into having a conference with Billy's teacher even though his report card looks all right.

People who are anxious enough keep their car insurance up, have the brakes checked, don't take a second drink when they have to drive, are careful where they go and with whom they drive on holidays. People who are too anxious either refuse to go into cars at all—and so complicate the ordinary course of life—or drive so tensely and overcautiously that they help cause accidents. People who aren't anxious enough take chance after chance, which increases the terrible death toll of the roads.

On balance, our age of anxiety represents a large advance over savage and peasant cultures. Out of a productive system of technology drawing upon enormous resources, we have created a nation in which anxiety has replaced terror and despair, for all except the severely disturbed. The specter of hunger means something only to those Americans who can identify themselves with the millions of hungry people on other continents. The specter of terror may still be roused in some by a knock at the door in a few parts of the South, or in those who have just escaped from a totalitarian regime or who have kin still behind the Curtains.

But in this twilight world which is neither at peace nor at war, and where there is insurance against certain immediate, downright, personal disasters, for most Americans there remains only anxiety over what may happen, might happen, could happen.

This is the world out of which grows the hope, for the first time in history, of a society where there will be freedom from want and freedom from fear. Our very anxiety is born of our knowledge of what is now possible for each and for all. The number of people who consult psychiatrists today is not, as is sometimes felt, a symptom of increasing mental ill health, but rather the precursor of a world in which the hope of genuine mental health will be open to everyone, a world in which no individual feels that he need be hopelessly broken-hearted, a failure, a menace to others or a traitor to himself.

But if, then, our anxieties are actually signs of hope, why is there such a voice of discontent abroad in the land? I think this comes perhaps because our anxiety exists without an accompanying recognition of the tragedy which will always be inherent in human life, however well we build our world. We may banish hunger, and fear of sorcery, violence, or secret police; we may bring up children who have learned to trust life and who have the spontaneity and curiosity necessary to devise ways of making trips to the moon; we cannot—as we have tried to do—banish death itself.

Americans who stem from generations which left their

old people behind and never closed their parents' eyelids in death, and who have experienced the additional distance from death provided by two world wars fought far from our shores are today pushing away from them both a recognition of death and a recognition of the tremendous significance—for the future—of the way we live our lives. Acceptance of the inevitability of death, which, when faced, can give dignity to life, and acceptance of our inescapable role in the modern world, might transmute our anxiety about making the right choices, taking the right precautions, and the right risks into the sterner stuff of responsibility, which ennobles the whole face rather than furrowing the forehead with the little anxious wrinkles of worry.

Worry in an empty context means that men die daily little deaths. But good anxiety—not about the things that were left undone long ago, but which return to haunt and harry men's minds, but active, vivid anxiety about what must be done and that quickly—binds men to life with an intense concern.

This is still a world in which too many of the wrong things happen somewhere. But this is a world in which we now have the means to make a great many more of the right things happen everywhere. For Americans, the generalization which a Swedish social scientist made about our attitudes on race relations is true in many other fields: anticipated change which we feel is right and necessary but difficult makes us unduly anxious and apprehensive, but such change, once consummated, brings a glow of relief. We are still a people who—in the literal sense—believe in making good.

IDEAS

1. How does Mead carefully define *anxiety* so that it is not confused with other similar terms? What, for instance, is the difference between being anxious and being frightened?

2. How can a bomb in an unknown city half a world away ruin "one's carefully planned education in law school"?

3. What is her purpose in shifting to an illustration about driving? How does this example relate to her thesis?

4. Mead seems to suggest that anxiety can exist only in a world where there is the possibility for good. Do you agree with this idea?

5. Mead once said that American society misses something by not having its young people grow up with its old people. She argued that there were valuable lessons to be learned by the young if their aging grandparents lived in the home with them rather than in a nursing home. How does this idea relate to what she is saying about "good anxiety" in this essay?

6. How can one distinguish real fear from good anxiety? What, for instance, is the difference between being afraid to walk the city streets at night and being anxious about that walk? Does Mead offer any suggestions, or is this something we must decide for ourselves?

ORGANIZATION AND STYLE

1. What is the specific function of paragraphs two, three, four, and five? How do they help the author develop her ideas?

2. Mead confronts opposing ideas in the paragraph beginning "This is not to say that there isn't plenty to worry about in our world today." In what other paragraphs does she acknowledge opposing views? What transition word does she often use in these instances?

3. To what extent is the next-to-last paragraph a miniature of the entire essay? Is this an effective technique?

4. Mead's essay is a general statement of philosophy. Are there any parts of it that you feel could have been improved by specific examples? Why do you suppose Mead did not include more examples?

WRITING

1. Write a rebuttal to Mead's ideas, suggesting that anxiety is not good and that happy people are people without anxieties. Design your essay as a dialectical swinger, an essay pro and con. Pick up brief quotations or ideas from Mead's essay and counter them with your own ideas and evidence.

   If you can meet the opposition in one swing, do so in your second paragraph as you begin your "middle," immediately after setting your thesis, on the following pattern:

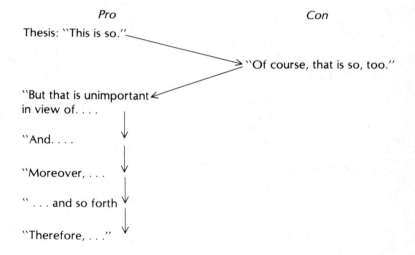

Pro   Con

Thesis: "This is so."

"Of course, that is so, too."

"But that is unimportant in view of. . . ."

"And. . . ."

"Moreover, . . .

" . . . and so forth

"Therefore, . . ."

Your con, your *"Of course,* the opposition," which is the subordinate part of your argument, reflects exactly its subordinate position in your thesis—in your thoughts: "Although Mead would say. . . ." "Of course, Mead would say. . . ."

If your argument demands more swinging from pro to con, do not hesitate to swing more than once. Suppose you were writing about your own attitudes toward funerals. You might write a thesis asserting: "Funerals are inappropriate remnants from barbaric times." You then admit your first con: "Of course, some people still need the comfort of the ritual." You then swing back to your pro side with "But these needs can be met without public display and embarrassing pomp." You then find another con: "I admit that anyone's life deserves some acknowledgment, some tribute in conclusion." Then go back to your pro side: "But let us eliminate all empty show." Such a complex or multiple pro-con would follow a structure something like this:

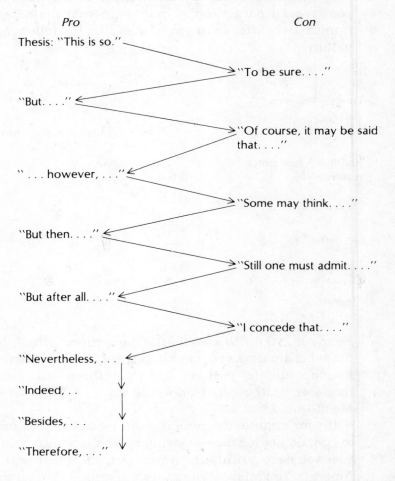

2. Write a dialectical essay in which you take a decided position on some controversial topic that interests you.

Think through your ideas carefully and anticipate the opposition. Make yourself a thesis—one sentence that concedes something to the opposition, then asserts your pro: "Although many highway deaths result from teenagers who are drinking, establishing a national drinking age of twenty-one is unreasonable." Swing your pros and cons on one of the two patterns suggested.

The Black Mind on the American Campus

JULIAN BOND

———————•———————

From his perspective as a black politician, Bond sees the racial issues on college campuses as microcosms of a much larger macrocosm: the entire fabric of modern society. His recognition of the loyal opposition is everywhere present in his essay, questioning the attitudes of complacent blacks and racially prejudiced whites alike. His ultimate indictment against American education raises frightening questions for the future of peoples of all races.

The crisis in race that exists on the college campus is of course only a reflection of a larger, more serious crisis in the country and, indeed, throughout the world.

The roots of the crisis are as old as the world itself; they involve the continuing failure of the white minority of peoples of the world to share power and wealth with the nonwhite majority.

That struggle has been in the streets of every city in this country, both violently and non-violently. It is part of the struggle that inspired Fidel Castro to overthrow a dictator in Cuba, and it is the same struggle that is inspiring the patriots of Vietnam to continue, successfully, it seems, their twenty-year-old struggle to resist foreign domination of their homeland.

That it should come to the college campus is not at all unusual; here, after all, are the people who have been told since the day they graduated from high school that the earth is theirs for taking, that they are the inheritors of tomorrow. Who is to blame if they believe it? That it is spreading downward into high schools, and even elementary schools is not surprising either.

It ought not to be surprising that young people who learned how to organize the poor and powerless in the Mississippi Delta would transfer their expertise to the powerless at Berkeley and Cornell.

And it ought not be surprising that race has played a large part in the continuing struggle of man against man.

To tie today's on-campus unrest only to yesterday's off-campus protests is unreal. However, there is a great deal more at stake than that.

A great deal has been made by some scholars and pollsters of the difference in the demands of black and white student activists. The whites want revolution, the experts say, while all the blacks want, despite their revolutionary rhetoric, is reform, a chance to bend the established system to their own ends, which are as safe and as ordinary as those shared by the rest of middle-class America.

Therein lies, I think, the conflict present in the black mind on the American campus. The black student is torn between the need for a regular, formal education, part of the socialization process that we are told everyone needs in order to seek an acceptable role in society, and his need to carve out a new education experience, one that is meaningful to him as a black person.

A young girl, a student at Tougaloo College in Mississippi, summed up this feeling when she wrote of her reaction to learning that Tougaloo and Brown University had entered into an education compact, with Brown acting as big brother.

"We argued," she wrote, "that Tougaloo could do better, that we did not have to pattern ourselves after Brown or any of the Ivy League schools, that we have a unique opportunity to make Tougaloo a revolutionary institute of learning. We questioned the notion that places like Brown offered a superior education; we felt in fact that they dealt in mis-education. We felt that if schools like Brown had been truly educating their students then the state of the country and the world would be a lot different."

CHANGE THE TOUGALOOS

The dilemma of whether to change the Tougaloos of the world or to get what can be gotten from the Browns is the continuing one among young blacks.

The demand for a black dorm or an Afro-American center is a part of this dilemma. The unscholarly attacks on black educational institutions by scholars who should know better are a part of that dilemma.

So the current and future course for those blacks interested in solving—or rather eliminating—the crisis of race is unclear.

One has to realize that it is educated and civilized man who has put us where we are today. The rape of Vietnam was not begun by high school dropouts, but by liberally educated men. The pollution of the air and water is not carried out by fools and idiots, but by men educated at the best scientific and technical centers. The ability to shape a society that spends nearly $100 billion on conquering space and dominating the globe militarily comes from men of genius, not from men whose minds are limited.

Civilized man, or educated man, is supposed to solve his problems in a civilized manner.

But the problems of the twentieth century are so vast that many have quite properly been urged to seek uncivilized solutions to them. These problems include the poisoning of the air and water; the rape of the land; the new colonization of peoples, both here and abroad; the new imperialism practiced by Western democracy, and the continuing struggle of those who have not against those who have.

BIRTH OF THE COLOSSUS

With the birth, two hundred years ago, of the colossus called the United States, rational and educated men began to believe that civilization stretched to its highest order had begun. Building on a heritage of revolution, expressing a belief in the equality of most, if not all men, this new democracy was to be the highest elevation of man's relations, one to the other, and a new beginning of decency between nations.

Civilization, as it was then defined, included imposing limitations on war between nations, encouraging the spread of industrialization, the civilizing of so-called heathen elements, the harnessing of nature for the benefit and pleasure of man. It was believed generally that man's better nature would triumph over his base desire to conquer and rule and make war, and that intellect, reason, and logic would share equally with morality in deciding man's fate.

Of course it has not been so. Man still makes war. He still insists that one group subordinate its wishes and desires to that of another. He still insists on gathering material wealth at the expense of his fellows and his environment.

Men and nations have grown arrogant, and the struggle of the twentieth century has continued.

And while the struggle has continued, the university has remained aloof, a center for the study of why man behaves as he does, but never a center for the study of how to make man behave in a civilized manner.

Robert M. Hutchins, former chancellor of the University of Chicago, describes the present-day university thus: It was hoped "it would lead the way to national power and prosperity . . . become the central factory of the knowledge industry, the foundation of our future. [But it became] . . . the national screening device through which individuals were to be put in the proper productive relationship to the national program of power and prosperity.

"[But] the world has moved too fast for the university. The leaders of the younger generations see that the problem is not to get wealth and power. [Nations] have enough of those already. The problem is justice, or what to do with wealth and power. An institution that evidently has little interest in this question cannot command the allegiance of the young."

That the allegiance of some of the young is not with the

university but with the oppressed and downtrodden is evident. Every continent has seen its young rise up against the evils the university is supposed to teach them how to destroy, and many have risen up against the university itself.

Despite its goal of producing individuals who know their relationship to be managers of the new industrial and technological society, the university has thankfully, probably against its desires, produced a new crop of people, a group of activists whose current demands on the university will hopefully be expanded to include assaults on the foundations of a society which has perverted education to reinforce inequity.

ENTIRE FABRIC ATTACKED

So then it is the entire fabric of education that is being attacked, its purpose, its ends. All black students have done is allowed their demands to be colored by their race.

Why should we not demand amnesty, the young ask, when you have allowed amnesty for over three hundred years? Why should we negotiate, they ask, when you have received it since you came to power? Why should we not use weapons, when you have used them time and time again against us? Why should we be accused of tearing down the university and having nothing to put in its place, when you have torn down Vietnam and left the ghetto standing?

Why should we not have a black house on campus, the blacks ask, when the Methodists, Episcopalians, Jews, and Catholics often have theirs?

Why shouldn't we take over a building and evict the deans? Isn't every big-city university, in connivance with urban renewal, doing the same thing to entire families on a permanent basis every day?

Why should we not learn about ourselves, the blacks ask? Haven't we been made to learn more than we ever wanted to know about you?

Why shouldn't any and every black high school graduate be admitted freely to this college, the blacks ask? Aren't they being taught by your graduates, and therefore shouldn't they have learned what it takes to fit in here?

Why should Dow Chemical or ROTC be on campus, the students ask? We are not here to learn to make napalm or to learn how to be soldiers. This is not a vocational school for *any* employer. Or at least it should not be.

This ought to be, the students say, a center for the shaping of civilized man; a center for the study of not just why man behaves as he does, but also a center for the study of how to make him behave better.

To do this, the university must rid itself of several old notions. First of all, higher education can no longer be regarded as a privilege for a few, but must be seen as a right for the many. None of the rhetoric of the past several years about an education for everyone really approaches this aim; higher education is still an elitist and largely white preserve in America today.

In an age when education itself is being questioned, to permit or even to require that everyone receive a piece of parchment which will establish that he knows what millions of people already know with little profit to mankind will not suffice; it is simply not enough and simply will not do.

What is it then that is lacking? What is there beyond four years of compressing all the world's knowledge from lecture notes to the little blue book?

For the blacks, it must be more than Swahili lessons and Afro-American centers, although these have their place. For white universities, it must be more than raiding Southern black schools and taking their most talented faculty and students. For the black school it must be more than pride in blackness.

A writer in *The Center Magazine* described the school's failing action. He wrote: "Students are encouraged to relinquish their own wills, their freedom of volition: they are taught that value and culture reside outside oneself, and must be acquired from the institutions, and almost everything in their education is designed to discourage them from activity, from the wedding of idea and act. It is almost as if we hoped to discourage them from thought itself, by making ideas so lifeless, so hopeless, that their despair would be enough to make them manipulable and obedient."

While the university may have bred despair, it thankfully has not bred obedience. Violence occurs where there is no politics; while there is no politics of race, or rather while there is no anti-racist politics in the university, violence—physical and intellectual—will flourish.

THE UNIVERSITY IN DOUBT

Until the university develops a politics or, in better terms perhaps for this gathering, a curriculum and a discipline that stifles war and poverty and racism, until then, the university will be in doubt.

If education is a socializing process, in our society it has prepared white people to continue enjoying privileged traditions and positions, while black people, through it, have been programmed for social and economic oblivion.

Today's black and white students see this. They see the university nurturing war and directing counter-revolution; they see their professors employed in the Pentagon; they see their presidents serving on commission after commission investigating and recommending last year's solution to the last century's problems; they see the university recruit ghetto students with substandard backgrounds and then submit these students to standards of white, middle-class America.

They believe, as does the Tougaloo student I quoted from earlier, that "the task for black students and black Americans is much greater than trying to change white institutions and their white counterparts in the South. The task is to create revolutionary institutes of learning. The act of trying to be a better person, of trying to imagine and create humane institutions is formidable, but we have no other alternative. We must have a prototype from which to build a good society.

"The point which I make is an old one: that revolution is not only the seizure of power, but is also the building of a society that is qualitatively better than the one we presently live in."

But perhaps what the university's response ought to be in sentiments like that is best expressed in the words of the late W.E.B. Du Bois, words written almost fifty years ago.

Dr. Du Bois said: ". . . We believe that the vocation of man in a modern civilized land includes not only the technique of his actual work but intelligent comprehension of his elementary duties as a father, citizen, maker of public opinion . . . a conserver of the public health, an intelligent follower of moral customs, and one who can appreciate if not partake something of the higher spiritual life of the world.

"We do not pretend that this can be taught to each individual in school, but it can be put into social environment, and the more that environment is restricted and curtailed the more emphatic is the demand that . . . [man] shall be trained and trained thoroughly in these matters of human development if he is to share the surrounding civilization." Or, indeed, if there is to be any civilization at all.

IDEAS

1. Have educators been wrong in telling students that "the earth is theirs for the taking"? Has this bred a false sense of security that ultimately leads to disappointment and hostility?

2. Examine the two extremes of education presented by Bond in the ninth paragraph ("Therein lies, I think. . . ."). What are the possibilities and frustrations at both extremes? Which of the two do you feel is the most important one in today's society?

3. Evaluate the statement made by the student from Tougaloo. Is her position valid, or is a compromise between Tougaloo and Brown a better solution?

4. Carefully evaluate the statement from W.E.B. Du Bois that ends this selection. What is the range of its implications? Has American education made any progress toward this goal in the half-century since Du Bois?

ORGANIZATION AND STYLE

1. Bond does not present his thesis until the ninth paragraph ("Therein lies, I think...."). What is the function of the first eight paragraphs? Would the essay have been more effective if it had begun with the ideas in that ninth paragraph?

2. The third paragraph contains two sentences beginning with "That it...." What is the stylistic effect of these inverted sentences?

3. Why do you think Bond has so many very short paragraphs in this essay?

4. Bond's first recognition of his opposition is in the fourth paragraph, "A great deal has been made...." At what other places in the essay does he recognize and refute opposing views?

5. The author includes a series of paragraphs all beginning with *Why.* What is he doing in these paragraphs other than developing a series of parallel beginnings? That is, what is the purpose of these paragraphs? How effective is this technique?

6. Bond ends the essay with a very short (eleven words) sentence that follows the DuBois quotation. Is this an effective ending? What would have happened had he written a much longer sentence (or maybe even a final paragraph) to end the selection?

WRITING

1. Some educators argue that American colleges are now becoming too concerned about preparing students for jobs. They argue that a *real* college education trains

the mind and acquaints students with the great thoughts and thinkers of the past. These educators particularly cite the absence of required courses in history, philosophy, and literature.

Write an essay in which you argue for what you feel to be the ideal college education for today's world. Using an organization framework similar to that on page 83, confront your opposition as you develop support for your ideas.

2. Select one of the following topics and develop an essay in which you argue the specific merits (or lack of merits) for this type of educational environment: a church-related college, an all male (or female) college, a dormitory (or commuter) college, an all black (or integrated) college. Don't forget to confront your opposition by using a scheme somewhat like that on page 84.

Black Colleges Redefined

CHARLES V. WILLIE

———————— ● ————————

*Willie, an educator, boldly asserts that "black colleges
and universities have kept alive interest in the pursuit of honesty, justice, and altruism in higher education," taking on such formidable opponents as Daniel
Patrick Moynihan and Michael Meyers. Indeed, presenting the opposing view and then refuting it to
move along to his own ideas is Willie's essential organization pattern. Every paragraph has a kind of miniature dialectic pattern.*

The minority is a curious reflection of the majority. I say
curious because in the human social system the minority
provides a double reflection: It indicates what the society
has been and what it can be. Richard Wright recognized
this several decades ago when he wrote, "We black folk,
our history and our present being, are a mirror of all the
manifold experiences of America." Whites, he said, can
better understand themselves as the majority by coming to
know the minority.

I begin this discussion on the future of black colleges
and universities by emphasizing the *function* of minorities in society in the hope of replacing the frame of reference used by national leaders such as Daniel Patrick
Moynihan. He suggested that the progress of the minority
is seriously retarded when its way of life "is out of line
with the rest of American society." This implies that
minorities should be other-directed, that their behavior
should be imitative, that they should be remade in the
image of whites. And Christopher Jencks and David Ries-
man, in a 1967 *Harvard Educational Review* article, "The
American Negro College," called the black college of the

mid-twentieth century "an ill-financed, ill-staffed caricature of white higher education."

Michael Meyers of the NAACP has attempted to dismiss
the argument for the continuation of black colleges as an
"outcry of emotionalism, ethnic chauvinism, and pater-
nalism." He summed up his view with this statement: "No
matter what else is taught or how well it is taught, the fact
that a school is segregated teaches that there is a qualita-
tive difference between students in black and white colleges." Clearly Meyers's assumption is that the black colleges are second rate.

Apparently, any approach to education that differs for
blacks does not make sense to Meyers or Moynihan. In this
respect, they are bedfellows. The logic of positing a different educational approach for the minority is lost on both
critics. Meyers has formulated the question wrongly in
assuming that "the issue at stake in the current controversy over all-black colleges is segregation." Others believe that the issue is education!

With this kind of criticism coming from the friends of
black institutions, it is difficult for these colleges to get a
hearing regarding what they can, could, and should do not
only for blacks but for the education of the nation. Yet our
national history offers evidence that the approach of the
minority may in the end be of great value to the majority.
W.E.B. Du Bois said that the public school system in most
southern states began with the enfranchisement of blacks.
The idea that the masses should be educated to effectively
participate in public decision making was formulated by
Thomas Jefferson several decades before the Civil War, but
was not implemented until blacks became members of
southern state legislatures during Reconstruction. In the
early 1800s there was no public educational system in the
South, except perhaps in North Carolina. In his study,
Black Reconstruction in America, Du Bois said that education was regarded by poor whites before the Civil War "as a
luxury connected with wealth." In Thomas Jefferson's Virginia, for example, "less than one half of the poor white
children were attending any school." The laws passed in

South Carolina between 1856 and 1870 that authorized tax-supported schools open to all were described in the book as "the most beneficial legislation the state . . . has ever enacted." These laws were initiated and supported by black lawmakers.

One could say of Reconstruction black legislators that the progeny of the former slaves fulfilled for all people the slave owner's dream of publicly supported education in the South. In contemporary times, blacks have continued to link legislation and the idea of liberation in a way that has improved education for members of their own race and for whites. Each day before he leaves home for his classes, Allan Bakke should thank God that there are racial minorities in America whose political action resulted in a law that guarantees his right to attend medical school. That law is the Civil Rights Act of 1964.

John Monro of Tougaloo College . . . has said that if more white colleges used readings from black authors, readings that develop a full and accurate awareness of the American black experience, this country would be much better off. He acknowledged, however, that "the white colleges are not going to do it, or anything like it—which is one reason sensible people prefer to teach in black colleges." A research project on the techniques of the best teachers at black colleges would be a valuable contribution from the black experience. The findings of such a study would benefit all colleges—selective ones that are developing more diversified student bodies and community colleges or other open-door institutions where more than a third of all higher education students now matriculate.

The qualities that educators praise in community college teaching have long been the way of life for instructors in black four-year colleges. Daniel Thompson, provost and vice president of Dillard University, told the Black College Conference at Harvard that "the work of talented, dedicated, persevering teachers has substantiated the claim of black colleges that they can take certain students who are rejected by most or all of the affluent, high ranking, prestigious white colleges and produce a relatively large proportion of topflight college graduates." This can be done, Thompson pointed out, because "teachers in black colleges . . . are more concerned with classroom activities, personal counseling, sponsoring organizations." He described the interaction between students and teachers at black colleges as "many sided, sustained, and personal." The top faculty often teach lower-division students because "they want to lay as solid a foundation as possible at the start of the college career so that academic development will be sound and continuous."

Some policy makers and educators have seized on this asset of black colleges and have tried by way of reductionism to turn it into a liability. They have suggested that the future of higher education would be served best if most black colleges became two-year institutions. This fails to recognize the other goals that these colleges fulfill.

To state it bluntly, black colleges and universities have kept alive interest in the pursuit of honesty, justice, and altruism in higher education. They have helped the nation recognize the difference between information and knowledge on the one hand and virtue and wisdom on the other. W. B. Schrader, in a College Entrance Examination Board study, reported the findings of Junius Davis on the qualities college teachers value in students. In addition to intellectual quickness, creativity, and motivation to achieve, the teachers valued honesty, open-mindedness, pleasantness, self-understanding, and altruism. Black colleges and universities have emphasized these values through the sit-ins and freedom rides and civil rights demonstrations led by their students and graduates, and through instruction and other means.

During the past few years the president of Harvard University and other academic leaders have wrestled with the moral and ethical issues arising from their institutions' investments in corporations that transact business in South Africa. After a great deal of soul searching, President Derek Bok said—and I report this so that it may be compared with the position taken by the leader of a black college several years earlier—"Injustice and suffering are plainly matters of grave concern. We may justly feel impelled to give our time and effort as individuals to the struggle against these evils. We may also expect the university not to act deliberately to increase the suffering of others. But the principal issue before us is whether we should go further and use the university as a means of expressing moral disapproval or as a weapon in our fight against injustice even if we threaten to injure the academic functions of the institution. . . . Universities are designed to achieve particular purposes. Their special mission is the discovery and transmission of knowledge. . . . Their institutional goal is not to reform society in specific ways. Universities have neither the mandate nor the competence to administer foreign policy, set our social and economic priorities, enforce standards of conduct in the society, or carry out other social functions apart from learning and discovery." Moreover, the Harvard president asserted: "We should also recognize that very rarely will the institutional acts of a single university—or even universities as a group—have any substantial possibility of putting an end to the misfortunes that exist in society."

Back in 1945, when Martin Luther King, Jr., was completing his freshman year at Morehouse College, the president of that school said in a radio address, "It will not be sufficient for Morehouse College . . . to produce clever graduates, men fluent in speech and able to argue their way through; but rather honest men, men who are sensitive to the wrongs, the sufferings, and the injustices of society and who are willing to accept responsibility for correcting the ills." Ten years later, in the Montgomery bus boycott of 1955–56, King acted out the words he had heard from his college president, Benjamin Mays. Both presidents mentioned the efforts of individuals. But one emphasized analysis and the other action.

Historian L. D. Reddick described Morehouse as a place where "teachers encouraged their students to explore and search for solutions to campus and world problems," a place where "nobody on the faculty seemed to be afraid to think and speak out," a place where the president "was willing to be counted." Clearly King's dedication to social justice was bound up with his Morehouse College education. Black colleges have been more concerned with racial advancement than with individual success, and they have placed greater emphasis on participation in the processes of democracy than have most white institutions. There is no paradox in this; those who are denied the rights of democratic citizenship are likely to value them more highly than those who can take them for granted.

What Morehouse did for King other black colleges have done for their graduates. Gregory Kannerstein, who studied the self-concepts of several black colleges, concluded that "perhaps the greatest and most distinctive contribution of black colleges to the American philosophy of higher education has been to emphasize and legitimate public and community service as a major objective of colleges and universities." Kannerstein said that statements of the purpose of most black colleges reveal a "litany of 'education-citizenship-leadership-democracy' that affirms a belief in the democratic process and in the ability of colleges, students, and alumni to influence it."

While the black college that King attended emphasized service and citizenship, it also provided him with a good academic education. In fact, one tenth of its baccalaureates have earned doctorate degrees. Thus a focus on service and citizenship need not result in neglect of other areas. Most black colleges have provided their students with a comprehensive education.

Black colleges are also flexible enough to combine classical and career education at a time when a growing number of white as well as black students are insisting that college should equip them with sufficient skills to get a good job upon graduation. This synthesis of the liberal arts and vocationally oriented courses first emerged in black colleges and universities and placed these institutions in the vanguard of higher education; it grew out of the Booker T. Washington-W.E.B. Du Bois debate at the beginning of the twentieth century on the nature of higher education appropriate for blacks. At the time the discussion was ignored as merely a fuss between two blacks. But by the turbulent 1960s white colleges realized that teaching students how to survive and to do things with their hands was as important as teaching courses in the liberal arts tradition.

Another area in which black colleges excel is that of integrating the races. They have demonstrated how to do this from their beginning. The Office for Advancement of Public Negro Colleges of the National Association of State Universities and Land-Grant Colleges has reported that "approximately 15 percent of the total number of students graduating from historically black public colleges are classified as nonblack." Few predominantly white colleges have desegregated to that extent. Black colleges, though they were segregated by law, have never been segregat*ing;* they have always had white faculty members. They could and should teach other institutions how to become pluralistic.

My own studies have revealed that in order to make an educational impact a racial minority must constitute about 20 percent of the student body. Black colleges that have 15 percent white enrollment are within striking distance of this goal. The ideal minimum is a population of at least one third that differs from the predominant group.

Thus one possible future function for black colleges is that of serving as settings in which whites may enroll as the minority. There is nothing intrinsically good about being the majority or intrinsically bad about being the minority. In a pluralistic and cosmopolitan society everyone may be part of a minority in one context or another at some time; so it is well that, in school, whites should learn not to fear the consequences of minority status, and blacks and browns should learn to be comfortable with the responsibilities of majority status.

This idea grew out of my experience as a member of a court-appointed panel in the 1974 Boston school desegregation case *Morgan et al.* v. *Kerrigan et al.* The plan we proposed veered from the requirement of an equal ratio of black, white, and other minorities in each school and recommended that the student bodies be diversified rather than strictly balanced. In other words, some schools would have a majority of whites in the student body with a sufficient minority of blacks to have educational impact on the total system. Other schools would have a majority of blacks with a sufficient minority of whites to have a meaningful influence. This proposal for elementary and secondary public schools is certainly appropriate for public and private colleges. But whites can experience minority status only if there are predominantly black institutions in which to enroll. Thus the retention of predominantly black colleges and universities is for the benefit of whites as well as blacks.

In the past blacks have helped to enrich the nation through state systems of public education; the future is theirs if they will seize it in an other-centered, self-directed way—not in a self-centered, other-directed way. They have been pioneers in demonstrating how to integrate higher education faculties. Similar ingenuity could be used to desegregate college and university student bodies so that the outcome is beneficial to all. But black colleges and universities must refuse to cooperate in their own oppression; they must never try to be exclusive. A self-centered attempt to save black institutions for blacks would be as damaging as an other-directed effort to remake them in the image of whites. Both actions ultimately would end in defeat. Black colleges and universities must be preserved for their value to society as a whole. A higher education system with a Harvard but not a Hampton is incomplete. Black colleges and universities have a *future* in our society because of their *function*.

IDEAS

1. Do you agree with Willie's opening sentence, "The minority is a curious reflection of the majority"? In what aspects of life do you find this statement to be true? Are

there other aspects of life which you feel vary from the thesis made here?

2. John Monro of Tougaloo College argues that students at "white colleges" need to read the works of black authors to "develop a full and accurate awareness of the American black experience." Do you agree or disagree with this statement? Relate your response, if possible, to what you have read that was authored by blacks.

3. Daniel Thompson argues that good teachers are those who become personally involved with their students as individuals. How does this square with your experience?

4. Harvard University President Derek Bok argues that universities exist to discover and transmit knowledge and that they should not become involved with social and political issues. Is this a valid stance? Is this position affected at all by Bok's suggestion that universities "are designed to achieve particular purposes"? Might some institutions have "particular purposes" that are completely different from those at other institutions?

5. Is Willie's argument affected at all by his suggestion that black colleges are really not exclusively black, that they often have a significant number of white faculty members and students?

6. Compare the argument made in this essay with the one made in the previous selection by Julian Bond. What philosophic points do they have in common? What differences?

ORGANIZATION AND STYLE

1. How does the sentence "In this respect, they are bedfellows" (paragraph four) relate to the opening sentence of the essay and serve as a kind of framing technique for the introduction?

2. This essay offers an excellent example of dialectic organization. Prepare a chart similar to that on page 84 in which you show the dialectic swings in paragraph five.

3. Willie makes reference to a large number of people, frequently quoting from them to get an idea going. Find several examples. How effectively does Willie make this organizational pattern work? Do you feel he uses it too often? Can you tell in every instance whether he agrees or disagrees with the statement that he is quoting?

4. The final section of the essay ("Another area in which black colleges. . . .") is separated from the rest of the selection by additional space above it. How connected are the ideas in that last section to those in the first part? Does this final section offer a valid conclusion to Willie's earlier arguments? Notice, especially, how often Willie uses the idea from his first sentence to develop his thoughts in this final section.

5. Compare the organization and style of this selection with Bond's in the previous essay. What similarities and differences do you find? Can you, for instance, find evidence that Bond is a politician and that Willie is an educator?

WRITING

1. Write your own dialectic essay on the role of education in American society as you perceive it. Use several quotations from this essay to introduce an idea; then spring from that idea to other views. Although you may certainly present your own concerns on black versus white colleges, you need not be limited to that topic. Willie's quotations address a large number of issues in education and, if carefully read, should provide you with the possibility for a range of ideas.

2. After carefully reading the essays by Bond and Willie, imagine what would happen if the two men met and held a discussion on the role of education, especially as it affects black students. Write an essay in which you describe the way you feel that conversation would go. You might even wish to write a dialogue:

BOND: I have a couple of serious questions about your interpretation of Bok's remarks. First, you say that. . . .

WILLIE: Well, Julian, I agree in part with what you are suggesting. However, it seems to me that you are confusing. . . .

BOND: But, Charles, you seem to be forgetting what I wrote in my own essay about that very same concept. I said that. . . .

Man Against Darkness

W. T. STACE

———————— ● ————————

Stace asserts, and explains, the modern view of a purposeless universe. His opening paragraph sets his thesis: the idea of a godless, chaotic, meaningless universe is true. He fronts several quite different degrees and kinds of opposition, from the bishops, with whom he opens, to the personal attitude of Mr. Russell, one of the strongest supporters of his own position. Notice early in Stace's essay how an opposition—the bishops—can well serve as an opener to set up one's thesis. Notice how he brings in more support before differing first with Russell's attitude then with modern assumptions about how science has changed everything, Stace merely correcting at this stage rather than disagreeing. Plato, Aristotle, and medieval Christianity, his major opposition, come rather late in his layout. As you read, underline Stace's favorite marker of conceding to the opposition: "It is true." And note where he returns to his own line of argument with But. *See if you can mark all of his dialectic swings from side to side as he argues his case.*

1

The Catholic bishops of America recently issued a statement in which they said that the chaotic and bewildered state of the modern world is due to man's loss of faith, his abandonment of God and religion. For my part I believe in no religion at all. Yet I entirely agree with the bishops. It is no doubt an oversimplification to speak of the cause of so complex a state of affairs as the tortured condition of the world today. Its causes are doubtless multitudinous. Yet allowing for some element of oversimplification, I say that the bishops' assertion is substantially true.

M. Jean-Paul Sartre, the French existentialist philosopher, labels himself an atheist. Yet his views seem to me plainly to support the statement of the bishops. So long as there was believed to be a God in the sky, he says, men could regard him as the source of their moral ideals. The universe, created and governed by a fatherly God, was a friendly habitation for man. We could be sure that, however great the evil in the world, good in the end would triumph and the forces of evil would be routed. With the disappearance of God from the sky, all this has changed. Since the world is not ruled by a spiritual being, but rather by blind forces, there cannot be any ideals, moral or otherwise, in the universe outside us. Our ideals, therefore, must proceed only from our own minds; they are our own inventions. Thus the world which surrounds us is nothing but an immense spiritual emptiness. It is a dead universe. We do not live in a universe which is on the side of our values. It is completely indifferent to them.

Years ago Mr. Bertrand Russell, in his essay *A Free Man's Worship,* said much the same thing.

> Such in outline, but even more purposeless, more void of meaning, is the world which Science presents for our belief. Amid such a world, if anywhere, our ideals henceforward must find a home. . . . Blind to good and evil, reckless of destruction, omnipotent matter rolls on its relentless way; for man, condemned today to lose his dearest, tomorrow himself to pass through the gate of darkness, it remains only to cherish, ere yet the blow falls, the lofty thoughts that ennoble his little day; . . . to worship at the shrine his own hands have built; . . . to sustain alone, a weary but unyielding Atlas, the world that his own ideals have fashioned despite the trampling march of unconscious power.

It is true that Mr. Russell's personal attitude to the disappearance of religion is quite different from either that of M. Sartre or the bishops or myself. The bishops think it a calamity. So do I. M. Sartre finds it "very distressing." And he berates as shallow the attitude of those who think that without God the world can go on just the same as before, as if nothing had happened. This creates for mankind, he thinks, a terrible crisis. And in this I agree with him. Mr. Russell, on the other hand, seems to believe that religion has done more harm than good in the world, and that its disappearance will be a blessing. But his picture of the world, and of the modern mind, is the same as that of M. Sartre. He stresses the *purposelessness* of the universe, the facts that man's ideals are his own creations, that the universe outside him in no way supports them, that man is alone and friendless in the world.

Mr. Russell notes that it is science which has produced this situation. There is no doubt that this is correct. But the way in which it has come about is not generally understood. There is a popular belief that some particular scientific discoveries or theories, such as the Darwinian theory of evolution, or the views of geologists about the age of the earth, or a series of such discoveries, have done the damage. It would be foolish to deny that these discoveries have had a great effect in undermining religious dogmas. But this account does not at all go to the root of the matter. Religion can probably outlive any scientific discoveries which could be made. It can accommodate itself to them. The root cause of the decay of faith has not been any particular discovery of science, but rather the general spirit of science and certain basic assumptions upon which modern science, from the seventeenth century onwards, has proceeded.

2

It was Galileo and Newton—notwithstanding that Newton himself was a deeply religious man—who destroyed the old comfortable picture of a friendly universe governed by spiritual values. And this was effected, not by Newton's discovery of the law of gravitation nor by any of Galileo's brilliant investigations,* but by the general picture of the

*The experiments of Galileo Galilei (1564–1642), though his writings were eventually banned, or indexed, by the Catholic authorities in Rome, led to the work of Isaac Newton (1642–1727) with gravity and planetary motion, for which Newton invented the calculus.

world which these men and others of their time made the basis of the science, not only of their own day, but of all succeeding generations down to the present. That is why the century immediately following Newton, the eighteenth century, was notoriously an age of religious skepticism. Skepticism did not have to wait for the discoveries of Darwin and the geologists in the nineteenth century. It flooded the world immediately after the age of the rise of science.

Neither the Copernican hypothesis nor any of Newton's or Galileo's particular discoveries were the real causes. Religious faith might well have accommodated itself to the new astronomy. The real turning point between the medieval age of faith and the modern age of unfaith came when the scientists of the seventeenth century turned their backs upon what used to be called "final causes." The final cause of a thing or event meant the purpose which it was supposed to serve in the universe, its cosmic purpose. What lay back of this was the presupposition that there is a cosmic order or plan and that everything which exists could in the last analysis be explained in terms of its place in this cosmic plan, that is, in terms of its purpose.

Plato and Aristotle believed this, and so did the whole medieval Christian world. For instance, if it were true that the sun and the moon were created and exist for the purpose of giving light to man, then this fact would explain why the sun and the moon exist. We might not be able to discover the purpose of everything, but everything must have a purpose. Belief in final causes thus amounted to a belief that the world is governed by purposes, presumably the purposes of some overruling mind. This belief was not the invention of Christianity. It was basic to the whole of Western civilization, whether in the ancient pagan world or in Christendom, from the time of Socrates to the rise of science in the seventeenth century.

The founders of modern science—for instance, Galileo, Kepler, and Newton—were mostly pious men who did not doubt God's purposes. Nevertheless they took the revolutionary step of consciously and deliberately expelling the idea of purpose as controlling nature from their new science of nature. They did this on the ground that inquiry into purposes is useless for what science aims at: namely, the prediction and control of events. To predict an eclipse, what you have to know is not its purpose but its causes. Hence science from the seventeenth century onwards became exclusively an inquiry into causes. The conception of purpose in the world was ignored and frowned on. This, though silent and almost unnoticed, was the greatest revolution in human history, far outweighing in importance any of the political revolutions whose thunder has reverberated through the world.

For it came about in this way that for the past three hundred years there has been growing up in men's minds, dominated as they are by science, a new imaginative picture of the world. The world, according to this new picture, is purposeless, senseless, meaningless. Nature is nothing but matter in motion. The motions of matter are governed, not by any purpose, but by blind forces and laws. Nature in this view, says Whitehead—to whose writings I am indebted in this part of my paper—is "merely the hurrying of material, endlessly, meaninglessly." You can draw a sharp line across the history of Europe dividing it into two epochs of very unequal length. The line passes through the lifetime of Galileo. European man before Galileo—whether ancient pagan or more recent Christian—thought of the world as controlled by plan and purpose. After Galileo European man thinks of it as utterly purposeless. This is the great revolution of which I spoke.

It is this which has killed religion. Religion could survive the discoveries that the sun, not the earth, is the center; that men are descended from simian ancestors; that the earth is hundreds of million of years old. These discoveries may render out of date some of the details of older theological dogmas, may force their restatement in new intellectual frameworks. But they do not touch the essence of the religious vision itself, which is the faith that there is plan and purpose in the world, that the world is a moral order, that in the end all things are for the best. This faith may express itself through many different intellectual dogmas, those of Christianity, of Hinduism, of Islam. All and any of these intellectual dogmas may be destroyed without destroying the essential religious spirit. But that spirit cannot survive destruction of belief in a plan and purpose of the world, for that is the very heart of it. Religion can get on with any sort of astronomy, geology, biology, physics. But it cannot get on with a purposeless and meaningless universe.

If the scheme of things is purposeless and meaningless, then the life of man is purposeless and meaningless too. Everything is futile, all effort is in the end worthless. A man may, of course, still pursue disconnected ends, money, fame, art, science, and may gain pleasure from them. But his life is hollow at the center. Hence the dissatisfied, disillusioned, restless, spirit of modern man.

The picture of a meaningless world, and a meaningless human life, is, I think, the basic theme of much modern art and literature. Certainly it is the basic theme of modern philosophy. According to the most characteristic philosophies of the modern period from Hume* in the eighteenth century to the so-called positivists of today, the world is just what it is, and that is the end of all inquiry. There is no reason for its being what it is. Everything might just as well have been quite different, and there would have been no reason for that either. When you have stated what things are, what things the world contains, there is nothing more which could be said, even by an omniscient being. To ask any question about why things are thus, or what purpose their being so serves, is to ask a senseless question, because they serve no purpose at all. For instance, there is for modern philosophy no such thing as the ancient problem of evil. For this once famous question pre-supposes that pain and misery, though they seem

---

*David Hume (1700–1776), Scottish philosopher and economist, who attacked empirical theories by arguing that we have no rational grounds for our ideas of objective reality, or even for believing that things continue to exist when out of sight, beyond customary associations in the imagination.

so inexplicable and irrational to us, must ultimately sub-
serve some rational purpose, must have their places in the
cosmic plan. But this is nonsense. There is no such overruling rationality in the universe. Belief in the ultimate
irrationality of everything is the quintessence of what is
called the modern mind.

It is true that, parallel with these philosophies which
are typical of the modern mind, preaching the meaning-
lessness of the world, there has run a line of idealistic
philosophies whose contention is that the world is after all
spiritual in nature and that moral ideals and values are
inherent in its structure. But most of these idealisms were
simply philosophical expressions of romanticism, which
was itself no more than an unsuccessful counterattack of
the religious against the scientific view of things. They
perished, along with romanticism in literature and art,
about the beginning of the present century, though of
course they still have a few adherents.

At the bottom these idealistic systems of thought were
rationalizations of man's wishful thinking. They were
born of the refusal of men to admit the cosmic darkness.
They were comforting illusions within the warm glow of
which the more tender-minded intellectuals sought to
shelter themselves from the icy winds of the universe.
They lasted a little while. But they are shattered now, and
we return once more to the vision of a purposeless world.

3

Along with the ruin of the religious vision there went the
ruin of moral principles and indeed of all values. If there
is a cosmic purpose, if there is in the nature of things a
drive towards goodness, then our moral systems will derive their validity from this. But if our moral rules do not
proceed from something outside us in the nature of the
universe—whether we say it is God or simply the universe
itself—then they must be our own inventions. Thus it
came to be believed that moral rules must be merely an
expression of our own likes and dislikes. But likes and

dislikes are notoriously variable. What pleases one man, people, or culture displeases another. Therefore morals are wholly relative.

This obvious conclusion from the idea of a purposeless world made its appearance in Europe immediately after the rise of science, for instance in the philosophy of Hobbes.* Hobbes saw at once that if there is no purpose in the world there are no values either. "Good and evil," he writes, "are names that signify our appetites and aversions; which in different tempers, customs, and doctrines of men are different. . . . Every man calleth that which pleaseth him, good; and that which displeaseth him, evil."

This doctrine of the relativity of morals, though it has recently received an impetus from the studies of anthropologists, was thus really implicit in the whole scientific mentality. It is disastrous for morals because it destroys their entire traditional foundation. That is why philosophers who see the danger signals, from the time at least of Kant, have been trying to give to morals a new foundation, that is, a secular or nonreligious foundation. This attempt may very well be intellectually successful. Such a foundation, independent of the religious view of the world, might well be found. But the question is whether it can ever be a *practical* success, that is, whether apart from its logical validity and its influence with intellectuals, it can ever replace among the masses of men the lost religious foundation. On that question hangs perhaps the future of civilization. But meanwhile disaster is overtaking us.

The widespread belief in "ethical relativity" among philosophers, psychologists, ethnologists, and sociologists is the theoretical counterpart of the repudiation of principle which we see all around us, especially in international

*Thomas Hobbes (1588–1679), English philosopher, best known for *Leviathan* (1651), a discourse on government as the protector of the individual. Hobbes favored the monarchy as the most effective means of fulfilling this obligation, and rejected a role for the church in government. Without strong government, human life would inevitably be "solitary, poor, nasty, brutish, and short."

affairs, the field in which morals have always had the weakest foothold. No one any longer effectively believes in moral principles except as the private prejudices either of individual men or of nations or cultures. This is the inevitable consequence of the doctrine of ethical relativity, which in turn is the inevitable consequence of believing in a purposeless world.

Another characteristic of our spiritual state is loss of belief in the freedom of the will. This also is a fruit of the scientific spirit, though not of any particular scientific discovery. Science has been built up on the basis of determinism, which is the belief that every event is completely determined by a chain of causes and is therefore theoretically predictable beforehand. It is true that recent physics seems to challenge this. But so far as its practical consequences are concerned, the damage has long ago been done. A man's actions, it was argued, are as much events in the natural world as is an eclipse of the sun. It follows that men's actions are as theoretically predictable as an eclipse. But if it is certain now that John Smith will murder Joseph Jones at 2.15 P.M. on January 1, 1963, what possible meaning can it have to say that when that time comes John Smith will be *free* to choose whether he will commit the murder or not? And if he is not free, how can he be held responsible?

It is true that the whole of this argument can be shown by a competent philosopher to be a tissue of fallacies—or at least I claim that it can. But the point is that the analysis required to show this is much too subtle to be understood by the average entirely unphilosophical man. Because of this, the argument against free will is generally swallowed whole by the unphilosophical. Hence the thought that man is not free, that he is the helpless plaything of forces over which he has no control, has deeply penetrated the modern mind. We hear of economic determinism, cultural determinism, historical determinism. We are not responsible for what we do because our glands control us, or because we are the products of environment or heredity. Not moral self-control, but the doctor, the psychiatrist, the educationist, must save us from doing evil. Pills and injections in the future are to do what Christ and the prophets have failed to do. Of course I do not mean to deny that doctors and educationists can and must help. And I do not mean in any way to belittle their efforts. But I do wish to draw attention to the weakening of moral controls, the greater or less repudiation of personal responsibility which, in the popular thinking of the day, result from these tendencies of thought.

4

What, then, is to be done? Where are we to look for salvation from the evils of our time? All the remedies I have seen suggested so far are, in my opinion, useless. Let us look at some of them.

Philosophers and intellectuals generally can, I believe, genuinely do something to help. But it is extremely little. What philosophers can do is to show that neither the relativity of morals nor the denial of free will really follows from the grounds which have been supposed to support them. They can also try to discover a genuine secular basis for morals to replace the religious basis which has disappeared. Some of us are trying to do these things. But in the first place philosophers unfortunately are not agreed about these matters, and their disputes are utterly confusing to the non-philosophers. And in the second place their influence is practically negligible because their analyses necessarily take place on a level on which the masses are totally unable to follow them.

The bishops, of course, propose as remedy a return to belief in God and in the doctrines of the Christian religion. Others think that a new religion is what is needed. Those who make these proposals fail to realize that the crisis in man's spiritual condition is something unique in history for which there is no sort of analogy in the past. They are thinking perhaps of the collapse of the ancient Greek and Roman religions. The vacuum then created was easily filled by Christianity, and it might have been filled by

Mithraism* if Christianity had not appeared. By analogy they think that Christianity might now be replaced by a new religion, or even that Christianity itself, if revivified, might bring back health to men's lives.

But I believe that there is no analogy at all between our present state and that of the European peoples at the time of the fall of paganism. Men had at that time lost their belief only in particular dogmas, particular embodiments of the religious view of the world. It had no doubt become incredible that Zeus and the other gods were living on the top of Mount Olympus. You could go to the top and find no trace of them. But the imaginative picture of a world governed by purpose, a world driving towards the good— which is the inner spirit of religion—had at that time received no serious shock. It had merely to re-embody itself in new dogmas, those of Christianity or some other religion. Religion itself was not dead in the world, only a particular form of it.

But now the situation is quite different. It is not merely that particular dogmas, like that of the virgin birth, are unacceptable to the modern mind. That is true, but it constitutes a very superficial diagnosis of the present situation of religion. Modern skepticism is of a wholly different order from that of the intellectuals of the ancient world. It has attacked and destroyed not merely the outward forms of the religious spirit, its particularized dogmas, but the very essence of that spirit itself, belief in a meaningful and purposeful world. For the founding of a new religion a new Jesus Christ or Buddha would have to appear, in itself a most unlikely event and one for which in any case we cannot afford to sit and wait. But even if a new prophet and a new religion did appear, we may predict that they would fail in the modern world. No one for long would believe in them, for moderm men have lost the vision, basic to all religion, of an ordered plan and purpose of the world. They have before their minds the picture of a

*From Mithras, the Persian god of light and the sun. Mithraism had a very large following throughout the Roman world until the early fourth century, when it was suppressed by the newly Christian empire.

puposeless universe, and such a world-picture must be fatal to any religion at all, not merely to Christianity.

We must not be misled by occasional appearances of a revival of the religious spirit. Men, we are told, in their disgust and disillusionment at the emptiness of their lives, are turning once more to religion, or are searching for a new message. It may be so. We must expect such wistful yearnings of the spirit. We must expect men to wish back again the light that is gone, and to try to bring it back. But however they may wish and try, the light will not shine again—not at least in the civilization to which we belong.

Another remedy commonly proposed is that we should turn to science itself, or the scientific spirit, for our salvation. Mr. Russell and Professor [John] Dewey both make this proposal, though in somewhat different ways. Professor Dewey seems to believe that discoveries in sociology, the application of scientific method to social and political problems, will rescue us. This seems to me to be utterly naïve. It is not likely that science, which is basically the cause of our spiritual troubles, is likely also to produce the cure for them. Also it lies in the nature of science that, though it can teach us the best means for achieving our ends, it can never tell us what ends to pursue. It cannot give us any ideals. And our trouble is about ideals and ends, not about the means for reaching them.

5

No civilization can live without ideals, or to put it in another way, without a firm faith in moral ideals. Our ideals and moral ideas have in the past been rooted in religion. But the religious basis of our ideals has been undermined, and the superstructure of ideals is plainly tottering. None of the commonly suggested remedies on examination seems likely to succeed. It would therefore look as if the early death of our civilization were inevitable.

Of course we know that it is perfectly possible for individual men, very highly educated men, philosophers, scientists, intellectuals in general, to live moral lives without any religious convictions. But the question is whether a whole civilization, a whole family of peoples, composed almost entirely of relatively uneducated men and women, can do this.

It follows, of course, that if we could make the vast majority of men as highly educated as the very few are now, we might save the situation. And we are already moving slowly in that direction through the techniques of mass education. But the critical question seems to concern the time-lag. Perhaps in a few hundred years most of the population will, at the present rate, be sufficiently highly educated and civilized to combine high ideals with an absence of religion. But long before we reach any such stage, the collapse of our civilization may have come about. How are we to live through the intervening period?

I am sure that the first thing we have to do is to face the truth, however bleak it may be, and then next we have to learn to live with it. Let me say a word about each of these two points. What I am urging as regards the first is complete honesty. Those who wish to resurrect Christian dogmas are not, of course, consciously dishonest. But they have that kind of unconscious dishonesty which consists in lulling oneself with opiates and dreams. Those who talk of a new religion are merely hoping for a new opiate. Both alike refuse to face the truth that there is, in the universe outside man, no spirituality, no regard for values, no friend in the sky, no help or comfort for man of any sort. To be perfectly honest in the admission of this fact, not to seek shelter in new or old illusions, not to indulge in wishful dreams about this matter, this is the first thing we shall have to do.

I do not urge this course out of any special regard for the sanctity of truth in the abstract. It is not self-evident to me that truth is the supreme value to which all else must be sacrificed. Might not the discoverer of a truth which would be fatal to mankind be justified in suppressing it, even in teaching men a falsehood? Is truth more valuable than goodness and beauty and happiness? To think so is to invent yet another absolute, another religious delusion in which Truth with a capital T is substituted for God. The reason why we must now boldly and honestly face the truth that the universe is non-spiritual and indifferent to goodness, beauty, happiness, or truth is not that it would be wicked to suppress it, but simply that it is too late to do so, so that in the end we cannot do anything else but face it. Yet we stand on the brink, dreading the icy plunge. We need courage. We need honesty.

Now about the other point, the necessity of learning to live with the truth. This means learning to live virtuously and happily, or at least contentedly, without illusions. And this is going to be extremely difficult because what we have now begun dimly to perceive is that human life in the past, or at least human happiness, has almost wholly depended upon illusions. It has been said that man lives by truth, and that the truth will make us free. Nearly the opposite seems to me to be the case. Mankind has managed to live only by means of lies, and the truth may very well destroy us. If one were a Bergsonian one might believe that nature deliberately puts illusions into our souls in order to induce us to go on living.

The illusions by which men have lived seem to be of two kinds. First, there is what one may perhaps call the Great Illusion—I mean the religious illusion that the universe is moral and good, that it follows a wise and noble plan, that it is gradually generating some supreme value, that goodness is bound to triumph in it. Secondly, there is a whole host of minor illusions on which human happiness nourishes itself. How much of human happiness notoriously comes from the illusions of the lover about his beloved? Then again we work and strive because of the illusions connected with fame, glory, power, or money. Banners of all kinds, flags, emblems, insignia, ceremonials, and rituals are invariably symbols of some illusion or other. The British Empire, the connection between mother country and dominions, is partly kept going by illusions surrounding the notion of kingship. Or think of the vast amount of human happiness which is derived from the illusion of supposing that if some nonsense sylla-ble, such as "sir" or "count" or "lord," is pronounced in conjunction with our names, we belong to a superior order of people.

There is plenty of evidence that human happiness is almost wholly based upon illusions of one kind or another. But the scientific spirit, or the spirit of truth, is the enemy of illusions and therefore the enemy of human happiness. That is why it is going to be so difficult to live with the truth.

There is no reason why we should have to give up the host of minor illusions which render life supportable. There is no reason why the lover should be scientific about the loved one. Even the illusions of fame and glory may persist. But without the Great Illusion, the illusion of a good, kindly, and purposeful universe, we shall *have* to learn to live. And to ask this is really no more than to ask that we become genuinely civilized beings and not merely sham civilized beings.

I can best explain the difference by a reminiscence. I remember a fellow student in my college days, an ardent Christian, who told me that if he did not believe in a future life, in heaven and hell, he would rape, murder, steal, and be a drunkard. That is what I call being a sham civilized being. On the other hand, not only could a [Thomas] Hux-ley, a John Stuart Mill, a David Hume, live great and fine lives without any religion, but a great many others of us, quite obscure persons, can at least live decent lives with-out it.

To be genuinely civilized means to be able to walk straightly and to live honorably without the props and crutches of one or another of the childish dreams which have so far supported men. That such a life is likely to be ecstatically happy I will not claim. But that it can be lived in quiet content, accepting resignedly what cannot be helped, not expecting the impossible, and thankful for small mercies, this I would maintain. That it will be diffi-cult for men in general to learn this lesson I do not deny.

But that it will be impossible I would not admit since so many have learned it already.

Man has not yet grown up. He is not adult. Like a child he cries for the moon and lives in a world of fantasies. And the race as a whole has perhaps reached the great crisis of its life. Can it grow up as a race in the same sense as individual men grow up? Can man put away childish things and adolescent dreams? Can he grasp the real world as it actually is, stark and bleak, without its romantic or religious halo, and still retain his ideals, striving for great ends and noble achievements? If he cannot, he will probably sink back into the savagery and brutality from which he came, taking a humble place once more among the lower animals.

IDEAS

1. What exactly does Stace mean when he writes "We do not live in a universe which is on the side of our values"?

2. Stace quotes Russell on man's building his own shrine and then, wearily, sustaining alone "the world that his own ideals have fashioned." Can you give some examples of these shrines and this world fashioned from these self-generated ideals?

3. What is Stace's distinction between cause and purpose? Explain what he calls "the greatest revolution in human history."

4. Stace argues that in the new scientific picture of the world "all effort is in the end worthless." He also says tha man will sink back among the lower animals unless he can "retain his ideal, striving for great ends and noble achievements." Where does Stace stand? Can you reconcile these statements in Stace's terms, or in your own? What is the purpose of writing an essay in a purposeless universe?

ORGANIZATION AND STYLE

1. Stace effectively balances extremely short sentences against longer, more stylistically sophisticated ones. Find examples throughout the essay. What kinds of ideas does Stace most often relegate to those shorter sentences?

2. Prepare a chart similar to the one on page 84 in which you show the dialectic swings in the paragraph beginning "Mr. Russell notes that it is science. . . ."

3. Stace introduces a large number of people and their ideas. Can you determine his organizational pattern or patterns (chronological, ascending importance, thematic)?

4. The essay has five numbered sections. What specific idea is Stace developing in each section? With what subheadings might you, as an editor, designate those five sections?

5. How effective are Stace's rhetorical questions in the final paragraph? To what extent do those questions summarize ideas in his essay?

WRITING

1. Stace argues that we must "be able to walk straightly and to live honorably without the props and crutches of one or another of the childish dreams which have so far supported men." Write your own dialectic essay in which you either agree or disagree with this thesis. Be certain to examine both sides of the argument. You might wish to use some quotations from Stace as you organize your ideas.

2. Carefully compare Stace's ideas with Margaret Mead's. As with Bond and Willie, write an essay or dialogue in which you imagine Stace and Mead discussing life in today's world.

3

PARAGRAPHS: BEGINNING, MIDDLE, END

Here we look at paragraphing as it implements the essay's two powers: (1) idea and (2) structure. The thesis formulates the idea that penetrates the whole, like a skewer, through all its various bits of detail and meat. The structure arranges that whole in meaningful display. Paragraphs group the details for clearer comprehension. As we read, we begin to see an irradiated pattern. The essay has traced an inevitable beginning, middle, and end. Its paragraphs have evolved into a more or less uniform thickness. But beginning paragraphs and end paragraphs have evolved two opposite and distinct patterns. As the following three very different essays show, the writer's instinct, in its individual way, inevitably traces something of this ideal geometry.

Thus these essays illustrate, with natural variations, the

three essential kinds of paragraph: (1) the beginning paragraph, (2) the end paragraph, and (3) the middle paragraph—the standard one, the norm. Think of the beginning paragraph as a funnel that begins somewhat broadly with an opening invitation and then narrows down sharply to state the thesis at its end. Think of the end paragraph as the funnel inverted, starting with a sentence restating the essay's thesis, then opening out to wider and deeper implications, with a touch of fervor and finality.

Think of the middle paragraph as a standard frame of four or five sentences, and as a miniature of the essay as a whole, with its own small beginning, middle, and end. Its beginning is its *topic sentence*—its own small thesis, which the middle of the paragraph then unfolds and illustrates. Its end sentence should have some sense of conclusion, like the entire essay's end paragraph.

These are the three ideal forms of the paragraph, the forms-in-the-head, which writers use and vary as the flow of language and subject demand. Each of the essays in this section is ably paragraphed. Each writer, as if working from a preconceived norm, measures his or her thoughts more or less into equal paragraphs, sometimes coming up short for emphasis, sometimes expanding for clarity. Notice how most paragraphs begin with some kind of topic sentence. Notice, too, the transitional guides that help the reader from one paragraph to the next: *Since then, These, But, Though, By this time.* Finally, notice beginnings and endings. Asimov uses the inductive, questioning approach to organize his essay and develop his paragraphs. Thomas also follows the scientist's inductive impulse, taking six introductory paragraphs to build his beginning—the point from which he will argue his thesis—and then building his argument point by point, paragraph by paragraph, with frequent inductive questions. *The New Yorker*'s anonymous horsewoman tethers her autobiographical meditation in a perfect circle with her beginning and ending paragraphs.

The Ultimate Speed Limit

ISAAC ASIMOV

————————●————————

*Asimov makes his thesis a question—*Or won't it?*—
following two preliminary questions that introduce
the con, or opposing side, of his argument, like the
subordinate* Although *in a positive statement. His
title has already pretty well stated his belief in an
ultimate cosmic speed limit. But his thesis-question
sets up an* inductive *procedure, which, after all, is the
way of science—an essay "leading into" the answer
rather than the usual* deductive *procedure of Jefferson and most other essayists: stating the thesis, then
demonstrating the evidence to persuade the reader it
is right. Asimov must first lead his reader by careful
steps to grasp some simple ideas of physics that most
find bewildering. Then he begins to handle his cons
with* Nor is this just theory. *Then he faces the cons of
science fiction before his final firm conclusion, his
essential thesis:* the speed limit remains. *Note how he
moves in brief paragraphs to clarify his technical explanation, step by step, and how his paragraphs
lengthen when he reaches easier expository ground.*

If you push something hard enough, it begins to move. If
you continue to push it while it moves, it accelerates; that
is, it keeps moving faster and faster. Is there a limit to how
fast it can move? If we just keep on pushing and pushing,
will it go faster and faster and faster? Or won't it?

When something moves, it has kinetic energy. The quantity of kinetic energy possessed by a moving object depends
upon its velocity and its mass. Velocity is a straightforward
property that is easy to grasp. To be told something is moving at a high or a low velocity brings a clear picture to mind.
Mass, however, is a little more subtle.

Mass is related to the ease with which an object can be accelerated. Suppose you have two baseballs; one is conventional, and the other is an exact imitation in solid steel. It would take much more effort to accelerate the steel ball to a particular speed by throwing it than it would the ordinary baseball. The steel ball, therefore, has more mass.

Gravitational pull also depends on mass. The steel ball is attracted more strongly to the earth than the baseball because the steel ball has more mass. In general, then, on the surface of the earth, a more massive object is heavier than a less massive one. In fact, it is common (but not really correct) to say "heavier" and "lighter" when we mean "more massive" and "less massive."

But back to our moving object with kinetic energy that depends on both velocity and mass. If our moving object is made to move more rapidly by means of that push we're talking about, then its kinetic energy increases. This increase is reflected both in an increase in velocity and in an increase in mass, the two factors on which kinetic energy depends.

At low velocities, the ordinary velocities in the world about us, most of the increase in kinetic energy goes into increase in velocity and very little into increase in mass. In fact, the increase in mass is so tiny at ordinary velocities that it could not be measured. It was assumed that as an object gained kinetic energy, *only* the velocity increased—the mass remained unchanged.

As a result, mass was often incorrectly defined as simply the quantity of matter in a particular object, something that obviously couldn't change with velocity.

In the 1890s, however, theoretical reasons arose for considering the possibility that mass increased as velocity increased. Then, in 1905, Albert Einstein explained the matter exactly in his Special Theory of Relativity. He presented an equation that described just how mass increased as velocity increased.

Using this equation, you can calculate that an object with a mass of 1 kilogram when it is at rest has a mass of

1.005 kilograms when it is moving at 30,000 kilometers a second. (A velocity of 30,000 kilometers per second—about 18,600 miles per second—is far greater than any velocity measured prior to the twentieth century, and even then the increase in mass is only half of 1 percent. It's no surprise that the mass increase was never suspected until the 1890s.)

As velocity continues to increase, the mass begins to increase more rapidly. At 150,000 kilometers per second, an object that has a "rest mass" of 1 kilogram has a mass of 1.15 kilograms. At 270,000 kilometers per second, the mass has risen to 2.29 kilograms.

As the mass increases, however, the difficulty of further accelerating the object—making it move still faster—also increases. (That's the definition of mass.) A push of a given size becomes less and less effective as a way of increasing the object's velocity and more and more effective as a way of increasing its mass. By the time velocity has increased to 299,000 kilometers per second, almost all the energy gained by an object through further pushes goes into an increase in mass and very little goes into an increase in velocity. This is just the opposite of the situation at very low or "normal" velocities.

As we approach a velocity of 299,792.5 kilometers per second, just about *all* the extra energy derived from a push goes into additional mass and almost *none* goes into additional velocity. If a velocity of 299,792.5 kilometers per second could actually be reached, the mass of any moving object with a rest mass greater than zero would be infinite. No push, however great, could then make it move faster.

As it happens, 299,792.5 kilometers per second (about 186,000 miles per second) is the speed of light. Thus what Einstein's Special Theory of Relativity tells us is that it is impossible for any object with mass to be accelerated to speeds equal to or greater than the speed of light. The speed of light (in a vacuum) is the absolute speed limit for objects with mass, objects such as ourselves and our spaceships.

Nor is this just theory. Velocities at very nearly the

speed of light have been measured since the Special Theory was announced, and the increase in mass was found to be exactly as predicted. The Special Theory predicted all sorts of phenomena that have since been observed with great accuracy, and there seems to be no reason to doubt the theory or to doubt the fact that the speed of light is the speed limit for all objects with mass.

But let's get more fundamental. All objects with mass are made up of combinations of subatomic particles that themselves possess mass; for example, the proton, the electron, and the neutron. Such particles must always move at speeds less than that of light. They are called "tardyons," a name invented by physicist Olexa-Myron Bilaniuk and his co-workers.

There also are particles that at rest would have no mass at all—a rest mass of zero. However, these particles are never at rest, so the value of the rest mass must be determined indirectly. Bilaniuk therefore suggested the term "proper mass" be used to replace rest mass in order to avoid speaking of the rest mass of something that is never at rest.

It turns out that any particle with a proper mass of zero *must* travel at the speed of 299,792.5 kilometers per second, no more, no less. Light is made up of photons, particles that have a proper mass of zero. This is why light travels at 299,792.5 kilometers per second and why this speed is known as the "speed of light." Other particles with proper mass of zero, such as neutrinos and gravitons, also travel at the speed of light. Bilaniuk suggested that all such zero mass particles be termed "luxons" from a Latin word for "light."

This celestial speed limit, the speed of light, has been of particular annoyance to writers of science fiction because it has seriously limited the scope of their stories. The nearest star, Alpha Centauri, is 25 trillion miles away. Traveling at the speed of light, it would take 4.3 years (earthtime) to go from earth to Alpha Centauri, and another 4.3 years to come back. Special Relativity's speed limit therefore means that a minimum of 8.6 years must pass on earth before anything can make a round trip to even the nearest star. A minimum of 600 years must pass before anything can get to the Pole Star and back. A minimum of 150,000 years must pass before anything can get to the other end of the Galaxy and back. A minimum of 5 million years must pass before anything can get to the Andromeda Galaxy and back.

Taking these *minimum* time lapses into account (and remembering that the actual time lapse would be much larger under any reasonable conditions) would make any science fiction story involving interstellar travel extraordinarily complicated. Science fiction writers who wished to avoid these complications would find themselves confined to the solar system only.

What can be done? To begin with, science fiction writers might ignore the whole thing and pretend there is no limit. That, however, is not real science fiction; it is just fairy tales. On the other hand, science fiction writers can sigh and accept the speed limit with all its complications. L. Sprague de Camp did so routinely, and Poul Anderson recently wrote a novel, *Tau Zero,* that accepted the limit in a very fruitful manner. Finally, science fiction writers might find some more or less plausible way of getting around the speed limit. Thus, Edward E. Smith, in his series of intergalactic romances, assumed some device for reducing the inertia of any object to zero. With zero inertia, any push can produce infinite acceleration, and Smith reasoned that any velocity up to the infinite would therefore become possible.

Of course, there is no known way of reducing inertia to zero. Even if there were a way, inertia is completely equivalent to mass and to reduce inertia to zero is to reduce mass to zero. Particles without mass *can* be accelerated with infinite ease, but only to the speed of light. Smith's zero-inertia drive would make possible travel *at* the speed of light but not *faster* than light.

A much more common science fictional device is to imagine an object leaving our universe altogether.

To see what this means, let's consider a simple analogy.

Suppose that a person must struggle along on foot across very difficult country—mountainous and full of cliffs, declivities, torrential rivers, and so on. He might well argue that it was completely impossible to travel more than two miles a day. If he has so long concentrated on surface travel as to consider it the only form of progress conceivable, he might well come to imagine that a speed limit of two miles per day represents a natural law and an ultimate limit under all circumstances.

But what if he travels through the air, not necessarily in a powered device such as a jet plane or rocket, but in something as simple as a balloon? He can then easily cover two miles in an hour or less, regardless of how broken and difficult the ground beneath him is. In getting into a balloon, he moved outside the "universe" to which his fancied ultimate speed limit applied. Or, speaking in dimensions, he derived a speed limit for two-dimensional travel along a surface, but it did not apply to travel in three dimensions by way of a balloon.

Similarly, the Einsteinian limit might be conceived of as applying only to our own space. In that case, what if we could move into something beyond space, as our balloonist moved into something beyond surface? In the region beyond space, or "hyperspace," there might be no speed limit at all. You could move at any velocity, however enormous, by the proper application of energy and then, after a time lapse of a few seconds, perhaps, re-enter ordinary space at some point that would have required two centuries of travel in the ordinary fashion.

Hyperspace, expressly stated or quietly assumed, has been part of the stock in trade of science fiction writers for several decades now.

Few, if any, science fiction writers supposed hyperspace and faster-than-light travel to be anything more than convenient fiction that made it simpler to develop the intricacies and pathways of plots on a galactic and super-galactic scale. Yet, surprisingly enough, science seemed to come to their rescue. What science fiction writers were groping toward by means of pure imagination was something that, in a way, seemed to have justification after all in Special Relativity.

Suppose we imagine an object with a rest mass of 1 kilogram moving at 425,000 kilometers per second, nearly half again as fast as the speed of light. We might dismiss this as impossible but, for a moment, let's not. Rather, let us use Einstein's equation to calculate what its mass would be if it did reach this speed.

It turns out that, according to Einstein's equation, an object with a rest mass of 1 kilogram moving at 425,000 kilometers per second has a mass equal to $\sqrt{-1}$ kilograms. The expression $\sqrt{-1}$ is what mathematicians call an "imaginary number." Such numbers are not really imaginary and have important uses, but they are not the kind of numbers ordinarily considered appropriate for measuring mass. The general feeling would be to consider an imaginary mass as "absurd" and let it go at that.

In 1962, however, Bilaniuk and his co-workers decided to check into the matter of imaginary mass and see if it might be given meaning. Perhaps an imaginary mass merely implied a set of properties that were different from those possessed by objects with ordinary mass. For instance, an object with ordinary mass speeds up when pushed and slows down when it makes its way through a resisting medium. What if an object with imaginary mass slowed down when it was pushed and speeded up when it made its way through a resisting medium? On the same line of thought, an object with ordinary mass has more energy the faster it goes. What if an object with imaginary mass has *less* energy the faster it goes?

Once such concepts were introduced, Bilaniuk and his associates were able to show that objects with imaginary mass, traveling faster than the speed of light, did not *violate* Einstein's Special Theory of Relativity. In 1967, physicist Gerald Feinberg, in discussing these faster-than-light particles, called them "tachyons" from a Greek word meaning "speed."

However, tachyons have their own limitations. As they gain energy by being pushed, they slow down. As they move slower and slower, it becomes more and more difficult to make them move still slower. When they approach the speed of light, they cannot be made to go any more slowly.

There are, then, three classes of particles: (1) *Tardyons,* which have a proper mass greater than zero and which can move at any velocity *less* than the speed of light, but can never move at the speed of light or faster; (2) *Luxons,* which have a proper mass of zero and which can move *only* at the speed of light; and (3) *Tachyons,* which have an imaginary proper mass and which can move at any velocity *greater* than the speed of light, but can never move at the speed of light or slower.

Granted that this third class, the tachyons, can exist without violating Special Relativity, do they *actually* exist? It is a common rule in theoretical physics, one accepted by many physicists, that anything not forbidden by the basic laws of nature *must* take place. If the tachyons are not forbidden, then they must exist. But can we detect them?

In theory, there is a way of doing so. When a tachyon passes through a vacuum at more than the speed of light (as it must), it leaves a flash of light trailing behind it. If this light were detected, one could, from the light's properties, identify and characterize the tachyon that has passed. Unfortunately, a tachyon moving at more than the speed of light remains in a particular vicinity—say, in the neighborhood of a detecting device—for only an incredibly small fraction of a second. The chances of detecting a tachyon are therefore incredibly small, and none have as yet been detected. (But that doesn't prove they don't exist.)

It is perfectly possible to convert a particle from one class to another. For example, an electron and a positron, both of which are tardyons, can combine to form gamma rays. Gamma rays are composed of luxons and can be converted back into electrons and positrons. There would seem, then, to be no theoretical objection to the conversion of tardyons to tachyons and back again, if the proper procedure could be found.

Suppose, then, that it were possible to convert all the tardyons in a spaceship, together with its contents, both animate and inanimate, into equivalent tachyons. The tachyon-spaceship, with no perceptible interval of acceleration, would be moving at perhaps 1,000 times the speed of light and would get to the neighborhood of Alpha Centauri in a little over a day. There it would be reconverted into tardyons.

It must be admitted that this is a lot harder to do than to say. How does one convert tardyons into tachyons while maintaining all the intricate interrelationships between the tardyons, say, in a human body? How does one control the exact speed and direction of travel of the tachyons? How does one convert the tachyons back into tardyons with such precision that everything is returned exactly to the original without disturbing that delicate phenomenon called life?

But suppose it could be done. In that case, going to the distant stars and galaxies by way of the tachyon-universe would be exactly equivalent to the science fictional dream of making the trip by way of hyperspace. Would the speed limit then be lifted? Would the universe, in theory at least, be at our feet?

Maybe not. In an article I wrote in 1969, I suggested that the two universes that are separated by the "luxon wall," ours of the tardyons and the other of the tachyons, represented a suspicious asymmetry. It seemed to me that the laws of nature were basically symmetrical, and to imagine speeds less than light on one side of the wall and speeds greater than light on the other wasn't right.

Properly speaking, I suggested (without any mathematical analysis at all and arguing entirely from intuition) that whichever side of the luxon wall you were on would seem to be the tardyon universe and it would always be the other side that was the tachyon universe. In that way there would be perfect symmetry: Both sides would be tardyon to themselves; both sides tachyon to the other. In an article entitled "Space-Time" in the 1971 issue of the *McGraw-Hill Yearbook of Science and Technology,* Bilaniuk subjected the matter to careful mathematical analysis. He found that there *was* just this symmetry between the two universes.

If this is so, the speed limit remains. No matter how spaceships shift back and forth between universes, they are always tardyon, and it is always the other universe that is going faster than the speed of light. Science fiction writers must, after all, look elsewhere for their hyper-space.

IDEAS

1. Does Asimov provide sufficient explanations and examples to keep you interested in his ideas despite their technical nature?

2. What exactly is the ultimate speed limit? Do you think that modern space exploration has, perhaps, outdated Asimov's thesis?

3. Asimov states that many theoretical physicists accept the idea "that anything not forbidden by the basic laws of nature *must* take place." Does his conclusion about tachyons bear this out?

ORGANIZATION AND STYLE

1. How effective is Asimov's opening paragraph? Is it funneled to a point? In what way does it help to set the tone for the essay?

2. In several places Asimov moves from one idea to another with one-sentence paragraphs. Is this effective? Would those transitional sentences be just as effective at the end of the previous paragraph or the beginning of the next? Why or why not?

3. Throughout the essay Asimov asks rhetorical questions. Sometimes they address his reader directly, involving the reader in his ideas. Sometimes they are transitions, changing his direction. Sometimes they re-

fute his opposition. Isolate several of these rhetorical questions and discuss their particular function.

4. Isolate several of Asimov's paragraphs and evaluate the transitional word or phrase—his *this, of course,* his repeated word or idea.

5. In what way does Asimov's final paragraph take the reader back to his opening paragraph?

WRITING

1. Use Asimov's opening sentence—"When you push something hard enough, it begins to move"—as a thesis sentence for an essay of your own. Instead of arguing a scientific topic, however, argue a social one. If you push someone—a parent, a teacher, a boyfriend or girlfriend, a husband or wife—hard enough, does that person really move as you intend? If not, why not?

2. Write a critique of some science fiction work (a short story, book, or film) with which you are familiar. Use Asimov's ideas as a part of your discussion. Is maintaining the speed limit necessary to fiction? Consider converting "tardyons into tachyons while maintaining all the interrelationships between tardyons, say, in a human body." (Incidentally, would *among* have been a better word? Why?)

The Hazards of Science

LEWIS THOMAS

———————— ● ————————

Like Asimov, Thomas follows the scientist's inductive impulse. Yet he also manages it within the lines of deductive paragraphing, setting up hubris *as a partial thesis in his introductory paragraph and building up to his* flat no *in his sixth. His frequent questions continue to mark his inductive cast of mind until his concluding paragraph ultimately discards* hubris *as a misnomer for science and a mistake.*

The code word for criticism of science and scientists these days is "hubris."* Once you've said that word, you've said it all; it sums up, in a word, all of today's apprehensions and misgivings in the public mind—not just about what is perceived as the insufferable attitude of the scientists themselves but, enclosed in the same word, what science and technology are perceived to be doing to make this century, this near to its ending, turn out so wrong.

"Hubris" is a powerful word, containing layers of powerful meaning, derived from a very old word, but with a new life of its own, growing way beyond the limits of its original meaning. Today, it is strong enough to carry the full weight of disapproval for the cast of mind that thought up atomic fusion and fission as ways of first blowing up and later heating cities as well as the attitudes which led to strip mining, offshore oil wells, Kepone, food additives, SST's, and the tiny spherical particles of plastic recently discovered clogging the waters of the Sargasso Sea.

The biomedical sciences are now caught up with physi-

*Overbearing pride (from Greek).

cal science and technology in the same kind of critical judgment, with the same pejorative word. Hubris is responsible, it is said, for the whole biological revolution. It is hubris that has given us the prospects of behavior control, psychosurgery, fetal research, heart transplants, the cloning of prominent politicians from bits of their own eminent tissue, iatrogenic disease, overpopulation, and recombinant DNA. This last, the new technology that permits the stitching of one creature's genes into the DNA of another, to make hybrids, is currently cited as the ultimate example of hubris. It is hubris for man to manufacture a hybrid on his own.

So now we are back to the first word again, from "hybrid" to "hubris," and the hidden meaning of two beings joined unnaturally together by man is somehow retained. Today's joining is straight out of Greek mythology: it is the combining of man's capacity with the special prerogative of the gods, and it is really in this sense of outrage that the word "hubris" is being used today. This is what the word has grown into, a warning, a code word, a shorthand signal from the language itself: if man starts doing things reserved for the gods, deifying himself, the outcome will be something worse for him, symbolically, than the litters of wild boars and domestic sows were for the ancient Romans.

To be charged with hubris is therefore an extremely serious matter, and not to be dealt with by murmuring things about antiscience and anti-intellectualism, which is what many of us engaged in science tend to do these days. The doubts about our enterprise have their origin in the most profound kind of human anxiety. If we are right and the critics are wrong, then it has to be that the word "hubris" is being mistakenly employed, that this is not what we are up to, that there is, for the time being anyway, a fundamental misunderstanding of science.

I suppose there is one central question to be dealt with, and I am not at all sure how to deal with it, although I am quite certain about my own answer to it. It is this: are there some kinds of information leading to some sorts of knowledge that human beings are really better off not having? Is there a limit to scientific inquiry not set by what is knowable but by what we *ought* to be knowing? Should we stop short of learning about some things, for fear of what we, or someone, will do with the knowledge? My own answer is a flat no, but I must confess that this is an intuitive response, and I am neither inclined nor trained to reason my way through it.

There has been some effort, in and out of scientific quarters, to make recombinant DNA into the issue on which to settle this argument. Proponents of this line of research are accused of pure hubris, of assuming the rights of gods, of arrogance and outrage; what is more, they confess themselves to be in the business of making live hybrids with their own hands. The mayor of Cambridge [Massachusetts—site of both Harvard University and the Massachusetts Institute of Technology] and the attorney general of New York have both been advised to put a stop to it, forthwith.

It is not quite the same sort of argument, however, as the one about limiting knowledge, although this is surely part of it. The knowledge is already here, and the rage of the argument is about its application in technology. Should DNA for making certain useful or interesting proteins be incorporated into *E. coli* plasmids or not? Is there a risk of inserting the wrong sort of toxins or hazardous viruses, and then having the new hybrid organisms spread beyond the laboratory? Is this a technology for creating new varieties of pathogens, and should it be stopped because of this?

If the argument is held to this level, I can see no reason why it cannot be settled, by reasonable people. We have learned a great deal about the handling of dangerous microbes in the last century, although I must say that the opponents of recombinant-DNA research tend to downgrade this huge body of information. At one time or another, agents as hazardous as those of rabies, psittacosis, plague, and typhus have been dealt with by investigators in secure laboratories, with only rare instances of self-infection of the investigators themselves, and no instances at all of epidemics. It takes some high imagining to postulate the creation of brand-new pathogens so wild and voracious as to spread from equally secure laboratories to endanger human life at large, as some of the arguers are now maintaining.

But this is precisely the trouble with the recombinant-DNA problem: it has become an emotional issue, with too many irretrievably lost tempers on both sides. It has lost the sound of a discussion of technological safety, and begins now to sound like something else, almost like a religious controversy, and here it is moving toward the central issue: are there some things in science we should not be learning about?

There is an inevitably long list of hard questions to follow this one, beginning with the one which asks whether the mayor of Cambridge should be the one to decide, first off.

Maybe we'd be wiser, all of us, to back off before the recombinant-DNA issue becomes too large to cope with. If we're going to have a fight about it, let it be confined to the immediate issue of safety and security, of the recombinants now under consideration, and let us by all means have regulations and guidelines to assure the public safety wherever these are indicated or even suggested. But if it is possible let us stay off that question about limiting human knowledge. It is too loaded, and we'll simply not be able to cope with it.

By this time it will have become clear that I have already taken sides in the matter, and my point of view is entirely prejudiced. This is true, but with a qualification. I am not so much in favor of recombinant-DNA research as I am opposed to the opposition of this line of inquiry. As a longtime student of infectious-disease agents, I do not take kindly the declarations that we do not know how to keep from catching things in laboratories, much less how to keep them from spreading beyond the laboratory walls. I believe we learned a lot about this sort of thing, long ago. Moreover, I regard it as a form of hubris-in-reverse to claim that man can make deadly pathogenic microorganisms so easily. In my view, it takes a long time and a great deal of interliving before a microbe can become a successful pathogen. Pathogenicity is, in a sense, a highly skilled trade, and only a tiny minority of all the numberless tons of microbes on the earth has ever been involved itself in it; most bacteria are busy with their own business, browsing and recycling the rest of life. Indeed, pathogenicity often seems to be a sort of biological accident in which signals are misdirected by the microbe or misinterpreted by the host, as in the case of endotoxin, or in which the intimacy between host and microbe is of such long standing that a form of molecular mimicry becomes possible, as in the case of diphtheria toxin. I do not believe that by simply putting together new combinations of genes one can create creatures as highly skilled and adapted for dependence as a pathogen must be, any more than I have ever believed that microbial life from the moon or Mars could possibly make a living on this planet.

But, as I said, I'm not at all sure this is what the argument is really about. Behind it is that other discussion, which I wish we would not have to become enmeshed in.

I cannot speak for the physical sciences, which have moved an immense distance in this century by any standard, but it does seem to me that in the biological and medical sciences we are still far too ignorant to begin making judgments about what sorts of things we should be learning or not learning. To the contrary, we ought to be grateful for whatever snatches we can get hold of, and we ought to be out there on a much larger scale than today's, looking for more.

We should be very careful with that word "hubris," and make sure it is not used when not warranted. There is a great danger in applying it to the search for knowledge. The application of knowledge is another matter, and there is hubris in plenty in our technology, but I do not believe that looking for new information about nature, at whatever level, can possibly be called unnatural. Indeed, if there is any single attribute of human beings, apart from language, which distinguishes them from all other creatures on earth, it is their insatiable, uncontrollable drive to learn things and then to exchange the information with others of the species. Learning is what we do, when you think about it. I cannot think of a human impulse more difficult to govern.

But I can imagine lots of reasons for trying to govern it. New information about nature is very likely, at the outset, to be upsetting to someone or other. The recombinant-DNA line of research is already upsetting, not because of the dangers now being argued about but because it is disturbing, in a fundamental way, to face the fact that the genetic machinery in control of the planet's life can be fooled around with so easily. We do not like the idea that anything so fixed and stable as a species line can be changed. The notion that genes can be taken out of one genome and inserted in another is unnerving. Classical mythology is peopled with mixed beings—part man, part animal or plant—and most of them are associated with tragic stories. Recombinant DNA is a reminder of bad dreams.

The easiest decision for society to make in matters of this kind is to appoint an agency, or a commission, or a subcommittee within an agency to look into the problem and provide advice. And the easiest course for a committee to take, when confronted by any process that appears to be disturbing people or making them uncomfortable, is to recommend that it be stopped, at least for the time being.

I can easily imagine such a committee, composed of unimpeachable public figures, arriving at the decision that the time is not quite ripe for further exploration of the transplantation of genes, that we should put this off for a while, maybe until next century, and get on with other affairs that make us less discomfited. Why not do science on something more popular, say, how to get solar energy more cheaply? Or mental health?

The trouble is, it would be very hard to stop once this line was begun. There are, after all, all sorts of scientific inquiry that are not much liked by one constituency or another, and we might soon find ourselves with crowded rosters, panels, standing committees, set up in Washington for the appraisal, and then the regulation, of research. Not on grounds of the possible value and usefulness of the new knowledge, mind you, but for guarding society against scientific hubris, against the kinds of knowledge we're better off without.

It would be absolutely irresistible as a way of spending time, and people would form long queues for membership. Almost anything would be fair game, certainly anything to do with genetics, anything relating to population control, or, on the other side, research on aging. Very few fields would get by, except perhaps for some, like mental health, in which nobody really expects anything much to happen, surely nothing new or disturbing.

The research areas in the greatest trouble would be those already containing a sense of bewilderment and surprise, with discernible prospects of upheaving present dogmas.

It is hard to predict how science is going to turn out, and if it is really good science it is impossible to predict. This is in the nature of the enterprise. If the things to be found are actually new, they are by definition unknown in advance, and there is no way of telling in advance where a really new line of inquiry will lead. You cannot make choices in this matter, selecting things you think you're going to like and shutting off the lines that make for discomfort. You either have science or you don't, and if you have it you are obliged to accept the surprising and disturbing pieces of information, even the overwhelming and upheaving ones, along with the neat and promptly useful bits. It is like that.

The only solid piece of scientific truth about which I feel totally confident is that we are profoundly ignorant about nature. Indeed, I regard this as the major discovery of the past hundred years of biology. It is, in its way, an illuminating piece of news. It would have amazed the brightest minds of the eighteenth-century Enlightenment to be told by any of us how little we know, and how bewildering seems the way ahead. It is this sudden confrontation with the depth and scope of ignorance that represents the most significant contribution of twentieth-century science to the human intellect. We are, at last, facing up to it. In earlier times, we either pretended to understand how things worked or ignored the problem, or simply made up stories to fill the gaps. Now that we have begun exploring in earnest, doing serious science, we are getting glimpses of how huge the questions are, and how far from being answered. Because of this, these are hard times for the human intellect, and it is no wonder that we are depressed. It is not so bad being ignorant if you are totally ignorant; the hard thing is knowing in some detail the reality of ignorance, the worst spots and here and there the not-so-bad spots, but no true light at the end of any tunnel nor even any tunnels that can yet be trusted. Hard times, indeed.

But we are making a beginning, and there ought to be some satisfaction, even exhilaration, in that. The method works. There are probably no questions we can think up that can't be answered, sooner or later, including even the matter of consciousness. To be sure, there may well be questions we can't think up, ever, and therefore limits to the reach of human intellect which we will never know about, but that is another matter. Within our limits, we should be able to work our way through to all our answers, if we keep at it long enough, and pay attention.

I am putting it this way, with all the presumption and confidence that I can summon, in order to raise another, last question. Is this hubris? Is there something fundamentally unnatural, or intrinsically wrong, or hazardous for the species in the ambition that drives us all to reach a comprehensive understanding of nature, including ourselves? I cannot believe it. It would seem to me a more unnatural thing, and more of an offense against nature, for us to come on the same scene endowed as we are with curiosity, filled to overbrimming as we are with questions, and naturally talented as we are for the asking of clear questions, and then for us to do nothing about it or, worse, to try to suppress the questions. This is the greater danger for our species, to try to pretend that we are another kind of animal, that we do not need to satisfy our curiosity, that we can get along somehow without inquiry and exploration and experimentation, and that the human mind can rise above its ignorance by simply asserting that there are things it has no need to know. This, to my way of thinking, is the real hubris, and it carries danger for us all.

IDEAS

1. What does Thomas's term *code word,* at the start, indicate about his underlying thesis?

2. The root behind the Greek *hubris* and the Latin *hybrid* is the Indo-European *ud* (modern "out" and "uttermost") that lends the Greek word its meaning "outrage," in pride and anger, and the Latin word its meaning "out of the ordinary." Comment on Thomas's paragraph beginning with the topic sentence "So now we are back to the first word again, from 'hybrid' to 'hubris'. . . ."

3. What is Thomas's distinction between hubris in the search for knowledge and in the application of knowledge? What illustration can you offer to distinguish between the two?

4. Some have charged that research physicians (for instance, the surgeons who performed the heart transplant on Barney Clark) are guilty of hubris. Do you agree or disagree? To what extent are medical advances dependent upon hubris? Are any safeguards needed to protect the patient or society?

5. What exactly does Thomas define as the "real hubris" in his final paragraph?

ORGANIZATION AND STYLE

1. Thomas's first six paragraphs introduce his subject and lead up to his thesis. Is this much background necessary to prove his point?

2. Unlike Asimov, Thomas writes in the first person. How does his purpose justify this approach?

3. Four of the paragraphs in this rather short essay begin with "But. . . ." What is the purpose of those paragraphs?

4. The only paragraph without some supporting detail is the single-sentence one beginning "The research areas in the greatest trouble. . . ." Why does Thomas not include detail in this paragraph?

5. With which paragraph does Thomas begin his conclusion?

WRITING

1. Select one area of scientific research—for instance, organ transplants, the testing of new drugs, space exploration, or nuclear energy—and develop an essay in which you discuss the necessity for certain built-in controls that will protect society. You might wish to use some of Thomas's ideas about hubris as you develop your ideas. Or try an essay on the "satisfaction, even exhilaration," or the hazards in learning something out of curiosity—observing ants, tinkering with a motor.

2. *Hubris* is defined as overbearing pride, but everyone recognizes that a certain amount of pride is essential to one's sense of worth. How does one distinguish constructive pride from overbearing pride? Develop an essay in which you explore the differences. Be certain to offer specific examples of each.

Changing Horses in Mid-Dream

ANONYMOUS

———————●———————

An anonymous horsewoman (a "correspondent" for
The New Yorker) *sets up a dialectic contrast in a neat*
opening paragraph with a thesis so clear that half of
her contrast, the cat, can then vanish—only to reap-
pear and make her point with an equally neat ending
paragraph, in this wonderland of an essay. Notice
how her middle paragraphs swell in length as her
troubles and enthusiasms require.

Sometimes I make scientific discoveries that I would like
to share with the world, but because I don't have the sort
of proof scientific journals require, my findings, I know,
would not be accepted. Nevertheless, I write them down
just to see how they look on paper. A recent discovery has
to do with an important difference between the minds of
cats (predators) and horses (herbivores). Herbivores live
in the present. For predators, the future is all.

I have two horses. One of them, Sunny, is a pinto pony
about fourteen hands high. I got him fifteen years ago,
when my son went away to school and I was lonely. The
pony is very pretty, with flashy chestnut-and-white mark-
ings and a neck that can arch like those of the horses in
Greek marbles. But he is small and has faults—a balky
disposition and a jolting trot, owing to his short stride.
After I'd had Sunny a few years, I was invited to ride a
friend's mare, Maisie, and fell in love with her. She was
considerably bigger—a nice-looking eighteen-year-old
chestnut with smooth gaits and a responsiveness that
made riding her an easy thing, like dancing with a good
dancer. I bought Maisie and retired Sunny. They have
spent a peaceful decade grazing in my pasture. They look

beautiful together. The chestnut patches on Sunny's sleek hide match Maisie's coat perfectly, and Sunny's white mane and tail heighten the whiteness of the daisies in June and the Queen Anne's lace later in the summer.

However, ten years passed, and Maisie was twenty-eight. She still looked fine, but the summer before last, when I rode her, I found that though she still had plenty of life—at a light touch, she would, as always, break into her airy trot—there were also unexpected little near-mishaps along the trail that had never happened before. A root would trip her. She would lurch, and I would lurch. We always recovered together, but it was a little scary all the same. The vet came and looked her over. She was remarkably sound, he said, but twenty-eight years is a lot of years.

I like this vet. He is a tall, casual young man, friendly and kind. He doesn't scorn to make calls on what they call in the trade "a backyard horse," whereas a lot of vets won't come unless you have a string of valuable show horses. I stood holding Maisie in the bright stable yard and chatted with the vet. He pointed out that riding a horse that stumbles has its dangers. Sooner or later, she might go down. "You can ride her very slow, on level ground," he said. "Or else"—and here I was aware of a faintly quizzical smile as he gazed at the two of us—"you might look for another horse."

The summer of 1979 was a difficult summer for me. I had little time for anything except a long, grueling piece of work that kept me grinding away at the typewriter day after day. I seldom rode. The work was so filled with tension that at night it took a long time to go to sleep. To pass the time and try to relax, I revived a childhood habit of deliberately turning my thoughts to something beautiful, something wonderful to contemplate, something I wanted very much. Now my choice was a horse. Next summer, when my work was finished and I was free again, I would buy a new horse. I feel about beautiful animals the way some people feel about art—enraptured and covetous. I decided I would buy a very beautiful horse. This must, after all, be my last horse. A horse aged eight or ten (when horses begin to be sensible) would last the rest of my riding days. Therefore, I would get the most beautiful horse I could find. Money wouldn't matter. I began to picture what I would like most. The image that became fixed in my mind was a white mare—possibly an Arab. She would have a delicate head, small, perfect feet, a lovely conformation, smooth gaits. She must be small, so that mounting wouldn't be difficult. I was able to picture her completely—a white horse grazing in a green pasture—and feel her under me as I imagined riding her through the fields and into the woods. Night after night, these thoughts put me to sleep.

This spring, I made a phone call to a man who breeds horses and asked him what he had to sell. I didn't mention my fantasy horse, because in the light of day it sounded absurd to shop for something so specific. He described a number of unsuitable horses and then said, "I do have a brood mare I'm thinking of selling. She may be a bit high-priced for you, but she's a real beauty." I asked what sort of horse she was, and he said she was an Arab, with elegant conformation and gaits. "How big?" I asked. "On the small side," he replied. "About fourteen two." I had an almost eerie feeling as I asked what color the mare was. He answered, "White." I made an appointment to see her the next day.

When I got to the farm, the owner took me into the stable where the mare, named Rassi, was. She was in a box stall. At the sight of us, she was on her toes—ears forward, nostrils quivering. She was lovely. The man snapped a shank to her halter and brought her out. She snorted and danced a little in the aisle. When I patted her neck, she shied nervously. "That doesn't mean anything," the man said. "She's really gentle, but she hasn't been handled much lately. Wait until you see her move. This mare has wings on her feet." Rassi's owner picked up a lunge line, and we walked out to the meadow. She arched her neck like a horse in a Grecian marble—she was the color of marble, too—and her small black hooves, neat and perfect, danced on the green turf. She tossed her head, looking at everything, and the owner—a strong man—took a tight grip on the shank. I could see his muscles strain as he held her. In the center of the meadow, at the crest of a little hill, he let out the line and Rassi took off, trotting in a wide circle at the end of the tether. She had been lovely before. Now she was breathtaking. Just as the owner had said, she had wings on her feet. As she extended her trot, she seemed hardly to touch the ground. Her head high, ears pricked, she fixed her gaze on the horizon as though if released she would simply soar across the meadow and into the woods. She cantered, then galloped. Her mane and tail had the grace of flowing water: the enchanted horse.

Rassi's owner slowed her down and pulled her in. "What do you think?" he asked. "Did you ever see such power? When you're on her, it's just like floating." Then he explained that though he would like me to ride her, he had no bridle or saddle—all his tack had been sent off to a horse show. He suggested I come back. I said I would telephone him and make a date. He led Rassi to a pasture, where other horses were grazing. The moment he unsnapped the lead, she was off like an arrow. She galloped around once and then, with the quick change of mood characteristic of horses, settled down to graze. A horse's thoughts center on the present: a mouthful of grass, then another; sudden alarm at something unexpected, such as a rabbit starting up; then quietness again when the danger is over. It makes sense for herbivores to think that way. They have no need to scheme or to plan. They have only one need—to evade the predator as long as possible. For them, each moment is sufficient unto itself.

I said goodbye and drove home, thinking, of course, about Rassi. She remained as clear in my mind's eye as the white mare of my fantasy with which this quest had begun. But there was now an added element in the picture: her hot, nervous temperament and the man's arm muscles straining as he held her. By the time I got home, I had made my decision. I knew that I wanted her even more now that she was real, but I was afraid of her. Ten years ago, I could have handled her, but not now. With all that power and spirit, anything might happen, and I wouldn't be strong enough, quick enough, brave enough to cope. Rassi was ideal for someone young, but not for me.

It was late afternoon, and I made a drink and took it out on the porch and tried to read the paper. The air was soft and calm, and the sun slanted beautifully through the leaves of overhanging trees, but the birds were noisy and distracting. I couldn't read. I thought, It is very foolish to get a new horse and risk your neck. Any new horse could give you trouble. And, face it, you don't ride that much anymore. Stick with Maisie and just go out for long, slow walks. If you only walk her, she'll be good for some years yet. While I was thinking these things, my black cat was in my lap. Like Maisie, she has slowed down lately. She used to hunt far out in the meadow, but now she knows her limitations and sticks pretty close to the shelter of the house. I was a little surprised when she jumped off my lap and went out on the lawn. As I watched, she walked purposefully over to the well, where a rambler rose makes a weedy thicket. At the edge of it, she arranged herself in a comfortable crouch and settled down to stare with steadfast patience into the leafy depths, whence, she no doubt had good reason to hope, some incautious mouse might at any moment emerge.

I turned back to the newspaper, in spite of the distracting birds and the distracting beauty of the trees and grass and sunshine. At the same time, wordless thoughts flowed through the back of my mind. After a while, I was aware that, without conscious thought, I had made a new decision. I would buy a horse after all. I would look for an older horse—maybe ten or fifteen—well-schooled and with a placid disposition; a horse that I could ride quietly and effortlessly. She would be a white mare, perhaps an Arab, with a flowing mane and tail. I saw her grazing in the pasture—Grecian marble in the green grass. It might take a long time to find her, but I would keep looking. I would find her.

I glanced out at the rosebush and saw my cat, still motionless after all that time, her lemon-yellow gaze unwaveringly fixed on the motionless leaves, and I thought, She is enjoying herself because she is thinking of the moment when the mouse will emerge. She is a predator, and predators wait, anticipate. Herbivores live in the present. For predators, the future is all. My cat and I, we live in our dreams.

IDEAS

1. What image do you get of the author after reading her essay? Why?

2. How does the author use her cat, mentioned in the first paragraph and not picked up again until near the end, to underscore her meaning?

3. What, exactly, is the author saying about our dreams? To what extent are they what keep us going? To what extent are we really afraid to have them come true?

ORGANIZATION AND STYLE

1. How does the author set up her thesis in her tightly developed first paragraph?

2. The essay is filled with short sentences, many only four or five words long and with *I* as the subject. How effective are these for the meaning of the essay? To what extent do they develop a bond between the author and the reader?

3. Why is the paragraph beginning "The summer of 1979 . . ." so important to the entire essay? In what way is it stylistically different from the other paragraphs?

4. Compare the first and last paragraphs as to theme and style. What do they have in common?

WRITING

1. The author clearly admits that she lives in her dream. Do you? In the writer's terms, do you see yourself as a *predator* or a *herbivore?* Do you live in the future or the present? What strengths or possible weaknesses do you see in your philosophic position?

2. This essay begins by taking unofficial scientific evidence, as observed by the author, and shaping that evidence into a thesis. You, too, have made similar empirical discoveries, which you can shape into a thesis. Perhaps you have reached a conclusion about why your two dogs have totally different personalities or why two of your best friends never really like each other. Write a light-hearted essay examining your discoveries. You might find the first paragraph of "Changing Horses" a helpful model to get your paper going.

4

TACTICS OF
DEVELOPMENT

We develop our ideas—and our essays to persuade others—
in a kind of alternating current basic to all thought:
separating likes from unlikes. Everything we know begins in comparison. Is this like, or unlike, that? Wet or
dry? Friend or foe? Tree or stone? The processes of dis-
cerning cause and effect, of comparing and contrasting,
of classifying, and of defining simply follow these neural
lines along which we think and survive. We employ their
essential tactics as we try, in our essays, to make our
thoughts survive. We employ their essential tactics to
persuade others to think as we think, to believe as we
believe.

Cause and Effect

The three essays that follow illustrate the flow and the ebb of this alluvial perception. Reeves looks at the present as cause, and suggests what the scary effects may all too probably be. Loeb examines various cause-to-effect concepts and, in the end, lets the reader make a decision about their reliability. Ward discusses what once was and what is now, while implying some causes and their effects along the way.

Vulnerable

RICHARD REEVES

———————————— ● ————————————

This essay on the paradox Los Angeles, a smog-bound former desert still burgeoning with new and newer houses and inhabitants, illustrates nicely the tactics of cause and effect. As the title suggests, Reeves's general direction is from present scene to probable future effects, but, to explain both the present and the future, he also looks from the present effect—Los Angeles, now—to past causes, or prior causes, such as geology, winds, greed, and love of nature.

It was midafternoon when I arrived at Los Angeles International Airport on October 23, 1978, but the sky was already dark. Driving home along the Pacific Ocean, I could see black to the north and west—boiling clouds of smoke coming off the Santa Monica Mountains. By six o'clock, I was standing in front of my house, in Pacific Palisades, watching waves of orange flame break over the mountains. Houses in the path of the waves exploded silently just before the flames reached them. I counted eight—puffs of bright gas, and then the houses were gone. By seven o'clock, I was packing the car—family photograph albums and insurance policies first—and listening to a radio report of tires melting as people tried to escape the fire in automobiles. At eight o'clock, the winds—the fierce desert winds called Santa Anas—suddenly died down, and the waves of fire spent themselves north of Sunset Boulevard, five blocks away. In places, the fire had been moving at fifty miles an hour.

My first earthquake was on New Year's Day of 1979. A friend and I were having a late lunch in a little place called the Inn of the Seventh Ray, in Topanga Canyon. There was a heavy jolt, and the floor vibrated. I thought a truck had hit the building. But the floor did not stop vibrating, as it would have if the building had been struck. I was confused. Actions seemed to be taking place in slow motion. People pushed chairs and tables aside, stood up, and began running toward the door. I realized that there was a sound—a steady roaring, as if a freight train were coming into the room. Outside, I still heard the sound and felt the vibration. Stones were clattering down a hillside into the roadway. The next day's Los Angeles *Times* reported that the quake was "small"—4.6 on the Richter scale. It had lasted less than ten seconds, and there were twenty smaller aftershocks. While it was happening, there was no way of knowing that this thing would be judged small by instruments at the California Institute of Technology.

I had already begun to wonder whether God intended for people to live in Los Angeles. Certainly He never meant for millions of them to live there. One of the first Europeans who saw the place—Father Juan Crespi, a Spanish missionary who passed through in August of 1769—wrote that the area was beautiful and a perfect place for a mission settlement. But he also noticed the signs of alternating drought and "great floods," and felt earthquake after earthquake, "which astonishes us." The men who followed Crespi defied God, defied nature, living in air they regularly poisoned, rerouting the rivers, levelling the hills, filling the canyons, building thousands and thousands of homes among the gnarled little trees and bushes —the "brush" in brushfires—that burn periodically and so make room for new growth, on slopes that continually slide back into canyons, above earthquake fault lines veined deep into the earth. Now I knew: Nature wanted Los Angeles back.

"There would be very few people in Los Angeles if they had to live with the energy, the wood, and the water that are naturally here," Richard Lillard, a retired professor of American studies and English at California State University, Los Angeles, told me not long ago. "Everything is imported. Four-fifths of the water in Los Angeles comes from other places—from as far away as four hundred and forty-four miles to the north. Nature has been pushed further here—a long way indeed—than almost anyplace on earth." Lillard has spent a professional lifetime thinking and writing about the ecology of Southern California, and in 1966 he put his thoughts together in a book titled *Eden in Jeopardy.* He wrote then, "Southern California speeds from one brilliant improvisation to another, valuing means, neglecting ends . . . the sun never rises and sets twice on the same landscape."

We sat talking last summer on the deck of Lillard's house, in the Hollywood Hills, overlooking, on a rare clear day, thirty miles of Los Angeles and the Pacific Ocean. "The city is a triumph of American genius and greed," he said. "What we're looking at was once a grassy plain. There were deer and antelope out there, and the Los Angeles River flowed through. It's been rerouted, of course, but it flowed through there"—he pointed to West Hollywood—"and nature remembers. There was a big rain in 1969, the spring of '69, and water began coming up near houses on Melrose and La Cienega. The original springs under La Cienega had begun to rise again."

West Hollywood is on the "City" side of Los Angeles, between the Pacific and forty miles of the Santa Monica Mountains. The Hollywood Hills are part of the southern slope of the Santa Monicas, a range with peaks that reach up to three thousand feet. To the north of the Santa Monicas is "the Valley"—the San Fernando Valley, flatland that stretches more than ten miles to the San Gabriel Mountains and was desert before water was pumped to it from farther north. When we talked about Los Angeles, we were talking about the basin of the Los Angeles River—roughly a thousand square miles between the San Gabriels and the sea, from Malibu in the north to Long Beach in the south. Politically, the area is a collage of cities—the City of Los Angeles, Santa Monica, Beverly Hills, and others—and communities scattered through the southern part of Los Angeles County. Perhaps six million people live in that basin.

"This is a city built by Yankee ingenuity," Lillard said. "The mud flats at the end of the continent were turned into harbors, marinas were dredged, the hills were levelled and nicked, and the canyons filled in. The water is imported. Even the air is imported, by the Santa Anas from the desert. Otherwise, no one could breathe the air that civilization has brought to the basin. The changes in nature have made us all vulnerable. The '61 fire, the Bel Air fire, almost got me in Beverly Glen—my desk furniture was smoldering from the heat—but the flames stopped about twenty feet from the house. Up there"—he pointed to the hills—"that's been bulldozed and filled; it's held up by cement pylons, but the earth still has a tendency to obey the law of gravity. We haven't had 'the storm of the century' yet—that's a geologists' term. The last one was in the eighteen-eighties. A lot of water will come—twelve inches in twenty-four hours, say. It would tear out half of what you and I are looking at right now."

John D. Weaver is also a Los Angeles writer, the author of a book on the city titled *El Pueblo Grande.* He and his wife, Harriett, are active in the Federation of Hillside and Canyon Associations, a conglomeration of citizen groups that monitors hillside development in thirty-one communities. Standing behind his house, in Sherman Oaks, recently, Weaver pointed to the west and said, "That ridge over there is above Stone Canyon. That's where the Bel Air fire started in 1961. They think a bulldozer backfired or struck a spark. There were—let's see if I can remember. Harriett, how many acres burned in the Bel Air fire?"

Harriett Weaver is considered one of Los Angeles' experts on brushfires. She has many titles, among them chairperson of the Mayor's Brush Clearance Committee. "Six thousand and ninety acres burned," she said. "Four hundred and eighty-four homes were destroyed, and the total property loss was about twenty-five million dollars." She continued, "The fires are a natural part of the ecological system. Dead growth has to burn off to continue the life cycle of the chaparral on these hills. The problem came with urbanization in the middle of the brush. A third of the city is in brush. In Los Angeles County, they joke that they don't need fire maps, because the whole thing would be red—'extremely hazardous.' We are just asking for it. The deadwood underneath the green that you see out there is soaked with resin and oils. It literally explodes. An acre of brush is the fuel equivalent of fifteen hundred to two thousand gallons of gasoline. Ernie Hanson, a fire chief in Los Angeles, got a lot of attention a few years ago by calculating that a hundred acres of brush five feet high can produce the same amount of heat as the atomic bomb that was dropped on Hiroshima."

I asked Mrs. Weaver about the fire I had seen in Mandeville Canyon, in the Santa Monicas, on October 23, 1978. She said that it had burned sixty-one hundred acres. Another fire that day, fifteen miles to the north, had burned twenty-five thousand three hundred and eighty-five acres between Agoura and Malibu. The two fires together damaged or destroyed two hundred and seventy houses and caused forty million dollars' worth of property damage. Two persons were killed in the Agoura fire. "The thing that was remarkable about October 23rd was the speed with which the fires moved," Mrs. Weaver said. "It all happened within twenty-four hours, and the Santa Anas were above thirty-five miles an hour. If the wind hadn't died down there wouldn't have been a prayer of keeping the Mandeville fire from jumping Sunset Boulevard." I had been standing on the other side, the south side, of Sunset. "Someday there will be a holocaust in this town," she added.

John Weaver said, "Not too far from our house, they built some houses that sold for around two hundred thousand dollars." He pointed again to the ridge west of us. "That view was a selling point. They didn't tell the buyers that they're planning to cut the top off the ridge and use the dirt to fill that little canyon—that they want to flatten out the view to build more houses. They're taking fifty feet off the top of the ridge and putting a hundred and sixty-five feet of fill in the canyon." He pointed to a slope and said, "Those homes down there will be flooded out unless the area gets adequate drainage. That's how it works."

"Floods and landslides are a real problem in the hills," Mrs. Weaver said. "A house half a block down the street lost its front yard in the last rain, and the whole thing is likely to go anytime. The brush is important—you need to leave enough to hold the hills against erosion but not enough to form a fire canopy. Worst of all, the developers cut out the toe of hills to get in that extra house. Much of the soil here is clay, and sooner or later, usually when they're wet, the geological planes slide out like cards from a deck. People aren't aware of the dangers—particularly people from the East. That's who they sell these houses to."

The Weavers talked on about the danger of slides, showing me clippings from the Los Angeles *Times.* In one story, about slides in Tarzana during April of 1978, John O. Robb, chief of the city's Grading Division, the section of the Department of Building and Safety that regulates the preparation of land for development, was quoted as saying that homeowners might be responsible for much of their own trouble. "One problem is educating hillside homeowners to maintain their property," Robb said. "Many mudslides have been caused by stopped drains and the overwatering of plants and other kinds of neglect."

"Overwatering of plants?" I said. "Are the hills that unstable?"

"They can be," John Weaver said. "You have to be careful of gopher holes, too."

He showed me some Polaroid snapshots a neighbor had taken of a house in a nearby canyon which had been caved in by a mudslide in March of 1978. "They've put the house back together now," he said. "You'd come out from New York and buy that house tomorrow. It looks fine. What you wouldn't know is that Los Angeles is not at peace with nature—that's why we get these periodic punishments. It's a man-made city, a tribute to rapacity and tenacity. There were people who could make money by putting a city here—the last place there should have been one. Hell, most of Los Angeles was just a swath of desert between great harbors in San Francisco and San Diego."

The next day, I went over to Tarzana, four miles west of Sherman Oaks, to meet a friend of the Weavers', Irma Dobbyn, who is also active in the Federation of Hillside and Canyon Associations. "They're building in steeper and steeper territory," Mrs. Dobbyn said. "Let me show you something." She took me out to her patio and pointed. We were looking at a bare beige pyramid that was flat-topped and terraced. "They've scraped that down to put in fifty-five houses," she said.

"How long will it look like that?" I asked.

"Probably only about three years," she said. "Plants can be slapped on, and they grow very quickly, with our twelve-month season. These pine trees"—she pointed at thirty-foot-high Aleppo and Monterey pines behind her house—"were planted when we came here, fifteen years ago."

We got into my car and drove around the corner to Conchita Way, a street of two-hundred-thousand-dollar homes. "You see the cracks in the streets," she said. "The city would come out to patch them when we complained that something was very wrong out here. They said everything was fine, and let the building continue. Then heavy rains came in the spring of 1978, and houses started coming down in April. Mudslides. The Smith house, up there, broke in half and started down the hill. That empty lot a little lower down was a rabbi's house; it just toppled on its front into the street. The Palmers there are suing for the damages to their house. Two men owned that vacant one next door. I think they just walked away from it when the cracks started appearing. That one"—she pointed to another vacant lot—"went in an earlier slide, eight or ten years ago. They're building there again now. See the foundation?"

The rabbi's name, I found out, was Michael Roth. "It looked like a normal house to us," Roth told me when I called on him. "There was a little hill behind us, but it's not there anymore. I was in Philadelphia when it happened, and my daughter called me and said, 'I don't want you to be shocked. If you watch the news on television tonight, you might see a house in the street. It's yours.'" The Roths are suing. "We're suing them all," he said. "The developer, the city, everybody."

Mrs. Dobbyn, like the Weavers, had pointed out earthmovers clanking along on the ridge that forms the base of Mulholland Drive, the long, winding road dividing the City and the Valley. Lil Melograno, who is an assistant to the area's city councilman and also a realtor, took me along the ridge, which is the peak line of the Santa Monicas. "There are a hundred and twenty-six acres in this tract," she said as we walked along terraces carved in the crumbly beige clay. "It's a pretty steep slope—parts of it might be as much as fifty per cent—and the city is allowing ninety-three houses. The developers originally wanted four hundred and thirty-eight houses, but we cut them down. That's what the Federation and people like me do. The lots start at three hundred thousand dollars apiece, so, with houses, the cost of most of the properties will be well over a million dollars. The developers cut fifty feet from the mountaintop over there and about a hundred feet here. The fill dumped in the canyon will eventually be two hundred and eighty-five feet deep. The city says it'll be a safe development, but no one knows for sure. No one has enough knowledge or control over the elements, the geology. We can't keep up with the technology of earthmoving and building. In the last fifteen years, the developers have learned to carve the mountains up into flatlands. These are just flatland developments with a view." The view was truly spectacular. In places, we were overlooking both the City and the Valley—Beverly Hills to the south, Studio City to the north.

"That's called Benedict Hills," Mrs. Melograno said after we had driven a few miles west along Mulholland. We were gazing out over hundreds of pseudo-Tudor homes. "Prices start at four hundred and fifty thousand dollars. The developer wanted to build five hundred and fifty houses, but we got him down to three hundred and forty. They're still building."

"It's a nice setting," I said, and she looked at me strangely.

"It used to be a lot nicer," she said. "They moved six million cubic yards of earth here beginning in 1970. There was a mountain there." She pointed into the air above a cluster of thirty houses. "They cut off a hundred and sixty-five feet of it to get more houses in. That's when the mudslides began. I spent one Christmas Eve shovelling mud out of the house of a friend. There's not much that the city can do. We don't do any testing work ourselves. We evaluate the reports of private geologists. We have to take their word, and, of course, most of them are hired by the developers. The only way to stop this would be for the city to buy the land, and it doesn't have the money."

"Is there corruption involved?" I asked. "Is somebody making enormous amounts of money here?"

"No," she said. "I don't think there's much of that. Basically, it's the American way—the attitude that a man has a right to do whatever he pleases with his own property. Even if it's dangerous for him and for everybody else. And it *is* dangerous. Anyone who wants to live on a hillside here faces the same hazards—fire, water, and earth. People are willing to take the chance because there's peace and quiet, they're still closer to nature, and the air is cleaner up here. They accept the chance that something will happen. They live with danger."

"Are you one of them?" I asked.

"Yes."

The flight to the hills was no doubt another attempt to outwit nature. The air is cleaner because many of the hillside homes are above the smog that sometimes blankets the flatlands of both the City and the Valley. The day Mrs. Melograno and I stood on Mulholland Drive—September 12th—was one of the worst days for breathing in Los Angeles history. The city was alive with "Stage 2" smog alerts. The day was one of eight consecutive Stage 2 days— a record unmatched since 1955—and admissions to local hospitals because of chronic lung disorders were increasing by fifty percent a day. The basin is routinely in a state of inversion; that is, a pool of stagnant, humid air is trapped above the city by a lid of warmer, drier air that forms north of Hawaii and drifts eastward until it is trapped by the Santa Monicas and the San Gabriels. Pollution, particularly from automobiles, pumps into the stagnant mass until ocean breezes or Santa Anas wash away the whiskey-colored gases. The hills, however, are usually above the inversion level, which often reaches only three hundred feet above sea level.

As I drove west along Mulholland Drive after talking to Mrs. Melograno, I watched helicopters chattering toward Sepulveda Pass, a cut through the Santa Monicas. They dropped, quite accurately, columns of water on a brushfire climbing up the hills along the San Diego Freeway. The fire was stopped after it had covered ten acres. Los Angeles is very good at that sort of thing. It has to be. Disaster—"holocaust," Harriett Weaver had said—is always near. "Disaster control" has real meaning here, and the city office charged with that function is the Office of Civil Defense, in City Hall East—or, rather, under City Hall East. I drove down four levels below the ground, parked my car, and then took an elevator down another level before being admitted—by buzzer—through eight-foot-high steel vault doors that lead to the office of the director, Michael J. Regan. He is a pudgy Irishman, sixty-two years old, who was a patrolman in the Los Angeles Police Department for twenty-one years and then police chief of a small town called Arvin. In 1970, he came to his present job. He told me that he had been the first police officer at the scene of a "killer slide" in Pacific Palisades, down the street from my house. That was in 1956, when part of the palisade overlooking the Pacific Coast Highway had slid over the roadway—something like that happens every couple of weeks in the winter, with houses and patios hanging over the highway—and pushed a small foreign car almost into the Pacific. "You never saw two people as scared or muddy as the two men in that car," Regan said. "The next day, a highway inspector was on the slope. He was signalling that everything was O.K. when a second slide came and buried him. Killed him."

As we talked, two women carrying rolled maps under their arms walked through Regan's office.

"We're really talking about ongoing preparations for an earthquake," one said.

"It's like a bomb," the other said. "If it drops, everything is gone. If we predict it and it doesn't happen, no one will pay attention the next time."

"Earthquake," Regan said, shaking his head. "That's what the public worries about. But for us it's not so bad.

There's nothing you can do about the first shock. But then you can race in and save people before the aftershocks hit. Floods are the thing we worry about most—they're the scariest. There's not a heck of a lot you can do about flash floods, and there's no warning. The ones we get push around boulders the size of vans. And a lot of people are living in certain flood paths."

He paused, and continued, "I'm not sure it makes a big difference. Darned near everybody living in Los Angeles is vulnerable to something. Flood, fire, slides, earthquake. If you live in Bel Air or Brentwood, you could be in a fire-storm canyon. People living in houses on stilts—I just shake my head. People in Tujunga, Sunland—they're in a natural flood path."

"What about you?" I asked.

"Me, too," he said. "I live in Verdugo Hills. A flood would wash me off. An earthquake would flip me off. You can't think about it too much. You'd shudder all the time, because you know these things are going to happen again."

Earthquakes are certainly going to happen again. There were four around Los Angeles in June of this year. What the city is worried about is a big one, and that is what the women I saw were working on that day, with the city's Task Force on Earthquake Prediction. No one is yet sure whether there actually is a science of earthquake prediction—the Chinese reportedly predicted a large quake in 1976 and evacuated hundreds of thousands of citizens from the threatened area before tremors began—but the need for such capability is obvious. The "General Background" section of the Task Force's October, 1978, Consensus Report began:

> In mid-February, 1976, the U.S. Geological Survey an-
> nounced the discovery of a major uplift of the earth cover-
> ing a large area that is centered approximately on the San
> Andreas fault in Southern California. Because of its large
> size and its alignment along a segment of the San Andreas
> fault that is known to have been "locked" since Southern

California's last great earthquake, in 1857, scientists expressed the concern that the "Palmdale Bulge," or "Southern California Uplift," may foreshadow the next great earthquake in the region. . . .

In mid-March, 1976, the U.S. Geological Survey noted the potential significance of the Southern California Uplift, and issued a warning: "If an earthquake similar to that in 1857 occurred today in the region about thirty miles north of Los Angeles, the probable losses in Orange and Los Angeles Counties alone are estimated as follows: 40,000 buildings would collapse or be seriously damaged. 3,000 to 12,000 people would be killed. 12,000 to 48,000 people would be hospitalized. $15 billion to $25 billion in damage would occur. Failure of one of the larger dams could leave 100,000 homeless, and tens of thousands dead."

If such a disaster occurred, Los Angeles might be run from a complex of rooms visible through a glass wall behind Michael Regan's desk. The emergency-operations center is encased in concrete, and it contains food, water, generators, and dormitories designed to sustain three hundred people for two weeks. "This is supposed to withstand a war," Regan said. It looked as if it could. The heart of the center is a cross-shaped "war room." One arm of the cross (Regan's office) would be the working area of the mayor and the chiefs of the Police and Fire Departments and their staffs. The other arm, interestingly, is reserved for the press, on the theory that what is most important—the operations center has already been used for fire and rain emergencies—is providing a panicked public with quick, accurate information. The main room, twenty-eight by fifty feet, lined with glass walls, maps, charts, and blackboards marked "Status" and "Deployment," is essentially a communications center, filled with twenty-button telephones and radio consoles, including a setup to commandeer every municipal radio frequency.

The Fire Department's Operations Control Division headquarters is down a long hall. It is an even more impressive room, two stories high, looking very much like the set of the television series *Star Trek*. Under a flashing "Quiet" light, men wearing white shirts, black pants, and ties sit in five-foot-high rust-colored leather swivel chairs before peach-and-cream-colored keyboards, screens, and microphone consoles. Towering over them are two huge maps, and display panels with flashing, moving colored lights that monitor equipment and personnel deployment. It was one of the most extraordinary rooms I have ever seen, but several people told me it does not work very well—the equipment, they said, is always breaking down.

Aboveground, the manipulation of the landscape was proceeding as usual. KFWB, an all-news radio station, was reporting that North Hollywood homeowners were protesting plans by MCA, Incorporated, to level three hills to provide flatland for parking and movie sets at its Universal City Studios. The company wanted to level sixty-seven acres, providing enough fill to cover a football field to a depth of eleven hundred and twenty-five feet. MCA, it was reported, was willing to give each of the homeowners six thousand dollars for their acquiescence. But one resident, identified as Billie Varga, was quoted as saying, "The hill we're on is going to go if they take down that one over there." Billie Varga said she was worried about "slide creep"—the geological phenomenon that Harriett Weaver had likened to cards sliding out of a deck.

A month later, I was driving north along the Pacific Coast Highway to visit Helen Funkhouser, a seventy-six-year-old woman who had moved back into the Santa Monica Mountains after losing her home in the Agoura fire of October 23, 1978. KFWB was reporting that twenty-seven hundred acres were burning near Pasadena. I passed a steel wall being constructed in what used to be one lane of the highway. The wall is supposed to hold back the crumbling, sliding palisades above Malibu.

Then I turned into Kanan-Dume Road, past a sign that said:

KANAN-DUME ROAD
SLIDE REMOVAL AREA
UP TO 20 MIN DELAYS
8:30 A.M. TO 4 P.M.
WEEKDAYS

Mrs. Funkhouser is an impressive woman. She was a state legislator in New Hampshire before coming to California, in 1961, with her husband, James, a chemistry professor. They were reading in the ten-foot-wide mobile-home units they had bought to replace their house—two were attached, to give them twenty feet of width—when I arrived at their isolated homesite, just north of Malibu, almost at the point where the Santa Monicas meet the Pacific. "We beat the fire by five minutes," Mrs. Funkhouser said. "We lost everything. Paintings, books, antiques. But Jim did manage to get his cello. We thought we would be safe, because we had built a system literally pouring water on every bit of the house and property, but they say the temperature of the fire was between twenty-five hundred and three thousand degrees. Here. This was my chicken-cooking pot." Jim Funkhouser handed me a flattened blob of aluminum. "It takes a certain kind of person to live here," she said. "We came back. We all came back. We're damn fools, but the trees come back, and so do we. It's a constant battle. Nature keeps trying to take over here. But it's beautiful, and it's where we want to be."

IDEAS

1. Do you agree with Reeves's thesis that the problems in Los Angeles are the results of people trying to live in an environment never intended for habitation?

2. What makes Los Angeles so vulnerable?

3. What are the causes of brush fires? Of landslides? Pick some passages to illustrate (1) the present effect of past causes, and (2) the present predicament as cause for future effects.

4. What is the force of *nature remembers* for the essay as a whole, considering that the man who says it lives in the Hollywood Hills?

5. Do people have a right to do anything they please with their property? With themselves?

ORGANIZATION AND STYLE

1. Observe how Reeves's first paragraph sets the pattern for chronological development. What are his transition markers? Find similar transition markers in the first five paragraphs.

2. Beginning with the sixth paragraph ("West Hollywood is on the. . . ."), Reeves breaks from this chronological pattern. Why does his subject matter dictate such a break here?

3. Reeves supports his thesis by quoting various people. How does he establish their credibility before quoting them?

4. How does Reeves constantly reinforce his thesis about the efforts of human beings "to outwit nature"? Find as many rephrasings of this thesis as you can.

5. Reeves writes in the first person. Would Reeves gain or lose by rewriting this as a third-person essay?

WRITING

1. Look around for some current "lost city" within your experience: a cluttered lounge on campus, a decayed neighborhood, a wrecked playground, an organization falling apart. Write an essay adducing the probable

causes of this effect, arguing inductively "This should not be," or, like Reeves, implying it in an inductive presentation.

2. Reeves argues that problems in Los Angeles are the results of trying to outwit nature. Select another situation in which you believe that trying to go contrary to nature has caused negative results. Develop your essay inductively, as Reeves does.

They Also Wait Who Stand and Serve Themselves

ANDREW WARD

———————— ● ————————

How does the past determine the present? How will the present affect the future? These are questions raised—perhaps a bit tongue-in-cheek—by Ward. He carefully describes his old neighborhood gas station and its almost hostile owner; then he reflects on the new self-service station in a manner that makes clear his fondness for Sal and the old station. Only slightly beneath the surface throughout the essay is his respect for the human touch in life and his fear of a universe populated by gadgets.

Anyone interested in the future of American commerce should take a drive sometime to my neighborhood gas station. Not that it is or ever was much of a place to visit. Even when I first moved here, five years ago, it was shabby and forlorn: not at all like the garden spots they used to feature in the commercials, where trim, manicured men with cultivated voices tipped their visors at your window and asked what they could do for you.

Sal, the owner, was a stocky man who wore undersized, popped-button shirts, sagging trousers, and oil-spattered work shoes with broken laces. "Gas stinks" was his motto, and every gallon he pumped into his customers' cars seemed to take something out of him. "Pumping gas is for morons," he liked to say, leaning indelibly against my rear window and watching the digits fly on the pump register. "One of these days I'm gonna dump this place on a Puerto Rican, move to Florida, and get into something nice, like hero sandwiches."

He had a nameless, walleyed assistant who wore a studded denim jacket and, with his rag and squeegee, left a milky film on my windshield as my tank was filling. There was a fume-crazed, patchy German shepherd, which Sal kept chained to the air pump, and if you followed Sal into his cluttered, overheated office next to the service bays, you ran a gauntlet of hangers-on, many of them Sal's brothers and nephews, who spent their time debating the merits of the driving directions he gave the bewildered travelers who turned into his station for help.

"I don't know," one of them would say, pulling a bag of potato chips off the snack rack, "I think I would have put 'em onto 91, gotten 'em off at Willow, and then—Bango!— straight through to Hamden."

Sal guarded the rest room key jealously and handed it out with reluctance, as if something in your request had betrayed some dismal aberration. The rest room was accessible only through a little closet littered with tires, fan belts, and cases of oil cans. Inside, the bulb was busted and there were never any towels, so you had to dry your hands on toilet paper—if Sal wasn't out of toilet paper, too.

The soda machine never worked for anyone except Sal, who, when complaints were lodged, would give it a contemptuous kick as he trudged by, dislodging warm cans of grape soda which, when their pop-tops were flipped, gave off a fine purple spray. There was, besides the snack rack in the office, a machine that dispensed peanuts on behalf of the Sons of Garibaldi. The metal shelves along the cinderblock wall were sparsely stocked with cans of cooling system cleaner, windshield de-icer, antifreeze, and boxed head lamps and oil filters. Over the battered yellow wiper case, below the Coca Cola clock, and half hidden by a calendar from a janitorial supply concern, hung a little brass plaque from the oil company, awarded in recognition of Salvatore A. Castallano's ten-year business association.

I wish for the sake of nostalgia that I could say Sal was a craftsman, but I can't. I'm not even sure he was an honest man. I suspect that when business was slow he may have cheated me, but I never knew for sure because I don't know anything about cars. If I brought my Volvo in because it was behaving strangely, I knew that as far as Sal was concerned it could never be a simple matter of tightening a bolt or re-attaching a hose. "Jesus," he'd wearily exclaim after a look under the hood. "Mr. Ward, we got problems." I usually let it go at that and simply asked him when he thought he could have it repaired, because if I pressed him for details he would get all worked up. "Look, if you don't want to take my word for it, you can go someplace else. I mean, it's a free country, you know? You got spalding on your caps, which means your dexadrometer isn't charging, and pretty soon you're gonna have hairlines in your flushing drums. You get hairlines in your flushing drums and you might as well forget it. You're driving junk."

I don't know what Sal's relationship was with the oil company. I suppose it was pretty distant. He was never what they call a "participating dealer." He never gave away steak knives or NFL tumblers or stuffed animals with his fill-ups, and never got around to taping company posters on his windows. The map rack was always empty, and the company emblem, which was supposed to rotate thirty feet above the station, had broken down long before I first laid eyes on it, and had frozen at an angle that made it hard to read from the highway.

If, outside of television, there was ever such a thing as an oil company service station inspector, he must have been appalled by the grudging service, the mad dog, the sepulchral john. When there was supposed to have been an oil shortage a few years ago, Sal's was one of the first stations to run out of gas. And several months ago, during the holiday season, the company squeezed him out for good.

I don't know whether Sal is now happily sprinkling olive oil over salami subs somewhere along the Sun Belt. I only know that one bleak January afternoon I turned into his station to find him gone. At first, as I idled by the no-lead pump, I thought the station had been shut down completely. Plywood had been nailed over the service bays,

Sal's name had been painted out above the office door, and all that was left of his dog was a length of chain dangling from the air pump's vacant mast.

But when I got out of the car I spotted someone sitting in the office with his boots up on the counter, and at last caught sight of the "Self-Service Only" signs posted by the pumps. Now, I've always striven for a degree of self-sufficiency. I fix my own leaky faucets and I never let the bellboy carry my bags. But I discovered as I squinted at the instructional sticker by the nozzle that there are limits to my desire for independence. Perhaps it was the bewilderment with which I approach anything having to do with the internal combustion engine; perhaps it was my conviction that fossil fuels are hazardous; perhaps it was the expectation of service, the sense of helplessness, that twenty years of oil company advertising had engendered, but I didn't want to pump my own gas.

A mongrel rain began to fall upon the oil-slicked tarmac as I followed the directions spelled out next to the nozzle. But somehow I got them wrong. When I pulled the trigger on the nozzle, no gas gushed into my fuel tank, no digits flew on the gauge.

"Hey, buddy," a voice sounded out of a bell-shaped speaker overhead. "Flick the switch."

I turned toward the office and saw someone with Wild Bill Hickok hair leaning over a microphone.

"Right. Thanks," I answered, and turned to find the switch. There wasn't one. There was a bolt that looked a little like a switch, but it wouldn't flick.

"The switch," the voice crackled in the rain. "Flick the switch."

I waved back as if I'd finally understood, but I still couldn't figure out what he was talking about. In desperation, I stuck the nozzle back into my fuel tank and pulled the trigger. Nothing.

In the office I could see that the man was now angrily pulling on a slicker. "What the hell's the matter with you?" he asked, storming by me. "All you gotta do is flick the switch."

"I couldn't find the switch," I told him.

"Well, what do you call this?" he wanted to know, pointing to a little lever near the pump register.

"A lever," I told him.

"Christ," he muttered, flicking the little lever. The digits on the register suddenly formed neat rows of zeros. "All right, it's set. Now you can serve yourself," the long-haired man said, ducking back to the office.

As the gas gushed into my fuel tank and the fumes rose to my nostrils, I thought for a moment about my last visit to Sal's. It hadn't been any picnic: Sal claimed to have found something wrong with my punting brackets, the German shepherd snapped at my heels as I walked by, and nobody had change for my ten. But the transaction had dimension to it: I picked up some tips about color antennas, entered into the geographical debate in the office, and bought a can of windshield wiper solvent (to fill the gap in my change). Sal's station had been a dime a dozen, but it occurred to me, as the nozzle began to balk and shudder in my hand, that gas stations of its kind were going the way of the village smithy and the corner grocer.

I got a glob of grease on my glove as I hung the nozzle back on the pump, and it took me more than a minute to satisfy myself that I had replaced the gas cap properly. I tried to whip up a feeling of accomplishment as I headed for the office, but I could not forget Sal's dictum: Pumping gas is for morons.

The door to the office was locked, but a sign directed me to a stainless steel teller's drawer which had been installed in the plate glass of the front window. I stood waiting for a while with my money in hand, but the long-haired man sat inside with his back to me, so at last I reached up and hesitantly knocked on the glass with my glove.

The man didn't hear me or had decided, in retaliation for our semantic disagreement, to ignore me for a while. I reached up to knock again, but noticed that my glove had left a greasy smear on the window. Ever my mother's son, I reflexively reached into my pocket for my handkerchief and was about to wipe the grease away when it hit me: at last the oil industry had me where it wanted me—standing in the rain and washing its windshield.

IDEAS

1. What is the collective image that Ward paints of the old-styled gas station? What are his stereotypes?

2. Is Ward implying that the new self-service stations have emerged as a result of the inefficiency of the older stations run by Sal and his like?

3. Do you feel that the newer self-service stations are an improvement over the older stations like Sal's? How representative are his contrasting pictures?

4. What other "improvements" in service (automatic banking machines, fast-food restaurants) can you think of? Are they better or worse? Are they for the convenience of the customer or the industry? Are they, in any way, brought about by problems in the old system?

ORGANIZATION AND STYLE

1. Ward's first sentence serves as his thesis. Does he develop it sufficiently? At what point does he restate it in different words?

2. Which paragraph of the "Sal section" (first six paragraphs) presents the most pictorial details? How important are they to Ward's thesis?

3. The "Sal section" presents several causes and effects. What are they?

4. The "Sal section" and the final part of the essay differ in tone. How does Ward's language let the reader know that he really was fond of Sal and his old station? What language suggests that he feels alienated or threatened by the new station?

WRITING

1. Select one of the "improvements" you earlier identified. Write an essay in which you discuss how things were at one time and how they are now. Let your language work for you to imply which you feel was better.

2. The last part of this essay presents a person frustrated and unable to cope with a new technique. Select a time in your own experience when you had similar problems—the first time you tried to work the automatic bank machine, or entered an automated parking garage, or tried to use a computer. Present, first, your anticipations; then show what really happened. Organize your essay to emphasize the causes for your frustration.

If the Moon Controls the Tide, Just Think What It Does to You

MARGARET LOEB

●

*After declaring in her first sentence that the influence
of the moon "is eternally mysterious," Loeb sets up an
organizational scheme that works something like
this: The moon may control human behavior, but it
may not. Some people say it does, but some say it does
not. Finally, she leaves the reader free to decide the
question. Perhaps the moon does, indeed, affect those
who believe in its power, and perhaps it has no effect
at all on those who do not believe. What do you believe?*

Its influence is eternally mysterious. Exposure to it has
variously been credited with removing freckles and warts
and curing leprosy. And it has been blamed for causing
everything from madness to blindness. "It" is the moon.
And its real or imagined effects on mankind have been
remarked upon from time immemorial.

Ancient Jewish teachings warn against certain activities in the moonlight. Ancient Greeks thought the full
moon was a lucky time to marry. Even today, fourteen
years after man first set foot on its surface, the moon remains mysterious. If anything is as constant as the moon's
phases for instance, it is man's superstitions about the
effects of the full moon.

Is it more than superstition? You can judge for yourself,
since there is a full moon this very night. But full-moon
lunacy is attested to by many who have to deal with it—
from hospital workers to law-enforcement officers.

"I've been known to call in sick when it's a full moon,
because it's so weird," says Richard Vivian, a San Fran-

cisco waiter. When it's possible, he says, "I don't come to work, and I try not to go out. I'll just stay in and be happy I'm not dealing with people."

A police officer in the same town says the full moon is accompanied by more accidents, drinking, and fights. "All kinds of crazy stuff happens," she says, including people jumping off buildings.

Although scientific studies may support many such conclusions, it's difficult to say anything with certainty about the effects of the full moon. At least one researcher suggests that magnetic interaction between the Earth and moon affects the minerals in the human body. Others suggest, less convincingly, that if the moon can turn the tides it can also affect the human body, which is 80% water.

With even less-convincing logic, it is suggested that if the moon moves oceans, perhaps it also moves the stock market. In his market letter "Deliberations," Ian McAvity, a Toronto investment analyst, told subscribers to be wary of the full moon.

"You could argue that the market tends to lose points around full moon, and gains during the new," he says. "In theory, you should short the day before a full moon, and cover the third day after." And "you should go long the fifth day before a new moon and sell the fifth day after," he adds. But he concedes that the moon-market correlation is so slight that his advice might be better used at a cocktail party than with a broker, and yesterday's market gain would seem to indicate caution.

Full-moon lore, of course, extends far beyond human and stock-market behavior. Carl Chapman, an Atlanta veterinarian, says the full moon brings him more four-legged patients. And Annie Collier, a farmer in Lawrence County, Tennessee, relates the moon to her vocation. "If you want mustard and turnip greens to have large leaves," she says, "plant after the moon fulls—after the moon gets round like a plate and starts back. But when the moon news, go out and sow your hay." Mrs. Collier knows a lot about these matters. She is the daughter of slaves, and has been farming for eighty-two of her eighty-eight years.

Both new moons and full moons occur when the sun, moon, and Earth are lined up. In a full moon, the Earth is between the moon and the sun, so the moon's surface appears awash in sunlight. New moons occur when the moon is between the sun and Earth. The far side of the moon is bathed in sunlight, while the side facing the Earth is dark. During both full and new moons, ocean tides are at their highest.

Some theories about the moon have waxed and waned over the years. The theories relating lunar phases to the weather have largely fallen by the wayside, according to William Donn, senior research scientist at Lamont-Doherty Geological Observatory in Palisades, New York. Other theories suggesting a link to earthquakes or volcanoes, he asserts, haven't been proved.

By far the most prevalent theories, however, are those linking full moons to bizarre behavior, increased illness, or even accelerated birth rates.

In his book "The Lunar Effect: Biological Tides and Human Emotions," Arnold L. Lieber traced 1,887 homicides in Dade County, Florida, between 1956 and 1970. A graph he devised plotting the murder rate showed "a striking correlation with the lunar phase cycle," Dr. Lieber said. "The homicides peaked at full moon."

In Chicago, Ralph Morris, a professor at the University of Illinois College of Pharmacy, says his research "indicates a correlation between the week of the full moon and a greater incidence of bleeding ulcer attacks, as well as coronary attacks in angina patients." He concludes that "stress-related diseases are most likely to have their crises, whether behavioral or physical."

Some researchers are reluctant to discuss their lunar-linked findings, lest they be considered astrologers or alchemists. Indeed some early alchemists prescribed blood-letting based on the phases of the moon, and some scientists think today's moon lore is just as suspect.

"We haven't found anything that shows an increase in admissions or an increase of referrals" at the time of the full moon, says Edwin Robbins, associate director of psychiatry at Bellevue Hospital Center in New York. "We studied this for many years," he adds. "I never wrote it up, because it's so stupid."

But that is unlikely to convince those who have observed the lunacy of man and beast. Toni Garcia, a former security guard at the San Diego Zoo, says elephants more often frolic in their swimming pools on full-moon evenings. Contrary to myth, however, the zoo's wolves don't howl at the moon—full or otherwise, she says.

Men are another story. When the moon is full, says Mark Hews, a driver with Park Cadillac Limousine Service in Palm Beach, Florida, "people tend to be crazier." He adds, "Maybe they drink too much. A lot of weird things seem to happen on full moons."

IDEAS

1. What are your feelings about the moon's effects on people? What stories have you heard about the moon's effects? Do they seem valid? What other causes are possible?

2. If the moon does not affect human behavior, how do you explain some of Loeb's evidence?

3. Some believe that other natural phenomena also affect human behavior: people drive crazily just before a thunder storm; people get depressed when barometric pressure falls. What other effects of this type have you heard of? Do you know any instances?

ORGANIZATION AND STYLE

1. The first three paragraphs are introductory. What is each paragraph's purpose?

2. Examine Loeb's contrasts pro and con. Can you detect any bias?

3. What are Loeb's organizational units—behavior of people, behavior of animals? Does she have a system?

4. Where does her conclusion begin? Is it a valid concluding section? Why does she not take a stand for one side or the other?

WRITING

1. Psychologists say that belief, even if superstition, affects behavior. Select one of your own beliefs (you never do well on tests on Friday; changes in the weather swing your moods; wearing your green sweater brings you luck) and develop an essay analyzing causes and effects. Consider the pros and cons!

2. Pick an outcome for which you can trace the causes: a lost love, a failed test, a smashed car, a winning campaign or contest. Make your thesis. Begin your essay with a thesis sentence something like "Something caused _____." Then present your causes, either in chronological order or order of importance.

Comparison and Contrast

All exposition reflects modes of thought, and comparing and contrasting is one of our basic modes. We compare things point by point so that we can see their shared similarity and appreciate their contrasting distinctions. Similarity is essential. Comparing eggs to trees, let us say, or even two short stories with nothing in common, makes no sense and draws no interest. But in our comparisons we may see and wish to emphasize the distinctions within the similarity, as Murray Ross does with our two most popular national sports. Both Talese and Menen contrast the familiar with the unfamiliar, opening our eyes to what we thought we knew about everyday New York, grandmothers, and the human race.

Football Red and Baseball Green

MURRAY ROSS

————————— ● —————————

Ross draws on his literary knowledge to contrast two sports alike in their tremendous popular appeal, and alike in their indicating something significant in the American character, but as different as red and green, as the epic heroics of battle and the pastoral dream of green fields.

The 1970 Superbowl, the final game of the professional football season, drew a larger television audience than either the moonwalk or Tiny Tim's wedding. This revelation is one way of indicating just how popular spectator sports are in this country. Americans, or American men anyway, seem to care about the games they watch as much as the Elizabethans cared about their plays, and I suspect for some of the same reasons. There is, in sport, some of the rudimentary drama found in popular theater: familiar plots, type characters, heroic and comic action spiced with new and unpredictable variations. And common to watching both activities is the sense of participation in a shared tradition and in shared fantasies. If it is true that sport exploits these fantasies without significantly transcending them, it seems no less satisfying for all that.

It is my guess that sport spectating involves something more than the vicarious pleasures of identifying with athletic prowess. I suspect that each sport contains a fundamental myth which it elaborates for its fans, and that our pleasure in watching such games derives in part from belonging briefly to the mythic world which the game and its players bring to life. I am especially interested in baseball and football because they are so popular and so uniquely *American;* they began here and unlike basketball they have not been widely exported. Thus whatever can be said, mythically, about these games would seem to apply directly and particularly to our own culture.

Baseball's myth may be the easier to identify since we have a greater historical perspective on the game. It was an instant success during the Industrialization, and most probably it was a reaction to the squalor, the faster pace and the dreariness of the new conditions. Baseball was old-fashioned right from the start; it seems conceived in nostalgia, in the resuscitation of the Jeffersonian dream. It established an artificial rural environment, one removed from the toil of an urban life, which spectators could be admitted to and temporarily breathe in. Baseball is a *pastoral* sport, and I think the game can be best understood as this kind of art. For baseball does what all good pastoral does—it creates an atmosphere in which everything exists in harmony.

Consider, for instance, the spatial organization of the game. A kind of controlled openness is created by having everything fan out from home plate, and the crowd sees the game through an arranged perspective that is rarely violated. Visually this means that the game is always seen as a constant, rather calm whole, and that the players and the playing field are viewed in relationship to each other. Each player has a certain position, a special area to tend, and the game often seems to be as much a dialogue between the fielders and the field as it is a contest between the players themselves: will that ball get through the hole? Can that outfielder run under that fly? As a moral genre, pastoral asserts the virtue of communion with nature. As a competitive game, baseball asserts that the team which best relates to the playing field (by hitting the ball in the right places) will be the team which wins.

I suspect baseball's space has a subliminal function too, for topographically it is a sentimental mirror of older America. Most of the game is played between the pitcher and the hitter in the extreme corner of the playing area. This is the busiest, most sophisticated part of the ball park, where something is always happening, and on which all subsequent action depends. From this urban corner we move to a supporting infield, active but a little less crowded, and from there we come to the vast stretches of the outfield. As is traditional in American lore, danger increases with distance, and the outfield action is often the most spectacular in the game. The long throw, the double off the wall, the leaping catch—these plays take place in remote territory, and they belong, like most legendary feats, to the frontier.

Having established its landscape, pastoral art operates to eliminate any references to that bigger, more disturbing, more real world it has left behind. All games are to some extent insulated from the outside by having their own rules, but baseball has a circular structure as well which furthers its comfortable feeling of self-sufficiency. By this I mean that every motion of extension is also one of return—a ball hit outside is a *home* run, a full circle. Home—familiar, peaceful, secure—it is the beginning and end of everything. You must go out and you must come back, for only the completed movement is registered.

Time is a serious threat to any form of pastoral. The genre poses a timeless world of perpetual spring, and it does its best to silence the ticking of clocks which remind us that in time the green world fades into winter. One's sense of time is directly related to what happens in it, and baseball is so structured as to stretch out and ritualize whatever action it contains. Dramatic moments are few, and they are almost always isolated by the routine texture of normal play. It is certainly a game of climax and drama, but it is perhaps more a game of repeated and predictable action: the foul balls, the walks, the pitcher fussing around on the mound, the lazy fly ball to centerfield. This is, I think, as it should be, for baseball exists as an alternative to a world of too much action, struggle, and change. It is a merciful release from a more grinding and insistent tempo, and its time, as William Carlos Williams suggests, makes a virtue out of idleness simply by providing it:

> *The crowd at the ball game*
> *is moved uniformly*
> *by a spirit of uselessness*
> *which delights them . . .*

Within this expanded and idle time, the baseball fan is at liberty to become a ceremonial participant and a lover of style. Because the action is normalized, how something is done becomes as important as the action itself. Thus baseball's most delicate and detailed aspects are often, to the spectator, the most interesting. The pitcher's windup, the anticipatory crouch of the infielders, the quick waggle of the bat as it poises for the pitch—these subtle miniature movements are as meaningful as the homeruns and the strikeouts. It somehow matters in baseball that all the tiny rituals are observed: the shortstop must kick the dirt and the umpire must brush the plate with his pocket broom. In a sense, baseball is largely a continuous series of small gestures, and I think it characteristic that the game's most treasured moment came when Babe Ruth pointed to the place where he subsequently hit a home run.

Baseball is a game where the little things mean a lot, and this, together with its clean serenity, its open space, and its ritualized action is enough to place it in a world of yesterday. Baseball evokes for us a past which may never have been ours, but which we believe was, and certainly that is enough. In the Second World War, supposedly, we fought for "Baseball, Mom, and Apple Pie," and considering what baseball means that phrase is a good one. We fought then for the right to believe in a green world of tranquillity and uninterrupted contentment, where the little things would count. But now the possibilities of such a world are more remote, and it seems that while the entertainment of such a dream has an enduring appeal, it is no longer sufficient for our fantasies. I think this may be why baseball is no longer our preeminent national pastime, and why its myth is being replaced by another more appropriate to the new realities (and fantasies) of our time.

Football, especially professional football, is the embodiment of a newer myth, one which in many respects is opposed to baseball's. The fundamental difference is that football is not a pastoral game; it is a heroic one. One way of seeing the difference between the two is by the juxtaposition of Babe Ruth and Jim Brown, both legendary players in their separate genres. Ruth, baseball's most powerful hitter, was a hero maternalized (his name), an epic figure destined for a second immortality as a candy bar.* His image was impressive but comfortable and altogether

*Editors' note—We are grateful to Professor Robert H. Henigan, Southern Missouri State University, for the information that the Baby Ruth candy bar was named not for the baseball player but for President Grover Cleveland's daughter, Ruth, who was born on October 3, 1891, and died of diphtheria on January 7, 1904. As George Herman Ruth's fame rose with both his pitching and his batting average, popular fancy linked him with the candy bar. In 1921, the Curtiss Company mounted an advertising campaign to exploit that linkage. Ruth protested in vain, then tried to establish the George H. Ruth Candy Company and to register "Ruth's Home Run Bar" with the U.S. Patent Office. The Curtiss Company claimed infringement of their patent, and the Patent Office rejected Ruth's application. See David Quentin Voigt, *American Baseball* (Norman: University of Oklahoma Press, 1970), vol. III, p. 158; Robert W. Creamer, *Babe: The Legend Comes to Life* (New York: Simon & Schuster, 1974), p. 274; Marshall Smelser, *The Life that Ruth Built* (New York: Quadrangle, 1975), pp. 207–208.

human: round, dressed in a baggy uniform, with a school-boy's cap and a bat which looked tiny next to him. His spindly legs supported a Santa-sized torso, and this comic disproportion would increase when he was in motion. He ran delicately, with quick, very short steps, since he felt that stretching your stride slowed you down. This sort of superstition is typical of baseball players, and typical too is the way in which a personal quirk or mannerism mitigates their awesome skill and makes them poignant and vulnerable.

There was nothing funny about Jim Brown. His muscular and almost perfect physique was emphasized further by the uniform which armoured him. Babe Ruth had a tough face, but boyish and innocent; Brown was an expressionless mask under the helmet. In action, he seemed invincible, the embodiment of speed and power in an inflated human shape. One can describe Brown accurately only with superlatives, for as a player he was a kind of Superman, undisguised.

Brown and Ruth are caricatures, yet they represent their games. Baseball is part of a comic tradition which insists that its participants be humans, while football, in the heroic mode, asks that its players be more than that. Football converts men into gods, and suggests that magnificence and glory are as desirable as happiness. Football is designed, therefore, to impress its audience rather differently than baseball, as I think comparison will show.

As a pastoral game, baseball attempts to close the gap between the players and the crowd. It creates the illusion, for instance, that with a lot of hard work, a little luck, and possibly some extra talent, the average spectator might well be playing, not watching. For most of us can do a few of the things the ballplayers do: catch a pop-up, field a ground ball, and maybe get a hit once in a while. Chance is allotted a good deal of play in the game. There is no guarantee, for instance, that a good pitch will not be looped over the infield, or that a solidly batted ball will not turn into a double play. In addition to all of this, almost every fan feels he can make the manager's decision for him, and not entirely without reason. Baseball's statistics are easily calculated and rather meaningful; and the game itself, though a subtle one, is relatively lucid and comprehensible.

As a heroic game, football is not concerned with a shared community of near-equals. It seeks almost the opposite relationship between its spectators and players, one which stresses the distance between them. We are not allowed to identify directly with Jim Brown any more than we are with Zeus, because to do so would undercut his stature as something more than human. The players do much of the distancing themselves by their own excesses of speed, size, and strength. When Bob Brown, the giant all-pro tackle, says that he could "block King Kong all day," we look at him and believe. But the game itself contributes to the players' heroic isolation. As George Plimpton has graphically illustrated in *Paper Lion,* it is almost impossible to imagine yourself in a professional football game without also considering your imminent humiliation and possible injury. There is scarcely a single play that the average spectator could hope to perform adequately, and there is even a difficulty in really understanding what is going on. In baseball, what happens is what meets the eye, but in football each action is the result of eleven men acting simultaneously against eleven other men, and clearly this is too much for the eye to totally comprehend. Football has become a game of staggering complexity, and coaches are now wired in to several "spotters" during the games so that they too can find out what is happening.

If football is distanced from its fans by its intricacy and its "superhuman" play, it nonetheless remains an intense spectacle. Baseball, as I have implied, dissolves time and urgency in a green expanse, thereby creating a luxurious and peaceful sense of leisure. As is appropriate to a heroic enterprise, football reverses this procedure and converts space into time. The game is ideally played in an oval stadium, not in a "park," and the difference is the elimination of prespective. This makes football a perfect television game, because even at first hand it offers a flat, perpetually moving foreground (wherever the ball is). The eye in baseball viewing opens up; in football it zeroes in. There is no democratic vista in football, and spectators are not asked to relax, but to concentrate. You are encouraged to watch the drama, not a medley of ubiquitous gestures, and you are constantly reminded that this event is taking place in time. The third element in baseball is the field; in football this element is the clock. Traditionally heroes do reckon with time, and football players are no exceptions. Time in football is wound up inexorably until it reaches the breaking point in the last minutes of a close game. More often than not it is the clock which emerges as the real enemy, and it is the sense of time running out that regularly produces a pitch of tension uncommon in baseball.

A further reason for football's intensity, surely, is that the game is played like a war. The idea is to win by going through, around or over the opposing team and the battle lines, quite literally, are drawn on every play. Violence is somewhere at the heart of the game, and the combat quality is reflected in football's army language ("blitz," "trap," "zone," "bomb," "trenches," etc.). Coaches often sound like generals when they discuss their strategy. Woody Hayes of Ohio State, for instance, explains his quarterback option plays as if it had been conceived in the Pentagon: "You know," he says, "the most effective kind of warfare is siege. You have to attack on broad fronts. And that's all the option is—attacking on a broad front. You know General Sherman ran an option right through the South."

Football like war is an arena for action, and like war football leaves little room for personal style. It seems to be a game which projects "character" more than personality, and for the most part football heroes, publicly, are a rather similar lot. They tend to become personifications rather than individuals, and, with certain exceptions, they are easily read emblematically as embodiments of heroic qualities such as "strength," "confidence," "perfection," etc.—clichés really, but forceful enough when represented by the play of a Dick Butkus, a Johnny Unitas, or a Bart Starr. Perhaps this simplification of personality results in part from the heroes' total identification with their mission, to the extent that they become more characterized by their work than by what they intrinsically "are." At any rate, football does not make allowances for the idiosyncrasies that baseball actually seems to encourage, and as a result there have been few football players as uniquely crazy or human as, say, Casey Stengel or Dizzy Dean.

A further reason for the underdeveloped qualities of football personalities, and one which gets us to the heart of the game's modernity, is that football is very much a game of modern technology. Football's action is largely interaction, and the game's complexity requires that its players mold themselves into a perfectly coordinated unit. Jerry Kramer, the veteran guard and author of *Instant Replay,* writes how Lombardi would work to develop such integration:

> He makes us execute the same plays over and over, a hundred times, two hundred times, until we do every little thing automatically. He works to make the kickoff team perfect, the punt-return team perfect, the field-goal team perfect. He ignores nothing. Technique, technique, technique, over and over and over, until we feel like we're going crazy. But we win.

Mike Garratt, the halfback, gives the player's version:

> After a while you train your mind like a computer—put the idea in, digest it, and the body acts accordingly.

As the quotations imply, pro football is insatiably preoccupied with the smoothness and precision of play execution, and most coaches believe that the team which makes the fewest mistakes will be the team that wins. Individual identity thus comes to be associated with the team or unit that one plays for to a much greater extent than in baseball. To use a reductive analogy, it is the difference between *Bonanza* and *Mission Impossible.* * Ted Williams is mostly Ted Williams, but Bart Starr is mostly the Green Bay Packers. The latter metaphor is a precise one, since football heroes stand out not because of purely individual acts, but because they epitomize the action and style of the groups they are connected to. Kramer cites the obvious if somewhat self-glorifying historical precedent: "Perhaps," he writes, "we're living in Camelot." Ideally a football team should be what Camelot was supposed to have been, a group of men who function as equal parts of a larger whole, entirely dependent on each other for their total meaning.

The humanized machine as hero is something very new in sport, for in baseball anything approaching a machine has always been suspect. The famous Yankee teams of the fifties were almost flawlessly perfect and never very popular. Their admirers took pains to romanticize their precision into something more natural than plain mechanics—Joe DiMaggio, for instance, was the "Yankee Clipper." Even so, most people hoped fervently the Brooklyn Dodgers (the "bums") would thrash them in every World Series. To take a more recent example, the victory of the Mets last year was so compelling largely because it was at the expense of a superbly homogenized team, the Baltimore Orioles, and it was accomplished by a somewhat random collection of inspired leftovers. In baseball, machinery seems tantamount to villainy, whereas in football this smooth perfection is part of the expected integration a championship team must attain.

It is not surprising, really, that we should have a game which asserts the heroic function of a mechanized group, since we have become a country where collective identity is a reality. Football as a game of groups is appealing to us as a people of groups, and for this reason football is very much an "establishment" game—since it is in the corpo-

---

*Television serials, the first about cattle-ranching in the old West, the second about dangerous missions too difficult for official governmental agencies, hence carried out by a small private commando group.

rate business and governmental structures that group America is most highly developed. The game comments on the culture, and vice-versa:

> President Nixon, an ardent football fan, got a football team picture as an inaugural anniversary present from his cabinet. . . .
>
> Superimposed on the faces of real gridiron players were the faces of Cabinet members. (A.P.)

This is not to say that football appeals only to a certain class, for group America is visible everywhere. A sign held high in the San Francisco Peace Moratorium last November read: "49er Fans against war, poverty, and the Baltimore Colts."

Football's collective pattern is only one aspect of the way in which it seems to echo our contemporary environment. The game, like our society, can be thought of as a cluster of people living under great tension in a state of perpetual flux. The potential for sudden disaster or triumph is as great in football as it is in our own age, and although there is something ludicrous in equating interceptions with assassinations and long passes with moonshots, there is also something valid and appealing in the analogies. It seems to me that football does successfully reflect those salient and common conditions which affect us all, and it does so with the end of making us feel better about them and our lot. For one thing, it makes us feel that something can be released and connected in all this chaos; out of the accumulated pile of bodies something can emerge—a runner breaks into the clear or a pass finds its way to a receiver. To the spectator, plays such as these are human and dazzling. They suggest to the audience what it has hoped for (and been told) all along, that technology is still a tool and not a master. Fans get living proof of this every time a long pass is completed; they see at once that it is the result of careful planning, perfect integration and an effective "pattern," but they see too that it is human and that what counts as well is man, his desire, his natural skill, and his "grace under pressure." Football metaphysically yokes heroic action and technology together by violence to suggest that they are mutually supportive. It's a doubtful proposition, but given how we live it has its attractions.

Football, like the space program, is a game in the grand manner, yet is a rather sober sport and often seems to lack that positive, comic vision of which baseball's pastoral is a part. It is a winter game, as those fans who saw the Minnesota Vikings play the Detroit Lions last Thanksgiving were graphically reminded. The two teams played in a blinding snowstorm, and except for the small flags in the corners of the end zones, and a patch of mud wherever the ball was downed, the field was totally obscured. Even through the magnified television lenses the players were difficult to identify; you saw only huge shapes come out of the gloom, thump against each other and fall in a heap. The movement was repeated endlessly and silently in a muffled stadium, interrupted once or twice by a shot of a bare-legged girl who fluttered her pom-poms in the cold. The spectacle was by turns pathetic, compelling, and absurd, a kind of theater of oblivion.

Games such as this are by no means unusual, and it is not difficult to see why, for many, football is a gladiatorial sport of pointless bludgeoning played by armoured monsters. However accurate this description may be, I still believe that even in the worst of circumstances football can be a liberating activity. In the game I have just described, for instance, there was one play, the turning point of the game, which more than compensated for the sluggishness of most of the action. Jim Marshall, the huge defensive end (who hunts on dogsleds during the off season), intercepted a pass deep in his own territory and rumbled upfield like a dinosaur through the mud, the snow, and the opposing team, lateraling at the last minute to another lineman who took the ball in for a touchdown. It was a supreme moment because Marshall's principal occupation is falling on quarterbacks, not catching the ball

196

and running with it. His triumphant jaunt, something that went unequaled during the rest of that dark afternoon, was a hearty burlesque of the entire sport, an occasion for epic laughter in bars everywhere (though especially in Minnesota), and it was more than enough to rescue the game from the snowbound limbo it was buried in.

In the end, I suppose both football and baseball could be seen as varieties of decadence. In its preoccupation with mechanization, and in its open display of violence, football is the more obvious target for social moralists, but I wonder if this is finally more "corrupt" than the seductive picture of sanctuary and tranquility that baseball has so artfully drawn for us. Almost all sport is vulnerable to such criticism because it is not strictly ethical in intent, and for this reason there will always be room for puritans like the Elizabethan John Stubbes who howled at the "wanton fruits which these cursed pastimes bring forth." As a long time dedicated fan of almost anything athletic, I confess myself out of sympathy with most of this; which is to say, I guess, that I am vulnerable to those fantasies which these games support, and that I find happiness in the company of people who feel as I do.

A final note. It is interesting that the heroic and pastoral conventions which underlie our most popular sports are almost classically opposed. The contrasts are familiar: city vs. country, aspiration vs. contentment, activity vs. peace, and so on. Judging from the rise of professional football, we seem to be slowly relinquishing that unfettered rural vision of ourselves that baseball so beautifully mirrors, and we have come to cast ourselves in a genre more reflective of a nation confronted by constant and unavoidable challenges. Right now, like the Elizabethans, we seem to share both heroic and pastoral yearnings, and we reach out to both. Perhaps these divided needs account in part for the enormous attention we as a nation now give to spectator sports. For sport provides one place, at least, where we can have our football and our baseball too.

IDEAS

1. What does Ross mean when he says that "each sport contains a fundamental myth which it elaborates for its fans"?

2. What definition of *pastoral* can you make from Ross's statements about baseball?

3. What significance do you see in the terms *fielders, field, ball park, urban corner, infield,* and *outfield*?

4. What is the significance of *time* in Ross's contrastive comparison?

5. What definition of *heroic* can you make from Ross's statements about football?

6. What distinction does Ross make between personality and character?

7. What present-day names would you substitute for Ross's stars of a decade ago?

8. How valid do you find the author's "doubtful proposition" that heroic action and technology linked by violence characterize the modern world?

ORGANIZATION AND STYLE

1. How many paragraphs are in the introduction to this essay? At what point does Ross state his thesis?

2. What is the purpose of the miniature comparison that Ross introduces in the first paragraph?

3. Find Ross's inductive definition of *pastoral.* Is his method of defining the word better than a straightforward definition would have been?

4. Ross organizes his essay by wholes, devoting one section completely to baseball, then another to football. In the football section, however, he occasionally makes contrastive statements about baseball. Why is this useful there? Why would it not have worked for him to mention football in the baseball section?

5. Does Ross provide sufficient transition to his football section? Would you have preferred one of the more traditional markers? If so, which one(s)?

6. In his conclusion (the final two paragraphs), Ross backs off from his comparison to develop final supporting arguments for his thesis. How does he nevertheless continue his contrastive comparison?

WRITING

1. Using Ross's distinction between the pastoral and the heroic, write your own comparison-contrast essay about two other sports or other activities—golf-tennis, gardening-cooking, fishing-rowing—which you feel can be discussed under those headings. Try to follow an organizational scheme similar to Ross's.

2. Some readers have suggested that Ross's description of baseball, now over a decade old, is dated, that baseball is now more heroic than pastoral. If you agree with this position, develop an essay to support your ideas. Consider the earlier parks, players, owners, and fans; then show how these items look today.

New York

GAY TALESE

———————●———————

Beginning with a thesis sentence that declares, "New York is a city of things unnoticed," Talese then sets about to notice the unnoticed. This is not a descriptive account of the parks, buildings, and streets to which the typical tourist to New York might be attracted. It is a contrasting picture, filled with interesting specific details, of scenes that most people fail to see. Through extensive detail, Talese makes even the unnoticed scenes attractive and interesting.

New York is a city of things unnoticed. It is a city with cats sleeping under parked cars, two stone armadillos crawling up St. Patrick's Cathedral, and thousands of ants creeping on top of the Empire State Building. The ants probably were carried up there by wind or birds, but nobody is sure; nobody in New York knows any more about the ants than they do about the panhandler who takes taxis to the Bowery; or the dapper man who picks trash out of Sixth Avenue trash cans; or the medium in the West Seventies who claims, "I am clairvoyant, clairaudient, and clairsensuous."

New York is a city for eccentrics and a center for odd bits of information. New Yorkers blink twenty-eight times a minute, but forty when tense. Most popcorn chewers at Yankee Stadium stop chewing momentarily just before the pitch. Gumchewers on Macy's escalators stop chewing momentarily just before they get off—to concentrate on the last step. Coins, paper clips, ball-point pens, and little girls' pocketbooks are found by workmen when they clean the sea lion's pool at the Bronx Zoo.

A Park Avenue doorman has parts of three bullets in his head—there since World War I. Several young gypsy daughters, influenced by television and literacy, are running away from home because they don't want to grow up and become fortune-tellers. Each month a hundred pounds of hair is delivered to Louis Feder on 545 Fifth Avenue, where blond hairpieces are made from German women's hair; brunette hairpieces from Italian women's hair; but no hairpieces from American women's hair which, says Mr. Feder, is weak from too frequent rinses and permanents.

Some of New York's best informed men are elevator operators, who rarely talk, but always listen—like doormen. Sardi's doormen listen to the comments made by Broadway's first-nighters walking by after the last act. They listen closely. They listen carefully. Within ten minutes they can tell you which shows will flop and which will be hits.

On Broadway each evening a big, dark, 1948 Rolls-Royce pulls into Forty-sixth Street—and out hop two little ladies armed with Bibles and signs reading, "The Damned Shall Perish." These ladies proceed to stand on the corner screaming at the multitudes of Broadway sinners, sometimes until three A.M., when their chauffeur in the Rolls picks them up and drives them back to Westchester.

By this time Fifth Avenue is deserted by all but a few strolling insomniacs, some cruising cabdrivers, and a group of sophisticated females who stand in store windows all night and day wearing cold, perfect smiles. Like sentries they line Fifth Avenue—these window mannequins who gaze onto the quiet street with tilted heads and pointed toes and long rubber fingers reaching for cigarettes that aren't there.

At five A.M. Manhattan is a town of tired trumpet players and homeward-bound bartenders. Pigeons control Park Avenue and strut unchallenged in the middle of the street. This is Manhattan's mellowest hour. Most *night* people are out of sight—but the *day* people have not yet appeared. Truck drivers and cabs are alert, yet they do not disturb the mood. They do not disturb the abandoned Rockefeller

Center, or the motionless night watchmen in the Fulton Fish Market, or the gas-station attendant sleeping next to Sloppy Louie's with the radio on.

At five A.M. the Broadway regulars either have gone home or to all-night coffeeshops where, under the glaring light, you see their whiskers and wear. And on Fifty-first Street a radio press car is parked at the curb with a photographer who has nothing to do. So he just sits there for a few nights, looks through the windshield, and soon becomes a keen observer of life after midnight.

"At one A.M.," he says, "Broadway is filled with wise guys and with kids coming out of the Astor Hotel in white dinner jackets—kids who drive to dances in their fathers' cars. You also see cleaning ladies going home, always wearing kerchiefs. By two A.M. some of the drinkers are getting out of hand, and this is the hour for bar fights. At three A.M. the last show is over in the nightclubs, and most of the tourists and out-of-town buyers are back in hotels. And small-time comedians are criticizing big-time comedians in Hanson's Drugstore. At four A.M., after the bars close, you see the drunks come out—and also the pimps and prostitutes who take advantage of drunks. At five A.M., though, it is mostly quiet. New York is an entirely different city at five A.M."

At six A.M. the early workers begin to push up from the subways. The traffic begins to move down Broadway like a river. And Mrs. Mary Woody jumps out of bed, dashes to her office, and phones dozens of sleepy New Yorkers to say in a cheerful voice, rarely appreciated: "Good morning. Time to get up." For twenty years, as an operator of Western Union's Wake-Up Service, Mrs. Woody has gotten millions out of bed.

By seven A.M. a floridly robust little man, looking very Parisian in a blue beret and turtleneck sweater, moves in a hurried step along Park Avenue visiting his wealthy lady friends—making certain that each is given a brisk, before-breakfast rubdown. The uniformed doormen greet him warmly and call him either "Biz" or "Mac" because he is Biz Mackey, a ladies' masseur *extraordinaire*. He never reveals the names of his customers, but most of them are middle-aged and rich. He visits each of them in their apartments, and has special keys to their bedrooms; he is often the first man they see in the morning, and they lie in bed waiting for him.

The doormen that Biz passes each morning are generally an obliging, endlessly articulate group of sidewalk diplomats who list among their friends some of Manhattan's most powerful men, most beautiful women, and snootiest poodles. More often than not, the doormen are big, slightly Gothic in design, and the possessors of eyes sharp enough to spot big tippers a block away in the year's thickest fog. Some East Side doormen are as proud as grandees, and their uniforms, heavily festooned, seem to come from the same tailor who outfitted Marshal Tito.

Shortly after seven-thirty each morning hundreds of people are lined along Forty-second Street waiting for the eight A.M. opening of the ten movie houses that stand almost shoulder-to-shoulder between Times Square and Eighth Avenue. Who are these people who go to the movies at eight A.M.? They are the city's insomniacs, night watchmen, and people who can't go home, do not want to go home, or have no home. They are derelicts, homosexuals, cops, hacks, truck drivers, cleaning ladies, and restaurant men who have worked all night. They are also alcoholics who are waiting for eight A.M. to pay their forty cents for a soft seat and to sleep in the dark, smoky theatre. And yet, aside from being smoky, each of Times Square's theatres has a special quality, or lack of quality, about it. At the Victory Theatre one finds horror films, while at the Times Square Theatre they feature only cowboy films. There are first-run films for forty cents at the Lyric, while at the Selwyn there are always second-run films for thirty cents. But if you go to the Apollo Theatre you will see, in addition to foreign films, people in the lobby talking with their hands. These are deaf-and-dumb movie fans who patronize the Apollo because they read the subtitles. The Apollo probably has the biggest deaf-and-dumb movie audience in the world.

New York is a city of 38,000 cabdrivers, 10,000 bus drivers, but only one chauffeur who has a chauffeur. The wealthy chauffeur can be seen driving up Fifth Avenue each morning, and his name is Roosevelt Zanders. He earns $100,000 a year, is a gentleman of impeccable taste and, although he owns a $23,000 Rolls-Royce, does not scorn his friends who own Bentleys. For $150 a day, Mr. Zanders will drive anyone anywhere in his big, silver Rolls. Diplomats patronize him, models pose next to him, and each day he receives cables from around the world urging that he be waiting at Idlewild, on the docks, or outside the Plaza Hotel. Sometimes at night, however, he is too tired to drive anymore. So Bob Clarke, his chauffeur, takes over and Mr. Zanders relaxes in the back.

New York is a town of 3,000 bootblacks whose brushes and rhythmic ragsnaps can be heard up and down Manhattan from midmorning to midnight. They dodge cops, survive rainstorms, and thrive in the Empire State Building as well as on the Staten Island Ferry. They usually wear dirty shoes.

New York is a city of headless men who sit obscurely in subway booths all day and night selling tokens to people in a hurry. Each weekday more than 4,500,000 riders pass these money changers who seem to have neither heads, faces, nor personalities—only fingers. Except when giving directions, their vocabulary consists largely of three words: "How many, please?"

In New York there are 200 chestnut vendors, and they average $25 on a good day peddling soft, warm chestnuts. Like many vendors, the chestnut men do not own their own rigs—they borrow or rent them from pushcart makers such as David Amerman.

Mr. Amerman, with offices opposite a defunct public bathhouse on the Lower East Side, is New York's master builder of pushcarts. His father and grandfather before him were pushcart makers, and the family has long been a household word among the city's most discriminating junkmen, fruit vendors, and hotdog peddlers.

In New York there are 500 mediums, ranging from

semi-trance to trance to deep-trance types. Most of them live in New York's West Seventies and Eighties, and on Sundays some of these blocks are communicating with the dead, vibrating to trumpets, and solving all problems.

The Manhattan Telephone Directory has 776,300 names, of which 3,316 are Smith, 2,835 are Brown, 2,444 are Williams, 2,070 are Cohen—and one is Mike Krasilovsky. Anyone who doubts this last fact has only to look at the top of page 876 where, in large black letters, is this sign: "There is only one Mike Krasilovsky. Sterling 3-1990."

In New York the Fifth Avenue Lingerie shop is on Madison Avenue; the Madison Pet Shop is on Lexington Avenue; the Park Avenue Florist is on Madison Avenue; and the Lexington Hand Laundry is on Third Avenue. New York is the home of 120 pawnbrokers and it is where Bishop Sheen's brother, Dr. Sheen, shares an office with one Dr. Bishop.

New York is a town of thirty tattooists where interest in mankind is skindeep, but whose impressions usually last a lifetime. Each day the tattooists go pecking away over acres of anatomy. And in downtown Manhattan, Stanley Moskowitz, a scion of a distinguished family of Bowery skin-peckers, does a grand business.

When it rains in Manhattan, automobile traffic is slow, dates are broken and, in hotel lobbies, people slump behind newspapers or walk aimlessly about with no place to sit, nobody to talk to, nothing to do. Taxis are harder to get; department stores do between fifteen and twenty-five percent less business, and the monkeys in the Bronx Zoo, having no audience, slouch grumpily in their cages looking more bored than the lobby-loungers.

While some New Yorkers become morose with rain, others prefer it, like to walk in it, and say that on rainy days the city's buildings seem somehow cleaner—washed in an opalescence, like a Monet painting. There are fewer suicides in New York when it rains. But when the sun is shining, and New Yorkers seem happy, the depressed person sinks deeper into depression, and Bellevue Hospital gets more suicide calls.

New York is a town of 8,485 telephone operators, 1,364 Western Union messenger boys, and 112 newspaper copyboys. An average baseball crowd at Yankee Stadium uses over ten gallons of liquid soap per game—an unofficial high mark for cleanliness in the major leagues; the stadium also has the league's top number of ushers (360), sweepers (72), and men's rooms (34).

New York is a town in which the brotherhood of Russian Bath Rubbers, the only union advocating sweatshops, appears to be heading for its last rubdown. The union has been going in New York City for years, but now most of the rubbers are pushing seventy and are deaf—from all the water and the hot temperatures.

Each afternoon in New York a rather seedy saxophone player, his cheeks blown out like a spinnaker, stands on the sidewalk playing *Danny Boy* in such a sad, sensitive way that he soon has half the neighborhood peeking out of windows tossing nickels, dimes, and quarters at his feet. Some of the coins roll under parked cars, but most of them are caught in his outstretched hand. The saxophone player is a street musician named Joe Gabler; for the past thirty years he has serenaded every block in New York and has sometimes been tossed as much as $100 a day in coins. He is also hit with buckets of water, empty beer cans and eggs, and chased by wild dogs. He is believed to be the last of New York's ancient street musicians.

New York is a town of nineteen midget wrestlers. They all can squeeze into the Hotel Holland's elevator, six can sleep in one bed, eight can be comfortably transported to Madison Square Garden in the chauffeur-driven Cadillac reserved for the midget wrestlers.

In New York from dawn to dusk to dawn, day after day, you can hear the steady rumble of tires against the concrete span of George Washington Bridge. The bridge is never completely still. It trembles with traffic. It moves in the wind. Its great veins of steel swell when hot and contract when cold; its span often is ten feet closer to the Hudson River in summer than in winter. It is an almost restless structure of graceful beauty which, like an irresistible seductress, withholds secrets from the romantics who gaze upon it, the escapists who jump off it, the chubby girl who lumbers across its 3,500-foot span trying to reduce, and the 100,000 motorists who each day cross it, smash into it, shortchange it, get jammed up on it.

When street traffic dwindles and most people are sleeping in New York, some neighborhoods begin to crawl with cats. They move quickly through the shadows of buildings; night watchmen, policemen, garbage collectors, and other nocturnal wanderers see them—but never for long.

There are 200,000 stray cats in New York. A majority of them hang around the fish market, or in Greenwich Village, and in the East and West Side neighborhoods where garbage cans abound. No part of the city is without its strays, however, and all-night garage attendants in such busy neighborhoods as Fifty-fourth Street have counted as many as twenty of them around the Ziegfeld Theatre early in the morning. Troops of cats patrol the waterfront piers at night searching for rats. Subway trackwalkers have discovered cats living in the darkness. They seem never to get hit by trains, though some are occasionally liquidated by the third rail. About twenty-five cats live seventy-five feet below the west end of Grand Central Terminal, are fed by the underground workers, and never wander up into the daylight.

New York is a city in which large, cliff-dwelling hawks cling to skyscrapers and occasionally zoom to snatch a pigeon over Central Park, or Wall Street, or the Hudson River. Bird watchers have seen these peregrine falcons circling lazily over the city. They have seen them perched atop tall buildings, even around Times Square. About twelve of these hawks patrol the city, sometimes with a wingspan of thirty-five inches. They have buzzed women on the roof of the St. Regis Hotel, have attacked repairmen on smokestacks, and, in August, 1947, two hawks jumped women residents in the recreation yard of the Home of the New York Guild for the Jewish Blind. Maintenance men at the Riverside Church have seen hawks dining on pigeons in the bell tower. The hawks remain there for only a little while. And then they fly out to the river, leaving pigeons' heads for the Riverside maintenance men to clean up. When the hawks return, they fly in quietly— *unnoticed,* like the cats, the headless men, the ants, the ladies' masseur, the doorman with three bullets in his head, and most of the other offbeat wonders in this town without time.

IDEAS

1. Is the image of New York presented in this essay essentially positive or negative? Do you think Talese likes or dislikes the city? What clues can you find in the essay?

2. Talese begins his essay by referring to New York as "a city of things unnoticed," and he develops his essay by looking at those unnoticed things and people. How might the essay have been different if he had focused on things noticed such as the large buildings, major stores, or prominent people? Would the essay have been as effective with this type of development? Why or why not?

3. How does this picture of New York meet with your own image of the city, either from knowing it personally or from reading about it?

4. If you could meet one of the individuals or groups that Talese writes about, who would it be? Why?

5. If you were developing a travel brochure designed to attract tourists to New York, which paragraphs from this essay might you wish to include?

ORGANIZATION AND STYLE

1. The essay is organized by using the catalog technique. Talese introduces a type or category and then develops each paragraph by listing or cataloging specific details in individual sentences, but he does not develop any of

those details very completely. How effective is this system for an essay of this type? Would you have preferred several paragraphs, for instance, about a specific doorman and what secrets he knew?

2. The middle part of the essay is developed chronologically. Does this system work? Can you think of any other way that the author could have organized the same material?

3. The sentences of this essay are generally short, and the author makes little use of such sophistications of style as lengthy parallel structures, participial beginnings, and so forth. Why do you think Talese elected to write this piece in such a simple, straightforward style?

4. What word in the final sentence of the essay ties that conclusion back to the opening sentence? How effective is this conclusion?

5. Why do you suppose the essay is entitled simply "New York"? Would a more specific title such as "New York from Dawn to Dusk" or "A Quick Glimpse at New York Scenes and People" have been equally effective?

6. How does Talese use comparison and contrast to write about New York at different times of the day? To portray the desirable parts of New York with the undesirable? To suggest an implied contrast between New York and other cities? Between New Yorkers and people from other cities?

WRITING

1. Write an essay in which you focus on the unnoticed things and people of your own city or neighborhood. Do not focus on the obvious; look for everyday scenes and activities that most people never see. Try using the same type of catalog detail that Talese uses.

2. Select one individual from "New York" who most fascinates you, perhaps the doorman, the elevator opera-

tor, or the pushcart vendor. Try to imagine what that person sees and hears in the course of several hours on the job. Write an imaginative essay in which that individual tells his or her own story about life on the job in New York. Let the structure of your essay work to highlight the contrasts among the different scenes that you describe.

My Grandmother and the Dirty English

AUBREY MENEN

———————●———————

Menen amusingly contrasts his Indian grand-mother's assumptions about decent conduct and the English against his English and American readers' unstated obverse assumptions about India, affirming something, with quiet irony, for both sides.

My grandmother, like Michelangelo, had *terribilità*. She had a driving will, she would not be balked, and whatever she did was designed to strike the spectator with awe. She was also something of a stick. She rarely spoke to anyone who was not of her own social station, and she received guests formally with her breasts completely bare. Even in her time, women were growing lax about this custom, in Malabar. But my grandmother insisted on it. She thought that married women who wore blouses and pretty saris were Jezebels; in her view, a wife who dressed above her waist could only be aiming at adultery.

My grandmother had several sons who obeyed her and one who did not—my father. He had been sent to England to take the degree of Bachelor of Medicine. He applied himself to medicine but found being a bachelor less to his liking. He fell in love with a lady of celebrated Irish beauty and married her. He settled in England and there, some two years later, I was born.

My grandmother took no notice of my existence until I was twelve years old, when she suddenly demanded that I be brought and shown to her. On the arrival of her message I was incontinently taken by my parents half across the earth, from London to south of Calicut. When my grandmother heard that my mother intended to come, she gave orders for a special house to be put in repair for my mother's accommodation. It was on the farthest confines of the family property. This was her solution of a difficult problem: My mother, being foreign, was ritually unclean, and therefore, whenever she entered the family house, she would defile it. The house would have to be purified each time, and so would every caste Hindu in it. It followed logically that if my mother stayed in the house, it would be continually in a state of defilement, and continually in a state of being ritually cleaned. Since this ceremony involved drums and conch shells, my mother's visit foreshadowed a prolonged uproar. All this was avoided by putting her up in a separate building, to which we were conducted on our arrival. My father stayed there with us for a while, but he was soon called away on urgent affairs of his own and could play no part in the battle that followed.

I cannot say that my grandmother was rude to my mother, though she never referred to her by name but always as "the Englishwoman." This is not necessarily an insulting expression, but my mother has Irish blood in her veins, and, what with this and the isolated house and some other pinpricks in our first week's stay, her temper rose. She ordered a quantity of medical stores from Calicut, and when they arrived she set up a free dispensary on the veranda, to which the peasants flocked. It was an admirably devised counterstroke. My grandmother had shut the door in my mother's face; she now had the galling experience of seeing my mother industriously cleaning up the doorstep. As my mother well knew, each drop of iodine she dispensed stung not only the grateful patient but also my grandmother's conscience.

My grandmother brooded for a few days and then sent my mother a bag of golden sovereigns. My mother sent it back, taking it to be, at the worst, a bribe to desist or, at the best, a tip. She was wrong. It was a peace offering. The sovereigns were sent again next day, accompanied by the family goldsmith, who sat, slept, and ate on the veranda for a week, during which he made them (with tweezers and a charcoal fire) into a great gold collar that my mother still, on occasion, wears.

When, fourteen years earlier, my father had written from England to say that he was getting married to a white woman, my grandmother was far from giving the union her blessing. But it would be wrong to say that she objected to it. If an American boy of twenty-two wrote home from foreign parts to say that he had taken to cannibalism, his parents would not object; they would be so revolted that a mere objection would never meet the case.

My grandmother had never met the English, but she knew all about them. She knew they were tall, fair, given to strong drink, and good soldiers, and that they had conquered her native country. She also knew that they were incurably dirty in their personal habits. She respected them but wished they would keep their distance. It was very much the way a Roman matron must have looked upon the Goths.

My father's eldest brother had been in England for two years, and on one occasion, in my presence, he spoke up for the English. He told his mother that while the Hindus were undoubtedly the most civilized race on earth and had been civilized a thousand years before the English, nevertheless the English were now the masters of the Hindus. My grandmother's reply to this was that the English were masters of the Hindus only because "nobody would listen to *us.*" By this she meant that our family, along with others of the same caste, had strongly objected to Vasco da Gama's being allowed to land in Calicut. They had, in fact, done their best to get him and his sailors massacred, but the country was not behind the plan, and he escaped. Everything, my grandmother argued, not without reason, had started then.

However, her chief complaint was that the English were dirty, and this was rather a poser for my uncle. When she asked if, like decent people, they took a minimum of two baths a day, my uncle, who could not lie to his mother without committing a disgraceful sin, said, well, no, but a few took one bath and the habit was spreading. He could go no further than that, though he added that my grandmother should remember England had a cold climate. This she loyally did, and when she discussed with me the question of bathing, she was able to treat it lightly, as one does the disgusting but rational liking of the Eskimos for eating blubber.

As for English eating, she did not have all the usual Hindu prejudices. She did not think it strange that they ate ham and beef; the outcaste hill tribes, called Todas, who made the family's straw mats and cleaned the latrines, ate anything. She was not disturbed, either, about the religion of the English, once my uncle had assured her that they had practically none. Their manners, however, she abominated. If she did not mind their eating meat, she considered their way of eating it beyond the pale of decent society. In her home, each person ate his meal separately, preferably in a secluded corner. The thought that English people could sit opposite each other and watch each other thrust food into their mouths, masticate, and swallow it made my grandmother wonder if there was anything that human beings would not do when left to their own devices.

She was not surprised to hear, therefore, that in England a woman could have more than one husband, particularly (and this was the crowning paradox) if she was a widow. To the day of her death, my grandmother never understood how people could call themselves civilized and yet allow widows to marry again. For her, the very foundation stone of society was that a child should have only one father. Nobody ever dared her wrath sufficiently to explain the position of women in English society. She was intensely proud of the standards of her house and she permitted no lewd talk to defile them.

Against this background, then, my grandmother's peace offering was a substantial victory for my mother, especially since the gold collar the goldsmith had been told to make was the characteristic jewelry of a Malabar bride.

The way was now open for me. I could go and see my grandmother. I had waited about three weeks.

I had many meetings with my grandmother—a dozen, perhaps, each of an hour's length, and at the end of the set time I would be courteously dismissed, as one is dismissed from the presence of royalty. I used to visit her in considerable state. The distance from my mother's house—the isolation wing, so to speak—to the main family mansion was more than a mile, and that was too far to walk in the Malabar sun. I went by palanquin—a hammock of red cloth, with rather worn embroidery of gold thread, swung on a black pole that had silver ornaments at either end. Four virtually naked men, two in front and two behind, carried the palanquin at a swift trot. There was a good deal of art in this. If the four men trotted just as they pleased, the hammock would swing in a growing arc until it tipped the passenger out. Consequently, the men trotted according to a complicated system, which I never really understood; watching them and trying to follow it was as difficult as trying to determine the order in which a horse puts its hoofs down. The men kept their rhythm by chanting. I used to fall asleep on the way, listening to them. It must have presented an interesting spectacle—the red palanquin, the sweating men, and a sleeping boy wearing an English school blazer that had stitched to its pocket a badge gained by infantile prowess in some sport I do not now remember.

The family house was vast and cool and, in my view, unfurnished. To my grandmother's eye, it was very elegant. There was nothing but the floor to sit on. She disliked chairs and thought them vulgar. What use were they, except for ostentation? There were no tables and no tablecloths. In my grandmother's house, if anybody dared eat in any fashion but off a fresh plantain leaf, his next meal would be served in the kitchen, where the servants were allowed to eat without ceremony. She approved of beds but insisted that the mattress be made of taut string; nothing else was considered clean. She also had a taste for handsome brassbound boxes. So beds, boxes, and oil lamps were the sole furniture of the innumerable rooms of the house.

My grandmother usually received me in her boudoir,

sitting by her favorite box. She made an unforgettable picture. She had great black eyes, a shock of white hair, and lips as lush and curved as those of a girl of eighteen. The skin of her bosom—bare, as I have said—was quite smooth. I sat on the floor in front of her, in my school blazer, and since my father had never taught me Malayalam (wishing me to be brought up like any other English boy), we talked through one of my uncles.

Many of the things my grandmother said to me were puzzling at the time, but I have come to understand them better. Much as she looked down on the English, I think that had she met some of them—had she overcome her well-bred fastidiousness and actually mixed with them—she would have found that she and they had much in common. Her compelling passion, like theirs, was racial pride. She believed—and this made her character—that she belonged to the cleverest family of the cleverest class of the cleverest people on earth. According to Lord Russell, this was also the firm faith of Mrs. Beatrice Webb, who used to repeat it to herself in moments when she might have felt inferior, such as when she made her entry into a distinguished party. Though my grandmother never went to parties, I'm sure that she, too, repeated the formula to stiffen her already formidable morale.

She felt that she was born of a superior race, and she had all the marks of her belief. For instance, she deplored the plumbing of every nation but her own. She would often say to me, through my uncle, "Never take a bath in one of those contraptions in which you sit in dirty water like a buffalo. Always bathe in running water. If you have servants to pour it over you, that's best; but otherwise you must stand under a tap or pour the water over yourself. A really nice person does not even glance at his own bath water, much less sit in it." Here she would laugh to herself—not an unkind laugh but a pitying one—as she thought of the backwardness of the white man's bathroom.

Another such mark—I have met it in many nations—was that she believed foreign sexual morals permitted and encouraged all sorts of abominations from which a civilized person shrank. She spoke to me with great freedom on this point; I was, after all, at puberty. I could not always follow the drift of her remarks, but I did gather that she felt strongly on one point. Why, if the English wanted their offspring to grow up decently, and not lewdly, did they not marry them off when they were children? There was something sinister in the neglect. A child should grow up knowing that all that side of his life was settled according to the best available advice and in the best possible manner for his welfare. When he was eighteen or twenty, the marriage could be consummated. Till then, he did not have to worry his head about women—or if he did worry, he would know he was slipping morally.

History, I have discovered, is on my grandmother's side. The great majority of civilized peoples have always agreed with her. In antiquity, romance and love and such things were for slaves. Respectable people arranged marriages as my grandmother had always wished to arrange those of her children. To take a single example, my grandmother and Brutus would fully have understood each other; she felt hurt that she had not been consulted about my father's marriage, while among the many side lights we have on Brutus is a letter in which he complains at being left out of the bargaining that went on preceding the betrothal of a close friend's daughter—"my dear little Attica"—who was nine years old.

Still a grandson was a grandson, even though my grandmother's permission had not been sought to bring him into the world, and she set about being not only a grandmother to me but a mother as well. She knew that soon I would go back among the heathen to finish my education, and she wanted me to go back knowing who and what I was. On one of my visits to her house, she gave me a small book in which were written all my duties and privileges as a member of my caste. The book was written on dried palm leaves, strung together with a cord between two covers of wood. It began with a prayer to God, thanking Him for creating us—our caste, that is—so much superior in every respect to the great majority of human beings.

My grandmother explained the contents of the book several times and with much emphasis, for she wanted to imprint it on my memory. Our family belongs to the caste called Nayars. The Nayars of Malabar are as old as Indian history, and therefore, it can be assumed, a good deal older. My grandmother told me that, traditionally, we had two obligations to society. We were warriors when there was fighting to do, and when there was not, we had the duty, on certain holy days, of carrying flowers to the temple. I remember that I thought this very romantic at the time and could not understand why my grandmother spoke of it prosaically; to me, warriors, flowers, and temples conjured up a picture of some Oriental Round Table. But my grandmother was right to be matter-of-fact. Our caste is a commonplace; it exists everywhere. In England, it is scattered all over the countryside. The men are what is called Army, and the women take not only flowers but fruit to the temple on the occasion of the Harvest Festival. It is curious, and inexplicable, that the combination of these two activities, whether in the shires or in the coconut groves of Malabar, produces the most ferocious snobs.

My grandmother explained to me that, as a Nayar, I should always be careful to keep my dignity when dealing with Brahmans. Brahmans are priests. The priests who had the cure of the souls of my grandmother's family were treated as domestic chaplains. Since their temples were on our property, my grandmother had several "livings," so to speak, at her disposal. Priests were, therefore, expected to make themselves agreeable, in return for which they were regularly fed. They were expected to mind their own business, which was to perform weekly ceremonies and to direct their preaching at the lower orders, particularly the servants. The Anglican settlement in England was much more elaborate, but, reduced to what it meant to the average priest in the vestry, it came to much the same thing, and provides one more reason why I wish my grandmother had visited the country of my birth.

She was quite ignorant of these striking resemblances, however, and begged me to remember myself when moving among the English. "They will look up to you, as a Nayar, to set an example," she would say. "They know that you have two thousand years' advantage over them, and they will be willing to learn. Show them this book. They will be very interested in it. It was written when they still went about naked. And I will give you some trinkets which you can hand out as gifts—some amulets, and some things made of sandalwood, which is very rare in England, so I am told, and much sought after. They will help you to make friends. But remember, it is your *example* that will count more than anything."

My grandmother gave me the things she had promised, and, as she had foretold, they were much admired in England. Some of them, I believe, are still in my school museum. She also gave me her blessing, which was what I had been brought across the world to get. Then, at long last, she agreed to see my mother. The meeting was formal. It lasted three minutes and took place on a conveniently outlying veranda of the family house. My grandmother politely spoke of another meeting, but she was saved by the monsoon. It broke the next day with such unprecedented violence that the paths were flooded and the palanquin bearers could not use them. It rained until the day of our departure.

When I thought over my grandmother's advice, back in England, I was in some confusion. Before my trip, my headmaster, wishing me goodbye and good luck, had said much the same thing. "Let them see by your example," he had said, "that you have been trained in an *English* school. Wherever you go, it is for *you* to set the tone." He had not given me any sandalwood, but I had been impressed. I had also been impressed with what my grandmother had said.

In my dilemma, I remembered that I had another

grandmother. She had always been a mysterious figure to me. I knew that she had been born in Killarney, and that she had been as beautiful as my mother. I also knew that she had gone to England to live. But she had died before I was born.

I asked my mother about her. She told me many things, but one in particular struck me. "My mother was never really happy in England," she said. "Sometimes, when things became unbearably tiresome, she would heave a long, deep sigh, close her eyes, and think about Killarney."

This seemed to me to be the neutral ground that I was looking for. I told my mother that whenever I found the English were what my Indian grandmother said they were, I would copy my other grandmother. I would close my eyes and remember I wasn't really Indian, and I wasn't English. I would remember that I was descended from the Irish, and do my best to stay out of the quarrel.

"You might try," my mother said, "but I don't think you will find it a great deal of help."

She was right. When I grew up, I went to Killarney to search for traces of my Irish ancestry. I found them. Several of my forebears had been hanged. The records called them brigands; the Irish called them patriots. They had taken to some mountains called Macgillicuddy's Reeks and had lived there for a century or more. I believe I also learned what it was my Irish grandmother had seen when she closed her eyes.

She saw, I think, those still remembered raids, when my Irish ancestors came bellowing and leaping down the Reeks to harry the detested English.

IDEAS

1. Is this essay really about the author's grandmother, different social customs, the generation gap, or just what?

2. What stereotypes of the English does Menen project? Of Indians? Of Irish?

3. Can you summarize the author's attitude toward the grandmother with a single word, perhaps with a qualifying adjective? What evidence supports your choice?

4. What do you learn here about the Indian caste system?

ORGANIZATION AND STYLE

1. Essentially, Menen contrasts the Indian and English peoples. What specific habits and assumptions (eating habits, bathing habits, clothing) carry his contrast?

2. With which paragraph does the essay's conclusion begin? What specifically does it accomplish?

3. How do Menen's comments about his other grandmother fit into his basic comparison and contrast? What do the last six paragraphs contribute to the essay's meaning?

4. What other "mini-comparisons" or "mini-contrasts" does Menen make? How do they merge into the whole to make the essay work?

WRITING

1. Though this essay concerns social and cultural differences, part of it also necessarily concerns the generation gap. Recall an incident when you were alone with your grandparents (or someone representing their generation) and when the conversation made you painfully aware of the differences between your generations. Write an essay that will examine, as Menen's does, several layers of the problem.

2. Menen focuses on his Indian grandmother and, near the end, reflects on his Irish one, suggesting an inherited debt to both. Examine the similarities and differences between your two sets of grandparents or perhaps your parents. Design your essay to show that you are indebted to each of them.

Classification

Classification is another basic process. Indeed, we cannot begin to think, or to compare and contrast, without it. Our ability to classify seems innate, aroused from birth by the world around us, as we begin to distinguish comfort from discomfort, warmth from coldness, light from dark. Before too long, we know a dog when we see one, having automatically acquired the idea of *dog,* the classification, from several sightings of this Pekingese and that Great Dane. Classification is simply a comparing and grouping of similars, and a separating of dissimilars into further subclasses of similars. Thus we can perceive this world around us, and begin to think about it.

The following two essayists both clarify parts of that world by classifying its diversities. Gould debates the evolutionary function of three biological classifications: the species, the individual, and the gene. Alexander examines how married couples fight and classifies their styles of combat.

Caring Groups and Selfish Genes

STEPHEN JAY GOULD

———————— ● ————————

Gould lays out his essay, like a scientist, inductively. How soon do you learn which side he is on? Is his case at all misleading? Would he have been stronger if he had set a deductive thesis at the end of his introductory remarks?

The world of objects can be arranged as a hierarchy, box within box. Molecules are made of atoms, crystals are made of molecules, and so on, to minerals, to rocks, the earth, the solar system, the galaxy made of stars, and the universe of galaxies. Different forces work at different levels. Rocks fall by gravity. At the atomic and molecular level, gravity is so weak that standard calculations ignore it.

Life, too, has many levels, and each has its role in the evolutionary process. Consider three major levels: genes, organisms, and species. Genes are blueprints for organisms; organisms are the building blocks of species. Evolution requires variation, for natural selection cannot operate without alternatives to choose among. Mutation is the ultimate source of variation, and genes are the unit of variation. Individual organisms are the units of selection. But individuals do not evolve—they can only grow, reproduce, and die. Evolutionary change occurs in groups of interacting organisms; species are the unit of evolution. In short, as philosopher David Hull writes, genes mutate, individuals are selected, and species evolve. Or so the orthodox, Darwinian view proclaims.

The identification of individuals as the unit of selection is a central theme in Darwin's thought. This idea underlies his most radical claim: that evolution is purposeless and without inherent direction. As I argued in my column for April 1977,* Darwin's theory transfers to biology the individualism of Adam Smith's laissez faire economics.† Smith had argued that a well-regulated economy, apparently harmonious and stable, would arise as a natural result of untrammeled self-interest, actively pursued by all. Many would lose and fall by the wayside, while winners would check and balance each other. Darwin contended

---

*"This View of Life," in *Natural History* magazine.

†Charles Darwin (1809–1882), naturalist, who established the theory of evolution that continues to underlie the life sciences; Adam Smith (1723–1790), Scottish economist, author of *The Wealth of Nations* (1776), the "bible" of free enterprise.

that the exquisite balance of nature had no "higher" cause. Evolution does not recognize the "good of the ecosystem" or even the "good of the species." Any harmony or stability is only an indirect result of individuals relentlessly pursuing their own self-interest—in modern parlance, getting more of their genes into future generations by greater reproductive success. Individuals are the unit of selection; the "struggle for existence" is a matter among individuals.

In the last fifteen years, however, challenges to Darwin's focus on individuals have sparked some lively debates among evolutionists. These challenges have come from above and below. From above, Scottish biologist V. C. Wynne-Edwards raised orthodox hackles fifteen years ago by arguing that groups, not individuals, are units of selection, at least for the evolution of social behavior. From below, English biologist Richard Dawkins has recently raised my hackles with his claim that genes themselves are units of selection, and individuals merely their temporary receptacles.

Wynne-Edwards presented his defense of "group selection" in a long book entitled *Animal Dispersion in Relation to Social Behavior* (New York: Hafner, 1962). He began with a dilemma: Why, if individuals only struggle to maximize their reproductive success, do so many species seem to maintain their populations at a fairly constant level, well matched to the resources available? The traditional Darwinian answer invoked external constraints of food, climate, and predation: only so many can be fed, so the rest starve (or freeze or get eaten) and numbers stabilized. Wynne-Edwards, on the other hand, argued that animals regulate their own populations by gauging the restrictions of their environment and regulating their own reproduction accordingly. He recognized right away that such a theory contravened Darwin's insistence on "individual selection," for it required that many individuals limit or forgo their own reproduction for the good of their group.

Wynne-Edwards postulated that a species is divided

into many more-or-less discrete groups. Some groups never evolved a way to regulate their reproduction. Within these groups, individual selection reigned supreme. In good years, populations rose and the groups flourished; in bad years, the group could not regulate itself and faced a severe crash and even extinction. Other groups developed systems of regulation in which many individuals sacrificed their reproduction for the group's benefit (an impossibility if selection can only encourage individuals to seek their own advantage). These groups survived the good and the bad. Evolution is a struggle among groups, not individuals. And groups survive if they regulate their populations by the altruistic acts of individuals. "It is necessary," Wynne-Edwards wrote, "to postulate that social organizations are capable of progressive evolution and perfection as entities in their own right."

Wynne-Edwards reinterpreted most animal behavior in this light. The environment, if you will, prints only so many tickets for reproduction. Animals then compete for tickets through elaborate systems of conventionalized rivalry. In territorial species, each parcel of land has a ticket and animals (usually males) posture for the parcels. Losers accept gracefully and retreat to peripheral celibacy for the good of all. (Wynne-Edwards, of course, does not impute conscious intent to winners and losers. He imagines that some unconscious hormonal mechanism underlies the good grace of losers.)

In species with dominance hierarchies, tickets are allotted to the appropriate number of places, and animals compete for rank. Competition is by bluff and posture, for animals must not destroy each other by fighting like gladiators. They are, after all, only competing for tickets to benefit the group. The contest is more of a lottery than a test of skills; an allotment of the right number of tickets is far more important than who wins. "The conventionalization of rivalry and the foundation of society are one and the same thing," Wynne-Edwards proclaimed.

But how do animals know the number of tickets? Clearly, they cannot, unless they can census their own populations. In his most striking hypothesis, Wynne-Edwards suggested that flocking, swarming, communal singing, and chorusing evolved through group selection as an effective device for censusing. He included "the singing of birds, the trilling of katydids, crickets, and frogs, the underwater sounds of fish, and the flashing of fireflies."

Darwinians came down hard on Wynne-Edwards in the decade following his book. They pursued two strategies. First, they accepted most of Wynne-Edward's observations, but reinterpreted them as examples of individual selection. They argued, for example, that *who* wins is what dominance hierarchies and territoriality are all about. If the sex ratio between males and females is near 50:50 and if successful males monopolize several females, then not all males can breed. Everyone competes for the Darwinian prize of passing more genes along. The losers don't walk away with grace, content that their sacrifices increase the common good. They have simply been beaten; with luck, they will win on their next try. The result may be a well-regulated population, but the mechanism is individual struggle. Adam Smith's invisible hand operates again—order and harmony from the pursuit of personal gain alone.

Virtually all Wynne-Edwards's examples of apparent altruism can be rephrased just as well as tales of individual selfishness. In many flocks of birds, for example, the first individual that spots a predator utters a warning cry. The flock scatters, but, according to group selectionists, the crier has saved his flockmates by calling attention to himself—self-destruction (or at least danger) for the good of the flock. Groups with altruist criers prevailed in evolution over all-selfish, silent groups, despite the danger to individual altruists. But the debates have brought forth at least a dozen alternatives that interpret crying as beneficial for the crier. The cry may put the flock in random motion, thus befuddling the predator and making it less likely that he will catch anyone, including the crier. Or the crier may wish to retreat to safety but dares not break rank to do it alone, lest the predator detect an individual out of step. So he cries to bring the flock along with him. As the crier, he may be disadvantaged relative to flockmates (or he may not, as the first to safety), but he may still be better off than if he had kept silent and allowed the predator to take someone (perhaps himself) at random.

The second strategy against Wynne-Edwards reinterprets apparent acts of disinterested altruism as selfish devices to propagate genes through surviving kin—the theory of kin selection. Siblings, on average, share half their genes. If you die to save three sibs, you pass on 150 percent of yourself through their reproduction. Again, you have acted for your own evolutionary benefit, if not for your corporeal continuity. Kin selection is a form of Darwinian individual selection.

These alternatives do not disprove group selection, for they merely retell its stories in the more conventional Darwinian mode of individual selection. The dust has yet to settle on this contentious issue but a consensus (perhaps incorrect) seems to be emerging. Most evolutionists would now admit that group selection can occur in certain special situations (species made of many very discrete, socially cohesive groups in direct competition with each other). But they regard such situations as uncommon if only because discrete groups are often kin groups, leading to a preference for kin selection as an explanation of altruism within the group.

Yet, just as individual selection emerged relatively unscarred after its battle from above with group selection, some other evolutionists launched an attack from below. Genes, they argue, not individuals are the units of selection. They begin by recasting Butler's famous aphorism that a hen is merely the egg's way of making another egg. An animal, they argue, is only DNA's way of making more DNA. Richard Dawkins has put the case most forcefully in his recent book *The Selfish Gene* (New York: Oxford University Press, 1976). "A body," he writes, "is the genes' way of preserving the genes unaltered."

For Dawkins, evolution is a battle among genes, each seeking to make more copies of itself. Bodies are merely the places where genes aggregate for a time. Bodies are temporary receptacles, survival machines manipulated by genes and tossed away on the geologic scrapheap once genes have replicated and slaked their insatiable thirst for more copies of themselves in bodies of the next generation. He writes:

"We are survival machines—robot vehicles blindly programmed to preserve the selfish molecules known as genes. . . .

"They swarm in huge colonies, safe inside gigantic lumbering robots . . . they are in you and me; they created us, body and mind; and their preservation is the ultimate rationale for our existence."

Dawkins explicitly abandons the Darwinian concept of individuals as units of selection: "I shall argue that the fundamental unit of selection, and therefore of self-interest, is not the species, nor the group, nor even, strictly, the individual. It is the gene, the unit of heredity." Thus, we should not talk about kin selection and apparent altruism. Bodies are not the appropriate units. Genes merely try to recognize copies of themselves wherever they occur. They act only to preserve copies and make more of them. They couldn't care less which body happens to be their temporary home.

I begin my criticism by stating that I am not bothered by what strikes most people as the most outrageous component of these statements—the imputation of conscious action to genes. Dawkins knows as well as you and I do that genes do not plan and scheme; they do not act as witting agents of their own preservation. He is only perpetuating, albeit more colorfully than most, a metaphorical shorthand used (perhaps unwisely) by all popular writers on evolution, including myself (although sparingly, I hope). When he says that genes strive to make more copies of themselves, he means that "selection has operated to favor genes that, by chance, varied in such a way that more copies survived in subsequent generations." The second is quite a mouthful; the first is direct and acceptable as metaphor although literally inaccurate.

Still, I find a fatal flaw in Dawkins's attack from below. No matter how much power Dawkins wishes to assign to genes, there is one thing that he cannot give them—direct visibility to natural selection. Selection simply cannot see genes and pick among them directly. It must use bodies as an intermediary. A gene is a bit of DNA hidden within a cell. Selection views bodies. It favors some bodies because they are stronger, better insulated, earlier in their sexual maturation, fiercer in combat, or more beautiful to behold.

If, in favoring a stronger body, selection acted directly upon a gene for strength, then Dawkins might be vindicated. If bodies were unambiguous maps of their genes, then battling bits of DNA would display their colors externally and selection might act upon them directly. But bodies are no such thing.

There is no gene "for" such unambiguous bits of morphology as your left kneecap or your fingernail. Bodies cannot be atomized into parts, each constructed by an individual gene. Hundreds of genes contribute to the building of most body parts and their action is channeled through a kaleidoscopic series of environmental influences: embryonic and postnatal, internal and external. So parts are not translated genes, and selection doesn't even work directly on parts. It accepts or rejects entire organisms because suites of parts, interacting in complex ways, confer advantages. The image of individual genes, plotting the course of their own survival, bears little relationship to developmental genetics as we understand it. Dawkins will need another metaphor: genes caucusing, forming alliances, showing deference for a chance to join a pact, gauging probable environments. But when you amalgamate so many genes and tie them together in hierarchical chains of action mediated by environments, we call the resultant object a body.

Moreover, Dawkins's vision requires that genes have an influence upon bodies. Selection cannot see them unless they translate to bits of morphology, physiology, or behavior that make a difference to the success of an organism. Not only do we need a one-to-one mapping between gene and body (criticized in the last paragraph), we also need a one-to-one *adaptive* mapping. Ironically, Dawkins's theory comes just at a time when more and more evolutionists are rejecting the panselectionist claim that all bits of the body are fashioned in the crucible of natural selection. It may be that many, if not most, genes work equally well (or at least well enough) in all their variants and that selection does not choose among them. If most genes do not present themselves for review, then they cannot be the unit of selection.

I think, in short, that the fascination generated by Dawkins's theory arises from some bad habits of Western scientific thought—from attitudes (pardon the jargon) that we call atomism, reductionism, and determinism. The idea that wholes should be understood by decomposition into "basic" units; that properties of microscopic units can generate and explain the behavior of macroscopic results; that all events and objects have definite, predictable, determined causes. These ideas have been successful in our study of simple objects, made of few components, and uninfluenced by prior history. I'm pretty sure that my stove will light when I turn it on (it did). The gas laws build up from molecules to predictable properties of larger volumes. But organisms are much more than amalgamations of genes. They have a history that matters; their parts interact in complex ways. Organisms are built by genes acting in concert, influenced by environments, translated into parts that selection sees and parts invisible to selection. Atoms that determine the properties of water are poor analogues for genes and bodies. I may not be the master of my fate, but my intuition of wholeness probably reflects a biological truth.

IDEAS

1. Gould states that "Evolution requires variation, for natural selection cannot operate without alternatives

to choose among." Can you explain that point more fully—perhaps adding some outside information about horseshoe crabs and early primates?

2. How is the species "the unit of evolution"?

3. Do you expect Gould to be pro-Darwin or anti-Darwin from his statement "Or so the orthodox, Darwinian view proclaims"? What does he turn out to be?

4. Wynne-Edwards says that groups, not individuals, are the units of selection; Gould, that the species is the unit of selection. How do their classifications differ?

5. How do you explain the "altruist" theory of selection?

6. How do Darwinians argue against the altruist theory?

7. What is "kin" selection?

8. According to Gould, why cannot genes be units of selection?

ORGANIZATION AND STYLE

1. Gould organizes his essay around three classifications: the species, the individual, and the gene. Find the sections treating each of these groups. With which is he the most concerned? Why?

2. The essay begins with an analogy, comparing the universe to the arrangement within a hierarchy. With what other analogies does Gould develop his ideas?

3. Classification invites words like *class, group, category, division, level,* or *type.* What are Gould's terms of this nature? How frequently, and where, does he use them? What does this suggest about his ability as a writer?

4. A part of this essay, beginning with the fourth paragraph, is a comparison-contrast of the ideas of Darwin and Wynne-Edwards. How does Gould fortify his own thesis in this section?

5. What features of a dialectic argument appear in this essay?

WRITING

1. To what extent is the human being a programmed survival machine? What instinctive reactions can you think of that support this theory? Develop an essay organized around several classes of instincts or responses.

2. Biologists argue that survival of the fittest is a fundamental law that works among animals and plants. Does it also work in social or business areas of life? What kinds of students tend to survive? What types of businesses, governments, neighborhoods? Using several different classes for your evidence, write an essay in which you argue for or against the survival of the fittest in the nonbiological world.

The Fine Art of Marital Fighting

SHANA ALEXANDER

———————— ● ————————

After first carefully showing how poorly most married couples fight (she refers to "native cowardice and abysmal crudity of American domestic fighting style"), Alexander then draws from the work of psychologist George R. Bach to classify bad fighters. Her argument is that if husbands and wives can recognize their class and its inherent weaknesses, they might become more talented combatants.

In the morning, his secretary quits; in the afternoon, his archrival at the office gets a promotion; when he gets home that evening he finds out his wife has put a dent in the new car. He drinks four martinis before dinner, and then calls his wife a lousy cook. She says how can he tell with all that gin in him, and he says she is getting as mean-tempered as her stupid mother, and she says at least her mother wasn't stupid enough to marry a phony slob, by which time he is bellowing like an enraged moose, she is shrieking and hurling dishes, the baby is screaming, the dogs are yapping, the neighbors are pounding on the walls, and the cops are on their way. Suddenly a car screeches to the curb and a little man with a tape recorder under his arm hops out and dashes inside.

This scene is a recurrent dream of George R. Bach, Ph.D., a Los Angeles clinical psychologist and West Coast chairman of the American Academy of Psychotherapy. For him, it is not a nightmare but a rosy fantasy of things to come. His great ambition is to set up a Los Angeles Municipal Fight Center which any embattled husband or wife, regardless of race, creed, or hour of the night, could telephone and get a fair hearing. Trained marriage counselors would man the switchboards, referee the disputes, tape-record the hubbub for analysis by dawn's early light, and if necessary, dispatch a mobile referee on a house call.

It is Bach's dream to become that referee. He studies human aggression, and he loves his work. Over the last twenty-five years, he has professionally analyzed 23,000 marital fights, including, he figures, at least 2,500 of his own. Gifted marital gladiators in action thrill him as the sunset does the poet.

Unfortunately, his clinical practice yields so few sunsets that Bach feels the future of American family life is gravely threatened. He recently told a startled audience of newsmen and psychiatrists at the annual meeting of the Ortho-Psychiatric Association that a primary aim of psychotherapy and marriage counseling should be "to teach couples to have more, shorter, *more constructive* fights." Along with a growing number of his colleagues, he says, he has come to believe that proper training in "the fine art of marital fighting" would not only improve domestic tranquillity, it could reduce divorces by up to 90 per cent.

What dismays the doctor is not bloodshed per se; it is the native cowardice and abysmal crudity of American domestic fighting style. Most husbands and wives, he has found, will avail themselves of any sneaky excuse to avoid a fight in the first place. But if cornered, they begin clobbering away at one another like dull-witted Neanderthals. They are clumsy, weak-kneed, afflicted with poor aim, rotten timing, and no notion of counterpunching. What's more, they fight dirty. Their favorite weapons are the low blow and the rock-filled glove.

The cause of the shoddy, low estate of the marital fight game is a misunderstanding of aggression itself, says the fight doctor. "Research has established that people always dream, and *my* research has established that people are always to some degree angry. But today they are ashamed of this anger. To express hostile feelings toward a loved one is considered impolite, just as the expression of sexual feelings was considered impolite before Freud."

What Freud did for sex, Bach, in his own modest way, would like to do for anger, which is almost as basic a human impulse. "We must remove the shame from aggression," he exhorts in a soft, singsong German accent much like Peter Lorre's. "Don't repress your aggressions—program them!"

When primitive man lived in the jungle, surrounded by real, lethal enemies, the aggressive impulse is what kept him alive. For modern man, the problem gets complicated because he usually encounters only what the psychologist calls "intimate enemies"—wives, husbands, sweethearts, children, parents, friends, and others whom he sometimes would like to kill, but toward whom he nonetheless feels basic, underlying goodwill.

When he gets mad at one of these people, modern man tends to go to pieces. His jungle rage embarrasses, betrays, even terrifies him. "He forgets that real intimacy *demands* that there be fighting," Bach says. He fails to realize that "nonfighting is only appropriate between strangers—people who have nothing worth fighting about. When two people begin to really *care* about each other, they become emotionally vulnerable—and the battles start."

Listening to Bach enumerate the many destructive, "bad" fight styles is rather like strolling through a vast Stillman's gym of domestic discord. Over there, lolling about on the canvas, watching TV, walking out, sitting in a trancelike state, drinking beer, doing their nails, even falling asleep, are the "Withdrawal-Evaders," people who will not fight. These people, Bach says, are very sick. After counseling thousands of them, he is convinced that "falling asleep causes more divorces than any other single act."

And over *there,* viciously flailing, kicking, and throwing knives at one another, shouting obnoxious abuse, hitting below the belt, deliberately provoking anger, exchanging meaningless insults (You stink! *You* doublestink!)—simply needling or battering one another for the hell of it—are people indulging in "open noxious attack." They are the "Professional Ego-Smashers," and they are almost as sick—but not quite—as the first bunch.

An interesting subgroup here are the "Chain-Reactors," specialists in what Bach once characterized as "throwing in the kitchen sink from left field." A chain-reacting husband opens up by remarking, "Well, I see you burned the toast again this morning." When his wife begins to make new toast, he continues, "And another thing . . . that no-good brother of yours hasn't had a job for two years." This sort of fight, says Bach, "usually pyramids to a Valhalla-type of total attack."

The third group of people are all smiling blandly and saying, "Yes, dear." But each one drags after him a huge gunnysack. These people are the "Pseudo-Accommodators," the ones who pretend to go along with the partner's point of view for the sake of momentary peace, but who never really mean it. The gunnysacks are full of grievances, reservations, doubts, secret contempt. Eventually the overloaded sacks burst open, making an awful mess.

The fourth group are "Carom Fighters," a sinister lot. They use noxious attack not directly against the partner but against some person, idea, activity, value, or object which the partner loves or stands for. They are a whiz at spoiling a good mood or wrecking a party, and when they *really* get mad, they can be extremely dangerous. Bach once made a study of one hundred intimate murders and discovered that two-thirds of the killers did not kill their partner, but instead destroyed someone whom the partner loved.

Even more destructive are the "Double Binders," people who set up warm expectations but make no attempt to fulfill them or, worse, deliver a rebuke instead of the promised reward. This nasty technique is known to some psychologists as the "mew phenomenon": "Kitty mews for milk. The mother cat mews back warmly to intimate that kitty should come and get it. But when the kitten nuzzles up for a drink, he gets slashed in the face with a sharp claw instead." In human terms, a wife says, for example, "I have nothing to wear." Her husband says, "Buy yourself a new dress—you deserve it." But when she comes home wearing the prize, he says, "What's that thing supposed to be, a paper bag with sleeves?"—adding, "Boy, do you look fat!"

The most irritating bad fighters, according to Bach, are the "Character Analysts," a pompous lot of stuffed shirts who love to explain to the mate what his or her real, subconscious, or hidden feelings are. This accomplishes nothing except to infuriate the mate by putting him on the defensive for being himself. This style of fighting is common among lawyers, members of the professional classes, and especially psychotherapists. It is presumptuous, highly alienating, and never in the least useful except in those rare partnerships in which husband and wife are equally addicted to a sick, sick game which Bach calls "Psychoanalytic Archaeology—the earlier, the farther back, the deeper, the better!"

In a far corner of Bach's marital gym are the "Gimmes," overdemanding fighters who specialize in "overloading the system." They always want more; nothing is ever enough. New car, new house, more money, more love, more understanding—no matter what the specific demand, the partner never can satisfy it. It is a bottomless well.

Across from them are found the "Withholders," stingily restraining affection, approval, recognition, material things, privileges—anything which could be provided with reasonable effort or concern and which would give pleasure or make life easier for the partner.

In a dark, scary back corner are the "Underminers," who deliberately arouse or intensify emotional insecurities, reinforce moods of anxiety or depression, try to keep the partner on edge, threaten disaster, or continually harp on something the partner dreads. They may even wish it to happen.

The last group are the "Benedict Arnolds," who not only fail to defend their partners against destructive, dangerous, and unfair situations, forces, people, and attacks but actually encourage such assaults from outsiders.

Husbands and wives who come to Psychologist Bach for help invariably can identify themselves from the categories he lists. If they do not recognize themselves, at least they recognize their mate. Either way, most are desperate to know what can be done. Somewhere, they feel, there must be another, sunnier, marital gym, a vast Olympic Games perhaps, populated with nothing but agile, happy, bobbing, weaving, superbly muscled, and incredibly sportsmanlike gladiators.

IDEAS

1. Do you believe that most couples try at first to avoid a fight and then, if provoked further, fight poorly?

2. Are there some instances when it might be better to be quiet and not argue an issue, or is it always better to say what you are really feeling?

3. Do marriage counselors really help to save troubled marriages? If so, what do you perceive to be their role?

4. Do the classes of marital fighting fit only in the husband-wife relationship? If extended into the social and business world, must other categories also be presented?

ORGANIZATION AND STYLE

1. Alexander begins her essay with a one-paragraph illustration. What is the tone of that paragraph? How does it help to shape the tone for the entire essay?

2. In the second paragraph, Alexander writes about a center to which "any embattled husband or wife, regardless of race, creed, or hour of the night, could telephone and get a fair hearing." What does the phrase "regardless of race, creed, or the hour of the night" contribute to the tone? At what other points in the essay does Alexander blend serious and colloquial language?

3. Alexander does not begin classifying marital fighters until about midway ("Listening to Bach enumerate. . . ."). What is the purpose of all that comes before this section? In what way does Alexander also classify in that earlier material?

WRITING

1. Alexander writes about how one man proposes to help troubled marriages. What other sources of "help"— family, friends, clergy, hypnotists, astrologists—are available? Write an essay in which you classify some of these different sources and discuss their relative merits. You might, like Alexander, wish to adopt a tone that will let you grin a bit at what you are writing.

2. Become an observer of human nature. You might watch the way students conduct themselves in the cafeteria or the football stadium, in long queues, or on a playground. Write an essay in which you analyze their different types of behavior. Try beginning your essay with a one-paragraph illustration, as does Alexander, that will set the tone for what is to follow.

Definition

As we have seen, definition is an aspect of classification. It establishes one class, like *evolutionary unit, democracy, history,* or *social science,* by drawing its limits and naming its ingredients, by excluding what it *is not,* and itemizing what it *is.* To establish the *is,* writers usually need several of the tactics we have already considered. They may need to describe causes and effects if they are defining a process, or something partaking of process, like *evolution, barometer, rocket,* or *good government.* They may need to compare and contrast *democracy,* let us say, with other systems and other uses and abuses of the term. They may need to define *character* by placing it under several classifications like *courage, integrity, compassion,* and the like. They may need examples and analogies to show what *justice* is, or is like, or is not like. Garver defines violence by separating it into four specific types, with examples for each. Hofstadter defines an intellectual by balancing traits that do not mark a person as intellectual against those that do.

Four Kinds of Violence

NEWTON GARVER

————————— ● —————————

Garver classifies violence to define it. Distinguishing personal from institutionalized violence, he separates these once again into overt and covert types, illustrating with concrete examples. Not all violence, he argues, is equal, and not all is readily detected. But, he continues, knowing more about its different types "will enable us to recognize more readily the many sorts of violence that surround our lives."

Violence can be usefully classified into four different kinds based on two criteria whether the violence is personal or institutionalized and whether the violence is overt or a kind of covert or quiet violence.

Overt physical assault of one person on the body of another is the most obvious form of violence. Mugging, rape, and murder are the flagrant "crimes of violence," and when people speak of the danger of violence in the streets it is usually visions of these flagrant cases that float before their minds. I share the general concern over the rising rate of these crimes, but at the same time I deplore the tendency to cast our image of violence just in the mold of these flagrant cases. These are cases where an attack on a human body is also clearly an attack on a person and clearly illegal. We must not tie these characteristics in too tight a package, for some acts of violence are intended as a defense of law or a benefit to the person whose body is beaten—for example, ordinary police activity (not "police brutality")[1] and the corporal punishment of children by parents and teachers. The humbler cases are violence too, although the fact that policemen, teachers, and parents have socially defined roles which they invoke when they resort to violence indicates that these cases have institutional aspects that overshadow the purely personal ones. These institutional overtones make a great deal of difference, but they cannot erase that there is violence done. Of course not all cases are so clear: I leave to the reader to ponder whether all sex acts are acts of violence, or just how to distinguish in practical terms those that are from those that are not. Whenever you do something to another person's body without his consent you are attacking not just a physical entity—you are attacking a person. You are doing something by force, so the violence in this case is something that is easily visible, has long been recognized as violence, and is a case of overt, personal violence.

[1] A persuasive account of the extent to which law itself can be a form of violence, rather than an alternative to it, is to be found in E. Z. Friedenberg's essay "A Violent Country" in the *New York Review,* October 20, 1966. [Garver's note]

In cases of war, what one group tries to do to another group is what happens to individuals in cases of mugging and murder. The soldiers involved in a war are responsible for acts of violence against "the enemy," at least in the sense that the violence would not have occurred if the soldiers had refused to act. (Of course some other violence might have occurred. But in any case I do not wish to try to assess blame or lesser evils.) The Nuremberg trials after World War II attempted to establish that individual soldiers are responsible morally and legally too, but this attempt overlooked the extent to which the institutionalization of violence changes its moral dimension. On the one hand, an individual soldier is not acting on his own initiative and responsibility, and with the enormous difficulty in obtaining reliable information and making a timely confrontation of government claims, not even U.S. Senators, let alone soldiers and private citizens, are in a good position to make the necessary judgments about the justice of a military engagement. On the other hand, a group does not have a soul and cannot act except through the agency of individual men. Thus there is a real difficulty in assigning responsibility for such institutional violence. The other side of the violence, its object, is equally ambiguous, for "the enemy" are being attacked as an organized political force rather than as individuals, and yet since a group does not have a body any more than it has a soul "the enemy" is attacked by attacking the bodies of individual men (and women and children). Warfare, therefore, because it is an institutionalized form of violence, differs from murder in certain fundamental respects.

Riots are another form of institutionalized violence, although their warlike character was not widely recognized until the publication of the report of the President's National Advisory Commission on Civil Disorders (the "Riot" Commission). In a riot, as in a war, there are many instances of personal violence, and some persons maintain that the civil disorders are basically massive crime waves. But on the other hand there is also much of a warlike character. One of the characteristics of the Watts riot, as

242

any will know who have read Robert Conot's very interesting book, *The Rivers of Blood, Years of Darkness,* is that in that riot the people who were supposed to be controlling the situation, the Los Angeles police and their various reinforcements, simply did not know basic facts about the community. In particular they did not know who was the person who could exercise a sort of leadership if the group were left alone and that person's hand was strengthened. One incident illustrates the sort of thing that happened. A Negro policeman was sent in plain clothes into the riot area and told to call back into the precinct whenever there was anything to report. He was told, furthermore, not to identify himself as a policeman under any conditions for fear of jeopardizing himself. At one point, he tried to intervene when some cops were picking on just altogether the wrong person, and he ended up getting cursed and having his head bashed in by one of his fellow members of the Los Angeles police force. The police were in such a state that they couldn't even refrain from hitting a Negro policeman who was sent on a plainclothes assignment into that area. In effect, the Los Angeles police and their various allies conducted what amounted to a kind of a war campaign. They acted like an army going out to occupy a foreign territory where they didn't know the people and didn't speak the language. The result was that their actions had the effect of breaking down whatever social structure there might have been. And the breakdown of the social structure then had the effect of releasing more and more overt violence. The military flavor of our urban disturbances has increased over the years, and 1967 saw the appearance not only of machine guns and automatic rifles but also of tanks and armored personnel carriers in Newark and Detroit, in what the Kerner Commission characterized as "indiscriminate and excessive use of force." For that reason the urban disorders that we've been having in recent summers are really a kind of institutionalized violence where there are two sides in combat with one another. It is quite different from a normal criminal situation where police act against individual miscreants.

Since these overt forms of violence are, on the whole, fairly easily recognized, let us go on to consider the other forms of violence, the quiet forms which do not necessarily involve any overt physical assault on anybody's person or property. There are both personal and institutional forms of quiet violence, and I would like to begin with a case of what we might call psychological violence, where individuals are involved as individuals and there are not social institutions responsible for the violation of persons that take place. Consider the following news item.[2]

> Phoenix, Ariz., Feb. 6 (AP)—Linda Marie Ault killed herself, policemen said today, rather than make her dog Beauty pay for her night with a married man.
>
> The police quoted her parents, Mr. and Mrs. Joseph Ault, as giving this account:
>
> Linda failed to return home from a dance in Tempe Friday night. On Saturday she admitted she had spent the night with an Air Force lieutenant.
>
> The Aults decided on a punishment that would "wake Linda up." They ordered her to shoot the dog she had owned about two years.
>
> On Sunday, the Aults and Linda took the dog into the desert near their home. They had the girl dig a shallow grave. Then Mrs. Ault grasped the dog between her hands, and Mr. Ault gave his daughter a .22-caliber pistol and told her to shoot the dog.
>
> Instead, the girl put the pistol to her right temple and shot herself. The police said there were no charges that could be filed against the parents except possibly cruelty to animals.

Obviously, the reason there can be no charges is that the parents did no physical damage to Linda. But I think your reaction might be the same as mine—that they really did terrible violence to the girl by the way they behaved in this situation. Of course one must agree that Linda did violence to herself, but that is not the whole account of the violence in this case. The parents did far more violence to the girl than the lieutenant, and the father recognized that

[2]*New York Times,* February 7, 1968. [Garver's note]

when he said to a detective, "I killed her. I killed her. It's just like I killed her myself." If we fail to recognize that there is really a kind of psychological violence that can be perpetrated on people, a real violation of their autonomy, their dignity, their right to determine things for themselves, their right to be humans rather than dogs, then we fail to realize the full dimension of what it is to do violence to one another.

One of the most obvious transition cases between overt personal violence and quiet personal violence is the case of a threat. Suppose a robber comes into a bank with a pistol, threatens to shoot one of the tellers, and walks out with money or a hostage or both. This is a case of armed robbery, and we rightly lump it together with cases of mugging and assault, morally and legally speaking, even if everybody emerges from the situation without any bruises or wounds. The reason is that there is a clear threat to do overt physical violence. By means of such a threat a person very often accomplishes what he might otherwise accomplish by actual overt violence. In this case the robber not only gets as much loot but he also accomplishes pretty much the same thing with respect to degrading the persons he is dealing with. A person who is threatened with being shot and then does something which he certainly would never otherwise do is degraded by losing his own autonomy as a person. We recognize that in law and morals: If a person who is threatened with a revolver takes money out of a safe and hands it to the robber we don't say that the person who has taken the money out of the safe has stolen it. We say that that person acted under compulsion, and hence the responsibility for what is done does not lie with him but with the person who threatened him.

It is very clear, and very important, that in cases where there is a threat of overt physical violence that we acknowledge that a person acting under that sort of a threat loses his autonomy. Of course, he needn't surrender his autonomy: he could just refuse to hand over the loot. There can be a great deal of dignity in such a refusal, and one of the messages of Sartre's moral philosophy, his existentialism, is that whenever you act other than with full responsibility yourself for your own actions that you are acting in bad faith. Now that is a very demanding philosophy, but it is one which puts a great deal of emphasis upon autonomy and dignity in human action and is not to be lightly dismissed. Nevertheless, we do not expect that people will act with such uncompromising strength and dignity. To recognize that people can be broken down by threats and other psychological pressures, as well as by physical attack, and that to have acted under threat or duress is as good an excuse before the law as physical restraint—these recognitions constitute acknowledgement of the pertinence of the concept of psychological violence.

Psychological violence often involves manipulating people. It often involves degrading people. It often involves a kind of terrorism one way or another. Perhaps these forms that involve manipulation, degradation, and terror are best presented in George Orwell's book, *1984.* In that book, the hero is deathly afraid of being bitten by a rat. He never is bitten by the rat, but he is threatened with the rat and the threat is such as to break down his character in an extraordinary way. Here what might be called the phenomenology of psychological violence is presented in as convincing a form as I know.

Apart from these cases of terror and manipulation and degradation, there are certain other forms of psychological violence. One of the most insidious is what might be called the "Freudian rebuff."[3] The Freudian rebuff works something like this. A person makes a comment on the Vietnam war or on civil rights or on some other current topic. The person he is talking to then says, "Well, you're just saying that because of your Oedipal relations with your father." The original speaker naturally objects, "Don't be silly. Of course I had a father and all that. But look at the facts." And then he starts bringing out the jour-

---

[3]Of course this is an aspect of cocktail-party Freudianism rather than of psychoanalytic theory, and what Freud invented was not this little ploy but the concepts that were later distorted into it. [Garver's note]

nals and newspapers and presents facts and statistics from them. "You must have a terrible Oedipal complex; you're getting so excited about this." And the person then says, "Look, I've had some fights with my father, but I'm not hung-up on him. I just have normal spats and affection. I've read the paper and I have an independent interest in the civil rights question. It has nothing to do with my relations with my father." To which the response is, "Well, your denial just proves how deep your Oedipal complex is." This type of Freudian rebuff has the effect of what John Henry Newman[4] called "poisoning the wells." It gives its victim just no ground to stand on. If he tries to stand on facts and statistics, they are discounted and his involvement is attributed to Freudian factors. If he tries to prove that he doesn't have the kind of psychological aberration in question, his very attempt to prove that he doesn't have it is taken to be evidence that he does. He can't get out of the predicament. It is like a quagmire in which the victim sinks deeper no matter which way he moves. So long as the proffered definition of the situation is imposed on him, a person has no way to turn: there is no possible sort of response that can extricate him from that charge laid upon him. To structure a situation against a person in such a manner does violence to him by depriving him of his dignity: no matter what he does, there is no way at all, so long as he accepts the problem in the terms in which it is presented, for him to make a response that will allow him to emerge with honor.

Although this sort of cocktail-party Freudianism is not very serious in casual conversations, where the definition of the situation can be challenged or the whole matter just shrugged off, it must be kept in mind that there are many forms of this ploy and that sometimes the whole life and character of a person may be involved. A classic literary and religious version is the dispute between Charles Kingsley and John Henry Newman in the nineteenth century, in

---

[4]In his famous debate with Charles Kingsley. See his *Apologia Pro Vita Sua,* conveniently available in a paperback edition, Garden City, Doubleday, 1956. [Garver's note]

which Kingsley challenged Newman's integrity and ended up losing his stature as a Protestant spokesman, and which is written up in fascinating detail in Newman's *Apologia.* A political variation is the Marxian rebuff where, of course, it is because of your class standing that you have such and such a view, and if you deny that the class standing is influencing you in that way your very denial shows how imbued you are with the class ideology. Between parent and child as well as between husband and wife there are variations of this ploy which turn around the identification (by one insistent party) of love with some particular action or other, so that the other party must either surrender his autonomy or acknowledge his faithfulness.

The cases where this sort of psychological violence are damaging are those where the person structuring the situation is in some position of special authority. Another form particularly virulent in urban schools—and probably suburban schools too—is the teacher's rebuff. An imaginative child does something out of the ordinary, and the teacher's response is that he is a discipline problem. It now becomes impossible for the child to get out of being a problem. If he tries to do something creative he will be getting out of line and thereby "confirm" that he is a discipline problem. If he stays in line he will be a scholastic problem, thereby "confirming" that he did not have potential for anything but mischief. The result is a kind of stunted person typical of schools in large urban areas, where it is common for a child to enter the public schools half a year behind according to standard tests. Such a child has undoubtedly been a discipline problem during this time, and the teacher has spent her effort trying to solve the discipline problem and keep him from getting out of line—that is, from learning anything.[5]

This last variation of the psychological rebuff brings us

[5]Among the many works commenting on this aspect of public education, I have found those of Edgar Friedenberg and Paul Goodman most instructive. See Paul Goodman, *Compulsory Miseducation,* New York, Horizon, 1964; Edgar Z. Friedenberg, *The Vanishing Adolescent,* Boston, Beacon Press, 1959, and *Coming of Age in America,* New York, Knopf, 1963. [Garver's note]

to the fourth general category of violence, institutionalized quiet violence. The schools are an institution, and teachers are hired not so much to act on their own in the classroom as to fulfill a predetermined role. Violence done by the teacher in the classroom may therefore not be personal but institutional, done while acting as a faithful agent of the educational system. The idea of such institutional violence is a very important one.

A clearer example of quiet institutional violence might be a well-established system of slavery or colonial oppression or the life of contemporary American ghettos. Once established, such a system may require relatively little overt violence to maintain it. It is legendary that Southerners used to boast, "We understand our nigras. They are happy here and wouldn't want any other kind of life,"— and there is no reason to doubt that many a Southerner, raised in the system and sheltered from the recurrent lynchings, believed it quite sincerely. In that sort of situation, it is possible for an institution to go along placidly, as we might say, with no overt disturbances and yet for that institution to be one that is terribly brutal and that does great harm to its victims and which, incidentally, at the same time brutalizes people who are on top, since they lose a certain measure of their human sensitivity.

There is more violence in the black ghettos than there is anywhere else in America—even when they are quiet. At the time of the Harlem riots in 1964, the Negro psychologist, Kenneth Clark, said that there was more ordinary, day-to-day violence in the life of the ghettos than there was in any day of those disturbances. I'm not sure exactly what he meant. The urban ghettos are places where there is a great deal of overt violence, much of it a kind of reaction to the frustrations of ghetto life. Fanon describes the similar phenomenon of the growth of violence within the oppressed community in th colonial situation in Algeria.[6] When people are suppressed by a colo-

---

[6]Frantz Fanon, *The Wretched of the Earth,* New York, Grove Press, 1966. [Garver's note]

nial regime, when they lack the opportunities which they see other people, white people, around them enjoying, then they become frustrated and have great propensities to violence. The safest target for such angry, frustrated people are their own kind. The Algerians did their first violence to other Algerians, in part because it wasn't safe to do it to a Frenchman. And the same is largely true of the situation that has developed in our urban ghettos. It isn't safe for a person living in the ghettos, if he is feeling frustrated and at the point of explosion, to explode against somebody outside the ghetto; but he can do it to his own kids, his wife, his brother, and his neighbor, and society will tend to look the other way. So there is a good deal of overt violence in the black ghettos. Perhaps, that is what Clark meant.

But we also have to recognize that there is sometimes a kind of quiet violence in the very operation of the system. Bernard Lafayette, who has worked in urban areas for both the American Freinds Service Committee and the Southern Christian Leadership Conference, speaks angrily of the violence of the status quo: "The real issue is that part of the 'good order of society' is the routine oppression and racism committed against millions of Americans every day. That is where the real violence is."[7] The fact is that there is a black ghetto in most American cities which operates very much like any system of slavery. Relatively little violence is needed to keep the institution going and yet the institution entails a real violation of the human beings being involved, because they are systematically denied the options which are obviously open to the vast majority of the members of the society in which they live. A systematic denial of options is one way to deprive men of autonomy. If I systematically deprive a person of the options that are normal in our society, then he is no longer in a position to decide for himself what to do. Any institution which systematically robs certain people of rightful

[7]In *Soul Force,* February 15, 1968. [Garver's note]

options generally available to others does violence to those people.

Perhaps denying options would not do violence to people if each individual person was an island unto himself and individuality were the full truth about human life. But it is not. We are social beings. Our whole sense of what we are is dependent on the fact that we live in society and have open to us socially determined options. I am now writing. As I write I make many choices about what to say, some having to do with whole paragraphs, some with single words, and some with punctuation. These choices are dependent upon a social institution, language. Unless I knew the language, and unless there were a society of language speakers, I would have no options at all about what to say. The options open to us by language are very important, but language is only one part of our society. There are many sorts of options which are open to us and important to us as individuals. It is how we act, how we choose with respect to socially defined options, that constitutes what we really are as human beings.

What we choose to do with respect to our socially defined options is much more important than which language or which system of property rights we inherit at birth—provided we have access to the options defined in the system. By suppressing options, you deprive a person of the opportunity to be somebody because you deprive him of choices. The institutional form of quiet violence operates when people are deprived of choices in a systematic way by the very manner in which transactions normally take place, without any individual act being violent in itself or any individual decision being responsible for the system.

These, then, are the main types of violence that I see. By recognizing those types of violence we begin to get the whole question of violence into a much richer perspective than when we hear the Chief of Police deplore violence. Such a richer perspective is vitally necessary, because we cannot do anything about the violence in our society unless we can see it, and most of us do not see it very well.

Conceptions and perceptions are closely dependent on one another, and perhaps having a better idea of what violence is will enable us to recognize more readily the many sorts of violence that surround our lives.

IDEAS

1. What exactly are the four kinds of violence Garver identifies?

2. Among the different kinds of violence, which do you consider to be the most dangerous to contemporary society?

3. This essay was first printed in 1968. Are its definitions of the kinds of violence still adequate? Would you now add other categories?

ORGANIZATION AND STYLE

1. Garver begins his essay with a very brief, businesslike first paragraph. How does this type of introduction set the mood for the entire essay?

2. How do the footnotes function to reinforce the general tone of the essay?

3. Examine each discussion of a kind of violence. Notice how Garver begins each by defining each kind, then illustrates with actual examples. Do you see any other common patterns of organization among the four distinct parts of the essay?

4. How, exactly, does Garver's purpose for writing this essay become clear in his concluding paragraph?

WRITING

1. Select one of Garver's kinds of violence; then develop an essay defining that violence through several different examples from the immediate present.

2. Select a word such as *love, hate, God, parents* that invites definition into different categories. Write an essay defining the different kinds of _____. Use Garver's pattern of identifying the category and then making it specific by a series of concrete examples.

What Is an Intellectual?

RICHARD HOFSTADTER

———————●———————

*Hofstadter works into his definition of an intellectual
by progressively setting aside the apparent to establish the true, living off ideas as against living for
ideas, the workaday practical as against the higher
practicality of the intellectual's mental play, then
naming the essential qualities that define the intellectual: mental play, piety, balance.*

But what is an intellectual, really? This is a problem of
definition that I found, when I came to it, far more elusive
than I had anticipated. A great deal of what might be
called the journeyman's work of our culture—the work of
engineers, physicians, newspapermen, and indeed of most
professors—does not strike me as distinctively intellectual, although it is certainly work based in an important
sense on ideas. The distinction that we must recognize,
then, is one originally made by Max Weber between living
for ideas and living *off* ideas. The intellectual lives for
ideas; the journeyman lives off them. The engineer or the
physician—I don't mean here to be invidious—needs to
have a pretty considerable capital stock in frozen ideas to
do his work; but they serve for him a purely instrumental
purpose; he lives off them, not for them. Of course he may
also be, in his private role and his personal ways of
thought, an intellectual, but it is not necessary for him to
be one in order to work at his profession. There is in fact
no profession which demands that one be an intellectual.
There do seem to be vocations, however, which almost
demand that one be an anti-intellectual, in which those
who live off ideas seem to have an implacable hatred for

those who live for them. The marginal intellectual workers and the unfrocked intellectuals who work in journalism, advertising, and mass communication are the bitterest and most powerful among those who work at such vocations.

It will help, too, to make the further distinction between living for ideas and living for *an idea.* History is full of cases of great men with good minds, a capacity to deal with abstractions, and a desire to make systems of them— all qualities we associate with the intellectual. But when, as it has in many of them, this concern with ideas, no matter how dedicated and sincere, reduces in the end to the ingenious use of them for a central preconception, however grand, then I think we have very little intellectualism and a great deal of something else. A good historical illustration is that of Lenin, who, as his more theoretical works show, had in him a powerful element of intellectuality; but this intellectuality was rendered thin by his all-absorbing concern with certain very limiting political values. His book on philosophy, *Materialism and Empirio-Criticism,* a shrill work and an extremely depressing one to read, makes it altogether clear that the politician in him swallowed up the intellectual. I choose the illustration of Lenin because it helps me to make another point that seems unfortunately necessary because of the present tendency to identify intellectuals with subversives. That point is that the idea of a party line and political messianism is inherently inconsistent with intellectualism, and those few intellectuals who have in some way survived that tension are few, pitiable, and on the whole sterile.

The journeyman of ideas, and the janizary* who makes a somewhat complicated but highly instrumental use of ideas, provide us with two illustrations of people who work with ideas but are not precisely intellectuals, as I understand the term. What, then, are the differences between

*Turkish elite guards, renowned for their fierceness in battle. Later, subservient officials.

the men who work with ideas but are *not* intellectuals and the men who work with ideas and *are* intellectuals?

Two things, that seem in fact to be mutually at odds, mark off the intellectual from the journeyman of ideas; one is playfulness, the other is piety.

Certainly the intellectual, if he is nothing else, is one who relishes *the play of the mind* for its own sake, for whom it is one of the major ends of life. The intellectual has a full quotient of what Veblen called "idle curiosity." His mind, instead of falling to rest when it has provided him with his girl and his automobile and his dinner, becomes even more active. Indeed if we had to define him in physiological terms, we might define him as the creature whose mind is *most* likely to be active after dinner.

I speak of playfulness too because of the peculiar nature of the relationship, in the intellectual's mind, between ideas and practicality. To the journeyman of ideas the be-all and end-all of ideas lies in their practical efficacy. Now the intellectual, by contrast, is not necessarily impractical; I can think of some intellectuals like Thomas Jefferson and Robert Owen and John Maynard Keynes* who have been eminently practical, and I consider the notion that the intellectual is inherently impractical to be one of the most contemptible of the delusions with which the anti-intellectual quiets his envy—the intellectual is not impractical but primarily concerned with a quality of ideas that does not depend upon their practicality. He neither reveres nor disdains practical consequences; for him they are either marginal or irrelevant. And when he does talk about the practicality or the "relevance" of ideas, the kind of practicality that he is concerned with is itself somewhat different from the practicality of building a bridge, curing a disease, or making a profit—it is practical relevance to spiritual values themselves.

The best illustration of the intellectual's view of the purely practical that has recently come to my attention is

*Robert Owen (1771–1858), Welsh social reformer, and John Maynard Keynes (1883–1946), British economist and proponent of state stimulation of demand to break depressions.

the reaction of Clerk Maxwell, the great nineteenth-century mathematician and theoretical physicist, to the invention of the telephone. Maxwell was asked to give a lecture on the workings of this wonderful new instrument, which he began by saying how difficult it was to believe, when the word first came from America, that such a thing had actually been devised. But then, he said, "when at last this little instrument appeared, consisting, as it does, of parts, every one of which is familiar to us, and capable of being put together by an amateur, the disappointment arising from its humble appearance was only partially relieved on finding that it was really able to talk." Perhaps, then, this regrettable appearance of simplicity might be redeemed by the presence somewhere of "recondite physical principles, the study of which might worthily occupy an hour's time of an academic audience." But no; Maxwell had not met a single person who could not understand the physical processes involved, and even the science reporters for the daily press had almost got it right! The thing was a disappointing bore; it was not recondite, it was not profound, it was not complex, it was not *intellectually* new.

To be sure, what this illustration suggests is not merely that the telephone disappointed Maxwell as a pure scientist and an intellectual, but that the strain of intellectuality in him was not as broadly developed as it might have been. The telephone might well excite not merely the commercial imagination but the historical imagination. But my point is, after all, not that Maxwell was a universal intellectual, but that he was displaying the attitude of the intellectual in his particular sphere of interest.

The second element in intellectualism is its religious strain, the note of piety. What I mean by this is simply that for the intellectual the whole world of moral values becomes attached to ideas and to the life dedicated to ideas. The life given over to the search for truth takes on for him a primary moral significance. Intellectualism, although hardly confined to doubters, is often the sole piety of the skeptic. A few years ago a distinguished sociologist asked me to read a brief manuscript which he had written primarily for students planning to go on to advanced work in his field, the purpose of which was to illustrate various ways in which the life of the mind might be cultivated. The essay had about it a little too much of the how-to-do books, and my friend abandoned it. But the nub of the matter from the standpoint of our present problem was that I found myself to be reading a piece of devotional literature, comparable perhaps to Cotton Mather's *Essays to do Good* or Richard Steele's *The Tradesman's Calling.** My friend was trying to communicate his sense of dedication to the life of ideas, which he conceived much in the fashion of the old Protestant writers as a *calling.* To work is to pray. Yes, and for this kind of man, to think—really to think—is to pray. What he knows best, when he is at his best, is the pursuit of truth; but *easy* truths bore him. What he is certain of becomes unsatisfactory always; the meaning of his intellectual life lies in the quest for new uncertainties.

In a bygone day when men lived even more by dogma than they do now, there were two kinds of men whose special office it was to seek for and utter the truth; and they symbolize these two sides of the intellectual's nature. One was the angelic doctor, the learned schoolman, the conserver of old orthodoxies but also the maker of the new, and the prodder at the outer limits of received truths. The other was the jester, the professional fool, who had license to say on occasion for the purposes of amusement and release those things that bordered on lèse majesté and could not be uttered by others who were accounted serious men.

The fool and the schoolman are very far apart. No doubt you will ask whether there is not a contradiction between these two qualities of the intellectual, piety and playfulness. Certainly there is great tension between them; human beings are tissues of contradictions, and the life even of the intellectual is not logic, to borrow from Holmes, but experience. If you will think of the intellectu-

---

*Cotton Mather (1663–1728), New England clergyman, and Richard Steele (1672–1725), English dramatist and essayist.

als you know, some will occur to you in whom the note of playfulness seems stronger, others who are predominantly pious. But I believe that in all intellectuals who have any stability as intellectuals—and that includes the angelic doctors of the Middle Ages—each of these characteristics is at some point qualified by the other. Perhaps the tensile strength of the intellectual can be gauged by his ability to maintain a fair equipoise between these aspects of himself. At one end of the scale, an excess of playfulness leads to triviality, to dilettantism, to cynicism, to the failure of all sustained creative effort. At the other, an excess of piety leads to fanaticism, to messianism, to ways of life that may be morally magnificent or morally mean, but in either case are not quite the ways of intellectualism. It is of the essence of the intellectual that he strikes a balance.

IDEAS

1. Do you disagree with any parts of Hofstadter's definition? If so, why?

2. How is living for *an idea* rather than for *ideas* anti-intellectual?

3. Hofstadter writes, "to think—really to think—is to pray." If this is true, *to pray* must be defined in a way broader than usual. How would you define *to pray* to include Hofstadter's statement?

4. Summarize the author's definition in one statement of what an intellectual *is,* and another statement of what an intellectual *is not.*

ORGANIZATION AND STYLE

1. Hofstadter begins his essay with a rhetorical question, and asks another at the end of the third paragraph. How do these rhetorical questions function to pull the reader into and through the essay?

2. What is the effect of the author's metaphor *frozen ideas* (first paragraph)?

3. How does Hofstadter exclude engineers, physicians, journalists, advertisers, and mass-communicators from his definition? How does this exclusion clarify his definition?

4. In the very middle of the essay, the author makes a transition with a one-sentence paragraph. How effective is this? What does the author do differently in the latter half of his essay?

WRITING

1. Several words in this essay—*implacable, efficacy, recondite,* and *equipoise,* for example—may not be a part of your normal vocabulary. Write carefully developed one-sentence definitions for these and any other words in the essay with which you are not familiar.

2. Select some acquaintance you consider an intellectual. Using Hofstadter's ideas as organizing points, develop an essay in which you show how this person qualifies as an intellectual.

3. Taking Hofstadter as a model, write an essay defining a *teacher,* a *student,* a *friend,* a *leader,* an *athlete,* or the like.

Description and Narration

Description and narration—showing and telling—are essential to each of the tactics we have considered. Without them, our writers could not have presented the causes and effects at work in changing ethnic neighborhoods, the comparisons and contrasts in baseball and football; could not have classified phases in technology or evolution; could not have defined an intellectual. In essence, description is spatial and narration is temporal. Description narrates the details of how something appears in space, as if photographed—the house hanging at the edge of the washed-out cliff. Narration describes the sequence of events as one makes a long river journey or watches the circus come to town. No essay can illustrate its points without some touch of both. But, as you will see in the five that follow, some subjects—and authors—generate extensive uses of one or the other.

Snow

FARLEY MOWAT

———————— ● ————————

Mowat's poetic description sweeps us through time and space, from pole to pole, from Canada to Siberia, from Greenland to the cosmic void. Such description takes narration, as the snow people form their domes of ice or spear seals through films of snow, and we end in warm laughter, snug in the igloos Mowat's description builds for us.

When Man was still very young he had already become aware that certain elemental forces dominated the world womb. Embedded on the shores of their warm sea, the Greeks defined these as Fire and Earth and Air and Water. But at first the Greek sphere was small and circumscribed and the Greeks did not recognize the fifth elemental.

About 330 B.C., a peripatetic Greek mathematician named Pytheas made a fantastic voyage northward to Iceland and on into the Greenland Sea. Here he encountered the fifth elemental in all of its white and frigid majesty, and when he returned to the warm blue Mediterranean, he described what he had seen as best he could. His fellow countrymen concluded he must be a liar since even their vivid imaginations could not conceive of the splendour and power inherent in the white substance that sometimes lightly cloaked the mountain homes of their high-dwelling Gods.

Their failure to recognize the immense power of snow was not entirely their fault. We who are the Greeks' inheritors have much the same trouble comprehending its essential magnitude.

How do *we* envisage snow?

It is the fragility of Christmas dreams sintering through azure darkness to the accompaniment of the sound of sleigh bells.

It is the bleak reality of a stalled car and spinning wheels impinging on the neat time schedule of our self-importance.

It is the invitation that glows ephemeral on a woman's lashes on a winter night.

It is the resignation of suburban housewives as they skin wet snowsuits from runny-nosed progeny.

It is the sweet gloss of memory in the failing eyes of the old as they recall the white days of childhood.

It is the banality of a TV advertisement pimping Coca Cola on a snowbank at Sun Valley.

It is the gentility of utter silence in the muffled heart of a snow-clad forest.

It is the brittle wind-rush of skis; and the bellicose chatter of snowmobiles.

Snow is these things to us, together with many related images; yet all deal only with obvious aspects of a multi-faceted, kaleidoscopic, and protean element.

Snow, which on our planet is a phoenix continually born again from its own dissolution, is also a galactic and immortal presence. In the nullity of outer space, clouds of snow crystals, immeasurably vast, drift with time, unchanged since long before our world was born, unchangeable when it will be gone. For all that the best brains of science and the sharpest of the cyclopean eyes of astronomers can tell, the glittering crystals flecking the illimitable void are as one with those that settle on our hands and faces out of the still skies of a December night.

Snow is a single flake caught for an instant on a windowpane. But it is also a signboard in the solar system. When astronomers peer up at Mars they see the Red Planet as a monochromatic globe—except for its polar caps from which gleaming mantles spread toward the equatorial regions. As the antelope flashes its white rump on the dun prairies, so does Mars signal to worlds beyond it with the brilliance of our common sun reflected from its plains of snow.

And so does Earth.

When the first star voyager arcs into deep space, he will watch the greens and blues of our seas and lands dissolve and fade as the globe diminishes until the last thing to beacon the disappearing Earth will be the glare of our own polar heliographs. Snow will be the last of the elementals in his distant eye. Snow may provide the first shining glimpse of our world to inbound aliens ... if they have eyes with which to see.

Snow is crystalline dust, tenuous amongst the stars; but on Earth it is, in yet another guise, the Master Titan. To the south it holds the entire continent of Antarctica in absolute thrall. To the north it crouches heavily upon mountain ranges; and the island subcontinent of Greenland literally sags and sinks beneath its weight. For glaciers are but another guise of snow.

Glaciers are born while the snow falls; fragile, soft, and almost disembodied . . . but falling steadily without a thawing time. Years pass, decades, centuries, and the snow falls. Now there is weight where there was none. At the surface of an undulating white waste, there seems to be no alteration, but in the frigid depths the crystals are deformed; they change in structure, interlock with increasing intimacy, and eventually meld into black, lightless ice.

Four times during Earth's most recent geological age snow fell like this across much of the northern half of our continent and in Europe and Asia too. Each time, snow altered the face of almost half a world. A creeping glacial nemesis as much as two miles thick oozed outward from vast central domes, excoriating the planet's face, stripping it of life and soil, ripping deep wounds into the primordial rock, and literally depressing Earth's stone mantle hundreds of feet below its former level. The snow fell, softly, steadily, until countless millions of tons of water had vanished from the seas, locked up within the glaciers; and the seas themselves withdrew from the edges of the continents.

There is no natural phenomenon known to us that can surpass the dispassionate power of a great glacier. The rupturing of Earth during its most appalling earthquake cannot compare with it. The raging water of the seas in their most violent moments cannot begin to match it. Air, howling in the dementia of hurricanes, is nothing beside it. The inner fire that blows a mountain to pieces and inundates the surrounding plains with floods of flaming lava is weak by comparison.

A glacier is the macrocosmic form of snow. But in its microscopic forms, snow epitomizes ethereal beauty. It is a cliché to say that no two snowflakes are identical, but it is a fact that each single snowflake that has fallen throughout all of time, and that will fall through what remains of time, has been—will be—a unique creation in symmetry and form.

I know of one man who has devoted most of his adult life to the study of this transient miracle. He has built a special house fitted with a freezing system, instead of heating equipment. It is a house with a gaping hole in its roof. On snowy days and nights he sits in icy solitude catching the falling flakes on plates of pre-chilled glass and hurriedly photographing them through an enlarging lens. For him the fifth elemental in its infinite diversity and singularity is beauty incarnate, and a thing to worship.

Few of us would be of a mind to share his almost medieval passion. In truth, modern man has insensibly begun to develop a schizophrenic attitude toward the fifth elemental. Although we may remember our childhood experience of it with nostalgia, more and more we have begun to think of snow with enmity. We cannot control snow, nor bend it to our will. The snow that fell harmlessly and beneficiently upon the natural world our forefathers lived in has the power to inflict chaos on the mechanical new world we have been building. A heavy snowfall in New York, Montreal, Chicago, produces a paralytic stroke. Beyond the congealed cities it chokes the arteries of our highways, blocks trains, grounds aircraft, fells power and telephone cables. Even a moderate snowfall causes heavy inconvenience—if smashed cars, broken bodies, and customers for the undertakers are only inconveniences.

We will probably come to like snow even less. Stories about the good old-fashioned winters when snow mounted to the eaves of houses and horse-hauled sleighs were galloped over drifts at tree-top level are not just old wives' tales. A hundred years ago such happenings were commonplace. However, during the past century our climate has experienced a warming trend, an upswing (from our point of view), in the erratic cyclic variations of the weather. It has probably been a short-term swing and the downswing may soon be upon us. And where will we be then, poor things, in our delicately structured artificial world? Will we still admire snow? More likely we will curse the very word.

However, when that time comes there may still be men alive who will be unperturbed by the gentle, implacable downward drift. They are the true people of the snows.

They live only in the northern hemisphere because the realm of snow in the southern hemisphere—Antarctica—will not permit the existence of any human life unless equipped with a panoply of protective devices not far short of what a spaceman needs. The snow people ring the North Pole. They are the Aleuts, Eskimos, and Athapascan Indians of North America; the Greenlanders; the Lapps, Nensi, Chukchee, Yakuts, Yukagirs and related peoples of Eurasia and Siberia.

Cocooned in the machine age, we smugly assume that because these people live unarmoured by our ornate technology, they must lead the most marginal kind of existence, faced with so fierce a battle to survive that they have no chance to realize the "human potential." Hard as it may strike into our dogmatic belief that technology offers the only valid way of life, I can testify from my own experiences with many of the snow people that this assumption is wrong. They mostly lived good lives, before our greed and our megalomaniac arrogance impelled us to meddle in their affairs. That is, if it be good to live at peace with oneself and one's fellowmen, to be in harmony with one's environment, to laugh and love without restraint, to know fulfilment in one's daily life, and to rest from birth to death upon a sure and certain pride.

Snow was these people's ally. It was their protection and their shelter from abysmal cold. Eskimos built complete houses of snow blocks. When heated only with simple animal-oil lamps, these had comfortable interior temperatures, while outside the wind screamed unheard and the mercury dropped to fifty degrees or more below zero. Compacted snow provides nearly perfect insulation. It can be cut and shaped much more easily than wood. It is light to handle and strong, if properly used. A snowhouse with an inner diameter of twenty feet and a height of ten feet can be built by two men in two hours. On special occasions Eskimos used to build snowhouses fifty feet in diameter and, by linking several such together, formed veritable snow mansions.

All of the snow people use snow for shelter in one way or another. If they are sedentary folk possessing wooden houses, they bank their homes with thick snow walls in wintertime. Some dig a basement in a snowdrift and roof it with reindeer skins. As long as snow is plentiful, the peoples of the far north seldom suffer serious discomfort from the cold.

Snow also makes possible their transportation system. With dog sleds and reindeer sleds, or afoot on snowshoes or trail skis, they can travel almost anywhere. The whole of the snow world becomes a highway. They can travel at speed, too. A dog or reindeer team can move at twenty miles an hour and easily cover a hundred miles a day.

The mobility snow gives them, combined with the way snow modifies the behaviour of game animals, ensures that—other things being equal—the snow people need not go hungry. Out on the arctic ice a covering of snow gives the seals a sense of false security. They make breathing holes in the ice, roofed by a thin layer of snow. The Chukchee or Eskimo hunter finds these places and waits beside them until, at a signal from a tell-tale wand of ivory or wood inserted in the roof, he plunges his spear down into the unseen animal below.

In wooded country, moose, elk, and deer are forced by deep snow to "yard" in constricted areas where they can be killed nearly as easily as cattle in a pen. Most important of all, every animal, save those with wings and those who live beneath the snow, leaves tracks upon its surface. From bears to hares they become more vulnerable to the human hunter as soon as the first snow coats the land.

The snow people know snow as they know themselves. In these days our scientists are busy studying the fifth elemental, not so much out of scientific curiosity but because we are anxious to hasten the rape of the north or fear we may have to fight wars in the lands of snow. With vast expenditures of time and money, the scientists have begun to separate the innumerable varieties of snow and to give them names. They could have saved themselves the trouble. Eskimos have more than a hundred compound words to express different varieties and conditions of snow. The Lapps have almost as many. Yukagir reindeer herdsmen on the arctic coast of Siberia can tell the depth of snow cover, its degree of compactness, and the amount of internal ice crystallization it contains simply by glancing at the surface.

The northern people are happy when snow lies heavy on the land. They welcome the first snow in autumn, and often regret its passing in the spring. Snow is their friend. Without it they would have perished or—almost worse from their point of view—they would long since have been driven south to join us in our frenetic rush to wherever it is that we are bound.

Somewhere, on this day, the snow is falling. It may be sifting thinly on the cold sands of a desert, spreading a strange pallidity and flecking the dark, upturned faces of a band of Semitic nomads. For them it is in the nature of a miracle; and it is certainly an omen and they are filled with awe and chilled with apprehension.

It may be whirling fiercely over the naked sweep of frozen plain in the Siberian steppe, or on the Canadian prairies, obliterating summer landmarks, climbing in scimitar drifts to wall up doors and windows of farmhouses. Inside, the people wait in patience. While the blizzard blows, they rest; when it is over, work will begin again. And in the spring the melted snows will water the new growth springing out of the black earth.

It may be settling in great flakes on a calm night over a vast city; spinning cones of distorted vision in the headlights of creeping cars and covering the wounds, softening the suppurating ugliness inflicted on the earth by modern man. Children hope it will continue all night long so that no buses, street cars, or family automobiles will be able to carry the victims off to school in the morning. But adult men and women wait impatiently, for if it does not stop soon the snow will smother the intricate designs that have been ordained for the next day's pattern of existence.

Or the snow may be slanting swiftly down across a cluster of tents huddled below a rock ridge on the arctic tundra. Gradually it enfolds a pack of dogs who lie, noses thrust under bushy tails, until the snow covers them completely and they sleep warm. Inside the tents men and women smile. Tomorrow the snow may be deep enough and hard enough so that the tents can be abandoned and the welcome domes of snowhouses can rise again to turn winter into a time of gaiety, of songs, of leisure and lovemaking.

Somewhere the snow is falling.

IDEAS

1. Why does Mowat begin with the early Greeks to discuss snow?

2. After asking how "we envisage snow," Mowat answers with a series of paragraphed sentences, each a metaphor. Which of these most fits your own attitude toward snow?

3. In what way is snow like a phoenix? Like the Master Titan?

4. What justifies Mowat's reference to the man who has spent his life studying the shapes of snow flakes as demonstrating "almost medieval passion"?

5. What is Mowat's definition of "the true people of the snows"?

6. In what ways has snow always served as man's ally?

ORGANIZATION AND STYLE

1. How does the third paragraph function as a bridge between the two introductory paragraphs and the body of the essay?

2. Is Mowat's series of paragraphed sentences, each with its metaphor, effective? What would have happened had he grouped these sentences into one longer paragraph?

3. How does the one-sentence paragraph, "And so does the Earth," function?

4. Mowat contrasts snow's potential destruction with its contributions to civilization. What are the organizational components of that argument?

5. Throughout, Mowat works with miniature comparisons and contrasts, as in the paragraph beginning, "There is no natural phenomenon known to us. . . ." At what other points in the essay do you find similar comparisons and contrasts? How effective are they?

6. Which paragraph begins the conclusion?

7. Mowat's concluding sentences are almost poetic. What details of metaphor, diction, and syntax convey this quality?

WRITING

1. Develop an essay describing your first serious experience with snow (or fog, torrential rains, 100-degree weather, and the like). Contrast what you had anticipated with what you discovered.

2. Mowat writes about the good life of the snow people: "To live at peace with oneself and one's fellowmen, to be in harmony with one's environment, to laugh and love without restraint, to know fulfilment in one's daily life, and to rest from birth to death upon a sure and certain pride." Does this concept of happiness, echoing Rousseau's noble savage, still exist in the latter part of the twentieth century? Write an essay in which you focus on a person or a group of people generally thought unhappy and unfulfilled but whom you know are perfectly content, like Mowat's snow people.

From *Life on the Mississippi*

MARK TWAIN

———————— ● ————————

Twain's memorable account of steamboating on the Mississippi is highly narrative, as the flowing river naturally draws us through narrative time. Twain begins with narrating how the swollen river "brought a new world" before his eyes. He recounts what happened "Once" when a fallen tree blocked the available passage. He tells at length the story of the pilot, Mr. X. But notice how indispensable are those touches and stretches of description that bring before our eyes the wretched little farms, the dim and shoreless sea of the overflowed river, the pilot-house at night.

As I have said, the big rise brought a new world under my vision.* By the time the river was over its banks we had forsaken our old paths and were hourly climbing over bars that had stood ten feet out of water before; we were shaving stumpy shores, like that at the foot of Madrid Bend, which I had always seen avoided before; we were clattering through chutes like that of 82, where the opening at the foot was an unbroken wall of timber till our nose was almost at the very spot. Some of these chutes were utter solitudes. The dense, untouched forest overhung both banks of the crooked little crack, and one could believe that human creatures had never intruded there before. The swinging grapevines, the grassy nooks and vistas glimpsed as we swept by, the flowering creepers waving their red blossoms from the tops of dead trunks, and all the spendthrift richness of the forest foliage, were wasted and thrown away there. The chutes were lovely places to steer

*Twain is observing the Mississippi as an apprentice pilot in 1857.

in; they were deep, except at the head; the current was gentle; under the "points" the water was absolutely dead, and the invisible banks so bluff that where the tender willow thickets projected you could bury your boat's broadside in them as you tore along, and then you seemed fairly to fly.

Behind other islands we found wretched little farms, and wretcheder little log cabins; there were crazy rail fences sticking a foot or two above the water, with one or two jeans-clad, chills-racked, yellow-faced male miserables roosting on the top rail, elbows on knees, jaws in hands, grinding tobacco and discharging the result at floating chips through crevices left by lost teeth; while the rest of the family and the few farm animals were huddled together in an empty wood-flat riding at her moorings close at hand. In this flatboat the family would have to cook and eat and sleep for a lesser or greater number of days (or possibly weeks), until the river should fall two or three feet and let them get back to their log cabins and their chills again—chills being a merciful provision of an all-wise Providence to enable them to take exercise without exertion. And this sort of watery camping out was a thing which these people were rather liable to be treated to a couple of times a year: by the December rise out of the Ohio, and the June rise out of the Mississippi. And yet these were kindly dispensations, for they at least enabled the poor things to rise from the dead now and then, and look upon life when a steamboat went by. They appreciated the blessing, too, for they spread their mouths and eyes open and made the most of these occasions. Now what *could* these banished creatures find to do to keep from dying of the blues during the low-water season!

Once, in one of these lovely island chutes, we found our course completely bridged by a great fallen tree. This will serve to show how narrow some of the chutes were. The passengers had an hour's recreation in a virgin wilderness, while the boat-hands chopped the bridge away; for there was no such thing as turning back, you comprehend.

From Cairo* to Baton Rouge, when the river is over its banks, you have no particular trouble in the night; for the thousand-mile wall of dense forest that guards the two banks all the way is only gapped with a farm or woodyard opening at intervals, and so you can't "get out of the river" much easier than you could get out of a fenced lane; but from Baton Rouge to New Orleans it is a different matter. The river is more than a mile wide, and very deep—as much as two hundred feet, in places. Both banks, for a good deal over a hundred miles, are shorn of their timber and bordered by continuous sugar-plantations, with only here and there a scattering sapling or row of ornamental China trees. The timber is shorn off clear to the rear of the plantations, from two to four miles. When the first frost threatens to come, the planters snatch off their crops in a hurry. When they have finished grinding the cane, they form the refuse of the stalks (which they call *bagasse*) into great piles and set fire to them, though in other sugar countries the bagasse is used for fuel in the furnaces of the sugarmills. Now the piles of damp bagasse burn slowly, and smoke like Satan's own kitchen.

An embankment ten or fifteen feet high guards both banks of the Mississippi all the way down that lower end of the river, and this embankment is set back from the edge of the shore from ten to perhaps a hundred feet, according to circumstances; say thirty or forty feet, as a general thing. Fill that whole region with an impenetrable gloom of smoke from a hundred miles of burning bagasse piles, when the river is over the banks, and turn a steamboat loose along there at midnight and see how she will feel. And see how you will feel, too: You find yourself away out in the midst of a vague, dim sea that is shoreless, that fades out and loses itself in the murky distances; for you

---

*Cairo, Illinois (pronounced "CAY-row"), at the tip of a peninsula where the Ohio River joins the Mississippi, featured in *Huckleberry Finn* as the point Huck and Jim, drifting downstream on their raft, hope to hit, to gain a steamboat passage up the Ohio and complete freedom from slavery for Jim.

cannot discern the thin rib of embankment, and you are always imagining you see a straggling tree when you don't. The plantations themselves are transformed by the smoke, and look like a part of the sea. All through your watch you are tortured with the exquisite misery of uncertainty. You hope you are keeping in the river, but you do not know. All that you are sure about is that you are likely to be within six feet of the bank *and* destruction, when you think you are a good half-mile from shore. And you are sure, also, that if you chance suddenly to fetch up against the embankment and topple your chimneys overboard, you will have the small comfort of knowing that it is about what you were expecting to do. One of the great Vicksburg packets darted out into a sugar-plantation one night, at such a time, and had to stay there a week. But there was no novelty about it; it had often been done before.

I thought I had finished this chapter, but I wish to add a curious thing, while it is in my mind. It is only relevant in that it is connected with piloting. There used to be an excellent pilot on the river, a Mr. X, who was a somnambulist. It was said that if his mind was troubled about a bad piece of river, he was pretty sure to get up and walk in his sleep and do strange things. He was once fellow-pilot for a trip or two with George Ealer, on a great New Orleans passenger-packet. During a considerable part of the first trip George was uneasy, but got over it by and by, as X seemed content to stay in his bed when asleep. Late one night the boat was approaching Helena, Ark.; the water was low, and the crossing above the town in a very blind and tangled condition. X had seen the crossing since Ealer had, and as the night was particularly drizzly, sullen, and dark, Ealer was considering whether he had not better have X called to assist in running the place, when the door opened and X walked in. Now, on very dark nights, light is a deadly enemy to piloting; you are aware that if you stand in a lighted room, on such a night, you cannot see things in the street to any purpose; but if you put out the lights and stand in the gloom you can make out objects in the street pretty well. So, on very dark nights, pilots do not smoke; they allow no fire in the pilot-house stove, if there is a crack which can allow the least ray to escape; they order the furnaces to be curtained with huge tarpaulins and the skylights to be closely blinded. Then no light whatever issues from the boat. The undefinable shape that now entered the pilot-house had Mr. X's voice. This said:

"Let me take her, George; I've seen this place since you have, and it is so crooked that I reckon I can run it myself easier than I could tell you how to do it."

"It is kind of you, and I swear *I* am willing. I haven't got another drop of perspiration left in me. I have been spinning around and around the wheel like a squirrel. It is so dark I can't tell which way she is swinging till she is coming around like a whirligig."

So Ealer took a seat on the bench, panting and breathless. The black phantom assumed the wheel without saying anything, steadied the waltzing steamer with a turn or two, and then stood at ease, coaxing her a little to this side and then to that, as gently and as sweetly as if the time had been noonday. When Ealer observed this marvel of steering, he wished he had not confessed! He stared, and wondered, and finally said:

"Well. I thought I knew how to steer a steamboat, but that was another mistake of mine."

X said nothing, but went serenely on with his work. He rang for the leads;* he rang to slow down the steam; he worked the boat carefully and neatly into invisible marks, then stood at the center of the wheel and peered blandly out into the blackness, fore and aft, to verify his position; as the leads shoaled more and more, he stopped the engines entirely, and the dead silence and suspense of "drifting" followed; when the shoalest water was struck, he cracked on the steam, carried her handsomely over, and then began to work her warily into the next system of

---

*Ropes, with lead weights at the end, dipped into the water by "leadsmen" in the boat's bow to measure the depth. They were marked by bits of leather or cloth at 2, 3, 5, 7, 10, 13, 15, 17, 20, and 25 fathoms (a fathom equaling 6 feet). Clemens took his pen name from the leadsman's cry "mark twain" (i.e., "at mark two"), signifying the last mark as the steamboat moved into shallow water and trouble.

shoal-marks; the same patient, heedful use of leads and engines followed, the boat slipped through without touching bottom, and entered upon the third and last intricacy of the crossing; imperceptibly she moved through the gloom, crept by inches into her marks, drifted tediously till the shoalest water was cried, and then, under a tremendous head of steam, went swinging over the reef and away into deep water and safety!

Ealer let his long-pent breath pour in a great relieving sigh, and said:

"That's the sweetest piece of piloting that was ever done on the Mississippi River! I wouldn't believe it could be done, if I hadn't seen it."

There was no reply, and he added:

"Just hold her five minutes longer, partner, and let me run down and get a cup of coffee."

A minute later Ealer was biting into a pie, down in the "texas," and comforting himself with coffee. Just then the night watchman happened in, and was about to happen out again, when he noticed Ealer and exclaimed:

"Who is at the wheel, sir?"

"X."

"Dart for the pilot-house, quicker than lightning!"

The next moment both men were flying up the pilot-house companionway, three steps at a jump! Nobody there! The great steamer was whistling down the middle of the river at her own sweet will! The watchman shot out of the place again; Ealer seized the wheel, set an engine back with power, and held his breath while the boat reluctantly swung away from a "towhead," which she was about to knock into the middle of the Gulf of Mexico!

By and by the watchman came back and said:

"Didn't that lunatic tell you he was asleep, when he first came up here?"

"No."

"Well, he was. I found him walking along on top of the railings, just as unconcerned as another man would walk a pavement; and I put him to bed; now just this minute there he was again, away astern, going through that sort of tight-rope deviltry the same as before."

"Well, I think I'll stay by next time he has one of those fits. But I hope he'll have them often. You just ought to have seen him take this boat through Helena crossing. *I* never saw anything so gaudy before. And if he can do such gold-leaf, kid-glove, diamond-breastpin piloting when he is sound asleep, what *couldn't* he do if he was dead!"

IDEAS

1. Twain wrote this selection at a time when travel pieces were popular, since few people traveled much beyond the county seat. These travel pieces gave them a glimpse of another world. How well does this selection share a part of the country with someone who has never been there?

2. With what kinds of details does Twain seem the most fascinated? Can you explain why?

3. In paragraph five, Twain writes about being "tortured with the exquisite misery of uncertainty." What does he mean? Is Twain painting a negative picture of the river and its peoples, or is he fascinated by their native will to endure?

4. What is the purpose of the narrative that ends this selection?

ORGANIZATION AND STYLE

1. Twain proceeds spatially, moving his description along as though it were a camera, capturing new sights as they appear. Where are his major movements to a "different picture"? With what kinds of transitions does he aid the reader?

2. The author begins his second paragraph "Behind other islands. . . ." Considering this and what he says

in his first and third paragraphs, how would you describe a *chute?*

3. What does Twain mean by "take exercise without exertion" (second paragraph)?

4. The word *wretched* sets the tone for the second paragraph. What other specific words in the paragraph are equally negative?

5. Observe Twain's effective verbs near the end of the essay. He writes, "imperceptibly she moved through the gloom, crept by inches into her marks, drifted tediously till the shoalest water was cried. . . ." Where else in the essay do you find well-chosen verbs?

6. What fully explicit thesis might serve for Twain's descriptive narrative?

WRITING

1. See if you can imitate Twain's manner and humor in an account of some apprenticeship of your own: your first day on a new job, your first day at college, your first meeting with a date's parents. You might even begin with a variation of Twain's opening sentence: "The first hour working in the diner brought a new world under my vision." Try to give your readers an ample descriptive picture, and then try to find a short, framing narrative anecdote, with a touch of dialogue, to make your point.

2. Twain provides a brush-stroke description of his travel down a narrow part of the river. Select your own narrow path and develop a descriptive essay that will capture the sights, sounds, and moods for your readers. You might focus on a section of a favorite street, a short stretch of highway, or even a walk down the corridors of your college.

The Spider and the Wasp

ALEXANDER PETRUNKEVITCH

———————————— ● ————————————

In this lucid scientific account* of a strange natural phenomenon, description and narration blend so effectively as to be almost indistinguishable, except for the longer narrative passages.

In the feeding and safeguarding of their progeny insects and spiders exhibit some interesting analogies to reasoning and some crass examples of blind instinct. The case I propose to describe here is that of the tarantula spiders and their archenemy, the digger wasps of the genus *Pepsis.* It is a classic example of what looks like intelligence pitted against instinct—a strange situation in which the victim, though fully able to defend itself, submits unwittingly to its destruction.

Most tarantulas live in the tropics, but several species occur in the temperate zone and a few are common in the southern U.S. Some varieties are large and have powerful fangs with which they can inflict a deep wound. These formidable looking spiders do not, however, attack man; you can hold one in your hand, if you are gentle, without being bitten. Their bite is dangerous only to insects and small mammals such as mice; for man it is no worse than a hornet's sting.

Tarantulas customarily live in deep cylindrical burrows, from which they emerge at dusk and into which they retire at dawn. Mature males wander about after dark in search of females and occasionally stray into houses. After mating, the male dies in a few weeks, but a female lives much longer and can mate several years in succession. In a Paris museum is a tropical specimen which is said to have been living in captivity for twenty-five years.

A fertilized female tarantula lays from 200 to 400 eggs at a time; thus it is possible for a single tarantula to produce several thousand young. She takes no care of them beyond weaving a cocoon of silk to enclose the eggs. After they hatch, the young walk away, find convenient places in which to dig their burrows and spend the rest of their lives in solitude. The eyesight of tarantulas is poor, being limited to a sensing of change in the intensity of light and to the perception of moving objects. They apparently have little or no sense of hearing, for a hungry tarantula will pay no attention to a loudly chirping cricket placed in its cage unless the insect happens to touch one of its legs.

But all spiders, and especially hairy ones, have an extremely delicate sense of touch. Laboratory experiments prove that tarantulas can distinguish three types of touch: pressure against the body wall, stroking of the body hair, and riffling of certain very fine hairs on the legs called trichobothria. Pressure against the body, by the finger or the end of a pencil, causes the tarantula to move off slowly for a short distance. The touch excites no defensive response unless the approach is from above, where the spider can see the motion, in which case it rises on its hind legs, lifts its front legs, opens its fangs and holds this threatening posture as long as the object continues to move.

The entire body of a tarantula, especially its legs, is thickly clothed with hair. Some of it is short and wooly, some long and stiff. Touching this body hair produces one of two distinct reactions. When the spider is hungry, it responds with an immediate and swift attack. At the touch of a cricket's antennae the tarantula seizes the insect so swiftly that a motion picture taken at the rate of sixty-four frames per second shows only the result and not the process of capture. But when the spider is not hungry, the stimulation of its hairs merely causes it to shake the touched limb. An insect can walk under its hairy belly unharmed.

The trichobothria, very fine hairs growing from disk-like membranes on the legs, are sensitive only to air movement. A light breeze makes them vibrate slowly, without disturbing the common hair. When one blows gently on the trichobothria, the tarantula reacts with a quick jerk of its four front legs. If the front and hind legs are stimulated at the same time, the spider makes a sudden jump. This reaction is quite independent of the state of its appetite.

These three tactile responses—to pressure on the body wall, to moving of the common hair, and to flexing of the trichobothria—are so different from one another that there is no possibility of confusing them. They serve the tarantula adequately for most of its needs and enable it to avoid most annoyances and dangers. But they fail the spider completely when it meets its deadly enemy, the digger wasp *Pepsis.*

These solitary wasps are beautiful and formidable creatures. Most species are either a deep shiny blue all over, or deep blue with rusty wings. The largest have a wing span of about four inches. They live on nectar. When excited, they give off a pungent odor—a warning that they are ready to attack. The sting is much worse than that of a bee or common wasp, and the pain and swelling last longer. In the adult stage, the wasp lives only a few months. The female produces but a few eggs, one at a time at intervals of two or three days. For each egg the mother must provide one adult tarantula, alive but paralyzed. The mother wasp attaches the egg to the paralyzed spider's abdomen. Upon hatching from the egg, the larva is many hundreds of times smaller than its living but helpless victim. It eats no other food and drinks no water. By the time it has finished its single Gargantuan meal and become ready for wasp-hood, nothing remains of the tarantula but its indigestible chitinous skeleton.

The mother wasp goes tarantula-hunting when the egg in her ovary is almost ready to be laid. Flying low over the ground late on a sunny afternoon, the wasp looks for its victim or for the mouth of a tarantula burrow, a round hole edged by a bit of silk. The sex of the spider makes no difference, but the mother is highly discriminating as to species. Each species of *Pepsis* requires a certain species of tarantula, and the wasp will not attack the wrong species. In a cage with a tarantula which is not its normal prey, the wasp avoids the spider and is usually killed by it in the night.

Yet when a wasp finds the correct species, it is the other way about. To identify the species, the wasp apparently must explore the spider with her antennae. The tarantula shows an amazing tolerance to this exploration. The wasp crawls under it and walks over it without evoking any hostile response. The molestation is so great and so persistent that the tarantula often rises on all eight legs, as if it were on stilts. It may stand this way for several minutes. Meanwhile the wasp, having satisfied itself that the victim is of the right species, moves off a few inches to dig the spider's grave. Working vigorously with legs and jaws, it excavates a hole eight to ten inches deep with a diameter slightly larger than the spider's girth. Now and again, the wasp pops out of the hole to make sure that the spider is still there.

When the grave is finished, the wasp returns to the tarantula to complete her ghastly enterprise. First she feels it all over once more with her antennae. Then her behavior becomes more aggressive. She bends her abdomen, protruding her sting, and searches for the soft membrane at the point where the spider's legs join its body—the only spot where she can penetrate the horny skeleton. From time to time, as the exasperated spider slowly shifts ground, the wasp turns on her back and slides along with the aid of her wings, trying to get under the tarantula for a shot at the vital spot. During all this maneuvering, which can last for several minutes, the tarantula makes no move to save itself. Finally the wasp corners it against some obstruction and grasps one of its legs in her powerful jaws. Now at last the harassed spider tries a desperate but vain defense. The two contestants roll over and over on the ground. It is a terrifying sight, and the outcome is always the same. The wasp finally manages to thrust her sting into the soft spot and holds it there for a few seconds while she pumps in the poison. Almost immediately the tarantula falls paralyzed on its back. Its legs stop twitching; its heart stops beating. Yet it is not dead, as is shown by the fact that if taken from the wasp it can be restored to some sensitivity by being kept in a moist chamber for several months.

After paralyzing the tarantula, the wasp cleans herself by dragging her body along the ground and rubbing her feet, sucks the drop of blood oozing from the wound in the spider's abdomen, then grabs a leg of the flabby, helpless animal in her jaws and drags it down to the bottom of the grave. She stays there for many minutes, sometimes for several hours, and what she does all that time in the dark we do not know. Eventually she lays her egg and attaches it to the side of the spider's abdomen with a sticky secretion. Then she emerges, fills the grave with soil carried bit by bit in her jaws, and finally tramples the ground all around to hide any trace of the grave from prowlers. Then she flies away, leaving her descendant safely started in life.

In all this, the behavior of the wasp evidently is qualitatively different from that of the spider. The wasp acts like an intelligent animal. This is not to say that instinct plays no part or that she reasons as man does. But her actions are to the point; they are not automatic and can be modified to fit the situation. We do not know for certain how she identifies the tarantula—probably it is by some olfactory or chemo-tactile sense—but she does it purposefully and does not blindly tackle a wrong species.

On the other hand, the tarantula's behavior shows only confusion. Evidently the wasp's pawing gives it no pleasure, for it tries to move away. That the wasp is not simulating sexual stimulation is certain because male and female tarantulas react in the same way to its advances. That the spider is not anesthetized by some odorless secretion is easily shown by blowing lightly at the tarantula and making it jump suddenly. What, then, makes the tarantula behave as stupidly as it does?

No clear, simple answer is available. Possibly the stimulation by the wasp's antennae is masked by a heavier pressure on the spider's body, so that it reacts as when prodded by a pencil. But the explanation may be much more complex. Initiative in attack is not in the nature of tarantulas; most species fight only when cornered so that escape is impossible. Their inherited patterns of behavior apparently prompt them to avoid problems rather than attack them. For example, spiders weave their webs in three dimensions, and when a spider finds that there is insufficient space to attach certain threads in the third dimension, it leaves the place and seeks another, instead of finishing the web in a single plane. This urge to escape seems to arise under all circumstances, in all phases of life, and to take the place of reasoning. For a spider to change the pattern of its web is as impossible as for an inexperienced man to build a bridge across a chasm obstructing his way.

In a way, the instinctive urge to escape is not only easier but often more efficient than reasoning. The tarantula does exactly what is most efficient in all cases except in an encounter with a ruthless and determined attacker dependent for the existence of her own species on killing as many tarantulas as she can lay eggs. Perhaps in this case the spider follows its usual pattern of trying to escape, instead of seizing and killing the wasp, because it is not aware of its danger. In any case, the survival of the tarantula species as a whole is protected by the fact that the spider is much more fertile than the wasp.

IDEAS

1. Petrunkevitch does not explain why the tarantula evolved such specialized sensing devices as its fine hairs, the trichobothria. Can you suggest explanations for this odd evolutionary feature?

2. The author says that the wasp hunts for tarantulas "late on a sunny afternoon." What does he leave unexplained in the puzzle of how tarantulas survive in the evolutionary struggle of the fittest?

3. In what ways does the wasp seem rational? The spider irrational?

4. What kind of people resemble *Pepsis* wasps? What kind tarantulas? Would you rate either kind higher on the evolutionary scale?

4. Although this essay was first published in a scientific journal, it is extremely interesting to read. What qualities in Petrunkevitch's writing make his essay so enjoyable?

ORGANIZATION AND STYLE

1. In the topic sentences, what words, ideas, and phrases refer transitionally to each preceding paragraph?

2. Paragraphs five through eight all deal with aspects of the same topic. What is the author's principle for paragraphing here? For organizing his ideas?

3. The final sentence in paragraph eight is transitional. Why is it more effective at the end of this paragraph than it would be at the beginning of paragraph nine?

4. Since narration moves through time, see how many "timing" words and phrases—*when, often, meanwhile*—you can find in the major narrative passage beginning "Yet when a wasp finds the correct species. . . ."

5. The first sentence suggests a division of activities analogous to the opposition of reasoning and blind instinct. Does this division organize later parts of the essay?

WRITING

1. If you happen to know some interesting natural phenomenon—how turtles, or fish, or frogs perpetuate

their species, for instance—see if you can emulate the author's narrative of the wasp and the tarantula in an essay of your own. Try to blend descriptive and narrative passages effectively as Petrunkevitch does.

2. Develop a descriptive narrative in which you illustrate how students enter a particular classroom, how the lunch hour goes in the cafeteria, or how people behave at a party. Blend the descriptive and narrative sequences of your writing so that they complement each other.

Circus at Dawn

THOMAS WOLFE

———————●———————

*Wolfe works from the axiom that good descriptive
writing has appeal to all five senses: seeing, hearing,
feeling, smelling, and tasting. Working from Wordsworth's concept of "recollections in tranquility," he
describes the circus of his youth in such intricate detail that his readers can share his childhood joy.*

There were times in early autumn—in September—when
the greater circuses would come to town—the Ringling
Brothers, Robinson's, and Barnum and Bailey shows, and
when I was a route-boy on the morning paper, on those
mornings when the circus would be coming in I would
rush madly through my route in the cool and thrilling
darkness that comes just before break of day, and then I
would go back home and get my brother out of bed.

Talking in low excited voices we would walk rapidly
back toward town under the rustle of September leaves, in
cool streets just grayed now with that still, that unearthly
and magical first light of day which seems suddenly to
re-discover the great earth out of darkness, so that the
earth emerges with an awful, a glorious sculptural stillness, and one looks out with a feeling of joy and disbelief,
as the first men on this earth must have done, for to see this
happen is one of the things that men will remember out
of life forever and think of as they die.

At the sculptural still square where at one corner, just
emerging into light, my father's shabby little marble shop
stood with a ghostly strangeness and familiarity, my
brother and I would "catch" the first street-car of the day
bound for the "depot" where the circus was—or sometimes

we would meet someone we knew, who would give us a lift in his automobile.

Then, having reached the dingy, grimy, and rickety depot section, we would get out, and walk rapidly across the tracks of the station yard, where we could see great flares and steamings from the engines, and hear the crash and bump of shifting freight cars, the swift sporadic thunders of a shifting engine, the tolling of bells, the sounds of great trains on the rails.

And to all these familiar sounds, filled with their exultant prophecies of flight, the voyage, morning, and the shining cities—to all the sharp and thrilling odors of the trains—the smell of cinders, acrid smoke, of musty, rusty freight cars, the clean pine-board of crated produce, and the smells of fresh stored food—oranges, coffee, tangerines and bacon, ham and flour and beef—there would be added now, with an unforgettable magic and familiarity, all the strange sounds and smells of the coming circus.

The gay yellow sumptuous-looking cars in which the star performers lived and slept, still dark and silent, heavily and powerfully still, would be drawn up in long strings upon the tracks. And all around them the sounds of the unloading circus would go on furiously in the darkness. The receding gulf of lilac and departing night would be filled with the savage roar of the lions, the murderously sudden snarling of great jungle cats, the trumpeting of the elephants, the stamp of the horses, and with the musty, pungent, unfamiliar odor of the jungle animals: the tawny camel smells, and the smells of panthers, zebras, tigers, elephants, and bears.

Then, along the tracks, beside the circus trains, there would be the sharp cries and oaths of the circus men, the magical swinging dance of lanterns in the darkness, the sudden heavy rumble of the loaded vans and wagons as they were pulled along the flats and gondolas, and down the runways to the ground. And everywhere, in the thrilling mystery of darkness and awakening light, there would be the tremendous conflict of a confused, hurried, and yet orderly movement.

The great iron-gray horses, four and six to a team, would be plodding along the road of thick white dust to a rattling of chains and traces and the harsh cries of their drivers. The men would drive the animals to the river which flowed by beyond the tracks, and water them; and as first light came one could see the elephants wallowing in the familiar river and the big horses going slowly and carefully down to drink.

Then, on the circus grounds, the tents were going up already with the magic speed of dreams. All over the place (which was near the tracks and the only space of flat land in the town that was big enough to hold a circus) there would be this fierce, savagely hurried, and yet orderly confusion. Great flares of gaseous circus light would blaze down on the seared and battered faces of the circus toughs as, with the rhythmic precision of a single animal—a human riveting machine—they swung their sledges at the stakes, driving a stake into the earth with the incredible instancy of accelerated figures in a motion picture. And everywhere, as light came, and the sun appeared, there would be a scene of magic, order, and of violence. The drivers would curse and talk their special language to their teams, there would be the loud, gasping and uneven labor of a gasoline engine, the shouts and curses of the bosses, the wooden riveting of driven stakes, and the rattle of heavy chains.

Already in an immense cleared space of dusty beaten earth, the stakes were being driven for the main exhibition tent. And an elephant would lurch ponderously to the field, slowly lower his great swinging head at the command of a man who sat perched upon his skull, flourish his gray wrinkled snout a time or two, and then solemnly wrap it around a tent pole big as the mast of a racing schooner. Then the elephant would back slowly away, dragging the great pole with him as if it were a stick of match-wood. . . .

Meanwhile, the circus food-tent—a huge canvas top without concealing sides—had already been put up, and now we could see the performers seated at long trestled tables underneath the tent, as they ate breakfast. And the savor of the food they ate—mixed as it was with our strong excitement, with the powerful but wholesome smells of the animals, and with all the joy, sweetness, mystery, jubilant magic and glory of the morning, and the coming of the circus—seemed to us to be of the most maddening and appetizing succulence of any food that we had ever known or eaten.

We could see the circus performers eating tremendous breakfasts, with all the savage relish of their power and strength: they ate big fried steaks, pork chops, rashers of bacon, a half dozen eggs, great slabs of fried ham and great stacks of wheat-cakes which a cook kept flipping in the air with the skill of a juggler, and which a husky-looking waitress kept rushing to their tables on loaded trays held high and balanced marvellously on the fingers of a brawny hand. And above all the maddening odors of the wholesome and succulent food, there brooded forever the sultry and delicious fragrance—that somehow seemed to add a zest and sharpness to all the powerful and thrilling life of morning—of strong boiling coffee, which we could see sending off clouds of steam from an enormous polished urn, and which the circus performers gulped down, cup after cup.

And the circus men and women themselves—these star performers—were such fine-looking people, strong and handsome, yet speaking and moving with an almost stern dignity and decorum, that their lives seemed to us to be as splendid and wonderful as any lives on earth could be. There was never anything loose, rowdy, or tough in their comportment, nor did the circus women look like painted whores, or behave indecently with the men.

Rather, these people in an astonishing way seemed to have created an established community which lived an ordered existence on wheels, and to observe with a stern fidelity unknown in towns and cities the decencies of family life. There would be a powerful young man, a handsome and magnificent young woman with blonde hair and the figure of an Amazon, and a powerfully-built, thick-set man of middle age, who had a stern, lined, responsible-looking face and a bald head. They were probably the members of a trapeze team—the young man and woman would leap through space like projectiles, meeting the grip of the older man and hurling back again upon their narrow perches, catching the swing of their trapeze in mid-air, and whirling thrice before they caught it, in a perilous and beautiful exhibition of human balance and precision.

But when they came into the breakfast tent, they would speak gravely yet courteously to other performers, and seat themselves in a family group at one of the long tables, eating their tremendous breakfasts with an earnest concentration, seldom speaking to one another, and then gravely, seriously and briefly.

And my brother and I would look at them with fascinated eyes: my brother would watch the man with the bald head for a while and then turn toward me, whispering:

"D-d-do you see that f-f-fellow there with the bald head? W-w-well he's the heavy man," he whispered knowingly. "He's the one that c-c-c-catches them! That f-f-fellow's got to know his business! You know what happens if he m-m-misses, don't you?" said my brother.

"What?" I would say in a fascinated tone.

My brother snapped his fingers in the air.

"Over!" he said. "D-d-done for! W-w-why, they'd be d-d-d-dead before they knew what happened. Sure!" he said, nodding vigorously. "It's a f-f-f-fact! If he ever m-m-m-misses it's all over! That boy has g-g-g-got to know his s-s-s-stuff!" my brother said. "W-w-w-why," he went on in a low tone of solemn conviction, "it w-w-w-wouldn't surprise me at all if they p-p-p-pay him s-s-seventy-five or a hundred dollars a week! It's a fact!" my brother cried vigorously.

And we would turn our fascinated stares again upon these splendid and romantic creatures, whose lives were so different from our own, and whom we seemed to know with such familiar and affectionate intimacy. And at length, reluctantly, with full light come and the sun up, we would leave the circus grounds and start for home.

And somehow the memory of all we had seen and heard that glorious morning, and the memory of the food-tent with its wonderful smells, would waken in us the pangs of such a ravenous hunger that we could not wait until we got home to eat. We would stop off in town at lunch-rooms and, seated on tall stools before the counter, we would devour ham-and-egg sandwiches, hot hamburgers red and pungent at their cores with coarse spicy sanguinary beef, coffee, glasses of foaming milk and doughnuts, and then go home to eat up everything in sight upon the breakfast table.

IDEAS

1. Among the scenes Wolfe describes, which one makes the most vivid impression on you? Why?

2. What stereotypes of circus performers does Wolfe attempt to negate?

3. How old do you suspect Wolfe and his brother were when they made these observations? Do you think they really observed all of these things as young boys, or is the description here a kind of "glorified recall" by an adult looking back at the event?

4. Does the dialogue at the end of this piece interrupt the descriptive process or reinforce it?

ORGANIZATION AND STYLE

1. The first three paragraphs of this selection are clearly the introduction and the final paragraph the conclusion. What principle of organization can you find for the body of the narrative?

2. Find examples that focus on each of the five senses: seeing, hearing, smelling, feeling, tasting.

3. Wolfe's sentences are usually quite long. The second paragraph, for instance, is one long sentence. Is this effective in writing of this type? Why or why not?

4. Find examples in the essay of alliteration ("sculptural still square," for instance) and onomatopoeia ("crash and bump of shifting freight cars" or "tolling of bells," for instance). What do these poetic techniques contribute to the entire selection?

5. Find Wolfe's references to night and day, darkness and emerging light. How do they serve as transitions to move the narrative along?

WRITING

1. Recall some fascinating childhood experience—a circus, a trip by car or train or boat, a country fair. Try to emulate Wolfe in setting it before your reader in pictorial and sensory detail, showing your reader things, not simply telling about them.

2. The purpose of Wolfe's narrative piece is to make his reader feel a part of the scene and share in its emotional impact. A journalist, on the other hand, is concerned with straight, factual reporting. Assume that you are a journalist assigned to write a 400–500-word report on the arrival of the circus in town. Rewrite appropriate parts of Wolfe's narrative in journalistic style. Present just the facts and avoid the stylistic flourishes appropriate for descriptive writing but not for news stories.

Shooting an Elephant

GEORGE ORWELL

———————●———————

Again, description and narration support the writer's task, showing their inescapable kinship and their indispensable power. "Shooting an Elephant" may be the best autobiographical essay ever written. It is a classic. It demonstrates superbly how a personal anecdotal narrative can illustrate a general argumentative point—imperialism is evil—a thesis that might have been developed at length in a conventional essay, with illustrations from history and testimony from other observers. Orwell does it all with narrative, reinforced by vivid description that keeps the picture before our eyes, especially in descriptive metaphors: as neatly as one skins a rabbit, like a huge rock toppling, grandmotherly air. *Don't fail to notice how Orwell's stringent honesty about his feelings enforces his thesis, that which he knows is right.*

In Moulmein, in Lower Burma, I was hated by large numbers of people—the only time in my life that I have been important enough for this to happen to me. I was sub-divisional police officer of the town, and in an aimless, petty kind of way anti-European feeling was very bitter. No one had the guts to raise a riot, but if a European woman went through the bazaars alone somebody would probably spit betel juice over her dress. As a police officer I was an obvious target and was baited whenever it seemed safe to do so. When a nimble Burman tripped me up on the football field and the referee (another Burman) looked the other way, the crowd yelled with hideous laughter. This happened more than once. In the end the sneering yellow faces of young men that met me everywhere, the insults hooted after me when I was at a safe distance, got badly on my nerves. The young Buddhist priests were the worst of all. There were several thousands of them in the town and none of them seemed to have anything to do except stand on street corners and jeer at Europeans.

All this was perplexing and upsetting. For at that time I had already made up my mind that imperialism was an evil thing and the sooner I chucked up my job and got out of it the better. Theoretically—and secretly, of course—I was all for the Burmese and all against their oppressors, the British. As for the job I was doing, I hated it more bitterly than I can perhaps make clear. In a job like that you see the dirty work of Empire at close quarters. The wretched prisoners huddling in the stinking cages of the lockups, the grey, cowed faces of the long-term convicts, the scarred buttocks of the men who had been flogged with bamboos—all these oppressed me with an intolerable sense of guilt. But I could get nothing into perspective. I was young and ill-educated and I had had to think out my problems in the utter silence that is imposed on every Englishman in the East. I did not even know that the British Empire is dying, still less did I know that it is a great deal better than the younger empires that are going to supplant it. All I knew was that I was stuck between my hatred of the empire I served and my rage against the evil-spirited little beasts who tried to make my job impossible. With one part of my mind I thought of the British Raj as an unbreakable tyranny, as something clamped down, *in saecula saeculorum,* upon the will of prostrate peoples; with another part I thought that the greatest joy in the world would be to drive a bayonet into a Buddhist priest's guts. Feelings like these are the normal by-products of imperialism; ask any Anglo-Indian official, if you can catch him off duty.

One day something happened which in a roundabout way was enlightening. It was a tiny incident in itself, but it gave me a better glimpse than I had before of the real nature of imperialism—the real motives for which despotic governments act. Early one morning the sub-inspector at a police station the other end of the town rang me up on the 'phone and said that an elephant was ravaging the bazaar. Would I please come and do something about it? I did not know what I could do, but I wanted to see what was happening and I got on to a pony and started out. I took my rifle, an old .44 Winchester and much too small to kill an elephant, but I thought the noise might be useful *in terrorem.* Various Burmans stopped me on the way and told me about the elephant's doings. It was not, of course, a wild elephant, but a tame one which had gone "must." It had been chained up, as tame elephants always are when their attack of "must" is due, but on the previous night it had broken its chain and escaped. Its mahout, the only person who could manage it when it was in that state, had set out in pursuit, but had taken the wrong direction and was now twelve hours' journey away, and in the morning the elephant had suddenly reappeared in the town. The Burmese population had no weapons and were quite helpless against it. It had already destroyed somebody's bamboo hut, killed a cow and raided some fruitstalls and devoured the stock; also it had met the municipal rubbish van and, when the driver jumped out and took to his heels, had turned the van over and inflicted violences upon it.

The Burmese sub-inspector and some Indian constables were waiting for me in the quarter where the elephant had been seen. It was a very poor quarter, a labyrinth of squalid bamboo huts, thatched with palmleaf, winding all over a steep hillside. I remember that it was a cloudy, stuffy morning at the beginning of the rains. We began questioning the people as to where the elephant had gone and, as usual, failed to get any definite information. That is invariably the case in the East; a story always sounds clear enough at a distance, but the nearer you get to the scene of events the vaguer it becomes. Some of the people said that the elephant had gone in one direction, some said that he had gone in another, some professed not even to have heard of any elephant. I had almost made up my mind that the whole story was a pack of lies, when we heard yells a little distance away. There was a loud, scandalized cry of "Go away, child! Go away this instant!" and an old woman with a switch in her hand came round the corner of a hut, violently shooing away a crowd of naked children. Some more women followed, clicking their tongues and exclaiming; evidently there was something that the children ought not to have seen. I rounded the hut and saw a man's dead body sprawling in the mud. He was an Indian, a black Dravidian coolie, almost naked, and he could not have been dead many minutes. The people said that the elephant had come suddenly upon him round the corner of the hut, caught him with its trunk, put its foot on his back and ground him into the earth. This was the rainy season and the ground was soft, and his face had scored a trench a foot deep and a couple of yards long. He was lying on his belly with arms crucified and head sharply twisted to one side. His face was coated with mud, the eyes wide open, the teeth bared and grinning with an expression of unendurable agony. (Never tell me, by the way, that the dead look peaceful. Most of the corpses I have seen looked devilish.) The friction of the great beast's foot had stripped the skin from his back as neatly as one skins a rabbit. As soon as I saw the dead man I sent an orderly to a friend's house nearby to borrow an elephant rifle. I had already sent back the pony, not wanting it to go mad with fright and throw me if it smelt the elephant.

The orderly came back in a few minutes with a rifle and five cartridges, and meanwhile some Burmans had arrived and told us that the elephant was in the paddy fields below, only a few hundred yards away. As I started forward practically the whole population of the quarter flocked out of the houses and followed me. They had seen the rifle and were all shouting excitedly that I was going to shoot the elephant. They had not shown much interest in the elephant when he was merely ravaging their homes, but it was different now that he was going to be shot. It was a bit of fun to them, as it would be to an English crowd; besides they wanted the meat. It made me vaguely uneasy. I had no intention of shooting the elephant—I had merely sent for the rifle to defend myself if necessary— and it is always unnerving to have a crowd following you.

I marched down the hill, looking and feeling a fool, with the rifle over my shoulder and an ever-growing army of people jostling at my heels. At the bottom, when you got away from the huts, there was a metalled road and beyond that a miry waste of paddy fields a thousand yards across, not yet ploughed but soggy from the first rains and dotted with course grass. The elephant was standing [eighty]* yards from the road, his left side towards us. He took not the slightest notice of the crowd's approach. He was tearing up bunches of grass, beating them against his knees to clean them and stuffing them into his mouth.

I had halted on the road. As soon as I saw the elephant I knew with perfect certainty that I ought not to shoot him. It is a serious matter to shoot a working elephant—it is comparable to destroying a huge and costly piece of machinery—and obviously one ought not to do it if it can possibly be avoided. And at that distance, peacefully eating, the elephant looked no more dangerous than a cow. I thought then and I think now that his attack of "must" was already passing off; in which case he would merely wander harmlessly about until the mahout came back and caught him. Moreover, I did not in the least want to shoot him. I decided that I would watch him for a little while to make sure that he did not turn savage again, and then go home.

But at that moment I glanced round at the crowd that had followed me. It was an immense crowd, two thousand at least and growing every minute. It blocked the road for a long distance on either side. I looked at the sea of yellow faces above the garish clothes—faces all happy and excited over this bit of fun, all certain that the elephant was going to be shot. They were watching me as they would watch a conjurer about to perform a trick. They did not like me, but with the magical rifle in my hands I was momentarily worth watching. And suddenly I realized that I should have to shoot the elephant after all. The people expected it of me and I had got to do it; I could feel their two thousand wills pressing me forward, irresistibly. And it was at this mo-

---

*Original and all reprints say "eight," an obvious typographical error.

ment, as I stood there with the rifle in my hands, that I first grasped the hollowness, the futility of the white man's dominion in the East. Here was I, the white man with his gun, standing in front of the unarmed native crowd—seemingly the leading actor of the piece; but in reality I was only an absurd puppet pushed to and fro by the will of those yellow faces behind. I perceived in this moment that when the white man turns tyrant it is his own freedom that he destroys. He becomes a sort of hollow, posing dummy, the conventionalized figure of a sahib. For it is the condition of his rule that he shall spend his life in trying to impress the "natives," and so in every crisis he has got to do what the "natives" expect of him. He wears a mask, and his face grows to fit it. I had got to shoot the elephant. I had committed myself to doing it when I sent for the rifle. A sahib has got to act like a sahib; he has got to appear resolute, to know his own mind and do definite things. To come all that way, rifle in hand, with two thousand people marching at my heels, and then to trail feebly away, having done nothing— no, that was impossible. The crowd would laugh at me. And my whole life, every white man's life in the East, was one long struggle not to be laughed at.

But I did not want to shoot the elephant. I watched him beating the bunch of grass against his knees, with that preoccupied grandmotherly air that elephants have. It seemed to me that it would be murder to shoot him. At that age I was not squeamish about killing animals, but I had never shot an elephant and never wanted to. (Somehow it always seems worse to kill a *large* animal.) Besides, there was the beast's owner to be considered. Alive, the elephant was worth at least a hundred pounds; dead, he would only be worth the value of his tusks, five pounds, possibly. But I had got to act quickly. I turned to some experienced-looking Burmans who had been there when we arrived, and asked them how the elephant had been behaving. They all said the same thing: he took no notice of you if you left him alone, but he might charge if you went too close to him.

It was perfectly clear to me what I ought to do. I ought

to walk up to within, say, twenty-five yards of the elephant and test his behavior. If he charged, I could shoot; if he took no notice of me, it would be safe to leave him until the mahout came back. But also I knew that I was going to do no such thing. I was a poor shot with a rifle and the ground was soft mud into which one would sink at every step. If the elephant charged and I missed him, I should have about as much chance as a toad under a steamroller. But even then I was not thinking particularly of my own skin, only of the watchful yellow faces behind. For at that moment, with the crowd watching me, I was not afraid in the ordinary sense, as I would have been if I had been alone. A white man mustn't be frightened in front of "natives"; and so, in general, he isn't frightened. The sole thought in my mind was that if anything went wrong those two thousand Burmans would see me pursued, caught, trampled on and reduced to a grinning corpse like that Indian up the hill. And if that happened it was quite probable that some of them would laugh. That would never do. There was only one alternative. I shoved the cartridges into the magazine and lay down on the road to get a better aim.

The crowd grew very still, and a deep, low, happy sigh, as of people who see the theatre curtain go up at last, breathed from innumerable throats. They were going to have their bit of fun after all. The rifle was a beautiful German thing with cross-hair sights. I did not then know that in shooting an elephant one would shoot to cut an imaginary bar running from ear-hole to ear-hole. I ought therefore, as the elephant was sideways on, to have aimed straight at his ear-hole; actually I aimed several inches in front of this, thinking the brain would be further forward.

When I pulled the trigger I did not hear the bang or feel the kick—one never does when a shot goes home—but I heard the devilish roar of glee that went up from the crowd. In that instant, in too short a time, one would have thought, even for the bullet to get there, a mysterious terrible change had come over the elephant. He neither stirred nor fell, but every line of his body had altered. He looked suddenly stricken, shrunken, immensely old, as though the frightful impact of the bullet had paralysed him without knocking him down. At last, after what seemed a long time—it might have been five seconds, I dare say—he sagged flabbily to his knees. His mouth slobbered. An enormous senility seemed to have settled upon him. One could have imagined him thousands of years old. I fired again into the same spot. At the second shot he did not collapse but climbed with desperate slowness to his feet and stood weakly upright, with legs sagging and head drooping. I fired a third time. That was the shot that did for him. You could see the agony of it jolt his whole body and knock the last remnant of strength from his legs. But in falling he seemed for a moment to rise, for as his hind legs collapsed beneath him he seemed to tower upwards like a huge rock toppling, his trunk reaching skywards like a tree. He trumpeted, for the first and only time. And then down he came, his belly towards me, with a crash that seemed to shake the ground even where I lay.

I got up. The Burmans were already racing past me across the mud. It was obvious that the elephant would never rise again, but he was not dead. He was breathing very rhythmically with long rattling gasps, his great mound of a side painfully arising and falling. His mouth was wide open—I could see far down into caverns of pale pink throat. I waited a long time for him to die, but his breathing did not weaken. Finally I fired my two remaining shots into the spot where I thought his heart must be. The thick blood welled out of him like red velvet, but still he did not die. His body did not even jerk when the shots hit him, the tortured breathing continued without a pause. He was dying, very slowly and in great agony, but in some world remote from me where not even a bullet could damage him further. I felt that I had got to put an end to that dreadful noise. It seemed dreadful to see the great beast lying there, powerless to move and yet powerless to die, and not even to be able to finish him. I sent back for my small rifle and poured shot after shot into his heart and down his throat. They seemed to make no impression. The tortured gasps continued as steadily as the ticking of a clock.

In the end I could not stand it any longer and went away. I heard later that it took him half an hour to die. Burmans were bringing dahs and baskets even before I left, and I was told they had stripped his body almost to the bones by the afternoon.

Afterwards, of course, there were endless discussions about the shooting of the elephant. The owner was furious, but he was only an Indian and could do nothing. Besides, legally I had done the right thing, for a mad elephant has to be killed, like a mad dog, if its owner fails to control it. Among the Europeans opinion was divided. The older men said I was right, the young men said it was a damn shame to shoot an elephant for killing a coolie, because an elephant was worth more than any damn Coringhee coolie. And afterwards I was very glad that the coolie had been killed; it put me legally in the right and it gave me a sufficient pretext for shooting the elephant. I often wondered whether any of the others grasped that I had done it solely to avoid looking a fool.

IDEAS

1. How does Orwell's opening statement—"I was hated by large numbers of people"—set the action for his essay?

2. What do you learn, almost incidentally, about the Burmese social system?

3. What function does the dead coolie play in Orwell's thoughts and essay—especially in "any damn Coringhee coolie" and "I was very glad"?

ORGANIZATION AND STYLE

1. How does the word *guts* function in Orwell's first two paragraphs? From Orwell's context, what do you understand by *in saecula saeculorum,* even with no knowledge of Latin? How about *in terrorem?*

2. Where does Orwell state his thesis most directly? Can you formulate a fully explicit thesis for this essay? (See how it would work, beginning with a *But,* at the end of the first paragraph.) Keep Orwell's procedure in mind when we consider induction and deduction in the next section.

3. What is the effect of "inflicted violences upon it" at the end of the third paragraph?

4. Which of Orwell's descriptive metaphors seem especially effective? Why?

5. What is the effect of Orwell's sentence "I got up"?

WRITING

1. Orwell admits that he shot the elephant because of pressure from the crowd, not because shooting it was right. Select a time in your life when you responded to similar pressure and did something wrong. Write an essay with enough detail for your reader to understand your internal conflict, to see you wrestling with your own conscience while listening to the crowd.

2. Write an autobiographical essay about some incident that taught you something significant, as Orwell's shooting of the elephant did him. Try for a clearer thesis than his, something like "One day something happened that taught me the real nature of robbery: that you really steal more from yourself than from others." Then make the whole body of your essay a vivid descriptive narrative, with detail after detail and an occasional illustrative metaphor, to lay out the sequence of the time you were in an automobile accident or stole your best friend's toy cannon or doll or broke a promise.

5

●

FOUNDATIONS: DEALING
WITH EVIDENCE

●

Evidence supports the essayist's ideas, and helps to refute those of the opposition. Statistical figures, descriptive or narrative examples, statements by authorities, citations from the daily news—all help to persuade the reader that what the thesis asserts as true is true indeed. Several pieces of evidence, preferably of different kinds, are more persuasive than one. But too much evidence overwhelms the point and the reader, as if the writer, in thinking the reader dull, seems also to be something of a dullard. On the other hand, one vivid descriptive or narrative example, like Orwell's shooting the elephant, may persuade us beyond all doubt.

Assumptions and Fallacies

All of the essayist's theses, and the evidence that supports them, rest on unstated, or unargued, assumptions—that tyranny is evil, life is good, the universe works, love is better than hate, freedom is better than servitude, for example. All of our statements spring from some assumptions below the surface. And here the essayist may run into fallacies. He or she misses other interpretations, other assumptions, from the evidence. Oddly enough, *all* evidence rests on the most basic of logical fallacies: *one* does not equal *all; some* does not equal *every.* No amount of evidence, the logicians tell us, can guarantee an assumption, because some can never equal all. That the sun has gotten up on time every morning so far is, they say, no logical guarantee that it will do so tomorrow. So much for logic. We can sleep peacefully on our common sense, satisfied with as much evidence as we want. Enough is as good as a feast. But we should watch for an essayist's unexamined assumptions, especially those that take the evidence to point one way, when it might just as well point in another. Schiefelbein, for instance, builds her case for the movement from the city to the smaller community by using a large number of assumptions, many of which may not stand up to close scrutiny. Greene's entire essay is predicated upon his assumption that the past differs significantly from the present. He may be guilty of confusing the *some* with the *every.*

Return of the Native

SUSAN SCHIEFELBEIN

───────────●───────────

Major cities are losing population to small towns and rural communities. This is a recognized fact, supported by many statistical studies. A far more complicated issue, however, is why people are moving from city to country. Schiefelbein analyzes the why, *but in doing so she makes some assumptions you might wish to challenge.*

LADY in a (theater) box: "Is there any culture . . . in Grover's Corners?"
MR. WEBB: "Well, ma'am, there ain't much. . . . Maybe this is the place to tell you that we've got a lot of pleasures of a kind here: we like the sun comin' up over the mountain in the morning, and we all notice a good deal about the birds . . . and we watch the change of seasons. . . ."

OUR TOWN

For the first time in fifty years, more Americans are moving to small towns than to cities. In the three decades prior to 1970, nine million people left small towns and moved to urban areas; but in three short years after 1970, 1.5 million left metropolitan areas behind and headed for homes in small towns. Clearly, the once magical attractions of cosmopolitan life—the arts, the sophistication, the promise of success—no longer have the allure of those simple country "pleasures of a kind" so dear to Mr. Webb.

This trend is far too significant to be dismissed—along with organic gardens and communes—as nothing but a stale leftover from the Sixties. True, people who are moving from city to country are younger—by about seventeen years—than those who are staying put; but statistics also show that they earn about $1,500 more annually, they have higher-status jobs, and they have on the average two years more education than their cohorts who have chosen to remain in urban areas. Nor are movers simply spilling over from city to suburb: People are heading for small towns that are independent of cities. Although some of these areas are within commuting distance of cities and suburbs, the most spectacular growth is taking place in towns far from urban centers.

What is most important about this trend, however, is not so much the types of people and towns involved as the fact that the shift represents an abrupt and dramatic break with the American tradition of urban expansion. For an entire century, people have abandoned the rustic amenities of country living in favor of urban sophistication and convenience. By the Sixties, city life seemed so important to our culture that the President's Commission on Rural Poverty called its report "The People Left Behind." Indeed they were: Some two hundred counties had lost more than half their population to cities, and hundreds of others had dwindled almost as dramatically.

In the sociological literature, country folk have seemed not so much "the people left behind" as the people entirely forgotten—as evidenced by the titles that line library shelves: *The Urbanization of America; The Making of Urban America; The Urban Prospect.* Even Robert and Helen Lynd's classic *Middletown* (1929) and *Middletown in Transition* (1937)—both recognized as being among the most valuable records on an American community ever written—deal not with a small town but with a small city— Muncie, Indiana, thinly disguised. During the ten years in which the Lynds scrutinized "Middletown," its population grew from 36,000 to 50,000.

But even though the Lynds dealt with a middling-big town, they said a lot about small ones in between the lines. In *Middletown,* rural America slowly became an anachronism as the town began to pulse with life, thanks to a natural gas boom and the advent of the auto and radio.

Then in *Transition* the Lynds began to note the many admirable qualities of life Middletown's people had sacrificed in their rush to urbanization. " 'Progress'; 'growing' wealth and power; 'bigger and better' everything—these are some of the symbols that live daily in the skins of Middletown folk," the Lynds wrote. "People tend to lose each other. . . . One 'lives in' a town, 'makes one's money there,' . . . rather than necessarily being an integral part of the town."

Despite the isolation that characterized city life, however, decades passed and the small-town exodus and concurrent urban explosion continued. People examined their options and chose to buck cosmopolitan problems rather than wrestle with rural ones.

The choice was not altogether irrational. The problems that plague small towns remain serious even today. Health facilities are the worst of the lot: In 1970 there were half as many doctors per 100,000 people in nonmetropolitan areas as there were in metropolitan areas. Chronic disease and infant mortality have far higher incidence in small towns, and old people who live in them have so many health problems—and find it so difficult to reach a doctor—that life for many of them ranges from the unpleasant to the unbearable.

Income is another problem. Nonmetropolitan residents earn only three fourths as much as city dwellers, and the difference is not wholly made up, as one might expect, in the lower cost of living. Worse, jobs are scarce: Should a factory close down outside a small town, there isn't another one a few blocks away to soak up the unemployed. Twice as many of the nation's poor live in nonmetropolitan areas as in cities. Finally, people who live in rural areas are less educated, and their attitudes are often very fundamental and conservative—partly because, sociologists say, they don't have the city dweller's exposure to many different ideas. As a result, small-town people may appear naïve or narrow-minded to city dwellers who are considering a move to the country.

Why then, with all the problems and after all these

years, are so many city people now moving to small towns? Some reasons are obvious: Industries and businesses are moving to small towns, so more jobs are available. Better communications and transportation make for easier access to the city's benefits. The crime rates in cities have soared to such heights that many people are simply afraid to stay; the incidence of aggressive assault is twice as high in cities as in small towns, and the rate of robberies is thirteen times as high. Another factor is pollution. Too many cities have taken shortcuts in their race to profits, refusing to spend the money necessary to make their products or produce their energy in a safe, clean way. The environmental mess is no longer just a rallying point for people who are enamored of causes; statistics show that many of the people who are fleeing cities have lung and heart diseases caused by pollution and are too sick to take any more chances.

Sociological theories tell us more about the move to small towns than do any of the random factual or statistical explanations. In an article published in *The Geographical Review,* Wilbur Zelinsky hypothesizes that the more progressive a society becomes, the less the people flock toward traditional symbols of progress. As a society advances, he writes, economic features are not as important to them as human values, pleasures, and physical surroundings.

Another theory about the country's magnetic pull is developed with elaborate detail and admirable expertise in an issue of *The Annals of the American Academy* devoted to the "New Rural America" (January 1977). The numerous sociologists who contributed to this issue suggest that Americans have never wanted to live in the city at all; that the economic factor did not influence their choice—it *forced* their choice. Now that many Americans have achieved financial well-being, the *Annals* symposium suggests, they are concentrating on other needs—and are fulfilling these needs by moving to small towns. This theory is supported by Angus Campbell, whose studies show that although urban dwellers are satisfied with the specifics of life—hospitals, garbage collection, and so forth—they usually are not happy about life in toto. Rural people, on the other hand, are satisfied more with the whole of their life than with any of its parts. Another telling statistic from the *Annals* report: Six out of ten city dwellers want to move from the metropolitan areas; but nine out of ten small-town people wouldn't trade their life for any other.

Because the urban exodus of recent years began so suddenly, the sociological analysis of small-town living is currently more an art than a science. Besides examining the changing attitudes and values of Americans, sociologists have yet to address themselves to other pressing questions raised by the new preference for small towns: How can they avoid the problems that plague the cities? How, for instance, can they cope with the population influx? Who should assume the high cost of providing services for rural areas? Few minorities move to small towns; how can villages avoid being characterized as racially and socially exclusive?

Social scientists will, for some time to come, be writing and publishing furiously on these topics. In the meantime, the Americans who have left the urban rat race and settled down in the countryside can finally concentrate, not on earning a living, but on savoring life itself.

> STAGE MANAGER: *"And this is Mrs. Webb's garden. Just like Mrs. Gibbs's, only it's got a lot of sunflowers, too. Right here's a big butternut tree...."* He looks at the audience for a minute. *"Nice town, y'know what I mean?"*

IDEAS

1. Do you agree or disagree with Schiefelbein's assessments of city and noncity living?

2. What factors—other than those the author discusses—can you think of that might determine what kind of community a person chooses to live in?

3. If you had to live in a community different from your own, what problems would you expect to encounter? How would you anticipate dealing with them?

4. Schiefelbein says that the younger people moving to nonmetropolitan areas are better educated and make more money than do those who stay in cities. She also says that nonmetropolitan residents "earn only three fourths as much as city dwellers." How do you reconcile these statements? What do you predict for the future?

5. If salary and expenses were equal, would you choose to live in a city or in a smaller community? Why?

ORGANIZATION AND STYLE

1. Schiefelbein frames her essay with quotations from Thornton Wilder's play *Our Town.* How effective is this? How do the ideas in those quotations introduce and subsequently reinforce the author's thesis? What assumptions do those quotations make?

2. What different kinds of evidence does the author cite? Does she lean more to one type than another? Might she have improved her essay by including a brief narrative description of someone who has moved out of a city?

3. Schiefelbein makes many assumptions in this essay. She assumes, for instance, that people were originally drawn to city living by the attraction of "the arts, the sophistication, the promise of success." Later she cites a social scientist who suggests that people are moving out of the city to meet personal needs now that they have achieved financial well-being. Are these assumptions valid? What other assumptions are in the essay? Are they valid?

4. Apart from the assumptions, what clearly factual evidence does the author give? Should she have included more?

WRITING

1. Develop an essay describing the kind of community you would elect to live in if you had complete freedom of choice. Consider social, economic, and employment conditions in your community. Support your ideas with several kinds of evidence.

2. Schiefelbein suggests that rural people are more happy with their lives as a whole than with its parts, implying that city people are perhaps more happy with the parts of their lives than with the whole. Do you agree or disagree with this position? Can one, for instance, enjoy the fine music and outstanding restaurants available in a city and still hate living there? Or can one enjoy the peace and safety of a rural community and still be frustrated by the lack of social and cultural events? Do the parts equal the whole, or can they be separated? Write an essay in which you analyze this problem from your own experience. Support your ideas with appropriate evidence.

Permanent Record—A Big Paper Tiger

BOB GREENE

———————●———————

Anytime an author claims to reduce "thousands of theories" "down to one simple thing," you can be certain that some very broad assumptions are going to be made. Greene, a popular newspaper columnist, has fun with some of those assumptions in his brief essay. Beneath his discussion of the permanent record, however, is a rather broadly implied social judgment. What is it?

There are thousands of theories about what's gone wrong with the world, but I think it comes down to one simple thing:

The death of the Permanent Record.

You remember the Permanent Record. When you were in elementary school, junior high school, and high school, you were constantly being told that if you screwed up, news of that screw-up would be sent down to the principal's office, and would be placed in your Permanent Record.

Nothing more needed to be said. No one had ever seen a Permanent Record; that didn't matter. We knew they were there. We all imagined a steel filing cabinet, crammed full of Permanent Records—one for each kid in the school. I think we always assumed that when we graduated our Permanent Record was sent on to college with us, and then when we got out of college our Permanent Record was sent to our employer—probably with a duplicate copy sent to the U.S. government.

I don't know if students are still threatened with the promise of unpleasant things included in their Permanent Record, but I doubt it. I have a terrible feeling that mine was the last generation to know what a Permanent Record was—and that not only has it disappeared from the schools of the land, but it has disappeared as a concept in society as a whole.

There once was a time when people really stopped before they did something they knew was deceitful, immoral, or unethical—no matter how much fun it might sound. They didn't stop because they were such holy folks. They stopped because—no matter how old they were— they had a nagging fear that if they did it, it would end up on their Permanent Record.

At some point in the last few decades, I'm afraid, people wised up to something that amazed them: There is no Permanent Record. There probably never was.

They discovered that regardless of how badly you fouled up your life or the lives of others, there was nothing permanent about it on your record. You would always be forgiven, no matter what; no matter what you did, other people would shrug it off.

So pretty soon men and women—instead of fearing the Permanent Record—started laughing at the idea of the Permanent Record. The kinds of things that they used to be ashamed of—the kinds of things that they used to secretly cringe at when they thought about them—now became "interesting" aspects of their personalities.

If those "interesting" aspects were weird enough—if they were the kinds of things that would have really jazzed up the Permanent Record—the people sometimes wrote books confessing those things, and the books became best sellers. And the people found out that other people—far from scorning them—would line up in the bookstores to get their autographs on the inside covers of the books.

The people started going on talk shows to discuss the things that, in decades past, would have been included in their Permanent Records. The talk-show hosts would say,

"Thank you for being so honest with us; I'm sure the people in our audience can understand how much guts it must take for you to tell us these things." The Permanent Records were being opened up for the whole world to see—and the sky did not fall in.

If celebrities had dips in their careers, all they had to do to guarantee a new injection of fame was to admit the worst things about themselves—the Permanent Record things—and the celebrity magazines would print those things, and the celebrities would be applauded for their candor and courage. And they would become even bigger celebrities.

As Americans began to realize that there was no Permanent Record, and probably never had been, they deduced for themselves that any kind of behavior was permissible. After all, it wasn't as if anyone was keeping track; all you would have to do—just like the men and women with the best sellers and on the talk shows and in the celebrity magazines—would be to say, "That was a real crazy period in my life." All would be forgiven; all would be erased from the Permanent Record, which, of course, was no longer permanent.

And that is where we are today. Without really thinking about it, we have accepted the notion that no one is, indeed, keeping track. No one is even *allowed* to keep track. I doubt that you can scare a school kid today by telling him the principal is going to inscribe something on his Permanent Record; the kid would probably file a suit under the Freedom of Information Act, and gain possession of his Permanent Record by recess. Either that, or the kid would call up his Permanent Record on his computer terminal, and purge any information he didn't want to be there.

As for us adults—it has been so long since we have believed in the Permanent Record that the very mention of it today probably brings a nostalgic smile to our faces. We feel naive for ever having believed that a Permanent Record was ever really down there in the principal's office, anyway.

And who really knows if our smiles may freeze on some distant day—the day it is our turn to check out of this earthly world, and we are confronted with a heavenly presence greeting us at the gates of our new eternal home—a heavenly presence sitting there casually leafing through a dusty, battered volume of our Permanent Record as we come jauntily into view.

IDEAS

1. Is Greene simply writing about the Permanent Record, or is he making a broader social judgment? If so, what is it?

2. Did you grow up in an era when the Permanent Record was discussed? If so, how did it affect your conduct?

3. What other things—threats to tell your mother or father what you had done, threats of burning in hell, fear of getting your name in the local paper for some mischievous prank—were used to try to control your behavior? Were these effective? Would they be effective for today's adolescents?

ORGANIZATION AND STYLE

1. What assumptions does Greene make in his essay?

2. The author begins with a clear statement of his thesis, devotes several paragraphs to the former use of the Permanent Record, and then analyzes the present situation. Find those organizational divisions in the essay. How does Greene introduce them?

3. Examine the large number of sentences in which the author uses dashes. Are they effective? Are there too many of them? Might some of his dashed phrases be contained by the commas of more formal style?

4. In what way is Greene's final paragraph ironic? Does this irony support the author's major ideas?

WRITING

1. Select a time in your life when you were told that you must not do a particular thing because, if you did, you would carry the weight of your deed for the rest of your life. Develop an essay in which you analyze the proposed deed, the advice you were given, and your reaction to this Permanent Record syndrome. Introduce as much specific evidence as possible.

2. Many states now have laws that erase the criminal record of a person who has "gone straight" for a designated time. Some people feel that these are just laws, that one misdeed should not cloud a person's career. Others argue that erasure weakens law enforcement and increases crime. Write an essay arguing for one of these positions, with as much evidence as possible from newspapers, magazines, textbooks, experience, and the like.

Induction and Deduction

We have already looked at these two essential and opposite ways of thinking, and of laying out one's evidence, the inductive leading into one's central point and the deductive declaring of one's thesis and then leading away from it with evidence and explanation, the essayist's more usual and clearer—though less suspenseful—procedure, followed by most of the essayists in this book.

Here are three examples that proceed inductively, although each also has its deductive parts. Archibald Mac-Leish blends the two modes effectively, in what might be called a deductive-inductive essay. Alan Paton recounts inductively how he came to realize the gaps in his childhood certainties. Robert Heilbroner's essay is also almost purely inductive, though separate paragraphs are deductive, as indeed any paragraph with a good topic sentence must be, with the evidence following through. Notice, again, that the question is the mark of induction.

Why Do We Teach Poetry?

ARCHIBALD MacLEISH

———————— ● ————————

Like Virginia Woolf's "How Should One Read a Book?", MacLeish's title implies its deductive answer: "We should teach poetry because it is valuable, and in a specific way." We learn what that way is after Mac-Leish has inductively considered and set aside several alternate reasons as if he had been asking "Is it this?—No—Then this?—Well, not exactly—Then how about this?" Then with his assertion that teaching poetry as art is the only way to teach poetry as knowledge, we have a firm deductive thesis, and his evi-

*dence and persuasion follow the usual order, but with
frequent inductive questionings. As you read, notice
their frequency, and how each question-and-answer
sustains the inductive mood set by his title as it also
reinforces his deductive point.*

It is a relief to come upon someone who feels no defensiveness whatever about the teaching of poetry, someone who is perfectly certain that poetry ought to be taught now as at any other time and who is perfectly certain also that he knows why. The paragon I have in mind is a young friend of mine, a devoted teacher, who was recently made headmaster of one of the leading American preparatory schools, and who has been taking stock, for some time past, of his curriculum and his faculty. Poetry, as he sees it, ought to be taught "as a most essential form of human expression as well as a carrier throughout the ages of some of the most important values in our heritage." What troubles him is that few teachers, at least in the schools he knows, seem to share his conviction. He is not too sure that teachers themselves have "an abiding and missionary faith in poetry" which would lead them to see it as a great clarifier—a "human language" capable of competing with the languages of mathematics and science.

But though teachers lack the necessary faith, the fault, as my young friend sees it, is not wholly theirs. The fault is the fault of modern criticism, which has turned poetry into something he calls "poetry itself"—meaning, I suppose, poetry for poetry's sake. "Poetry itself" turns out to be poetry with its meanings distilled away, and poetry with its meanings distilled away is difficult if not impossible to teach in a secondary school—at least *his* secondary school. The result is that secondary school teachers have gone back, as to the lesser of two evils, to those historical and anecdotal practices sanctified by American graduate schools in generations past. They teach "poets and not poetry." With the result that "students become acquainted with poets from Homer to MacLeish" (quite a distance no matter how you measure it!) "but the experience doesn't necessarily leave them with increased confidence in what poetry has to offer." I can well believe it.

The reason why modern criticism has this disastrous effect, the reason why it produces "an almost morbid apathy toward 'content' or 'statement of idea,' " is its excessive "preoccupation with aesthetic values." Modern criticism insists that poems are primarily works of art; and when you insist that poems are primarily works of art you cannot, in my friend's view, teach them as carriers "throughout the ages of some of the most important values in our heritage." What is important about Homer and Shakespeare and the authors of the Bible is that they were "realists with great vision . . . whose work contains immensely valuable constructions of the meaning of life"; and if you talk too much about them as artists, those constructions of the meaning of life get lost.

Now this, you will observe, is not merely another walloping of the old horse which was once called the New Criticism. It goes a great deal farther. It is a frontal attack upon a general position maintained by many who never accepted the New Criticism or even heard of it. It is an attack upon those who believe—as most poets, I think, have believed—that a poem *is* primarily a work of art and must be read as a work of art if it is to be read at all. It is a highminded and disinterested attack but an attack notwithstanding. What it contends is that an approach to poetry which insists that a poem is a work of art blocks off what the poem has to say, whereas what the poem has to say is the principal reason for teaching it.

I can understand this argument and can respect the reasons for making it. Far too many of those who define poetry in exclusively artistic terms use their definition as a limiting and protective statement which relieves them of all obligation to drive the poem's meaning beyond the meanings of the poem: beyond the mere translation of the symbols and metaphors and the classical or other references—the whole apparatus of *explication du texte.* Far too many, indeed, of those who have to do with literature generally in our time, and particularly with modern literature, consider that meanings in any but a literary (which includes a Freudian) sense are not only outside, but beneath, their proper concern—that the intrusion of questions of morality and religion into the world of art is a kind of trespass and that works of literary art not only should but *can* be studied in a moral vacuum.

But although I can understand this argument, and although I can respect its reasons, and although I believe it raises a true issue and an important issue, I cannot accept it; for it rests, or seems to me to rest, on two quite dubious assumptions. The first is the assumption, familiar in one form or another to all of us, that the "idea" of a work of art is somehow separable from the work of art itself. The most recent—and most egregious—expression of this persistent notion comes from a Dean of Humanities in a great institution of learning who is reported by the *New York Times* to have argued in a scholarly gathering that "the idea which the reader derives from Ernest Hemingway's *The Old Man and The Sea* comes after the reader has absorbed some 60,000 words. This takes at least an hour. . . . A similar understanding could come after a few minutes' study of a painting by a skillful artist." Precisely, one imagines, as the Doré illustrations gave one the "idea" of the *Inferno* in a few easy looks!

It is the second assumption, however, which divides me most emphatically from my young friend. For the second assumption seems to be that "art" and "knowledge" are somehow opposite and irreconcilable conceptions so that if you teach a poem as work of art you cannot teach it as instrument of perception. This too, of course, is a fairly familiar notion in our world: it is a commonplace with us that knowledge is the exclusive domain of science and that poetry has nothing to do with it. "Whatever," says Bertrand Russell, "can be known can be known by means of science." But because the notion is generally accepted does not necessarily mean that it is true. For the fact is that poetry also is capable of knowledge; that poetry, indeed, is capable of a kind of knowledge of which science is not capable; that it is capable of that knowledge *as poetry;* and that the teaching of poetry as poetry, the teaching of poem as work of art, is not only not incompatible with the teaching of poetry as knowledge but is, indeed, the only possible way of teaching poetry as knowledge.

To most of us, brought up as we have been in the world of abstractions which science has prepared for us, and in the kind of school which that world produces—schools in which almost all teaching is teaching of abstractions—the notion of poetry as knowledge, the notion of art as knowledge, is a fanciful notion. Knowledge by abstraction we understand. Science can abstract ideas about apple from apple. It can organize those ideas into knowledge about apple. It can then introduce that knowledge into our heads—possibly because our heads are abstractions also. But poetry, we know, does not abstract. Poetry presents. Poetry presents the thing as the thing. And that it should be possible to *know* the thing *as the thing it is*—to *know* apple *as* apple—this we do not understand; this, the true child of the time will assure you, cannot be done. To the true child of abstraction you can't know apple as apple. You can't know tree as tree. You can't know man as man. All you can *know* is a world dissolved by analyzing intellect into abstraction—not a world composed by imaginative intellect into itself. And the result, for the generations of abstraction, is that neither poetry nor art can be a means to knowledge. To inspiration, yes: poetry can undoubtedly lead to that—whatever it is. To revelation, perhaps: there may certainly be moments of revelation in poetry. But to knowledge, no. The only connection between poetry and knowledge we can see is the burden of used abstractions—adages and old saws—which poetry, some poetry, seems to like to carry—adages most of which we knew before and some of which aren't even true.

But if all this is so, what then is the "experience of art"—the "experience of poetry"—which all of us who think about these things at all have known? What is the experience of *realization* which comes over us with those

apples on a dish of Cézanne's or those three pine trees?
What is the experience of realization which comes over us
with Debussy's *Nuages?** What is the experience of realization which comes over us when Coleridge's robin sits
and sings

> *Betwixt the tufts of snow on the bare branch*
> *Of mossy apple-tree, while the nigh thatch*
> *Smokes in the sun thaw; . . .*

or when his eave-drops fall

> *Heard only in the trances of the blast,*
> *Or if the secret ministry of frost*
> *Shall hang them up in silent icicles,*
> *Quietly shining to the quiet Moon.*

And if all this is so, why does one of the most effective of
modern definitions of poetry (Arnold's in his letter to Maurice de Guérin) assign to that art the peculiar "power of so
dealing with *things* as to awaken in us a wonderfully full,
and new and intimate sense of them and of our relation
with them"?

The answer is, of course, that the children of abstraction are wrong—and are impoverished by their error, as
our entire time is impoverished by it. They are wrong on
both heads. They are wrong when they think they *can*
know the world through its abstractions: nothing can be
known through an abstraction but the abstraction itself.
They are wrong also when they think they *cannot* know
the world as the world: the whole achievement of art is a
demonstration to the contrary. And the reason they are
wrong on both heads is the reason given, quite unintentionally, by Matthew Arnold. They are wrong because they
do not realize that all true knowledge is a matter of relation: that we *really* know a thing only when we are filled
with "a wonderfully full, new and intimate sense of

*Paul Cézanne (1839–1906), French painter; Claude Debussy (1862–1918),
French composer.

it" and, above all, of "our relation with" it. This sense—
this *knowledge* in the truest meaning of the word knowledge—art can give but abstraction cannot.

There are as many proofs as there are successful works
of art. Take, for obvious example, that unseen mysterious
phenomenon, the wind. Take any attempt, by the familiar
process of abstraction, to "know" the wind. Put beside it
those two familiar lines of George Meredith:

> *Mark where the pressing wind shoots javelin-like*
> *Its skeleton shadow on the broad back'd wave!*

What will be the essential difference between the two?
Will it not be that the first, the analytical, statement is or
attempts to be a wholly objective statement made without
reference to an observer (true everywhere and always),
whereas an observer—*one's self* as observer!—is involved
in the second? And will not the consequential difference be
that a relation involving one's self is created by the second
but not by the first? And will not the end difference be that
the second, but not the first, will enable us to know the
thing itself—to know what the thing is *like?*

It would be quite possible, I suppose, to semanticize this
difference between knowledge by poetry and knowledge
by abstraction out of existence by demonstrating that the
word, know, is being used in two different senses in the two
instances, but the triumph would be merely verbal, for the
difference is real. It is indeed the realest of all differences,
for what it touches is the means by which we come at
reality. How are we to find the knowledge of reality in the
world without, or in the shifting, flowing, fluid world
within? Is all this a task for the techniques of abstraction—for science as it may be or as it is? Is it through
abstraction alone that we are to find what is real in our
experience of our lives—and so, conceivably, what is real
in ourselves? Or do we need another and a different way
of knowing—a way of knowing which will make that
world out there, this world in here, available to us, not by
translating them into something else—into abstractions of

quantity and measure—but by bringing us ourselves to confront them as they are—man and tree face to face in the shock of recognition, man and love face to face?

The question, I beg you to see, is not what we *ought* to do. There is no ought. A man can "live" on abstractions all his life if he has the stomach for them, and many of us have—not the scientists only, but great numbers of the rest of us in this contemporary world, men whose days are a web of statistics and names, and business deals, held together by the parentheses of a pair of commuting trains with three Martinis at the close. The question is not what we ought to do. The question is what we have the choice of doing—what alternatives are open to us. And it is here and in these terms that the issue presents itself to the teacher of poetry.

Colleges and universities do not exist to impose duties but to reveal choices. In a civilization like ours in which one choice has all but overwhelmed the other, a civilization dominated by abstraction, in which men are less and less able to deal with their experience of the world or of themselves unless experience and self have first been translated into abstract terms—a civilization like a foreign language—in such a civilization the need for an understanding of the alternative is urgent. What must be put before the generation of the young is the possibility of knowledge of experience *as* experience, of self *as* self; and that possibility only the work of art, only the poem, can reveal. That it is so rarely, or so timidly, presented in our schools is one of the greatest failures of our educational system. Young men and young women graduate from American schools and colleges by the hundreds of thousands every year to whom science is the only road to knowledge, and to whom poetry is little more than a subdivision of something called "literature"—a kind of writing printed in columns instead of straight across the page and primarily intended to be deciphered by girls, who don't read it either.

This sort of thing has consequences. Abstractions are wonderfully clever tools for taking things apart and for arranging things in patterns, but they are very little use in putting things together and no use at all when it comes to determining what things are *for.* Furthermore abstractions have a limiting, a dehumanizing, a dehydrating effect on the relation to things of the man who must live with them. The result is that we are more and more left, in our scientific society, without the means of knowledge of ourselves as we truly are or of our experience as it actually is. We have the tools, all the tools—we are suffocating in tools—but we cannot find the actual wood to work or even the actual hand to work it. We begin with one abstraction (something we think of as ourselves) and a mess of other abstractions (standing for the world) and we arrange and rearrange the counters, but who we are and what we are doing we simply do not know—above all what we are doing. With the inevitable consequence that we do not know either what our purpose is or our end. So that when the latest discoveries of the cyclotron are reported we hail them with the cry that we will now be able to control nature better than ever before—but we never go on to say for what purpose, to what end, we will control her. To destroy a city? To remake a world?

It was something of this kind, I imagine, that Adlai Stevenson had in mind when he startled a Smith Commencement by warning his newly graduated audience of prospective wives that the "typical Western man—or typical Western husband—operates well in the realm of means, as the Roman did before him. But outside his specialty, in the realm of ends he is apt to operate poorly or not at all. . . . The neglect of the cultivation of more mature values," Mr. Stevenson went on, "can only mean that his life, and the life of the society he determines, will lack valid purpose, however busy and even profitable it may be."

As he had so often done before, Mr. Stevenson there found words for an uneasiness which has been endemic but inarticulate in the American mind for many years— the sense that we are getting nowhere far too fast and that, if something doesn't happen soon, we may arrive. But when he came to spell out the causes for "the neglect of the cultivation of more mature values," Mr. Stevenson failed, or so it seems to me, to identify the actual villain. The contemporary environment in America, he told his young listeners, is "an environment in which 'facts,' the data of the senses, are glorified and value judgments are assigned inferior status as 'mere matters of opinion.' It is an environment in which art is often regarded as an adornment of civilization rather than a vital element of it, while philosophy is not only neglected but deemed faintly disreputable because 'it never gets you anywhere.' " It is true that philosophy is neglected, and even truer that art is regarded in this country generally as it seems to be regarded by the automobile manufacturers of Detroit: as so much enamel paint and chromium to be applied for allegedly decorative purposes to the outside of a car which would run better without it. But the explanation is not, I think, that we set facts—even facts in quotation marks—above values, or that we glorify the data of the senses, unless one means by that latter phrase not what the senses tell us of the world we live in but what the statistics that can be compiled out of the data of the senses would tell us if we were ever in touch with our senses.

In few civilizations have the senses been less alive than they are with us. Look at the cities we build and occupy— but look at them!—the houses we live in, the way we hold ourselves and move; listen to the speaking voices of the greater part of our women. And in no civilization, at least in recorded time, have human beings been farther from the *facts* if we mean by that word, facets of reality. Our indifference to ends is the result of our obsession with abstractions rather than facts: with the ideas of things rather than with things. For there can be no concern for ends without a hunger for reality. And there can be no hunger for reality without a sense of the real. And there can be no sense of the real in the world which abstraction creates, for abstraction is incapable of the real: it can neither lay hold of the real itself nor show us where to find it. It cannot, that is to say, create the *relation* between reality and ourselves which makes *knowledge* of reality possible, for neither reality nor ourselves exist in abstraction. Everything in the world of abstraction is object. And, as George Buttrick pointedly says, *we* are not objects: we are subjects.

But all this is a negative way of saying what a defender of poetry should not be afraid of saying positively. We have lost our concern with ends because we have lost our touch with reality and we have lost our touch with reality because we are estranged from the means to reality which is the poem—the work of art. To most members of our generation this would seem an extravagant statement, but it is not extravagant in fact and would not have seemed so in another time. In ancient China the place of poetry in men's lives was assumed as a matter of course; indeed, the polity was based on it. The three hundred and five odes or songs which make up the Song-word Scripture survived to the fourth century B.C., when Confucius is said to have collected them, because they were part of the government records preserved in the Imperial Archive. For thousands of years the examinations for the Chinese civil service were examinations in poetry, and there is no record that the results were more disappointing to the throne than examinations of a different character might have been.

It was not for nothing Confucius told his disciples that the three hundred and five songs of the Song-word Scripture could be boiled down to the commandment: "Have no twisty thoughts." One can see, not only in the three hundred and five songs, but in Chinese poetry of other periods, what Confucius meant. Consider two Chinese poems of the second century B.C. and the sixth of our era, both written by Emperors. The first is a poem of grief—of the sense of loss of someone loved: a poem therefore of that inward world of feeling, of emotion, which seems to us most nearly ourselves and which, because it is always in flux, always shifting and changing and flowing away, is, of all parts of our experience of our lives, most difficult to know. We cannot know it through science. We cannot know it by knowing things *about* it—even the shrewdest and most intelligent things. We cannot know it either by merely feeling it—by uttering its passing urgencies. How then can we know it?

The Emperor Wu-ti wrote (this is Arthur Waley's beautiful translation):

> *The sound of her silk skirt has stopped.*
> *On the marble pavement dust grows.*
> *Her empty room is cold and still.*
> *Fallen leaves are piled against the doors.*
>
> *Longing for that lovely lady*
> *How can I bring my aching heart to rest?*

Four images, one of sound, two of sight, one of feeling, each like a note plucked on a stringed instrument. Then a question like the chord the four would make together. And all at once we *know.* We know this grief which no word could have described, which any abstraction the mind is capable of would have destroyed. But we know more than this grief: we know our own—or will when it shall visit us—and so know something of ourselves.

The second is a poem of delight: youth and delight—the morning of the world—the emotion, of all emotions, most difficult to stop, to hold, to see. "Joy whose hand is ever at his lips bidding adieu." How would you *know* delight in yourself and therefore yourself delighting? Will the psychiatrists tell you? Is there a definition somewhere in the folios of abstraction which will capture it for you? The Emperor Ch'ien Wen-ti (again Waley's translation) knew that there is only one mirror which will hold that vanishing smile: the mirror of art, the mirror of the poem.

> *A beautiful place is the town of Lo-yang:*
> *The big streets are full of spring light.*
> *The lads go driving out with harps in their hands:*
> *The mulberry girls go out to the fields with their*
>   *baskets.*
> *Golden whips glint at the horses' flanks,*
> *Gauze sleeves brush the green boughs.*
> *Racing dawn the carriages come home—*
> *And the girls with their high baskets full of fruit.*

In this world within, you see, this world which is ourselves, there is no possibility of knowing by abstracting the meaning out—or what we hope will be the meaning. There we must know things *as* themselves and it must be *we* who know them. Only art, only poetry, can bring about that confrontation.

Why do we teach poetry in this scientific age? To present the great alternative, not to science but to that knowledge by abstraction which science has imposed. And what is this great alternative? Not the "messages" of poems, their interpreted "meanings," for these are abstractions also—abstractions far inferior to those of science. Not the explications of poetic texts, for the explication of a poetic text which goes no farther ends only in abstraction.

No, the great alternative is the poem as itself, the poem as a poem, the poem as a work of art—which is to say, the poem in the context in which alone the work of art exists: the context of the world, of the man and of the thing, of the infinite relationship which is our lives. To present the great alternative is to present the poem not as a message in a bottle, and not as an object in an uninhabited landscape, but as an action in the world, an action in which we ourselves are actors and our lives are known.

IDEAS

1. From MacLeish's opening evidence concerning his friend, the headmaster, what do you expect his point to be? Are you surprised (pleased, disappointed) when you find out? What does this suggest about induction?

2. Do you believe that a poem is primarily a work of art, or is it a "carrier" for important ideas? Are these two extreme views of the poem incompatible? Can you think of a poem that accomplishes both objectives?

3. What does MacLeish seem to mean by an "obligation to drive the poem's meaning beyond the meaning of the poem"?

4. MacLeish implies that the poetic statement including "*one's self* as observer" is not "true everywhere and always." Does this strengthen or weaken his case for poetry?

5. To what extent does MacLeish's argument rest on his definition of *abstractions*? What is that definition?

6. Can you make a case for stating the "messages," the interpreted "meanings," of poems from MacLeish's own remarks? From your own point of view?

7. If you followed MacLeish's recommendations, how would you try to teach poetry?

ORGANIZATION AND STYLE

1. How does the title establish an inductive pattern for the essay? What would have been different had MacLeish entitled his essay "Proven Methods for Teaching Poetry"?

2. MacLeish often repeats words in his essay. Look, for example, at the second paragraph. Are these repetitions effective? Would other words have been better? In what other paragraphs does he repeat noticeably?

3. Examine the three parallel *although*-clauses that begin the fifth paragraph. How do they organize what is to follow. Where else does the author parallel similarly?

4. What is the effect of the first-person point of view in this essay? Is it especially effective because MacLeish himself is a recognized poet?

5. Trace the question-answer motif throughout the essay. What principles of a dialectic argument are at work in these mini-units?

6. What exactly does the author accomplish in his conclusion (the last two paragraphs)? What has prepared the reader for this extremely brief summary?

WRITING

1. Take a poem that you like and write an essay illustrating, or qualifying, what MacLeish and Mathew Arnold mean by the "power of so dealing with *things* as to awaken in us a wonderfully full, and new and intimate sense of them and our relation with them" (page 326). Consider, especially, MacLeish's emphasis on the relation between ourselves and things as necessary to knowledge.

2. Select a current course (or series of courses)—Urban Survival Skills, Feminist Literature, Investment Strategies, Pet Training—offered at your college. Write an essay beginning with the title "Why Do We Teach _____?" Try to emulate MacLeish's effective question-answer scheme.

The Challenge of Fear

ALAN PATON

───────────────●───────────────

*Paton moves inductively to explore the growth of his
knowledge of the world and the curious realization,
in MacLeish's term, of the general precepts he had
learned from his parents and his early religious
teaching. His awareness of fear came late in the process, as it does in his essay, to become central to his
understanding of society's defects and of the countervailing power of love.*

One of the big lessons that life has taught me is that my
earlier understanding of man and his society was wretch-
edly inadequate. An extraordinary thing, is it not, that one
should begin to acquire an understanding of them both
when one is drawing near to the end of his acquaintance
with them? The richer one grows in wisdom, the shorter
becomes the time in which to use it.

Just how it happened that my understanding was so
inadequate, I don't quite know. My parents certainly never
taught me that man was growing better and better and
that the future was therefore in some way assured. They
certainly taught me to seek after righteousness, but they
never taught me that righteousness would in a temporal
and political sense be successful. Nor did I ever learn this
at school. Yet that is what I grew up believing. Why should
this be so?

I can only think that it was taught to me after all, not by
father or mother or teacher or priest, but because it was a
basic assumption of the pre-1914 society into which I was
born. I am surprised to find that this view of man and life
was shared by many all over the world who were born at
that time. I am surprised because my own particular

world was a very particular one indeed. It was the town of Pietermaritzburg, Natal, founded by the Afrikaner trekkers, but intensely British at the time of my birth in 1903, most of the trekkers having gone to the Transvaal after the British annexation of Natal. My world was intensely pro-Empire, devoted to the Royal Family, moved to excitement and pride when the red-coated soldiers of the British garrison marched down the street past our home, with arms swinging and drums beating and fifes blowing, to the old Polo Ground to parade for the King's birthday.

There were 30,000 people in Pietermaritzburg in my boyhood, more than half of them Africans and Indians, of whose existence we knew and of whose lives we did not. They were not persons. The Africans were servants, or they dug up the roads. The Indians sold fruit and vegetables, in baskets fastened one to the front and the other to the back end of a flexible strip of bamboo carried on the shoulder, the baskets swaying up and down with a springy motion.

This faulty understanding of man and life has been called by some the romantic illusion, and can be entertained in different places and at different times in history, but in our illusion the might of the British Empire, the indomitable British Navy, and the *Pax Britannica* were particular elements. The world was good, and it was going to stay good, perhaps even become better.

I had no conception at that age of the way in which man could create tremendous, noble-sounding slogans, and could shout them aloud while doing ignoble actions; and what is more, the louder the shout, the greater the ignobleness could be. I had no conception of the need of so much of mankind, while it was actually employed in self-seeking and self-securing, to cling simultaneously to unself-centered religion and altruistic ethics. Nor did I realize that man could so easily deceive himself that his highest religious and ethical values were identical with his own self-interest. And there must have been a great many people like me; otherwise why did George Orwell's *1984* create such a sensation among us?

The extraordinary thing about all this is that I ought to have known it. My parents gave me a religious upbringing, and the reading of the gospel story should have prepared me better for the world with its scribes and pharisees and the crucifixion of Jesus through the instruments of church and state. I take that story seriously, for I believe that in some societies one cannot be true to one's highest beliefs without paying for it in suffering. This is more true in the totalitarian and the semitotalitarian societies (of which Nazi Germany is an example of the first and South Africa an example of the second) than in countries such as America and Britain. In South Africa, one may say with safety that apartheid is misguided, but it is dangerous to say that it is cruel or to oppose it too vigorously.

Not only the Gospel, but history also should have taught me to know better. There is, for one thing, the tale of man's innumerable wars, and of his inhumanity to other men. The early Christians were persecuted by the state, but when Christianity became a state religion, it was not long before the church began persecuting and burning heretics. For centuries, the Jews suffered unspeakably at the hands of Christians, who had no difficulty in believing that they were doing a good thing, and doing it in the name of Christ, who taught that one must love one's neighbor as oneself and had made it very clear who one's neighbor was.

Not even the World War of 1914 shattered my pre-1914 world, though today to read of the terrible and useless slaughter of the bright youth of Britain, France, and Germany leaves one appalled. It was Adolf Hitler who finally destroyed for me—and for many others—the romantic illusion. Dachau, Belsen, Auschwitz—these places gave me an education which was not available in Pietermaritzburg. So one suddenly learns in age the truth of a saying heard in youth; namely, that life is the greatest teacher of them all.

What Hitler taught me about man and nature was sobering enough, but life taught me two further lessons. The first was that, whatever Hitler had taught me about man,

I must on no account forget that all over the world men and women, both young and old, would offer their lives in the fight against totalitarian rule and the doctrine of race superiority because they believed them to be evil. The second lesson was quite different, and that was that some of these same men and women twenty years later would begin to support the very things that they had fought against, and to approve of the punishment without trial of those who opposed the doctrine of apartheid, but had committed no known offense.

And why do they behave like this? Have they suddenly, or even gradually, become corrupted? And if so, why? Surely the answer is that the nature of their security—and that means the nature of their self-interest—has changed. In 1939, their security was the British Empire and the Navy. In 1967, amid the turbulence and uncertainties of modern Africa, their security appears to them to lie in white supremacy and apartheid. With the change of one's self-interest, there comes also a change in one's ideology, one's values, one's principles.

This discovery of the complexity of human nature was accompanied by another—the discovery of the complexity and irrationality of human motive, the discovery that one could love and hate simultaneously, be honest and cheat, be arrogant and humble, be any pair of opposites that one had supposed to be mutually exclusive. This, I believe, is not common knowledge and would be incomprehensible to many. It has always been known, of course, by the dramatists and the novelists. It is, in fact, a knowledge far more disturbing to other people than to writers, for to writers it is the grist to their mills.

Nor was I aware when I was young (both as boy and as man) how powerful a motive is fear, even though I myself had many fears. As I write this, I am searching for an explanation of the fact that under some circumstances men readily admit fear, and under other circumstances do not. I assume that readiness to admit fear is part of a general readiness to look at the world as it is, and therefore at oneself as one is, while unwillingness to admit fear may be a strong element in self-esteem. One does not readily admit to a fear of which one is ashamed.

Now, while fear has its important uses, such as causing an outflow of adrenalin which helps one run away faster, it is a wretched determinant of conduct. There is nothing more pitiable than a human being whose conduct is largely determined by fear. Furthermore, it is a destroyer of reason and the rational life. What can be done to control it, check it, or even eliminate it?

Here I must use language which will be out of fashion for some, and I must use reasoning which will seem quite unreal to others. Life has taught me that John uttered the plain and simple truth when he wrote that there is no fear in love, but that perfect love casts out fear. In one sense, the opposite of fear is courage, but in the dynamic sense the opposite of fear is love, whether this be love of man or love of justice.

It is clearly not enough to tell a fearful man that if he would only love more, he would fear less. In an age when leprosy was feared much more than it is today, that rich and spoiled young man, Francis of Assisi, impelled by some sudden and irresistible emotion, got down from his gaily caparisoned horse and embraced a leper in the road. From that day, he feared nothing, and taught thousands of others to fear nothing. Yet few of us are visited by such irresistible emotion.

How does one help ordinary men and women, if not to eliminate fear, at least to keep it within bounds, so that reason may play a stronger role in the affairs of men and nations and so that men may cease to pursue policies which must lead to the very disasters they fear? To me, this is the most important question that confronts the human race.

I note that it is more and more widely held that poverty and inequality of opportunity are among the greatest causes of tension between man and man, between race and race, and between nation and nation. I believe that race tension in my own country would be amazingly abated if the disparity between average white income and average black income were not so overwhelming. I believe that tension between America and Russia has declined since Russia became one of the productive nations. Yet when men are ruled by fear, they strive to prevent the very changes that will abate it.

Fear of change is, no doubt, in all of us, but it most afflicts the man who fears that any change must lead to loss of his wealth and status. When this fear becomes inordinate, he will, if he has political power, abrogate such things as civil rights and the rule of law, using the argument that he abrogates them only to preserve them. In my own country, the government, in order to preserve Christian civilization, uses methods incompatible with Christianity and abrogates values which are essential to any civilization which calls itself Christian. If only a man would say, "I do this because I'm afraid," one could bear it; but when he says, "I do this because I'm good," that is a bit too much.

I see no hope for the peace of society or the peace of the world so long as this fear of change is so powerful. And this fear will remain powerful so long as the one side has so much to gain and the other so much to lose.

I should like to make one point clear, and that is that I do not believe that a more equitable distribution of wealth will automatically bring the Great Society. The point I am trying to make is that if it is not done, there will never be any Great Society. Nor will there be any peace for the world.

Can a school prepare our children for the complexity and waywardness of man? Is it not more likely that these lessons can be taught only by living? There would be the danger that some children might learn to believe a contrary illusion, namely, that man is cruel, cunning, and deceitful. If I remember my childhood and boyhood correctly, and perhaps even my experience as a young teacher, one actually protected children against knowing too much of the worse sides of man's nature. My readers know, no doubt, the story of the businessman who put his young son on the roof of the house, and, standing below, said, "Jump, son, and Daddy will catch you." So the boy jumped, and Daddy didn't catch him, but instead said to him, "Son, that will teach you to trust nobody." One could hardly do that. But one could, while holding up the goals of honesty, kindness, loyalty, tolerance, integrity, tell children a bit of what the world is like. I would also assume that the children of 1967 know far more about man and his nature and society than did the children of the pre-1914 days; it must be almost impossible for children of today to cherish the old romantic illusion.

One must not suppose, however, that because children have lost the romantic illusion and look upon life and the world and their parents with a more calculating eye that they are now free of illusions. In South Africa, many white children cherish the illusion that they are, in many important ways, superior to other children, and I regret to add that many non-white children entertain the illusion that they are, in many important ways, inferior to white children. Another powerful illusion handed down to many white children is that their country is perfect and their government wholly just and benign, so that they lose all faculty for self-criticism.

I have known people who, when their romantic illusion is finally destroyed, cease to believe anything except that man is bad and life intolerable; who feel that they have come, to use Thomas Wolfe's magnificent words, from the prison of their mothers' flesh "into the unspeakable and incommunicable prison of this earth." I presume they would say that this is what life has taught them. It is my fortune to be able to say that though life destroyed my romantic illusion, she did not teach me the contrary illusion. It would appear either that she does not teach the same lessons to everybody, or that other factors operate besides experience, such as temperament, character, religious faith, and sheer luck and good fortune.

I certainly had good fortune in marriage and children and friends—especially those friends who, with me, have challenged the beliefs and practices of a color-bar society—and it is these personal relationships that have saved me from the melancholy that besets the wholly disillusioned. I call this my luck because it is very difficult, and perhaps impossible, to achieve such a state by act of will. You may say to a friend, "Don't worry; worry changes nothing," but that in itself will not stop him from worrying. Life has taught me—and this is my luck—that active loving saves one from a morbid preoccupation with the shortcomings of society and the waywardness of men.

I should again make it clear at this point that I am not saying that human society is unimprovable. What I am saying is that the problems of creating the Great Society are immensely greater than many of us were taught to believe and that we would have been better equipped to deal with them if we had understood their nature and difficulty better. To give up the task of reforming society is to give up one's responsibility as a free man. The task itself is endless, and large parts of it, sometimes the whole of it, must be performed anew by each succeeding generation.

Now, while life was teaching me these lessons, she was leading me in what would appear to be a quite contrary or at least contradictory direction. Here I must refer directly to my own local and particular situation as a white South African. While, on the one hand, I was discarding the romantic illusion about men and society, on the other I was beginning to rebel against the man-made barriers of race and color that divided man from man and to cherish a new ideal of society, which would be judged by some to be an illusion no less romantic than the one it was replacing.

When I first set out in this direction, the road was certainly unusual, whereas later it was to become dangerous, owing to the coming to power of a government which took to itself supra-legal powers enabling it to banish, silence, confine to small areas, debar from certain occupations and from attending any social or political gathering, any person who in the opinion of the Minister was "furthering the aims of Communism." Many non-Communists were dealt with in this way, without charge, trial, or sentence; some of these were my own fellow liberals, whose only offenses had been that they had ignored conventional race barriers or had been active in providing legal defense for political prisoners and aid for their dependents.

Whereas South Africa teaches many of its people to fear and to hate racial mixing (and I use the word "mixing" in its widest, not its narrowest sense), here it was teaching me the opposite, and teaching me to see our future as being that of one nonracial society and not a collection of strictly separated and individual race groups. The whole philosophy of apartheid is based on the fundamental assumption that there can be no such thing as a nonracial society, and that each individual realizes himself only through his membership in his own racial group, and that, therefore, it is the duty of the government to preserve these racial differences, in language, education, sex, marriage, sport, entertainment, and so on and so on. The apostle of apartheid would further declare that it is only another romantic illusion to imagine that an Afrikaner Calvinist, an English-speaking Anglican (Episcopalian), a colored (that is, of mixed blood) Roman Catholic, an African Methodist, an African ancestor-worshipper, an Indian Hindu, and an Indian Muslim—not to mention those who profess no particular faith—could operate a common nonracial society. The apostle of apartheid says he is a realist and that a person like myself is a sentimental idealist. But when this apostle is angry with me he would call me dangerous, and could, if he wished, restrict my freedom in the ways I have mentioned above.

He will, almost certainly in 1968, make it an offense to operate a nonracial (and multiracial) political party. One learns the lesson at first hand that the practice of the art of political persuasion can be made impossible by the state. One learns how the whole character of a people can be changed by a powerful state. Having Germany in mind, I do not say fundamentally changed; but even if the change is not fundamental, it is terrible enough.

Yet, in spite of all this one goes on believing in a nonracial unity that can transcend racial difference. This is something that one has come to believe through experience of personal relationships, and it may be that what is possible in personal relationships is not possible in society. There have been many examples in history where two individuals from mutually hostile groups have greatly loved one another.

Now, is it possible or is it not possible to realize in society what one has realized in personal relationships? I believe one cannot answer the question. All that one can say is that there is within one an impulse to try to realize it, that this impulse is an integral part of one's self, and that it must be obeyed, for to disobey it is to do damage to the integrity of one's self. And what is more, one has fortunately already learned the lesson that a failure, or a measure of failure, to realize some social or political aim can be compensated for to a tremendous degree by the depth and warmth of one's personal relationships.

What has life then taught me after all? She has taught me not to expect too much, though not in the sense of the cynical beatitude, "Blessed is he who expecteth nothing, for he shall not be disappointed." Life has not taught me to expect nothing, but she has taught me not to expect success to be the inevitable result of my endeavors. She has taught me to seek sustenance from the endeavor itself, but to leave the result to God. And the strange thing is that my parents taught me all this more than half a century ago. It is a lesson that—for me—had to be learned at least twice. When I learned it in my youth, it meant Sir Galahad and the Holy Grail. When I learned it in my age, it meant Christ and the road to Golgotha. And looking back upon it all, I would not wish it otherwise. Indeed, I cannot see how it could have been otherwise.

To try to be free of self-deception, to try to see with clear eyes oneself and others and the world, does not necessarily bring an undiluted kind of happiness. Yet it is something I would not exchange for any happiness built on any other foundation. There is only one way in which one can endure man's inhumanity to man and that is to try, in one's own life, to exemplify man's humanity to man. "Teach me, oh Lord, to seek not so much to be consoled as to console."

IDEAS

1. What, precisely, is "the romantic illusion" to which Paton refers?

2. George Orwell's *1984* pictures an imaginary totalitarian society. From Paton's remarks about values and self-interest, what would you say Paton sees as the center of Orwell's picture, even if you have not read the book?

3. What part does man's "inhumanity to other men" play in Paton's essay?

4. Explain Paton's point about fears and values.

5. How has Paton experienced the truth of John's saying that "perfect love casts out fear"?

6. What does Paton mean by racial mixing "in its widest, not its narrowest sense"?

7. Can you explain what Paton means by his contrast of Galahad and the Holy Grail with Christ and Golgotha? How does this change the picture of his "the endeavor itself"?

ORGANIZATION AND STYLE

1. Why does Paton devote so much space at the beginning to analyze man and society? How does this analysis work to set up his thesis?

2. Paton's sentences frequently develop his ideas by negatives. Look, for example, at: "Just how it happened that my understanding was so inadequate, I *don't* quite know." "I had *no* conception of the need of so much of mankind . . . to cling simultaneously to unself-centered religion and altruistic ethics." *"Not* only the Gospel, but history also should have taught me to know better." *"Not* even the World War of 1914. . . ." What is the effect of these sentences on his style? Why, do you suppose, did Paton select this style?

3. Throughout the essay, Paton makes certain points with comparisons or contrasts. What specific things does he compare or contrast? How do these miniature rhetorical units contribute to the whole of the essay?

4. Where do Paton's rhetorical questions move us from one thought to another? Are these rhetorical questions more effective than simple transitional words or phrases might have been?

5. With which paragraph does Paton begin his conclusion?

WRITING

1. Write an essay on a thesis something like "Alan Paton is right when he says . . . ," with most of your evidence your own parallel experiences of growing and learning.

2. Margaret Mead writes about anxiety (p. 77), and Alan Paton writes about fear. What common thread, if any, runs through their two essays? What differences? Which author offers the sanest advice for coping with your individual world?

The Eye of the Needle

ROBERT HEILBRONER

———————————— ● ————————————

Heilbroner sets up his first paragraph with what looks like a thesis: mankind has always been ambivalent about riches. This gives his essay an orderly shape. It also launches the inductive question about how we should evaluate our acquisitive drive. But here, in good deductive order, Heilbroner presents the historic evidence for our long suspicion, ending with: "All this by way of introduction." Now induction again flows in as Heilbroner unpeels the question layer by layer until we reach the nub, which turns out to be a whole change in our economics. Note his inductive questions, which lead us from layer to layer.

I have taken as my title a phrase that expresses a certain skepticism as to the rich man's chances of entering heaven,* and while I do not propose to settle the theological merits of that argument, the Eye of the Needle serves me in good stead as a point of reference. For I wish to discuss a well-known and yet little-discussed problem—a problem with which we are all familiar and which is yet somehow embarrassing to vent in public. It is the problem of the ambivalence of our feelings about wealth—the mixture of envy and disdain, admiration and disrepute with which riches have always been surrounded.

I do not know if I need to document this curious ambivalence, but a few shorthand references to the critique of wealth may serve to highlight the problem. We all know the age-old Biblical injunctions against wealth, "Woe unto

*Matthew xix:24: "And again I say unto you, It is easier for a camel to go through the eye of a needle, than for a rich man to enter into the kingdom of God."

you that are rich," says the Sermon on the Mount, "for ye have received your reward." All through the Bible from Deuteronomy to the New Testament runs the theme of a theological suspicion and rejection of wealth, for reasons that we will examine shortly. But the disdain for riches is not just a theological concern, dismissible as mere pietism. We hear a similar charge levied by nontheological writers whom we might call professional "students of human nature"—meaning by that phrase not alone the psychologists and psychiatrists of our generation, but the novelists, dramatists, and essayists of all generations. One has only to think of Shylock, or Père Grandet, or of Dickens's gallery of characters, or to turn to the pages of clinical journals to recognize a secular version of the theological warning that the pursuit of wealth, when carried too far, can warp the person and even destroy life.

All of us are familiar with and, as I have said, made faintly uncomfortable by such warnings. But there is a second and even more penetrating critique. This one also has its churchly setting, although its rationale is no longer theological but social. It is eloquently stated by Ambrose, the magnificent fourth-century bishop of Milan, who thundered: "Think you that you commit no injustice by keeping to yourself alone what would be the means of life to many? It is the bread of the hungry you cling to; it is the clothing of the naked you lock up; the money you bury is the redemption of the poor."

I need hardly dwell on the secular extension of this argument. Beginning with the earliest communistic experiments of the Church Fathers themselves, it bursts forth in the nineteenth and twentieth centuries as the central theme of socialism. For whatever the other purposes of socialism, the inner core of the socialist critique has always been simple. It has attacked the institutions of a society that has permitted the accumulation of private wealth, because it has identified wealth—as did Ambrose—with injustice.

Yet even this example does not yet fully underscore my initial point. Just as we can shrug off the theological indictment of wealth-seeking because it is, after all, "only" religious, so we can discount the socialist critique of the pursuit of wealth because it is socialist. But there is a last argument that gives us no such easy out. It lies, curiously, in the very discipline to which we resort when we come to the intellectual defense of wealth—economics. Economics is, of course, very polite in the face of the theological and socialist criticisms of acquisitiveness and the system that encourages it, but it has an answer we all know very well. "If you want a society to increase its output," says the economist, "then you must give the acquisitive drive its head. The profit motive may not represent man at his noblest, but it nonetheless serves society better than any other motive force."

We shall have to look into this defense more carefully, both as to its strengths and weaknesses. But at the start there is something to note that attests, from this unimpeachable source, as to the curiously mixed regard in which the accumulation of wealth is held. Having given their full blessing to the motivation of acquisitiveness, the economists now cunningly design an economic system that places every possible obstacle in the way of realizing that motivation in fact. For at least in the ideal economy envisioned in their textbooks, the economists proceed to hamper the accumulation of private wealth by insisting that the acquisitive drive be exercised only in an environment of pure competition, the purpose of which is to prevent "monopoly gains," and to temper the licit "competitive profits" to a point at which economists have to use a theoretical microscope to find them at all. Thus even the economic sanction of wealth-seeking turns out to be an implicit condemnation of wealth-getting. Indeed, in the extraordinary frustrations that it imposes, the economist's endorsement of acquisitiveness is like some eugenic enthusiast's plan for improving the race by the encouragement of uninhibited sexuality—a plan that was to be realized by such an arduous program of physical fitness that the successful participants would be much too exhausted to put their prowess to the test.

All this by way of introduction. The ambivalence of our regard for wealth, the ambiguity of our sanctions for wealth-gathering are evidently deeper-rooted than we like to admit. What is to be asked now is what we can say about the substance of the charges that have been brought. What do we know about the relation of wealth and personality? Of wealth and injustice?

Surprisingly little has been written about the complex phenomenon of the drive to amass wealth.[1] Yet it is clear that the activity of wealth-seeking has more than one root. At its base it would seem that men seek wealth because they must eat and clothe themselves and shelter their bodies from the elements, so that reduced to its fundamentals the drive for wealth becomes nothing but the social expression of the drive for self-preservation.

Yet, although it may be true as far as it goes, this is clearly an inadequate answer. For one of the commonest observations of social anthropologists is that people in poorer countries do not show the insatiable desire to improve their standards of living characteristic of people in so-called "advanced" countries. Homeostasis, not maximization, is the descriptive word for the attitude of the peasants of the world. The peasant may be avaricious, stingy, greedy; but in the sense in which it refers to a drive to enjoy an ever-larger income, he is not acquisitive.

No doubt it will be rejoined that he is not acquisitive because he cannot be. Precisely. The point is that the drive to amass wealth is a *social* manifestation, whatever its psychological basis. There are, of course, acquisitive types even in the poorest nations. But to find the acquisitive orientation as the normal mode of *behavior* we have to turn to the developed economies, and particularly to those with highly developed market systems.

Why do men behave acquisitively in market systems? In part, because they have to. At every level of society we are taught and trained to try to "make money"—and the

[1]The single most comprehensive article is still, to my knowledge, Otto Fenichel, "The Drive to Amass Wealth," *Psychoanalytic Quarterly,* VI (January 1938). [Heilbroner's note]

environment reinforces these lessons with severe punishments if we ignore or forget that we live in a world where each man is for himself and devil take the hindmost.

Yet here we come full circle. There is certainly an element of self-preservation that motivates the actors in a market system, but it does not explain their actions fully. For just as the peasants of the world fail to display much of an acquisitive behavior pattern, so the normal participant in the developed economies goes far beyond the requirements imposed by sheer need. Indeed, it is a typical observation that the more we have, the more we want—that the more successful we are at making money, the more whetted, not satiated, becomes our appetite.

Thus, if there is an inextricable social element in acquisitiveness, there is also an indissoluble psychological element as well. What do we know about it? No one has described it better than William James in his *Principles of Psychology* in 1890:

> It is clear that between what a man calls me and what he simply calls *mine,* the line is very difficult to draw. We feel and act about certain things that are ours very much as we feel and act about ourselves. . . . In its widest possible sense, a man's Self is the sum total of all that he can call his, not only his body and his psychic powers, but his clothes and his house, his wife and his children, his ancestors and his friends, his reputation and his works, his land and horses and yacht and bank account. If they wax and prosper, he feels triumphant, if they dwindle and die away, he feels cast down—not necessarily in the same degree for each thing, but in much the same way for all.[2]

There is more than psychology that is interesting in James's statement, as we shall see later. But James has made very clear the basic psychological mechanism at work in all acquisitive processes. Acquisitiveness is a means of fortifying and enlarging the Self by projecting it into objects that will expand in social value. In a peasant's

[2]William James, *Principles of Psychology* (New York: Holt, Rinehart and Winston, 1890), pp. 291–292. [Heilbroner's note].

world this may be his children, which are all he has. In a market world it is apt to be money.

There is no doubt that students of human nature have known about this projective capability long before James's time; Plato wrote about "the makers of fortunes [who] have a second love of money as a creation of their own, resembling the love of authors for their own poems, or of parents for their children." Contemporary psychoanalysis brings some additional enlightenment to the problem, however. It has discovered for us the persistence of the child encapsulated in the adult, and has taught us to look for infantile meanings and origins and symbols in acts that we would otherwise judge solely in adult terms. Thus, modern psychology emphasizes the ease with which the accumulation of wealth becomes the vehicle for the expression of childhood needs and longings, whether for love or security or for other primitive satisfactions. Behind the voracious acquisitor we now see not a wicked adult, but a hungry and importunate child.

This symbolic aspect of acquisitiveness helps explain more fully the dangers that the theologian and the student of human nature have both sensed in the wealth-oriented individual. The typical obsessive-compulsive attributes of the money-oriented character, with its social blindness and its self-destructiveness, can now be seen, not in moralistic terms, but as symptoms of a personality that has not overcome its infantile demands and which therefore pursues external goals with a childish selfishness or with a near-autistic intensity. In the same way, psychoanalytic insight helps explain our own ambivalent feelings toward acquisitiveness. It is not only the rich man's money that we envy, but the uncurbed expression of his infantile megalomania, the memory of which can be roused in everyone. And it is not only the moral meaning of his acquisitive acts that we reject, but his right to unleash an infantile trait that we have painfully mastered.

There is, I suspect, not too much objection to this psychiatric commentary on an ancient antipathy. Certainly the contemporary businessman looks with as much distaste as any churchman on the more pathological expressions of the acquisitive drive. He is even prepared to admit that an ordinary degree of acquisitiveness exacts its psychological price—that the drive to make money, even when it does not reach grotesque limits, brings out an unlovely side of human nature.

Yet this general line of criticism against the quest for wealth does not deeply trouble him. More and more, he would maintain, businessmen are interested in the creative or administrative aspects of business rather than in sheer money-making—indeed, the waning of the very competitive discipline that the economists prescribe has permitted a much more relaxed and unacquisitive style of business. And then, perhaps even more important, the businessman is prepared to defend the psychological cost of acquisitiveness as a lesser burden for society than the costs of some alternative driving motivation. Although it may seem like the Devil quoting Scripture, the businessman could call on John Maynard Keynes to confirm his view:

> Dangerous human proclivities can be canalised into comparatively harmless channels by the existence of opportunities for money-making and private wealth, which, if they cannot be satisfied in this way, may find their outlet in cruelty, the reckless pursuit of personal power and authority, and other forms of self-aggrandizement. It is better that a man should tyrannise over his bank balance than over his fellow-citizen; and whilst the former is sometimes denounced as but a means to the latter, sometimes at least it is an alternative.[3]

Finally the defender of the acquisitive motivation sets a last string to his bow. He points out that neither clergyman nor social critic nor economist objects to the effort to gain wealth when it is exercised by the poor. The "honest workingman" seeking a rise in pay, the underdeveloped coun-

[3] John Maynard Keynes, *The General Theory of Employment, Interest, and Money* (New York: Harcourt Brace Jovanovich, 1936), p. 374. [Heilbroner's note]

try trying to increase its gross national product, do not incur the opprobrium of the critics of the acquisitive drive. It is only after some indefinitely located middle ground has been crossed that the criticism begins. But this leads to hypocritical results, says the businessman. Why is an attitude that is encouraged in the poor man or the poor nation to be condemned in the rich? Is not the critic of the quest for wealth logically bound to urge an asceticism on poor as well as rich, or else to recommend acquisitiveness for the rich as well as for the poor?

The defense is well taken. There *have* been those who have urged a universal abnegation of riches—Christ was one—and there are those who have taken the opposite tack and glorified acquisitiveness as the universal standard—I think of Ayn Rand. But I think it is fair to state that neither view, however logically consistent, has commanded much general respect. Whether it is psychologically in their best interests or not, we *do* commend the effort to gain wealth on the part of the poor; and whether it is morally or logically consistent or not, we *do* look with reservations on the same drive on the part of the rich.

How can this be? The very illogicality of the psychological argument gives us the key. It is that we see the acquisitive drive not only as a personal activity to be judged by its inner consequences, but as an activity inextricably mixed into the social world where it is to be judged as part of the whole scheme of social relationships. And here the ambivalence of our view about the same drive in the rich and the poor reveals a feeling that is deeply imbedded within us. It is the reverberatory echo of Bishop Ambrose's accusation, the lingering conviction that the juxtaposition of rich and poor, whether men or nations, is a condition that is fundamentally unjust. From there it follows that every step that widens the gap between rich and poor—that is, every act of the rich to grow richer—worsens a condition that is already profoundly wrong.

There is no accusation that so deeply offends the businessman as this one. He will accept the charge that he may be ruining his character by running after money, just as we all accept the risk that we may be ruining our health by smoking. But tell the businessman that in pursuing wealth he is undertaking an activity that is in itself unjust and he will rise up in righteous indignation.

Furthermore, he makes a very plausible case for his anger. Far from grinding the faces of the poor, he insists, the wealth-seeker is releasing the force that will ultimately free the poor from their poverty. For if the great escape from poverty is to be made, it will surely require the massive accumulation of capital, and the most effective way of amassing that capital, he will tell you, is through the activities of individual private accumulators, each striving for his own enrichment.

Moreover, says the businessman, the process of amassing private wealth in a dynamic economy is basically different from that in a static one, such as that described in the Bible. In the latter situation, one man's riches were very likely squeezed from another's poverty, through consumption loans or onerous rents. Indeed, the businessman will gladly admit that poverty is the other side of riches in any society where the sum total of the social product remains the same. But once the terrible stasis of underdevelopment is broken and a process of economic increase is inaugurated, we leave behind the situation of "I win—you lose." In the expanding economy of the wealth-driven society it is possible for rich and poor to gain together, and indeed for the poor to gain more rapidly than the rich.

Finally the defense goes further still. Not only is the drive for wealth justifiable as the necessary means to the abolition of poverty, but the system that promotes the individual search for wealth also provides an invaluable framework for the achievement of other no less desired goals, high among them social mobility and political liberty. The market system, in other words, not only gives us economic efficiency, but by virtue of its self-regulating, unsupervised operation, it sets the stage for other kinds of freedoms. Indeed, these freedoms can be asserted to depend not only on a market system but on the careful restriction of firms to a single goal of money-making and on their exclusion from noneconomic activities. As one staunch defender of the acquisitive society has written, "Few trends would so thoroughly undermine the very foundations of our free society as the acceptance by corporate officials of a social responsibility other than to make as much money for their stockholders as they possibly can."[4]

Like the tempered defense of the acquisitive drive, the worldly defense of the acquisitive society is impressive. I think a valid case *can* be made for the usefulness of the money-making system as an instrument for social accumulation, at least in certain stages of history and in certain social settings. Unquestionably it did the trick for the West. I think as well that the acquisitive drive in an expanding economy does lead to results different from those in a static, zero-sum world, and that in the capitalist market systems the poor have grown richer, together with and faster than the rich, predictions of Karl Marx to the contrary notwithstanding. And whereas I believe that the equation of economic freedom and political freedom is a vast oversimplification of a very complex problem, I am even prepared to concede that there is a certain protective value for personal freedom in the refuge provided by a market system for those who do not wish to join the approved institutions of society in order to make their livings.

Yet however reasonable, indeed however true, these counterarguments, I do not think they quite come to grips with the problem that wealth and wealth-seeking stubbornly impose. After all the doubts associated with the pursuit of wealth have been smoothed away, the canker of unease remains. There is something about the acquisitive drive, and perhaps even more important, something about the nature of the system erected on the foundation of that

[4]Milton Friedman, *Capitalism and Freedom* (Chicago: University of Chicago Press, 1962), p. 133. [Heilbroner's note]

drive, that continues to trouble us. In the remainder of this essay, let me try to voice what these lingering and recalcitrant problems are.

One problem is relatively simple to diagnose. It is a peculiar moral opacity that afflicts a society that is dependent on the continuous exercise of the acquisitive propensity as the very precondition for its economic cohesion.

It is certainly not difficult to find examples of this opacity at work. The Market System, as every student of economics knows, is essentially a rationing mechanism, an institution for the efficient distribution of scarce resources among claimants. By virtue of its self-enforcing dynamics, its speed and clarity of operation, its usefulness in solving the difficult tasks of production and distribution, it has proved indispensable for complex industrial economic systems. Nonetheless, *the market mechanism solves its tasks efficiently just because it applies to the varied and tangled needs of a human community one and only one criterion—the criterion of wealth.* Those who have the requisite wealth may, if they wish, exercise their claims on the resources to be divided. Those who do not, may not.

I have already admitted that the market mechanism, operating under the crude but efficient calculus of wealth, brings many advantages in its wake. Nonetheless, with each cut of its blade, it imposes a rule of allocation that is utterly without considerations of a noneconomic kind. Wants, needs, just deserts or ill-gotten gains play no part in the market's distribution of goods. Thus the acquisitive society is one that caters to every whim of the rich but that ignores the elemental requirements of the poor.

But the issue posed by this enthronement of the market principle is not that it calls its particular solution to the rationing problem "just." It is that it submerges *all* considerations of justice under the cloak of economic calculus. I have often remarked on this in connection with the reconstruction of Park Avenue in New York City. In the twenty-five years since the war, a row of apartment houses from 46th Street to 59th Street, formerly the undistinguished-looking buildings in which the rich lived, have been torn down and replaced by the very distinguished-looking buildings in which the rich work. There has been considerable comment on the architectural achievements and failures of this multi-hundred-million-dollar transformation. Yet, so far as I know, not a single voice has pointed out a grotesque failure, an unbelievable misallocation, that occurred here. *The buildings were built in the wrong place.* As every citizen of New York knows, the crying need for the steel and glass, concrete and brick, that went into Park Avenue from 46th to 59th streets was fifty blocks up that avenue where Harlem begins in all its overcrowded misery.

Now, had the Gosplanners* in Russia committed a similar mistake—had they squandered the scarce resources of steel and concrete on fancy offices for themselves while the majority of Moscow slept four to a room—one can picture the satisfaction with which we would have pointed out the moral turpitude of the Soviets. But in our own case, the exact self-same misallocation was removed entirely from the realm of moral considerations by the overriding calculus of the market.

Or take another case, that of advertising. There is much hue and cry as to the aesthetics of advertising. But the fuss over the raucous quality of commercials misses the moral point. It is that advertising represents an effort on the part of some individuals to persuade other individuals—quite without any knowledge of their circumstances, desires, or problems—to take certain actions in life, i.e., to acquire certain possessions or to expend their wealth in certain ways. Were this outrageous intrusion into private life taken for any other purpose, it would be regarded as intolerable. But under the obscuring shadow of the economic

---

*Bureaucrats responsible for devising and executing long-term economic and social policies.

calculus we do not consider what violations we perform on the human being when we reduce him to the unidimensionality of a "consumer."

I do not think I need labor the point. The injustice of a market society is not that of the rich abusing the poor or snatching bread from their mouths. It is rather the peculiar screening effect that economic considerations cast over life, causing us to act in ways or acquiesce in actions that, were they not justified by the money-making principle, would be judged out of hand as wrong.

This is one source, I believe, of the uneasiness that afflicts an acquisitive society. But there is another, also passed over silently in the usual cogent defenses of the usefulness of the acquisitive drive. It concerns the historic relevance of the social system that emerges as a result of that drive.

Here again I refer to William James's explication of the possessive Self. What James fails to note—and his failure is itself revealing of the preconceptions of an acquisitive society—are the different meanings in the word "his" with which he illustrates a man's projective propensities. When James speaks of the relationship between a person and "his" body, or "his" wife, or "his" land and horses, yacht and bank account, he is confusing physical, social, and legal meanings of the possessive pronoun. No doubt there is a certain universality in the projection of our psyches into the physical and familiar world. But as we have already noted, its projection into *economic property* is not a psychological but a social phenomenon. The ability or the permission to accumulate material wealth (in which one may therefore vest one's psyche) is not found in all societies. The acquisitive society is not therefore the inevitable embodiment of an imperious psychological drive, but a historical social structure in which that drive is allowed or encouraged to vent itself in the accumulation of economic goods and resources.

Thus the acquisitive manifestation cannot be considered without reference to the entire social structure that has been built upon it and around it—a structure that entails not alone the freedom of acquisitive action on the marketplace, but the extension of acquisitive action to the personal "ownership" of vast assemblages of productive assets. In a word, we cannot appraise the acquisitive drive unless we take into account the entire system of private ownership of the means of production that we call capitalism.

To render a judgment on capitalism is far too complex a task to be attempted here. But I think all would agree where its strengths lie. Indeed, we have already enumerated them. Above all, capitalism is justified by the enormous powers of production that it generates. There are of course other strengths, including the economic freedom it permits, and there are as well flaws—some of them having to do with the moral opacity I have just discussed; others, of perhaps greater functional seriousness, related to the dangers of fortresses of private economic power, or of property-oriented ideologies. Yet, to the extent that these flaws are excused or excusable, it is always by reference to the overriding consideration of capitalism as an unsurpassed engine of production. *As economists and social philosophers from Marx to the most conservative have always agreed, the historic task of capitalism is to produce.*

But what if production is no longer the central historic requirement? What if the technological virtuosity of the capitalist nations has now reached the point at which satiety and superfluity rather than scarcity are the impending problems? Let us bear in mind the trajectory of our present economic growth. It has been calculated that if the rate of real output per capita continues to increase by two percent a year, as it has since the mid-nineteenth century, our average family income (in terms of today's purchasing power) by the end of the century will be almost $15,000. Twenty-five years later it will have grown to over $30,000. A century ahead—say, at the time when our great-grandchildren go to work—it will have reached a level of well over $100,000 per family.

I do not offer these mechanical calculations as indicating anything more than the general orders of magnitude as to what is technologically possible. But it is important to consider what such a prospect offers by way of affecting the historic relevance of an acquisitive society. If there is one thing that is unmistakably implicit in the vista of impending affluence, it is the increasing pointlessness of an economic system whose main claim to historic worth has been its ability to produce.

To be sure, the world may still be poor a century hence, so that our huge productive powers could be put to good use. The question then is whether an equitable and efficient distribution of wealth from rich nations to poorer ones will be made under the aegis of a society that still abides by the calculus of wealth, or whether it will not require the emergence of new pillars of social belief and new directions of social motivation more closely attuned to the problems of an age of the administration, rather than the acquisition, of wealth.

The attainment of that age lies still in the future, although not so far as to be merely a vision at the horizon. Already the first embarrassments of an age of partial abundance are upon us, and already its arrival challenges the paraphernalia of capitalism to the very core. The economic agencies, the class privileges, the social conceptions of a society whose main purpose has been the accumulation of wealth are put to the test in an age that begins to seek the private realizations and the public attainments that are only possible in—but that go counter to the grain of—a society of wealth.*

Beyond that, the social usefulness of the underlying drive itself begins to wane in a society in which the advance and mastery of a gigantic technology will clearly be the first order of business. Acquisitiveness, not as a psychological propensity but as a social form of activity, thus begins to display its historic irrelevancy, just as the new

---

*Since writing this essay, the ecological crisis has challenged the acquisitive drive of capitalism from another quarter [on which Heilbroner elaborates in a later chapter].

drives of scientific and technical discovery and administration begin to assert their historic paramountcy. If the rich man—or better yet, the rich society—finally wins admission to heaven, I suspect it will be not because capitalists have pure hearts, but because scientists will have succeeded in breeding exceptionally thin and agile camels, and because technology has succeeded in making needles with very large and very wide eyes.

IDEAS

1. Heilbroner's title is a biblical reference, and his essay is filled with biblical quotations and allusions. How effective are these? Do they limit the impact of the essay in any way?

2. How does James lessen the guilt of acquisitiveness? How does the modern psychologist?

3. What is Keynes's justification? The businessman's? The social justification?

4. Do you agree with the statement that wealth is a social manifestation?

5. Heilbroner admits that some people "have urged a universal abnegation of riches," and he gives Christ as an example. What modern examples can you think of? What, instead of wealth and ownership, makes these people happy?

6. Can you describe in your own terms and from your own experience what the author means by the moral opacity that inflicts an acquisitive society?

ORGANIZATION AND STYLE

1. What exactly has Heilbroner accomplished up to the paragraph beginning "All this by way of introduction"? What is the function of the series of questions with which that paragraph ends?

2. How would you describe the author's expository tactic when he says, "In the remainder of this essay, let me try. . . ."?

3. Heilbroner writes, "Finally the defender of the acquisitive motivation sets a last string to his bow." What is meant by this metaphor? Where else does the author make a point with metaphor?

4. Examine the large number of paragraphs beginning "There is. . . ." Are these beginnings stylistically effective? Do the several of them, scattered throughout the essay, form a kind of rhetorical unit?

5. Carefully examine the final sentence. What are its stylistic parts? How do they fit together? How do they effectively summarize Heilbroner's thesis?

WRITING

1. Write an essay illustrating and supporting or attacking something Heilbroner says about the acquisitive drive from your own experience or observation, how it makes for those unheavenly drives or opacities concerning injustice and other harmful behavior, or how it accents the positive in one's self-esteem and effectiveness as a member of society. Consider some satisfactions you have known from a job and competitive success, or from selfless work in social service.

2. Select someone you know to be very happy or very unhappy. To what extent are wealth (or its absence) and possessions (or their absence) a part of the formula? Develop an essay in which you attempt to analyze what makes this person so happy or so unhappy. Examine the various layers of experience, constantly coming back, for reinforcement, to the role played by wealth and possessions.

6

SENTENCES: THE
RHYTHM OF THOUGHT

As we grasp a writer's central idea, and follow, or disagree with, its development, moving through the structure of his display, we also respond to his style, his language. We sense a rhythm in his thinking. We recognize a personality moving distinctively sentence by sentence, from short, hard declarations to long and longer expanses, perhaps brought short again with a snap. Each writer or personality, however capable of variety, will favor one kind of sentence. Some writers are *paratactic,* favoring sentences all on the same level; others are *hypotactic,* with many sentence-ideas tucked under a dominant one as supporting clauses and phrases. The paratactic writer favors simple sentences and *coordination;* the hypotactic writer, *subordination* and *parallelism.*

I. COORDINATION

Here we find straightforward statements, all in a row, either separately, in short sentences, or joined together by semicolons or conjunctions such as *and* or *but*.

> All men are beasts. They feed, couple, sleep, and die; they satisfy only themselves. But they have souls too, and these can move them to greatness.

The quality here is forcefulness, like a hammer on an anvil. This mode frequently produces the short epigrammatic sentence: "Writing makes thought visible."

II. SUBORDINATION

Here you attach a number of statements to one principal statement, putting them in a "sub" order to it, tying them in with prepositions, relative pronouns, adverbs, or any other subordinating word—*with, in, who, which, when, after.*

> Man of today, the atomic manipulator, the aeronaut who flies faster than sound, has precisely the same brain and body as his ancestors of twenty thousand years ago who painted the last Ice Age mammoths on the walls of caves in France.*

The main statement is *Man has the same brain and body;* all the rest is *subordinate* to it.

III. PARALLELISM

You put parallel thoughts in parallel constructions. Witness the following example of introductory phrases in parallel:

*Loren Eiseley, "The Real Secret of Piltdown," *The Immense Journey* (New York: Random House, 1955).

Having studied hard,
having gone to bed early,
having reviewed the main points in the morning,
    she still wrote a poor exam.

Or you may use paralleling coordinators such as *either/or,*
not only/but also, first/second/third.

> He is *either* an absolute piker *or* a fool.
> This is true *not only* of the young voters *but also* of their
> parents.

All in all, the richest style is one that can move among
these three modes to vary the short and emphatic sentence
against the long and interestingly subordinated one.

    The essayists in this group nicely bring the sentence to
our attention—Canby, specifically, as he writes about Thoreau's sentence-making. Thoreau seems to have had an
essentially paratactic mind, one prone to short and pithy
statement. But his thoughts also swell in remarkable
subordinations and parallels and afterthoughts, producing a prose rich in meditative rhythms of short and long
and longer sentences, frequently brought short and pungent again. White, like Canby an admirer of Thoreau,
seems also to have a paratactic bent, more relaxed and
chatty than Thoreau's, with many *ands* keeping his sen-
tence-thoughts flowing along at the same level. But he, too,
is a master of subordination and parallel and rhythmic
variation. As you read these three writers, notice the contrasts of short and long. You may absorb some of their
variations into your own verbal rhythms.

Where I Lived, and What I Lived For

HENRY DAVID THOREAU

—————————— ● ——————————

In this chapter from Walden, *Thoreau explains his wish to discover and experience the essentials of life, which the routine rounds of existence always seem to carpet with comfortable trivialities or wearisome and unnecessary labors. He is the world's most famous dropout, as he tries to drop in on the vital center of being. Do you see what he means? Does he reflect impulses of your own? To enjoy his meaty power over words, underline his puns and metaphors. Note the imaginative punster at work in his opening passage as he plays with the* idea *of buying a farm, with the fact that one really possesses a thing only in one's consciousness and imagination.* Season *takes on a strong agricultural climate;* survey *means both to look over and to measure;* price *means a cost not only financial but also spiritual. Can you unravel the punning dynamics of* deed?

At a certain season of our life we are accustomed to consider every spot as the possible site of a house. I have thus surveyed the country on every side within a dozen miles of where I live. In imagination I have bought all the farms in succession, for all were to be bought, and I knew their price. I walked over each farmer's premises, tasted his wild apples, discoursed on husbandry with him, took his farm at his price, at any price, mortgaging it to him in my mind; even put a higher price on it,—took every thing but a deed of it,—took his word for his deed, for I dearly love to talk,—cultivated it, and him too to some extent, I trust, and withdrew when I had enjoyed it long enough, leaving

him to carry it on. This experience entitled me to be regarded as a sort of real-estate broker by my friends. Wherever I sat, there I might live, and the landscape radiated
from me accordingly. What is a house but a *sedes,* a seat?—
better if a country seat. I discovered many a site for a
house not likely to be soon improved, which some might
have thought too far from the village, but to my eyes the
village was too far from it. Well, there I might live, I said;
and there I did live, for an hour, a summer and a winter
life; saw how I could let the years run off, buffet the winter
through, and see the spring come in. The future inhabitants of this region, wherever they may place their houses,
may be sure that they have been anticipated. An afternoon
sufficed to lay out the land into orchard, woodlot, and pasture, and to decide what fine oaks or pines should be left
to stand before the door, and whence each blasted tree
could be seen to the best advantage; and then I let it lie,
fallow perchance, for a man is rich in proportion to the
number of things which he can afford to let alone.

My imagination carried me so far that I even had the
refusal of several farms,—the refusal was all I wanted,—
but I never got my fingers burned by actual possession.
The nearest that I came to actual possession was when I
bought the Hollowell place, and had begun to sort my
seeds, and collected materials with which to make a
wheelbarrow to carry it on or off with; but before the
owner gave me a deed of it, his wife—every man has such
a wife—changed her mind and wished to keep it, and he
offered me ten dollars to release him. Now, to speak the
truth, I had but ten cents in the world, and it surpassed my
arithmetic to tell, if I was that man who had ten cents, or
who had a farm, or ten dollars, or all together. However,
I let him keep the ten dollars and the farm too, for I had
carried it far enough; or rather, to be generous, I sold him
the farm for just what I gave for it, and, as he was not a
rich man, made him a present of ten dollars, and still had
my ten cents, and seeds, and materials for a wheelbarrow
left. I found thus that I had been a rich man without any

damage to my poverty. But I retained the landscape, and I have since annually carried off what it yielded without a wheelbarrow. With respect to landscapes,—

I am monarch of all I survey,
*My right there is none to dispute.**

I have frequently seen a poet withdraw, having enjoyed the most valuable part of a farm, while the crusty farmer supposed that he had got a few wild apples only. Why, the owner does not know it for many years when a poet has put his farm in rhyme, the most admirable kind of invisible fence, has fairly impounded it, milked it, skimmed it, and got all the cream, and left the farmer only the skimmed milk.

The real attractions of the Hollowell farm, to me, were: its complete retirement, being about two miles from the village, half a mile from the nearest neighbor, and separated from the highway by a broad field; its bounding on the river, which the owner said protected it by its fogs from frosts in the spring, though that was nothing to me; the gray color and ruinous state of the house and barn, and the dilapidated fences, which put such an interval between me and the last occupant; the hollow and lichen-covered apple trees, gnawed by rabbits, showing what kind of neighbors I should have; but above all, the recollection I had of it from my earliest voyages up the river, when the house was concealed behind a dense grove of red maples, through which I heard the house-dog bark. I was in haste to buy it, before the proprietor finished getting out some rocks, cutting down the hollow apple trees, and grubbing up some young birches which had sprung up in the pasture, or, in short, had made any more of his improvements. To enjoy these advantages I was ready to carry it on; like Atlas, to take the world on my shoulders,—I never

*The opening lines of "Verses Supposed to be Written by Alexander Selkirk During His Solitary Abode in the Island of Juan Fernandez" (1782), by William Cowper (1731–1800). Selkirk (1676–1721) had been the model for Daniel Defoe's Robinson Crusoe (1719).

heard what compensation he received for that,—and do all those things which had no other motive or excuse but that I might pay for it and be unmolested in my possession of it; for I knew all the while that it would yield the most abundant crop of the kind I wanted if I could only afford to let it alone. But it turned out as I have said.

All that I could say, then, with respect to farming on a large scale (I have always cultivated a garden) was, that I had had my seeds ready. Many think that seeds improve with age. I have no doubt that time discriminates between the good and the bad; and when at last I shall plant, I shall be less likely to be disappointed. But I would say to my fellows, once for all, As long as possible live free and uncommitted. It makes but little difference whether you are committed to a farm or the county jail.

Old Cato,* whose "De Re Rustica" is my "Cultivator," says,—and the only translation I have seen makes sheer nonsense of the passage,—"When you think of getting a farm, turn it thus in your mind, not to buy greedily; nor spare your pains to look at it, and do not think it enough to go round it once. The oftener you go there the more it will please you, if it is good." I think I shall not buy greedily, but go round and round it as long as I live, and be buried in it first, that it may please me the more at last.

The present was my next experiment of this kind, which I propose to describe more at length, for convenience, putting the experience of two years into one. As I have said, I do not propose to write an ode to dejection, but to brag as lustily as chanticleer in the morning, standing on his roost, if only to wake my neighbors up.

When first I took up my abode in the woods, that is, began to spend my nights as well as days there, which, by accident, was on Independence day, or the fourth of July, 1845, my house was not finished for winter, but was merely a defense against the rain, without plastering or chimney, the walls being of rough, weather-stained boards, with

*Marcus Porcius Cato (234–149 B.C.), Roman soldier and statesman, who worked for the reform of Roman institutions. He farmed between military campaigns, or when resting from his many public commissions.

wide chinks, which made it cool at night. The upright white hewn studs and freshly planed door and window casings gave it a clean and airy look, especially in the morning, when its timbers were saturated with dew, so that I fancied that by noon some sweet gum would exude from them. To my imagination it retained throughout the day more or less of this auroral character, reminding me of a certain house on a mountain which I had visited the year before. This was an airy and unplastered cabin, fit to entertain a travelling god, and where a goddess might trail her garments. The winds which passed over my dwelling were such as sweep over the ridges of mountains, bearing the broken strains, or celestial parts only, of terrestrial music.*The morning wind forever blows, the poem of creation is uninterrupted; but few are the ears that hear it. Olympus* is but the outside of the earth everywhere.

The only house I had been the owner of before, if I except a boat, was a tent, which I used occasionally when making excursions in the summer, and this is still rolled up in my garret; but the boat, after passing from hand to hand, has gone down the stream of time. With this more substantial shelter about me, I had made some progress toward settling in the world. This frame, so slightly clad, was a sort of crystallization around me, and reacted on the builder. It was suggestive somewhat as a picture in outlines. I did not need to go out-doors to take the air, for the atmosphere within had lost none of its freshness. It was not so much within-doors as behind a door where I sat, even in the rainiest weather. The Harivamsa says, "An abode without birds is like a meat without seasoning."† Such was not my abode, for I found myself suddenly neighbor to the birds; not by having imprisoned one, but having caged myself near them. I was not only nearer to

*Mount Olympus, in Greece, revered in ancient times as the "abode of the gods."

†The *Harivaṁśa* ("Geneology of Hari," the Hindu god Vishnu), a Sanskrit epic (fifth century A.D.) dealing chiefly with the deeds of Krishna (whose name means "black"), the eighth avatar, or earthly incarnation, of Vishnu.

some of those which commonly frequent the garden and the orchard, but to those wilder and more thrilling song-sters of the forest which never, or rarely, serenade a vil-lager,—the wood-thrush, the veery, the scarlet tanager, the field-sparrow, the whippoorwill, and many others.

I was seated by the shore of a small pond, about a mile and a half south of the village of Concord and somewhat higher than it, in the midst of an extensive wood between that town and Lincoln, and about two miles south of that our only field known to fame, Concord Battle Ground; but I was so low in the woods that the opposite shore, half a mile off, like the rest, covered with wood, was my most distant horizon. For the first week, whenever I looked out on the pond it impressed me like a tarn high up on the side of a mountain, its bottom far above the surface of other lakes, and, as the sun arose, I saw it throwing off its nightly clothing of mist, and here and there, by degrees, its soft ripples or its smooth reflecting surface was revealed, while the mists, like ghosts, were stealthily withdrawing in every direction into the woods, as at the breaking up of some nocturnal conventicle. The very dew seemed to hang upon the trees later into the day than usual, as on the sides of mountains.

This small lake was of most value as a neighbor in the intervals of a gentle rain storm in August, when, both air and water being perfectly still, but the sky overcast, mid-afternoon had all the serenity of evening, and the wood-thrush sang around, and was heard from shore to shore. A lake like this is never smoother than at such a time; and the clear portion of the air above it being shallow and darkened by clouds, the water, full of light and reflections, becomes a lower heaven itself so much the more impor-tant. From a hill top near by, where the wood had been recently cut off, there was a pleasing vista southward across the pond, through a wide indentation in the hills which form the shore there, where their opposite sides sloping toward each other suggested a stream flowing out in that direction through a wooded valley, but stream there was none. That way I looked between and over the near green hills to some distant and higher ones in the horizon, tinged with blue. Indeed, by standing on tiptoe I could catch a glimpse of some of the peaks of the still bluer and more distant mountain ranges in the north-west, those true-blue coins from heaven's own mint, and also of some portion of the village. But in other directions, even from this point, I could not see over or beyond the woods which surrounded me. It is well to have some water in your neighborhood, to give buoyancy to and float the earth. One value even of the smallest well is, that when you look into it you see that earth is not continent but insular. This is as important as that it keeps butter cool. When I looked across the pond from this peak toward the Sudbury meadows, which in time of flood I distinguished elevated perhaps by a mirage in their seething valley, like a coin in a basin, all the earth beyond the pond appeared like a thin crust insulated and floated even by this small sheet of intervening water, and I was reminded that this on which I dwelt was but *dry land.*

Though the view from my door was still more contracted, I did not feel crowded or confined in the least. There was pasture enough for my imagination. The low shrub-oak plateau to which the opposite shore arose, stretched away toward the prairies of the West and the steppes of Tartary, affording ample room for all the roving families of men. "There are none happy in the world but beings who enjoy freely a vast horizon,"—said Damodara, when his herds required new and larger pastures.*

Both place and time were changed, and I dwelt nearer to those parts of the universe and to those eras in history which had most attracted me. Where I lived was as far off as many a region viewed nightly by astronomers. We are wont to imagine rare and delectable places in some remote and more celestial corner of the system, behind the constellation of Cassiopeia's Chair, far from noise and disturbance. I discovered that my house actually had its site in

---

*Also from the *Harivaṁśa,* which Thoreau has quoted three paragraphs earlier. "Damadora" is one of Krishna's many names in the poem.

such a withdrawn, but forever new and unprofaned, part of the universe. If it were worth the while to settle in those parts near to the Pleiades or the Hyades, to Aldebaran or Altair, then I was really there, or at an equal remoteness from the life which I had left behind, dwindled and twinkling with as fine a ray to my nearest neighbor, and to be seen only in moonless nights by him. Such was that part of creation where I had squatted;—

> *There was a shepherd that did live,*
> *And held his thoughts as high*
> *As were the mounts whereon his flocks*
> *Did hourly feed him by.*

What should we think of the shepherd's life if his flocks always wandered to higher pastures than his thoughts?

Every morning was a cheerful invitation to make my life of equal simplicity, and I may say innocence, with Nature herself. I have been as sincere a worshiper of Aurora as the Greeks. I got up early and bathed in the pond; that was a religious exercise, and one of the best things which I did. They say that characters were engraven on the bathing tub of king Tching-thang to this effect: "Renew thyself completely each day; do it again, and again, and forever again." I can understand that. Morning brings back the heroic ages. I was as much affected by the faint hum of a mosquito making its invisible and unimaginable tour through my apartment at earliest dawn, when I was sitting with door and windows open, as I could be by any trumpet that ever sang of fame. It was Homer's requiem; itself an Iliad and Odyssey in the air, singing its own wrath and wanderings. There was something cosmical about it; a standing advertisement, till forbidden, of the everlasting vigor and fertility of the world. The morning, which is the most memorable season of the day, is the awakening hour. Then there is least somnolence in us; and for an hour, at least, some part of us awakes which slumbers all the rest of the day and night. Little is to be expected of that day, if it can be called a day, to which we are

not awakened by our Genius, but by the mechanical nudg-
ings of some servitor, are not awakened by our newly-
acquired force and aspirations from within, accompanied
by the undulations of celestial music, instead of factory
bells, and a fragrance filling the air—to a higher life than
we fell asleep from; and thus the darkness bear its fruit,
and prove itself to be good, no less than the light. That man
who does not believe that each day contains an earlier,
more sacred, and auroral hour than he has yet profaned,
has despaired of life, and is pursuing a descending and
darkening way. After a partial cessation of his sensuous
life, the soul of man, or its organs rather, are reinvigorated
each day, and his Genius tries again what noble life it can
make. All memorable events, I should say, transpire in
morning time and in a morning atmosphere. The Vedas
say, "All intelligences awake with the morning." Poetry
and art, and the fairest and most memorable of the actions
of men, date from such an hour. All poets and heroes, like
Memnon, are the children of Aurora, and emit their music
at sunrise. To him whose elastic and vigorous thought
keeps pace with the sun, the day is a perpetual morning.
It matters not what the clocks say or the attitudes and
labors of men. Morning is when I am awake and there is
a dawn in me. Moral reform is the effort to throw off sleep.
Why is it that men give so poor an account of their day if
they have not been slumbering? They are not such poor
calculators. If they had not been overcome with drowsi-
ness they would have performed something. The millions
are awake enough for physical labor; but only one in a
million is awake enough for effective intellectual exertion, only one in a hundred millions to a poetic or divine
life. To be awake is to be alive. I have never yet met a man
who was quite awake. How could I have looked him in the
face?

We must learn to reawaken and keep ourselves awake,
not by mechanical aids, but by an infinite expectation of
the dawn, which does not forsake us in our soundest sleep.
I know of no more encouraging fact than the unquestionable ability of man to elevate his life by a conscious en-

deavor. It is something to be able to paint a particular picture, or to carve a statue, and so to make a few objects beautiful; but it is far more glorious to carve and paint the very atmosphere and medium through which we look, which morally we can do. To affect the quality of the day, that is the highest of arts. Every man is tasked to make his life, even in its details, worthy of the contemplation of his most elevated and critical hour. If we refused, or rather used up, such paltry information as we get, the oracles would distinctly inform us how this might be done.

I went to the woods because I wished to live deliberately, to front only the essential facts of life, and see if I could not learn what it had to teach, and not, when I came to die, discover that I had not lived. I did not wish to live what was not life, living is so dear; nor did I wish to practice resignation, unless it was quite necessary. I wanted to live deep and suck out all the marrow of life, to live so sturdily and Spartan-like as to put to rout all that was not life, to cut a broad swath and shave close, to drive life into a corner, and reduce it to its lowest terms, and, if it proved to be mean, why then to get the whole and genuine meanness of it, and publish its meanness to the world; or if it were sublime, to know it by experience, and be able to give a true account of it in my next excursion. For most men, it appears to me, are in a strange uncertainty about it, whether it is of the devil or of God, and have *somewhat hastily* concluded that it is the chief end of man here to "glorify God and enjoy him forever."

Still we live meanly, like ants; though the fable tells us that we were long ago changed into men; like pygmies we fight with cranes; it is error upon error, and clout upon clout, and our best virtue has for its occasion a superfluous and evitable wretchedness. Our life is frittered away by detail. An honest man has hardly need to count more than his ten fingers, or in extreme cases he may add his ten toes, and lump the rest. Simplicity, simplicity, simplicity! I say, let your affairs be as two or three, and not a hundred or a thousand; instead of a million count half a dozen, and keep your accounts on your thumb nail. In the midst of this chopping sea of civilized life, such are the clouds and storms and quicksands and thousand-and-one items to be allowed for, that a man has to live, if he would not founder and go to the bottom and not make his port at all, by dead reckoning, and he must be a great calculator indeed who succeeds. Simplify, simplify. Instead of three meals a day, if it be necessary eat but one; instead of a hundred dishes, five; and reduce other things in proportion. Our life is like a German Confederacy, made up of petty states, with its boundary forever fluctuating, so that even a German cannot tell you how it is bounded at any moment.* The nation itself, with all its so-called internal improvements, which, by the way, are all external and superficial, is just such an unwieldy and overgrown establishment, cluttered with furniture and tripped up by its own traps, ruined by luxury and heedless expense, by want of calculation and a worthy aim, as the million households in the land; and the only cure for it as for them is in a rigid economy, stern and more than Spartan simplicity of life and elevation of purpose. It lives too fast. Men think that it is essential that the *Nation* have commerce, and export ice, and talk through a telegraph, and ride thirty miles an hour, without a doubt, whether *they* do or not; but whether we should live like baboons or like men, is a little uncertain. If we do not get our sleepers, and forge rails, and devote days and nights to the work, but go to tinkering upon our *lives* to improve *them,* who will build railroads? And if railroads are not built, how shall we get to heaven in season? But if we stay at home and mind our business, who will want railroads? We do not ride on the railroad; it rides upon us. Did you ever think what those sleepers are that underlie the railroad? Each one is a man, an Irishman, or a Yankee man. The rails are laid on them, and they are covered with sand,

---

*Otto von Bismarck (1815–1898), in effective control of Prussia's diplomatic and military establishments, "corrected" this condition by causing, through wars with Austria and France in 1866 and 1871, the unification of the various states of the Confederation with Prussia to create the German Empire, which lasted until 1918.

and the cars run smoothly over them. They are sound sleepers, I assure you. And every few years a new lot is laid down and run over; so that, if some have the pleasure of riding on a rail, others have the misfortune to be ridden upon. And when they run over a man that is walking in his sleep, a supernumerary sleeper in the wrong position, and wake him up, they suddenly stop the cars, and make a hue and cry about it, as if this were an exception. I am glad to know that it takes a gang of men for every five miles to keep the sleepers down and level in their beds as it is, for this is a sign that they may sometime get up again.

Why should we live with such hurry and waste of life? We are determined to be starved before we are hungry. Men say that a stitch in time saves nine, and so they take a thousand stitches to-day to save nine tomorrow. As for *work,* we haven't any of any consequence. We have the Saint Vitus' dance, and cannot possibly keep our heads still. If I should only give a few pulls at the parish bellrope, as for a fire, that is, without setting the bell, there is hardly a man on his farm in the outskirts of Concord, notwithstanding that press of engagements which was his excuse so many times this morning, nor a boy, nor a woman, I might almost say, but would forsake all and follow that sound, not mainly to save property from the flames, but, if we will confess the truth, much more to see it burn, since burn it must, and we, be it known, did not set it on fire,— or to see it put out, and have a hand in it, if that is done as handsomely; yes, even if it were the parish church itself. Hardly a man takes a half hour's nap after dinner, but when he wakes he holds up his head and asks, "What's the news?" as if the rest of mankind had stood his sentinels. Some give directions to be waked every half hour, doubtless for no other purpose; and then, to pay for it, they tell what they have dreamed. After a night's sleep the news is as indispensable as the breakfast. "Pray tell me any thing new that has happened to a man anywhere on this globe," —and he reads it over his coffee and rolls, that a man has had his eyes gouged out this morning on the Wachito

River; never dreaming the while that he lives in the dark unfathomed mammoth cave of this world, and has but the rudiment of an eye himself.

For my part, I could easily do without the post-office. I think that there are very few important communications made through it. To speak critically, I never received more than one or two letters in my life—I wrote this some years ago—that were worth the postage. The penny-post is, commonly, an institution through which you seriously offer a man that penny for his thoughts which is so often safely offered in jest. And I am sure that I never read any memorable news in a newspaper. If we read of one man robbed, or murdered, or killed by accident, or one house burned, or one vessel wrecked, or one steamboat blown up, or one cow run over on the Western Railroad, or one mad dog killed, or one lot of grasshoppers in the winter,—we never need read of another. One is enough. If you are acquainted with the principle, what do you care for myriad instances and applications? To a philosopher all *news,* as it is called, is gossip, and they who edit and read it are old women over their tea. Yet not a few are greedy after this gossip. There was such a rush, as I hear, the other day at one of the offices to learn the foreign news by the last arrival, that several large squares of plate glass belonging to the establishment were broken by the pressure,—news which I seriously think a ready wit might write a twelvemonth or twelve years beforehand with sufficient accuracy. As for Spain, for instance, if you know how to throw in Don Carlos and the Infanta, and Don Pedro and Seville and Granada, from time to time in the right proportions,—they may have changed the names a little since I saw the papers,—and serve up a bull-fight when other entertainments fail, it will be true to the letter, and give us as good an idea of the exact state or ruin of things in Spain as the most succinct and lucid reports under this head in the newspapers: and as for England, almost the last significant scrap of news from that quarter was the revolution of 1649; and if you have learned the history of her crops for an average year, you never need attend to that thing again, unless your speculations are of a merely pecuniary character. If one may judge who rarely looks into the newspapers, nothing new does ever happen in foreign parts, a French revolution not excepted.

What news! how much more important to know what that is which was never old! "Kieou-he-yu (great dignitary of the state of Wei) sent a man to Khoung-tseu to know his news. Khoung-tseu caused the messenger to be seated near him, and questioned him in these terms: What is your master doing? The messenger answered with respect: My master desires to diminish the number of his faults, but he cannot come to the end of them. The messenger being gone, the philosopher remarked: What a worthy messenger! What a worthy messenger!" The preacher, instead of vexing the ears of drowsy farmers on their day of rest at the end of the week,—for Sunday is the fit conclusion of an ill-spent week, and not the fresh and brave beginning of a new one,—with this one other draggle-tail of a sermon, should shout with thundering voice,—"Pause! Avast! Why so seeming fast, but deadly slow?"

Shams and delusions are esteemed for soundest truths, while reality is fabulous. If men would steadily observe realities only, and not allow themselves to be deluded, life, to compare it with such things as we know, would be like a fairy tale and the Arabian Nights' Entertainments. If we respected only what is inevitable and has a right to be, music and poetry would resound along the streets. When we are unhurried and wise, we perceive that only great and worthy things have any permanent and absolute existence, —that petty fears and petty pleasures are but the shadow of the reality. This is always exhilarating and sublime. By closing the eyes and slumbering, and consenting to be deceived by shows, men establish and confirm their daily life of routine and habit everywhere, which still is built on purely illusory foundations. Children, who play life, discern its true law and relations more clearly than men, who fail to live it worthily, but who think that they are wiser by experience, that is, by failure. I have read in a Hindoo book, that "there was a king's son, who, being expelled in infancy from his native city, was brought up by a forester, and, growing up to maturity in that state, imagined himself to belong to the barbarous race with which he lived. One of his father's ministers having discovered him, revealed to him what he was, and the misconception of his character was removed, and he knew himself to be a prince. So soul," continues the Hindoo philosopher, "from the circumstances in which it is placed, mistakes its own character, until the truth is revealed to it by some holy teacher, and then it knows itself to be *Brahme.*" I perceive that we inhabitants of New England live this mean life that we do because our vision does not penetrate the surface of things. We think that that *is* which *appears* to be. If a man should walk through this town and see only the reality, where, think you, would the "Mill-dam" go to? If he should give us an account of the realities he beheld there, we should not recognize the place in his description. Look at a meetinghouse, or a courthouse, or a jail, or a shop, or a dwellinghouse, and say what that thing really is before a true gaze, and they would all go to pieces in your account of them. Men esteem truth remote, in the outskirts of the system, behind the farthest star, before Adam and after the last man. In eternity there is indeed something true and sublime. But all these times and places and occasions are now and here. God himself culminates in the present moment, and will never be more divine in the lapse of all the ages. And we are enabled to apprehend at all what is sublime and noble only by the perpetual instilling and drenching of the reality that surrounds us. The universe constantly and obediently answers to our conceptions; whether we travel fast or slow, the track is laid for us. Let us spend our lives in conceiving then. The poet or the artist never yet had so fair and noble a design but some of his posterity at least could accomplish it.

Let us spend one day as deliberately as Nature, and not be thrown off the track by every nutshell and mosquito's wing that falls on the rails. Let us rise early and fast, or break fast, gently and without perturbation; let company come and let company go, let the bells ring and the children cry,—determined to make a day of it. Why should we knock under and go with the stream? Let us not be upset and overwhelmed in that terrible rapid and whirlpool called a dinner, situated in the meridian shallows. Weather this danger and you are safe, for the rest of the way is down hill. With unrelaxed nerves, with morning vigor, sail by it, looking another way, tied to the mast like Ulysses. If the engine whistles, let it whistle till it is hoarse for its pains. If the bell rings, why should we run? We will consider what kind of music they are like. Let us settle ourselves, and work and wedge our feet downward through the mud and slush of opinion, and prejudice, and tradition, and delusion, and appearance, that alluvion which covers the globe, through Paris and London, through New York and Boston and Concord, through church and state, through poetry and philosophy and religion, till we come to a hard bottom and rocks in place, which we can call *reality,* and say, This is, and no mistake; and then begin, having a *point d'appui,* below freshet and frost and fire, a place where you might found a wall or a state, or set a lamp-post safely, or perhaps a gauge, not a Nilometer, but a Realometer, that future ages might know how deep a freshet of shams and appearances had gathered from time to time. If you stand right fronting and face to face to a fact, you will see the sun glimmer on both its surfaces, as if it were a cimeter, and feel its sweet edge dividing you through the heart and marrow, and so you will happily conclude your mortal career. Be it life or death, we crave only reality. If we are really dying, let us hear the rattle in our throats and feel cold in the extremities; if we are alive, let us go about our business.

Time is but the stream I go a-fishing in. I drink at it; but while I drink I see the sandy bottom and detect how shallow it is. Its thin current slides away, but eternity remains. I would drink deeper; fish in the sky, whose bottom is pebbly with stars. I cannot count one. I know not the first letter of the alphabet. I have always been regretting that I was not as wise as the day I was born. The intellect is a cleaver; it discerns and rifts its way into the secret of things. I do not wish to be any more busy with my hands than is necessary. My head is hands and feet. I feel all my best faculties concentrated in it. My instinct tells me that my head is an organ for burrowing, as some creatures use their snout and fore-paws, and with it I would mine and burrow my way through these hills. I think that the richest vein is somewhere hereabouts; so by the divining rod and thin vapors I judge; and here I will begin to mine.

IDEAS

1. How is a man rich in proportion to what he can afford to let alone? How does Thoreau *retain* the landscape?

2. What is Thoreau's point in his statement, "As long as possible live free and uncommitted"? Was this perhaps easier to do a hundred years ago than it is today?

3. Why is it important to see "that the earth is not continent but insular"? How do *coins* work in Thoreau's description here?

4. Thoreau writes in several places about attitudes of being awake and of being asleep, about things that go on in our conscious as well as our subconscious mind. What are the implications of these statements?

5. How can you explain Thoreau's criticism of the railroad? How might you translate *railroad* into a modern equivalent which you feel Thoreau would also criticize?

6. What is Thoreau's point about time in the last paragraph? How could a stream have a bottom "pebbly with stars"?

7. Thoreau is called a Transcendentalist, one of a New England movement whose thinking, like Plato's, transcended everyday reality to reach permanent ideals and concepts above the ordinary world. From Thoreau's metaphors "wedge our feet downward," "drink deeper," "burrowing," and the like, how might he more aptly be named?

ORGANIZATION AND STYLE

1. Along with *season, surveyed, price,* and *deed,* what are the dynamics in Thoreau's *cultivated,* in his opening sentence?

2. In the first paragraph, Thoreau has a sentence that reads in part, "Well, there I might live, I said; and there I did live, for an hour, a summer and a winter life." Find other similar sentences in which the author summarizes attitudes toward time in this imaginative way.

3. What does Thoreau mean by "brag as lustily as chanticleer"? What are some other effective metaphors?

4. How does the author pun to achieve a part of his purpose?

5. Like poets, prose writers can alliterate effectively. Find several sentences in which Thoreau's alliterative patterns help to create a smooth rhythm.

6. What can you say about the flow of his sentences in the last two paragraphs? Look especially at the ones leading into and away from the long sentence beginning "Let us settle ourselves, . . ."

WRITING

Whatever you choose to write, try varying your sentences from short to long, with a metaphor for good measure, as Thoreau does. Try for a touch of Thoreau's informal diction among sophistications: "crusty farmer," "let it alone," "thrown off the track." Try for a pithy Thoreauvian epigram: "To be awake is to be alive."

To warm up and expand your control of the sentence try this time-tested exercise and have some fun with it. See if you can write a hundred-word sentence with everything subordinated to one main statement, using any subject, the more playful the better. Here is a useful pattern:

Having (Although, After, When) ,
   having _____ ,
   having _____ ,
   having _____ ,
    she got up
     because _____ ,
     because _____ ,
     and because _____ .

You can use other subordinating words, of course, and you can spin out your statements by inserting still further subordinations: "because she, *who had slept for forty-eight hours, and who never got up before noon anyway,* now realized. . . ." You can place your main statement early or late, but if you let it in too soon you sometimes run out of gas.

1.   Write an essay demonstrating that Thoreau, who preferred the cowbell to the churchbell, is essentially religious, that his work contains, as E. B. White says, religious feeling without religious images.

2.   Write an essay showing that Thoreau's opinions about travel and material satisfactions are proving relevant in our current problems with energy and environmental conservation.

3.   Write an essay illustrating Thoreau's "Morning is when I am awake and there is dawn in me." Or on some other Thoreauvian idea, perhaps "Let us spend one day as deliberately as Nature. . . ." (this might be a wonderful opening for humor—the shoes full of water, the sandwiches full of ants).

Sentence-Maker

HENRY SEIDEL CANBY

———————————— ● ————————————

This selection from Canby's Thoreau *gets to the heart of both Thoreau and our present concern: the sentence. Sentences are where we live, in prose, and where we think. The thesis sentence shapes the essay. The topic sentence shapes the paragraph. The sentence nets our thought. As Canby suggests, the writer's sentences are the writer's very self, engaging his subject and trying to engage his general reader in it. Notice the flow and subordinating richness of Canby's own sentences as he describes those of the more epigrammatic person he admires.*

Thoreau's writing was to an unusual extent a by-product of his experience. His profession was living, yet, as with all those born to be men of letters, his life seemed incomplete until he had got it described satisfactorily in words. "You . . . have the best of me in my books," he wrote to an admirer in Michigan, Calvin H. Greene, and of course he was right. Therefore, as was natural, he took his writing seriously, and was rich in self-criticism as all writers should be, but are not.

It took him most of the 1840's to get rid of [Thomas] Carlyle's religio-mystical view of literature, which made preachers of the young men of Thoreau's generation. When, in the fifties, his reading swung from literature toward science, he shrugged off this stale generalizing, for there was neither time nor inclination for it. It is only rarely that, after 1850, he writes about a literary masterpiece, for he was no longer studying in that school. Yet it is precisely in this last decade of his life that he makes the shrewdest comments on the art of writing—which is natural, for he had then matured his own. And here he is worth listening to, as is any first-rate writer who tries to analyze his own processes. Not the most philosophic perhaps, but certainly the most valuable, criticism we have is the occasional comment of a good writer on how to write—which means almost invariably how he writes himself.

It was a decade, as we have already seen, of crowded experiences for him with men, women, nature, and the state. There was plenty to write about, so that his Journal sometimes has sudden expansions for a day's thought and adventure which must have taken hours to set in order and express. The whole into which he hoped to fit his parts eluded his grasp, but his faith was firm that if he could reduce his observations to perfect sentences, somehow they would see the light, reach their mark, accomplish their destiny. This optimism has been justified, but only by the labor of many editors, and the enthusiasm of readers searching the trackless Journal for his best.

It was the sentence—a *sententia*—that most occupied his thought. The sentence was his medium—whatever he does and writes about, however often he rewrites or enriches, the fruit of it can be found ripened in a sentence. In the revision of *Walden* for the press, it was doubtful sentences that he threw out, then looked them over, and took back the good ones. They smelled right, as he says, using quaintly his keenest sense as if it could extend itself to words. Naturally he writes best about writing when he is writing about sentences, and these remarks have a biographical value, for they describe as no one else can do the man's mind at work. Only in those deeply impassioned pages about his Sister [the wife of his friend Emerson], so strongly felt as to be scarcely articulate, does he fail to get sentences equal to the emotional intensity or the intellectual insight of his experience. And these, of course, were not meant for publication. With Bacon, Shakespeare, Pope, Doctor Johnson, the makers of the English Bible, and Benjamin Franklin, he belongs among the great makers of the English sentence. Therefore his account of his own practice is interesting.

Two principles, especially, guided him in his writing as, sitting under a pasture oak, he set down his things seen or thought about, or, upstairs in the house on Main Street, worked his notes into his Journal. The first principle might be called intuition made articulate, a favorite idea with all the romantic Transcendentalists [a group of New England writers devoted to a philosophy stressing the importance of individual spiritual perception]:

> April 1. Sunday. 1860 . . . The fruit a thinker bears is *sentences,*—statements or opinions. He seeks to affirm something as true. I am surprised that my affirmations or utterances come to me ready-made,—not fore-thought,—so that I occasionally awake in the night simply to let fall ripe a statement which I had never consciously considered before, and as surprising and novel and agreeable to me as anything can be. As if we only thought by sympathy with the universal mind, which thought while we were asleep. There is such a necessity [to] make a definite statement that our minds at length do it without our consciousness, just as we carry our food to our mouths. This occurred to me last night, but I was so surprised by the fact which I have just endeavored to report that I have entirely forgotten what the particular observation was.

That is the difficulty, of course, with these flashes from a mind in which the heat of long brooding turns to light— if they are not recorded on some sensitive film they are lost and gone, often irrevocably. It was Thoreau's practice to wait for the flash and then anxiously develop the impression until a sentence was made that was true to the original inspiration, yet communicable to the reader. "There is no more Herculean task than to think a thought about this life and then get it expressed." To write that way is dangerous, since the flow of thought is checked while expression is made perfect; yet it is hard not to believe that here is the secret of Thoreau's durability. The rifle is more penetrating than the shotgun; the line is remembered when the poem is forgot.

But these sudden luminosities of thought or irradiations of experience were seldom made articulate at the first trial:

Jan. 26. 1852 . . . Whatever wit has been produced on the spur of the moment will bear to be reconsidered and reformed with phlegm. The arrow had best not be loosely shot. The most transient and passing remark must be . . . made sure and warranted, as if the earth had rested on its axle to back it, and all the natural forces lay behind it. The writer must direct his sentences as carefully and leisurely as the marksman his rifle. . . . If you foresee that a part of your essay will topple down after the lapse of time, throw it down now yourself.

Inspiration pricking him on, he writes several such sentences as these lines describe: "I feel the spur of the moment thrust deep into my side. The present is an inexorable rider." Then, with a shift of theme: "The truest account of heaven is the fairest, and I will accept none which disappoints expectation." Here are other comments:

Nov. 12. 1851 . . . Those sentences are good and well discharged which are like so many little resiliences from the spring floor of our life. . . . Sentences uttered with your back to the wall. . . . Sentences in which there is no strain.

Aug. 22. 1851 . . . It is the fault of some excellent writers —De Quincey's first impressions on seeing London suggest it to me—that they express themselves with too great fullness and detail. They . . . lack moderation and sententiousness. They . . . say all they mean. Their sentences are not concentrated and nutty. Sentences which suggest far more than they say, which have an atmosphere about them, which do not merely report an old, but make a new, impression . . . to frame these, that is the *art* of writing. Sentences which are expensive, towards which so many volumes, so much life, went; which lie like boulders on the page, up and down or across; which contain the seed of other sentences, not mere repetition, but creation; which a man might sell his grounds and castles to build. If De Quincey had suggested each of his pages in a sentence and passed on, it would have been far more excellent writing. His style is nowhere kinked and knotted up into something hard and significant, which you could swallow like a diamond, without digesting.

That last sentence describes the way Thoreau wrote, and the reason for reading him deliberately. To skim his pages, except in parts of *Cape Cod* or in *The Maine Woods* or in some of the *Excursions,* is like walking rapidly down a gallery of fine paintings. Even with every assistance from theme and narrative, as in *Walden,* Thoreau's work reads slowly—which is not always a virtue, but often a fault, like the faults of paradox and exaggeration, of which he accused himself. He favored his best sentences at the expense of his chapters and paragraphs. They contained the most of him.

His second principle of writing was native to a man who put the art of life ahead of the art of literature. It was, to be vital:

> Sept. 2. 1851 . . . We cannot write well or truly but what we write with gusto. The body, the senses, must conspire with the mind. Expression is the act of the whole man, that our speech may be vascular. The intellect is powerless to express thought without the aid of the heart and liver and of every member.

> Jan. 30. Friday. 1852 . . . It is in vain to write on chosen themes. We must wait till they have kindled a flame in our minds. There must be the copulating and generating force of love behind every effort destined to be successful. The cold resolve gives birth to, begets, nothing. . . . Obey, report.

> July 14. 1852. A writer who does not speak out of a full experience uses torpid words, wooden or lifeless words, such words as "humanitary," which have a paralysis in their tails.

And finally, by way of warning, the original of Barrett Wendell's often quoted phrase, "a diarrhoea of words and constipation of thought":

> Dec. 31. 1851 . . . The . . . creative moment . . . in the case of some too easy poets . . . becomes mere diarrhoea, mud and clay relaxed. The poet must not have something pass his bowels merely; that is women's poetry. He must have something pass his brain and heart and bowels, too. . . . So he gets delivered.

The rhetorical quality that many feel, even in Thoreau's best writing, is sometimes only a tone and attitude which he sustains, like a good lecturer, through all of such a book as the *Week* or *Walden.* Yet I think that the difficulty which the modern reader finds in what seems to him the stylized writing of *Walden,* or even of the *Excursions,* has a more important source in this habit of the packed and intensely expressive sentence. Our education in science, or its derivatives, has made us more inductive in our mental processes than were our immediate ancestors. We are accustomed to the kind of writing—especially in newspapers and magazines—that assembles facts, which we call news. The packed statement, which is a deduction handed over for our thinking, is unfamiliar and inspires distrust. Our writing escapes the dogmatic by being dilute and often inconclusive. It is easy to abbreviate, as the success of such magazines as *The Reader's Digest* has shown. We write, not by sentences, not even by paragraphs, but in a stream directed at one outlet. The reading of poetry has decreased in proportion to the increase of this homeopathic way of writing, for the effectiveness of poetry is an effectiveness of charged words and lines. If it is not to have high specific gravity, it would be better to write it in prose. Thoreau suffers from this changed habit of reading, since his sentences, with their backs to the wall, and their feet on Mother Earth, differ from poetry in this respect only in a freer rhythm.

Yet there is no intentional obscurity. "I am thinking," he wrote one day, "by what long discipline and at what cost a man learns to speak simply at last." Nor was there any literary affectation in his creed, although it cannot be denied that, like his contemporaries, he let his words strut and crow now and then with the *Walden* cock. "Why, the roots of *letters,*" he says aptly, "are *things.* Natural objects and phenomena are the original symbols or types which express our thoughts and feelings, and yet American scholars, having little or no root in the soil, commonly strive with all their might to confine themselves to the imported symbols alone. All the true growth and experience, the living speech, they would fain reject as 'Americanisms.' " "It is a great art in the writer to improve from day to day just that soil and fertility which he has. . . ." "Your mind must not perspire,"—which last, if said of walking out-of-doors, was surely meant for writing indoors also.

The art of writing is much broader and more complex than Thoreau's remarks on sentence-making imply. There is no doubt, however, that his particular art has a survival value much greater than any novelty in his ideas. But, inevitably, it became a perfectionist art, and so a curb upon free writing. Whoever writes by sentences writes slowly, and will often follow his own nose instead of his theme. And being perfectionist, this art made the completion of any whole exceedingly difficult, because each sentence had to be a finished production. He used the spot light instead of the flood. No wonder, then, that, as a student of nature trying to put between the covers of a book an account of that age-old Concord scene in which man had found a new home, Thoreau's work was left half done. Nevertheless, he mopped up his trenches as he crossed them, and left a noble sentence for each significant experience.

IDEAS

1. Canby suggests that, at least in part, Thoreau wrote so well because he was writing out of his personal experience. How true is this statement for you as writer? What is the difference between writing about one of your personal experiences and writing about major implications of some world problem?

2. Canby says Thoreau kept only those sentences that "smelled right." What does this mean? How can you tell when a sentence works and when it doesn't?

ORGANIZATION AND STYLE

1. Around what two points does Canby organize his essay?

2. How effectively does Canby quote Thoreau to support his points?

3. Like Thoreau, Canby is fond of metaphors. Find some of these and evaluate their effectiveness.

4. How effective are Canby's own sentences? How are they different from Thoreau's? How can you explain those differences in terms of audience and purpose?

WRITING

1. Canby quotes Thoreau, "We cannot write well or truly but when we write with gusto." Develop an essay in which you analyze your own writing in two different situations, one when you were writing on a topic about which you felt very deeply and one when you were not. How did you approach the two different tasks? If you still have those two papers, quote some of your sentences to show differences in your style.

2. Select a writer (or speaker) with whom you are familiar and who you feel is guilty of "a diarrhoea of words and constipation of thought." What evidence do you have for this indictment? What do you suspect prompted this style? Write an essay in which you evaluate the dangers of this kind of writing that tends to touch only the emotions and leave the intellect alone.

A Slight Sound at Evening

E. B. WHITE

———————●———————

In White's admiration of Thoreau, we can see one source of his own quiet magic: a love of words and their wily ways in catching at the simple wonders of life, together with a protective humor to keep from going overboard. Like Thoreau, White is a playful alluder, slipping in phrases from other writers on the assumption that his readers are so knowledgeable they will recognize and enjoy them. As you read, mark White's allusions, especially those echoes from Thoreau's piece. Notice his coupling of complex words with the commonplace—inspirational puffballs—*his admixture of slangy words*—Nature Boy, whack, show-off, ruckus—*and his phrases from commercial America*—vitamin-enriched, in-town location.*

In his journal for July 10–12, 1841, Thoreau wrote: "A slight sound at evening lifts me up by the ears, and makes life seem inexpressibly serene and grand. It may be in Uranus, or it may be in the shutter." The book into which he later managed to pack both Uranus and the shutter was published in 1854, and now, a hundred years having gone by, *Walden,* its serenity and grandeur unimpaired, still lifts us up by the ears, still translates for us that language we are in danger of forgetting, "which all things and events speak without metaphor, which alone is copious and standard."

Walden is an oddity in American letters. It may very well be the oddest of our distinguished oddities. For many it is a great deal too odd, and for many it is a particular bore. I have not found it to be a well-liked book among my acquaintances, although usually spoken of with respect, and one literary critic for whom I have the highest regard can find no reason why anyone gives *Walden* a second thought. To admire the book is, in fact, something of an embarrassment, for the mass of men have an indistinct notion that its author was a sort of Nature Boy.

I think it is of some advantage to encounter the book at a period in one's life when the normal anxieties and enthusiasms and rebellions of youth closely resemble those of Thoreau in that spring of 1845 when he borrowed an axe, went out to the woods, and began to whack down some trees for timber. Received at such a juncture, the book is like an invitation to life's dance, assuring the troubled recipient that no matter what befalls him in the way of success or failure he will always be welcome at the party—that the music is played for him, too, if he will but listen and move his feet. In effect, that is what the book is—an invitation, unengraved; and it stirs one as a young girl is stirred by her first big party bid. Many think it a sermon; many set it down as an attempt to rearrange society; some think it an exercise in nature-loving; some find it a rather irritating collection of inspirational puffballs by an eccentric show-off. I think it none of these. It still seems to me the best youth's companion yet written by an American, for it carries a solemn warning against the loss of one's valuables, it advances a good argument for traveling light and trying new adventures, it rings with the power of positive adoration, it contains religious feeling without religious images, and it steadfastly refuses to record bad news. Even its pantheistic note is so pure as to be noncorrupting—pure as the flutenote blown across the pond on those faraway summer nights. If our colleges and universities were alert, they would present a cheap pocket edition of the book to every senior upon graduating, along with his sheepskin, or instead of it. Even if some senior were to take it literally and start felling trees, there could be worse mishaps: the axe is older than the Dictaphone and it is just as well for a young man to see what kind of chips he leaves before listening to the sound of his own voice. And even if some were to get no farther than the table of contents, they would learn how to name eighteen chapters by the use of only thirty-nine words and would see how sweet are the uses of brevity.

If Thoreau had merely left us an account of a man's life in the woods, or if he had simply retreated to the woods and there recorded his complaints about society, or even if he had contrived to include both records in one essay, *Walden* would probably not have lived a hundred years. As things turned out, Thoreau, very likely without knowing quite what he was up to, took man's relation to nature and man's dilemma in society and man's capacity for elevating his spirit and he beat all these matters together, in a wild free interval of self-justification and delight, and produced an original omelette from which people can draw nourishment on a hungry day. *Walden* is one of the first of the vitamin-enriched American dishes. If it were a little less good than it is, or even a little less queer, it would be an abominable book. Even as it is, it will continue to baffle and annoy the literal mind and all those who are unable to stomach its caprices and imbibe its theme. Certainly the plodding economist will continue to have rough going if he hopes to emerge from the book with a clear system of economic thought. Thoreau's assault on the Concord society of the mid-nineteenth century has the quality of a modern Western: he rides into the subject at top speed, shooting in all directions. Many of his shots ricochet and nick him on the rebound, and throughout the melee there is a horrendous cloud of inconsistencies and contradictions, and when the shooting dies down and the air clears, one is impressed chiefly by the courage of the rider and by how splendid it was that somebody should have ridden in there and raised all that ruckus.

When he went to the pond, Thoreau struck an attitude and did so deliberately, but his posturing was not to draw the attention of others to him but rather to draw his own attention more closely to himself. "I learned this at least by my experiment: that if one advances confidently in the direction of his dreams, and endeavors to live the life which he has imagined, he will meet with a success unexpected in common hours." The sentence has the power to resuscitate the youth drowning in his sea of doubt. I recall my exhilaration upon reading it, many years ago, in a time of hesitation and despair. It restored me to health. And now in 1954 when I salute Henry Thoreau on the hundredth birthday of his book, I am merely paying off an old score—or an installment on it.

In his journal for May 3–4, 1838—Boston to Portland—he wrote: "Midnight—head over the boat's side—between sleeping and waking—with glimpses of one or more lights in the vicinity of Cape Ann. Bright moonlight—the effect heightened by seasickness." The entry illuminates the man, as the moon the sea on that night in May. In Thoreau the natural scene was heightened, not depressed, by a disturbance of the stomach, and nausea met its match at last. There was a steadiness in at least one passenger if there was none in the boat. Such steadiness (which in some would be called intoxication) is at the heart of *Walden*—confidence, faith, the discipline of looking always at what is to be seen, undeviating gratitude for the life-everlasting that he found growing in his front yard. "There is nowhere recorded a simple and irrepressible satisfaction with the gift of life, any memorable praise of God." He worked to correct that deficiency. *Walden* is his acknowledgment of the gift of life. It is the testament of a man in a high state of indignation because (it seemed to him) so few ears heard the uninterrupted poem of creation, the morning wind that forever blows. If the man sometimes wrote as though all his readers were male, unmarried, and well-connected, it is because he gave his testimony during the callow years, and, for that matter, never really grew up. To reject the book because of the immaturity of the author and the bugs in the logic is to throw away a bottle of good wine because it contains bits of the cork.

Thoreau said he required of every writer, first and last, a simple and sincere account of his own life. Having delivered himself of this chesty dictum, he proceeded to ignore it. In his books and even in his enormous journal, he withheld or disguised most of the fact from which an understanding of his life could be drawn. *Walden,* subtitled "Life in the Woods," is not a simple and sincere account of a man's life, either in or out of the woods; it is an account of a man's journey into the mind, a toot on the trumpet to alert the neighbors. Thoreau was well aware that no one can alert his neighbors who is not wide awake himself, and he went to the woods (among other reasons) to make sure that he would stay awake during his broadcast. What actually took place during the years 1845–1847 is largely unrecorded, and the reader is excluded from the private life of the author, who supplies almost no gossip about himself, a great deal about his neighbors and about the universe.

As for me, I cannot in this short ramble give a simple and sincere account of my own life, but I think Thoreau might find it instructive to know that this memorial essay is being written in a house that, through no intent on my part, is the same size and shape as his own domicile on the pond—about ten by fifteen, tight, plainly finished, and at a little distance from my Concord. The house in which I sit this morning was built to accommodate a boat, not a man, but by long experience I have learned that in most respects it shelters me better than the larger dwelling where my bed is, and which, by design, is a manhouse not a boathouse. Here in the boathouse I am a wilder and, it would appear, a healthier man, by a safe margin. I have a chair, a bench, a table, and I can walk into the water if I tire of the land. My house fronts a cove. Two fishermen have just arrived to spot fish from the air—an osprey and a man in a small yellow plane who works for the fish company. The man, I have noticed, is less well equipped than the hawk, who can dive directly on his fish and carry it away, without telephoning. A mouse and a squirrel share the house with me. The building is, in fact, a multiple dwelling, a semidetached affair. It is because I am semidetached while here that I find it possible to transact this private business with the fewest obstacles.

There is also a woodchuck here, living forty feet away under the wharf. When the wind is right, he can smell my house; and when the wind is contrary, I can smell his. We both use the wharf for sunning, taking turns, each adjusting his schedule to the other's convenience. Thoreau once ate a woodchuck. I think he felt he owed it to his readers, and that it was little enough, considering the indignities they were suffering at his hands and the dressing-down they were taking. (Parts of *Walden* are pure scold.) Or perhaps he ate the woodchuck because he believed every man should acquire strict business habits, and the woodchuck was destroying his market beans. I do not know. Thoreau had a strong experimental streak in him. It is probably no harder to eat a woodchuck than to construct a sentence that lasts a hundred years. At any rate, Thoreau is the only writer I know who prepared himself for his great ordeal by eating a woodchuck; also the only one who got a hangover from drinking too much water. (He was drunk the whole time, though he seldom touched wine or coffee or tea.)

Here in this compact house where I would spend one day as deliberately as Nature if I were not being pressed by *The Yale Review,* and with a woodchuck (as yet uneaten) for neighbor, I can feel the companionship of the occupant of the pondside cabin in Walden woods, a mile from the village, near the Fitchburg right of way. Even my immediate business is no barrier between us: Thoreau occasionally batted out a magazine piece, but was always suspicious of any sort of purposeful work that cut into his time. A man, he said, should take care not to be thrown off the track by every nutshell and mosquito's wing that falls on the rails.

There has been much guessing as to why he went to the pond. To set it down to escapism is, of course, to misconstrue what happened. Henry went forth to battle when he took to the woods, and *Walden* is the report of a man torn by two powerful and opposing drives—the desire to enjoy the world (and not be derailed by a mosquito wing) and the urge to set the world straight. One cannot join these two successfully, but sometimes, in rare cases, something good or even great results from the attempt of the tormented spirit to reconcile them. Henry went forth to battle, and if he set the stage himself, if he fought on his own terms and with his own weapons, it was because it was his nature to do things differently from most men, and to act in a cocky fashion. If the pond and the woods seemed a more plausible site for a house than an in-town location, it was because a cowbell made for him a sweeter sound than a churchbell. *Walden,* the book, makes the sound of the cowbell, more than a churchbell, and proves the point, although both sounds are in it, and both remarkably clear and sweet. He simply preferred his churchbell at a little distance.

I think one reason he went to the woods was a perfectly simple and commonplace one—and apparently he thought so, too. "At a certain season of our life," he wrote, "we are accustomed to consider every spot as the possible site of a house." There spoke the young man, a few years out of college, who had not yet broken away from home. He hadn't married, and he had found no job that measured up to his rigid standards of employment, and like any young man, or young animal, he felt uneasy and on the defensive until he had fixed himself a den. Most young men, of course, casting about for a site, are content merely to draw apart from their kinfolks. Thoreau, convinced that the greater part of what his neighbors called good was bad, withdrew from a great deal more than family: he pulled out of everything for a while, to serve everybody right for being so stuffy, and to try his own prejudices on the dog.

The house-hunting sentence above, which starts the Chapter called "Where I Lived, and What I Lived For," is followed by another passage that is worth quoting here because it so beautifully illustrates the offbeat prose that Thoreau was master of, a prose at once strictly disciplined and wildly abandoned. "I have surveyed the country on every side within a dozen miles of where I live," continued this delirious young man. "In imagination I have bought all the farms in succession, for all were to be bought, and I knew their price. I walked over each farmer's premises, tasted his wild apples, discoursed on husbandry with him, took his farm at his price, at any price, mortgaging it to him in my mind; even put a higher price on it—took everything but a deed of it—took his word for his deed, for I dearly love to talk—cultivated it, and him too to some extent, I trust, and withdrew when I had enjoyed it long enough, leaving him to carry it on." A copydesk man would get a double hernia trying to clean up that sentence for the management, but the sentence needs no fixing, for it perfectly captures the meaning of the writer and the quality of the ramble.

"Wherever I sat, there might I live, and the landscape radiated from me accordingly." Thoreau, the home-seeker, sitting on his hummock with the entire State of Massachusetts radiating from him, is to me the most humorous of the New England figures, and *Walden* the most humorous of the books, though its humor is almost continuously subsurface and there is nothing funny anywhere, except a few weak jokes and bad puns that rise to the surface like a perch in the pond that rose to the sound of the maestro's flute. Thoreau tended to write in sentences, a feat not every writer is capable of, and *Walden* is, rhetorically speaking, a collection of certified sentences, some of them, it would now appear, as indestructible as they are errant. The book is distilled from the vast journals, and this accounts for its intensity: he picked out bright particles that pleased his eye, whirled them in the kaleidoscope of his content, and produced the pattern that has endured—the color, the form, the light.

On this its hundredth birthday, Thoreau's *Walden* is pertinent and timely. In our uneasy season, when all men unconsciously seek a retreat from a world that has got almost completely out of hand, his house in the Concord woods is a haven. In our culture of gadgetry and the multiplicity of convenience, his cry "Simplicity, simplicity, simplicity!" has the insistence of a fire alarm. In the brooding atmosphere of war and the gathering radioactive storm, the innocence and serenity of his summer afternoons are enough to burst the remembering heart, and one gazes back upon that pleasing interlude—its confidence, its purity, its deliberateness—with awe and wonder, as one would look upon the face of a child asleep.

"This small lake was of most value as a neighbor in the intervals of a gentle rain-storm in August, when, both air and water being perfectly still, but the sky overcast, midafternoon had all the serenity of evening, and the woodthrush sang around, and was heard from shore to shore." Now, in the perpetual overcast in which our days are spent, we hear with extra perception and deep gratitude that song, tying century to century.

I sometimes amuse myself by bringing Henry Thoreau back to life and showing him the sights. I escort him into a phone booth and let him dial Weather. "This is a delicious evening," the girl's voice says, "when the whole body is one sense, and imbibes delight through every pore." I show him the spot in the Pacific where an island used to be, before some magician made it vanish. "We know not where we are," I murmur. "The light which puts out our eyes is darkness to us. Only that day dawns to which we are awake." I thumb through the latest copy of *Vogue* with him. "Of two patterns which differ only by a few threads more or less of a particular color," I read, "the one will be sold readily, the other lie on the shelf, though it frequently happens that, after the lapse of a season, the latter becomes the most fashionable." Together we go outboarding on the Assabet, looking for what we've lost—a hound, a bay horse, a turtledove. I show him a distracted farmer who is trying to repair a hay baler before the thunder shower breaks. "This farmer," I remark, "is endeavoring to solve the problem of a livelihood by a formula more complicated than the problem itself. To get his shoe strings he speculates in herds of cattle."

I take the celebrated author to Twenty-One [in New York] for lunch, so the waiters may study his shoes. The proprietor welcomes us. "The gross feeder," remarks the proprietor, sweeping the room with his arm, "is a man in the larva stage." After lunch we visit a classroom in one of those schools conducted by big corporations to teach their superannuated executives how to retire from business without serious injury to their health. (The shock to men's systems these days when relieved of the exacting routine of amassing wealth is very great and must be cushioned.) "It is not necessary," says the teacher to his pupils, "that a man should earn his living by the sweat of his brow, unless he sweats easier than I do. We are determined to be starved before we are hungry."

I turn on the radio and let Thoreau hear [Walter] Winchell beat the red hand around the clock. "Time is but the stream I go a-fishing in," shouts Mr. Winchell, rattling his telegraph key. "Hardly a man takes a half hour's nap after dinner, but when he wakes he holds up his head and asks, 'What's the news?' If we read of one man robbed, or murdered, or killed by accident, or one house burned, or one vessel wrecked, or one steamboat blown up, or one cow run over on the Western Railroad, or one mad dog killed, or one lot of grasshoppers in the winter—we need never read of another. One is enough."

I doubt that Thoreau would be thrown off balance by the fantastic sights and sounds of the twentieth century. "The Concord nights," he once wrote, "are stranger than the Arabian nights." A four-engined air liner would merely serve to confirm his early views on travel. Everywhere he would observe, in new shapes and sizes, the old predicaments and follies of men—the desperation, the impedimenta, the meanness—along with the visible capacity for elevation of the mind and soul. "This curious world which we inhabit is more wonderful than it is convenient; more beautiful than it is useful; it is more to be admired and enjoyed than used." He would see that today ten thousand engineers are busy making sure that the world shall be convenient if they bust doing it, and others are determined to increase its usefulness even though its beauty is lost somewhere along the way.

At any rate, I'd like to stroll about the countryside in Thoreau's company for a day, observing the modern scene, inspecting today's snowstorm, pointing out the sights, and offering belated apologies for my sins. Thoreau is unique among writers in that those who admire him find him uncomfortable to live with—a regular hairshirt of a man. A little band of dedicated Thoreauvians would be a sorry sight indeed: fellows who hate compromise and have compromised, fellows who love wildness and have lived tamely, and at their side, censuring them and chiding them, the ghostly figure of this upright man, who long ago gave corroboration to impulses they perceived were right and issued warnings against the things they instinctively knew to be their enemies. I should hate to be called a Thoreauvian, yet I wince every time I walk into the barn I'm pushing before me, seventy-five feet by forty, and the author of *Walden* has served as my conscience through the long stretches of my trivial days.

Hairshirt or no, he is a better companion than most, and I would not swap him for a soberer or more reasonable friend even if I could. I can reread his famous invitation with undiminished excitement. The sad thing is that not more acceptances have been received, that so many decline for one reason or another, pleading some previous engagement or ill health. But the invitation stands. It will beckon as long as this remarkable book stays in print—which will be as long as there are August afternoons in the intervals of a gentle rainstorm, as long as there are ears to catch the faint sounds of the orchestra. I find it agreeable to sit here this morning, in a house of correct proportions, and hear across a century of time his flute, his frogs, and his seductive summons to the wildest revels of them all.

IDEAS

1. Do you pick up any allusive echo in White's "sweet are the uses of brevity"? If so, why is it appropriate?

2. What tribute does White pay to "the sentence" in this essay?

3. What is the effect of White's autobiographical report, in the midst of his "short ramble" on Thoreau?

4. Why does White characterize Thoreau's cabin as being "a mile from the village, near the Fitchburg right of way"?

5. What is White's point about the churchbell? What do you think Thoreau's was?

6. What is White's point about the Pacific island "some magician made vanish"?

7. What is White's point about engineers busy to make the world convenient and useful?

ORGANIZATION AND STYLE

1. How many subordinate clauses can you find in White's second paragraph? Does the flow seem paratactic or hypotactic?

2. How would you classify the sentence beginning "Many think it a sermon" (third paragraph)? How about the next two sentences?

3. How apt is White's phrase "to act in a cocky fashion"?

4. What is the effect of White's "a world that has got almost completely out of hand"? How might a more conventional writer have phrased it?

5. In the same passage, what is the force of "that pleasing interlude"? Of "the perpetual overcast"?

6. How does *invitation* work in White's concluding paragraph, and in his essay? (Look back at the outset of his third paragraph.)

WRITING

1. Write an essay about where you might live, perhaps about building a tree house, or setting up housekeeping in a basement corner. Quote from both Thoreau and White for support.

2. White writes, "I sometimes amuse myself by bringing Henry Thoreau back to life and showing him the sights," adding later, "I doubt that Thoreau would be thrown off balance by the fantastic sights and sounds of the twentieth century." Write an essay in which you personally take Thoreau on a tour of twentieth-century sights. Where will you take him? What will be his reaction?

7

WORDS: THE SUBSTANCE
OF THOUGHT

As we have seen in Thoreau and Canby, words are the substance, the meaty particles, within our larger rhythms of thought. They picture the world as we see it. They describe, but they carry the colors of our spirits. If words lack character, they convey no reality. We cannot believe in anything, with nobody there. Thoreau, the sentence-smith, puts it another way, probably borrowing from Socrates in Plato's *Cratylus:* "Why, the roots of *letters* are *things.* Natural objects and phenomena are the original symbols or types which express our thoughts and feelings. . . ." Or again, he writes as if words were like seeds, common and unnoticed, just waiting to be awakened. But he failed to remark that his own personality was the sun of spring.

Nevertheless, he saw and enjoyed the essential energy in words. He saw the power of finding the natural object to express the thought, and the thought to express the natural object, connecting himself to the object and giving us the immediacy of both, as MacLeish might say. He also knew how to pun, to turn common abstractions back into their original metaphors: "I feel *the spur of the moment* thrust deep into my side. The present is an inexorable rider." Before we consider the physical *spurs* and abstract *inexorabilities* of words in the following selections, perhaps we had better review this figurative dimension. A figurative word like *spur* condenses an imaginative comparison, an *as if.* The urgency of the present moment feels *as if* it were the spur on the heel of an actual horseman. In Coles's essay, we will find an old woman obliquely comparing herself and her husband to the adobe bricks of their house as they sit soaking in the sun. We can extend this comparison to illustrate the four kinds of metaphor, the transference of qualities from one thing to another:

Simile: We are *like* adobe bricks.
We are baked *as* adobe bricks are baked.
We feel *as if* we were adobe bricks.
Plain Metaphor: We *are* adobe bricks.
Implied Metaphor: Our common clay and straw make us strong.
Dead Metaphor: He is a real brick [a splendid fellow].

To awaken that dead metaphor, an alert writer would simply exhume the idea, as Thoreau did with *spur* by bringing it to light again: "He is a real brick, solid, dependable, enduring: you could build a city with people like him."

As you read Coles, Orwell, Schlesinger, and Davis, you might keep an eye, and pencil, sharp for these metaphorical shadings, and indeed for the Latinate *inexorables,* which have certain powers of their own, particularly as they blend with the brief and pithy, as in Coles's "dull, dreary, *ponderous,* smug," or Orwell's *"prefabricated* hen-house," or *"continuous temptation,* a packet of aspirins." In his essay, Davis points up the dangers of using language as a social or racial means to isolate and control people.

Two Languages, One Soul

ROBERT COLES

———————●———————

*Coles gives us the vivid metaphorical expression, in
mixed Spanish and English, of an unlettered person
who has drawn her life, and soul, from the living
world around her, from the sermons she has heard,
and the Bible she has heard read—in the naturally
figurative language of a Hebrew pastoral culture not
greatly unlike her own.*

Here are the words of a quite elderly woman who has had
virtually no schooling and speaks a mixture of Spanish
(which I have translated) and terse but forceful English.
She lives in a small isolated mountain community well to
the north of Santa Fe and enjoys talking with her visitor:

"Sometimes I have a moment to think. I look back and
wonder where all the time has gone to—so many years; I
cannot say I like to be reminded how many. My sister is
three years older, eighty this May. She is glad to talk of her
age. I don't like to mention mine. Maybe I have not her
faith in God. She makes her way every day to Church. I go
only on Sundays. Enough is enough; besides, I don't like
the priest. He points his finger too much. He likes to accuse
us—each week it is a different sin he charges us with. My
mother used to read me Christ's words when I was a
girl—from the old Spanish Bible her grandmother gave to
her on her deathbed. I learned that Christ was a kind man:
He tried to think well of people, even the lowest of the low,
even those at the very bottom who are in a swamp and
don't know how to get out, never mind find for themselves
some high, dry land.

"But this priest of ours gives no one the benefit of a

doubt. I have no right to find fault with him; I know that. Who am I to do so? I am simply an old lady, and I had better watch out: the Lord no doubt punishes those who disagree with His priests. But our old priest who died last year was so much finer, so much better to hear on a warm Sunday morning. Every once in a while he would even lead us outside to the courtyard, and talk with us there, give us a second sermon. I felt so much better for listening to him. He was not in love with the sound of his own voice, as this new priest is. He did not stop and listen to the echo of his words. He did not brush away dust from his coat, or worry if the wind went through his hair. He was not always looking for a paper towel to wipe his shoes. My husband says he will buy this priest a dozen handkerchiefs and tell him they are to be used for his shoes only. Here when we get rain we are grateful, and it is not too high a price to pay, a little mud to walk through. Better mud that sticks than dust that blows away.

"Well, I should not go on so long about a vain man. We all like to catch ourselves in the mirror and find ourselves good to look at. Here I am, speaking ill of him, yet I won't let my family celebrate my birthdays any more; and when I look at myself in the mirror a feeling of sadness comes over me. I pull at my skin and try to erase the lines, but no luck. I think back: all those years when my husband and I were young, and never worried about our health, our strength, our appearance. I don't say we always do now; but there are times when we look like ghosts of ourselves. I will see my husband noticing how weak and tired I have become, how hunched over. I pretend not to see, but once the eyes have caught something, one cannot shake the picture off. And I look at him, too; he will straighten up when he feels my glance strike him, and I quickly move away. Too late, though; he has been told by me, without a word spoken, that he is old, and I am old, and that is our fate, to live through these last years.

"But it is not only pity we feel for ourselves. A few drops of rain, and I feel grateful; the air is so fresh afterwards. I love to sit in the sun. We have the sun so often here, a regular visitor, a friend one can expect to see often and trust. I like to make tea for my husband and me. In mid-day we take our tea outside and sit on our bench, our backs against the wall of the house. Neither of us wants pillows; I tell my daughters and sons that they are soft—those beach chairs of theirs. Imagine beach chairs here in New Mexico, so far from any ocean! The bench feels strong to us, not uncomfortable. The tea warms us inside, the sun on the outside. I joke with my husband, I say we are part of the house: the adobe gets baked, and so do we. For the most part we say nothing, though. It is enough to sit and be part of God's world. We hear the birds talking to each other, and are grateful they come as close to us as they do; all the more reason to keep our tongues still and hold ourselves in one place. We listen to cars going by and wonder who is rushing off. A car to us is a mystery. The young understand a car. They cannot imagine themselves not driving. They have not the interest we had in horses. Who is to compare one lifetime with another, but a horse is alive and one loves a horse and is loved by a horse. Cars come and go so fast. One year they command all eyes. The next year they are a cause for shame. The third year they must be thrown away without the slightest regret. I may exaggerate, but not much!

"My moods are like the Church bell on Sunday: way up, then down, then up again—and often just as fast. I make noises, too; my husband says he can hear me smiling and hear me turning sour. When I am sour I am really sour—sweet milk turned bad. Nothing pleases me. I am more selfish than my sister. She bends with the wind. I push my heels into the ground and won't budge. I know enough to frown at myself, but not enough to change. There was a time when I tried hard. I would talk to myself as if I was the priest. I would promise myself that tomorrow I would be different. I suppose only men and women can fool themselves that way; an animal knows better. Animals are themselves. We are always trying to be better—and often we end up even worse than we were to start with.

"But now, during the last moments of life, I think I have

learned a little wisdom. I can go for days without an upset. I think I dislike our priest because he reminds me of myself. I have his long forefinger, and I can clench my fist like him and pound the table and pour vinegar on people with my remarks. It is no good to be like that. A man is lucky; it is in his nature to fight or preach. A woman should be peaceful. My mother used to say all begins the day we are born: some are born on a clear, warm day; some when it is cloudy and stormy. So, it is a consolation to find myself easy to live with these days. And I have found an answer to the few moods I still get. When I have come back from giving the horses each a cube or two of sugar, I give myself the same. I am an old horse who needs something sweet to give her more faith in life!

"The other day I thought I was going to say good-bye to this world. I was hanging up some clothes to dry. I love to do that, then stand back and watch and listen to the wind go through the socks or the pants or the dress, and see the sun warm them and make them smell fresh. I had dropped a few clothespins, and was picking them up, when suddenly I could not catch my breath, and a sharp pain seized me over my chest. I tried hard to stand up, but I couldn't. I wanted to scream, but I knew there was no one nearby to hear. My husband had gone to the store. I sat down on the ground and waited. It was strong, the pain; and there was no one to tell about it. I felt as if someone had lassoed me and was pulling the rope tighter and tighter. Well here you are, an old cow, being taken in by the good Lord; that is what I thought.

"I looked at myself, sitting on the ground. For a second I was my old self again—worrying about how I must have appeared there, worrying about my dress, how dirty it would get to be. This is no place for an old lady, I thought— only for one of my little grandchildren, who love to play out here, build their castles of dirt, wetted down with water I give to them. Then more pain; I thought I had about a minute of life left. I said my prayers. I said good-bye to the house. I pictured my husband in my mind: fifty-seven years of marriage. Such a good man! I said to myself that I might not see him ever again; surely God would take him into Heaven, but as for me, I have no right to expect that outcome. Then I looked up to the sky and waited.

"My eye caught sight of a cloud. It was darker than the rest. It was alone. It was coming my way. The hand of God, I was sure of it! So that is how one dies. All my life, in the spare moments a person has, I wondered how I would go. Now I knew. Now I was ready. I thought I would soon be taken up to the cloud and across the sky I would go, and that would be that. But the cloud kept moving, and soon it was no longer above me, but beyond me; and I was still on my own land, so dear to me, so familiar after all these years. I can't be dead, I thought to myself, if I am here and the cloud is way over there, and getting further each second. Maybe the next cloud—but by then I had decided God had other things to do. Perhaps my name had come up, but He had decided to call others before me, and get around to me later. Who can ever know His reasons? Then I spotted my neighbor walking down the road, and I said to myself that I would shout for him. I did, and he heard. But you know, by the time he came I had sprung myself free. That is right, the pain was all gone.

"He helped me up, and he was ready to go find my husband and bring him back. No, I told him no; I was all right, and I did not want to risk frightening my husband. He is excitable. He might get some kind of attack himself. I went inside and put myself down on our bed and waited. For an hour—it was that long, I am sure—my eyes stared at the ceiling, held on to it for dear life. I thought of what my life had been like: a simple life, not a very important one, maybe an unnecessary one. I am sure there are better people, men and women all over the world, who have done more for their neighbors and yet not lived as long as I have. I felt ashamed for a few minutes: all the complaints I'd made to myself and to my family, when the truth has been that my fate has been to live a long and healthy life, to have a good and loyal husband, and to bring two sons and three daughters into this world. I thought of the five children we had lost, three before they had a chance to take a breath. I wondered where in the universe they were. In the evening sometimes, when I go to close loose doors that otherwise complain loudly all night, I am likely to look at the stars and feel my long-gone infants near at hand. They are far off, I know; but in my mind they have become those stars—very small, but shining there bravely, no matter how cold it is so far up. If the stars have courage, we ought have courage; that is what I was thinking, as I so often have in the past—and just then he was there, my husband, calling my name and soon looking into my eyes with his.

"I'm all right, I told him. He didn't know what had happened; our neighbor had sealed his lips, as I told him to do. But my husband knows me, so he knew I looked unusually tired; and he couldn't be easily tricked by me. The more I told him I'd just worked too hard, that is all, the more he knew I was holding back something. Finally, I pulled my ace card. I pretended to be upset by his questions and by all the attention he was giving me. I accused him: why do you make me want to cry, why do you wish me ill, with those terrible thoughts of yours, I am not ill! If you cannot let me rest without thinking I am, then God have mercy on you for having such an imagination! God have mercy! With the second plea to our Lord, he was beaten and silent. He left me alone. I was about to beg him to come back, beg his forgiveness. But I did not want him to bear the burden of knowing: he would not rest easy by day or by night. This way he can say to himself: she has always been cranky, and she will always be cranky, so thank God her black moods come only now and then—a spell followed by the bright sun again.

"I will say what I think happened: I came near going, then there was a change of heart up there in Heaven, so I have a few more days, or weeks, or months, or years— who knows? As for a doctor, I have never seen one, so why start now? Here we are so far away from a hospital. We have no money. Anglos don't like us, anyway: we are the poor ones, the lost ones. My son tells me the Anglos look down on us—old people without education and up in the hills, trying to scrape what we can from the land, and helped only by our animals. No matter; our son is proud of us. He is proud to stay here with us. He says that if he went to the city he would beg for work and be told no, no, no: eventually he might be permitted to sweep someone's floor. Better to hold on to one's land. Better to fight it out with the weather and the animals.

"Again I say it: doctors are for others. My mother and my aunt delivered my children. I once went to see a nurse; she worked for the school and she told me about my children— the diseases they get. Thank you, I said. Imagine: she thought I knew nothing about bringing up children, or about the obstacles God puts in their way to test them and make them stronger for having gone through a fever, a rash, some pain. No, I will see no nurse and no doctor. They are as far from here as the stars. Oh, that is wrong: they are much farther. The stars I know and recognize and even call by name. They are my names, of course; I don't know what others call the stars. Is it wrong to do that? Perhaps I should ask the priest. Perhaps the stars are God's to name, not ours to treat like pets—by addressing them familiarly. But it is too late; my sins have been recorded, and I will soon enough pay for each and every one of them."

True, I have pulled together remarks made over a stretch of months. And again, I have translated her Spanish into plain, understandable English, or at least I hope I have done so. I have even "cleaned up" her English to an extent: that is, I have eliminated some of the repetitive words or phrases she uses—as we all do when we talk informally to a visitor in our homes. On the other hand, I have made every effort to keep faithful to the spirit, and mostly the letter of her remarks. I have found that her Spanish is as bare, unaffected, and strong as her English. I have found that in both languages she struggles not only to convey meaning, but to enliven her words with her heart's burden or satisfactions. I have found that she struggles not only with her mind but her body, her whole being, to express herself. Nor is she alone, some peculiar or specially gifted person whose manner of expression is thoroughly idiosyncratic. She is one of a number of aged Spanish-speaking men and women of New Mexico I have been privileged to meet and visit in their homes. And she certainly can be saddled with negatives, however compelling her way of speaking. She is uneducated. She is superstitious. She never has attended any bilingual classes. She is poor. Maybe some doctor would find her at times forgetful, a little "senile." She and others like her are rural people; they belong to a social and economic "system" that we all know is "out-of-date," whereas the future of America is to be found in cities like Albuquerque and their suburbs. Or so we are told.

Nor is she saintly. She can be morose, and at times quite cranky and reticent. Once she asked me this: "What is the point of trying to talk to those who are deaf?" She had in mind some Anglo county officials who refused a needy cousin of hers food stamps. She had in mind an Anglo teacher or two, and yes, a Spanish-speaking teacher or two; they had said rude things to her grandchildren and to their parents, her children. So, she becomes bitter and tense, and after a while she explodes. She admits it is not in her "nature" to hold in her beliefs, her feelings. She must have her say. And when she does her hands move, her body sways a bit, and sometimes, when she is especially worked up, there is a lurch forward from the chair, so that suddenly she is standing—giving a sermon, almost like the priests she has listened to all these years. A hand goes out, then is withdrawn. The head goes up, then is lowered. A step is taken forward, then back she goes—and soon she is seated again, ready to sew and continue the conversation on a less intense level. When she searches for a word, be it in Spanish or English, she drops her needle and thread, drops a fork or spoon, drops anything she may have in her hands. She needs those old, arthritic fingers of hers. They flex and unflex; it is as if before her is a sandpile of words, and she must push and probe her way through it, until she has found what she is looking for. Then the fingers can stop, the hands can relax and go back to other business or simply be allowed a rest on her lap.

The more time I spend with this woman and her husband and their friends and neighbors and relatives, the more confused I become by much of what I read about them and their so-called "cultural disadvantage." I have no inclination to turn such people into spotless, utterly flawless human beings, yet another highly romanticized group, to be used as bludgeons against the rest of the country. They can be mean and narrow at times; the woman I have been quoting says things about "hippies," and even at times about Anglos, that I disagree with or find exaggerated, unfair, distorted. As for her own disposition, she makes clear her personal limitations. Still, she and her kind are at best pitied by many who have described their "plight." If there are grounds for pity (poverty, substantial unemployment, a degree of prejudice even in New Mexico, never mind Texas or California), there are also grounds for respect and admiration—maybe even envy. Some of us who have gone through all those schools and colleges and graduate schools, who have plenty of work and who live comfortable upper-middle-class lives, might want to stop and think about how *we* talk.

Occasionally I come home from a day spent with Chicano families or Indian families and pick up a psychiatric journal, or for that matter, the daily newspaper. Or I happen to go to a professional meeting and hear papers presented, or afterwards, people talking in lobbies or corridors or restaurants—all those words, all those ideas, spoken by men and women who have no doubt about their importance, their achievements, and certainly, their ability to "communicate." No one is proposing that jargon-filled scholars of one sort or another overcome their "cultural disadvantage." Few are examining ever so closely the rhetoric of various business and professional people, or their elected leaders—the phony, deceiving, dull, dreary, ponderous, smug, deadly words and phrases such people use and use and use. Relatively few are looking at the way such people are taught in elementary school and high school and beyond. Who is to be pitied, the old lady who can't recognize a possible coronary seizure, and instead sees the hand of God approaching her, or some of us who jabber with our clichés and don't have the slightest idea how to use a metaphor or an image in our speech?

IDEAS

1. What does Coles's title mean?

2. What in the woman's account shows her more Christ-like than the priest?

3. What does her epigram about mud and dust (paragraph 3) reveal about her way of life? About her attitudes? About what one might value in life in general?

4. How do you imagine her as a young woman? Why?

5. What does her simile about the churchbell illustrate about her way of thought? Her metaphors of *old horse* and *old cow?* Her loving to hang up the laundry?

6. What significance is there in the grandchildren's "castles of dirt, wetted down with water I give them"?

ORGANIZATION AND STYLE

1. Do you find the woman's language "bare, unaffected, and strong"?

2. What do you think of Coles's metaphor "a sandpile of words"?

3. Why does Coles put *cultural disadvantage* in quotation marks?

4. What does Coles imply about images and metaphors?

5. Find the organizational units in the woman's narrative that move back and forth between the positive and the negative.

6. Does the one-paragraph introduction adequately prepare you for the direction this essay is going to take? Would it have been helpful to have had a bit of Coles's thesis revealed in that paragraph?

7. The last third of the essay is Coles's analysis of the woman, her language, and her world. How effective is it at underscoring his thesis? Would it have been better to have mixed some of her dialogue with some of his analysis throughout the essay?

WRITING

1. Either as a separate exercise or in your next essay, see what you can do with reviving a dead metaphor, on the model of Thoreau's *spur* or the *brick* discussed at the beginning of this section.

2. Coles presents an uneducated woman who speaks a mixture of Spanish and English and is considered disadvantaged. The opposite is obviously true. Write an essay comparing Coles's old woman's life and attitudes with those of someone you know, perhaps even your own.

3. Take some piece of writing from a professional journal or the daily newspaper (to experience Coles's shock in returning to urban civilization) or from a textbook or other inflated example. Rewrite it to simplify it and express it more concretely.

Politics and the English Language

GEORGE ORWELL

———————————— ● ————————————

This essay remains a classic on style. Its essential advice—to fend off all prefabricated phrases so one can find the accurate word for the thought—reflects Orwell's ingrained honesty, as did his commitment to a life that could find no satisfactory politics.

Most people who bother with the matter at all would admit that the English language is in a bad way, but it is generally assumed that we cannot by conscious action do anything about it. Our civilization is decadent and our language—so the argument runs—must inevitably share in the general collapse. It follows that any struggle against the abuse of language is a sentimental archaism, like preferring candles to electric light or hansom cabs to aeroplanes. Underneath this lies the half-conscious belief that language is a natural growth and not an instrument which we shape for our own purposes.

Now, it is clear that the decline of a language must ultimately have political and economic causes: it is not due simply to the bad influence of this or that individual writer. But an effect can become a cause, reinforcing the original cause and producing the same effect in an intensified form, and so on indefinitely. A man may take to drink because he feels himself to be a failure, and then fail all the more completely because he drinks. It is rather the same thing that is happening to the English language. It becomes ugly and inaccurate because our thoughts are foolish, but the slovenliness of our language makes it easier for us to have foolish thoughts. The point is that the

420

process is reversible. Modern English, especially written English, is full of bad habits which spread by imitation and which can be avoided if one is willing to take the necessary trouble. If one gets rid of these habits one can think more clearly, and to think clearly is a necessary first step towards political regeneration: so that the fight against bad English is not frivolous and is not the exclusive concern of professional writers. I will come back to this presently, and I hope that by that time the meaning of what I have said here will have become clearer. Meanwhile, here are five specimens of the English language as it is now habitually written.

These five passages have not been picked out because they are especially bad—I could have quoted far worse if I had chosen—but because they illustrate various of the mental vices from which we now suffer. They are a little below the average, but are fairly representative samples. I number them so that I can refer back to them when necessary:

1. I am not, indeed, sure whether it is not true to say that the Milton who once seemed not unlike a seventeenth-century Shelley had not become, out of an experience ever more bitter in each year, more alien [sic] to the founder of that Jesuit sect which nothing could induce him to tolerate.

   PROFESSOR HAROLD LASKI
   (ESSAY IN *Freedom of Expression*).

2. Above all, we cannot play ducks and drakes with a native battery of idioms which prescribes such egregious collocations of vocables as the Basic *put up with* for *tolerate* or *put at a loss* for *bewilder*.

   PROFESSOR LANCELOT HOGBEN
   (*Interglossa*).

3. On the one side we have the free personality: by definition it is not neurotic, for it has neither conflict nor dream. Its desires, such as they are, are transparent, for they are just what institutional approval keeps in the forefront of consciousness; another institutional pattern would alter their number and intensity; there is little in them that is natural, irreducible, or culturally

dangerous. But *on the other side,* the social bond itself is nothing but the mutual reflection of these self-secure integrities. Recall the definition of love. Is not this the very picture of a small academic? Where is there a place in this hall of mirrors for either personality or fraternity?

ESSAY ON PSYCHOLOGY IN *Politics* (NEW YORK).

4. All the "best people" from the gentlemen's clubs, and all the frantic fascist captains, united in common hatred of Socialism and bestial horror of the rising tide of the mass revolutionary movement, have turned to acts of provocation, to foul incendiarism, to medieval legends of poisoned wells, to legalize their own destruction of proletarian organizations, and rouse the agitated petty-bourgeoisie to chauvinistic fervor on behalf of the fight against the revolutionary way out of the crisis.

COMMUNIST PAMPHLET.

5. If a new spirit *is* to be infused into this old country, there is one thorny and contentious reform which must be tackled, and that is the humanization and galvanization of the BBC.* Timidity here will bespeak canker and atrophy of the soul. The heart of Britain may be sound and of strong beat, for instance, but the British lion's roar at present is like that of Bottom in Shakespeare's *Midsummer Night's Dream*—as gentle as any sucking dove. A virile new Britain cannot continue indefinitely to be traduced in the eyes, or rather ears, of the world by the effete languors of Langham Place, brazenly masquerading as "standard English." When the voice of Britain is heard at nine o'clock, better far and infinitely less ludicrous to hear aitches [*h*'s] honestly dropped than the present priggish, inflated, inhibited, schoolma'amish arch braying of blameless bashful mewing maidens!

LETTER IN *Tribune.*

Each of these passages has faults of its own, but, quite apart from avoidable ugliness, two qualities are common to all of them. The first is staleness of imagery; the other is lack of precision. The writer either has a meaning and cannot express it, or he inadvertently says something else, or he is almost indifferent as to whether his words mean

*British Broadcasting Corporation.

anything or not. This mixture of vagueness and sheer incompetence is the most marked characteristic of modern English prose, and especially of any kind of political writing. As soon as certain topics are raised, the concrete melts into the abstract and no one seems able to think of turns of speech that are not hackneyed: prose consists less and less of *words* chosen for the sake of their meaning, and more and more of *phrases* tacked together like the sections of a prefabricated hen-house. I list below, with notes and examples, various of the tricks by means of which the work of prose-construction is habitually dodged:

Dying metaphors. A newly invented metaphor assists thought by evoking a visual image, while on the other hand a metaphor which is technically "dead" (e.g. *iron resolution*) has in effect reverted to being an ordinary word and can generally be used without loss of vividness. But in between these two classes there is a huge dump of worn-out metaphors which have lost all evocative power and are merely used because they save people the trouble of inventing phrases for themselves. Examples are: *Ring the changes on, take up the cudgels for, toe the line, ride roughshod over, stand shoulder to shoulder with, play into the hands of, no axe to grind, grist to the mill, fishing in troubled waters, on the order of the day, Achilles' heel, swan song, hotbed.* Many of these are used without knowledge of their meaning (what is a "rift," for instance?), and incompatible metaphors are frequently mixed, a sure sign that the writer is not interested in what he is saying. Some metaphors now current have been twisted out of their original meaning without those who use them even being aware of the fact. For example, *toe the line* is sometimes written *tow the line.* Another example is *the hammer and the anvil,* now always used with the implication that the anvil gets the worst of it. In real life it is always the anvil that breaks the hammer, never the other way about: a writer who stopped to think what he was saying would be aware of this, and would avoid perverting the original phrase.

Operators or *verbal false limbs.* These save the trouble

of picking out appropriate verbs and nouns, and at the same time pad each sentence with extra syllables which give it an appearance of symmetry. Characteristic phrases are *render inoperative, militate against, make contact with, be subjected to, give rise to, give grounds for, have the effect of, play a leading part (role) in, make itself felt, take effect, exhibit a tendency to, serve the purpose of, etc., etc.* The keynote is the elimination of simple verbs. Instead of being a single word, such as *break, stop, spoil, mend, kill,* a verb becomes a *phrase,* made up of a noun or adjective tacked on to some general-purpose verb such as *prove, serve, form, play, render.* In addition, the passive voice is wherever possible used in preference to the active, and noun constructions are used instead of gerunds *(by examination of* instead of *by examining).* The range of verbs is further cut down by means of the *-ize* and *de-* formations, and the banal statements are given an appearance of profundity by means of the *not un-* formation. Simple conjunctions and prepositions are replaced by such phrases as *with respect to, having regard to, the fact that, by dint of, in view of, in the interests of, on the hypothesis that;* and the ends of sentences are saved from anticlimax by such resounding commonplaces as *greatly to be desired, cannot be left out of account, a development to be expected in the near future, deserving of serious consideration, brought to a satisfactory conclusion,* and so on and so forth.

Pretentious diction. Words like *phenomenon, element, individual* (as noun), *objective, categorical, effective, virtual, basic, primary, promote, constitute, exhibit, exploit, utilize, eliminate, liquidate,* are used to dress up simple statements and give an air of scientific impartiality to biased judgments. Adjectives like *epoch-making, epic, historic, unforgettable, triumphant, age-old, inevitable, inexorable, veritable,* are used to dignify the sordid processes of international politics, while writing that aims at glorifying war usually takes on an archaic color, its characteristic words being: *realm, throne, chariot, mailed fist, trident, sword, shield, buckler, banner, jackboot, clarion.*

Foreign words and expressions such as *cul de sac, ancient régime, deus ex machina, mutatis mutandis, status quo, gleichschaltung, weltanschauung,* are used to give an air of culture and elegance. Except for the useful abbreviations *i.e., e.g.,* and *etc.,* there is no real need for any of the hundreds of foreign phrases now current in English. Bad writers, and especially scientific, political and sociological writers, are nearly always haunted by the notion that Latin or Greek words are grander than Saxon ones, and unnecessary words like *expedite, ameliorate, predict, extraneous, deracinated, clandestine, subaqueous* and hundreds of others constantly gain ground from their Anglo-Saxon opposite numbers.[1] The jargon peculiar to Marxist writing (*hyena, hangman, cannibal, petty bourgeois, these gentry, lacquey, flunkey, mad dog, White Guard,* etc.) consists largely of words and phrases translated from Russian, German, or French; but the normal way of coining a new word is to use a Latin or Greek root with the appropriate affix and, where necessary, the *-ize* formation. It is often easier to make up words of this kind (*deregionalize, impermissible, extramarital, non-fragmentary* and so forth) than to think up the English words that will cover one's meaning. The result, in general, is an increase in slovenliness and vagueness.

Meaningless words. In certain kinds of writing, particularly in art criticism and literary criticism, it is normal to come across long passages which are almost completely lacking in meaning.[2] Words like *romantic, plastic, values,*

---

[1] An interesting illustration of this is the way in which the English flower names which were in use till very recently are being ousted by Greek ones, *snapdragon* becoming *antirrhinum, forget-me-not* becoming *myosotis,* etc. It is hard to see any practical reason for this change of fashion: it is probably due to an instinctive turning-away from the more homely word and a vague feeling that the Greek word is scientific. [Orwell's note]

[2] Example: "Comfort's catholicity of perception and image, strangely Whitmanesque in range, almost the exact opposite in aesthetic compulsion, continues to evoke that trembling atmospheric accumulative hinting at a cruel, an inexorably serene timelessness. . . . Wrey Gardiner scores by aiming at simple bull's-eyes with precision. Only they are not so simple, and through this contented sadness runs more than the surface bittersweet of resignation." *(Poetry Quarterly.)* [Orwell's note]

human, dead, sentimental, natural, vitality, as used in art criticism, are strictly meaningless, in the sense that they not only do not point to any discoverable object, but are hardly ever expected to do so by the reader. When one critic writes, "The outstanding feature of Mr. X's work is its living quality," while another writes, "The immediately striking thing about Mr. X's work is its peculiar deadness," the reader accepts this as a simple difference of opinion. If words like *black* and *white* were involved, instead of the jargon words *dead* and *living,* he would see at once that language was being used in an improper way. Many political words are similarly abused. The word *Fascism* has now no meaning except in so far as it signifies "something not desirable." The words *democracy, socialism, freedom, patriotic, realistic, justice,* have each of them several different meanings which cannot be reconciled with one another. In the case of a word like *democracy,* not only is there no agreed definition, but the attempt to make one is resisted from all sides. It is almost universally felt that when we call a country democratic we are praising it: consequently the defenders of every kind of régime claim that it is a democracy, and fear that they might have to stop using the word if it were tied down to any one meaning. Words of this kind are often used in a consciously dishonest way. That is, the person who uses them has his own private definition, but allows his hearer to think he means something quite different. Statements like *Marshal Pétain was a true patriot, The Soviet Press is the freest in the world, The Catholic Church is opposed to persecution,* are almost always made with intent to deceive. Other words used in variable meanings, in most cases more or less dishonestly, are: *class, totalitarian, science, progressive, reactionary, bourgeois, equality.*

Now that I have made this catalogue of swindles and perversions, let me give another example of the kind of writing that they lead to. This time it must of its nature be an imaginary one. I am going to translate a passage of good English into modern English of the worst sort. Here is a well-known verse from *Ecclesiastes:*

"I returned and saw under the sun, that the race is not to the swift, nor the battle to the strong, neither yet bread to the wise, nor yet riches to men of understanding, nor yet favour to men of skill; but time and chance happeneth to them all."

Here it is in modern English:

"Objective consideration of contemporary phenomena compels the conclusion that success or failure in competitive activities exhibits no tendency to be commensurate with innate capacity, but that a considerable element of the unpredictable must invariably be taken into account."

This is a parody, but not a very gross one. Exhibit (3), above, for instance, contains several patches of the same kind of English. It will be seen that I have not made a full translation. The beginning and ending of the sentence follow the original meaning fairly closely, but in the middle the concrete illustrations—race, battle, bread—dissolve into the vague phrase "success or failure in competitive activities." This had to be so, because no modern writer of the kind I am discussing—no one capable of using phrases like "objective consideration of contemporary phenomena"—would ever tabulate his thoughts in that precise and detailed way. The whole tendency of modern prose is away from concreteness. Now analyse these two sentences a little more closely. The first contains forty-nine words but only sixty syllables, and all its words are those of everyday life. The second contains thirty-eight words of ninety syllables: eighteen of its words are from Latin roots, and one from Greek. The first sentence contains six vivid images, and only one phrase ("time and chance") that could be called vague. The second contains not a single fresh, arresting phrase, and in spite of its ninety syllables it gives only a shortened version of the meaning contained in the first. Yet without a doubt it is the second kind of sentence that is gaining ground in modern English. I do not want to exaggerate. This kind of writing is not yet universal, and outcrops of simplicity will occur here and there in the worst-written page. Still, if you or I were told to write a few lines on the uncertainty of human fortunes, we should probably come much nearer to my imaginary sentence than to the one from *Ecclesiastes*.

As I have tried to show, modern writing at its worst does not consist in picking out words for the sake of their meaning and inventing images in order to make the meaning clearer. It consists in gumming together long strips of words which have already been set in order by someone else, and making the results presentable by sheer humbug. The attraction of this way of writing is that it is easy. It is easier—even quicker, once you have the habit—to say *In my opinion it is not an unjustifiable assumption that* than to say *I think.* If you use ready-made phrases, you not only don't have to hunt about for words; you also don't have to bother with the rhythms of your sentences, since these phrases are generally so arranged as to be more or less euphonious. When you are composing in a hurry— when you are dictating to a stenographer, for instance, or making a public speech—it is natural to fall into a pretentious, Latinized style. Tags like *a consideration which we should do well to bear in mind* or *a conclusion to which all of us would readily assent* will save many a sentence from coming down with a bump. By using stale metaphors, similes, and idioms, you save much mental effort, at the cost of leaving your meaning vague, not only for your reader but for yourself. This is the significance of mixed metaphors. The sole aim of a metaphor is to call up a visual image. When these images clash—as in *The Fascist octopus has sung its swan song, the jackboot is thrown into the melting pot*—it can be taken as certain that the writer is not seeing a mental image of the objects he is naming; in other words he is not really thinking. Look again at the examples I gave at the beginning of this essay. Professor Laski (1) uses five negatives in fifty-three words. One of these is superfluous, making nonsense of the whole passage, and in addition there is the slip *alien* for akin, making further nonsense, and several avoidable pieces of clumsiness which increase the general vagueness. Professor Hogben (2) plays ducks and drakes with a battery which is able to write prescriptions, and, while disapproving of the everyday phrase *put up with,* is unwilling to look *egregious* up in the dictionary and see what it means; (3), if one takes an uncharitable attitude towards it, is simply meaningless: probably one could work out its intended meaning by reading the whole of the article in which it occurs. In (4), the writer knows more or less what he wants to say, but an accumulation of stale phrases chokes him like tea leaves blocking a sink. In (5), words and meaning have almost parted company. People who write in this manner usually have a general emotional meaning—they dislike one thing and want to express solidarity with another—but they are not interested in the detail of what they are saying. A scrupulous writer, in every sentence that he writes, will ask himself at least four questions, thus: What am I trying to say? What words will express it? What image or idiom will make it clearer? Is this image fresh enough to have an effect? And he will probably ask himself two more: Could I put it more shortly? Have I said anything that is avoidably ugly? But you are not obliged to go to all this trouble. You can shirk it by simply throwing your mind open and letting the ready-made phrases come crowding in. They will construct your sentences for you—even think your thoughts for you, to a certain extent—and at need they will perform the important service of partially concealing your meaning even from yourself. It is at this point that the special connection between politics and the debasement of language becomes clear.

In our time it is broadly true that political writing is bad writing. Where it is not true, it will generally be found that the writer is some kind of rebel, expressing his private opinions and not a "party line." Orthodoxy, of whatever color, seems to demand a lifeless, imitative style. The political dialects to be found in pamphlets, leading articles, manifestos, White Papers, and the speeches of under-secretaries do, of course, vary from party to party, but they are all alike in that one almost never finds in them a fresh, vivid, home-made turn of speech. When one watches some tired hack on the platform mechanically repeating the familiar phrases—*bestial atrocities, iron heel, blood-stained tyranny, free peoples of the world, stand shoulder to shoulder*—one often has a curious feeling that one is not watching a live human being but some kind of dummy: a feeling which suddenly becomes stronger at moments when the light catches the speaker's spectacles and turns them into blank discs which seem to have no eyes behind them. And this is not altogether fanciful. A speaker who uses that kind of phraseology has gone some distance towards turning himself into a machine. The appropriate noises are coming out of his larynx, but his brain is not involved as it would be if he were choosing his words for himself. If the speech he is making is one that he is accustomed to make over and over again, he may be almost unconscious of what he is saying, as one is when one utters the responses in church. And this reduced state of consciousness, if not indispensable, is at any rate favorable to political conformity.

In our time, political speech and writing are largely the defence of the indefensible. Things like the continuance of British rule in India, the Russian purges and deportations, the dropping of the atom bombs on Japan, can indeed be defended, but only by arguments which are too brutal for most people to face, and which do not square with the professed aims of political parties. Thus political language has to consist largely of euphemism, question-begging and sheer cloudy vagueness. Defenceless villages are bombarded from the air, the inhabitants driven out into the countryside, the cattle machine-gunned, the huts set on fire with incendiary bullets: this is called *pacification.* Millions of peasants are robbed of their farms and sent trudging along the roads with no more than they can carry: this is called *transfer of population* or *rectification of frontiers.* People are imprisoned for years without trial, or shot in the back of the neck or sent to die of scurvy in Arctic lumber camps: this is called *elimination of unreliable elements.* Such phraseology is needed if one wants to name things without calling up mental pictures of them. Consider for instance some comfortable English professor defending Russian totalitarianism. He cannot say outright, "I believe in killing off your opponents when you can get good results by doing so." Probably, therefore, he will say something like this:

"While freely conceding that the Soviet régime exhibits certain features which the humanitarian may be inclined to deplore, we must, I think, agree that a certain curtailment of the right to political opposition is an unavoidable concomitant of transitional periods, and that the rigors which the Russian people have been called upon to undergo have been amply justified in the sphere of concrete achievement."

The inflated style is itself a kind of euphemism. A mass of Latin words falls upon the facts like soft snow, blurring the outlines and covering up all the details. The great enemy of clear language is insincerity. When there is a gap between one's real and one's declared aims, one turns as it were instinctively to long words and exhausted idioms, like a cuttlefish squirting out ink. In our age there is no such thing as "keeping out of politics." All issues are political issues, and politics itself is a mass of lies, evasions, folly, hatred, and schizophrenia. When the general atmosphere is bad, language must suffer. I should expect to find—this is a guess which I have not sufficient knowledge to verify—that the German, Russian, and Italian languages have all deteriorated in the last ten or fifteen years, as a result of dictatorship.

But if thought corrupts language, language can also corrupt thought. A bad usage can spread by tradition and imitation, even among people who should and do know better. The debased language that I have been discussing is in some ways very convenient. Phrases like *a not unjustifiable assumption, leaves much to be desired, would serve no good purpose, a consideration which we should do well to bear in mind,* are a continuous temptation, a packet of aspirins always at one's elbow. Look back through this essay, and for certain you will find that I have again and again committed the very faults I am protesting against. By this morning's post I have received a pamphlet dealing with conditions in Germany. The author tells me that he "felt impelled" to write it. I open it at random, and here is almost the first sentence that I see: "[The Allies] have an opportunity not only of achieving a radical transformation of Germany's social and political structure in such a way as to avoid a nationalistic reaction in Germany itself, but at the same time of laying the foundations of a cooperative and unified Europe." You see, he "feels impelled" to write—feels, presumably, that he has something new to say—and yet his words, like cavalry horses answering the bugle, group themselves automatically into the familiar dreary pattern. This invasion of one's mind by ready-made phrases *(lay the foundations, achieve a radical transformation)* can only be prevented if one is constantly on guard against them, and every such phrase anaesthetizes a portion of one's brain.

I said earlier that the decadence of our language is probably curable. Those who deny this would argue, if they produced an argument at all, that language merely reflects existing social conditions, and that we cannot influence its development by any direct tinkering with words and constructions. So far as the general tone or spirit of a language goes, this may be true, but it is not true in detail. Silly words and expressions have often disappeared, not through any evolutionary process but owing to the conscious action of a minority. Two recent examples were *explore every avenue* and *leave no stone unturned,* which were killed by the jeers of a few journalists. There is a long list of fly-blown metaphors which could similarly be got rid of if enough people would interest themselves in the job; and it should also be possible to laugh the *not un-*formation out of existence,[3] to reduce the amount of Latin and Greek in the average sentence, to drive out foreign phrases and strayed scientific words, and, in general, to make pretentiousness unfashionable. But all these are minor points. The defence of the English language im-

[3] One can cure oneself of the *not un-* formation by memorizing this sentence: *A not unblack dog was chasing a not unsmall rabbit across a not ungreen field.* [Orwell's note]

plies more than this, and perhaps it is best to start by saying what it does *not* imply.

To begin with it has nothing to do with archaism, with the salvaging of obsolete words and turns of speech, or with the setting up of a "standard English" which must never be departed from. On the contrary, it is especially concerned with the scrapping of every word or idiom which has outworn its usefulness. It has nothing to do with correct grammar and syntax, which are of no importance so long as one makes one's meaning clear, or with the avoidance of Americanisms, or with having what is called a "good prose style." On the other hand it is not concerned with fake simplicity and the attempt to make written English colloquial. Nor does it even imply in every case preferring the Saxon word to the Latin one, though it does imply using the fewest and shortest words that will cover one's meaning. What is above all needed is to let the meaning choose the word, and not the other way about. In prose, the worst thing one can do with words is to surrender to them. When you think of a concrete object, you think wordlessly, and then, if you want to describe the thing you have been visualizing you probably hunt about till you find the exact words that seem to fit it. When you think of something abstract you are more inclined to use words from the start, and unless you make a conscious effort to prevent it, the existing dialect will come rushing in and do the job for you, at the expense of blurring or even changing your meaning. Probably it is better to put off using words as long as possible and get one's meaning as clear as one can through pictures or sensations. Afterwards one can choose—not simply *accept*—the phrases that will best cover the meaning, and then switch round and decide what impression one's words are likely to make on another person. This last effort of the mind cuts out all stale or mixed images, all prefabricated phrases, needless repetitions, and humbug and vagueness generally. But one can often be in doubt about the effect of a word or a phrase, and one needs rules that one can rely on when instinct fails. I think the following rules will cover most cases:

(i.)   Never use a metaphor, simile or other figure of speech which you are used to seeing in print.

(ii.)   Never use a long word where a short one will do.

(iii.)   If it is possible to cut a word out, always cut it out.

(iv.)   Never use the passive where you can use the active.

(v.)   Never use a foreign phrase, a scientific word or a jargon word if you can think of an everyday English equivalent.

(vi.)   Break any of these rules sooner than say anything outright barbarous.

These rules sound elementary, and so they are, but they demand a deep change of attitude in anyone who has grown used to writing in the style now fashionable. One could keep all of them and still write bad English, but one could not write the kind of stuff that I quoted in those five specimens at the beginning of this article.

I have not here been considering the literary use of language, but merely language as an instrument for expressing and not for concealing or preventing thought. Stuart Chase and others have come near to claiming that all abstract words are meaningless, and have used this as a pretext for advocating a kind of political quietism. Since you don't know what Fascism is, how can you struggle against Fascism? One need not swallow such absurdities as this, but one ought to recognize that the present political chaos is connected with the decay of language, and that one can probably bring about some improvement by starting at the verbal end. If you simplify your English, you are freed from the worst follies of orthodoxy. You cannot speak any of the necessary dialects, and when you make a stupid remark its stupidity will be obvious, even to yourself. Political language—and with variations this is true of all political parties, from Conservatives to Anarchists—is designed to make lies sound truthful and murder respectable, and to give an appearance of solidity to pure wind. One cannot change this all in a moment, but one can at least change one's own habits, and from time to time one can even, if one jeers loudly enough, send some wornout and useless phrase—some *jackboot, Achilles' heel, hotbed, melting pot, acid test, veritable inferno* or other lump of verbal refuse—into the dustbin where it belongs.

IDEAS

1. How clear is it that "the decline of language must ultimately have political and economic causes"?

2. How can you illustrate Orwell's comment about "inventing phrases for themselves" from Thoreau and Coles?

3. What are the metaphors in *toe the line* and *tow the line?*

4. What single verb would you supply for each of the phrases in Orwell's list beginning *render inoperative?*

5. Can you "think up the English words" for *deregionalize, impermissible, extramarital,* and *non-fragmentary?*

6. Which of Laski's five negatives is superfluous?

7. What example can you provide to illustrate or challenge Orwell's statement that grammar and syntax are unimportant as long as meaning is clear?

8. How would you explain Orwell's point about escaping "the worst follies of orthodoxy"?

ORGANIZATION AND STYLE

1. What is the effect of Orwell's metaphor concerning the prefabricated hen house? See if you can explain his other metaphors as you go through the essay.

2. Why are gerunds preferable to noun constructions?

3. In Orwell's third example, why does he italicize *on the other side?*

4. Which is the more accurate: *can only be prevented if* or *can be prevented only if?*

5. Does Orwell's own writing in the essay avoid the pitfalls about which he warns?

6. Examine the beginnings of Orwell's paragraphs. What are his transitions linking each paragraph with what has come before it?

WRITING

1. Orwell charges that most modern writing is "sheer humbug," consisting of nothing more than "long strips of words which have already been set in order by someone else." Evaluate this statement in an essay in which you focus not on the writer of such humbug but on the reader. What does the acceptance of such meaningless writing say about today's readers? Do they want the real truth or do they prefer slick, stock responses? As you see them, what are the causes of this condition in our society?

2. Analyze some political statement, from a campus politician perhaps, or a national one. You might want to use Orwell's categories of dying metaphors, false verbal limbs, and pretentious diction as organizational units in your own essay.

Politics and the American Language

ARTHUR SCHLESINGER, JR.

———————————— ● ————————————

Schlesinger brings Orwell to the American language and a newer generation, drawing particularly on the alliance between reason and freedom in the political thinking that originated American politics.

In our time, political speech and writing are largely the defence of the indefensible.

George Orwell

It takes a certain fortitude to pretend to amend Orwell on this subject. But "Politics and the English Language"—which I herewith incorporate by reference—was written more than a generation ago. In the years since, the process of semantic collapse has gathered speed, verified all of Orwell's expectations, and added new apprehensions for a new age. Americans in particular have found this a painful period of self-recognition. In 1946 we comfortably supposed that Orwell was talking about other people—Nazis and Stalinists, bureaucrats and sociologists, Professor Lancelot Hogben and Professor Harold Laski. Now recent history has obliged us to extend his dispiriting analysis to ourselves.

Vietnam and Watergate: these horrors will trouble the rest of our lives. But they are not, I suppose, unmitigated horrors. "Every act rewards itself," said Emerson.* As Vietnam instructed us, at terrible cost, in the limit of our wisdom and power in foreign affairs, so Watergate in-

*Ralph Waldo Emerson (1803–1882), New England essayist and poet.

structed us, at considerably less cost, in the limits of wisdom and power in the presidency. It reminded us of the urgent need to restore the original balance of the Constitution—the balance between presidential power and presidential accountability. In doing this, it has, among other things, brought back into public consciousness the great documents under which the American government was organized.

The Constitution, the debates of the Constitutional Convention, *The Federalist Papers*—how many of us read them with sustained attention in earlier years? A few eccentrics like Justice Black and Senator Ervin pored over them with devotion. The rest of us regarded them, beyond an occasional invocation of the Bill of Rights or the Fourteenth Amendment, as documents of essentially historical interest and left them undisturbed on the shelf. Then, under the goad first of Vietnam and then of Watergate, legislators, editors, columnists, even political scientists and historians—everyone, it would seem, except for presidential lawyers—began turning the dusty pages in order to find out what [James] Madison said in the convention about the war-making power or how [Alexander] Hamilton defined the grounds for impeachment in the sixty-fifth Federalist. Vietnam and Watergate are hardly to be compared. One is high tragedy, the other low, if black, comedy. But between them they have given the American people a spectacular reeducation in the fundamentals of our constitutional order.

One cannot doubt that this experience will have abiding political significance. The effect of Vietnam in exorcising our illusions and chastening our ambitions in foreign affairs has long been manifest. Now we begin to see the effect of Watergate in raising the standards of our politics. But I am less concerned initially with the political than with the literary consequences of this return to our constitutional womb. For, in addition to their exceptional qualities of insight and judgment, the historic documents must impress us by the extraordinary distinction of their language.

This was the age of the Enlightenment in America. The cooling breeze of reason tempered the hot work of composition and argument. The result was the language of the Founding Fathers—lucid, measured, and felicitous prose, marked by Augustan virtues of harmony, balance, and elegance. People not only wrote this noble language. They also read it. The essays in defense of the Constitution signed Publius appeared week after week in the New York press during the winter of 1787–88; and the demand was so great that the first thirty-six Federalist papers were published in book form while the rest were still coming out in the papers. One can only marvel at the sophistication of an audience that consumed and relished pieces so closely reasoned, so thoughtful and analytical. To compare *The Federalist Papers* with their equivalents in the press of our own day—say, with the contributions to the Op Ed page of the *New York Times*—is to annotate the decay of political discourse in America.

No doubt the birth of a nation is a stimulus to lofty utterance. The Founding Fathers had a profound conviction of historical responsibility. "The people of this country, by their conduct and example," Madison wrote in *The Federalist,* "will decide the important question, whether societies of men are really capable or not of establishing good government from reflection and choice, or whether they are forever destined to depend for their political constitutions on accident and force." The substitution of reflection and choice for accident and force proposed a revolution in the history of government; and the authors of *The Federalist* were passionate exemplars of the politics of reason.

The Founding Fathers lived, moreover, in an age when politicians could say in public more or less what they believed in private. If their view of human nature was realistic rather than sentimental, they were not obliged to pretend otherwise. *The Federalist,* for example, is a work notably free of false notes. It must not be supposed, however, that even this great generation was immune to temptation. When the Founding Fathers turned to speak of and to the largest interest in a primarily agricultural nation, they changed their tone and relaxed their standards. Those who lived on the soil, Jefferson could inanely write, were "the chosen people of God . . . whose breasts He has made His peculiar deposit for substantial and genuine virtue." Such lapses from realism defined one of the problems of American political discourse. For, as society grew more diversified, new interests claimed their place in the sun; and each in time had to be courted and flattered as the Jeffersonians had courted and flattered the agriculturists. The desire for success at the polls thus sentimentalized and cheapened the language of politics.

And politics was only an aspect of a deeper problem. Society as a whole was taking forms that warred against clarity of thought and integrity of language. "A man's power to connect his thought with its proper symbol, and so to utter it," said Emerson, "depends on the simplicity of his character, that is, upon his love of truth, and his desire to communicate it without loss. The corruption of man is followed by the corruption of language. When simplicity of character and the sovereignty of ideas is broken up by the prevalence of secondary desires, the desire of riches, of pleasure, of power, and of praise . . . words are perverted to stand for things which are not."

"The prevalence of secondary desires," the desire of riches, pleasure, power, and praise—this growing social complexity began to divert the function of words from expression to gratification. No one observed the impact of a mobile and egalitarian society on language more acutely than Tocqueville.* Democracy, he argued, inculcated a positive preference for ambiguity and a dangerous addiction to the inflated style. "An abstract term," Tocqueville wrote, "is like a box with a false bottom; you may put in what you please, and take them out again without being observed." So words, divorced from objects, became in-

---

*Alexis Charles Henri Maurice-Clérel de Tocqueville (1805–1859), French politician, diplomat, and traveler, wrote, after extensive travels in America, the first analysis of American institutions and politics from a European perspective, *Democracy in America* (1835), still considered a shrewd appreciation of American democracy.

struments less of communication than of deception. Unscrupulous orators stood abstractions on their head and transmuted them into their opposites, aiming to please one faction by the sound and the contending faction by the meaning. They did not always succeed. "The word *liberty* in the mouth of [Daniel] Webster," Emerson wrote with contempt after the Compromise of 1850,* "sounds like the word *love* in the mouth of a courtezan." Watching Henry Kissinger babbling about his honor at his famous Salzburg press conference, one was irresistibly reminded of another of Emerson's nonchalant observations: "The louder he talked of his honor, the faster we counted our spoons."

Other developments hastened the spreading dissociation of words from meaning, of language from reality. The rise of mass communications, the growth of large organizations and novel technologies, the invention of advertising and public relations, the professionalization of education—all contributed to linguistic pollution, upsetting the ecological balance between words and their environment. In our own time the purity of language is under unrelenting attack from every side—from professors as well as from politicians, from newspapermen as well as from advertising men, from men of the cloth as well as from men of the sword, and not least from those indulgent compilers of modern dictionaries who propound the suicidal thesis that all usages are equal and all correct.

A living language can never be stabilized, but a serious language can never cut words altogether adrift from meanings. The alchemy that changes words into their opposites has never had more adept practitioners than it has today. We used to object when the Communists described dictatorships as "people's democracies" or North Korean aggression as the act of a "peace-loving" nation. But we are no slouches ourselves in the art of verbal metamorphosis. There was often not much that was "free" about many of the states that made up what we used to call, sometimes

*Which admitted California as a free state, but did not prohibit slavery in the New Mexico and Utah territories. It also strengthened the Fugitive Slave Act, to the South's advantage.

with capital letters, the Free World; as there is, alas, very often little that is gay about many of those who seek these days to kidnap that sparkling word for specialized use. Social fluidity, moral pretension, political and literary demagoguery, corporate and academic bureaucratization, and a false conception of democracy are leading us into semantic chaos. We owe to Vietnam and Watergate a belated recognition of the fact that we are in linguistic as well as political crisis and that the two may be organically connected. As Emerson said, "We infer the spirit of the nation in great measure from the language."

For words are not neutral instruments, pulled indifferently out of a jumbled tool kit. "Language," wrote Coleridge, "is the armoury of the human mind; and at once contains the trophies of its past, and the weapons of its future conquests." Language colors and penetrates the depths of our consciousness. It is the medium that dominates perceptions, organizes categories of thought, shapes the development of ideas, and incorporates a philosophy of existence. Every political movement generates its own language-field; every language-field legitimizes one set of motives, values, and ideals and banishes the rest. The language-field of the Founding Fathers directed the American consciousness toward one constellation of standards and purposes. The language-field of Vietnam and Watergate has tried to direct the national consciousness toward very different goals. Politics in basic aspects is a symbolic and therefore a linguistic phenomenon.

We began to realize this in the days of the Indochina War. In the middle 1960s Americans found themselves systematically staving off reality by allowing a horrid military-bureaucratic patois to protect our sensibilities from the ghastly things we were doing in Indochina. The official patter about "attrition," "pacification," "defoliation," "body counts," "progressive squeeze-and-talk" sterilized the frightful reality of napalm and My Lai. This was the period when television began to provide a sharper access to reality, and Marshall McLuhan ["The medium is the message"] had his day in court.

But the military-bureaucratic jargon could be blamed on generals, who, as General Eisenhower reminded us at every press conference, habitually speak in a dialect of their own. What we had not perhaps fully realized before Watergate was the utter debasement of language in the mouths of our recent civilian leaders. How our leaders really talk is not, of course, easy to discover, since their public appearances are often veiled behind speeches written by others. I know that President Kennedy spoke lucidly, wittily and economically in private. President Johnson spoke with force and often in pungent and inventive frontier idiom. President Nixon's fascinating contribution to oral history suggests, however, a recent and marked decline in the quality of presidential table talk. "A man cannot speak," said Emerson, "but he judges himself."

Groping to describe that degenerate mélange of military, public relations and locker-room jargon spoken in the Nixon White House, Richard N. Goodwin aptly wrote of "the bureaucratization of the criminal class." It was as if the Godfather spoke in the phrases of the secretary of health, education and welfare. When one read of "stroking sessions," of "running out of the bottom line," of "toughing it out," of going down "the hang-out road," or "how do you handle that PR-wise," one felt that there should be one more impeachable offense; and that is verbicide. But what was worse than the massacre of language, which after all displayed a certain low ingenuity, was the manipulation of meaning. The presidential speech preceding the release of the expurgated transcripts was syntactically correct enough. But it proclaimed in tones of ringing sincerity that the transcripts showed exactly the opposite of what in fact the transcripts did show. "He unveils a swamp," as the *New Yorker* well put it, "and instructs us to see a garden of flowers." In the Nixon White House, language not only fled the reality principle but became the servant of nightmare.

"The use of words," wrote Madison in the thirty-seventh *Federalist,* "is to express ideas. Perspicuity, therefore, requires not only that the ideas should be distinctly formed, but that they should be expressed by words distinctly and exclusively appropriate to them." Madison was under no illusion that this condition of semantic beatitude was easy to attain. "No language is so copious," he continued, "as to supply words and phrases for every complex idea, or so correct as not to include many equivocally denoting different ideas. . . . When the Almighty himself condescends to address mankind in their own language, his meaning, luminous as it must be, is rendered dim and doubtful by the cloudy medium through which it is communicated." Nevertheless, Madison and his generation thought the quest for precision worth the effort. It is an entertaining but morbid speculation to wonder what the Founding Fathers, returning to inspect the Republic on the eve of the two-hundredth anniversary of the independence they fought so hard to achieve, would make of the White House tapes.

The degradation of political discourse in America is bound to raise a disturbing question. May it be, as Tocqueville seemed to think, that such deterioration is inherent in democracy? Does the compulsion to win riches, pleasure, power, and praise in a fluid and competitive society make the perversion of meaning and the debasement of language inevitable? One can certainly see specific American and democratic traits that have promoted linguistic decay. But a moment's reflection suggests that the process is by no means confined to the United States nor to democracies. Language degenerates a good deal more rapidly and thoroughly in communist and fascist states. For the control of language is a necessary step toward the control of minds, as Orwell made so brilliantly clear in *1984.* Nowhere is meaning more ruthlessly manipulated, nowhere is language more stereotyped, mechanical, implacably banal, and systematically false, nowhere is it more purged of personal nuance and human inflection, than in Russia and China. In democracies the assault on language is piecemeal, sporadic, and unorganized. And democracy has above all the decisive advantage that the preservation of intellectual freedom creates the opportunity for counterattack. Democracy always has the chance to redeem its language. This may be an essential step toward the redemption of its politics.

One must add that it is idle to expect perfection in political discourse. The problem of politics in a democracy is to win broad consent for measures of national policy. The winning of consent often requires the bringing together of disparate groups with diverging interests. This inescapably involves a certain oracularity of expression. One remembers de Gaulle before the crowd in Algeria, when the *pieds-noirs* chanted that Algeria belonged to France, replying solemnly, "Je vous comprends, mes comarades"*—hardly a forthright expression of his determination to set Algeria free. Besides, oracularity may often be justified since no one can be all that sure about the future. The Founding Fathers understood this, which is why the Constitution is in many respects a document of calculated omission and masterful ambiguity whose "real" meaning—that is, what it would mean in practice—only practice could disclose. Moreover, as Lord Keynes, who wrote even economics in English, once put it, "Words ought to be a little wild, for they are an assault of thought upon the unthinking."

Keynes immediately added, however: "But when the seats of power and authority have been attained, there should be no more poetic license." Madison described the American experiment as the replacement of accident and force by reflection and choice in the processes of government. The responsibility of presidents is to define real choices and explain soberly why one course is to be preferred to another—and, in doing so, to make language a means not of deception but of communication, not an enemy but a friend of the reality principle.

Yet presidents cannot easily rise above the society they serve and lead. If we are to restore the relationship between words and meaning, we must begin to clean up the whole linguistic environment. This does not mean a cru-

---

*"I understand you, my comrades."

sade for standard English or a campaign to resurrect the stately rhythms of *The Federalist Papers*. Little could be more quixotic than an attempt to hold a rich and flexible language like American English to the forms and definitions of a specific time, class, or race. But some neologisms are better than others, and here one can demand, particularly in influential places, a modicum of discrimination. More important is that words, whether new or old, regain a relationship to reality. Vietnam and Watergate have given a good many Americans, I believe, a real hatred of double-talk and a hunger for bluntness and candor. Why else the success of the posthumous publication of President Truman's gaudy exercise in plain speaking?

The time is ripe to sweep the language-field of American politics. In this season of semantic malnutrition, who is not grateful for a public voice that appears to blurt out what the speaker honestly believes? A George Wallace begins to win support even among blacks (though ambition is already making Wallace bland, and blandness will do him in too). Here those who live by the word—I mean by the true word, like writers and teachers; not by the phony word, like public relations men, writers, and teachers— have their peculiar obligation. Every citizen is free under the First Amendment to use and abuse the words that bob around in the swamp of his mind. But writers and teachers have, if anyone has, the custodianship of the language. Their charge is to protect the words by which they live. Their duty is to expel the cant of the age.

At the same time, they must not forget that in the recent past they have been among the worst offenders. They must take scrupulous care that indignation does not lead them to the same falsity and hyperbole they righteously condemn in others. A compilation of political pronouncements by eminent writers and learned savants over the last generation would make a dismal volume. One has only to recall the renowned, if addled, scholars who signed the full page advertisement in the *New York Times* of October 15, 1972, which read, as the *New Yorker* would say, in its entirety: "Of the two major candidates for the

Presidency of the United States, we believe that Richard Nixon has demonstrated the superior capacity for prudent and responsible leadership. Consequently, we intend to vote for President Nixon on November 7th and we urge our fellow citizens to do the same."

The time has come for writers and teachers to meet the standards they would enforce on others and rally to the defense of the word. They must expose the attack on meaning and discrimination in language as an attack on reason in discourse. It is this rejection of reason itself that underlies the indulgence of imprecision, the apotheosis of usage, and the infatuation with rhetoric. For once words lose a stable connection with things, we can no longer know what we think or communicate what we believe.

One does not suggest that the restoration of language is all that easy in an age when new issues, complexities, and ambiguities stretch old forms to the breaking point.

> *. . . Words strain*
> *Crack and sometimes break, under the burden,*
> *Under the tension, slip, slide, perish,*
> *Decay with imprecision, will not stay in place,*
> *Will not stay still.**

Each venture is therefore the new beginning, the raid on the inarticulate with shabby equipment always deteriorating in the general mess of imprecision of feeling. Yet, as Eliot went on to say, "For us, there is only the trying. The rest is not our business."† As we struggle to recover what has been lost ("and found and lost again and again"), as we try our own sense of words against the decay of language, writers and teachers make the best contribution they can to the redemption of politics. Let intellectuals never forget that all they that take the word shall perish with the word. "Wise men pierce this rotten diction," said Emerson, "and fasten words again to visible things; so that

---

*T. S. Eliot, "Burnt Norton," sec. V, *Four Quartets.*
†"East Coker," sec. V, *Four Quartets.*

picturesque language is at once a commanding certificate that he who employs it, is a man in alliance with truth and God."

IDEAS

1. What is Schlesinger's metaphor concerning the "cooling breeze of reason"? How does his linkage of reason and clear language resemble Orwell's? How does it work throughout the essay?

2. Would he agree with Orwell that the decline of language has political and economic causes?

3. Do you agree with Schlesinger's assessment of our Founding Fathers? Were they as honest and noble as he suggests?

4. What is meant by the metaphor "Every political movement generates its own language-field"?

5. What do Schlesinger and Orwell mean by "standard English"? Are there other meanings?

6. What does Schlesinger's quotation from *The New York Times* illustrate? That teachers and writers are not protecting "the words by which they live"? That they are guilty of falsity and hyperbole? Can you see anything faulty in its language or construction?

7. Schlesinger refers to "the suicidal thesis that all usages are equal and all correct." In his next-to-last paragraph, how is "the apotheosis of usage" a "rejection of reason itself"?

ORGANIZATION AND STYLE

1. Where does Schlesinger's introduction end?

2. Why does he introduce the ideas of Vietnam and Watergate in the second paragraph when he follows this with several paragraphs about the beginnings of this nation?

3. What shift does the essay take with the paragraph beginning "A living language can never be stabilized. . . ."?

4. Examine Schlesinger's various sentence lengths. When does he tend to write unusually long sentences? When very short and direct ones?

5. The author is frequently metaphorical. Which of his metaphors are most effective. Do any overshout? Might metaphors, like clichés, obscure meaning rather than make it clear?

WRITING

1. Orwell comes down hard on Latinate words, overlooking the effectiveness and wit of such phrases as his own "sentimental archaism" or Schlesinger's "semantic malnutrition," especially when some big Latinity couples with something short and sharp "incomprehensibly smug," "outrageously dry," "prefabricated hen-house," (Orwell), "constitutional womb" (Schlesinger). In your next essay, try at least one such combination of Latin and Saxon words: you may discover some incomparable zip in your writing.

2. Write an essay in which you spin off from Schlesinger's "Little could be more quixotic than an attempt to hold a rich and flexible language like American English to the forms and definitions of a specific time, class, or race." Do you agree or disagree with this statement? What are the possibilities that language can become a tool of the power class? If there are no ultimate standards in using the language, what is the possibility that everyone may speak and write so diversely that no one will be able to understand anyone outside of his or her social, economic group?

3. The essays by Orwell and Schlesinger both came down rather severely on politicians, but what about other professions? Select another professional group—per-

haps educators, clergy, physicians, or computer engineers—and write an essay in which you show how members of that group use or misuse the language. Do you feel the way they use language is a deliberate attempt to manipulate others? A way to keep a special field of information exclusively to themselves?

The English Language Is My Enemy

OSSIE DAVIS

———————————— ● ————————————

Because they are the substance of thought, words may sway and control others positively or negatively. Sometimes this effect is unconscious; at other times it may be deliberate and, as Davis suggests, malicious.

A superficial examination of Roget's *Thesaurus of the English Language* reveals the following facts: the word WHITENESS has 134 synonyms; 44 of which are favorable and pleasing to contemplate, i.e., purity, cleanness, immaculateness, bright, shining, ivory, fair, blond, stainless, clean, clear, chaste, unblemished, unsullied, innocent, honorable, upright, just, straight-forward, fair, genuine, trustworthy (a white-man colloquialism). Only ten synonyms for WHITENESS appear to me to have negative implications—and these only in the mildest sense: gloss over, whitewash, gray, wan, pale, ashen, etc.

The word BLACKNESS has 120 synonyms, 60 of which are distinctly unfavorable, and none of them even mildly positive. Among the offending 60 were such words as: blot, blotch, smut, smudge, sully, begrime, soot, becloud, obscure, dingy, murky, low-toned, threatening, frowning, foreboding, forbidden, sinister, baneful, dismal, thundery, evil, wicked, malignant, deadly, unclean, dirty, unwashed, foul, etc. . . . not to mention 20 synonyms directly related to race, such as: Negro, Negress, nigger, darky, blackamoor, etc.

When you consider the fact that *thinking* itself is subvocal speech—in other words, one must use *words* in order to think at all—you will appreciate the enormous heritage of racial prejudgment that lies in wait for any child born into the English Language. Any teacher good or bad, white or black, Jew or Gentile, who uses the English Language as a medium of communication is forced, willy-nilly, to teach the Negro child 60 ways to despise himself, and the white child 60 ways to aid and abet him in the crime.

Who speaks to me in my Mother Tongue damns me indeed! . . . the English Language—in which I cannot conceive myself as a black man without, at the same time, debasing myself . . . my enemy, with which to survive at all I must continually be at war.

IDEAS

1. What is the difference between the denotative meaning of a word and its connotative meaning? Do all words have connotative meanings?

2. What is Davis's specific quarrel with the English language?

3. Davis does not say that all *whiteness* words are positive and all *blackness* words are negative. He comments on 44 (out of 134) in the first category and 60 (out of 120) in the latter. Examine Roget's *Thesaurus* and do your own analysis of the entire set of words. Does Davis's thesis still hold up?

4. Do *whiteness* words and *blackness* words have similar connotations in other languages? Why would humanity think negatively about night and darkness and positively about day and light?

ORGANIZATION AND STYLE

1. What is Davis's thesis? Is it effective in this position, or would it be more effective located at a different place in the brief essay?

2. What do you perceive as the difference in style between the first two paragraphs and the last two? How

can you account for this difference? What would have been the effect had Davis reversed the order of the paragraph sets?

WRITING

1. Select a minority group with which you are familiar, perhaps one to which you belong. Examine the power of language, as others might use it, to paint a negative picture of the group and its members. What words are especially offensive? Why?

2. Find an article in a current newspaper—maybe an editorial or a letter to the editor—in which the writer makes decided use of highly connotative words to achieve either a positive or a negative effect. Write an essay in which you analyze that article and its language. What words are connotative? How do they affect the final meaning? Do you think the author used them purposefully? What would have been the effect had all connotative words been eliminated?

8

SPECIAL FORMS

We have already seen something of what the five essays that follow exhibit: dramatic irony, as Ward's Sal disguises his mechanical ignorance in verbiage, for instance; verbal irony as White praises the Nature Boy, Thoreau. Orwell has already given us the supreme autobiographical essay. Virginia Woolf and MacLeish have deployed the critic's generalizing powers. And we have seen the lucidity of science in Asimov, Gould, and Petrunkevitch.

Yet the five essays in this concluding section attract special attention. Swift's is unique, a peculiar, unequalled masterpiece of irony, and Baker's, though much more lighthearted, is perhaps nearly as devastating in its implied judgments. Eiseley's personal illumination of Thoreau's depths is also unequalled, a rare blend of critical perception and personal admiration. Winn's critical analysis of the Beatles, with its perceptive and well-illustrated thesis, explains their achievement, and their attraction, as never before. Einstein leaves us humble before his own magnificent humility and intelligence, his clarity in explaining the awesome but simple calculations that describe our corner of the universe, and finally, his admirable tribute to both cosmic and human rationality.

The Ironic Essay

A *Modest Proposal for Preventing the Children of Ireland from Being a Burden to Their Parents or Country*

JONATHAN SWIFT

———————— ● ————————

Swift's Proposal is a masterpiece of dramatic irony, in which the dramatized speaker believes and expresses one thing but inadvertently conveys its ironic opposite to his wiser audience. Swift's caricatured speaker, or writer, urges what he thinks a reasonable solution to the horrors of Irish poverty under English domination and Anglo-Irish landlords. The ironic opposite is Swift's actual message: this exploitation is heartless, ghastly, and avoidable, to be mitigated by the "other expedients" the writer, in ironic despair, declares useless at the end.

The irony begins with the words "their dear native country" in the first paragraph, after a straight description of the actuality. The phrase would be direct verbal irony between two people fully aware of Irish feelings, mutually understanding each other—that is, if Swift himself were speaking directly to us. But it becomes dramatic irony on the caricatured speaker's lips because he is unaware of its untruth. He believes it literally and says it as an element to wring our hearts to accept what he thinks is a modest and reasonable proposal, his method for rendering the children "sound, useful members of the commonwealth" by killing them. At times, Swift nears the surface in direct verbal irony in phrases about landlords "devouring" their tenants whole, or about a certain country "glad to eat up our whole nation" with-

out salt. But, still, these touches only deepen the speaker's dramatic blindness to his position as he rises to try a little ironic wit, still blind to our larger ironic perception of the true situation and message.

It is a melancholy object to those who walk through this great town [Dublin], or travel in the country, when they see the streets, the roads, and cabin-doors, crowded with beggars of the female sex, followed by three, four, or six children, all in rags, and importuning every passenger for an alms. These mothers, instead of being able to work for their honest livelihood, are forced to employ all their time in strolling to beg sustenance for their helpless infants; who, as they grow up, either turn thieves for want of work, or leave their dear native country to fight for the Pretender in Spain, or sell themselves to the Barbadoes.

I think it is agreed by all parties, that this prodigious number of children in the arms, or on the backs, or at the heels of their mothers, and frequently of their fathers, is, in the present deplorable state of the kingdom, a very great additional grievance; and, therefore, whoever could find out a fair, cheap, and easy method of making these children sound, useful members of the commonwealth, would deserve so well of the public, as to have his statue set up for a preserver of the nation.

But my intention is very far from being confined to provide only for the children of professed beggars; it is of a much greater extent, and shall take in the whole number of infants at a certain age, who are born of parents in effect as little able to support them, as those who demand our charity in the streets.

As to my own part, having turned my thoughts for many years upon this important subject, and maturely weighed the several schemes of our projectors, I have always found them grossly mistaken in their computation. It is true, a child, just dropped from its dam, may be supported by her milk for a solar year, with little other nourishment; at most, not above the value of two shillings, which the mother may certainly get, or the value in scraps, by her lawful occupation of begging; and it is exactly at one year old that I proposed to provide for them in such a manner, as, instead of being a charge upon their parents, or the parish, or wanting food and raiment for the rest of their lives, they shall, on the contrary, contribute to the feeding and partly to the clothing, of many thousands.

There is likewise another great advantage in my scheme, that it will prevent those voluntary abortions, and that horrid practice of women murdering their bastard children, alas, too frequent among us! sacrificing the poor innocent babes, I doubt more to avoid the expense than the shame, which would move tears and pity in the most savage and inhuman breast.

The number of souls in this kingdom being usually reckoned one million and a half, of these I calculate there may be about two hundred thousand couple whose wives are breeders; from which number I subtract thirty thousand couple, who are able to maintain their own children, (although I apprehend there cannot be so many, under the present distresses of the kingdom;) but this being granted, there will remain a hundred and seventy thousand breeders. I again subtract fifty thousand, for those women who miscarry, or whose children die by accident or disease within the year. There only remain a hundred and twenty thousand children of poor parents annually born. The question therefore is, How this number shall be reared and provided for? which, as I have already said, under the present situation of affairs, is utterly impossible by all the methods hitherto proposed. For we can neither employ them in handicraft or agriculture; we neither build houses (I mean in the country,) nor cultivate land: they can very seldom pick up a livelihood by stealing, till they arrive at six years old, except where they are of towardly parts; although I confess they learn the rudiments much earlier; during which time they can, however, be properly looked upon only as probationers; as I have been informed by a principal gentleman in the county of Cavan, who protested to me, that he never knew above one or two instances under the age of six, even in a part of the kingdom so renowned for the quickest proficiency in that art.

I am assured by our merchants, that a boy or a girl before twelve years old is no saleable commodity; and even when they come to this age they will not yield above three pounds, or three pounds and half-a-crown at most, on the exchange; which cannot turn to account either to the parents or kingdom, the charge of nutriment and rags having been at least four times that value.

I shall now, therefore, humbly propose my own thoughts, which I hope will not be liable to the least objection.

I have been assured by a very knowing American of my acquaintance in London, that a young healthy child, well nursed, is, at a year old, a most delicious, nourishing, and wholesome food, whether stewed, roasted, baked, or boiled; and I make no doubt that it will equally serve in a fricassee or a ragout.

I do therefore humbly offer it to public consideration, that of the hundred and twenty thousand children already computed, twenty thousand may be reserved for breed, whereof only one-fourth part to be males; which is more than we allow to sheep, black-cattle, or swine, and my reason is, that these children are seldom the fruits of marriage, a circumstance not much regarded by our savages, therefore one male will be sufficient to serve four females. That the remaining hundred thousand may, at a year old, be offered in sale to the persons of quality and fortune through the kingdom; always advising the mother to let them suck plentifully in the last month, so as to render them plump and fat for a good table. A child will make two dishes at an entertainment for friends; and when the family dines alone, the fore or hind quarter will make a reasonable dish, and, seasoned with a little pepper or salt, will be very good boiled on the fourth day, especially in winter.

I have reckoned, upon a medium, that a child just born will weigh twelve pounds, and in a solar year, if tolerably nursed, will increase to twenty-eight pounds.

I grant this food will be somewhat dear, and therefore

very proper for landlords, who, as they have already devoured most of the parents, seem to have the best title to
the children.

Infant's flesh will be in season throughout the year, but
more plentifully in March, and a little before and after: for
we are told by a grave author, an eminent French physician, that fish being a prolific diet, there are more children
born in Roman Catholic countries about nine months after
Lent, than at any other season; therefore, reckoning a year
after Lent, the markets will be more glutted than usual,
because the number of Popish infants is at least three to
one in this kingdom; and therefore it will have one other
collateral advantage, by lessening the Papists among us.

I have already computed the charge of nursing a beg-
gar's child (in which list I reckon all cottagers, labourers,
and four-fifths of the farmers) to be about two shillings per
annum, rags included; and I believe no gentleman would
repine to give ten shillings for the carcass of a good fat
child, which, as I have said, will make four dishes of excellent nutritive meat, when he has only some particular
friend, or his own family, to dine with him. Thus the
squire will learn to be a good landlord, and grow popular
among his tenants; the mother will have eight shillings
net profit, and be fit for work till she produces another
child.

Those who are more thrifty (as I must confess the times
require) may flay the carcass; the skin of which, artifi-
cially dressed, will make admirable gloves for ladies, and
summer-boots for fine gentlemen.

As to our city of Dublin, shambles [slaughter houses]
may be appointed for this purpose in the most convenient
parts of it, and butchers, we may be assured, will not be
wanting; although I rather recommend buying the children alive, then dressing them hot from the knife, as we
do roasting pigs.

A very worthy person, a true lover of his country, and
whose virtues I highly esteem, was lately pleased, in dis-
coursing on this matter, to offer a refinement upon my
scheme. He said, that many gentlemen of this kingdom,

having of late destroyed their deer, he conceived that the want of venison might be well supplied by the bodies of young lads and maidens, not exceeding fourteen years of age, nor under twelve; so great a number of both sexes in every country being now ready to starve for want of work and service; and these to be disposed of by their parents, if alive, or otherwise by their nearest relations. But, with due deference to so excellent a friend, and so deserving a patriot, I cannot be altogether in his sentiments; for as to the males, my American acquaintance assured me, from frequent experience, that their flesh was generally tough and lean, like that of our schoolboys, by continual exercise, and their taste disagreeable; and to fatten them would not answer the charge. Then as to the females, it would, I think, with humble submission, be a loss to the public, because they soon would become breeders themselves: and besides, it is not improbable that some scrupulous people might be apt to censure such a practice, (although indeed very unjustly,) as a little bordering upon cruelty; which, I confess, has always been with me the strongest objection against any project, how well soever intended.

But in order to justify my friend, he confessed that this expedient was put into his head by the famous Psalmanazar,* a native of the island Formosa, who came from thence to London above twenty years ago; and in conversation told my friend, that in his country, when any young person happened to be put to death, the executioner sold the carcass to persons of quality as a prime dainty; and that in his time the body of a plump girl of fifteen, who was crucified for an attempt to poison the emperor, was sold to his imperial majesty's prime minister of state, and other great mandarins of the court, in joints from the gibbet, at four hundred crowns. Neither indeed can I deny, that, if

---

*George Psalmanazar (c.1679–1763), a Frenchman, who came to London pretending to be Japanese. The Bishop of London converted him and hired him to translate the catechism into what was presumed to be Japanese. He published a spurious *Historical and Geographical Description of Formosa* in 1704. He eventually confessed his frauds and lived an exemplary life, but never revealed his true name.

the same use were made of several plump young girls in this town, who, without one single groat to their fortunes, cannot stir abroad without a chair, and appear at playhouse and assemblies in foreign fineries which they never will pay for, the kingdom would not be the worse.

Some persons of a desponding spirit are in great concern about that vast number of poor people, who are aged, diseased, or maimed; and I have been desired to employ my thoughts, what course may be taken to ease the nation of so grievous an encumbrance. But I am not in the least pain upon that matter, because it is very well known, that they are every day dying, and rotting, by cold and famine, and filth and vermin, as fast as can be reasonably expected. And as to the young labourers, they are now in almost as hopeful a condition: they cannot get work, and consequently pine away for want of nourishment, to a degree, that if at any time they are accidentally hired to common labour, they have not strength to perform it; and thus the country and themselves are happily delivered from the evils to come.

I have too long digressed, and therefore shall return to my subject. I think the advantages by the proposal which I have made are obvious and many, as well as of the highest importance.

For first, as I have already observed, it would greatly lessen the number of Papists, with whom we are yearly over-run, being the principal breeders of the nation, as well as our most dangerous enemies; and who stay at home on purpose to deliver the kingdom to the Pretender,* hoping to take their advantage by the absence of so many good Protestants, who have chosen rather to leave their country than stay at home and pay tithes against their conscience to an Episcopal curate.

Secondly, The poorer tenants will have something valuable of their own, which by law may be made liable to distress, and help to pay their landlord's rent; their corn

---

*James Francis Edward Stuart (1688–1766), son of James II, deposed in 1688 for Catholicism, who claimed the right to the British throne from exile in France for the rest of his life.

and cattle being already seized, and money a thing unknown.

Thirdly, Whereas the maintenance of a hundred thousand children, from two years old and upwards, cannot be computed at less than ten shillings a piece per annum, the nation's stock will be thereby increased fifty thousand pounds per annum, beside the profit of a new dish introduced to the tables of all gentlemen of fortune in the kingdom, who have any refinement in taste. And the money will circulate among ourselves, the goods being entirely of our own growth and manufacture.

Fourthly, The constant breeders, beside the gain of eight shillings sterling per annum by the sale of their children, will be rid of the charge of maintaining them after the first year.

Fifthly, This food would likewise bring great custom to taverns; where the vintners will certainly be so prudent as to procure the best receipts for dressing it to perfection, and, consequently, have their houses frequented by all the fine gentlemen, who justly value themselves upon their knowledge in good eating: and a skilful cook, who understands how to oblige his guests, will contrive to make it as expensive as they please.

Sixthly, This would be great inducement to marriage, which all wise nations have either encouraged by rewards, or enforced by laws and penalties. It would increase the care and tenderness of mothers toward their children, when they were sure of a settlement for life to the poor babes, provided in some sort by the public, to their annual profit or expense. We should see an honest emulation among the married women, which of them could bring the fattest child to the market. Men would become as fond of their wives during the time of their pregnancy as they are now of their mares in foal, their cows in calf, their sows when they are ready to farrow; nor offer to beat or kick them (as is too frequent a practice) for fear of a miscarriage.

Many other advantages might be enumerated. For instance, the addition of some thousand carcasses in our exportation of barrelled beef; the propagation of swine's flesh, and improvement in the art of making good bacon, so much wanted among us by the great destruction of pigs, too frequent at our table; which are no way comparable in taste or magnificence to a well-grown, fat, yearling child, which, roasted whole, will make a considerable figure at a lord mayor's feast, or any other public entertainment. But this, and many others, I omit, being studious of brevity.

Supposing that one thousand families in this city would be constant customers for infants' flesh, beside others who might have it at merry-meetings, particularly at weddings and christenings, I compute that Dublin would take off annually about twenty thousand carcasses; and the rest of the kingdom (where probably they will be sold somewhat cheaper) the remaining eighty thousand.

I can think of no one objection, that will possibly be raised against this proposal, unless it should be urged, that the number of people will be thereby much lessened in the kingdom. This I freely own, and it was indeed one principal design in offering it to the world. I desire the reader will observe, that I calculate my remedy for this one individual kingdom of Ireland, and for no other that ever was, is, or I think ever can be, upon earth. Therefore let no man talk to me of other expedients: of taxing our absentees at five shillings a pound: of using neither clothes, nor household furniture, except what is our own growth and manufacture: of utterly rejecting the materials and instruments that promote foreign luxury: of curing the expensiveness of pride, vanity, idleness, and gaming in our women: of introducing a vein of parsimony, prudence and temperance: of learning to love our country, in the want of which we differ even from LAPLANDERS, and the inhabitants of TOPINAMBOO: of quitting our animosities and factions, nor acting any longer like the Jews, who were murdering one another at the very moment their city was taken:* of being a little cautious not to sell our country and conscience for

---

*Three rival factions were at war within Jerusalem when the beseiging Romans, under Titus, finally took the city and burned the Temple in A.D. 70, ending four years of rebellion.

nothing: of teaching landlords to have at least one degree of mercy toward their tenants: lastly, of putting a spirit of honesty, industry, and skill into our shopkeepers; who, if a resolution could now be taken to buy only our native goods, would immediately unite to cheat and exact upon us in the price, the measure, and the goodness, nor could ever yet be brought to make one fair proposal of just dealing, though often and earnestly invited to it.

Therefore I repeat, let no man talk to me of these and the like expedients, till he has at least some glimpse of hope, that there will be ever some hearty and sincere attempt to put them in practice.

But, as to myself, having been wearied out for many years with offering vain, idle, visionary thoughts, and at length utterly despairing of success, I fortunately fell upon this proposal; which, as it is wholly new, so it has something solid and real, of no expense and little trouble, full in our own power, and whereby we can incur no danger in disobliging ENGLAND. For this kind of commodity will not bear exportation, the flesh being of too tender a consistence to admit a long continuance in salt, although perhaps I could name a country, which would be glad to eat up our whole nation without it.

After all, I am not so violently bent upon my own opinion as to reject any offer proposed by wise men, which shall be found equally innocent, cheap, easy, and effectual. But before something of that kind shall be advanced in contradiction to my scheme, and offering a better, I desire the author, or authors, will be pleased maturely to consider two points. First, as things now stand, how they will be able to find food and raiment for a hundred thousand useless mouths and backs. And, secondly, there being a round million of creatures in human figure throughout this kingdom, whose whole subsistence put into a common stock would leave them in debt two millions of pounds sterling, adding those who are beggars by profession, to the bulk of farmers, cottagers, and labourers, with the wives and children who are beggars in effect; I desire those politicians who dislike my overture, and may perhaps be so bold as to attempt an answer, that they will first ask the parents of these mortals, whether they would not at this day think it a great happiness to have been sold for food at a year old, in the manner I prescribe, and thereby have avoided such a perpetual scene of misfortunes, as they have since gone through, by the oppression of landlords, the impossibility of paying rent without money or trade, the want of common sustenance, with neither house nor clothes to cover them from the inclemencies of the weather, and the most inevitable prospect of entailing the like, or greater miseries, upon their breed for ever.

I profess, in the sincerity of my heart, that I have not the least personal interest in endeavouring to promote this necessary work, having no other motive than the public good of my country, by advancing our trade, providing for infants, relieving the poor, and giving some pleasure to the rich. I have no children by which I can propose to get a single penny; the youngest being nine years old, and my wife past childbearing.

IDEAS

1. What specific Irish problems does the essay detail? What are the speaker's suggested solutions? Try to itemize them.

2. What is the dramatic irony in the reckoning concerning Lent?

3. What is the dramatic irony in the practice censured "(although indeed very unjustly,) as a little bordering on cruelty"? What, in the paragraph concerning the infirm, who are dying "as fast as can be reasonably expected"?

4. What is the country "perhaps I could name"?

5. What is your image of the speaker? How does he attempt to present himself favorably? How does the final paragraph function toward this purpose?

ORGANIZATION AND STYLE

1. Carefully examine the speaker's language. For instance, what is the effect of "just dropped from its dam" or "poor innocent babes"? How does Swift let language underscore either a positive or negative attitude?

2. At what point do you first become aware of the irony here? What are your clues?

3. What is the effect of the pronoun *I* throughout the essay?

4. How closely does the essay follow a rational organization—stating a problem, indicating a thesis, then proposing a solution?

WRITING

1. Write a parodic version of Swift's "Modest Proposal" about some current abuse you and your readers would have well in mind: unreasonable assignments or regulations; cafeteria food, infringement of, or insistence on, equal rights; curing inflation; handling noisy people in the library or impossible roommates; or the like, trying to capture Swift's ironic tones.

2. Swift's essay represents that form of satire which takes a lofty subject (human life) and treats it at a most common level. Another satiric form reverses the process, taking something ordinary and treating it in lofty prose. Select such a common object as your favorite pair of sneakers, your favorite shirt or blouse, or maybe just a nail file, comb, or toothbrush. Write an ironic essay in lofty language—"O superb adjuster of my hair and image"—making it the most important possession in your world. Explain how carefully you protect it, how you could not bear life without it, how constantly it is on your mind.

Drafting the Priority of Independence

RUSSELL BAKER

────────────── ● ──────────────

By imagining that Ronald Reagan joined Thomas Jefferson and others to draft the Declaration of Independence, Baker points up differences between two eras and two personalities, Reagan and Jefferson. Notice his light ironic language throughout the piece.

Thomas Jefferson, who had the usual writer's vanity about his own prose, had been vaguely unhappy ever since Ronald Reagan had replaced Benjamin Franklin on the committee writing the Declaration of Independence.

Reagan, who was older than Franklin, had pulled his seniority on the canny Pennsylvanian, justifying it on the ground that Franklin's scientific genius could be better used on the Militia Committee to develop lightning into a weapon that could blast the turrets off the Kremlin.

"But Russia is not the enemy," Franklin had said. This statement was publicized by Reagan's advisers, who said it showed Franklin was not tough enough to write a hard-nosed Declaration of Independence. Objections that Reagan was unaccustomed to writing anything were swept aside when he noted that he had a large advisory staff to do the writing for him.

Now, after weeks of working with Reagan, Jefferson was near tears. His unhappiness had begun the very first week. Having composed what he considered a masterly opening paragraph, he was dismayed when Reagan refused to accept it without first consulting his advisers.

Jefferson looked again at the revised version he had been forced to accept and started to read slowly to himself:

"When at that point in time which falls within the parameters of human events, it becomes a highly prioritized policy to effect a liquidation of obligations of a sociopolitical nature initially undertaken and subsequently implemented in good faith, and to . . ."

Jefferson's eyes were blinded with tears, which he dabbed with the feathered end of his quill. Then he read aloud:

"In order to maximize our share of the opinion input process and thereby increase our opportunities of winning the struggle for the hearts and opinions of both womankind and mankind . . ."

Was it any wonder that seven members of the Continental Congress who had seen the draft had fled Philadelphia, threatening to defect to King George III? Still, John Hancock had stood firm. Faithful John Hancock. Even now Hancock was scouring Philadelphia chicken coops, searching for a newborn chick with a quill so small that no one would be able to decipher his signature without a microscope.

"I don't mind being hanged for freedom," Hancock had told Jefferson, "but I see nothing heroic about being hanged for a highly prioritized policy."

And now Reagan was due in Jefferson's room at any moment to put the finishing touch on the document. Jefferson wished he could get angry with Reagan, but he could not.

Nobody could get angry with Reagan. Not even the hot-tempered Sam Adams. Reagan was too nice. There had been that moment last month when Reagan proposed that instead of going to war with Britain, the Colonies should enact immense tax loopholes for kings so that King George would move out of England and settle peaceably in Delaware.

It made Sam Adams so angry he had threatened to disguise himself as an Indian and throw Reagan's advisers into Philadelphia harbor. When he stormed off to confront Reagan, Jefferson thought his troubles were over.

Two hours later, Jefferson encountered the two laughing merrily together. "This Reagan is really the most charming fellow," Adams told him. "Tell him that story, Ron, about the time you played the second lead in 'Gammer Gurton's Needle.'"

"Hi, Phil." This greeting interrupted Jefferson's reverie.

"I'm not Phil. I'm Tom," said Jefferson.

Reagan smiled at him, and Jefferson felt terrible about correcting a fellow with such a nice smile. What kind of man was he becoming, that he became offended when a perfectly decent human being couldn't remember his name?

"But I'd be honored if you'd call me Phil," Jefferson said. Reagan rewarded him with a dazzling grin.

"These final words you've written," said Reagan. "I think they're just about some of the finest stuff you've come up with since you wrote 'Romeo and Juliet.'"

Jefferson accepted the compliment, even preened a bit, as he repeated his closing line aloud: "'We mutually pledge to each other our lives, our fortunes, and our sacred honor.' Do you really like it?"

"It's terrific. Everything but that 'lives, fortunes and sacred honor' business. I just want you to read this, and see how much it improves it."

Jefferson took the paper Reagan handed him and read it. "You think we ought to pledge to each other our lives, our sacred honor and an immediate tax cut?"

"And the tax cut could be highly prioritized." Reagan smiled. It was such a nice smile. Jefferson couldn't help smiling back. Reagan patted his shoulder. "I knew you'd like it, Harry," he said.

IDEAS

1. What is Baker's image of Reagan? Of Jefferson?

2. How do you expect the Declaration of Independence might have been written differently had Reagan (or any other contemporary politician) been one of the authors?

3. How do the final paragraphs develop a caricature of contemporary politicians?

ORGANIZATION AND STYLE

1. Carefully examine Baker's language presenting Jefferson. He dabs his eyes "with the feathered end of his quill" and submits eagerly to Reagan's calling him Phil. Now examine his language presenting Reagan. He is "too nice," and he rewards people with "dazzling" grins. How do these descriptive phrases project Baker's images of the two.

2. Look at the paragraph beginning "In order to maximize our share. . . ." Compare the language in this proposed introduction with that of the original (p. 41).

3. How does the final sentence underscore Baker's irony?

WRITING

1. Select a portion of the original Declaration of Independence and, following Baker's lead, rewrite it in contemporary political style.

2. Baker juxtaposes Jefferson against Reagan to make a statement about their respective times. Select another person whose work you have read recently (perhaps an essayist from this text) and similarly juxtapose him or her with someone representing highly different views.

You might, for instance, imagine a meeting between King (p. 64) and a prominent atheist, or between Thoreau (p. 364) and a contemporary militant activist. Try to treat each person's views honestly while highlighting their differences in amusing foolery.

The Autobiographical Essay

Thoreau's Unfinished Business

LOREN EISELEY

———————— ● ————————

Thoreau has proved to be the American conscience trying to fulfill Jefferson's pursuit of life, liberty, and happiness. Eiseley sees in him, as White and many another have done, a fellow spirit, but, from his anthropological perspective, Eiseley peers into Thoreau's bleak cosmic pursuit as no one else has done.

The life of Henry David Thoreau has been thoroughly explored for almost a century by critics and biographers, yet the mystery of this untraveled man who read travel literature has nowhere been better expressed than by his old walking companion Ellery Channing, who once wrote: "I have never been able to understand what he meant by his life. Why was he so disappointed with everybody else? Why was he so interested in the river and the woods . . . ? Something peculiar here I judge."

If Channing, his personal friend, was mystified, it is only to be expected that as Thoreau's literary stature has grown, the ever present enigma of his life and thought has grown with it. Wright Morris, the distinguished novelist and critic, has asked, almost savagely, the same questions in another form.

In a less personal context he quotes from Thoreau, who spent two years upon the Walden experiment and then abandoned it, "If we are alive let us go about our business." "But," counters Morris brutally, "what business?" Thoreau fails to inform us. In the words of Morris, Walden was the opening chapter of a life, one that enthralls us, but with the remaining chapters missing.

For more than a decade after *Walden* was composed, Thoreau continued his intensive exploration of Concord, its inhabitants and its fields, but upon the "business" for which he left Walden he is oddly cryptic. Once, it is true, he muses in his journal that "the utmost possible novelty would be the difference between me and myself a year ago." He must then have been about some business, even though the perceptive critic Morris felt he had already performed it and was at loose ends and groping. The truth is that the critic, in a timeless sense, can be right and in another way wrong, for looking is in itself the business of art.

Thoreau was indeed a spiritual wanderer through the deserts of the modern world. Almost by instinct he rejected that beginning wave of industrialism that was later to so entrance his century. He also rejected the peace he had found on the shores of Walden Pond, the alternate glazing and reflection of that great natural eye which impartially received the seasons. It was, in the end, too great for his endurance, too timeless. He was a restless pacer of fields, a reader who, in spite of occasional invective directed against those who presumed to neglect their homes for far places, nevertheless was apt with allusions drawn from travel literature and quick to discern in man uncharted spaces.

"Few adults," once remarked Emerson, Thoreau's one-time mentor and friend, "can see nature." Thoreau was one of those who could. Moreover he saw nature as another civilization, a thing of vaster laws and vagaries than that encompassed by the human mind. When he visited the Maine woods he felt its wind upon him like the closing of a dank door from some forgotten cellar of the past.

Was it some curious midnight impulse to investigate such matters that led Thoreau to abandon the sunny hut at Walden for "other business"? Even at Walden he had heard, at midnight, the insistent fox, the "rudimental man," barking beyond his lighted window in the forest. The universe was in motion, nothing was fixed. Nature was "a prairie for outlaws," violent, unpredictable. Alone in the environs of Walden, Thoreau wandered in the midst of that greater civilization he had discovered as surely as some monstrous edifice come suddenly upon in the Maya jungles. He never exclaimed about the Indian trails seen just at dusk in a winter snowfall—neither where they went nor upon what prairie they vanished or in what direction. He never ventured to tell us, but he was one of those great artist-scientists who could pursue the future through its past. This is why he lives today in the hearts of young and old alike, "a man of surfaces," but such surfaces—the arrowhead, the acorn, the oak leaf, the indestructible thought print headed toward eternity.

Thoreau, in his final journals, had said that the ancients with their gorgons and sphinxes could imagine more than existed. Modern men, by contrast, could not imagine so much as exists. For more than one hundred years that statement has stood to taunt us. Every succeeding year has proved Thoreau right. The one great hieroglyph, nature, is as unreadable as it ever was and so is her equally wild and unpredictable offspring, man. Like Thoreau, the examiner of lost and fragile surfaces of flint, we are only by indirection students of man. We are, in actuality, students of that greater order known as nature. It is into nature that man vanishes. "Wildness is a civilization other than our own," Thoreau had ventured. Out of it man's trail had wandered. He had come with the great ice, drifting before its violence, scavenging the flints it had dropped. Whatever he was now, the ice had made him, the breath from the dank door, great cold, and implacable winters.

Thoreau in the final pages of *Walden* creates a myth about a despised worm that surmounts death and bursts from its hidden chamber in a wooden table. Was the writer dreaming of man, man freed at last from the manacles of the ice? Is not the real business of the artist to seek for man's salvation, and by understanding his ingredients to make him less of an outlaw to himself, civilize him, in fact, back into that titanic otherness, that star's substance from which he had arisen? Perhaps encamped sufficiently in the great living web we might emerge again, not into the blind snow-covered eye of Walden's winter, but into the eternal spring man dreams of everywhere and nowhere finds.

Man, himself, is Walden's eye of ice and eye of summer. What now makes man an outlaw, with the fox urgent at his heels, is that one of his eyes is gray and wintry and blind, while with the other is glimpsed another world just tantalizingly visible and dismissed as an illusion. What we know with certainty is that a creature with such disparate vision cannot long survive. It was that knowledge that led Thoreau to strain his eyesight till it ached and to record all he saw. A flower might open a man's mind, a box tortoise endow him with mercy, a mist enable him to see his own shifting and uncertain configuration. But the alchemist's touchstone in Thoreau was to give him sight, not power. Only man's own mind, the artist's mind, can change the winter in man.

On July 14 of the year 1973, I awoke at dawn and saw above my head the chisel marks on an eighteenth-century beam in the Concord Inn. As I strolled up the street toward the cemetery I saw a few drifters, black and white, stirring from their illegal night's sleep among the gravestones. Later I came to the Thoreau family plot and saw the little yellow stone marked "Henry," which no one is any longer sure indicates the precise place where he lies. Perhaps there is justice in this obscurity because the critics are also unsure of the contradictions and intentions of his journal, even of the classic *Walden*. A ghost then, of shifting features, peers out from between the gravestones, unreal, perhaps uninterpreted still.

I turned away from the early morning damp for a glimpse of the famous pond which in the country of my youth would have been called a lake. It was still an unearthly reflection of the sky, even if here and there beer bottles were bobbing in the shallows. I walked along the tracks of the old railroad where Thoreau used to listen to

477

the telegraph wires. He had an eye for the sharp-edged artifact, I thought. He would have transmitted the bobbing bottles, the keys to beer cans, into cosmic symbols, just as he had sensed all past time in the odors of a swamp. "All the ages are represented still," he had said, with nostrils flaring above the vegetation-choked water, "and you can smell them out."

As for arrowheads, he says in a memorable passage, "You would say it had rained arrowheads for they lie all over the surface of America. They are sown like grain . . . over the earth. Each one yields me a thought. . . . It is humanity inscribed on the face of the earth. It is a footprint—rather a mindprint—left everywhere. . . . They are not fossil bones, but, as it were, fossil thoughts forever reminding me of the mind that shaped them. I am on the trail of mind."

Some time ago in a graduate seminar in honor of a visiting eminent prehistorian I watched the scholar and his listeners grapple with the significance of an anciently shaped stone. Not one of those present, involved as they were with semantic involutions, could render up so simple an expression as "mindprint." The lonely follower of the plow at Concord had provided both art and anthropology with an expression of horizon-reaching application that they have inexplicably chosen to ignore.

Mindprints are what the first men left, mindprints will be what the last man leaves, even if it is only a beer can dropped rolling from the last living hand or a sagging picture in a ruined house.

Thoreau had extended his thought prints to something beyond what we of this age would call the natural. He would read them into nature itself, see, in other words, some kind of trail through that prairie for outlaws that had always intimidated him. On mountaintops, he had realized a star's substance, sensed a nature "not bound to be kind to man." Nevertheless he confided firmly to his diary, "the earth which I have *seen* cannot bury me." He searches desperately, all senses alert, for a way to read these greater hieroglyphs in which the tiny interpretable minds of our forerunners are embedded. We, with a sharper knowledge of human limitations and a devotion to the empirical fact, may deny to ourselves the reality of this other civilization within whose laws and probabilities we exist. Thoreau reposed faith in the consistency of nature's habits, but only up to a point, for he was a student of change.

Now Thoreau was a stay-at-home who traveled much in his mind, both in travel literature and beside Walden Pond. I, by circumstance, directly after delivering a lecture at Concord and gazing in my turn at Walden, was forced immediately to turn and fly west to the badlands and dinosaur-haunted gulches of Montana, some of its natives wild, half-civilized still. As I followed our mixed-breed Cheyenne, as ambivalent toward us as the savage blood in his veins demanded, it came to me, as it must have come to many others, that seeing is not the same thing as understanding.

One man sees with indifference a leaf fall; another with the vision of Thoreau invokes the whole of that nostalgic world that we call autumn. One man sees a red fox running through a shaft of sunlight and lifts a rifle; another lays a restraining hand upon his companion's arm and says, "Please. There goes the last wild gaiety in the world. Let it live, let it run." This is the role of the alchemist, the true, if sometimes inarticulate, artist. He transmutes the cricket's song in an autumn night to an aching void in the heart; snowflakes become the flying years. And when, as archeologist, he lifts from the encrusting earth those forgotten objects Thoreau called "fossil thoughts," he is giving depth and tragedy and catharsis to the one great drama that concerns us most, the supreme mystery, man. Only man is capable of comprehending all he was and all that he has failed to be.

On those sun-beaten uplands over which we wandered, every chip of quartzite, every patinized flint gleamed in our eyes as large as the monuments of other lands. Our vision in that thin air was incredibly enhanced and prolonged. Thoreau had conceived of nature as a single reflecting eye, the Walden eye of which he strove to be a solitary part, to apprehend with all his being. It was chance that had brought me in the span of a day to the dinosaur beds of Montana. Thoreau would have liked that. He had always regarded such places as endowed with the vapors of Nox, places where rules were annulled. He had called arrowheads mindprints. What then would he have termed a tooth of *Tyrannosaurus rex** held in my palm? The sign of another civilization, another order of mind? Or that tiny Cretaceous† mammal that was a step on the way to ourselves? Surely it represented mind in embryo, our mind, but not of our devising. What would he have called it—that miracle of a bygone moment, the annulment of what had been, to be replaced by an eye, the artist's eye, that nature had never heretofore produced among her creatures? Would he have simply called it "nature," as we sometimes do, scarcely knowing how to interpret the looming inchoate power out of which we have been born? Or would he have labeled nature itself a mindprint beyond our power to read or to interpret?

A man might sketch *Triceratops,* ‡ but the alphabet from which it was assembled had long since disappeared. As for man, how had his own alphabet been constructed? The nature in which he momentarily resided was a journal in which the script was always changing, like the dancing footprints of the fox on icy Walden Pond. Here, exposed about me, was the great journal Thoreau had striven to read, the business, in the end, that had taken him beyond Walden. He would have been too wise, too close to earth, too intimidated, to have called such a journal human. It was palpably inscribed from a star's substance. Tiny and brief in that journal were the hieroglyphs of man. Like Thoreau, we had come to the world's end, but not to the end of nature, not to the end of time. All that

*A huge carnivorous dinosaur.

†The Cretaceous period in geology marked, 80 to 100 million years ago, the sunset of the dinosaurs' long dominance of earth, and the dawn for mammals.

‡A heavy armored and horned rhinoceros-like reptile, contemporary of *Tyrannosaurus rex.*

could be read was that we had a past; that was something no other life on the planet had learned. There was, we had also ascertained, a future.

In the meantime, Thoreau would have protested, there is the eye, the sun and the eye. "Nothing must be postponed; find eternity in each moment." But how few of us are endowed to sustain Thoreau's almost diabolical vision. Here and here alone the true alchemist must come to exist in each of us. It is ours to transmute, not iron, not copper, not gold, but our tracks through nature, see them finally attended by self-knowledge, by the vision of the universal eye—that faculty possessed by the alchemist at Walden Pond.

But why, why had he left the sunny doorway of his hut in Walden for unknown mysterious business? Had he not written as though he had settled down forever? Why had Channing chronicled Thoreau's grievous disappointments? What had he been seeking and how had it affected him? If Walden was the opening chapter of a life, might not there still be a lurking message, a termination, a final chapter beyond his recorded death?

It was evident that he had seen the whole of American culture as copper tinted by its antecedents, its people shadowy and gigantic as figures looming indistinctly in some Indian-summer haze. He had written of an old tree near Concord penetrated by a flying arrow with the shaft still attached. Some of the driving force of that flint projectile still persisted in his mind. Perhaps indeed those points that had once sung their message through every glade of the eastern woodland had spoken louder than the telegraph harp to which his ears had been attuned at Walden. Protest as he would, cultivate sauntering as he would, abhor as he would the rootless travelers whose works he read by lamplight, he was himself the eternal traveler. On the mountains of New Hampshire he had found "small and almost uninhabited ponds, apparently without fish, sources of rivers, still and cold, strange as condensed clouds." He had wandered without realizing it back into the time of the first continental ice recession.

"It is not worth the while to go around the world to count the cats in Zanzibar," he once castigated some luckless explorer, but why then this peering into lifeless tarns or engrossing himself with the meteoritic detritus of the Appalachians? Did he secretly wish to come to a place of no more life, where a man might stiffen into immobility as I had found myself freezing into the agate limbs of petrified trees in Montana? He admitted that he would gladly fall "into some crevice along with leaves and acorns." "There is no more fatal blunderer," he protested, "than he who consumes the greater part of life getting a living." He had emphasized that contemplative view at Walden, lived it, in fact, to the point where the world came finally to accept him as a kind of rural Robinson Crusoe whom, as the cities grew, it might prove wise to emulate.

"I sat in my sunny doorway," he ruminated, "from sunrise till noon, rapt in revery, amidst the pines and hickories and sumachs, in undisturbed solitude and stillness, while the birds sang around or flitted noiseless through the house, until by the sun falling in at my west window, or the noise of some traveler's wagon on the distant highway, I was reminded of the lapse of time. I grew in those seasons like corn in the night."

This passage would seem to stand for the serene and timeless life of an Oriental sage, a well-adjusted man, as the psychiatrists of our day would have it. Nevertheless this benign façade is deceptive. There is no doubt that Thoreau honestly meant what he said at the time he said it, but the man was storm-driven. He would not be content with the first chapter of his life; he would, like a true artist, dredge up dreams even from the bottom of a pond.

In the year 1837 Thoreau confided abruptly to his journal: "Truth strikes us from behind, and in the dark." Thoreau's life was to be comparatively short and ill-starred. Our final question must, therefore, revolve, not about wanderings in autumn fields, not the drowsing in pleasant doorways where time stood still forever, but rather upon the leap of that lost arrow left quivering in an ancient oak. It was, in symbol, the hurtling purposeful arrow of a seemingly aimless life. It has been overlooked by Thoreau's biographers, largely because they have been men of the study or men of the forest. They have not been men of the seashore or men gifted with the artist's eye. They have not trudged the naturalist's long miles through sea sand, where the war between two elements leaves even the smallest object magnified, as the bleached bone or broken utensil can be similarly magnified only on the dead lake beaches of the west.

Thoreau had been drawn to Cape Cod in 1849, a visit he had twice repeated. It was not the tourist resort it is today. It was still the country of men on impoverished farms, who went to sea or combed the beaches like wreckers seeking cargo. On those beaches, commented Thoreau, in a work that he was destined never to see in print, "a house was rarely visible . . . and the solitude was that of the ocean and the desert combined." Here, recorded the chronicler, was a wilder, less human nature. Objects on the beach, he noted, were always more grotesque and dilated than upon approach they proved to be. A cast-up pair of gloves suggested the reality of hands.

Thoreau's account, in *Cape Cod,* of the "charity house" to which his wanderings led him takes on a special meaning. I think it embodies something of a final answer to Channing's question about Thoreau's disappointment in his fellow men. Published two years after his death, it contains his formulation of the end of his business, or perhaps I should say, of his quest. Hidden in what has been dismissed as a mere book of travel is an episode as potentially fabulous as that of Melville's great white whale.

First, however, I must tell the story of another coast because it will serve to illuminate Thoreau's final perception. A man, a shore dweller on Long Island, told me of his discovery in a winter dawn. All night there had been a heavy surf and freezing wind. When he came to stroll along his beach at morning he had immediately seen a lifeboat cast upon the shingle and a still, black figure with the eastern sun behind it on the horizon. Gripped by a premonition he ran forward. The seaman in oilskins was alone and stiffly upright. A compass was clutched in his numb fingers. The man was sheeted in ice. Ice over his beard, his clothing, his hands, ice over his fixed, open eyes. Had he made the shore alive but too frozen to move? No one would ever know, just as no one would ever know his name or the sinking vessel from which he came. With desperate courage he had steered a true course through a wild night of breakers only to freeze within sight of help.

In those fishing days on Cape Cod, Thoreau came to know many such stories—vessels without weather warnings smashed in the winter seas, while, perhaps, a pittance of soaked men gained the shore. The sea, the intolerable sea, tumbled with total indifference the bodies of the dead or the living who were tossed up through the grinding surf of winter. These were common events in the days of sail.

The people who gained a scant living along that coast entertained, early in the nineteenth century, the thought that a few well-stocked sheds, or charity houses, might enable lost seamen who made the shore to warm and feed themselves among the dunes till rescued. The idea was to provide straw and matches and provender, supervised and checked at intervals by some responsible person. Impressed at first by this signal beneficence of landsmen, Thoreau noted the instructions set down for the benefit of mariners. Finally, he approached one such charity house. It appeared, he commented, "but a stage to the grave." The chimney had fallen. As he and his companion wished to gain an idea of a "humane house," they put their eyes, by turns, to a knothole in the door. "We had," Thoreau comments ironically, "some practice at looking inward—the pupil becomes enlarged. Nature is never so dark that a patient eye may not prevail over it."

So there, at last, he saw the end of his journey, of the business begun at Walden. He was peering into the charity house of man, upon a Cape Cod beach. For frozen, shipwrecked mariners he saw a fireplace with no matches, no provisions, no straw upon the floor. "We looked," he said, "into the bowels of mercy, and for bread we found a stone."

Shivering like castaways, "we looked through the knot-hole into that night without a star, until we concluded it was not a humane house at all." The arrow Thoreau had followed away from Walden had pierced as deep as Captian Ahab's lance.* No wonder the demoniacal foxes leaping at Thoreau's window had urged him to be gone. He had always looked for a crevice into the future. He had peered inward instead. It was ourselves who were rudimental men.

A hundred years after Thoreau's death people were still trying to understand what he was about. They were still trying to get both eyes open. They were still trying to understand that he had brought something to share with his fellows, something that, if they partook of it, might transpose them to another world.

I had thought, staring across an angular gravestone at Concord, and again as I held a wind-varnished flint in Montana, that "sharing" could be the word. It was appropriate, even though Thoreau in a final bitterness had felt sharing to be as impoverished as the charity house for sailors—a knothole glimpse into the human condition. How then should the artist see? By an eye applied to a knothole? By a magnification of sand-filled gloves washed up on a beach? Could this be the solitary business that led Thoreau on his deathbed to mutter, whether in irony or confusion, "One world at a time"?

This is the terror of our age. How should we see? In what world are we? For we have fallen out of nature and see sometimes more and sometimes less. We see the past, the looming future, and then, so fearfully is the eye confused, that it stares inverted into a charity house that appears to reflect a less than human heart. Is this Thoreau's final surrealist vision, his glance through the knothole into the humane house? It would appear at least to be a glimpse from one of those two great alternating eyes at Walden Pond from which in the end he had fled—the blind eye of

*With which Ahab, to his own destruction, spears Moby Dick (in Herman Melville's novel).

winter and that innocent blue pupil beside which he had once drowsed when time seemed endless. Both are equally real, as the great poets and prophets have always known, but it was Thoreau's tragic destiny to see, with eyes strained beyond endurance, man subsiding into two wrinkled gloves grasping at the edge of infinity. It is his final contribution to literature, the final hidden conclusion of an unwritten life whose first chapter Morris had rightly diagnosed as *Walden*.

There is an old biblical saying that our days are prolonged and every vision fails us. This I would dispute. The vision of the great artist does not fail. It sharpens and refines with age until everything extraneous is pared away. "Simplify," Thoreau had advocated. Two gloves, devoid of flesh, clutching the stones of the ebbing tide become, transmuted, the most dreadful object in the world.

"There has been nothing but the sun and eye from the beginning," Thoreau had written when his only business was looking and he grew, as he expressed it, "like corn in the night." The sun and the eye are the two aspects of nature that are irremediably linked. But the eye of man constitutes an awesome crystal whose diffractions are far greater than those of any Newtonian prism.*

We see, as artists, as scientists, each in his own way, through the inexorable lens we cannot alter. In a nature that Thoreau recognized as unfixed and lawless anything might happen. The artist's endeavor is to make it happen—the unlawful, the oncoming world, whether endurable or mad, but shaped always by the harsh angles of truth—the truth as glimpsed through the terrible crystal of genius. This is the one sure rule of that other civilization, which we have come to know is greater than our own. Thoreau called it, from the first, "unfinished business," when he turned and walked away from his hut at Walden Pond.

*Isaac Newton (1642–1727), English mathematician and physicist, and the formulator of the law of gravity, also was the first to break down sunlight into all its elemental colors by bending, or refracting, it through a prism.

IDEAS

1. Note Eiseley's phrases like "thought prints," "man's trail," "star's substance," and "arrowheads." How do these phrases accumulate meaning throughout the essay? (Keep "thought print" in mind when you read Einstein.)

2. How can you explain Eiseley's metaphor in the paragraph beginning "Man, himself, is Walden's eye. . . ."? Trace this idea through the essay.

3. What is Thoreau's final "unfinished business," which Eiseley unfolds in the "episode as potentially fabulous as that of Melville's great white whale"? What do the frozen man, the hut, and the gloves symbolize?

4. Eiseley raises a lot of questions about Thoreau and his motivations. Are all of these questions answered to your own satisfaction? Which ones, if any, do you think need further explanation?

5. What specific lessons does the author suggest that our generation might learn from Thoreau and his way of life?

ORGANIZATION AND STYLE

1. How exactly does the first paragraph set the pattern for Eiseley's essay?

2. The essay contains a large number of rhetorical questions. Just how does Eiseley use them? Are they too numerous? If so, why?

3. What is the purpose of the paragraph beginning "On July 14 of the year 1973. . . ."? Find other passages where Eisely writes from his personal experience. How does he introduce those sequences? How do they relate thematically to the entire essay?

4. Carefully examine the one-sentence paragraph beginning "Mindprints are what the first men left. . . ." To

what extent is this brief paragraph a miniature of the entire essay?

5. How does Eisley's metaphor of an arrow unify various parts of the essay?

WRITING

1. Eiseley writes, "Thoreau, in his final journals, had said that the ancients with their gorgons and sphinxes could imagine more than existed. Modern men, by contrast, could not imagine so much as exists. For more than one hundred years that statement has stood to taunt us." What exactly did Eiseley mean? Select some aspect of modern life and discuss ways in which you feel people today "cannot imagine so much as exists." Try to explain how we all are made smaller by the smallness of our imaginations.

2. Take some "mindprint" you have observed, whether some human artifact like a clay pot or stone bowl or something apparently instinctive like a hornet's nest, and write an essay on a thesis about "the mysterious harmony of nature," using whatever comes to hand from Eiseley, Thoreau, Petrunkevitch, and elsewhere.

The Critical Essay

The Beatles as Artists: A Meditation for December Ninth

JAMES A. WINN

———————— ● ————————

Winn's analysis of the Beatles is a masterful synthesis of social, musical, and, indeed, literary criticism as he follows their career from public mania to private melding of their unusual and varied gifts.

The stark white graphics on the television screen were terrible in both their symmetry and their finality: John Lennon: 1940–1980. If you had thought of him as permanently twenty-five, the knowledge that Lennon had reached age forty became a part of the larger, more horrifying news that he was dead. For even in separation and disarray, the Beatles served several generations as symbols on which to hang fantasies, aspirations, and not-yet-formed identities. And as they came to realize, first from the physically dangerous way their young fans pelted them with jelly beans and grabbed at their clothing, then from the grinding daily impossibility of achieving privacy, their status as symbols was a heavy burden indeed. Typically, it was John who found a way of expressing their plight, with a metaphor many found scandalous; in a song complaining about the way the press hounded him on his honeymoon (*The Ballad of John and Yoko,* 1969), he predicted with wry and eerie accuracy the final bloody cost of his notoriety:

Christ! You know it ain't easy,
you know how hard it can be.
The way things are going
they're going to crucify me.

Predictably, the first eulogies in the press concentrated
on the public aspects of Lennon's career: the mass hysteria
called Beatlemania, the admissions of drug use, the flirta-
tion with Eastern religions, the naive but touching bill-
board campaign for world peace. But I shall be arguing
here that the lasting accomplishment of Lennon and his
mates, their emergence as self-consciously artistic makers
of songs, was itself a response to and attempted escape
from the burdens of public notoriety. The Beatles gave
their last public concert on 29 August 1966; in that same
month, they issued the ironically-titled *Revolver,* an
album that signalled a new introspection and a greater
willingness to test and tease the hearer. Freed from the
exhausting and demeaning business of touring, they were
able to sustain their growing complexity and creativity for
four highly productive years, during which they produced
Sergeant Pepper's Lonely Hearts Club Band (1967), *Magical Mystery Tour* (1967), the double album called *The Beatles* (1968), *Abbey Road* (1969), and *Let It Be* (1970)—albums that expanded and apparently exhausted the
possibilities of the rock song.

This fruitful withdrawal from public performance necessarily followed at least a decade of frequent performance; indeed, in the early years of the group's development, the Beatles sought every opportunity to perform,
presumably because they craved money, success, and notoriety—not because they wished to make an artistic statement. John's wacky and deliberately inaccurate account
of their early history, written in 1961, dismisses the motives for their trip to Hamburg as purely monetary: "And
then a man with a beard cut off said—will you go to Germany and play mighty rock for the peasants for money?
And we said we would play mighty anything for money."
One thinks of Dr. Johnson's equally proud and practical

statements: "Sir, I could write a preface upon a broom-stick" or (even closer) "No man but a blockhead ever wrote, except for money." In both cases, the claim to be motivated by money is at once a declaration of professional pride and a rejection of more Romantic notions of the reasons for creativity. By declaring that one plays concerts or writes prefaces for money, one emphasizes the work involved and casts doubt on the notion that the making of music or literature is a mysterious, metaphysical, quasi-religious calling. By 1968, when "interpretations" of Beatles lyrics were a constant topic of journalism and party conversation, John would debunk the idea of his work as "art" in an even more savage way: "It's nice when people like it, but when they start 'appreciating' it, getting great deep things out of it, making a thing of it, then it's a lot of shit. It proves what we've always thought about most sorts of so-called art. It's all a lot of shit. It is depressing to realize we were right in what we always thought, all those years ago. Beethoven is a con, just like we are now. He was just knocking out a bit of work, that was all." For the young Beatles, playing concerts was basically "knocking out a bit of work," and getting paid meant being able to keep playing, avoiding the duller jobs as deliverymen and factory workers they had briefly held as teenagers. Thus money, as a way to escape the grim Liverpool life of their parents, was a motive they could acknowledge; the notion of making "so-called art," by contrast, was a ludicrous idea they actively rejected.

Fame fell somewhere in between. According to George Harrison, "we used to send up the idea of getting to the top. When things were a real drag and nothing happening, we used to go through this routine: John would shout, 'Where are we going, fellas?' We'd shout back, 'To the Top, Johnny!' Then he would shout, 'What Top?' 'To the Top-permost of the Poppermost, Johnny!' " But was this routine a "send-up," a completely ironic gesture of disdain, or was it a therapeutic way of pretending, as record company after record company turned them down, that getting to the top didn't matter, and thus ultimately a ritual of morale-boosting? If, as I suspect, the young Beatles desperately wanted to achieve fame, but had a concurrent need to pretend to disdain it, would it not be possible to extend that argument to cover their attitude toward "so-called art" as well? To be sure, they did not want to be thought of as pale aesthetes; John's remarks about Beethoven make that clear enough. But it was the same John Lennon who described his song *Because* (1969) as "the Moonlight Sonata backwards," and the introduction to that song does strongly suggest the harmonic motion of Beethoven's piece. So despite John's warnings against commentary couched in artistic language, and despite what must always have been their own powerful ambivalence about their status as "artists," the Beatles' tireless work at the making and recording of songs after their withdrawal from public performance was ultimately motivated by a quite subtle and impressive aesthetic sense, and by a driving need to create that they shared with many poets and composers. As John himself once said, "I can't retire. I've got these bloody songs to write."

This remark suggests not only a need to write songs but a sense of that writing as work; like the early story of the morale-boosting routine, it underscores the Beatles' determination and persistence, qualities that would serve them well when their musical ideas became so complex as to require hours of overdubbing and mixing. Even George Martin, the producer whose technical expertise had so much to do with the excellence of the later albums, has spoken admiringly of the Beatles' patient perfectionism, their capacity for hard work. The Beatles themselves, while sometimes disparaging their group as "an average band," were nonetheless careful to give themselves credit for putting out effort. Speaking of the pressure under which he and John often produced the last few songs to fill out an album, Paul McCartney once referred to such songs, written by "pure slog," as "not necessarily worse than ones done out of imagination," indeed "often better," and John extended this principle to a definition of "talent" as "believing you can do something." This notion of talent as confidence and effort, a curiously overlooked consequence of the Beatles' working-class origins, freed them from the crippling romantic notion of "originality" as "inspiration." Without knowing it, the Beatles were recovering a philosophy of art frequently encountered in the Renaissance and the eighteenth century, the simpler idea of the artist as artisan. Paul used to write proudly at the top of each of the hundreds of unrecorded songs they wrote as teenagers, "Another Original by Lennon and McCartney," but the songs were actually highly derivative, drawing on Elvis Presley, Chuck Berry, and the English music hall, among other sources. By turning out these imitative exercises, and by striving in their singing for flawless imitations of Elvis or Little Richard, the Beatles were putting themselves through an apprenticeship of the kind thought normal for poets and composers before the triumph of Romanticism: one thinks of Shakespeare's Plautine plays, or of Pope's derivative *Pastorals,* or of Beethoven's early exercises in a style overtly dependent on Haydn and Mozart. For these artists as for the Beatles, creation was hard work, and apprenticeship involved the mastering of idioms learned from earlier artists. At the level of vocal style, those imitated idioms remained with the Beatles as *personae:* as late as *Abbey Road* Paul was using his "Little Richard" voice for *Oh Darling,* and his "Elvis" voice for the barrel-house bridge of *You Never Give Me Your Money* ("Out of college, money spent . . .").

Beyond providing a poet or composer with a sense of what style *is* or a *persona* he may later employ with ironic effect, imitation may also be a way of developing the habit of making; having written their hundreds of teenage "originals," John and Paul were ready to flex those muscles in more personal ways when their chance came. In their very first English recording, made in November 1962, they display, at least in embryo, a distinct idiom as composers and singers, though their lyrics remain shamelessly conventional. They knew that the path "to the Toppermost of the Poppermost" would lead through the recording studios, and that their material for records would have to be different or arresting in some way besides the sheer volume on which they had relied in Hamburg. They also had the good fortune to begin recording at a moment when seeming new or different was not terribly difficult; American and English popular music were both in a period of stagnation. After a great burst of energy in the middle 1950s, largely the result of Elvis Presley's popularizing of a previously black "rhythm and blues" idiom, American "Top 40" hits had settled into a predictable pattern: chord changes were restricted to primary triads (usually I-VI-IV-V, in that order); guitar playing was almost always a mindless banging out of those chords, with very little linear interest; vocal harmony rarely involved anything more complex than the smooth thirds of the Everly Brothers; lyrics, rhythms, and melodies were equally dull. Only the Beach Boys, still at a very early stage, promised any development beyond this pattern. In England, where the top group was Cliff Richard and the Shadows, the situation was no better, indeed, as the antiseptic primness of that group's style suggested, probably worse.

The Beatles' first single *(Love Me Do* and *PS I Love You)* was palpably different. Their teenage fans, when referring to the "new sound" they heard in these songs, were probably responding first of all to the strong two-part singing of John and Paul, the most immediately obvious of a number of principles of contrast that would make their maturer work so musically interesting. Paul, a natural tenor with unusually clear, well-produced high notes, sounded quite unlike John, a natural baritone singing with obvious but expressive strain when reaching for his high notes. (Later, the Beatles would find uses for John's low range: he sings a low G in *I'm a Loser* and a low A in *Happiness is a Warm Gun.*) The frequent open fifths between the voices in *Love Me Do* emphasize this difference in vocal quality; unlike the Everly Brothers and others who sought an anonymously smooth blend, the Beatles had to be heard as individuals working together. Even in *Love Me Do,* first composed in their skiffle-group days, John and Paul constantly vary the vocal texture: they sing separately, in unison, in octaves, in fifths, in thirds, and even in contrary motion. This variety of texture, together with George's tight, witty guitar work and John's bluesy harmonica, gives a basically primitive song enough musical content to sustain our interest.

The desire for variety was a compositional principle, not merely a matter of performance. Remembering how they decided to proceed after their highly successful second single *(Please Please Me),* Paul says: "we decided we must do something different for the next song. We'd put on one funny hat, so we took it off and looked for another one to put on." Other groups were content to grind out follow-up songs in the mold of the last hit, but the Beatles had an almost obsessive need to "change hats"; it came to characterize their approach to composition, instrumental texture, electronic production, and form (both the form of individual songs and the larger forms they learned to construct on whole album sides). Groups with immediately identifiable but unchanging "sounds" (the Supremes, for example) had little difficulty producing individual hits, but their albums, which made the similarities between those hits painfully obvious, seemed pointless. The Beatles, with their rhetorical, hat-changing theory of style, were ideally suited to the album format. The strong contrasts between John and Paul, which extended well beyond mere vocal quality, helped them achieve continual variety. Paul began as a facile composer of melodies and bass lines, John as a writer of clever nonsense words, but even as teenagers theirs was no simple collaboration between tune man and word man. By their own account, John began writing tunes to keep up with Paul, and Paul would eventually be encouraged to improve his lyrics by his contact with John. By not rigorously dividing the tasks, one taking responsibility for words, the other for tunes, as other song-writing teams had done, they gained a much richer and more complex kind of collaboration. As they worked together, each constantly adding to, improving, and developing what the other had done, they achieved not one composite style but a kaleidoscopic series of styles.

John even thought of the composing process, verbal and musical, as a matter of linking up "bits"—the more different the "bits," the better, as in *I am the Walrus* or *Happiness is a Warm Gun.*

Another kind of variety important to the Beatles' later work, its rich harmonic language, is hardly apparent in *Love Me Do,* which uses only three chords. But following the principle of contrast, the other side, *PS I Love You,* employs augmented dominants and a deceptive cadence on the flatted sixth. Remembering their earliest days together, John once remarked that he and Paul took George into the group "because he knew more chords, a lot more than we knew. So we got a lot from him. Every time we learned a new chord, we'd write a song around it." This reminiscence provides another valuable glimpse into the Beatles' apprenticeship; their willingness to write songs *around* each new chord would prove more important than the chords themselves, which were complex only by comparison with the dull triads of American groups. By writing songs around chords, not merely using chords as ornamental flourishes, the Beatles gained a new principle of variety. Some of the earliest analytical pieces on their music noticed the frequency of major chords built on the flat sixth and the flat third; my point is that phrases moving through such harmonies may be effectively contrasted with phrases moving through more conventional "changes," as in *It Won't Be Long Now* (November 1963), a song in C major which juxtaposes a refrain moving through A minor against a verse moving through A-flat major. The Beatles were learning to use chord changes not only for variety but for wit, and even as expressive devices. *If I Fell* (August 1964), perhaps the most beautiful of the early songs, gains some of its tenderness by beginning in E-flat minor, with an uncertain and unsettled series of harmonies, while the speaker asks, "If I fell in love with you, would you promise to be true, and help me understand?" With his assertion that "love is more than just holding hands," the song finds D major, its true key; the modulation underscores the text, an early example of something the Beatles did continually in their mature period.

During the three years between their first single and the album called *Rubber Soul* (December 1965), despite a hectic schedule of tours and appearances, the Beatles managed to make steady progress as composers and musicians. They relied less and less on the conventional 32-bar AABA form in which pop songs had most often been written in previous decades, increasingly inventing new, less symmetrical forms; *Another Girl* (August 1965), in which a shortened chorus used as an introduction enjambs into the verse, provides one striking example. They also escaped the rock convention of the "fade out" ending; the endings of *A Hard Day's Night, And I Love Her,* and *We Can Work it Out,* each of which restates some harmonic or rhythmic motif of the song in a fresh and conclusive way, justify Leonard Bernstein's famous remark that the Beatles were "the greatest composers of codas since Beethoven." But as they improved and developed, they naturally began to seek effects in the studio which they could not reproduce in performance: the string quartet accompaniment to Paul's *Yesterday,* for example, or the technically difficult piano solo George Martin plays on *In My Life.* As George Harrison later put it, "we were held back in our development by having to go onstage all the time and do it, with the same old guitars, drums, and bass."

"Having to go onstage and do it" held the Beatles' development back in ways less obvious and more important than mere instrumentation. The chaotic conditions under which they performed made them understandably reluctant to try complex rhythms: a concert in a stadium, where the performers often had trouble hearing each other, was hardly the place to experiment with tricky rhythms, nor would such rhythms have been appreciated by fans who expected such concerts to provide a heavy "beat" as an aid to ritual hypnosis. Significantly, the first Beatles song involving a change of meter, John's *She Said She Said,* in which 4/4 slides into 3/4 in the third bar of the bridge, was first recorded on *Revolver,* at the point of the withdrawal

from public concerts. Once that breakthrough had occurred, effective metrical changes were frequent: the en-
ergetic 5/4 bars in *Good Morning, Good Morning* account
for some of that song's electricity, while the stumbling
alternation of 4/4 and 3/4 in *All You Need Is Love* keeps
the hearer off balance. Such innovations, while certainly
less complex than the rhythms of modern serious music or
those of the Indian music that came to fascinate George
Harrison, were previously unheard of in rock and roll, in
which one unbreakable rule had been regular dance
rhythm. ("It's got a good beat, Murray. You could dance to
it. I'd give it about 85.") And by breaking free of that rule,
the Beatles gained not only a new kind of variety, but the
ability to use regular rhythm ironically, again as a *persona.* In John's *Happiness is a Warm Gun,* for example,
the words of the title are sung to a slow, mindlessly regular
4/4 beat, while the harmonies move through the I-VI-IV-V
triadic pattern of the early 1960s, but that obviously parodic section is preceded by an irregularly accented section in triple time ("Mother Superior, jump the gun"), in
which the cross-rhythms suggest African drumming, not
American Bandstand. The juxtaposition enriches both
segments, and the implication is that the kind of listener
who would require that all music have a beat "you could
dance to" is the kind likely to respond to the American
hunting magazine ad from which John lifted the title.
"Mother Superior" is John's wife Yoko Ono, the Oriental
who "jumps the gun" by running traffic signals, so of
course her music is irregular, non-Western, and vigorous.

This kind of rhythmic complexity, especially when
rendered mimetic by a careful matching to words, requires a listener of a far different kind than the listener
addressed by *She Loves You.* If the early songs were designed to be heard over a public address system, the later
songs were produced to be heard through headphones. Despite the melodic and harmonic and formal progress the
Beatles were making during their lucrative years as the
"Fab Four," the conditions under which they performed
virtually arrested their development as lyricists. John

could hardly have projected the punning ambiguities of his later style when singing over the din of thousands of prepubescent girls who had come to hear such unambiguous messages as "I wanna hold your hand." But as the recording studio rather than the public stage became their arena, the Beatles' approach to lyrics began to change. An honest appraisal will have to admit that *Drive My Car, Norwegian Wood,* and *Nowhere Man,* all first recorded on the British version of *Rubber Soul,* are the first Beatles songs that can claim to have interesting lyrics; the contrast between these witty, fully shaped lyrics and those of the vapid early love songs is instructive.

In the early songs, the first-person speaker is usually a teenage lover: most often he talks to his girl ("Please please me oh yeh, like I please you"); sometimes he talks about her ("Well, she was just seventeen, And you know what I mean"); if he complains about her ("Well I gave you everything I had, But you left me sitting on my own"), it is only as part of a plea for reconciliation ("I beg you on my bended knees"). The situations dramatized by the songs were simple plots into which a teenage girl could project herself, casting her favorite Beatle as the devoted lover; this ploy was probably as important a cause of Beatlemania as Brian Epstein's aggressive press-agentry. But these songs merely set up situations; they never resolve them, leaving what happens *after* the speaker delivers his message to our imagination. Some of the songs on the album *Help!* (August 1965) have a little more bite: now the speaker responds to mistreatment with more resentment ("For I have got another girl, another girl who will love me to the end") and even addresses another male with a threat ("You're going to lose that girl"). But these situations were still simple; the fourteen-year-old girl apparently assumed as the listener needed only to cast herself as the "other girl" or the mistreated girl whose boyfriend would soon be replaced by a Beatle.

The more complicated songs on *Rubber Soul* make this kind of identification impossible by completing their stories, and by creating characters with whom no teenager would readily identify. In *Drive My Car,* for example, we meet a girl who is so confident that she is going to be "famous, a star of the screen" that she offers the speaker a job as her chauffeur:

> *"Baby, you can drive my car,*
> *Yes I'm gonna be a star.*
> *Baby, you can drive my car,*
> *and maybe I'll love you."*

The speaker is attracted but wary:

> *I told that girl that my prospects were good,*
> *She said, "Baby, It's understood.*
> *Working for peanuts is all very fine,*
> *But I can show you a better time."*
> *"Baby, you can drive my car, . . ." (etc.)*

So the speaker takes the bait, only to discover that a crucial element is missing:

> *I told that girl I could start right away,*
> *She said, "Baby I've got something to say.*
> *I got no car and it's breaking my heart,*
> *But I've found a driver, that's a start."*
> *"Baby, you can drive my car, . . ." (etc.)*

Unlike the early songs, this one does not seem designed to arouse sympathy or affection, nor is it simply a complaint, like *Day Tripper.* Both the girl, with her delusions of Hollywood, and the speaker, whose good "prospects" yield to a willingness to "start right away," are satirized, and *Drive My Car* marks the first time in the Beatles' development that a speaker is an object of satire. Indeed, he sounds like the kind of marginally employed Liverpool character the Beatles themselves might have been had they not become "stars of the screen," and the girl sounds suspiciously like someone eager to reach "the Toppermost of the Poppermost." By declaring that she wants to be famous, she is

able (for one brief moment) to enjoy one of the fruits of
fame, an amorous chauffeur. If talent is "believing you
can do something," she has it. She cannot create a car out
of thin air, but the Beatles do it for her in the exuberant
"Beep Beep" refrain that ends the song. If the song sati-
rizes the longings for fame and comfort of both its characters, it does so from the vantage point of people already
ambivalent about fame, though doubtless enjoying its
comforts. And it cannot be heard in the way audiences
presumably heard the early love songs. No teenage girl
would identify with the girl in the song, whose fantasies
are exposed as illusory; no teenage boy would identify
with the speaker, who is foolish enough to believe her. Nor
does the song encourage adulation of its makers as sex
objects. If we admire them, we must now admire them as
we admire the writers of stories, for the amusing shape
they have given their little tale and perhaps for the wry
and indirect way it dramatizes something about their own
lives, in this case their bemusement about their status as
"stars."

Norwegian Wood, another story about a failed encounter with a woman, features a series of absurdities and
ambiguities. In the very first line ("I once had a girl, or
should I say, she once had me"), a cliché is redefined in a
way that makes it ambiguous: in which of its many senses,
we wonder, is the word "had" being used? Like the girl in
Drive My Car this one is associated with a physical object,
apparently real this time, but never defined: "She showed
me her room, isn't it good Norwegian wood." If we think
that the Norwegian wood is her expensive modern furniture, we soon learn otherwise:

She asked me to stay and she told me to sit anywhere,
So I looked around and I noticed there wasn't a chair.

We never learn just what the wood is (panelling?), nor do
we learn why, after the speaker has "sat on a rug, biding
my time, drinking her wine," the girl apparently rejects
him:

*She told me she worked in the morning and started
  to laugh,*
I told her I didn't and crawled off to sleep in the bath.

Most mysterious of all, we are left to puzzle about what
really happens the next morning, when our hero wakes
up, finds himself alone, and lights a fire, adding the inevitable refrain, "Isn't it good, Norwegian wood." Perhaps he
burns her precious wood in the fireplace; perhaps he
merely has a smoke. But the song itself is the real act of
arson; its hint of destructiveness at the end dramatizes the
resentment a working-class youth (say, a singer from
Liverpool) might feel after an awkward social failure in
an upper-class *milieu.* Still, just as in *Drive My Car,* both
figures are satirized; if we sympathize with the speaker,
we surely also chuckle as he crawls off to sleep in the bath,
and John's ability to include himself in the satire saves the
song from being merely destructive. Perhaps it is even
another song about the limits of fame, if we may credit
John's claim that its story is autobiographical; perhaps he
learned from the real encounter here turned into fiction
that his fame and money were still insufficient to gain him
entry into the upper-class world, the world here symbol-
ized by a woman more interested in wood than in sex.

Similar class or political concerns do figure in the lyrics of the Beatles' maturity (John's *Revolution* and
George's *Taxman* and *Piggies* come immediately to
mind), but social commentary is finally less important
than the basic theme of failed communication established in *Norwegian Wood.* As in many later songs, the
withholding of information and uncertainty of reference
allow *Norwegian Wood* to enact its theme: our confusion
about the meaning of the refrain makes us like the
speaker, who must also wonder why the girl keeps talking about wood. *Nowhere Man,* the third striking lyric on
Rubber Soul, develops this theme of isolation without recourse to a story; here John invents a mythic figure, significantly described in the third person before being
compared to both listener and speaker:

> *He's a real Nowhere Man,*
> *Sitting in his Nowhere Land,*
> *Making all his nowhere plans for nobody.*
> *Doesn't have a point of view,*
> *Knows not where he's going to,*
> *Isn't he a bit like you and me?*

After describing Nowhere Man in that verse, the speaker addresses him directly in the bridge:

> *Nowhere Man, please listen,*
> *You don't know what you're missing*
> *Nowhere Man, the world is at your command.*

Then the alternation of description and address is recapitulated in even briefer compass:

> *He's as blind as he can be,*
> *Just sees what he wants to see,*
> *Nowhere Man, can you see me at all?*

By talking *about* Nowhere Man and then immediately talking *to* him, John gives the song's point of view a rich confusion. How can we project ourselves into this song? "Please listen, / You don't know what you're missing" sounds like a message to us about the growing complexity of Beatles music, but if we accept that identification of ourselves as Nowhere Man, the song is accusing us of blindness. John's account of the making of the song suggests an alternate possibility: "I was just sitting, trying to think of a song, and I thought of myself sitting there, doing nothing and getting nowhere. . . . Nothing would come. I was cheesed off and went for a lie down, having given up. Then I thought of myself as Nowhere Man—sitting in his nowhere land." But if John is Nowhere Man, then he is talking to himself in this song. By having it both ways ("Isn't he a bit like you *and* me"), the song ultimately shows us how uncertainty about identity and point of view leads to failed communication.

The complexity of these lyrics suggests a more intimate relationship between singer and hearer, and musically these songs are ill-suited to public performance: *Norwegian Wood* employs a sitar and quiet acoustic guitars, while *Nowhere Man* begins with four-part *a capella* singing (a chancy procedure in concert for singers used to instruments—especially Ringo). Musically and lyrically, these are "studio" songs, relying on us to listen carefully and repeatedly to their subtle effects; they are harbingers of the more sweeping changes coming on *Revolver*. On the one single issued between the two albums (*Paperback Writer*, June 1966), the Beatles seem to be musing about the meaning of those changes; Paul was the main composer, though the lyrics confirm John's remark that he "helped out." It is hard to escape the conclusion that beneath its satire, this song concerns the new relationship in which the Beatles were beginning to engage the public. This time the story takes the form of a letter:

> *Dear Sir or Madam will you read my book?*
> *It took me years to write, will you take a look?*
> *Based on a novel by a man named Lear*
> *And I need a job, so I want to be a paperback writer,*
>   *paperback writer.*

Here we have another satirized speaker, again in part a projection of John, whose own books *(In His Own Write* and *A Spaniard in the Works)* are indeed heavily influenced by the nonsense verse of Edward Lear. But the circles of self-consciousness are just beginning to spin; now the writer summarizes his plot:

> *It's the dirty story of a dirty man,*
> *And his clinging wife doesn't understand.*
> *His son is working for the Daily Mail;*
> *It's a steady job, but he wants to be a paperback writer,*
>   *paperback writer.*

Formally, this is a comic use of refrain, a trick as old as the medieval French *rondeau,* enforced by the high seventh chord on the second "paperback writer." Considered as narrative, the song constitutes a tiny example of the Quaker Oats box effect, since the characters in the proffered manuscript are little versions of its maker. But since that maker, the author of the manuscript and the letter, is in turn a version of John, what we finally have here is another consideration of the complex relationship between fame and communication. "Dear Sir or Madam will you read my book" is in many ways the same plea as "Nowhere Man, please listen," but the speaker's need for fame, his hope to be a "paperback writer" (or a "star of the screen" or a Beatle) makes him all too eager to alter his art to gain popularity and money. In the last verse, he is quick to assure the editor that he can write to order: "I can make it longer if you like the style, / I can change it 'round, and I want to be a paperback writer." The main reason why he urges acceptance of his manuscript is its sales potential: "It could make a million for you overnight."

Properly understood, the paperback writer is an even more complex *persona* than the Nowhere Man; he captures the Beatles' ambivalence about fame and communication at the very moment when they made their brave decision to withdraw from that public ritual of fame, the rock concert, a ritual they had come to see as an inferior form of communication—sexual, perhaps political, certainly dramatic, but not finally musical. Leaving the hot, physical communication of such concerts to The Rolling Stones and The Who, they deliberately chose the cooler, more writerly, ultimately more musical medium of the long-playing album, and from *Revolver* on, they made the goal of their work the production of albums: not performances or even individual songs, but whole, structured artifacts with cunning musical and lyrical relations between their parts. Conceived on this larger scale, the later albums demand of the hearer the kind of repeated, serious, analytical attention we normally reserve for high art.

Like high art they are impossible to paraphrase: even the published music, roughly accurate as to melodies and chord changes, is hopelessly inadequate as a transcription of *Sergeant Pepper* or *Abbey Road.* The album itself is the text, the finished product, the authority.

The songs on these later albums return to the theme of isolation, questioning whether meaningful communication can ever be achieved, but the albums themselves offer the best answer to that repeated question: they achieve a kind of communication not previously even attempted in popular music, a kind best understood by those fortunate enough to have been part of a successful musical ensemble. Nobody understands how a string quartet achieves perfect attacks and well-tuned chords, but everyone agrees that much of what is involved cannot be discussed verbally. The Beatles in 1966 had already experienced a decade of such privileged musical communication, and their ensemble in the studio years became even tighter. The film *Let it Be,* which preserves some moments from their last recording sessions, offers tantalizing glimpses of this musical communication even though the cohesiveness of the group is already suffering from the strains that would lead to their breakup. Still, we see Paul and Ringo communicating entirely with their eyes as they work out a coherent pattern for bass and drums, John adjusting the tempo of one of Paul's tunes, George working out guitar lines that reveal new features of melodies by the others. And in the case of John and Paul, musical communication was not merely a matter of tight performing ensemble; it extended to composition as well. One example of this uncanny rapport will have to suffice, John's account of the way a tune originally conceived by Paul alone ("Woke up, fell out of bed, dragged a comb across my head"), turned out to be exactly what was needed for the bridge of John's *A Day in the Life.* Increasingly aware of the special qualities of this rapport, its superiority as communication to small talk, newspaper interviews, *and concerts,* the Beatles became unable to go through the motions of writing teenage love songs and performing them on stage. That decision doubtless lost them that portion of their audience for whom they were only sex objects or symbols of youthful rebellion, but it gained them the continuing respect of musicians of all kinds.

As John explained in 1968, "We talk in code to each other as Beatles. We always did that, when we had so many strangers round us on tours. We never really communicated with other people. . . . Talking is the slowest form of communicating anyway. Music is much better. We're communicating to the outside world through our music." Indeed they were, and the careful listener to the later albums is not part of a mass audience, but a fortunate eavesdropper, allowed to witness the Beatles' own private kind of communication, and trusted to respond to it; that, I take it, is one meaning of the lines on *Sergeant Pepper* that say "You're such a lovely audience, We'd like to take you home with us." I have been arguing that collaboration was the crucial factor for the Beatles from the beginning, that by finding ways to bring their disparate voices and contrasting musical personalities together, they achieved a richer and more satisfying art than other groups. My point here is that their abandoning of the concert stage enriched their collaboration and extended it, that their communication with the listener, now more intimate and complex, became more like their communication with each other, and that the primary mode of communication, in both cases, was music.

Once we understand this fact, we can abandon the hopeless process of trying to understand the lyrics of John's most complex later songs as if they had exact, referential meaning. Some commentators imagine that it is sufficient to explain such songs as *Tomorrow Never Knows, Lucy in the Sky with Diamonds, I Am the Walrus, Strawberry Fields, Glass Onion,* and *Happiness is a Warm Gun* by making the obvious point that they seem connected to drug experiences. But even if drugs were a part of the genesis of some of the imagery in these songs, they cannot account for the way that imagery communicates to its hearers. A more serious approach might consider the ways these lyrics achieve the goal of French Symbolist poetry, the way they attain what Pater called "the condition of music." For even if the opaque and nonsensical phrases in these songs originally had some private meaning for the Beatles, we often cannot recover that original reference, so that a phrase like "a soap impression of his wife which he ate and donated to the National Trust" must communicate to us in the way that music *always* communicates to us: not as a series of sounds with precise, lexical meaning, but as a series of sounds rich with suggestion, pregnant with possibilities, resistant to paraphrase. Of the many ways poets have tried to attain "the condition of music," nonsense verse, which prefers rhyming to syntax, sound to logic, is one of the closest approaches. To be sure, part of the fun of nonsense—in Lear, Ionesco, or Lennon—comes from the way it frustrates our instinctive urge to make sense of it; our example is amusing because carving one's wife in soap is absurd, eating the soap carving is more absurd, and donating something one has already eaten is impossible. But pure sound plays a vital role as well; the internal chime of *"ate* and don-*ate*d" produces what W. K. Wimsatt, in his seminal essay on rhyme, called "an alogical pattern of implication." Because rhyming and punning depend on accidental rather than grammatical resemblances between sounds, they produce kinds of meaning which are purely contextual, unique to the phrase, poem, or song in which they occur. And *all* musical meaning is like that: the note G means nothing by itself, but in a given context, it may be a tonic, a leading tone, or (most like a pun) the pivot note for a modulation. The prevalence of punning on the later Beatle albums is another indication of the dominance there of musical kinds of meaning.

In these great albums, all the strengths we noticed in the Beatles' early work reach fulfillment. George's guitar improvisations move well beyond "riffing": his solo on

John's *Good Morning, Good Morning* is the most musically convincing use of distortion ever achieved on the electric guitar, and his conversational "fills" between the phrases of Paul's *She Came in Through the Bathroom Window* contribute wonderfully to that song's oddball comedy. The singing, both solo and background, improves much over that on the early albums, in part because each of the singers develops several distinct vocal styles. These include the *personae* already mentioned, but also softer kinds of singing not possible in concert, for example Paul's folk-like warbling on *Blackbird* or John's mournful chant in *Julia,* a song for his dead mother. Rhythmic and harmonic ideas, increasingly sophisticated on the small scale, begin to function on the large scale as well: on side two of *Abbey Road,* the songs actually have a continuous sequence of key relations like a Schubert song cycle; they are also related by repeating chord sequences used motivically and by proportional rhythmic schemes, most obviously in the closely connected sequence from *Mean Mr. Mustard* to *The End.* And in ways too subtle and various to list here, all the late albums develop connections between musical and verbal structure.

As any musician knows, the compromising of egos necessary to produce musical ensemble has its costs, and it seems reasonable to infer that when creation, not merely performance, is the goal, the costs are even higher. The talents and egos involved in the Beatles were strong, and sad as it was to witness those final quarrels over the spoils of fame—money, managers, corporations, copyrights—the real wonder is that the inevitable breakup did not occur earlier. Nor was there ever any real hope of a reunion, once the four members had gone their separate and musically disappointing ways. Yet the slightest rumor of some occasion on which they might meet was sufficient for a decade to send a thrill through many of us; the hope that they might somehow regroup, like the hope of the religious for a Second Coming, was a sustaining myth to be cherished in difficult times. As far as popular music is concerned, these are difficult times; in quite different ways, the two dominant styles are both radical rejections of the Beatles' kind of musical communication. Punk, which features crudely revolutionary lyrics, deliberately incompetent playing, and performers selected for their bizarre appearance alone, reduces rock to theatre, virtually eliminating music. Disco, which employs monotonously thick chords purged of expressive value, complex total attack rhythms laid on top of a deadly 4/4 thud, and performers selected for their slick anonymity, reduces rock to Muzak, eliminating any principle of contrast or expression. Faced with that kind of choice, many of us took comfort in the remote hope for a Beatles reunion, and drew sustenance from replaying our Beatle albums. John's death three years ago deprived us of that unrealistic hope; its anniversary may serve to remind us again of the sustenance.

CREDITS

IF I FELL, TELL ME WHY (John Lennon and Paul McCartney)
© 1964 Northern Songs Limited*

ANOTHER GIRL, DRIVE MY CAR, NORWEGIAN WOOD, NOWHERE MAN, YOU'RE GOING TO LOSE THAT GIRL (John Lennon and Paul McCartney)
© 1965 Northern Songs Limited*

PAPERBACK WRITER (John Lennon and Paul McCartney)
© 1967 Northern Songs Limited*

A DAY IN THE LIFE (John Lennon and Paul McCartney)
© 1967 Northern Songs Limited*

HAPPINESS IS A WARM GUN (John Lennon and Paul McCartney)
© 1968 Northern Songs Limited*

BALLAD OF JOHN AND YOKO, YOU NEVER GIVE ME YOUR MONEY (John Lennon and Paul McCartney)
© 1969 Northern Songs Limited*

IDEAS

1. In what way does Winn prove his thesis that the Beatles' success was "a response to and attempted escape from the burdens of public notoriety"?

2. Winn emphasizes the Beatles' monetary drives, their claims that they performed for money not art. Are these assertions valid? Do you suppose any artist is solely concerned with artistic worth, caring nothing about money? Have there been artists like this in the past? Do you think that Beethoven was "just knocking out a bit of work"?

3. What do you learn about class consciousness and social concerns from this essay?

4. Based upon information in Winn's review, do you feel that the Beatles were honest with their audiences, or do you think that they manipulated and used them?

5. In what specific ways did the collaboration about which Winn writes strengthen the Beatles as musicians?

6. Do you feel that Winn's harsh criticism of punk and disco music (last paragraph) is valid?

ORGANIZATION AND STYLE

1. For the most part, this essay is chronological. Why, then, does Winn begin with a discussion of Lennon's death?

2. How does Winn move the essay along through the various phases of the Beatles' development? His transitions are more sophisticated than *first, second, third* or *the following year, six months later, the next July.* How, exactly, does he achieve transition?

3. Does Winn do an effective job of working in quotations from the Beatles themselves? What about his excerpts from their songs? Are there too many of them? Not enough?

4. How does Winn let his organizational scheme work so that it highlights certain contrasts among members of the Beatles group? Among the group and their audiences?

5. Winn's essay focuses on the Beatles' gradual maturation. Interestingly, Winn's own sentences become more syntactically sophisticated as the essay progresses. Examine sentences in the early part of the essay and compare them with those in the latter part. What differences in syntactic patterns do you find?

WRITING

1. Winn suggests that the Beatles "served several generations as symbols on which to hang fantasies, aspirations, and not-yet-formed identities." Write an essay about hanging fantasies and identities on some contemporary artist (musician, writer, painter).

2. In the latter part of his essay, Winn analyzes the meaning and the potential social implications of selected Beatles songs. Write your own analysis, matching Winn in detail and quotation, of some currently popular song.

The Scientific Essay: Exposition of a Process

Johannes Kepler

ALBERT EINSTEIN

———————●———————

This essay is remarkable not only for its remarkable author but for the clarity with which he explains a scientific problem. His opening comments on faith and his concluding comments on empirical method and the human mind are no less memorable.

In anxious and uncertain times like ours, when it is difficult to find pleasure in humanity and the course of human affairs, it is particularly consoling to think of the serene greatness of a Kepler.* Kepler lived in an age in which the reign of law in nature was by no means an accepted certainty. How great must his faith in a uniform law have been, to have given him the strength to devote ten years of hard and patient work to the empirical investigation of the movement of the planets and the mathematical laws of that movement, entirely on his own, supported by no one and understood by very few! If we would honor his memory worthily, we must get as clear a picture as we can of his problem and the stages of his solution.

Copernicus† had opened the eyes of the most intelligent to the fact that the best way to get a clear grasp of the apparent movements of the planets in the heavens was by

---

*Johannes Kepler (1571–1630), German astronomer.
    †Nicolaus Copernicus (1473–1543), Polish astronomer, regarded as the founder of modern astronomy.

regarding them as movements around the sun conceived as stationary. If the planets moved uniformly in a circle around the sun, it would have been comparatively easy to discover how these movements must look from the earth. Since, however, the phenomena to be dealt with were much more complicated than that, the task was a far harder one. The first thing to be done was to determine these movements empirically from the observations of Tycho Brahe.* Only then did it become possible to think about discovering the general laws which these movements satisfy.

To grasp how difficult a business it was even to find out about the actual rotating movements, one has to realize the following. One can never see where a planet really is at any given moment, but only in what direction it can be seen just then from the earth, which is itself moving in an unknown manner around the sun. The difficulties thus seemed practically unsurmountable.

Kepler had to discover a way of bringing order into this chaos. To start with, he saw that it was necessary first to try and find out about the motion of the earth itself. This would simply have been impossible if there had existed only the sun, the earth and the fixed stars, but no other planets. For in that case one could ascertain nothing empirically except how the direction of the straight sun-earth line changes in the course of the year (apparent movement of the sun with reference to the fixed stars). In this way it was possible to discover that these sun-earth directions all lay in a plane stationary with reference to the fixed stars, at least according to the accuracy of observation achieved in those days, when there were no telescopes. By this means it could also be ascertained in what manner the sun-earth revolves round the sun. It turned out that the angular velocity of this motion went through regular change in the course of the year. But this was not of much use, as it was still not known how the distance from

---

*Tycho Brahe (1546–1601; pronounced BRAH-uh), Danish astronomer, the first modern recorder of systematic and accurate observations concerning motions of the sun and moon and the places of 777 fixed stars.

the earth to the sun alters in the course of the year. It was only when they found out about these changes that the real shape of the earth's orbit and the manner in which it is described were discovered.

Kepler found a marvelous way out of this dilemma. To begin with it was apparent from observations of the sun that the apparent path of the sun against the background of the fixed stars differed in speed at different times of the year, but that the angular velocity of this movement was always the same at the same point in the astronomical year, and therefore that the speed of rotation of the straight line earth-sun was always the same when it pointed to the same region of the fixed stars. It was thus legitimate to suppose that the earth's orbit was a self-enclosed one, described by the earth in the same way every year—which was by no means obvious *a priori.* For the adherent of the Copernican system it was thus as good as certain that this must also apply to the orbits of the rest of the planets.

This certainty made things easier. But how to ascertain the real shape of the earth's orbit? Imagine a brightly shining lantern M somewhere in the plane of the orbit. We know that this lantern remains permanently in its place and thus forms a kind of fixed triangulation point for determining the earth's orbit, a point which the inhabitants of the earth can take a sight on at any time of year. Let this lantern M be further away from the sun than the earth. With the help of such a lantern it was possible to determine the earth's orbit, in the following way:—

First of all, in every year there comes a moment when the earth E lies exactly on the line joining the sun S and the lantern M. If at this moment we look from the earth E at the lantern M, our line of sight will coincide with the line SM (sun-lantern). Suppose the latter to be marked in the heavens. Now imagine the earth in a different position and at a different time. Since the sun S and the lantern M can both be seen from the Earth, the angle at E in the triangle SEM is known. But we also know the direction of SE in relation to the fixed stars through direct solar observations, while the direction of the line SM in relation to the fixed stars was finally ascertained previously. But in the triangle SEM we also know the angle at S. Therefore, with the base SM arbitrarily laid down on a sheet of paper, we can, in virtue of our knowledge of the angles at E and S, construct the triangle SEM. We might do this at frequent intervals during the year; each time we should get on our piece of paper a position of the earth E with a date attached to it and a certain position in relation to the permanently fixed base SM. The earth's orbit would thereby be empirically determined, apart from its absolute size, of course.

But, you will say, where did Kepler get his lantern M? His genius and Nature, benevolent in this case, gave it to him. There was, for example, the planet Mars; and the length of the Martian year—i.e., one rotation of Mars around the sun—was known. It might happen one fine day that the sun, the earth and Mars lie absolutely in the same straight line. This position of Mars regularly recurs after one, two, etc., Martian years, as Mars has a self-enclosed orbit. At these known moments, therefore, SM always presents the same base, while the earth is always at a different point in its orbit. The observations of the sun and Mars at these moments thus constitute a means of determining the true orbit of the earth, as Mars then plays the part of our imaginary lantern. Thus it was that Kepler discovered the true shape of the earth's orbit and the way in which the earth describes it, and we who come after—Europeans, Germans, or even Swabians—may well admire and honor him for it.

Now that the earth's orbit had been empirically determined, the true position and length of the line SE at any moment was known, and it was not so terribly difficult for Kepler to calculate the orbits and motions of the rest of the planets too from observations—at least in principle. It was nevertheless an immense work, especially considering the state of mathematics at the time.

Now came the second and no less arduous part of Kepler's life work. The orbits were empirically known, but their laws had to be deduced from the empirical data. First he had to make a guess at the mathematical nature of the curve described by the orbit, and then try it out on a vast assemblage of figures. If it did not fit, another hypothesis had to be devised and again tested. After tremendous search, the conjecture that the orbit was an ellipse with the sun at one of its foci was found to fit the facts. Kepler also discovered the law governing the variation in speed during rotation, which is that the line sun-planet sweeps out equal areas in equal periods of time. Finally he also discovered that the square of the period of circulation around the sun varies as the cube of the major axes of the ellipse.

Our admiration for this splendid man is accompanied by another feeling of admiration and reverence, the object of which is no man but the mysterious harmony of nature into which we are born. As far back as ancient times people devised the lines exhibiting the simplest conceivable form of regularity. Among these, next to the straight line and the circle, the most important were the ellipse and the hyperbola. We see the last two embodied—at least very nearly so—in the orbits of the heavenly bodies.

It seems that the human mind has first to construct forms independently before we can find them in things. Kepler's marvelous achievement is a particularly fine example of the truth that knowledge cannot spring from experience alone but only from the comparison of the inventions of the intellect with observed fact.

IDEAS

1. What is the chaos that Kepler was to bring to order?

2. What is the import of Einstein's remark that Nature, "benevolent in this case," gave Kepler his lantern M? How would Eiseley concur?

3. Can you explain what Einstein means by this statement: "At these known moments, therefore, SM always presents the same base, while the earth is always at a different point in its orbit"? How did observations at these moments solve the problem?

4. Why does Einstein say "or even Swabians"? (Your encyclopedia will help.)

5. How do Eiseley and Einstein agree or disagree about "the mysterious harmony of nature into which we are born"?

6. How might the people of ancient times have derived their concepts of the simplest conceivable forms of regularity?

ORGANIZATION AND STYLE

1. The third sentence of the first paragraph is particularly stylized. What are its stylistic elements?

2. What is the function of the final sentence of the first paragraph?

3. Einstein organizes his essay by presenting a problem and then following with a solution. How many problem-solution sequences are there in this brief essay?

4. How do the final two paragraphs function as an effective conclusion?

WRITING

1. Develop an essay explaining some scientific concept, or some practical operation like that of a pump, an unusual engine (the Wankel, for instance), a dressmaker, or a carpenter, trying to attain the lucidity of Einstein on Kepler. You might wish to follow the problem-solution pattern.

2. Consider Einstein's statement "that knowledge cannot spring from experience alone but only from the comparison of the inventions of the intellect with observed fact" and Thoreau's statement that one should "elevate his life by conscious endeavor" and "carve and paint the very atmosphere and medium through which we look." See what some meditation about mind over matter, or in collaboration with matter, will produce.

Index

TAKING RIGHTS SERIOUSLY

Taking Rights Seriously

RONALD DWORKIN

DUCKWORTH

First published in 1977 by
Gerald Duckworth & Co. Ltd.
The Old Piano Factory
43 Gloucester Crescent, London NW1

© 1977 Ronald Dworkin

Cloth ISBN 0 7156 0715 4

Paper ISBN 0 7156 1174 7

7802

323. 4

Printed in Great Britain by
Bristol Typesetting Co. Ltd.
Barton Manor, St. Philips, Bristol

Contents

Introduction

The chapters of this book were written separately during a period of great political controversy about what law is and who must obey it and when. During the same period the political attitude called 'liberalism', once the posture of almost all politicians, seemed to lose a great deal of its appeal. The middle-aged blamed liberalism for permissiveness and the young blamed it for rigidity, economic injustice and the war in Vietnam. Uncertainty about law reflected uncertainty about a conventional political attitude.

The various chapters define and defend a liberal theory of law. They are nevertheless sharply critical of another theory that is widely thought to be a liberal theory. This theory has been so popular and influencial that I shall call it the ruling theory of law. The ruling theory has two parts, and insists on their independence. The first is a theory about what law is; in less dramatic language it is a theory about the necessary and sufficient conditions for the truth of a proposition of law. This is the theory of legal positivism, which holds that the truth of legal propositions consists in facts about the rules that have been adopted by specific social institutions, and in nothing else. The second is a theory about what the law ought to be, and how the familiar legal institutions ought to behave. This is the theory of utilitarianism, which holds that law and its institutions should serve the general welfare, and nothing else. Both parts of the ruling theory derive from the philosophy of Jeremy Bentham.

The critical portions of these essays criticize both parts of the theory, and also criticize the assumption that they are independent of one another. The constructive portions emphasize an idea that is also part of the liberal tradition, but that has no place in either legal positivism or utilitarianism. This is the old idea of individual human rights. Bentham called that idea 'nonsense on stilts'.

A general theory of law must be normative as well as conceptual. Its normative part must treat a variety of topics indicated by the following catalogue. It must have a theory of legislation, of adjudication, and of compliance; these three theories look at the normative questions of law from the standpoints of a lawmaker, a judge, and an ordinary citizen. The theory of legislation must contain a theory of legitimacy, which describes the circumstances under which a particular person or group is entitled to make law, and a theory of legislative justice, which describes the law they are entitled or obliged to make. The theory of adjudication must also be complex: it must contain a theory of controversy, which sets out standards that judges should use to decide hard cases at law, and a theory of jurisdiction, which explains why and when judges, rather than other groups or institutions, should make the decisions required by the theory of controversy. The theory of compliance must contrast and discuss two roles. It must contain a theory of deference, which discusses the nature and limits of the citizen's duty to obey the law in different forms of state, and under different circumstances, and a theory of enforcement, which identifies the goals of enforcement and punishment, and describes how officials should respond to different categories of crime or fault.

A general theory of law will comprehend subjects that do not fall within any of these categories, and a topic that falls within one may fall within others as well. The politically sensitive issue of constitutionalism is, for example, an issue in the theory of legitimacy. Why should the elected representatives of the majority ever be disabled from enacting law that seems to them fair and efficient? But a related question is also an issue in the conceptual part of a legal theory. Can the most fundamental principles of the constitution, which define who is competent to make law and how, themselves be considered as part of the law? That conceptual question plainly bears on other questions of legitimacy and jurisdiction. If the political principles embedded in the constitution are law, then the title of judges to decide what the constitution requires is, at least *prima facie*, confirmed; if these principles are law in spite of the fact that they are not the product of deliberate social or political decision, then the fact that law can be, in that sense, natural argues for the constraint on majority power that a constitution imposes. Both the conceptual question and the questions of jurisdiction and legitimacy bear in obvious ways on the theory of compliance; they bear, for example, on the issue of whether a dissident can plausibly or even coherently say that his idea of what the fundamental law of the constitution requires may be superior to that of the legislature and the judges.

The interdependencies of the various parts of a general theory of law are therefore complex. In the same way, moreover, a general theory of law will have many connections with other departments of philosophy. The normative theory will be embedded in a more general political and moral philosophy which may in turn depend upon philosophical theories about human nature or the objectivity of morality. The conceptual part will draw upon the philosophy of language and therefore upon logic and metaphysics. The issue of what propositions of law mean, and whether they are always true or false, for example, establishes immediate connections with very difficult and controverted questions in philosophical logic. A general theory of law must therefore constantly take up one or another disputed position on problems of philosophy that are not distinctly legal.

3.

Bentham was the last philosopher in the Anglo-American stream to offer a theory of law that is general in the way just described. One may find in his work a conceptual part and a normative part of a general theory of law, and one may find, within the latter, distinct theories of legitimacy, legislative justice, jurisdiction and controversy, all suitably related under a political and moral theory of utilitarianism and a more general metaphysical theory of empiricism. Each component of this general theory has been developed and refined, by different academic lawyers, but the ruling theory of law, in both British and American law schools, remains a Benthamite theory.

The conceptual part of his theory – legal positivism – has been much improved. The most powerful contemporary version of positivism is that proposed by H. L. A. Hart, and it is Hart's version which is criticized in this book. The normative part of Bentham's theory has been much refined through the use of economic analysis in legal theory. Economic analysis provides standards for identifying and measuring the welfare of the individuals who make up a community (though the nature of these standards is much in dispute) and holds that the normative questions of a theory of legitimacy, legislative justice, jurisdiction and controversy, as well as deference and enforcement, must all be answered by supposing that legal institutions compose a system whose overall goal is the promotion of the highest average welfare among these individuals. This general normative theory emphasizes what earlier versions of utilitarianism often neglected: that this overall goal might be advanced more securely by assigning different types of questions to different institutions according to some theory of institutional competence, rather than by supposing that all institutions are equally able to calculate the impact on overall welfare of any particular political decision.[1]

Since legal positivism and economic utilitarianism are complex doctrines, the ruling theory of law has many antagonists many of which are equally antagonistic to each other. The ruling theory is opposed, for

---

[1] See, for example, the influential teaching materials by H. M. Hart and A. Sachs, *The Legal Process* (mimeographed materials published by the Harvard Law School).

Introduction

...ample, by various forms of collectivism. Legal positivism assumes that law is made by explicit social practice or institutional decision; it rejects the more romantic and obscure idea that legislation can be the product of an implicit general or corporate will. Economic utilitarianism is also (though only to a degree) individualistic. It sets as a standard of justice in legislation, the goal of overall or average welfare, but it defines overall welfare as a function of the welfare of distinct individuals, and steadily opposes the idea that a community has, as a distinct entity, some independent interest or entitlement.

The ruling theory is also criticized because it is rationalistic. It teaches, in its conceptual part, that law is the product of deliberate and purposeful decision by men and women planning, through such decisions, to change the community through general obedience to the rules their decisions create. It commends, in its normative part, decisions based on such plans, and it therefore supposes that men and women in political office can have the skill, knowledge and virtue to make such decisions effectively under conditions of considerable uncertainty in highly complex communities.

Some of those who criticize the individualism and rationalism of the ruling theory represent what is often called, in political discussions, the 'left'. They believe that the formalism of legal positivism forces courts to substitute a thin sense of procedural justice, which serves conservative social policies, for a richer substantive justice that would undermine these policies. They believe that economic utilitarianism is unjust in its consequences, because it perpetuates poverty as a means to efficiency, and deficient in its theory of human nature, because it sees individuals as self-interested atoms of society, rather than as inherently social beings whose sense of community is an essential part of their sense of self.

Many other critics of the ruling theory, on the other hand, are associated with the political right.[1] They follow the curious philosophy of Edmund Burke, who has become newly popular in American political theory, and believe that the true law of the community is not simply the deliberate decisions that legal positivism takes to be exclusive, but also the diffuse customary morality that exercises a great influence on these decisions. They believe that economic utilitarianism, which insists that deliberate decisions contrary to conventional morality can improve the community's welfare, is hopelessly optimistic. They argue, with Burke, that the rules best suited to promote the welfare of a community will emerge only from experience of that community, so that more trust must be put in established social culture than in the social engineering of utilitarians who suppose that they know better than history.

---

[1] See, for example, Hayek, *Law, Liberty and Legislation*.

Neither of these very different critiques of the ruling theory chall
one specific feature of that theory I mentioned, however. Neither a
that the ruling theory is defective because it rejects the idea that in.___
duals can have rights against the state that are prior to the rights created
by explicit legislation. On the contrary, opposition from the left and the
right is united in condemning the ruling theory for its excessive concern,
as they take it to be, with the fate of individuals as individuals. The idea
of individual rights, in the strong sense in which that idea is defended
in this book, is for them simply an exaggerated case of the disease from
which the ruling theory already suffers.

4.

That idea has, of course, been advanced by many different philosophers
in many different forms, but the ruling theory rejects the idea in any
form. Legal positivism rejects the idea that legal rights can pre-exist
any form of legislation; it rejects the idea, that is, that individuals or
groups can have rights in adjudication other than the rights explicitly
provided in the collection of explicit rules that compose the whole of a
community's law. Economic utilitarianism rejects the idea that political
rights can pre-exist legal rights; that is, that citizens can justifiably
protest a legislative decision on any ground except that the decision does
not in fact serve the general welfare.

Much of the ruling theory's opposition to natural rights is the consequence of an idea Bentham promoted: that natural rights can have no
place in a respectably empirical metaphysics. Liberals are suspicious of
ontological luxury. They believe that it is a cardinal weakness in various
forms of collectivism that these rely on ghostly entities like collective wills
or national spirits, and they are therefore hostile to any theory of natural
rights that seems to rely on equally suspicious entities. But the idea of
individual rights that these essays defend does not presuppose any ghostly
forms; that idea is, in fact, of no different metaphysical character from
the main ideas of the ruling theory itself. It is, in fact, parasitic on the
dominant idea of utilitarianism, which is the idea of a collective goal of
the community as a whole.

Individual rights are political trumps held by individuals. Individuals
have rights when, for some reason, a collective goal is not a sufficient
justification for denying them what they wish, as individuals, to have or
to do, or not a sufficient justification for imposing some loss or injury
upon them. That characterization of a right is, of course, formal in the
sense that it does not indicate what rights people have or guarantee,
indeed, that they have any. But it does not suppose that rights have
some special metaphysical character, and the theory defended in these

essays therefore departs from older theories of rights that do rely on that supposition.

The theory requires a vocabulary for making distinctions among the different types of rights individuals have. A vocabulary is proposed in Chapter 4. The most important of the distinctions made there is the distinction between two forms of political rights : background rights, which are rights that hold in an abstract way against decisions taken by the community or the society as a whole, and more specific institutional rights that hold against a decision made by a specific institution. Legal rights may then be identified as a distinct species of a political right, that is, an institutional right to the decision of a court in its adjudicative function.

Legal positivism, in this vocabulary, is the theory that individuals have legal rights only insofar as these have been created by explicit political decisions or explicit social practice. That theory is criticised in Chapters 2 and 3 as an inadequate conceptual theory of law. Chapter 4 suggests an alternative conceptual theory which shows how individuals may have legal rights other than those created by explicit decision or practice; that is, that they may have rights to specific adjudicative decisions even in hard cases when no explicit decision or practice requires a decision either way.

The argument of Chapter 4 provides a bridge between the conceptual and the normative parts of the alternate theory. It provides a normative theory of adjudication, which emphasizes the distinction between arguments of principle and policy, and defends the claim that judicial decisions based on arguments of principle are compatable with democratic principles. Chapter 5 applies that normative theory of adjudication to the central and politically important cases of constitutional adjudication. It uses the theory to criticize the debate between what is called judicial activism and restraint in constitutional law, and defends the propriety of judicial review limited to arguments of principle, even in politically controversial cases.

Chapter 6 discusses the foundation of a theory of legislative rights. It argues, through an analysis of John Rawls's powerful and influential theory of justice, that our intuitions about justice presuppose not only that people have rights but that one right among these is fundamental and even axiomatic. This most fundamental of rights is a distinct conception of the right to equality, which I call the right to equal concern and respect.

Chapters 7 and 8 defend a normative theory of compliance. Chapter 7 considers cases in which an individual's legislative, though not necessarily his legal, rights are in dispute. It does not argue for any particular set of individual rights, but only for certain consequences of conceding that individuals have some legislative rights distinct from and prior to their legal rights. This theory of compliance does not, therefore, rest on any presumptions about the character of the background and legislative rights people actually have; it does not presuppose even the abstract conclusion of Chapter 6. It therefore fulfills an important requirement of any political theory that gives a prominent place to rights: it provides a theory of compliance under conditions of uncertainty and controversy about what rights people actually have.

Chapter 8 extends the analysis to cases of uncertainty and controversy about legal rights. It takes up two important and often neglected questions of a theory of compliance: What are the background rights and responsibilities of a citizen when his constitutional rights are uncertain, but he genuinely believes that the government has no legal right to compel him to do what he believes is wrong? What are the responsibilities of officials who believe that he is wrong but sincere in his opinion of what the law is?

Chapter 9 returns to the right to concern and respect described in Chapter 6. It shows how that conception of equality may be used to interpret the famous Equal Protection Clause of the Fourteenth Amendment to the United States Constitution, and how, used in that way, the conception confirms our intuitions about racial discrimination and supports the politically controversial practice called reverse discrimination.

Chapters 10, 11 and 12 consider the competing claims of a different right that has also been considered by many political philosophers to be the most fundamental of political rights; this is the so-called right to liberty, which is often thought not only to be a rival to the right to equality, but to be, in at least some cases, inconsistent with that right. Chapter 12 argues that there is no right to liberty as such; indeed that the idea of such a right is itself a confusion. It does not reject the idea that individuals have rights to certain distinct liberties, like the right to personal moral decisions discussed in Chapter 10, or the right to the liberties described in the Constitutional Bill of Rights. On the contrary, Chapter 12 argues that these conventional rights are derivative, not from a more abstract general right to liberty as such, but from the right to equality itself. The essays therefore contradict the popular and dangerous idea that individualism is the enemy of equality. That idea is the common mistake of libertarians who hate equality and egalitarians who hate liberty; each attacks his own ideal under its other name.

5.

The essays provide the main structure for a distinct theory of law. But though they were all written in pursuit of that theory, they were written separately and therefore contain, as a group, overlappings and differences in emphasis and detail. They do not anticipate all the objections that will be made to what is said, nor do they say all that I should like to say about many of the topics they consider.

It is no part of my theory, for example, that any mechanical procedure exists for demonstrating what political rights, either background or legal, a particular individual has. On the contrary, the essays emphasize that there are hard cases, both in politics and at law, in which reasonable lawyers will disagree about rights, and neither will have available any argument that must necessarily convince the other. It may be objected that in such circumstances it is nonsense to suppose that any rights exist at all. This objection presupposes a general philosophical theory according to which no proposition can be true unless some procedure exists, at least in principle, for demonstrating its truth in such a way that any rational person must concede that it is true. Chapter 13 argues that we have no reason to accept that general philosophical position and good reason to reject it, particularly insofar as it applies to arguments about rights.[1]

Someone might wish to object, however, that in any case, as a practical matter, there can be no point in making or arguing about claims of right unless these can be demonstrated to be true or false. That objection is misguided. We could not understand the important ideas of sincerity in political argument, or of responsibility in political decision, if that were so; nor, indeed, could we comprehend the commonplace practice, in which we all engage, of arguing about rights in hard cases. It is important, however, that a political theory recognize that many claims of right, including some very important claims, are not demonstrable, and therefore provide principles to govern official decision when rights are controversial. The theory of compliance developed in Chapters 7 and 8, as I have said, provides such principles.

Chapter 12 offers an argument in favor of recognizing certain specific background and institutional rights. It might be wise to repeat here what I say there, which is that neither the rights there described, nor the method used to argue for these rights, is meant to be exclusive of other rights or of other methods of argument. The general theory of rights allows that there may be different sorts of argument, each sufficient to establish some reason why a collective goal that normally provides a justification for a political decision does not justify a particular disadvantage to some individual.

The book nevertheless suggests one favored form of argument for

---

[1] See also 'No Right Answer', in *Law, Morality and Society: Essays in Honour of H. L. A. Hart*, London 1977.

political rights, which is the derivation of particular rights from the abstract right to concern and respect taken to be fundamental and axiomatic. Chapter 6 shows how a familiar argument for economic rights on behalf of the worst-off group can be traced to that abstract right, and Chapters 9 and 12 show how a different argument might generate the familiar civil rights from the same source. Chapter 12 suggests, moreover, that the right to concern and respect is fundamental among rights in a different way, because it shows how the idea of a collective goal may itself be derived from that fundamental right. If so, then concern and respect is a right so fundamental that it is not captured by the general characterization of rights as trumps over collective goals, except as a limiting case, because it is the source both of the general authority of collective goals and of the special limitations on their authority that justify more particular rights.

That promise of unity in political theory is indistinct in these essays, however. It must be defended, if at all, elsewhere. In particular it must be shown how the same conception of equal concern that justifies the trade-offs characteristic of economic collective goals also justifies exemption, in the form of economic rights, for those who suffer most from those trade-offs. Some conception of levels of need is needed here, so that it can be shown that while equal concern justifies trade-offs within needs of a given level of urgency, it does not permit sacrifices in needs at a more urgent level even for the sake of the fuller satisfaction of more needs that are less urgent.

Chapters 12 and 13 have not been published before. Chapters 2 and 6 were published originally in the *University of Chicago Law Review*; Chapters 3 and 10 in the *Yale Law Journal*; and Chapter 4 in the *Havard Law Review*. Chapters 1, 5, 7, 8, 9 and 11 were published in the *New York Review of Books*. In each case changes, sometimes including a change in title, have been made for this publication.

I

Jurisprudence

When lawyers argue cases, or advise clients, or draft laws to meet specific social goals, they face problems that are technical, in the sense that there is general agreement within the profession as to what sort of argument or evidence is relevant. But sometimes lawyers must deal with problems that are not technical in this sense, and there is no general agreement on how to proceed. One example is the ethical problem that is presented when a lawyer asks, not whether a particular law is effective, but whether it is fair. Another example is the conceptual puzzles that arise when lawyers try to describe the law in concepts that are unclear. A lawyer may want to say, for instance, that the law of torts holds men liable only for damage caused by their faults. Another lawyer may challenge this statement, and the issue between them may be a disagreement not about fact or doctrine, but about what fault means. Or two lawyers may disagree whether the Supreme Court, in the 1954 segregation case, was following established principles or making new law; and the issue between them may turn on what principles are and what it means to apply them. It is unclear how conceptual issues like these are to be resolved; certainly they lie beyond the ordinary techniques of the practicing lawyers.

Lawyers call these recalcitrant questions 'jurisprudential', and they disagree, as one would expect, on whether it is important to resolve them. Law schools generally provide special courses, called 'Jurisprudence' or 'Legal Theory' or something of the sort, devoted to their study, but since the distinguishing mark of these issues is just that there is no agreement on what sort of issues they are, and what techniques of study they require, these courses vary widely in the methods they use. The method chosen, moreover, influences the choice of the particular issues selected for study, though this choice is also affected by intellectual fashion and public affairs. Just now, for example, the question of whether men have a moral obligation to obey the law figures prominently in jurisprudence courses throughout the country; but two decades ago almost no one mentioned that issue.

Until recently the dominant approach to jurisprudence in England and America was what one might call a professional approach. The lawyers who taught jurisprudence recognized that jurisprudential questions, like those I have listed, were troublesome just because they were not amenable to ordinary legal techniques; but they proposed nevertheless to meet this difficulty by picking out those aspects of the questions that could be treated with these techniques while ignoring the rest. When lawyers deal with the technical questions I mentioned, they use a combination of three particular skills. Lawyers are trained to analyze statutes and judicial opinions to extract legal doctrine from these official sources. They are trained to analyze complex factual situations in order to summarize the essential facts accurately. And they are trained to think in tactical terms, to design statutes and legal institutions that will bring about particular social changes decided upon in advance. The professional approach to jurisprudence tried to reformulate jurisprudential issues so that one or more of these skills could be brought to bear. This approach produced only the illusion of progress, and left the genuinely important issues of principle in the law untouched.

To sustain this serious charge I must describe where jurisprudence stood at mid-century. In England the subject was taught out of standard textbooks like *Salmond on Jurisprudence* and *Paton on Jurisprudence*. Most of these texts were devoted to what they called analytical jurisprudence, which they carefully distinguished from 'ethical jurisprudence' or the study of what the law ought to be. By analytical jurisprudence they meant the careful elaboration of the meaning of certain terms (like 'fault', 'possession', 'ownership', 'negligence', and 'law') that are fundamental to law in the sense that they appear not just in one or another branch but throughout the range of legal doctrine. These concepts, like those I mentioned earlier, are troublesome because lawyers use them even though they do not understand exactly what they mean.

But the English texts attacked these concepts, not by elucidating their meaning in ordinary speech, but rather by using conventional doctrinal methods to demonstrate their specifically *legal* meaning as revealed in cases and statutes. They studied the opinions of judges and legal experts and extracted from them summaries of the various legal rules and doctrines in which these troublesome concepts appeared, but they did little to connect these rules with the various non-legal judgments about fault, possession, etc., that the layman makes.

If we ask *why* lawyers argue about these concepts, however, we can see why this emphasis on doctrine appears irrelevant. A lawyer worries about the concept of fault, not because he is unaware of how the courts have used the term, or what the rules for determining legal fault are, but because he uses the non-legal concept of fault to justify or criticize the law. He believes – as a matter of habit or conviction – that it is morally wrong to punish someone for something not his fault; he wants to know whether the law offends this moral principle in holding an employer liable for what his employee does, or in holding a negligent driver liable for the death of a man he ran down if the injury was slight but the victim was a haemophiliac. He knows these facts of legal doctrine very well, but he is unclear whether the facts clash with the principle. Is harm a man's fault if it is committed by someone under his charge, or if it results from his act because of circumstances he could not possibly foresee? These questions call for an analysis of the moral concept of fault, not the legal concept that the lawyer already understands; but it is just the moral use of the concept that the doctrinal approach of English jurisprudence ignored.

The record of American jurisprudence is more complex. It devoted itself largely to one issue that English theory had, in comparison, neglected : How do courts decide difficult or controversial lawsuits? Our courts had played a larger role than the English courts in reshaping nineteenth-century law to the needs of industrialization, and our constitution made legal issues out of problems that in England were political only. In England, for example, the issue of whether minimum wage legislation is fair was a political issue, but in America it was a constitutional, that is, judicial, issue as well. American lawyers were therefore pressed harder to furnish an accurate description of what the courts were doing, and to justify this if they could; the call was most urgent when the courts appeared to be making new and politically controversial law instead of simply applying old law as orthodox legal theory required.

Early in this century, John Chipman Gray and, later, Oliver Wendell Holmes published skeptical accounts of the judicial process, debunking the orthodox doctrine that judges merely apply existing rules. This skeptical approach broadened, in the 1920s and '30s, into the powerful intellectual movement called 'legal realism'. Its leaders (Jerome Frank, Karl Llewelyn, Wesley Sturges, and Morris and Felix Cohen, among others) argued that orthodox theory had gone wrong because it had taken a doctrinal approach to jurisprudence, attempting to describe what judges do by concentrating on the rules they mention in their decision. This is an error, the realists argued, because judges actually decide cases according to their own poltical or moral tastes, and then choose an appropriate legal rule as a rationalization. The realists asked for a 'scientific' approach that would fix on what judges do, rather than what they say, and the actual impact their decisions have on the larger community.

The main line of American jurisprudence followed this call for realism, and avoided the doctrinal approach of the English texts. It emphasized the two other professional skills – the lawyer's skills at marshalling facts and at designing tactics for social change. We can trace the later impact of realism more clearly if we distinguish these two techniques. The emphasis on facts developed into what Roscoe Pound of Harvard called sociological jurisprudence; he meant the careful study of legal institutions as social processes, which treats a judge, for example, not as an oracle of doctrine, but as a man responding to various sorts of social and personal stimuli. Some lawyers, like Jerome Frank and Pound himself, attempted to carry out this sort of study, but they discovered that lawyers do not have the training or statistical equipment necessary to describe complex institutions in other than an introspective and limited way. Sociological jurisprudence therefore became the province of sociologists.

The emphasis on tactics had a more lasting effect within the law schools. Scholars like Myres McDougal and Harold Lasswell at Yale, and Lon L. Fuller, Henry Hart, and Albert Sachs at Harvard, though different from one another, all insisted on the importance of regarding the law as an instrument for moving society toward certain large goals, and they tried to settle questions about the legal process instrumentally, by asking which solutions best advanced these goals.

But this emphasis on fact and strategy ended by distorting jurisprudential issues in much the same way as the English doctrinal approach distorted them, that is, by eliminating just those issues of moral principle that form their core. This failure emerges if we consider in greater detail the central problem that the sociologists and instrumentalists discussed : Do judges always follow rules, even in difficult and controversial cases, or do they sometimes make up new rules and apply them retroactively?

Lawyers have argued this issue for decades, not because they are ignorant of the sorts of decisions judges make or the reasons they give, but because they are unclear what the concept of following rules really means. In easy cases (when a man is charged with violating a statute that forbids driving over sixty miles an hour, for example) it seems right to say that the judge is simply applying a prior rule to a new case. But can we say this when the Supreme Court overturns precedent and orders the schools desegregated, or outlaws procedures that for decades the police have been using and the courts condoning? In these dramatic cases the Court gives reasons – it does not cite statutes, but it does appeal to principles of justice and policy. Does that mean that the Court is following rules after all, although of a more general and abstract quality? If so, where do these abstract rules come from, and what makes them valid? Or does it mean that the Court is deciding the case in accordance with its own moral and political beliefs?

The lawyers and laymen who ask these questions are not worrying aimlessly or out of idle curiosity; they know that judges wield great political power, and they are concerned with whether that power is justified, in general or in particular cases. They are not necessarily persuaded that judges who make up new rules are acting improperly. But they want to know how far the justification for judicial power available in easy cases – that the judge is applying standards already established – extends to hard ones, and therefore how much, and what sort of, supplementary justification these hard cases require.

The question of justification has important ramifications, because it affects not only how far judicial authority extends, but the extent of an individual's political and moral obligation to obey judge-made law. It also affects the grounds on which a controversial opinion may be challenged. If it makes sense to say that a judge should follow existing standards in hard cases, then it makes sense for a conscientious objector to argue that the judge has made a mistake in the law when he holds the draft constitutional. But if judges can only make new law in hard cases, that claim is nonsense. So though the question of whether judges follow rules may sound linguistic, it reveals concerns that are in the last degree practical.

I have spelled out these implications to show that here, as in the case of the concept of fault, there are issues of moral principle that lie beneath an apparently linguistic problem. Critics of law accept, again either by habit or through conviction, the principle that a judicial decision is fairer if it represents the application of established standards rather than the imposition of new ones. But they are unclear what counts as applying established standards, and they express this uncertainty by asking whether judges are really following rules, in some sense at least, even in novel cases. Jurisprudence should respond to this concern by exploring the nature of moral argument, trying to clarify the principle of fairness which the critics have in mind to see whether judicial practice does, in fact, satisfy that principle.

But American jurisprudence made no such attempt. The sociologists, for their part, refused to talk about following rules, on the ground that that concept was too vague to be studied in experimental or quantitative ways. The very fact that men are unable to agree on what following a rule means, they pointed out, disqualifies that concept for science; if each investigator were to use his own sense of the term, there would be no objective data and no joint progress. So sociologists like Glendon Schubert, C. Herman Pritchett, and Stuart Nagel substituted questions that seemed related and more precise : Do judges from particular economic or social backgrounds, or from particular sorts of legal practice, or with particular political affiliations, or particular value schemes, tend to decide in favor of corporate defendants? Do the judges in the Supreme Court form parties that stick together when cases involving race, or labor unions, or antitrust are decided? These empirical questions seemed relevant, because if social background or prior allegiance determines a judge's decision, this suggests that he is not following rules.

But in fact this information, though interesting and useful for other purposes, throws little light on the issues of principle that inspired the original question. Lawyers need no evidence to show that judges disagree, and that their decisions often reflect their background and temperament. They are puzzled, however, as to whether this means only that the judges differ on the nature and point of fundamental legal principles, or whether it demonstrates that there are no such principles. If it means the former, then this argues that judges are trying to follow rules, as they see them, and that people who disagree with their decisions may still be right on the law; if it means the latter then this argument, as I said, is absurd. The lawyers are also uncertain whether the fact of divergence, on either account, is to be regretted, or accepted as inevitable, or applauded as dynamic, and how all this connects with the crucial issues of political obligation and law enforcement that lawyers face. The sociological approach, in reframing the question, eliminated just those aspects that bear on all these issues.

The instrumental branch of post-realism also reframed the question, though in a different way. Henry Hart and Sachs, in their brilliant materials on the legal process, suggested that conceptual questions about rules could be bypassed by putting the issue this way: How should judges reach their decisions in order best to advance the goals of the legal process? But their hope that this would avoid the puzzles about rules was vain, because it proved impossible to state the goals of the legal process without those problems appearing at a later stage. If we state the goal of the process in some vacuous way (by saying that the law should do justice, or advance the just state) then the question is inescapable whether, as many suppose, justice requires decisions according to prior rules; and this question, in turn, requires an analysis of what it is to follow a rule. If we attempt to state some more particular or precise goal (that the legal process should increase the gross national product, for example) then the exercise loses its point, because there is no warrant for assuming that any such particular goal is the proper exclusive concern of law.

We may argue (as some writers did) that the law will be economically more efficient if judges are allowed to take the economic impact of their decision into account; but this will not answer the question of whether it is fair for them to do so, or whether we can regard economic standards as part of existing law, or whether decisions based on economic impact carry more or less moral weight for that reason. Suppose that a judge is persuaded, for example, that the automobile industry will prosper if he repeals an old rule and invents a new one for its benefit, and that the general economy will benefit if the automobile industry does. Is this a good reason for changing the rule? We cannot decide this sort of question by analysis that simply relates means to ends.

So the various branches of the professional approach to jurisprudence failed for the same underlying reason. They ignored the crucial fact that jurisprudential issues are at their core issues of moral principle, not legal fact or strategy. They buried these issues by insisting on a conventional legal approach. But if jurisprudence is to succeed, it must expose these issues and attack them as issues of moral theory.

This simple fact explains Professor H. L. A. Hart's importance and success. Hart is a moral philosopher; he has an instinct for issues of principle, and a marvelous lucidity in setting them out. In his first book, *The Concept of Law*, for example, he raised the issue of whether judges follow rules in a way that made plain the connection between this problem and the moral issue of when it is proper for one man to charge another with an obligation. He offered an analysis of the rules that our community follows, as a matter of convention, in making and criticizing arguments about moral obligation, and argued that judges follow much the same rules in reasoning about legal obligation. In another book, *Causation in the Law*, Hart and a co-author, A. M. Honore, discussed the conceptual puzzles about fault, which I mentioned earlier, but unlike Hart's predecessors, they undertook to explain the ordinary as well as the strictly legal meanings of that concept. Like Hart's colleagues in the Oxford school of philosophy, particularly J. L. Austin, they used the study of ordinary language to show the ways in which members of the community habitually ascribe fault and responsibility to one another; and they then used these conventional judgments to explain, for example, the legal rule that holds a man fully liable if he injures a haemophiliac.

They pointed out that ordinary language draws a distinction between unusual circumstances existing at the time a man acts and unlikely coincidences that arise afterward. It distinguishes, for example, the case in which the careless driver slightly injures a man who dies because he is haemophiliac from the case in which a careless driver slightly injures a man who dies of blood poisoning through a doctor's negligence. Most people would say that in the first case the careless driver caused the death and that it was his fault; but they would not say this in the second case. This distinction, in turn, reflects a popular conception of causation: the ordinary man distinguishes a causally effective act as an act that operates upon a stage already set; contemporaneous circumstances, like the blood disease, are part of the stage setting and not competing causes. But later events, like a doctor's negligence, are interventions that break the causal chain. So, the legal rule is comprehensible as an extension of popular theories of morality and cause.

But Hart has not been content simply to explain the law by showing how it incorporates the ordinary man's moral judgments. He views this sort of analysis as a necessary preliminary to a critical evaluation both of the law and of the popular morality on which it rests. Until we are clear what moral practice or judgment the law reflects, we cannot criticize it intelligently; but once we are clear about this it remains to ask whether this practice or judgment is sensible, or sound, or consistent with the other principles the law claims to serve.

Hart's more recent book, *Punishment and Responsibility,* is an excellent example of this process of criticism. The book reprints a series of his essays on jurisprudential issues in criminal law; most of these essays treat the problem of whether a man should be excused from liability for a criminal act because of his mental state. Should he be excused (or should his penalty be reduced) if his act was an accident, or if he acted negligently rather than deliberately, or if he was mentally ill? The law generally grants an excuse, or at least mitigates punishment, in such cases, but some contemporary critics argue that this policy is wrong.

If the criminal law aimed at vengeance and retribution, they say, the point of these mental defences would be obvious, for there is no satisfaction to be gained from taking revenge on someone who acted by mistake or was insane. But if the law's goals are only to prevent further harm by the criminal, and deter others by his example, the defenses seem counterproductive. We could prevent harm more by jailing the accident-prone driver than by jailing the man who murders his father for an inheritance; and we would increase the deterrent power of the law if we accepted no excuses whatever, and did not encourage potential criminals to hope that they could fake an insanity plea if caught. So the critics argue that the law should sharply limit these defenses, on the ground that the defenses increase the expense of trials and legal education, that they are abused, and that their purpose in an enlightened criminal system seems obscure.

Hart disagrees. He begins his response by reminding us that it is wrong to assume that the criminal law (or any other branch of the law) has a set of goals that are overriding, in the sense that every feature of the law must be tailored to these goals. The criminal law aims at preventing crime, to be sure, but it must pursue this aim subject to principles that may limit its efficiency in reaching them; it would be wrong to punish an innocent man as a hostage even if to do so would in fact reduce crime. We must understand the mental defenses in that light, so the fact that they may interfere with crime prevention is not a conclusive argument. But this point is only negative, and leaves open the question whether the mental defenses are in fact justified, or ought to be changed. Hart attacks this issue in the manner I described; he begins by asking whether the mental defenses reflect any moral tradition, or any general aim or policy, of the community.

He considers first the suggestion of some criminal lawyers, like Professor Jerome Hall, that the point of the mental defense is to insure that the law punishes as criminals only men who are morally blameworthy on conventional standards. This attractive notion has initial plausibility. In ordinary life we do not blame someone who has done harm if he acted unintentionally or inadvertently (unless, perhaps, he was also careless); nor do we do so if we believe that he is suffering from a serious mental disorder. It is therefore plausible to suppose that judges and legislators would carry these attitudes into the criminal law, in the form of a doctrine that men should not be punished under these conditions, even though it would be more efficient to do so.

Hart rejects this theory, however, on the ground that there are many crimes – for example, the failure to abide by the English rail transport regulations – which are not in themselves morally blameworthy. The existence of such crimes, he argues, shows that the law has no general purpose to condemn only blameworthy acts, and so proves this could not be the point of the mental defenses.

But Hart is wrong to dismiss the blameworthiness theory in this way; he is confusing, I think, two grounds on which a violation of law might be morally wrong. It might be wrong to break a law because the act the law condemns (killing, for example) is wrong in itself. Or it might be wrong, even though the act condemned is not wrong in itself, just because the law forbids it, and railroad legislation may be a case in point. Perhaps it is doubtful whether it is wise or fair for England to nationalize the railroads; it might still be true that once the law is passed everyone has a moral obligation to obey it.

Of course, it does not follow that a man is morally to blame every time he does what the law prohibits. He might not be blameworthy because the law is so unfair or unjust that the normal moral obligation to obey the law was lapsed, an argument that was made by some conscientious objectors to the draft. (It is arguable that the point of the due process and other clauses of the United States Constitution is to guard against a man's being punished in that case.) Or he may not be blameworthy because his act was committed by accident, or inadvertently, or because he had a mental disease and so was not responsible for his conduct. Professor Hall's argument, which Hart rejects too quickly, is that the point of the mental defenses is to guard against punishing a man in this case.

Even if Hall is right, however, the critical questions remain, because we must ask whether our conventional attitudes about blame and punishment are really relevant to the law. Those who doubt the value of the mental defenses argue that since the goal of the criminal law is to reform and deter, and not to punish, these conventions are irrelevant, and the mental defenses should be abandoned. They drive this point home by proposing to drop the word 'punishment', and speak of 'treatment' instead. If a man has committed a crime, they argue, then how society should treat him – whether he should be confined, or hospitalized, or released – should depend on which course would best prevent a repetition. It confuses the issue, on this account, as to whether he was morally blameworthy in doing what he did, because treatment might be unnecessary even if he was, and advisable even if he was not. We must ask whether the mental defenses serve any purpose that is relevant to this revised notion of the criminal law.

In one of the early essays, 'Legal Responsibility and Excuses', reprinted in the recent book, Hart offers this suggestion. The mental defenses increase each man's control over his own fate, by reducing the number of occasions on which the law will interfere with his freedom in a way he could not have predicted from his own deliberate acts. If the defenses were repealed, we would all have to live with the fact that some accident or piece of inadvertence would send us to jail, or involve us in a lengthy, expensive, and degrading trial. By virtue of the defenses, we can count on the fact that in general we will be prosecuted only for acts done with the awareness that prosecution might follow, which has the incidental benefit that those who are punished have had at least the satisfaction of taking and carrying out a decision to break the law.

But this is a weak argument, if it is addressed entirely to the increased personal security that the mental defenses afford, because this increased security is minimal. After all, the community has accepted a great many decisions that make life much more perilous, such as the decision to foster competition in commerce, to permit automobiles, and to wage war. These decisions vastly increase the likelihood that particular men will suffer harm which they could not foresee and which does not flow from their deliberate acts; but society still accepts these decisions, and runs these risks, for the sake of some goal of efficiency or profit or national policy. If, as Hart is willing to suppose, eliminating the mental defenses would increase the efficiency of the criminal law in preventing crime, then this would add to the ordinary citizen's personal safety and control over his own fate in a measure that would presumably outweigh the increased risk of his being subject to liability for an accident.

Hart is more successful, I think, when he provides a different and more general justification for the mental defenses in a later essay, 'Punishment and the Elimination of Responsibility' : 'Human society is a society of persons; and persons do not view themselves or each other merely as so many bodies moving in ways which are sometimes harmful and have to be prevented or altered. Instead persons interpret each other's movements as manifestations of intentions . . . .' Elsewhere, and in the same vein, he says that the law would treat people as means rather than ends if it abandoned these defenses.

These statements unite the legal doctrines with a wide range of moral traditions. The principle they urge is that the government must treat its citizens with the respect and dignity that adult members of the community claim from each other. The government may restrain a man for his own or the general good, but it may do so only on the basis of his behavior, and it must strive to judge his behavior from the same standpoint as he judges himself, that is, from the standpoint of his intentions, motives, and capacities. Men generally feel that they have chosen to act as they have, but they do not feel this to be so in particular circumstances of accident, compulsion, duress, or disease. And each of us makes this distinction not only for himself but in judging how to respond to others he regards with any respect. Even a dog, Holmes said, knows the difference between being kicked and being tripped over.

The criminal law might be more efficient if it disregarded this troublesome distinction, and jailed men or forced them to accept treatment whenever this seemed likely to decrease future crime. But that, as Hart's principle suggests, would cross the line that separates treating someone else as a fellow human being from treating him as a resource for the benefit of others, and there can be no more profound insult, under the conventions and practices of our community, than that. The insult is as great whether the process is called one of punishment or treatment. It is true that we sometimes restrain and give treatment to a man just because we believe that he does not have control over his conduct. We do this under civil commitment statutes and typically, after a man is acquitted of a serious crime on grounds of insanity. But we ought to recognize the compromise with principle that this policy involves; and should treat a man against his will only when the danger he presents is vivid, not whenever we calculate that it would probably reduce crime if we did.

Of course this line of argument raises more questions than it settles. Some philosophers think, on the basis of contemporary physiology and psychology, that this phenomenological distinction between choice and compulsion makes no sense. They believe that all human behavior is determined by factors beyond individual control, so that the feelings of free choice we often have are just illusions. But the scientific evidence for this is far from conclusive, and even those who think it weighty must decide how the law should respond until the case is proved (if it ever is or can be). If we accepted the view that all behavior is determined, for example, would it follow that we should abandon entirely the idea that human beings have rights that their government is morally bound to respect? If we chose not to go so far, either because the scientific evidence is inconclusive, or because we are reluctant to abandon the notion of rights in any event, would it not be inconsistent to abandon the mental defenses in the name of science? If, on the other hand, we retain these defenses, and accept as their basis the phenomenological distinction between choosing or not choosing to do something, as this argument suggests, how should that guide our approach to troublesome cases, like that of the psychopath? Is the psychopath in control of himself, according to conventional standards of behavior, or is his case a half-way house, which explains our confusion? There is no space here to pursue these issues (some of which Hart discusses), and I mention them only to show that the approach to jurisprudence that emphasizes principle cannot stop at simply showing the links between legal and social practice, but must continue to examine and criticize social practice against independent standards of consistency and sense.

The mental defenses are not the only controversial aspects of the criminal law include the protection of individual freedom as well as the rules of criminal procedure – regarding interrogation, confessions, and preventive detention, for example – that protect the alleged criminal at some cost to police efficiency. It might be useful to point out the value of a more philosophic approach to these issues than academic lawyers have yet provided. So far the liberal position has been presented chiefly in instrumental terms. The liberal argues that the proper goals of the criminal law include the protection of individual freedom as well as the prevention of crime, and that the procedural safeguards strike a balance between these two goals. But this way of putting the point suggests that a balance between the two goals is in order; it encourages others to ask why the majority of law-abiding citizens should not strike the balance further on the side of its own protection.

The liberal is placed in a difficult position by that question. He might reply that he, personally, values the liberty of others more than his own increased security, but he would have to admit that this is a minority position. He might argue that the majority would itself be better off in the long run by promoting freedom at the cost of a little security, but this argument, though popular with liberals, is plainly wrong. The criminal law presents more of a threat to the black narcotics addict than to the middle-class white, and there is little reason to suppose that interrogating the former without counsel, or locking him up pending trial, will even in the long run affect the latter's liberty.

Here again Hart's general approach is helpful. The liberal position should be argued, it would suggest, by emphasizing moral principles that act as constraints on the law rather than citing the law's conflicting goals. It should fix on legal doctrines that are embedded in our traditions (like the doctrines that no man may be forced to condemn himself, and that a man is presumed innocent until proved guilty) to support the claim that society has no right to interrogate a man without a lawyer, and that an accused suspect is entitled to be free before his trial, whether the majority benefits or not. Of course there may be conflicts between these principles and practical needs, but these are not occasions for fair compromise, but rather, if the principles must be dishonored, for shame and regret.

Those who take a different view, and want to increase police efficiency, accept the doctrines I mentioned, such as the privilege against self-incrimination, but deny that they guarantee the particular rights the liberals claim. They would argue that this privilege, for example, protects a man from being tortured to extract a confession, but does not entitle him to withdraw a voluntary confession just because it was given without reflection. So the controversy must be pressed in philosophical terms : does the use of unadvised confessions, or preventive detention, contradict the moral principles underlying the established doctrines? I think they do, but it remains for jurisprudence to construct the bridges between legal and moral theory that support that claim.

Perhaps the principle Hart cited, that the government must show the minimum of respect even to accused criminals and treat them as humans rather than as opportunities, will help establish that a contradiction exists. This principle, for example, informs the doctrine that a man is innocent until proved guilty, and helps to explain why it seems wrong to imprison a man awaiting trial on the basis of a prediction that he might commit further crimes if released on bail. For any such prediction, if it is sound, must be based on the view that an individual is a member of a class having particular features, which class is more likely than others to commit crime. The prediction, that is, must be actuarial, like the prediction an insurance company makes about the likelihood of teenagers to have automobile accidents. But it is unjust to put someone in jail on the basis of a judgment about a class, however accurate, because that denies his claim to equal respect as an individual.

B

2

The Model of Rules I

I. EMBARRASSING QUESTIONS

Lawyers lean heavily on the connected concepts of legal right and legal obligation. We say that someone has a legal right or duty, and we take that statement as a sound basis for making claims and demands, and for criticizing the acts of public officials. But our understanding of these concepts is remarkably fragile, and we fall into trouble when we try to say what legal rights and obligations are. We say glibly that whether someone has a legal obligation is determined by applying 'the law' to the particular facts of his case, but this is not a helpful answer, because we have the same difficulties with the concept of law.

We are used to summing up our troubles in the classic questions of jurisprudence: What is 'the law'? When two sides disagree, as often happens, about a proposition 'of law', what are they disagreeing about, and how shall we decide which side is right? Why do we call what 'the law' says a matter of legal 'obligation'? Is 'obligation' here just a term of art, meaning only what the law says? Or does legal obligation have something to do with moral obligation? Can we say that we have, in principle at least, the same reasons for meeting our legal obligations that we have for meeting our moral obligations?

These are not puzzles for the cupboard, to be taken down on rainy days for fun. They are sources of continuing embarrassment, and they nag at our attention. They embarrass us in dealing with particular problems that we must solve, one way or another. Suppose a novel right-of-privacy case comes to court, and there is no statute or precedent claimed by the plaintiff. What role in the court's decision should be played by the fact that most people in the community think that private individuals are 'morally' entitled to that particular privacy? Supposing the Supreme Court orders some prisoner freed because the police used procedures that the Court now says are constitutionally forbidden, although the Court's earlier decisions upheld these procedures. Must the Court, to be consistent, free all other prisoners previously convicted through these same procedures?[1] Conceptual puzzles about 'the law' and 'legal obligation'

[1] See *Linkletter v. Walker*, 381 U.S. 618 (1965).

become acute when a court is confronted with a problem like this.

These eruptions signal a chronic disease. Day in and day out we send people to jail, or take money away from them, or make them do things they do not want to do, under coercion of force, and we justify all of this by speaking of such persons as having broken the law or having failed to meet their legal obligations, or having interfered with other people's legal rights. Even in clear cases (a bank robber or a wilful breach of contract), when we are confident that someone had a legal obligation and broke it, we are not able to give a satisfactory account of what that means, or why that entitles the state to punish or coerce him. We may feel confident that what we are doing is proper, but until we can identify the principles we are following we cannot be sure that they are sufficient, or whether we are applying them consistently. In less clear cases, when the issue of whether an obligation has been broken is for some reason controversial, the pitch of these nagging questions rises, and our responsibility to find answers deepens.

Certain lawyers (we may call them 'nominalists') urge that we solve these problems by ignoring them. In their view the concepts of 'legal obligation' and 'the law' are myths, invented and sustained by lawyers for a dismal mix of conscious and subconscious motives. The puzzles we find in these concepts are merely symptoms that they are myths. They are unsolvable because unreal, and our concern with them is just one feature of our enslavement. We would do better to flush away the puzzles and the concepts altogether, and pursue our important social objectives without this excess baggage.

This is a tempting suggestion, but it has fatal drawbacks. Before we can decide that our concepts of law and of legal obligation are myths, we must decide what they are. We must be able to state, at least roughly, what it is we all believe that is wrong. But the nerve of our problem is that we have great difficulty in doing just that. Indeed, when we ask what law is and what legal obligations are, we are asking for a theory of how we use those concepts and of the conceptual commitments our use entails. We cannot conclude, before we have such a general theory, that our practices are stupid or superstitious.

Of course, the nominalists think they know how the rest of us use these concepts. They think that when we speak of 'the law' we mean a set of timeless rules stocked in some conceptual warehouse awaiting discovery by judges, and that when we speak of legal obligation we mean the invisible chains these mysterious rules somehow drape around us. The theory that there are such rules and chains they call 'mechanical jurisprudence', and they are right in ridiculing its practitioners. Their difficulty, however, lies in finding practitioners to ridicule. So far they have had little luck in caging and exhibiting mechanical jurisprudents

(all specimens captured – even Blackstone and Joseph Beale – have had to be released after careful reading of their texts.)

In any event, it is clear that most lawyers have nothing like this in mind when they speak of the law and of legal obligation. A superficial examination of our practices is enough to show this for we speak of laws changing and evolving, and of legal obligation sometimes being problematical. In these and other ways we show that we are not addicted to mechanical jurisprudence.

Nevertheless, we do use the concepts of law and legal obligation, and we do suppose that society's warrant to punish and coerce is written in that currency. It may be that when the details of this practice are laid bare, the concepts we do use will be shown to be as silly and as thick with illusion as those the nominalists invented. If so, then we shall have to find other ways to describe what we do, and either provide other justifications or change our practices. But until we have discovered this and made these adjustments, we cannot accept the nominalists' premature invitation to turn our backs on the problems our present concepts provide.

Of course the suggestion that we stop talking about 'the law' and 'legal obligation' is mostly bluff. These concepts are too deeply cemented into the structure of our political practices – they cannot be given up like cigarettes or hats. Some of the nominalists have half-admitted this and said that the myths they condemn should be thought of as Platonic myths and retained to seduce the masses into order. This is perhaps not so cynical a suggestion as it seems; perhaps it is a covert hedging of a dubious bet.

If we boil away the bluff, the nominalist attack reduces to an attack on mechanical jurisprudence. Through the lines of the attack, and in spite of the heroic calls for the death of law, the nominalists themselves have offered an analysis of how the terms 'law' and 'legal obligation' should be used which is not very different from that of more classical philosophers. Nominalists present their analysis as a model of how legal institutions (particularly courts) 'really operate'. But their model differs mainly in emphasis from the theory first made popular by the nineteenth century philosopher John Austin, and now accepted in one form or another by most working and academic lawyers who hold views on jurisprudence. I shall call this theory, with some historical looseness, 'legal positivism'. I want to examine the soundness of legal positivism, particularly in the powerful form that Professor H. L. A. Hart has given to it. I choose to focus on his position, not only because of its clarity and elegance, but because here, as almost everywhere else in legal philosophy, constructive thought must start with a consideration of his views.

2. POSITIVISM

Positivism has a few central and organizing propositions as its skeleton, and though not every philosopher who is called a positivist would subscribe to these in the way I present them, they do define the general position I want to examine. These key tenets may be stated as follows :

(a) The law of a community is a set of special rules used by the community directly or indirectly for the purpose of determining which behavior will be punished or coerced by the public power. These special rules can be identified and distinguished by specific criteria, by tests having to do not with their content but with their *pedigree* or the manner in which they were adopted or developed. These tests of pedigree can be used to distinguish valid legal rules from spurious legal rules (rules which lawyers and litigants wrongly argue are rules of law) and also from other sorts of social rules (generally lumped together as 'moral rules') that the community follows but does not enforce through public power.

(b) The set of these valid legal rules is exhaustive of 'the law', so that if someone's case is not clearly covered by such a rule (because there is none that seems appropriate, or those that seem appropriate are vague, or for some other reason) then that case cannot be decided by 'applying the law.' It must be decided by some official, like a judge, 'exercising his discretion,' which means reaching beyond the law for some other sort of standard to guide him in manufacturing a fresh legal rule or supplementing an old one.

(c) To say that someone has a 'legal obligation' is to say that his case falls under a valid legal rule that requires him to do or to forbear from doing something. (To say he has a legal right, or has a legal power of some sort, or a legal privilege or immunity, is to assert, in a shorthand way, that others have actual or hypothetical legal obligations to act or not to act in certain ways touching him.) In the absence of such a valid legal rule there is no legal obligation; it follows that when the judge decides an issue by exercising his discretion, he is not enforcing a legal right as to that issue.

This is only the skeleton of positivism. The flesh is arranged differently by different positivists, and some even tinker with the bones. Different versions differ chiefly in their description of the fundamental test of pedigree a rule must meet to count as a rule of law.

Austin, for example, framed his version of the fundamental test as a series of interlocking definitions and distinctions.[1] He defined having an obligation as lying under a rule, a rule as a general command, and a command as an expression of desire that others behave in a particular way, backed by the power and will to enforce that expression in the event of disobedience. He distinguished classes of rules (legal, moral or religious) according to which person or group is the author of the general command the rule represents. In each political community, he thought, one will find a sovereign – a person or a determinate group whom the rest obey habitually, but who is not in the habit of obeying anyone else. The legal rules of a community are the general commands its sovereign has deployed. Austin's definition of legal obligation followed from this definition of law. One has a legal obligation, he thought, if one is among the addressees of some general order of the sovereign, and is in danger of suffering a sanction unless he obeys that order.

Of course, the sovereign cannot provide for all contingencies through any scheme of orders, and some of his orders will inevitably be vague or have furry edges. Therefore (according to Austin) the sovereign grants those who enforce the law (judges) discretion to make fresh orders when novel or troublesome cases are presented. The judges then make new rules or adapt old rules, and the sovereign either overturns their creations or tacitly confirms them by failing to do so.

Austin's model is quite beautiful in its simplicity. It asserts the first tenet of positivism, that the law is a set of rules specially selected to govern public order, and offers a simple factual test – what has the sovereign commanded? – as the sole criterion for identifying those special rules. In time, however, those who studied and tried to apply Austin's model found it too simple. Many objections were raised, among which were two that seemed fundamental. First, Austin's key assumption that in each community a determinate group or institution can be found, which is in ultimate control of all other groups, seemed not to hold in a complex society. Political control in a modern nation is pluralistic and shifting, a matter of more or less, of compromise and cooperation and alliance, so that it is often impossible to say that any person or group has that dramatic control necessary to qualify as an Austinian sovereign. One wants to say, in the United States for example, that the 'people' are sovereign. But this means almost nothing, and in itself provides no test for determining what the 'people' have commanded, or distinguishing their legal from their social or moral commands.

Second, critics began to realize that Austin's analysis fails entirely to account for, even to recognize, certain striking facts about the attitudes

<hr />

[1] J. Austin, *The Province of Jurisprudence Determined* (1832).

we take toward 'the law.' We make an important distinction between law and even the general orders of a gangster. We feel that the law's strictures – and its sanctions – are different in that they are obligatory in a way that the outlaw's commands are not. Austin's analysis has no place for any such distinction, because it defines an obligation as subjection to the threat of force, and so founds the authority of law entirely on the sovereign's ability and will to harm those who disobey. Perhaps the distinction we make is illusory – perhaps our feelings of some special authority attaching to the law is based on religious hangover or another sort of mass self-deception. But Austin does not demonstrate this, and we are entitled to insist that an analysis of our concept of law either acknowledge and explain our attitudes, or show why they are mistaken.

H. L. A. Hart's version of positivism is more complex than Austin's, in two ways. First, he recognizes, as Austin did not, that rules are of different logical kinds. (Hart distinguishes two kinds, which he calls 'primary' and 'secondary' rules). Second, he rejects Austin's theory that a rule is a kind of command, and substitutes a more elaborate general analysis of what rules are. We must pause over each of these points, and then note how they merge in Hart's concept of law.

Hart's distinction between primary and secondary rules is of great importance.[1] Primary rules are those that grant rights or impose obligations upon members of the community. The rules of the criminal law that forbid us to rob, murder or drive too fast are good examples of primary rules. Secondary rules are those that stipulate how, and by whom, such primary rules may be formed, recognized, modified or extinguished. The rules that stipulate how Congress is composed, and how it enacts legislation, are examples of secondary rules. Rules about forming contracts and executing wills are also secondary rules because they stipulate how very particular rules governing particular legal obligations (*i.e.*, the terms of a contract or the provisions of a will) come into existence and are changed.

His general analysis of rules is also of great importance.[2] Austin had said that every rule is a general command, and that a person is obligated under a rule if he is liable to be hurt should he disobey it. Hart points out that this obliterates the distinction between being *obliged* to do something and being *obligated* to do it. If one is bound by a rule he is obligated, not merely obliged, to do what it provides, and therefore being bound by a rule must be different from being subject to an injury if one disobeys an order. A rule differs from an order, among other ways, by being *normative*, by setting a standard of behavior that has a call on

[1] See H. L. A. Hart, *The Concept of Law*, 89-96 (1961).
[2] *Id.* at 79-88.

its subject beyond the threat that may enforce it. A rule can never be binding just because some person with physical power wants it to be so. He must have *authority* to issue the rule or it is no rule, and such authority can only come from another rule which is already binding on those to whom he speaks. That is the difference between a valid law and the orders of a gunman.

So Hart offers a general theory of rules that does not make their authority depend upon the physical power of their authors. If we examine the way different rules come into being, he tells us, and attend to the distinction between primary and secondary rules, we see that there are two possible sources of a rule's authority :[1]

(a) A rule may become binding upon a group of people because that group through its practices *accepts* the rule as a standard for its conduct. It is not enough that the group simply conforms to a pattern of behavior : even though most Englishmen may go to the movies on Saturday evening, they have not accepted a rule requiring that they do so. A practice constitutes the acceptance of a rule only when those who follow the practice regard the rule as binding, and recognize the rule as a reason or justification for their own behavior and as a reason for criticizing the behavior of others who do not obey it.

(b) A rule may also become binding in quite a different way, namely by being enacted in conformity with some *secondary* rule that stipulates that rules so enacted shall be binding. If the constitution of a club stipulates, for example, that by-laws may be adopted by a majority of the members, then particular by-laws so voted are binding upon all the members, not because of any practice of acceptance of these particular by-laws, but because the constitution says so. We use the concept of *validity* in this connection : rules binding because they have been created in a manner stipulated by some secondary rule are called 'valid' rules.

Thus we can record Hart's fundamental distinction this way : a rule may be binding (a) because it is accepted or (b) because it is valid.

Hart's concept of law is a construction of these various distinctions.[2] Primitive communities have only primary rules, and these are binding entirely because of practices of acceptance. Such communities cannot be said to have 'law,' because there is no way to distinguish a set of legal rules from amongst other social rules, as the first tenet of positivism

---

[1] *Id.* at 97-107.
[2] *Id. passim*, particularly ch. 6.

requires. But when a particular community has developed a fundamental secondary rule that stipulates how legal rules are to be identified, the idea of a distinct set of legal rules, and thus of law, is born.

Hart calls such a fundamental secondary rule a 'rule of recognition'. The rule of recognition of a given community may be relatively simple ('What the king enacts is law') or it may be very complex (the United States Constitution, with all its difficulties of interpretation, may be considered a single rule of recognition). The demonstration that a particular rule is valid may therefore require tracing a complicated chain of validity back from that particular rule ultimately to the fundamental rule. Thus a parking ordinance of the city of New Haven is valid because it is adopted by a city council, pursuant to the procedures and within the competence specified by the municipal law adopted by the state of Connecticut, in conformity with the procedures and within the competence specified by the constitution of the state of Connecticut, which was in turn adopted consistently with the requirements of the United States Constitution.

Of course, a rule of recognition cannot itself be valid, because by hypothesis it is ultimate, and so cannot meet tests stipulated by a more fundamental rule. The rule of recognition is the sole rule in a legal system whose binding force depends upon its acceptance. If we wish to know what rule of recognition a particular community has adopted or follows, we must observe how its citizens, and particularly its officials, behave. We must observe what ultimate arguments they accept as showing the validity of a particular rule, and what ultimate arguments they use to criticize other officials or institutions. We can apply no mechanical test, but there is no danger of our confusing the rule of recognition of a community with its rules of morality. The rule of recognition is identified by the fact that its province is the operation of the governmental apparatus of legislatures, courts, agencies, policemen, and the rest.

In this way Hart rescues the fundamentals of positivism from Austin's mistakes. Hart agrees with Austin that valid rules of law may be created through the acts of officials and public institutions. But Austin thought that the authority of these institutions lay only in their monopoly of power. Hart finds their authority in the background of constitutional standards against which they act, constitutional standards that have been accepted, in the form of a fundamental rule of recognition, by the community which they govern. This background legitimates the decisions of government and gives them the cast and call of obligation that the naked commands of Austin's sovereign lacked. Hart's theory differs from Austin's also, in recognizing that different communities use different ultimate tests of law, and that some allow other means of creating law than the deliberate act of a legislative institution. Hart mentions 'long customary practice' and 'the relation [of a rule] to judicial decisions' as other criteria that are often used, though generally along with and subordinate to the test of legislation.

So Hart's version of positivism is more complex than Austin's, and his test for valid rules of law is more sophisticated. In one respect, however, the two models are very similar. Hart, like Austin, recognizes that legal rules have furry edges (he speaks of them as having 'open texture') and, again like Austin, he accounts for troublesome cases by saying that judges have and exercise discretion to decide these cases by fresh legislation.[1] (I shall later try to show why one who thinks of law as a special set of rules is almost inevitably drawn to account for difficult cases in terms of someone's exercise of discretion.)

3. RULES, PRINCIPLES, AND POLICIES

I want to make a general attack on positivism, and I shall use H. L. A. Hart's version as a target, when a particular target is needed. My strategy will be organized around the fact that when lawyers reason or dispute about legal rights and obligations, particularly in those hard cases when our problems with these concepts seem most acute, they make use of standards that do not function as rules, but operate differently as principles, policies, and other sorts of standards. Positivism, I shall argue, is a model of and for a system of rules, and its central notion of a single fundamental test for law forces us to miss the important roles of these standards that are not rules.

I just spoke of 'principles, policies, and other sorts of standards'. Most often I shall use the term 'principle' generically, to refer to the whole set of these standards other than rules; occasionally, however, I shall be more precise, and distinguish between principles and policies. Although nothing in the present argument will turn on the distinction, I should state how I draw it. I call a 'policy' that kind of standard that sets out a goal to be reached, generally an improvement in some economic, political, or social feature of the community (though some goals are negative, in that they stipulate that some present feature is to be protected from adverse change). I call a 'principle' a standard that is to be observed, not because it will advance or secure an economic, political, or social situation deemed desirable, but because it is a requirement of justice or fairness or some other dimension of morality. Thus the standard that automobile accidents are to be decreased is a policy, and the standard that no man may profit by his own wrong a principle. The distinction can be collapsed by construing a principle as stating a social goal (*i.e.*, the goal of a

---

[1] *Id.* ch. 7.

society in which no man profits by his own wrong), or by construing a policy as stating a principle (*i.e.*, the principle that the goal the policy embraces is a worthy one) or by adopting the utilitarian thesis that principles of justice are disguised statements of goals (securing the greatest happiness of the greatest number). In some contexts the distinction has uses which are lost if it is thus collapsed.[1]

My immediate purpose, however, is to distinguish principles in the generic sense from rules, and I shall start by collecting some examples of the former. The examples I offer are chosen haphazardly; almost any case in a law school casebook would provide examples that would serve as well. In 1889 a New York court, in the famous case of *Riggs v. Palmer*,[2] had to decide whether an heir named in the will of his grandfather could inherit under that will, even though he had murdered his grandfather to do so. The court began its reasoning with this admission: 'It is quite true that statutes regulating the making, proof and effect of wills, and the devolution of property, if literally construed, and if their force and effect can in no way and under no circumstances be controlled or modified, give this property to the murderer.'[3] But the court continued to note that 'all laws as well as all contracts may be controlled in their operation and effect by general, fundamental maxims of the common law. No one shall be permitted to profit by his own fraud, or to take advantage of his own wrong, or to found any claim upon his own iniquity, or to acquire property by his own crime.'[4] The murderer did not receive his inheritance.

In 1960, a New Jersey court was faced, in *Henningsen v. Bloomfield Motors, Inc.*[5] with the important question of whether (or how much) an automobile manufacturer may limit his liability in case the automobile is defective. Henningsen had bought a car, and signed a contract which said that the manufacturer's liability for defects was limited to 'making good' defective parts – 'this warranty being expressly in lieu of all other warranties, obligations or liabilities.' Henningsen argued that, at least in the circumstances of his case, the manufacturer ought not to be protected by this limitation, and ought to be liable for the medical and other expenses of persons injured in a crash. He was not able to point to any statute, or to any established rule of law, that prevented the manufacturer from standing on the contract. The court nevertheless agreed with Henningsen. At various points in the court's argument the

---

[1] See Chapter 4. See also Dworkin, 'Wasserstrom: The Judicial Decision', 75 *Ethics* 47 (1964), reprinted as 'Does Law Have a Function?', 74 *Yale Law Journal* 640 (1965).

[2] 115 N.Y. 506, 22 N.E. 188 (1889).

[3] *Id.* at 509, 22 N.E. at 189.

[4] *Id.* at 511, 22 N.E. at 190.

[5] 32 N.J. 358, 161 A.2d 69 (1960).

following appeals to standards are made : (a) '[W]e must keep in mind the general principle that, in the absence of fraud, one who does not choose to read a contract before signing it cannot later relieve himself of its burdens.'[1] (b) 'In applying that principle, the basic tenet of freedom of competent parties to contract is a factor of importance.'[2] (c) 'Freedom of contract is not such an immutable doctrine as to admit of no qualification in the area in which we are concerned.'[3] (d) 'In a society such as ours, where the automobile is a common and necessary adjunct of daily life, and where its use is so fraught with danger to the driver, passengers and the public, the manufacturer is under a special obligation in connection with the construction, promotion and sale of his cars. Consequently, the courts must examine purchase agreements closely to see if consumer and public interests are treated fairly.'[4] (e) ' "[I]s there any principle which is more familiar or more firmly embedded in the history of Anglo-American law than the basic doctrine that the courts will not permit themselves to be used as instruments of inequity and injustice ?" '[5] (f) ' "More specifically the courts generally refuse to lend themselves to the enforcement of a 'bargain' in which one party has unjustly taken advantage of the economic necessities of other . . . ." '[6]

The standards set out in these quotations are not the sort we think of as legal rules. They seem very different from propositions like 'The maximum legal speed on the turnpike is sixty miles an hour' or 'A will is invalid unless signed by three witnesses'. They are different because they are legal principles rather than legal rules.

The difference between legal principles and legal rules is a logical distinction. Both sets of standards point to particular decisions about legal obligation in particular circumstances, but they differ in the character of the direction they give. Rules are applicable in an all-or-nothing fashion. If the facts a rule stipulates are given, then either the rule is valid, in which case the answer it supplies must be accepted, or it is not, in which case it contributes nothing to the decision.

This all-or-nothing is seen most plainly if we look at the way rules operate, not in law, but in some enterprise they dominate – a game, for example. In baseball a rule provides that if the batter has had three strikes, he is out. An official cannot consistently acknowledge that this is an accurate statement of a baseball rule, and decide that a batter who has had three strikes is not out. Of course, a rule may have exceptions

---

[1] *Id.*, at 386, 161 A.2d at 84.
[2] *Id.*
[3] *Id.* at 388, 161 A.2d at 86.
[4] *Id.* at 387, 161 A.2d at 85.
[5] *Id.* at 389, 161 A.2d at 86 (quoting Frankfurter, J., in *United States v. Bethlehem Steel*, 315 U.S. 289, 326 [1942]).
[6] *Id.*

(the batter who has taken three strikes is not out if the catcher drops the third strike). However, an accurate statement of the rule would take this exception into account, and any that did not would be incomplete. If the list of exceptions is very large, it would be too clumsy to repeat them each time the rule is cited; there is, however, no reason in theory why they could not all be added on, and the more that are, the more accurate is the statement of the rule.

If we take baseball rules as a model, we find that rules of law, like the rule that a will is invalid unless signed by three witnesses, fit the model well. If the requirement of three witnesses is a valid legal rule, then it cannot be that a will has been signed by only two witnesses and is valid. The rule might have exceptions, but if it does then it is inaccurate and incomplete to state the rule so simply, without enumerating the exceptions. In theory, at least, the exceptions could all be listed, and the more of them that are, the more complete is the statement of the rule.

But this is not the way the sample principles in the quotations operate. Even those which look most like rules do not set out legal consequences that follow automatically when the conditions provided are met. We say that our law respects the principle that no man may profit from his own wrong, but we do not mean that the law never permits a man to profit from wrongs he commits. In fact, people often profit, perfectly legally, from their legal wrongs. The most notorious case is adverse possession – if I trespass on your land long enough, some day I will gain a right to cross your land whenever I please. There are many less dramatic examples. If a man leaves one job, breaking a contract, to take a much higher paying job, he may have to pay damages to his first employer, but he is usually entitled to keep his new salary. If a man jumps bail and crosses state lines to make a brilliant investment in another state, he may be sent back to jail, but he will keep his profits.

We do not treat these – and countless other counter-instances that can easily be imagined – as showing that the principle about profiting from one's wrongs is not a principle of our legal system, or that it is incomplete and needs qualifying exceptions. We do not treat counter-instances as exceptions (at least not exceptions in the way in which a catcher's dropping the third strike is an exception) because we could not hope to capture these counter-instances simply by a more extended statement of the principle. They are not, even in theory, subject to enumeration, because we would have to include not only these cases (like adverse possession) in which some institution has already provided that profit can be gained through a wrong, but also those numberless imaginary cases in which we know in advance that the principle would not hold. Listing some of these might sharpen our sense of the principle's weight (I shall mention that dimension in a moment), but it would not make for a more accurate or complete statement of the principle.

A principle like 'No man may profit from his own wrong' does not even purport to set out conditions that make its application necessary. Rather, it states a reason that argues in one direction, but does not necessitate a particular decision. If a man has or is about to receive something, as a direct result of something illegal he did to get it, then that is a reason which the law will take into account in deciding whether he should keep it. There may be other principles or policies arguing in the other direction – a policy of securing title, for example, or a principle limiting punishment to what the legislature has stipulated. If so, our principle may not prevail, but that does not mean that it is not a principle of our legal system, because in the next case, when these contravening considerations are absent or less weighty, the principle may be decisive. All that is meant, when we say that a particular principle is a principle of our law, is that the principle is one which officials must take into account, if it is relevant, as a consideration inclining in one direction or another.

The logical distinction between rules and principles appears more clearly when we consider principles that do not even look like rules. Consider the proposition, set out under '(d)' in the excerpts from the *Henningsen* opinion, that 'the manufacturer is under a special obligation in connection with the construction, promotion and sale of his cars'. This does not even purport to define the specific duties such a special obligation entails, or to tell us what rights automobile consumers acquire as a result. It merely states – and this is an essential link in the *Henningsen* argument – that automobile manufacturers must be held to higher standards than other manufacturers, and are less entitled to rely on the competing principle of freedom of contract. It does not mean that they may never rely on that principle, or that courts may rewrite automobile purchase contracts at will; it means only that if a particular clause seems unfair or burdensome, courts have less reason to enforce the clause than if it were for the purchase of neckties. The 'special obligation' counts in favor, but does not in itself necessitate, a decision refusing to enforce the terms of an automobile purchase contract.

This first difference between rules and principles entails another. Principles have a dimension that rules do not – the dimension of weight or importance. When principles intersect (the policy of protecting automobile consumers intersecting with principles of freedom of contract, for example), one who must resolve the conflict has to take into account the relative weight of each. This cannot be, of course, an exact measurement, and the judgment that a particular principle or policy is more important than another will often be a controversial one. Nevertheless, it is an integral part of the concept of a principle that it has this dimension, that it makes sense to ask how important or how weighty it is.

Rules do not have this dimension. We can speak of rules as being *functionally* important or unimportant (the baseball rule that three strikes are out is more important than the rule that runners may advance on a balk, because the game would be much more changed with the first rule altered than the second). In this sense, one legal rule may be more important than another because it has a greater or more important role in regulating behavior. But we cannot say that one rule is more important than another within the system of rules, so that when two rules conflict one supersedes the other by virtue of its greater weight.

If two rules conflict, one of them cannot be a valid rule. The decision as to which is valid, and which must be abandoned or recast, must be made by appealing to considerations beyond the rules themselves. A legal system might regulate such conflicts by other rules, which prefer the rule enacted by the higher authority, or the rule enacted later, or the more specific rule, or something of that sort. A legal system may also prefer the rule supported by the more important principles. (Our own legal system uses both of these techniques.)

It is not always clear from the form of a standard whether it is a rule or a principle. 'A will is invalid unless signed by three witnesses' is not very different in form from 'A man may not profit from his own wrong', but one who knows something of American law knows that he must take the first as stating a rule and the second as stating a principle. In many cases the distinction is difficult to make – it may not have been settled how the standard should operate, and this issue may itself be a focus of controversy. The first amendment to the United States Constitution contains the provision that Congress shall not abridge freedom of speech. Is this a rule, so that if a particular law does abridge freedom of speech, it follows that it is unconstitutional? Those who claim that the first amendment is 'an absolute' say that it must be taken in this way, that is, as a rule. Or does it merely state a principle, so that when an abridgement of speech is discovered, it is unconstitutional unless the context presents some other policy or principle which in the circumstances is weighty enough to permit the abridgement? That is the position of those who argue for what is called the 'clear and present danger' test or some other form of 'balancing'.

Sometimes a rule and a principle can play much the same role, and the difference between them is almost a matter of form alone. The first section of the Sherman Act states that every contract in restraint of trade shall be void. The Supreme Court had to make the decision whether this provision should be treated as a rule in its own terms (striking down every contract 'which restrains trade', which almost any contract does) or as a principle, providing a reason for striking down a contract in the absence of effective contrary policies. The Court construed the provision as a rule, but treated that rule as containing the word 'unreasonable', and as prohibiting only 'unreasonable' restraints of trade.[1] This allowed the provision to function logically as a rule (whenever a court finds that the restraint is 'unreasonable' it is bound to hold the contract invalid) and substantially as a principle (a court must take into account a variety of other principles and policies in determining whether a particular restraint in particular economic circumstances is 'unreasonable').

Words like 'reasonable', 'negligent', 'unjust', and 'significant' often perform just this function. Each of these terms makes the application of the rule which contains it depend to some extent upon principles or policies lying beyond the rule, and in this way makes that rule itself more like a principle. But they do not quite turn the rule into a principle, because even the least confining of these terms restricts the *kind* of other principles and policies on which the rule depends. If we are bound by a rule that says that 'unreasonable' contracts are void, or that grossly 'unfair' contracts will not be enforced, much more judgment is required than if the quoted terms were omitted. But suppose a case in which some consideration of policy or principle suggests that a contract should be enforced even though its restraint is not reasonable, or even though it is grossly unfair. Enforcing these contracts would be forbidden by our rules, and thus permitted only if these rules were abandoned or modified. If we were dealing, however, not with a rule but with a policy against enforcing unreasonable contracts, or a principle that unfair contracts ought not to be enforced, the contracts could be enforced without alteration of the law.

4. PRINCIPLES AND THE CONCEPT OF LAW

Once we identify legal principles as separate sorts of standards, different from legal rules, we are suddenly aware of them all around us. Law teachers teach them, lawbooks cite them, legal historians celebrate them. But they seem most energetically at work, carrying most weight, in difficult lawsuits like *Riggs* and *Henningsen*. In cases like these, principles play an essential part in arguments supporting judgments about particular legal rights and obligations. After the case is decided, we may say that the case stands for a particular rule (e.g., the rule that one who murders is not eligible to take under the will of his victim). But the rule does not exist before the case is decided; the court cites principles as its justification for adopting and applying a new rule. In *Riggs*, the court

[1] *Standard Oil v. United States*, 221 U.S. 1, 60 (1911); *United States v. American Tobacco Co.*, 221 U.S. 106, 180 (1911).

cited the principle that no man may profit from his own wrong as a background standard against which to read the statute of wills and in this way justified a new interpretation of that statute. In *Henningsen*, the court cited a variety of intersecting principles and policies as authority for a new rule respecting manufacturer's liability for automobile defects.

An analysis of the concept of legal obligation must therefore account for the important role of principles in reaching particular decisions of law. There are two very different tacks we might take :

(a) We might treat legal principles the way we treat legal rules and say that some principles are binding as law and must be taken into account by judges and lawyers who make decisions of legal obligation. If we took this tack, we should say that in the United States, at least, the 'law' includes principles as well as rules.

(b) We might, on the other hand, deny that principles can be binding the way some rules are. We would say, instead, that in cases like *Riggs* or *Henningsen* the judge reaches beyond the rules that he is bound to apply (reaches, that is, beyond the 'law') for extra-legal principles he is free to follow if he wishes.

One might think that there is not much difference between these two lines of attack, that it is only a verbal question of how one wants to use the word 'law'. But that is a mistake, because the choice between these two accounts has the greatest consequences for an analysis of legal obligation. It is a choice between two *concepts* of a legal principle, a choice we can clarify by comparing it to a choice we might make between two concepts of a legal rule. We sometimes say of someone that he 'makes it a rule' to do something, when we mean that he has chosen to follow a certain practice. We might say that someone has made it a rule, for example, to run a mile before breakfast because he wants to be healthy and believes in a regimen. We do not mean, when we say this, that he is *bound* by the rule that he must run a mile before breakfast, or even that he regards it as binding upon him. Accepting a rule as binding is something different from making it a rule to do something. If we use Hart's example again, there is a difference between saying that Englishmen make it a rule to see a movie once a week, and saying that the English have a rule that one must see a movie once a week. The second implies that if an Englishman does not follow the rule, he is subject to criticism or censure, but the first does not. The first does not exclude the possibility of a *sort* of criticism – we can say that one who does not see movies is neglecting his education – but we do not suggest that he is doing something wrong *just* in not following the rule.[1]

If we think of the judges of a community as a group, we could describe the rules of law they follow in these two different ways. We could say, for instance, that in a certain state the judges make it a rule not to enforce wills unless there are three witnesses. This would not imply that the rare judge who enforces such a will is doing anything wrong just for that reason. On the other hand we can say that in that state a rule of law requires judges not to enforce such wills; this does imply that a judge who enforces them is doing something wrong. Hart, Austin and other positivists, of course, would insist on this latter account of legal rules; they would not at all be satisfied with the 'make it a rule' account. It is not a verbal question of which account is right. It is a question of which describes the social situation more accurately. Other important issues turn on which description we accept. If judges simply 'make it a rule' not to enforce certain contracts, for example, then we cannot say, before the decision, that anyone is 'entitled' to that result, and that proposition cannot enter into any justification we might offer for the decision.

The two lines of attack on principles parallel these two accounts of rules. The first tack treats principles as binding upon judges, so that they are wrong not to apply the principles when they are pertinent. The second tack treats principles as summaries of what most judges 'make it a principle' to do when forced to go beyond the standards that bind them. The choice between these approaches will affect, perhaps even determine, the answer we can give to the question whether the judge in a hard case like *Riggs* or *Henningsen* is attempting to enforce pre-existing legal rights and obligations. If we take the first tack, we are still free to argue that because such judges are applying binding legal standards they are enforcing legal rights and obligations. But if we take the second, we are out of court on that issue, and we must acknowledge that the murderer's family in *Riggs* and the manufacturer in *Henningsen* were deprived of their property by an act of judicial discretion applied *ex post facto*. This may not shock many readers – the notion of judicial discretion has percolated through the legal community – but it does illustrate one of the most nettlesome of the puzzles that drive philosophers to worry about legal obligation. If taking property away in cases like these cannot be justified by appealing to an established obligation, another justification must be found, and nothing satisfactory has yet been supplied.

In my skeleton diagram of positivism, previously set out, I listed the doctrine of judicial discretion as the second tenet. Positivists hold that

[1] The distinction is in substance the same as that made by Rawls, 'Two Concepts of Rules', 64 *Philosophical Review* 3 (1955).

when a case is not covered by a clear rule, a judge must exercise his discretion to decide that case by what amounts to a fresh piece of legislation. There may be an important connection between this doctrine and the question of which of the two approaches to legal principles we must take. We shall therefore want to ask whether the doctrine is correct, and whether it implies the second approach, as it seems on its face to do. En route to these issues, however, we shall have to polish our understanding of the concept of discretion. I shall try to show how certain confusions about that concept and in particular a failure to discriminate different senses in which it is used, account for the popularity of the doctrine of discretion. I shall argue that in the sense in which the doctrine does have a bearing on our treatment of principles, it is entirely unsupported by the arguments the positivists use to defend it.

5. DISCRETION

The concept of discretion was lifted by the positivists from ordinary language, and to understand it we must put it back in *habitat* for a moment. What does it mean, in ordinary life, to say that someone 'has discretion?' The first thing to notice is that the concept is out of place in all but very special contexts. For example, you would not say that I either do or do not have discretion to choose a house for my family. It is not true that I have 'no discretion' in making that choice, and yet it would be almost equally misleading to say that I do have discretion. The concept of discretion is at home in only one sort of context; when someone is in general charged with making decisions subject to standards set by a particular authority. It makes sense to speak of the discretion of a sergeant who is subject to orders of superiors, or the discretion of a sports official or contest judge who is governed by a rule book or the terms of the contest. Discretion, like the hole in a doughnut, does not exist except as an area left open by a surrounding belt of restriction. It is therefore a relative concept. It always makes sense to ask, 'Discretion under which standards?' or 'Discretion as to which authority?' Generally the context will make the answer to this plain, but in some cases the official may have discretion from one stand-point though not from another.

Like almost all terms, the precise meaning of 'discretion' is affected by features of the context. The term is always colored by the background of understood information against which it is used. Although the shadings are many, it will be helpful for us to recognize some gross distinctions.

Sometimes we use 'discretion' in a weak sense, simply to say that for some reason the standards an official must apply cannot be applied mechanically but demand the use of judgment. We use this weak sense when the context does not already make that clear, when the background our audience assumes does not contain that piece of information. Thus we might say, 'The sergeant's orders left him a great deal of discretion', to those who do not know what the sergeant's orders were or who do not know something that made those orders vague or hard to carry out. It would make perfect sense to add, by way of amplification, that the lieutenant had ordered the sergeant to take his five most experienced men on patrol but that it was hard to determine which were the most experienced.

Sometimes we use the term in a different weak sense, to say only that some official has final authority to make a decision and cannot be reviewed and reversed by any other official. We speak this way when the official is part of a hierarchy of officials structured so that some have higher authority but in which the patterns of authority are different for different classes of decision. Thus we might say that in baseball certain decisions, like the decision whether the ball or the runner reached second base first, are left to the discretion of the second base umpire, if we mean that on this issue the head umpire has no power to substitute his own judgment if he disagrees.

I call both of these senses weak to distinguish them from a stronger sense. We use 'discretion' sometimes not merely to say that an official must use judgment in applying the standards set him by authority, or that no one will review that exercise of judgment, but to say that on some issue he is simply not bound by standards set by the authority in question. In this sense we say that a sergeant has discretion who has been told to pick any five men for patrol he chooses or that a judge in a dog show has discretion to judge airedales before boxers if the rules do not stipulate an order of events. We use this sense not to comment on the vagueness or difficulty of the standards, or on who has the final word in applying them, but on their range and the decisions they purport to control. If the sergeant is told to take the five most experienced men, he does not have discretion in this strong sense because that order purports to govern his decision. The boxing referee who must decide which fighter has been the more aggressive does not have discretion, in the strong sense, for the same reason.[1]

If anyone said that the sergeant or the referee had discretion in these cases, we should have to understand him, if the context permitted, as using the term in one of the weak senses. Suppose, for example, the

---

[1] I have not spoken of that jurisprudential favorite, 'limited' discretion, because that concept presents no special difficulties if we remember the relativity of discretion. Suppose the sergeant is told to choose from 'amongst' experienced men, or to 'take experience into account'. We might say either that he has (limited) discretion in picking his patrol, or (full) discretion to either pick amongst experienced men or decide what else to take into account.

lieutenant ordered the sergeant to select the five men he deemed most experienced, and then added that the sergeant had discretion to choose them. Or the rules provided that the referee should award the round to the more aggressive fighter, with discretion in selecting him. We should have to understand these statements in the second weak sense, as speaking to the question of review of the decision. The first weak sense – that the decisions take judgment – would be otiose, and the third, strong sense is excluded by the statements themselves.

We must avoid one tempting confusion. The strong sense of discretion is not tantamount to license, and does not exclude criticism. Almost any situation in which a person acts (including those in which there is no question of decision under special authority, and so no question of discretion) makes relevant certain standards of rationality, fairness, and effectiveness. We criticize each other's acts in terms of these standards, and there is no reason not to do so when the acts are within the center rather than beyond the perimeter of the doughnut of special authority. So we can say that the sergeant who was given discretion (in the strong sense) to pick a patrol did so stupidly or maliciously or carelessly, or that the judge who had discretion in the order of viewing dogs made a mistake because he took boxers first although there were only three airedales and many more boxers. An official's discretion means not that he is free to decide without recourse to standards of sense and fairness, but only that his decision is not controlled by a standard furnished by the particular authority we have in mind when we raise the question of discretion. Of course this latter sort of freedom is important; that is why we have the strong sense of discretion. Someone who has discretion in this third sense can be criticized, but not for being disobedient, as in the case of the soldier. He can be said to have made a mistake, but not to have deprived a participant of a decision to which he was entitled, as in the case of a sports official or contest judge.

We may now return, with these observations in hand, to the positivists' doctrine of judicial discretion. That doctrine argues that if a case is not controlled by an established rule, the judge must decide it by exercising discretion. We want to examine this doctrine and to test its bearing on our treatment of principles; but first we must ask in which sense of discretion we are to understand it.

Some nominalists argue that judges always have discretion, even when a clear rule is in point, because judges are ultimately the final arbiters of the law. This doctrine of discretion uses the second weak sense of that term, because it makes the point that no higher authority reviews the decisions of the highest court. It therefore has no bearing on the issue of how we account for principles, any more than it bears on how we account for rules.

The positivists do not mean their doctrine this way, because they say that a judge has no discretion when a clear and established rule is available. If we attend to the positivists' arguments for the doctrine we may suspect that they use discretion in the first weak sense to mean only that judges must sometimes exercise judgment in applying legal standards. Their arguments call attention to the fact that some rules of law are vague (Professor Hart, for example, says that all rules of law have 'open texture'), and that some cases arise (like *Henningsen*) in which no established rule seems to be suitable. They emphasize that judges must sometimes agonize over points of law, and that two equally trained and intelligent judges will often disagree.

These points are easily made; they are commonplace to anyone who has any familiarity with law. Indeed, that is the difficulty with assuming that positivists mean to use 'discretion' in this weak sense. The proposition that when no clear rule is available discretion in the sense of judgment must be used is a tautology. It has no bearing, moreover, on the problem of how to account for legal principles. It is perfectly consistent to say that the judge in *Riggs*, for example, had to use judgment, and that he was bound to follow the principle that no man may profit from his own wrong. The positivists speak as if their doctrine of judicial discretion is an insight rather than a tautology, and as if it does have a bearing on the treatment of principles. Hart, for example, says that when the judge's discretion is in play, we can no longer speak of his being bound by standards, but must speak rather of what standards he 'characteristically uses'.[1] Hart thinks that when judges have discretion, the principles they cite must be treated on our second approach, as what courts 'make it a principle' to do.

It therefore seems that positivists, at least sometimes, take their doctrine in the third, strong sense of discretion. In that sense it does bear on the treatment of principles; indeed, in that sense it is nothing less than a restatement of our second approach. It is the same thing to say that when a judge runs out of rules he has discretion, in the sense that he is not bound by any standards from the authority of law, as to say that the legal standards judges cite other than rules are not binding on them.

So we must examine the doctrine of judicial discretion in the strong sense. (I shall henceforth use the term 'discretion' in that sense.) Do the principles judges cited in cases like *Riggs* or *Henningsen* control their decisions, as the sergeant's orders to take the most experienced men or the referee's duty to choose the more aggressive fighter control the decisions of these officials? What arguments could a positivist supply to show that they do not?

[1] H. L. A. Hart, *The Concept of Law*, 144 (1961).

(1) A positivist might argue that principles cannot be binding or obligatory. That would be a mistake. It is always a question, of course, whether any particular principle is *in fact* binding upon some legal official. But there is nothing in the logical character of a principle that renders it incapable of binding him. Suppose that the judge in *Henningsen* had failed to take any account of the principle that automobile manufacturers have a special obligation to their consumers, or the principle that the courts seek to protect those whose bargaining position is weak, but had simply decided for the defendant by citing the principle of freedom of contract without more. His critics would not have been content to point out that he had not taken account of considerations that other judges have been attending to for some time. Most would have said that it was his duty to take the measure of these principles and that the plaintiff was entitled to have him do so. We mean no more, when we say that a *rule* is binding upon a judge, than that he must follow it if it applies, and that if he does not he will on that account have made a mistake.

It will not do to say that in a case like *Henningsen* the court is only 'morally' obligated to take particular principles into account, or that it is 'institutionally' obligated, or obligated as a matter of judicial 'craft', or something of that sort. The question will still remain why this type of obligation (whatever we call it) is different from the obligation that rules impose upon judges, and why it entitles us to say that principles and policies are not part of the law but are merely extra-legal standards 'courts characteristically use'.

(2) A positivist might argue that even though some principles are binding, in the sense that the judge must take them into account, they cannot determine a particular result. This is a harder argument to assess because it is not clear what it means for a standard to 'determine' a result. Perhaps it means that the standard *dictates* the result whenever it applies so that nothing else counts. If so, then it is certainly true that the individual principles do not determine results, but that is only another way of saying that principles are not rules. Only rules dictate results, come what may. When a contrary result has been reached, the rule has been abandoned or changed. Principles do not work that way; they incline a decision one way, though not conclusively, and they survive intact when they do not prevail. This seems no reason for concluding that judges who must reckon with principles have discretion because a set of principles *can* dictate a result. If a judge believes that principles he is bound to recognize point in one direction and that principles pointing in the other direction, if any, are not of equal weight, then he must decide accordingly, just as he must follow what he believes

to be a binding rule. He may, of course, be wrong in his assessment of the principles, but he may also be wrong in his judgment that the rule is binding. The sergeant and the referee, we might add, are often in the same boat. No one factor dictates which soldiers are the most experienced or which fighter the more aggressive. These officials must make judgments of the relative weights of these various factors; they do not on that account have discretion.

(3) A positivist might argue that principles cannot count as law because their authority, and even more so their weight, are congenitally *controversial*. It is true that generally we cannot *demonstrate* the authority or weight of a particular principle as we can sometimes demonstrate the validity of a rule by locating it in an act of Congress or in the opinion of an authoritative court. Instead, we make a case for a principle, and for its weight, by appealing to an amalgam of practice and other principles in which the implications of legislative and judicial history figure along with appeals to community practices and understandings. There is no litmus paper for testing the soundness of such a case – it is a matter of judgment, and reasonable men may disagree. But again this does not distinguish the judge from other officials who do not have discretion. The sergeant has no litmus paper for experience, the referee none for aggressiveness. Neither of these has discretion, because he is bound to reach an understanding, controversial or not, of what his orders or the rules require, and to act on that understanding. That is the judge's duty as well.

Of course, if the positivists are right in another of their doctrines – the theory that in each legal system there is an ultimate *test* for binding law like Professor Hart's rule of recognition – it follows that principles are not binding law. But the incompatibility of principles with the positivists' theory can hardly be taken as an argument that principles must be treated any particular way. That begs the question; we are interested in the status of principles because we want to evaluate the positivists' model. The positivist cannot defend his theory of a rule of recognition by fiat; if principles are not amenable to a test he must show some other reason why they cannot count as law. Since principles seem to play a role in arguments about legal obligation (witness, again, *Riggs* and *Henningsen*), a model that provides for that role has some initial advantage over one that excludes it, and the latter cannot properly be inveighed in its own support.

These are the most obvious of the arguments a positivist might use for the doctrine of discretion in the strong sense, and for the second approach to principles. I shall mention one strong counter-argument against that doctrine and in favor of the first approach. Unless at least some principles are acknowledged to be binding upon judges, requiring them as a set to reach particular decisions, then no rules, or very few rules, can be said to be binding upon them either.

In most American jurisdictions, and now in England also, the higher courts not infrequently reject established rules. Common law rules – those developed by earlier court decisions – are sometimes overruled directly, and sometimes radically altered by further development. Statutory rules are subjected to interpretation and reinterpretation, sometimes even when the result is not to carry out what is called the 'legislative intent.'[1] If courts had discretion to change established rules, then these rules would of course not be binding upon them, and so would not be law on the positivists' model. The positivist must therefore argue that there are standards, themselves binding upon judges, that determine when a judge may overrule or alter an established rule, and when he may not.

When, then, is a judge permitted to change an existing rule of law? Principles figure in the answer in two ways. First, it is necessary, though not sufficient, that the judge find that the change would advance some principle, which principle thus justifies the change. In *Riggs* the change (a new interpretation of the statute of wills) was justified by the principle that no man should profit from his own wrong; in *Henningsen* the previously recognized rules about automobile manufacturers' liability were altered on the basis of the principles I quoted from the opinion of the court.

But not any principle will do to justify a change, or no rule would ever be safe. There must be some principles that count and others that do not, and there must be some principles that count for more than others. It could not depend on the judge's own preferences amongst a sea of respectable extra-legal standards, any one in principle eligible, because if that were the case we could not say that any rules were binding. We could always imagine a judge whose preferences amongst extra-legal standards were such as would justify a shift or radical reinterpretation of even the most entrenched rule.

Second, any judge who proposes to change existing doctrine must take account of some important standards that argue against departures from established doctrine, and these standards are also for the most part principles. They include the doctrine of 'legislative supremacy', a set of principles that require the courts to pay a qualified deference to the acts of the legislature. They also include the doctrine of precedent, another set of principles reflecting the equities and efficiencies of consistency. The doctrines of legislative supremacy and precedent incline

[1] See Wellington and Albert, 'Statutory Interpretation and the Political Process: A Comment on Sinclair v. Atkinson', 72 *Yale L. J.* 1547 (1963).

toward the *status quo*, each within its sphere, but they do not command it. Judges are not free, however, to pick and choose amongst the principles and policies that make up these doctrines – if they were, again, no rule could be said to be binding.

Consider, therefore, what someone implies who says that a particular rule is binding. He may imply that the rule is affirmatively supported by principles the court is not free to disregard, and which are collectively more weighty than other principles that argue for a change. If not, he implies that any change would be condemned by a combination of conservative principles of legislative supremacy and precedent that the court is not free to ignore. Very often, he will imply both, for the conservative principles, being principles and not rules, are usually not powerful enough to save a common law rule or an aging statute that is entirely unsupported by substantive principles the court is bound to respect. Either of these implications, of course, treats a body of principles and policies as law in the sense that rules are; it treats them as standards binding upon the officials of a community, controlling their decisions of legal right and obligation.

We are left with this issue. If the positivists' theory of judicial discretion is either trivial because it uses 'discretion' in a weak sense, or unsupported because the various arguments we can supply in its defense fall short, why have so many careful and intelligent lawyers embraced it? We can have no confidence in our treatment of that theory unless we can deal with that question. It is not enough to note (although perhaps it contributes to the explanation) that 'discretion' has different senses that may be confused. We do not confuse these senses when we are not thinking about law.

Part of the explanation, at least, lies in a lawyer's natural tendency to associate laws and rules, and to think of 'the law' as a collection or system of rules. Roscoe Pound, who diagnosed this tendency long ago, though that English speaking lawyers were tricked into it by the fact that English uses the same word, changing only the article, for 'a law' and 'the law'.[1] (Other languages, on the contrary, use two words: 'loi' and 'droit', for example, and 'Gesetz' and 'Recht'.) This may have had its effect, with the English speaking positivists, because the expression 'a law' certainly does suggest a rule. But the principal reason for associating law with rules runs deeper, and lies, I think, in the fact that legal education has for a long time consisted of teaching and examining those established rules that form the cutting edge of law.

In any event, if a lawyer thinks of law as a system of rules, and yet recognizes, as he must, that judges change old rules and introduce new

---

[1] R. Pound, *An Introduction to the Philosophy of Law* 56 (rev. ed. 1954).

ones, he will come naturally to the theory of judicial discretion in the strong sense. In those other systems of rules with which he has experience (like games), the rules are the only special authority that govern official decisions, so that if an umpire could change a rule, he would have discretion as to the subject matter of that rule. Any principles umpires might mention when changing the rules would represent only their 'characteristic' preferences. Positivists treat law like baseball revised in this way.

There is another, more subtle consequence of this initial assumption that law is a system of rules. When the positivists do attend to principles and policies, they treat them as rules *manquées*. They assume that *if* they are standards of law they must be rules, and so they read them as standards that are trying to be rules. When a positivist hears someone argue that legal principles are part of the law, he understands this to be an argument for what he calls the 'higher law' theory, that these principles are the rules of a law about the law.[1] He refutes this theory by pointing out that these 'rules' are sometimes followed and sometimes not, that for every 'rule' like 'no man shall profit from his own wrong' there is another competing 'rule' like 'the law favors security of title', and that there is no way to test the validity of 'rules' like these. He concludes that these principles and policies are not valid rules of a law above the law, which is true, because they are not rules at all. He also concludes that they are extra-legal standards which each judge selects according to his own lights in the exercise of his discretion, which is false. It is as if a zoologist had proved that fish are not mammals, and then concluded that they are really only plants.

6. THE RULE OF RECOGNITION

This discussion was provoked by our two competing accounts of legal principles. We have been exploring the second account, which the positivists seem to adopt through their doctrine of judicial discretion, and we have discovered grave difficulties. It is time to return to the fork in the road. What if we adopt the first approach? What would the consequences of this be for the skeletal structure of positivism? Of course we should have to drop the second tenet, the doctrine of judicial discretion (or, in the alternative, to make plain that the doctrine is to be read merely to say that judges must often exercise judgment). Would we also have to abandon or modify the first tenet, the proposition that law is distinguished by tests of the sort that can be set out in a master rule like Professor Hart's rule of recognition? If principles of the *Riggs* and

[1] See, e.g., Dickinson, 'The Law Behind Law (pts. 1 & 2)', 29, *Columbia Law Review* 112, 254 (1929).

Henningsen sort are to count as law, and we are nevertheless to preserve the notion of a master rule for law, then we must be able to deploy some test that all (and only) the principles that do count as law meet. Let us begin with the test Hart suggests for identifying valid *rules* of law, to see whether these can be made to work for principles as well.

Most rules of law, according to Hart, are valid because some competent institution enacted them. Some were created by a legislature, in the form of statutory enactments. Others were created by judges who formulated them to decide particular cases, and thus established them as precedents for the future. But this test of pedigree will not work for the *Riggs* and *Henningsen* principles. The origin of these as legal principles lies not in a particular decision of some legislature or court, but in a sense of appropriateness developed in the profession and the public over time. Their continued power depends upon this sense of appropriateness being sustained. If it no longer seemed unfair to allow people to profit by their wrongs, or fair to place special burdens upon oligopolies that manufacture potentially dangerous machines, these principles would no longer play much of a role in new cases, even if they had never been overruled or repealed. (Indeed, it hardly makes sense to speak of principles like these as being 'overruled' or 'repealed'. When they decline they are eroded, not torpedoed.)

True, if we were challenged to back up our claim that some principle is a principle of law, we would mention any prior cases in which that principle was cited, or figured in the argument. We would also mention any statute that seemed to exemplify that principle (even better if the principle was cited in the preamble of the statute, or in the committee reports or other legislative documents that accompanied it). Unless we could find some such institutional support, we would probably fail to make out our case, and the more support we found, the more weight we could claim for the principle.

Yet we could not devise any formula for testing how much and what kind of institutional support is necessary to make a principle a legal principle, still less to fix its weight at a particular order of magnitude. We argue for a particular principle by grappling with a whole set of shifting, developing and interacting standards (themselves principles rather than rules) about institutional responsibility, statutory interpretation, the persuasive force of various sorts of precedent, the relation of all these to contemporary moral practices, and hosts of other such standards. We could not bolt all of these together into a single 'rule', even a complex one, and if we could the result would bear little relation to Hart's picture of a rule of recognition, which is the picture of a fairly stable master rule specifying 'some feature or features possession of which by a suggested rule is taken as a conclusive affirmative indication that it is a rule. . .'[1] ✗

Moreover, the techniques we apply in arguing for another principle do not stand (as Hart's rule of recognition is designed to) on an entirely different level from the principles they support. Hart's sharp distinction between acceptance and validity does not hold. If we are arguing for the principle that a man should not profit from his own wrong, we could cite the acts of courts and legislatures that exemplify it, but this speaks as much to the principle's acceptance as its validity. (It seems odd to speak of a principle as being valid at all, perhaps because validity is an all-or-nothing concept, appropriate for rules, but inconsistent with a principle's dimension of weight.) If we are asked (as we might well be) to defend the particular doctrine of precedent, or the particular technique of statutory interpretation, that we used in this argument, we should certainly cite the practice of others in using that doctrine or technique. But we should also cite other general principles that we believe support that practice, and this introduces a note of validity into the chord of acceptance. We might argue, for example, that the use we make of earlier cases and statutes is supported by a particular analysis of the point of the practice of legislation or the doctrine of precedent, or by the principles of democratic theory, or by a particular position on the proper division of authority between national and local institutions, or something else of that sort. Nor is this path of support a one-way street leading to some ultimate principle resting on acceptance alone. Our principles of legislation, precedent, democracy, or federalism might be challenged too; and if they were we should argue for them, not only in terms of practice, but in terms of each other and in terms of the implications of trends of judicial and legislative decisions, even though this last would involve appealing to those same doctrines of interpretation we justified through the principles we are now trying to support. At this level of abstraction, in other words, principles rather hang together than link together.

So even though principles draw support from the official acts of legal institutions, they do not have a simple or direct enough connection with these acts to frame that connection in terms of criteria specified by some ultimate master rule of recognition. Is there any other route by which principles might be brought under such a rule?

Hart does say that a master rule might designate as law not only rules enacted by particular legal institutions, but rules established by *custom* as well. He has in mind a problem that bothered other positivists, including Austin. Many of our most ancient legal rules were never

[1] H. L. A. Hart, *The Concept of Law* 92 (1961).

explicitly created by a legislature or a court. When they made their first appearance in legal opinions and texts, they were treated as already being part of the law because they represented the customary practice of the community, or some specialized part of it, like the business community. (The examples ordinarily given are rules of mercantile practice, like the rules governing what rights arise under a standard form of commercial paper.)[1] Since Austin thought that all law was the command of a determinate sovereign, he held that these customary practices were not law until the courts (as agents of the sovereign) recognized them, and that the courts were indulging in a fiction in pretending otherwise. But that seemed arbitrary. If everyone thought custom might in itself be law, the fact that Austin's theory said otherwise was not persuasive.

Hart reversed Austin on this point. The master rule, he says, might stipulate that some custom counts as law even before the courts recognize it. But he does not face the difficulty this raises for his general theory because he does not attempt to set out the criteria a master rule might use for this purpose. It cannot use, as its only criterion, the provision that the community regard the practice as *morally* binding, for this would not distinguish legal customary rules from moral customary rules, and of course not all of the community's long-standing customary moral obligations are enforced at law. If, on the other hand, the test is whether the community regards the customary practice as *legally* binding, the whole point of the master rule is undercut, at least for this class of legal rules. The master rule, says Hart, marks the transformation from a primitive society to one with law, because it provides a test for determining social rules of law other than by measuring their acceptance. But if the master rule says merely that whatever other rules the community accepts as legally binding are legally binding, then it provides no such test at all, beyond the test we should use were there no master rule. The master rule becomes (for these cases) a non-rule of recognition; we might as well say that every primitive society has a secondary rule of recognition, namely the rule that whatever is accepted as binding is binding. Hart himself, in discussing international law, ridicules the idea that such a rule could be a rule of recognition, by describing the proposed rule as 'an empty repetition of the mere fact that the society concerned . . . observes certain standards of conduct as obligatory rules'.[2]

[1] See Note, 'Custom and Trade Usage: Its Application to Commercial Dealings and the Common Law', 55 *Columbia Law Review* 1192 (1955), and materials cited therein at 1193 n.l. As that note makes plain, the actual practices of courts in recognizing trade customs follow the pattern of applying a set of general principles and policies rather than a test that could be captured as part of a rule of recognition.

[2] H. L. Hart, *The Concept of Law* 230 (1961). A master rule might specify some particular feature of a custom that is independent of the community's attitude; it

Hart's treatment of custom amounts, indeed, to a confession that there are at least some rules of law that are not binding because they are valid under standards laid down by a master rule but are binding – like the master rule – because they are accepted as binding by the community. This chips at the neat pyramidal architecture we admired in Hart's theory : we can no longer say that only the master rule is binding because of its acceptance, all other rules being valid under its terms.

This is perhaps only a chip, because the customary rules Hart has in mind are no longer a very significant part of the law. But it does suggest that Hart would be reluctant to widen the damage by bringing under the head of 'custom' all those crucial principles and policies we have been discussing. If he were to call these part of the law and yet admit that the only test of their force lies in the degree to which they are accepted as law by the community or some part thereof, he would very sharply reduce that area of the law over which his master rule held any dominion. It is not just that all the principles and policies would escape its sway, though that would be bad enough. Once these principles and policies are accepted as law, and thus as standards judges must follow in determining legal obligations, it would follow that *rules* like those announced for the first time in *Riggs* and *Henningsen* owe their force at least in part to the authority of principles and policies, and so not entirely to the master rule of recognition.

So we cannot adapt Hart's version of positivism by modifying his rule of recognition to embrace principles. No tests of pedigree, relating principles to acts of legislation, can be formulated, nor can his concept of customary law, itself an exception to the first tenet of positivism, be made to serve without abandoning that tenet altogether. One more possibility must be considered, however. If no rule of recognition can provide a test for identifying principles, why not say that principles are ultimate, and *form* the rule of recognition of our law? The answer to the general question 'What is valid law in an American jurisdiction?' would then require us to state all the principles (as well as ultimate constitutional rules) in force in that jurisdiction at the time, together with appropriate assignments of weight. A positivist might then regard the complete set of these standards as the rule of recognition of the jurisdiction. This

---

might provide, for example, that all customs of very great age, or all customs having to do with negotiable instruments count as law. I can think of no such features that in fact distinguish the customs that have been recognized as law in England or America, however. Some customs that are not legally enforceable are older than some that are, some practices relating to commercial paper are enforced and others not, and so forth. In any event, even if a distinguishing feature were found that identified all rules of law established by custom, it would remain unlikely that such a feature could be found for principles which vary widely in their subject matter and pedigree and some of which are of very recent origin.

solution has the attraction of paradox, but of course it is an unconditional surrender. If we simply designate our rule of recognition by the phrase 'the complete set of principles in force', we achieve only the tautology that law is law. If, instead, we tried actually to list all the principles in force we would fail. They are controversial, their weight is all important, they are numberless, and they shift and change so fast that the start of our list would be obsolete before we reached the middle. Even if we succeeded, we would not have a key for law because there would be nothing left for our key to unlock.

I conclude that if we treat principles as law we must reject the positivists' first tenet, that the law of a community is distinguished from other social standards by some test in the form of a master rule. We have already decided that we must then abandon the second tenet – the doctrine of judicial discretion – or clarify it into triviality. What of the third tenet, the positivists' theory of legal obligation?

This theory holds that a legal obligation exists when (and only when) an established rule of law imposes such an obligation. It follows from this that in a hard case – when no such established rule can be found – there is no legal obligation until the judge creates a new rule for the future. The judge may apply that new rule to the parties in the case, but this is *ex post facto* legislation, not the enforcement of an existing obligation.

The positivists' doctrine of discretion (in the strong sense) required this view of legal obligation, because if a judge has discretion there can be no legal right or obligation – no entitlement – that he must enforce. Once we abandon that doctrine, however, and treat principles as law, we raise the possibility that a legal obligation might be imposed by a constellation of principles as well as by an established rule. We might want to say that a legal obligation exists whenever the case supporting such an obligation, in terms of binding legal principles of different sorts, is stronger than the case against it.

Of course, many questions would have to be answered before we could accept that view of legal obligation. If there is no rule of recognition, no test for law in that sense, how do we decide which principles are to count, and how much, in making such a case? How do we decide whether one case is better than another? If legal obligation rests on an undemonstrable judgment of that sort, how can it provide a justification for a judicial decision that one party had a legal obligation? Does this view of obligation square with the way lawyers, judges and laymen speak, and is it consistent with our attitudes about moral obligation? Does this analysis help us to deal with the classical jurisprudential puzzles about the nature of law?

These questions must be faced, but even the questions promise more than positivism provides. Positivism, on its own thesis, stops short of just those puzzling, hard cases that send us to look for theories of law. When we read these cases, the positivist remits us to a doctrine of discretion that leads nowhere and tells nothing. His picture of law as a system of rules has exercised a tenacious hold on our imagination, perhaps through its very simplicity. If we shake ourselves loose from this model of rules, we may be able to build a model truer to the complexity and sophistication of our own practices.

3

The Model of Rules II

In Chapter 2 I argued that the central propositions of the legal theory I called positivism were in error and must be abandoned.[1] In particular, I argued that it is wrong to suppose, as that theory does, that in every legal system there will be some commonly recognized fundamental test for determining which standards count as law and which do not. I said that no such fundamental test can be found in complicated legal systems, like those in force in the United States and Great Britain, and that in these countries no ultimate distinction can be made between legal and moral standards, as positivism insists.

I might summarize the argument I made in this way. I said that the thesis that there exists some commonly recognized test for law is plausible if we look only at simple legal rules of the sort that appear in statutes or are set out in bold type in textbooks. But lawyers and judges, in arguing and deciding lawsuits, appeal not only to such black-letter rules, but also to other sorts of standards that I called legal principles, like, for example, the principle that no man may profit from his own wrong. This fact faces the positivist with the following difficult choice. He might try to show that judges, when they appeal to principles of this sort, are not appealing to legal standards, but only exercising their discretion. Or he might try to show that, contrary to my doubts, some commonly-recognized test always does identify the principles judges count as law, and distinguishes them from the principles they do not. I argued that neither strategy could succeed.

A number of lawyers have been kind enough to reply to my argument; an article by Dr. Raz is a distinguished example.[2] The chief points

---

[1] See p. 16 ff.

[2] Raz, 'Legal Principles and the Limits of Law', 81 *Yale L. J.* 823 (1972). See also G. Carrio, *Legal Principles and Legal Positivism* (1971); Christie, 'The Model of Principles', 1968, *Duke L. J.* 649; Gross, 'Jurisprudence', 1968/69 *Annual Survey of Am. L.* 575; Probert, 'The Right Way', *Human Rights* 163 (E. Pollack ed. 1971); Sartorius, 'Social Policy and Judicial Legislation', 8 *Am. Phil. Q.* 151 (1971); Tapper, 'A Note on Principles', 1971 *Modern L. Rev.* 628. For an earlier article, *see* Mac-Callum, 'Dworkin on Judicial Discretion', 60 *J. Phil.* 638 (1963). I do not attempt to reply to or even mention all the points and questions presented in these articles. I have selected for discussion those points made most often, or found most persuasive by students.

made against my argument seem to be these. (i) It is not clear, it is said, that my thesis really involves anything more than an amendment to the positivist's doctrine. If one reads carefully the work of Professor H. L. A. Hart, whose work I took to be the clearest example of a positivist theory, one will see that his theory is able to include my conclusions with only minor amendment.[1] (ii) It is said that my own arguments are inconsistent in this way: my argument against the theory of discretion supposes that in fact some principles do and some principles do not count as law, but if this is so then there must be a test for law of just the sort that I deny.[2] (iii) The arguments I make, moreover, suggest the form of this ultimate test. I said that judges identify principles at least in part by reference to the role that these principles have played in previous legal argument, and this kind of test, which I described as a test of 'institutional structure',[3] can supply the ultimate test for principles that I say cannot be found. (iv) My argument that judges do not have discretion in the matter of principles ignores the fact that judges may sometimes be *forced* to exercise discretion by virtue of the fact that it is not plain which principles count and for how much.[4] (v) The distinction between rules and principles, on which my argument seems to depend, is in fact untenable.[5]

There is a further objection, which might be made, but which I shall not try to answer. I have no answer to the argument that the term 'law' can be used in such a way as to make the positivist's thesis true by stipulation. It can be used, that is, in such a way that the speaker recognizes as 'legal' standards only those standards judges and lawyers cite which are in fact identified by some commonly-recognized test. No doubt 'law' can be used in that way, and perhaps some lawyers do so. But I was concerned with what I took to be an argument about the concept of law now in general employment, which is, I take it, the concept of the standards that provide for the rights and duties that a government has a duty to recognize and enforce, at least in principle, through the familiar institutions of courts and police. My point was that positivism, with its doctrine of a fundamental and commonly-recognized test for law, mistakes part of the domain of that concept for the whole.

Before I turn to the specific objections I listed, however, I want to consider one very general objection that I did not list, but which I believe, for reasons that will be clear, underlines several of those I did. This general objection depends on a thesis that Hart defended in *The*

---

[1] See, e.g., Carrio at 22.
[2] Sartorius at 155.
[3] *Id.* at 156.
[4] Raz at 843 ff., Carrio at 27; Christie at 669; MacCallum *loc. cit.*
[5] Raz at 834-54, Christie at 656 ff.

Concept of Law,[1] a thesis which belongs to moral as well as to legal philosophy. It argues, in its strongest form, that no rights or duties of any sort can exist except by virtue of a uniform social practice of recognizing these rights and duties. If that is so, and if law is, as I suppose, a matter of rights and duties and not simply of the discretion of officials, then there must be a commonly recognized test for law in the form of a uniform social practice, and my argument must be wrong.

In the first section of this essay I shall elaborate this powerful thesis, with special reference to the duty of judges to apply particular standards as law. I shall then argue that the thesis must be rejected. In the remaining sections I shall, on some occasions, recast my original arguments to show why they depend on rejecting it.

I. SOCIAL RULES

I shall begin by noticing an important distinction between two of the several types of concepts we use when we discuss our own or other people's behavior. Sometimes we say that on the whole, all things considered, one 'ought' or 'ought not' to do something. On other occasions we say that someone has an 'obligation' or a 'duty' to do something, or 'no right' to do it. These are different sorts of judgments: it is one thing, for example, simply to say that someone ought to give to a particular charity and quite another to say that he has a duty to do so, and one thing to say simply that he ought not to drink alcohol or smoke marijuana and quite another to say that he has no right to do so. It is easy to think of cases in which we should be prepared to make the first of each of these claims, but not the second.

Moreover, something might well turn, in particular cases, on which claim we did feel was justified. Judgments of duty are commonly much stronger than judgments simply about what one ought to do. We can demand compliance with an obligation or a duty, and sometimes propose a sanction for non-compliance, but neither demands nor sanctions are appropriate when it is merely a question of what one ought, on the whole, to do. The question of when claims of obligation or duty are appropriate, as distinct from such general claims about conduct, is therefore an important question of moral philosophy, though it is a relatively neglected one.

The law does not simply state what private citizens ought or ought not to do; it provides what they have a duty to do or no right to do. It does not, moreover, simply advise judges and other officials about the decisions they ought to reach; it provides that they have a duty to

---

[1] H. L. A. Hart, *The Concept of Law* 79-88 (1961).

recognize and enforce certain standards. It may be that in some cases a judge has no duty to decide either way; in this sort of case we must be content to speak of what he ought to do. This, I take it, is what is meant when we say that in such a case the judge has 'discretion'. But every legal philosopher, with the exception of the most extreme of the American legal realists, has supposed that in at least some cases the judge has a duty to decide in a particular way, for the express reason that the law requires that decision.

But it is a formidable problem for legal theory to explain why judges have such a duty. Suppose, for example, that a statute provides that in the event of intestacy a man's property descends to his next of kin. Lawyers will say that a judge has a duty to order property distributed in accordance with that statute. But what imposes that duty on the judge? We may want to say that judges are 'bound' by a general rule to the effect that they must do what the legislature says, but it is unclear where that rule comes from. We cannot say that the legislature is itself the source of the rule that judges must do what the legislature says, because that explanation presupposes the rule we are trying to justify. Perhaps we can discover a basic legal document, like a constitution, that says either explicitly or implicitly that the judges must follow the legislature. But what imposes a duty on judges to follow the constitution? We cannot say the constitution imposes that duty without begging the question in the same way.

If we were content to say merely that judges *ought* to follow the legislature, or the constitution, then the difficulty would not be so serious. We might provide any number of reasons for this limited claim; for example, that everyone would be better off in the long run, on balance, if judges behaved in this way. But this sort of reason is unpersuasive if we want to claim, as our concept of law seems to assume, that judges have a *duty* to follow the legislature or the constitution. We must then try to find, not just reasons why judges should do so, but grounds for asserting that duty, and this requires that we face the issue of moral philosophy I just named. Under what circumstances do duties and obligations arise?

Hart's answer may be summarized in this way.[1] Duties exist when social rules exist providing for such duties. Such social rules exist when the practice-conditions for such rules are met. These practice-conditions are met when the members of a community behave in a certain way; this behavior *constitutes* a social rule, and imposes a duty. Suppose that

---

[1] Hart's analysis, *loc. cit.*, is of the concept of 'obligation'. I use the word 'duty' here as well because it is more usual to speak of the judge's duty than of his obligation to impose the law, and because Hart means his analysis to apply to both terms; indeed he uses them almost interchangeably in *The Concept of Law*. See *id.* at 27, 238.

a group of churchgoers follows this practice : (a) each man removes his hat before entering church, (b) when a man is asked why he does so, he refers to 'the rule' that requires him to do so, and (c) when someone forgets to remove his hat before entering church, he is criticized and perhaps even punished by the others.[1] In those circumstances, according to Hart, practice-conditions for a duty-imposing rule are met. The community 'has' a social rule to the effect that men must not wear hats in church, and that social rule imposes a duty not to wear hats in church. That rule takes the issue of hat-wearing in church out of the general run of issues which men may debate in terms of what they ought to do, by creating a duty. The existence of the social rule, and therefore the existence of the duty, is simply a matter of fact.

Hart then applies this analysis to the issue of judicial duty. He believes that in each legal system the practice-conditions are met, by the behavior of judges, for a social rule that imposes a duty to identify and apply certain standards as law. If, in a particular community, these officials (a) regularly apply the rules laid down by the legislature in reaching their decisions, (b) justify this practice by appeal to 'the rule' that judges must follow the legislature, and (c) censure any official who does not follow the rule, then, on Hart's theory, this community can be said to have a social rule that judges must follow the legislature. If so, then judges in that community have a duty to do so. If we now ask why judges have a duty to follow social rules, after the fashion of our earlier quibbles, Hart will say that we have missed the point. It belongs to the concept of a duty, on his account, that duties are created by social rules of the sort he describes.

But Hart's theory, as so far presented, is open to an objection that might be put in the following way. When a sociologist says that a particular community 'has' or 'follows' a particular rule, like the no-hat-in-church rule, he means only to describe the behavior of that community in a certain respect. He means only to say that members of that community suppose that they have a particular duty, and not that he agrees. But when a member of the community himself appeals to a rule, for the purpose of criticizing his own or someone else's behavior, then he means not simply to describe the behavior of other people but to evaluate it. He means not simply that others believe that they have a certain duty, but that they *do* have that duty. We must therefore recognize a distinction between two sorts of statements each of which uses the concept of a rule. The sociologist, we might say, is asserting a *social* rule, but the

---

[1] Hart uses this example for a different purpose. See Hart, *op. cit.*, at 121. I have drafted the example so that the social rule here in play would be an obligation (or duty) imposing rule, e.g., by providing that the social pressures for conformity are severe.

churchgoer is asserting a *normative* rule. We might say that the sociologist's assertion of a social rule is true (or warranted) if a certain factual state of affairs occurs, that is, if the community behaves in the way Hart describes in his example. But we should want to say that the churchgoer's assertion of a normative rule is true (or warranted) only if a certain normative state of affairs exists, that is, only if individuals in fact do have the duty that they suppose they have in Hart's example. The judge trying a lawsuit is in the position of the churchgoer, not the sociologist. He does not mean to state, as a cold fact, simply that most judges believe that they have a duty to follow what the legislature has said; he means that they do in fact have such a duty and he cites that duty, not others' beliefs, as the justification for his own decision. If so, then the social rule cannot, without more, be the source of the duty he believes he has.

Hart anticipates this objection with an argument that forms the heart of his theory. He recognizes the distinction I have drawn between assertions of a 'social rule' and assertions of a 'normative rule', though he does not use these terms. However, he denies, at least as to the cases he discusses, that these two sorts of assertions can be said to assert two different sorts of rules. Instead, he asks us to distinguish between the *existence* of a rule and its *acceptance* by individual members of the community in question. When the sociologist asserts the existence of a social rule he merely asserts its existence : he says only that the practice-conditions for that rule have been met. When the churchgoer asserts its existence he also claims that these practice-conditions are met, but *in addition* he displays his *acceptance* of the rule as a standard for guiding his own conduct and for judging the conduct of others. He both identifies a social practice and indicates his disposition to conform his behavior to it. Nevertheless, insofar as each refers to a rule, it is the same rule, that is, the rule that is constituted by the social practice in question.

The difference between a statement of a social rule and a statement of a normative rule, then, is not a difference in the type of rule each asserts, but rather a difference in the attitude each displays towards the social rule it does assert. When a judge appeals to the rule that whatever the legislature enacts is law, he is taking an internal point of view towards a social rule; what he says is true because a social practice to that effect exists, but he goes beyond simply saying that this is so. He signals his disposition to regard the social practice as a justification for his conforming to it.

So Hart advances both a general theory about the concept of obligation and duty, and a specific application of that theory to the duty of judges to enforce the law. For the balance of this initial section, I shall be concerned to criticize the general theory, which I shall call the social rule theory, and I shall distinguish strong and weaker versions of that theory. On the strong version, whenever anyone asserts a duty he must be understood as presupposing the existence of a social rule and signifying his acceptance of the practice the rule describes. So if I say that men have a duty not to lie, I must mean at least that a social rule exists to that effect, and unless it does my statement must be false. On a weaker version, it is simply *sometimes* the case that someone who asserts a duty should be understood as presupposing a social rule that provides for that duty. For example, it might be the case that a churchgoer who says that men must not wear hats in church must be understood in that way, but it would not follow that the man who asserts a duty not to lie must be understood in the same way. He might be asserting a duty that does not in fact depend upon the existence of a social rule.

Hart does not make entirely plain, in the relevant pages of *The Concept of Law*, which version he means to adopt, though much of what he says suggests the strong version. But the application of his general theory to the problem of judicial duty will, of course, depend upon which version of the social rule theory he means to make out. If the strong version is right, then judges who speak about a fundamental duty to treat what the legislature says as law, for example, must presuppose a social rule to that effect. But if some weaker version of the social rule theory holds, then it simply might be the case that this is so, and further argument would be needed to show that it is.

The strong version of the theory cannot be correct if it proposes to explain all cases in which people appeal to duties, or even to all cases in which they appeal to rules as the source of duties. The theory must concede that there are some assertions of a normative rule that cannot be explained as an appeal to a social rule, for the reason that no corresponding social rule exists. A vegetarian might say, for example, that we have no right to kill animals for food because of the fundamental moral rule that it is always wrong to take life in any form or under any circumstance. Obviously no social rule exists to that effect : the vegetarian will acknowledge that very few men now recognize any such rule or any such duty and indeed that is his complaint.

However, the theory might argue that this use of the concepts of rule and duty designates a special case, and belongs in fact to a distinct kind of moral practice that is parasitic upon the standard practice the theory is designed to explain. The vegetarian must be understood, on this account, really to be saying not that men and women presently have a duty not to take life, but rather that since there are very strong grounds for saying that one *ought* not to take life, a social rule to that effect *ought to* exist. His appeal to 'the rule' might suggest that some such rule already does exist, but this suggestion is a sort of figure of speech, an attempt on his part to capture the imperative force of social rules, and extend that force to his own very different sort of claim.

But this defense misunderstands the vegetarian's claim. He wants to say, not simply that it is desirable that society rearrange its institutions so that no man ever has the right to take life, but that in fact, as things stand, no one ever does have that right. Indeed, he will want to urge the existence of a moral duty to respect life as a reason why society should have a social rule to that effect. The strong version of the social rule theory does not permit him to make that argument. So that theory can accommodate his statements only by insisting that he say something that he does not want to say.

If the social rule theory is to be plausible, therefore, it must be weakened at least to this extent. It must purport to offer an explanation of what is meant by a claim to duty (or an assertion of a normative rule of duty) only in one sort of case, namely, when the community is by-and-large agreed that some such duty does exist. The theory would not apply in the case of the vegetarian, but it would apply in the case of the churchgoer. This weakening would not much affect the application of the theory to the problem of judicial duty, because judges do in fact seem to follow much the same rules in deciding what to recognize as the law they are bound to enforce.

But the theory is not plausible even in this weakened form. It fails to notice the important distinction between two kinds of social morality, which might be called *concurrent* and *conventional* morality. A community displays a concurrent morality when its members are agreed in asserting the same, or much the same, normative rule, but they do not count the fact of that agreement as an essential part of their grounds for asserting that rule. It displays a conventional morality when they do. If the churchgoers believe that each man has a duty to take off his hat in church, but would not have such a duty but for some social practice to that general effect, then this is a case of conventional morality. If they also believe that each man has a duty not to lie, and would have this duty even if most other men did, then this would be a case of concurrent morality.

The social rule theory must be weakened so as to apply only to cases of conventional morality. In cases of concurrent morality, like the lying case, the practice-conditions Hart describes would be met. People would on the whole not lie, they would cite 'the rule' that lying is wrong as a justification of this behavior, and they would condemn those who did lie. A social rule would be constituted by this behavior, on Hart's theory, and a sociologist would be justified in saying that the community 'had a rule' against lying. But it would distort the claim that members of the community made, when they spoke of a duty not to lie, to suppose them to be *appealing* to that social rule, or to suppose that they count its existence necessary to their claim. On the contrary, since this is a case of concurrent morality, the fact is that they do not. So the social rule theory must be confined to conventional morality.

This further weakening of the theory might well reduce its impact on the problem of judicial duty. It may be that at least some part of what judges believe they must do represents concurrent rather than conventional morality. Many judges, for example, may believe that they have a duty to enforce decision of a democratically elected legislature on the grounds of political principles which they accept as having independent merit, and not simply because other judges and officials accept them as well. On the other hand, it is at least plausible to suppose that this is not so, and that at least the bulk of judges in typical legal systems would count some general judicial practice as an essential part of the case for any claim about their judicial duties.

However, the social rule theory is not even an adequate account of conventional morality. It is not adequate because it cannot explain the fact that even when people count a social practice as a necessary part of the grounds for asserting some duty, they may still disagree about the scope of that duty. Suppose, for example, that the members of the community which 'has the rule' that men must not wear hats in church are in fact divided on the question of whether 'that' rule applies to the case of male babies wearing bonnets. Each side believes that its view of the duties of the babies or their parents is the sounder, but neither view can be pictured as based on a social rule, because there is no social rule on the issue at all.

Hart's description of the practice-conditions for social rules is explicit on this point: a rule is constituted by the conforming behavior of the bulk of a population. No doubt he would count, as conforming behavior, behavior that everyone agrees would be required in a particular case even though the case has not arisen. So the social rule would 'cover' the case of a red-headed man, even if the community did not happen to include one as yet. But if half the churchgoers claim that babies are required to take off their bonnets and the other half denies any such requirement, what social rule does this behavior constitute? We cannot say either that it constitutes a social rule that babies must take off their bonnets, or a social rule that provides that they do not have that duty.

We might be tempted to say that the social rule about men wearing hats in church is 'uncertain' as to the issue of babies. But this involves confusion of just the sort that the social rule theory is meant to avoid. We cannot say that the social rule is uncertain when all the relevant facts about social behavior are known, as they are in this case, because that would violate the thesis that social rules are constituted by behavior.

A social rule about wearing hats in church might be said to be uncertain when the facts about what people did and thought had not yet been gathered, or, perhaps, if the question of babies had not yet arisen, so that it was unclear whether the bulk of the community would be of one mind or not. But nothing like this kind of uncertainty is present here; the case has arisen and we know that members of the community do not agree. So we must say, in this kind of case, not that the social rule about wearing hats in church is uncertain, but rather that the only social rule that the behavior of the community constitutes is the rule that prohibits grown men from wearing hats in church. The existence of that rule is certain, and it is equally certain that no social rule exists on the issue of babies at all.

But all this seems nearly fatal to the social rule theory, for this reason : when people assert normative rules, even in cases of conventional morality, they typically assert rules that differ in scope or in detail, or, in any event, that would differ if each person articulated his rule in further detail. But two people whose rules differ, or would differ if elaborated, cannot be appealing to the same social rule, and at least one of them cannot be appealing to any social rule at all. This is so even though they agree in most cases that do or might arise when the rules they each endorse are in play. So the social rule theory must be weakened to an unacceptable form if it is to survive at all. It must be held to apply only in cases, like some games, when it is accepted by the participants that if a duty is controversial it is no duty at all. It would not then apply to judicial duties.

The theory may try to avoid that conclusion in a variety of ways. It might argue, first, that when someone appeals to a rule, in a controversial case, what he says must be understood as having two parts : first, it identifies the social rule that does represent agreement within the community (that grown men must not wear hats in church) and then it urges that this rule *ought* to be extended to cover more controversial cases (babies in church). The theory might, in other words, take the same line towards all controversial appeals to rules as I said it might in the case of the vegetarian. But the objection I made in discussing the vegetarian's case could then be made, with much greater effect, as a general critique of the theory as a whole. People, at least people who live outside philosophy texts, appeal to moral standards largely in controversial circumstances. When they do, they want to say not that the standard ought to apply to the case in hand, whatever that would mean, but that the standard does apply; not that people ought to have the duties and responsibilities that the standard prescribed, but that they do have them. The theory could hardly argue that all these claims are special or parasitic employments of the concept of duty; if it did, it would limit its own application to the trivial.

The theory might be defended, alternatively, in a very different way : by changing the concept of a social rule that it employs. It might do this by fixing on the fact that, at least in the case of conventional morality, certain verbal formulations of a rule often become standard, like the form, 'men must take off their hats in church.' On the revised concept, a social rule exists when a community accepts a particular verbal formulation of its duties, and uses that formulation as a guide to conduct and criticism; the rule can then be said to be 'uncertain' to the degree that the community disagrees about the proper application of some one or more terms in the standard formulation, provided that it is agreed that the controversial cases must be decided on the basis of one or another interpretation of these terms. The revision would provide an answer to the argument I made. The churchgoers do accept one single social rule about their hat-wearing responsibilities, namely the rule that men must not wear hats in church. But that rule is uncertain, because there is disagreement whether 'men' includes male babies, or whether 'hats' includes bonnets.

But this revision of the concept places much too much weight upon the accident of whether members of the community in question are able to, or do in fact, locate their disagreements about duties as disagreements in the interpretation of some key word in a particular verbal formulation that has become popular. The churchgoers are able to put their disagreement in this form, but it does not follow that they all will. The verbal formulation of the rule might have been different without the underlying social facts having been different, as if people were in the habit of saying that only women may cover their heads in church; in that case the disagreement would have to be framed, not as a disagreement over whether 'women' includes 'male babies' but whether the popular version was a correct statement of the right normative rule.

Moreover, the theory would lose most of its original explanatory power if it were revised in this way. As originally presented it captured, though it misrepresented, an important fact, which is that social practice plays a central role in justifying at least some of our normative claims about individual responsibility or duty. But it is facts of consistent practice that count, not accidents of verbal behavior. Our moral practices are not exercises in statutory interpretation.

Finally, the social rule theory might retain Hart's original definition of a social rule, as a description of uniform practice, but retreat in a different way and cut its losses. It might give up the claim that social rules ever set the *limit* of a man's duties, but keep the idea that they set their *threshold*. The function of social rules in morality might then be said to be this : social rules distinguish what is settled by way of duties, not simply in the factual sense that they describe an area of consensus, but in the conceptual sense that when such consensus exists, it is undeniable that members of that community have at least the duties it embraces, though they may, and perhaps may properly, refuse to honor these duties. But the social rule does not settle that individuals have no rights or duties beyond its terms even in the area of conventional morality; the fact that the social rule does not extend to some case, like the case of babies in church, means rather that someone asserting a duty in that case must rely on arguments that go beyond a simple appeal to practice.

If the social rule theory is revised in this way it no longer supports Hart's thesis of a social rule of recognition in the way that the original theory I described does. If judges may have a duty to decide a case in a particular way, in spite of the fact that no social rule imposes that duty, then Hart's claim that social practice accounts for all judicial duty is lost. I should like to point out, however, the weakness that remains in even this revised form of the social rule theory. It does not conform with our moral practice to say even that a social rule stipulates the minimum level of rights and duties. It is generally recognized, even as a feature of conventional morality, that practices that are pointless, or inconsistent in principle with other requirements of morality, do not impose duties, though of course, when a social rule exists, only a small minority will think that this provision in fact applies. When a social rule existed, for example, that men extend certain formal courtesies to women, most people said that women had a right to them; but someone of either sex who thought these courtesies an insult would not agree.

This fact about conventional morality, which the social rule theory ignores, is of great importance because it points toward a better understanding of the connection between social practice and normative judgments than that theory provides. It is true that normative judgments often assume a social practice as an essential part of the case for that judgment; this is the hallmark, as I said, of conventional morality. But the social rule theory misconceives the connection. It believes that the social practice *constitutes* a rule which the normative judgment accepts; in fact the social practice helps to *justify* a rule which the normative judgment states. The fact that a practice of removing hats in church exists justifies asserting a normative rule to that effect – not because the practice constitutes a rule which the normative judgment describes and endorses, but because the practice creates ways of giving offense and gives rise to expectations of the sort that are good grounds for asserting a duty to take off one's hat in church or for asserting a normative rule that one must.

The social rule theory fails because it insists that a practice must somehow have the same *content* as the rule that individuals assert in its name. But if we suppose simply that a practice may justify a rule, then while the rule so justified may have the same content as the practice, it may not; it may fall short of, or go beyond it. If we look at the relationship between social practice and normative claims in this way, then we can account, smoothly, for what the social rule theory labors to explain. If someone finds a social practice pointless, or silly, or insulting, he may believe that it does not even in principle justify asserting any duties or normative rules of conduct, and in that case he will say, not that it imposes a duty upon him which he rejects, but that, in spite of what others think, it imposes no duty at all.

If a community has a particular practice, moreover, like the no-hat-in-church practice, then it will be likely, rather than surprising, that members will assert different normative rules, each allegedly justified by that practice. They will disagree about whether babies must wear bonnets because they will differ about whether, all things considered, the fact of the practice justifies asserting that duty. Some may think that it does because they think that the practice as a whole establishes a form of insult or disrespect that can be committed vicariously by an infant's parents. Others may disagree, for a variety of reasons. It is true that they will frame their dispute, even in this trivial case, as a dispute over what 'the rule' about hats in church requires. But the reference is not to the rule that is constituted by common behavior, that is, a social rule, but the rule that is justified by common behavior, that is, a normative rule. They dispute precisely about what *that* rule is.

It may be that judicial duty is a case of conventional morality. It does not follow that some social rule states the limit, or even the threshold, of judicial duty. When judges cite the rule that they must follow the legislature, for example, they may be appealing to a normative rule that some social practice justifies, and they may disagree about the precise content of that normative rule in a way that does not represent merely a disagreement about the facts of other judges' behavior. The positivist may be right, but he must make out his case without the short-cut that the social rule theory tries to provide.

2. DO I REALLY DISAGREE WITH HART?

It has been suggested that my disagreement with positivism, at least in the form presented by Hart, is not really so broad as I have claimed. Perhaps I have shown that a sensible account of law would have a place for principles as well as rules. But nothing in Hart's theory seems to deny this. It is true that he speaks only about rules, but he does not define 'rule' in the limited way in which I define that term in Chapter 2, and he might therefore be understood, when he speaks of rules, to include principles as well as rules in a narrow sense. Perhaps I have shown that any fundamental test for law, if it is to include principles as well as rules of law, must be more complex than the examples Hart offers as specimens of a rule of recognition. But Hart says that the rule of recognition may be complex; that it may be composed, indeed, of several criteria arranged in a hierarchy. His simple examples – like the rule that what the Queen in Parliament enacts is law – are intended to be merely examples.

Where then does the disagreement lie? It it true that Chapter 2 appears to deny Hart's thesis, that every legal system has a fundamental test for law in the form of a rule of recognition. But, as Professor Sartorius points out, I cannot really mean that a legal system can exist which has no fundamental test for identifying rules and principles of law.[1] It was part of my argument that some principles must be considered as law, and therefore figure in judicial argument, while others may not. But if that is true, then there must be some sort of test that can be used to distinguish the two. So my statement that no such fundamental rule exists must be understood as meaning merely that the fundamental test must be too complex to state in a simple rule. But since Hart never argued that the fundamental rule must be a simple one, this point of difference is limited.

So runs the first of the objections I want to consider. When I wrote Chapter 2 I thought that the positivist's thesis, that a fundamental test for law exists in every legal system, was sufficiently clear as to need very little elaboration. I thought that any ambiguities could be resolved by taking Professor Hart's careful formulation of that thesis as an example. The objection I have just described convinces me that I was wrong in this, and I shall now try to repair the damage by stating more clearly what I take the positivists' claim to be, and how that claim differs from claims that I myself would want to make.

I shall start by setting out three different theses, each of which has something to do with the idea of a fundamental test for law. In describing these different theses, I shall make use of the distinction I made in the last section, the distinction between describing social behavior through the concept of a social rule, on the one hand, and asserting a normative position through the concept of a normative rule, on the other. (i) The first thesis holds that, in every nation which has a developed legal system, some *social* rule or set of social rules exists within the community of its judges and legal officials, which rules settle

---

[1] Sartorius, *op. cit.* at 155.

the limits of the judge's duty to recognize any other rule or principle as law. The thesis would hold for England, for example, if English judges as a group recognized a duty to take into account, when determining legal rights and obligations, only rules or principles enacted by Parliament, or laid down in judicial decisions, or established by long standing custom, and recognized, as a group, that they had no duty to take into account anything else. Hart advances this first thesis; in fact, his theory that a social rule of recognition exists in every legal system may be regarded as one of the most important contributions he has made to the positivist tradition. (ii) The second thesis holds that in every legal system some particular *normative* rule or principle, or complex set of these, is the proper standard for judges to use in identifying more particular rules or principles of law. Someone who accepts this second thesis might believe, for example, that in England judges have a duty to recognize only statutes, precedents and clear customs as law, whether or not they actually reach their decisions in that fashion. (iii) The third thesis holds that in each legal system most of the judges accept *some* normative rule or theory governing their duty to count other standards as legal standards. This thesis argues that if one studies the patterns of decisions of the various English judges, for example, one would find that each judge, more or less consciously, follows a particular rule designating certain exclusive sources of law, or a more complex theory stipulating how law is to be found. It would not follow from this thesis, though it might also be true, that the bulk of the English judges follow the *same* rule or theory; if they did, then the first thesis would also be true of England, at least, but not otherwise.

The disagreement between Hart and myself is about the first of these three theses. He proposes that thesis, and I deny it. The issue is important; upon it hinges the orthodox idea that legal standards can be distinguished in principle and as a group from moral or political standards. If the first thesis is right, then in every legal system some commonly-accepted test does exist for law, in the shape of a social rule, and this is enough to distinguish legal from moral rules and principles. But if the first thesis is false, then no such test exists.

It is not enough that some version of the second or third thesis might be sound. Suppose that I myself accept a normative theory of law of the sort contemplated by the second thesis. My theory, if it is not shared by everyone else, will include controversial provisions; it might include, for example, a controversial theory of precedent that argues that courts must give more weight to recent than to out-of-date precedents. I would then be required to support the claim that my view of precedent correctly states a judge's duty, and I could do so only by deploying a further theory about the point or value of the institution of precedent. My case for this further theory would no doubt depend on controversial principles of political morality, principles, for example, about the proper place of a judiciary in a democracy. It is just this sort of dependence that positivism is most concerned to deny.

The distinctions I have drawn between these three different theses show why Sartorius's objection misses the point. He thinks that if I say that judges have a duty to use some principles but not others, or to assign a given weight to one principle but not a greater weight, it follows that I myself am committed to the idea that there is a fundamental test for law. It does follow that I am committed to some version of the second thesis, that is, that I myself think that a persuasive case can be made in support of one theory rather than some other about how judges must decide hard cases. But it does not follow that I must accept the first thesis, that some social rule exists among judges that settles that issue. That is Hart's thesis, but it is not, nor need it be, mine.

However, one feature of Hart's theory suggests that I attribute to him too rigid a theory. He is careful to say that a social rule of recognition might be uncertain in some cases, so that it does not settle every issue that might arise about what counts as law.[1] It is enough, for such a rule to exist, that it settles most such issues. He gives this example. There is no doubt, he says, that it is at least part of the rule of recognition of England that whatever Parliament enacts is law. It is nevertheless uncertain whether Parliament now has the power to bind future Parliaments, as it might try to do if, for example, it adopted a particular rule of law, and then entrenched both that rule and the entrenching provision by providing that neither could be repealed except by a two-thirds majority. If this happened, judges might well be divided as to the legal consequences of an attempt by a future Parliament to repeal these rules by a simple majority. If judges were so divided, this would show that the rule of recognition is uncertain on this point, and the issue could only then be settled, and the rule of recognition clarified, if some court made the decision one way or the other, and turned out to have the political power to make its decision stick.

So Hart, it might seem, is not committed to the notion that in every legal system some social rule exists that settles all issues of which standards count as law. It is enough to establish the first thesis, he might say, that a social rule is treated as *governing* all decisions of law, even though it is not so precise that what it requires is never open to dispute. He might then add that when judges are in fact divided (as they would be about entrenchment, or, to continue my own example, about the force

[1] Hart, *op. cit.* at 144.

to be given to older precedents) they reveal an area of uncertainty within a social rule that is for the most part certain.

But Hart's qualification, that the rule of recognition may be uncertain at particular points, does not simply add flexibility and sophistication to his theory. On the contrary, it undermines it, for reasons I tried to make plain in the last section. It simply does not fit the concept of a social rule, as Hart uses that concept, to say that a social rule may be uncertain in the sense that Hart now has in mind. If judges are in fact divided about what they must do if a subsequent Parliament tries to repeal an entrenched rule, then it is not uncertain whether any social rule governs that decision; on the contrary, it is certain that none does. The example simply shows that the statement, that in England a social rule exists among judges to the effect that whatever Parliament enacts is law, is strictly speaking inaccurate, though it might be accurate enough for most purposes.

A careful statement of the position, using the concept of a social rule, would have to be made along these lines. A social rule exists among judges to the effect that whatever Parliament enacts, short of a law purporting to bind future Parliaments, is law. No social rule exists on the issue of whether Parliament can bind future Parliaments; on this issue judges are divided. Some think that it can, and that they therefore have a duty not to recognize any purported repeal of an entrenched rule as law. Others think that it cannot and that they therefore have a duty to recognize repealing legislation as law. (This simple formulation ignores the more complex positions that different judges might in fact take.)

But, of course, putting the matter that way offers a counter-example to the claim of the first thesis, that some social rule always exists that stipulates necessary and sufficient conditions for what judges must recognize as law. If such disagreements among judges were limited only to extraordinary and rare cases, like entrenchment clauses, then such counter-examples would be few, and offer no real impediment to the claim. But if, as I suppose, disagreements among judges of this sort are very frequent, and indeed can be found whenever appellant tribunals attempt to decide difficult or controversial cases, then the general weakness this argument discloses is fatal.

It might now be said that I take too literally Hart's statement that the rule of recognition is a social rule constituted by the common behavior of the members of a particular community, like judges and other officials. He might want to revise that strict concept in the manner I suggested in the last section, to say that a rule of recognition exists as a social rule when judges accept a particular verbal formulation of their duty, like the verbal formulation, 'Whatever Parliament enacts is law'. If so, then

Hart may say that a social rule of recognition exists, but is nevertheless uncertain, when members of the community disagree about the proper application of that verbal formulation to particular cases. So the rule of recognition, that whatever Parliament does is law, exists as a social fact, but it is uncertain to the degree that judges disagree over particular cases like the case of entrenched statutes.

But this revision of the concept, as I said earlier, places too much weight upon accidents of language and history. The present example confirms this. It may be conventional to say that whatever Parliament enacts is law. But it is hardly possible to frame the disagreement about entrenched statutes as a disagreement about the proper interpretation of terms within that conventional formulation. No one would say that the controversy was over the meaning of 'whatever' or what force should be given to the term 'enacts'. Nor can many of the more pedestrian and numerous controversies I had in mind, like disagreement about the weight to be given to older precedents, be described as disagreements about the meaning of terms within some settled verbal formula.

Someone might take a different objection to my argument. He would remind me of the distinction I made on the last section, between statements about what judges ought to do and statements about what they have a duty to do. The first thesis does not claim that a social rule always exists that decides what judges *ought* to do in controversial cases like the entrenchment case. It claims only that a social rule stipulates what judges are *required* to do in such cases; the limit, that is, of their duties. If judges do disagree about whether to enforce a statute purporting to repeal an entrenched rule, the very fact of this disagreement, according to this objection, would show that judges have no duty either way. The matter would then be one that is left to their discretion, until some court, by the force of its decision one way or the other, encourages other judges to accept that decision as creating a duty.

If this were so, then the first thesis would be immune from the argument I made. But why should we suppose that it is so? The objection depends upon an assumption of moral philosophy. It assumes that duties cannot be controversial in principle. It assumes that if it is not plain what a judge's duty is, and not agreed what further evidence would decide the question, then he cannot have any duty, and we must only speak about what he ought to do. But that assumption is at least questionable. It does not square with the way we use the concept of duty in moral argument. The vegetarian need not accept that our duties are limited to what are uncontroversially or demonstrably our duties. It does not even square with how lawyers treat the issue of judicial duty. In the entrenchment clause dispute, for example, the one proposition that is common ground amongst the disputants is that the matter is not one in which judges are free to exercise discretion. Those who think that Parliament does have power to bind its successors believe that judges have no right to recognize a subsequent attempt at repeal. Those who believe that Parliament does not have this power believe that judges have a duty to recognize the subsequent repealer. It is true that some judges might be uncertain. But they are uncertain about their duties, not certain that they have none. Of course, if the strong version of the social rule theory were right, the assumption I described would be sound. But since that theory is false, some other support for the assumption must be found, and none, I think, can.

I hope that no one will want to say that in this sort of case judges are disagreeing about their political or moral duty as judges, but not about their legal duty. The only ground for this distinction is one which, in this context, plainly begs the question. The first thesis I distinguished is designed to explain the distinction the positivist draws between legal and other sorts of duties, and so it cannot assume that distinction. Hart himself says that the fundamental rule of recognition is a legal rule only in the sense in which the standard metre bar in Paris is one metre long;[1] if judges have a duty to enforce entrenchment clauses, that must be a legal duty in just that sense. But the question of terminology is beside the point. If judges may have a duty to apply some rule or principle in their determination of what the law requires, in spite of the fact that no social rule provides for that duty, then the first thesis is wrong, however that duty is described.

3. DOES 'INSTITUTIONAL SUPPORT' CONSTITUTE A RULE OF RECOGNITION?

In Chapter 2 I said that principles, like the principle that no man may profit from his own wrong, could not be captured by any simple rule of recognition, like the rule that what Parliament enacts is law. The positivist, I said, has this choice. He might argue that these principles are not part of the law, because the judge has no duty, but only a discretion, to take them into account. Or he might concede that they are law, and show how a more complicated social rule of recognition might be constructed that does capture such principles. Of course, the positivist might combine these strategies: he might argue that a more complex rule of recognition would capture some of the principles that judges cite, and then argue that judges have no duty to enforce any principles but these.

Dr Raz wishes to combine both strategies in that way. His principal

---

[1] Hart at 106.

reliance is on the argument, which I shall consider in the next section, that judges have a discretion, but no duty, to employ certain principles. But he believes that judges do have a duty to take into account at least some principles, and that these can be brought under something like a social rule of recognition, through the notion of what he calls a 'judicial custom'.[1] Suppose a particular principle is in fact cited by many judges over a period of time as a principle that must be taken into account. Then that very practice, he points out, would constitute a distinct social rule which would then stand, along with rules of recognition of the conventional sort that Hart had in mind, within a cluster of social rules that together provide a test for law.

But, for two reasons, this concept of judicial custom cannot carry the argument very far. First, the great bulk of the principles and policies judges cite are controversial, at least as to weight; the weight of the principle that no man may profit from his own wrong, for example, was sufficiently controversial to provoke a dissent in *Riggs v. Palmer*.[2] Second, a great many appeals to principle are appeals to principles that have not been the subject of any established judicial practice at all; this is true of several of the examples I gave from the decision in the *Henningsen* case, which included principles that had not in fact been formulated before, in anything like the same fashion, like the principle that automobile manufacturers have a special responsibility to the public.

So Raz's notion of judicial custom would not distinguish many of the principles that judges treat as principles they must take into account. We shall therefore have to consider very seriously his argument that judges in fact have no duty to give effect to principles that are not the subject of such a judicial custom. But first I want to consider a different and more complex idea of how the notion of a social rule of recognition can be adapted to capture principles as well as rules.

Professor Sartorius agrees with me in rejecting the idea that when judges appeal to principles in hard cases they do so in the exercise of some discretion.[3] If he wishes to embrace the first thesis I distinguished, therefore, he must describe a form of social rule that does in fact capture or at least provide for all these principles. This he attempts to do, and he proposes to use my own arguments against me. He admits that the development of a fundamental test for law would be extremely laborious, but he believes that it is in principle possible. He believes, further, that the nerve of any such ultimate test would lie in the concept of 'institutional support' that I developed in Chapter 2. He quotes the following passage from that chapter as authority for his own position :

[1] Raz at 852. Carrio at 25 uses the same term and concept.
[2] 115 N.Y. 506, 22 N.E. 188 (1889).
[3] Sartorius at 155.

[I]f we were challenged to back up our claim that some principle is a principle of law, we would mention any prior cases in which that principle was cited, or figured in the argument. We would also mention any statute that seemed to exemplify that principle (even better if the principle were cited in the preamble of the statute, or in the committee reports or other legislative documents that accompanied it). Unless we could find some such institutional support, we would probably fail to make out our case, and the more support we found the more weight we could claim for the principle.[1]

Of course Professor Sartorius would want to develop this doctrine of institutional support in much more detail than that. I myself should elaborate it in the following way,[2] and his article suggests that he might accept this elaboration. Suppose we were to gather together all the rules that are plainly valid rules of law in, for example, a particular American state, and add to these all the explicit rules about institutional competence that we relied upon in saying that the first set of rules were indeed valid rules of that jurisdiction. We would now have an imposing set of legal materials. We might then ask what set of principles taken together would be necessary to *justify* the adoption of the explicit rules of law and institutional rules we had listed. Suppose that each judge and lawyer of that state were to develop a 'theory of law' which described that set of principles and assigned relative weights to each (I ignore the fact that the labor of a lifetime would not be enough for a beginning). Each of them might then argue that his set of principles must count as principles of the legal system in question.

We might formulate the test for law that this story suggests in this way : a principle is a principle of law if it figures in the soundest theory of law that can be provided as a justification for the explicit substantive and institutional rules of the jurisdiction in question. Sartorius says, apparently with this sort of test in mind, that '[a]lthough perhaps it is a good way from Hart's version of positivism it is in accord with the fundamental positivist tenet as described by Dworkin, *viz.* that "the law of a community . . . can be identified and distinguished by specific criteria, by tests having to do not with . . . content but with . . . pedigree . . . ".'[3]

But some clarification is now needed. Sartorius could not mean that any particular lawyer's theory of law provides a *social* rule of recognition.

---

[1] *Id.* at 156, my Chapter 2 at 48.
[2] This elaboration is only a summary of the long argument of Chapter 4.
[3] Sartorius at 156, quoting my Chapter 2 at 17.

If I had developed a theory of law for a particular jurisdiction I might well hold that theory as a normative theory of judicial duty, in the spirit of the *second* thesis I distinguished. If most judges in the jurisdiction each had such a theory, then the *third* thesis would hold, for that jurisdiction. But each judge's theory would be more or less different from that of the next judge. Some of the principles he advanced would be different, and some of those that are the same would differ in weight. These differences insure that no one lawyer's theory can itself be taken as a complex social rule of the sort required by the *first* thesis.

So Sartorius must say, not that any particular lawyer's theory of law supplies a social rule of recognition, but rather that the test of institutional support *itself* is such a social rule. He might say, that is, that the social rule of recognition is just the rule that a principle must be applied as law if it is part of the soundest theory of law, and must be applied with the weight it is given by that theory. On this view, the different theories of law different lawyers would offer are simply different theories about how that social rule should be applied to particular cases.

But I do not see how one can put the matter that way, and still retain the idea that the test of institutional support provides 'specific criteria' of 'pedigree' rather than 'content'. The concept of a theory of law, in the way I described it, does not suppose that principles and policies explain the settled rules in the way in which a legal historian might explain them, by identifying the motives of those who adopted these rules, or by calling attention to the pressure groups which influenced their enactments. If a theory of law is to provide a basis for judicial duty, then the principles it sets out must try to *justify* the settled rules by identifying the political or moral concerns and traditions of the community which, in the opinion of the lawyer whose theory it is, do in fact support the rules. This process of justification must carry the lawyer very deep into political and moral theory, and well past the point where it would be accurate to say that any 'test' of 'pedigree' exists for deciding which of two different justifications of our political institutions is superior.

The simple example I gave earlier illustrates the point. If I disagree with another lawyer about the relative force to be given to older precedents, I will urge a theory of law that takes a view of the point of precedent that supports my case. I might say that the doctrine of precedent serves equality of treatment before the law, and that simplicity of treatment becomes less important and even perverse as the time elapsed between the two occasions increases. He might reply that the point of precedent is not so much equality as predictability of decision, which is best served by ignoring distinctions of age between precedents. Each of us will point to features of adjudication that support one view against the other. If one of us could find none, then, as I said in the quoted passage, his case would be weak. But the choice between our views will not depend only on the number of features each can find. It will depend as well on the moral case I can make for the duty of equal treatment that my argument presupposes, because the thesis that this duty justifies precedent assumes that the duty exists.

I do not mean to say that no basis can be found for choosing one theory of law over another. On the contrary, since I reject the doctrine of discretion described in the next section, I assume that persuasive arguments *can* be made to distinguish one theory as superior to another. But these arguments must include arguments on issues of normative political theory, like the nature of society's duty of equality, that go beyond the positivist's conception of the limits of the considerations relevant to deciding what the law is. The test of institutional support provides no mechanical or historical or morally neutral basis for establishing one theory of law as the soundest. Indeed, it does not allow even a single lawyer to distinguish a set of legal principles from his broader moral or political principles. His theory of law will usually include almost the full set of political and moral principles to which he subscribes; indeed it is hard to think of a single principle of social or political morality that has currency in his community and that he personally accepts, except those excluded by constitutional considerations, that would not find some place and have some weight in the elaborate scheme of justification required to justify the body of laws. So the positivist will accept the test of institutional settlement as filling the role of his ultimate test for law only at the cost of abandoning the rest of his script.

If that is so, then the consequences for legal theory are considerable. Jurisprudence poses the question : what is law? Most legal philosophers have tried to answer this question by distinguishing the *standards* that properly figure in arguments on behalf of legal rights and duties. But if no such exclusive list of standards can be made, then some other way of distinguishing legal rights and duties from other sorts of rights and duties must be found.

4. DO JUDGES HAVE TO HAVE DISCRETION?

I must now discuss, once again, the second of the two strategies for positivism that I distinguished at the beginning of the last section. This is the argument that when judges disagree about matters of principle they disagree not about what the law requires but about how their discretion should be exercised. They disagree, that is, not about where their duty to decide lies, but about how they ought to decide, all things considered, given that they have no duty to decide either way.

I tried to explain, in my original article, that this argument in fact depends upon a kind of ambiguity in the concept of discretion. We use that concept, in discussions about duty, in three different ways. First, we say that a man has discretion if his duty is defined by standards that reasonable men can interpret in different ways, as a sergeant has discretion if he is told to take the five most experienced men on patrol. Second, we say that a man has discretion if his decision is final, in the sense that no higher authority may review and set aside that decision, as when the decision whether a player is offside is left to the discretion of the linesman. Third, we say that a man has discretion when some set of standards which impose duties upon him do not in fact purport to impose any duty as to a particular decision, as when a clause in a lease gives the tenant the option in his discretion to renew.

It is plain that if no social rule unambiguously requires a particular legal decision, and the profession is split on what decision is in fact required, then judges will have discretion in the first of these senses, because they will have to exercise initiative and judgment beyond the application of a settled rule. It is also plain, if these judges form the highest court of appeal, that they will have discretion in the second sense. But, unless we accept the strongest form of the social rule theory, that duties and responsibilities can be generated only by social rules, it does not follow that these judges have discretion in the third sense. A judge may have discretion in both the first and second senses, and nevertheless properly regard his decision as raising an issue of what his duty as a judge is, an issue which he must decide by reflecting on what is required of him by the varying considerations that he believes are pertinent. If so, then this judge does not have discretion in the third sense, which is the sense a positivist needs to establish if he is to show that judicial duty is defined exclusively by an ultimate social rule or set of social rules.

Raz was not persuaded by my argument.[1] He repeats the distinction that I drew among these three senses of discretion, but having repeated that distinction he ignores it. He apparently thinks that I meant to argue as follows. (i) Judges have no discretion with respect to a decision when they all agree that a particular set of principles is decisive. (ii) That is sometimes the case even when no rule of law settles the case. (iii) Therefore it is never the case that judges have discretion when no rule settles the case.

That is a fallacious argument; fortunately it is not mine. Judges are

[1] Raz at 843 ff. See MacCallum, *loc. cit.*

sometimes united on a set of principles. But even when they are divided on principles they sometimes treat the issue as one of judicial responsibility, that is, as one that raises the question of what, as judges, they have a duty to do. In such a case they have discretion in the first sense I distinguished, but that is irrelevant. They nevertheless do not believe they have discretion in the third sense, which is the sense that counts.

Why should Raz ignore the distinctions I drew? He supposes that there are features of any legal system that have this consequence: If judges have discretion in the first sense, because no social rule directly or indirectly dictates the result they must reach, then they must also have discretion in the third sense, so that their decision cannot be a matter of judicial duty. Judges may be mistaken in this: they may inappropriately use the language of duty. But we must not, as Raz says, perpetuate mistakes just because they are popular. Still, it is necessary to show that they are mistakes, and Raz does not. What arguments might he make?

Raz's inclination, to convert discretion in the first into discretion in the third sense, is extraordinarily common among legal philosophers.[1] We must try to diagnose its source. When a judge faces a difficult decision he must suppose, before beginning his research, that there are in principle these three possibilities. The set of standards that he must take into account, taken together, require him to decide for the plaintiff, or require him to decide for the defendant, or require neither decision but permit either one. He must also recognize that he might be to some degree uncertain which of these three possibilities in fact holds; in that case he must decide on the basis of the case that seems to him the strongest. But that uncertainty might apply just as much to the third possibility as to the other two; the law might grant him a discretion, in the third sense, to reach either decision, but whether it does is a matter of what the legal materials, taken together, come to, and one may be as uncertain whether the materials justify *that* conclusion as either of the other two.

Raz apparently thinks that if it is uncertain whether the first or the second possibility is realized, then it follows that the third is. He thinks, that is, that if a judge is uncertain whether to decide for the plaintiff or defendant it follows that he should be certain that he has discretion to decide for either. I can think of only two arguments to support that extraordinary conclusion.

The first depends on the assumption of moral philosophy I described earlier, that duties cannot be controversial in principle. Raz makes that assumption, because he argues from the fact that judges may disagree

---

[1] It is displayed in all the articles referred to in note 6.

about principles, and particularly about their weight, to the conclusion that judges must have discretion in the sense I deny. That is a non sequitur unless something like that assumption holds, but we have no reason to suppose that it does, as I said, once we reject the strong version of the social rule theory.

The second argument relies on a different assumption, namely that every legal system contains a rule of decision which provides affirmatively that judges have discretion in hard cases. Some legal systems may employ such a rule. But the English and American systems do not. They contain no such explicit rule, nor as Raz agrees, does judicial behavior show that any such rule is recognized implicitly.

On the contrary, for us the proposition that judges have discretion in the third sense on some issue or other is a proposition that must be established affirmatively, on the balance of argument, and not simply by default. Sometimes judges do reach that conclusion; for example, when passing sentences under criminal statutes that provide a maximum and minimum penalty, or when framing equitable relief under a general equity jurisdiction. In such cases judges believe that no one has a right to any particular decision; they identify their task as selecting the decision that is best on the whole, all things considered, and here they talk not about what they must do but about what they should do. In most hard cases, however, judges take the different posture I described. They frame their disagreement as a disagreement about what standards they are forbidden or obliged to take into account, or what relative weights they are obliged to attribute to these, on the basis of arguments like the arguments I described in the last section illustrating the theory of institutional support. In such cases, some judges argue for the first possibility I mentioned, others for the second and others are undecided; but all exclude the third. There is plainly not even the beginnings of a social rule that converts the discretion that requires judgment into the discretion that excludes duty.

5. ARE RULES REALLY DIFFERENT FROM PRINCIPLES?

In Chapter 2 I distinguished rules from principles by distinguishing the different force that the two types of standards have in argument. My purpose was twofold: first, to call attention to a distinction which I thought was of importance in understanding how lawyers reason, and second, to call attention to the fact that some of the standards to which judges and lawyers appeal pose special problems for positivism, because these standards cannot be captured under a fundamental test for law like Hart's rule of recognition. These two purposes were distinct; even if the particular logical distinction that I claim between rules and principles can be shown to be spurious, it might still be that standards like those I mentioned, however identified, and whether or not classified as rules, cannot be captured by any such test. If I do not succeed in establishing my distinction between rules and principles, therefore, it by no means follows that the general argument I make against legal positivism is undermined.

Nevertheless, I do continue to think that the distinction that I drew between rules and principles is both genuine and important, and I should want to defend it. I do not mean, of course, that it is wrong to draw other sorts of distinctions among types of legal standards, or even that it is wrong or confusing to use the terms 'rule' and 'principle' to make these distinctions rather than the one I drew.

Raz's chief objection to my distinction might be put this way.[1] I argued that principles, like those I mentioned, conflict and interact with one another, so that each principle that is relevant to a particular legal problem provides a reason arguing in favor of, but does not stipulate, a particular solution. The man who must decide the problem is therefore required to assess all of the competing and conflicting principles that bear upon it, and to make a resolution of these principles rather than identifying one among others as 'valid'. Raz wishes to argue that it is not simply principles that properly conflict with one another in this way, but rules as well, and he believes that this fact undermines the distinction that I have drawn. He offers examples from both moral and legal argument. I shall consider each set of examples in turn.

Raz has it in mind that a man might accept, as moral rules for the guidance of his conduct, both the rule that one must never tell a lie and the rule that one must always keep his promises. He points out that on particular occasions these two rules might conflict, and require the man who accepts them both to choose between them on the basis of which under the circumstances has the greater weight, or importance, or on some other basis. He concludes that moral rules follow the logic that I described for principles, that is, that they point in one direction though they are not necessarily decisive of any moral issue.

But, in the first place, though it is possible that a man might accept moral rules for the guidance of his conduct in the way this argument assumes, it is far from the case that most men who take morality seriously do anything of the sort. For most people moral argument or decision is a matter of giving reasons for or against the morality of a certain course of conduct, rather than appealing to rules set down in advance whether by social or individual decision. It is true that a moral man may find himself in difficulty when he must choose between telling a lie or break-

---

[1] It is developed in Raz at 829 ff.

ing a promise, but it does not follow that he has accepted rules which come into conflict over the issue. He might simply have recognized that telling lies and breaking promises are both in principle wrong.

Of course we might describe his predicament by saying that he was forced to choose between two moral standards, even if he would not put the matter that way himself. But in that case, if we use the distinction I made, we should say that he was forced to resolve competing principles, not rules, because that would be the more accurate way of describing his situation. He recognizes that no moral consideration is by itself of overwhelming and overriding effect, and that any reason that counts against an act may in some circumstances have to yield to a competing consideration. Any philosopher or sociologist who wants to report his moral practices in terms of a code of standards must therefore say that for him morality is a matter of principle and not of rule.

But it is possible that some man might accept a moral rule for the guidance of his conduct in the way that Raz supposes. He might say, for example, that he has undertaken a personal commitment never to tell a lie. If he can accept one flat moral rule in this way, then he can accept others, and these may conflict in the way the example supposes. It would then be wrong to say, using my distinction, that this man has simply accepted a set of principles which might in principle conflict, because that wrongly describes his attitudes towards the several commitments he believes he has made. He believes he is committed to his different standards as rules, that is, as propositions which demand a particular course of conduct in the circumstances they name.

But I did not deny, in my original article, that conflicts in rules might exist. I said that in our legal system such conflicts would be occasions of emergency, occasions requiring a decision that would alter the set of standards in some dramatic way. Indeed this description fits the present non-legal example as well. Our moral hero, if he understands at all the concepts he has been using, cannot continue to say, after he has resolved his conflict, that he has been following both of his standards as flat rules. If he still wishes to present his morality as a consistent code, he may amend one or both of them to provide for the conflict, or he may revise his attitude towards one or both so as to convert them from rules into principles. He may do neither, but rather, when a conflict appears, announce himself to be in a state of moral dilemma, and do nothing, or flip a coin or decide in some other irrational way that the legal system does not permit. In any case, the distinction between rules and principles that I drew, so far from being called into question by the behavior of this unusual man, is in fact needed to explain it.

Raz takes his other examples from law. He calls our attention, for example, to rules of criminal law like the rule that prohibits an assault; this rule, he says, is in conflict with another rule which permits assault in self defense. Here, he concludes, we have two legal rules, both of them plainly valid, which are in conflict with one another. He believes that in particular cases, when these two rules do conflict, as they will when someone commits an assault in self defense, it is necessary for the judge to weigh the rules and decide to apply the more important, which will always be the rule that permits an assault in self defense. He offers this as an example of two rules which conflict acceptably, and with no sense of emergency, in the way that I said rules do not.

But this example surely rests on a bizarre notion of what a conflict is. If a criminal code contains a general rule to the effect that no one shall be criminally liable for an act committed in self defense, then that rule does not conflict with particular rules defining particular crimes, even if these particular rules make no mention of self defense. The general rule about self defense must be read to mean that notwithstanding the particular rules of criminal law, no act shall be a crime if committed in self defense. Indeed, rules providing general defenses are often drafted in just this way, but even when they are not, they are understood in that way. But a rule that provides an exception to another rule is not in conflict with that other rule, at least not in the sense that if a man accused of assault has proved a case of self-defense, the judge is then faced with two rules pulling in opposite directions, which he has somehow to weigh against one another in reaching his decision. The two rules taken together determine the result in a manner which does not require the judge to choose between them, or to determine their relative importance.

Why should Raz suppose that two rules are in conflict even when one has plainly the force of an exception to the other? The answer lies, I think, in what he says about the individuation of laws.[1] He supposes that I would want to answer his point, that the rule prohibiting assault conflicts with the rule permitting assault in self defense, by arguing that these two rules are really part of the same rule. He says that I could do that only at the price of accepting an unacceptable theory about the individuation of laws, and, anticipating such a mistake on my part, he says that I pay insufficient attention to the general problem of the individuation of laws. In this he is too generous for it would be more accurate to say that I pay no attention to that problem at all. I did not in fact rely upon the argument that a rule and its exception really count as one rule, but neither would I be disposed to argue that they must be in reality two rules.

[1] Raz at 825 ff.

Raz is of two minds about his theory of individuation of laws. Sometimes he treats a theory of individuation as a strategy of exposition, that is to say, a theory about the most illuminating way in which the legal system of a nation may be described. Plainly, the author of a textbook on criminal law, for example, needs a strategy of exposition. He needs to distinguish the doctrine of *mens rea* from the doctrine of necessity and to distinguish both of these general doctrines from the more particular rules which they cut across as qualifications and exemptions. But of course, though some strategies of exposition might be perverse or misguided, because they describe the law in an unmanageable or unassimilable form, a great many different strategies might be more or less equally competent.

At other times, however, Raz seems to think that the problem of individuation of laws has to do, not with any strategy of explaining what the law is to students or lawyers, but with the more philosophical question of what law is. He says that it is a problem about the formal structure of the law, which is of importance to the legal philosopher, and not to the author of a text. He poses the central problem in this way : 'What is to count as one complete law?', and he adopts Bentham's elaboration of this question. 'What is a law? What the part of a law? The subject of these questions, it is to be observed, is the *logical*, the *ideal*, the *intellectual* whole, not the *physical* one . . .'[1]

This sort of question carries us very far away from techniques of legal exposition : it carries us to the point at which, as Dr. Raz insists, theories of law may rise or fall depending upon the right answer to the question, 'What is to count as one complete law?'[2] That seems to me much too far. Suppose that you have read a long book about geology, and I ask you to tell me what information it contains. You will do so in a series of propositions of fact. But now suppose I ask you first how many propositions of fact the book contains, and what theory you used in counting them. You would think me mad, not simply because the question is preposterously difficult, as if I had asked you how many separate grains of sand there were in a particular beach, or because it requires a difficult conceptual discrimination, as if I had asked you how many human beings there were in a group that included a woman in early pregnancy. You would think me mad because I had asked entirely the wrong sort of question about the material at hand. The book contains a great deal of information; propositions are ways of presenting that information, but the number of propositions used will depend on considerations independent of the content of the information,

[1] Raz at 825.
[2] Raz at 825, 827-8.

such as, for example, whether one uses the general term 'rocks' or the names of particular sorts of rocks.

In the same way, lawyers use rules and principles to report legal information, and it is wrong to suppose that any particular statement of these is canonical. This is true even of what we call statutory rules, because it is a commonplace that lawyers will often misrepresent the rules that a statute enacted if they simply repeat the language that the statute used. Two lawyers might summarize the effect of a particular statute using different words, and one might use more rules than another; they might still both be saying the same thing.

My point was not that 'the law' contains a fixed number of standards, some of which are rules and others principles. Indeed, I want to oppose the idea that 'the law' is a fixed set of standards of any sort. My point was rather that an accurate summary of the considerations lawyers must take into account, in deciding a particular issue of legal rights and duties, would include propositions having the form and force of principles, and that judges and lawyers themselves, when justifying their conclusions, often use propositions which must be understood in that way. Nothing in this, I believe, commits me to a legal ontology that assumes any particular theory of individuation.

I did say that a 'full' statement of a legal rule would include its exceptions, and that a statement of a rule that neglected the exceptions would be 'incomplete'. I would not have put the point that way had I been aware of Raz's objection. I would have made plain that an exception can be stated in the form of a distinct rule, like the rule about self-defense, as well as in the form of a revised statement of the original rule. But if I had I would also have made plain that the difference is largely a matter of exposition. The distinction between rules and principles remains untouched. I might summarize a body of law by stating a rule, like the rule that an assault is a crime, and a list of established exceptions. If my summary is complete then anyone who commits an assault is guilty of a crime unless an exception I stated applies; if he is not guilty, then either I was wrong or the law has changed. It is otherwise in the case of a principle. Suppose I say that in principle someone may not profit from his own wrong but someone does. My statement need not be corrected, or even brought up-to-date, because someone may properly profit from his own wrong, as these terms must be understood, not only when a recognized exception applies, but when special features of his case invoke some other, newly-recognized, principle or policy that makes a difference.

It is his second, ontological, mood about the individuation of laws that leads Raz to his curious view about conflicts. If one takes seriously the idea that rules of law are in certain forms 'whole' and 'complete', then one may be tempted to think that whole and complete laws are also independent of one another, so that the rule defining assault must then be taken as a flat direction that men who do certain acts be punished. But if we take the statement of a rule of law as an attempt merely to describe the legal effect of certain institutional decisions, we are not tempted to suppose any such conflict. We shall then say merely that the rule about assault, like many of the rules about crimes, is subject to an exception in cases of self-defense; we shall not then worry about whether we have described one rule or two.

Raz has another argument against my distinction, which I do not fully understand. He argues that the distinction is undercut by the fact that rules may conflict with principles; the rules of adverse possession, for example, may be thought to conflict with the principle that no man may profit from his own wrong. I do not think it illuminating to describe the relationship between these rules and that principle as one of conflict. The fact that such rules exist, is, as I said, evidence that the principle about not profiting from one's wrong is indeed a principle and not a rule. If the rules of adverse possession are some day amended, either by explicit legislative enactment or by judicial reinterpretation, then one reason might be that the principle is then recognized as being more important than it was when the rules were adopted. Nevertheless, the rules governing adverse possession may even now be said to *reflect* the principle, rather than *conflict* with it, because these rules have a different shape than they would have had if the principle had not been given any weight in the decision at all. The long length of time generally required for acquiring title by adverse possession might have been much shorter, for example, had this not been thought to conflict with the principle. Indeed, one of my reasons for drawing the distinction between rules and principles was just to show how rules often represent a kind of compromise amongst competing principles in this way, and that point may be lost or submerged if we speak too freely about rules conflicting with principles.

In any event, I cannot see how this phenomenon casts doubt upon the distinction I want to draw between rules and principles. Raz thinks that it shows that rules as well as principles have weight, because he thinks that when rules and principles conflict a decision must be made as to which of them to prefer, and this decision must be made by assigning a weight to the rule which is then set against the weight of the principle. But this description surely misrepresents the interaction between rules and principles. Suppose a court decides to overrule an established common law rule that there can be no legal liability for negligent misstatements, and appeals to a number of principles to justify this decision, including the principle that it is unjust that one man suffer

D

because of another man's wrong. The court must be understood as deciding that the set of principles calling for the overruling of the established rule, including the principle of justice just mentioned, are as a group of greater weight under the circumstances than the set of principles, including the principle of stare decisis, that call for maintaining the rule as before. The court weighs two sets of principles in deciding whether to maintain the rule; it is therefore misleading to say that the court weighs the rule itself against one or the other set of these principles. Indeed, when Raz describes the weighing of either a legal or a moral rule, he in fact talks about weighing the principles and policies that the rule serves, because that must be what he means when he speaks of the 'goal' of the rule.

I cannot reply to all the further points of detail Raz makes in his article, but I should like to comment briefly on some of them.

(1) Raz endorses a different distinction between rules and principles from the one I drew.[1] He prefers a distinction according to which rules prescribe relatively specific acts and principles relatively unspecific acts.[2] 'An act is highly unspecific,' Raz says, 'if it can be performed on different occasions by the performance of a great many heterogeneous generic acts on each occasion.'[3] But this is unsatisfactory, for he fails to specify, except by example, his criteria for the heterogeneity of 'generic acts', and his examples confuse rather than illuminate. He says that the proposition that one must keep one's promises is a rule, and he uses that proposition to illustrate his thesis that rules may conflict with one another. But the most varied sorts of acts can each, in different circumstances, be acts that keep promises, because anything that a man may do he may also promise to do. Raz says, on the other hand, that 'a law instructing the courts and all public officials to protect freedom of speech' would be a principle. But the acts that officials would be required to perform in the light of this principle would all be acts of giving orders or casting votes, and those would seem more homogeneous, and certainly not less homogeneous, than the acts they would be required to do to keep all their promises as individuals. Of course, all acts of promise-keeping are alike in being acts of promise-keeping. But all acts of protecting free speech or even promoting equality are alike in the same way. Whether a group of acts is homogeneous depends upon the description under which they are considered, and until Raz offers a theory of canonical description his distinction is one we cannot use.

---

[1] Raz at 838 ff.
[2] Raz at 838.
[3] *Ibid.*

(2) Raz is right that some statements that begin 'It is a principle of our law that . . .' should be understood as merely summaries of other standards.[4] But he is wrong in supposing that a court's reference to the principle of freedom of contract, for example in the *Henningsen* case I discussed, should be understood in that way. On the contrary, these references recognize the force of a principle in determining particular legal rights and duties, and attempt to assess and sometimes to limit that force.

(3) Raz misunderstands the point I made about the use of words like 'reasonable' in rules.[1] I did not mean that it was the function of such words to 'immunize the law' against general considerations embodied in certain principles.[2] I meant rather that it was their function to open rules to the effect of certain principles, but only certain principles. The rule that unreasonable restraints of trade are invalid remains a rule if every restraint that is unreasonable is invalid, even if other reasons for enforcing it, not mitigating its unreasonableness, might be found. The principle that Raz cites as on all fours with such a rule, that the courts generally refuse to enforce unjust bargains, is by its own terms different in that sense. This principle contemplates that unjust bargains may indeed be enforced when unusual circumstances require; for example, perhaps, when no other way to protect innocent third parties can be found. It would be otherwise if the legislature had enacted a rule that unjust bargains are void and unenforceable.

(4) Raz is right in supposing that very few large communities share a consistent code of moral beliefs, but he misunderstands those judges who appeal to community morality, whom he accuses of propagating a harmful fiction.[3] He fails to distinguish between two concepts of the moral standards of a community. That phrase may refer to a consensus of belief about a particular issue, as might be elicited by a Gallup poll. Or it may refer to moral principles that underlie the community's institutions and laws, in the sense that these principles would figure in a sound theory of law of the sort discussed earlier in this chapter. Whether a principle is a principle of the community in this sense would be a matter for argument, not report, though typically the weight of the principle, not its standing, would be at issue. The judges Raz criticizes use the concept in this second sense, though they sometimes do so in language that is consistent with the first. Raz mistakes their failure to notice a sophisticated distinc-

---

[1] Raz at 837-8.
[2] See Raz at 837.
[3] Raz at 850-1.
[4] Raz at 828-9.

tion for hypocrisy. Is it far-fetched to suppose that his own failure to notice that distinction reflects his reliance on the social rule theory? If the strong version of that theory were right then one could not argue that a community was committed to any morality of duty, by its traditions and institutions, except the morality recognized in its uniform social practices, which generally embrace little of much significance. This is, I think, the most important consequence of the social rule theory for jurisprudence, and the most compelling reason for insisting that that theory is wrong.

4

Hard Cases

Legal positivism provides a theory of hard cases. When a particular lawsuit cannot be brought under a clear rule of law, laid down by some institution in advance, then the judge has, according to that theory, a 'discretion' to decide the case either way. His opinion is written in language that seems to assure that one or the other party had a pre-existing right to win the suit, but that idea is only a fiction. In reality he has legislated new legal rights, and then applied them retrospectively to the case at hand. In the last two chapters I argued that this theory of adjudication is wholly inadequate; in this chapter I shall describe and defend a better theory.

I shall argue that even when no settled rule disposes of the case, one party may nevertheless have a right to win. It remains the judge's duty, even in hard cases, to discover what the rights of the parties are, not to invent new rights retrospectively. I should say at once, however, that it is no part of this theory that any mechanical procedure exists for demonstrating what the rights of parties are in hard cases. On the contrary, the argument supposes that reasonable lawyers and judges will often disagree about legal rights, just as citizens and statesmen disagree about political rights. This chapter describes the questions that judges and lawyers must put to themselves, but it does not guarantee that they will all give these questions the same answer.

Some readers may object that, if no procedure exists, even in principle, for demonstrating what legal rights the parties have in hard cases, it follows that they have none. That objection presupposes a controversial thesis of general philosophy, which is that no proposition can be true unless it can, at least in principle, be demonstrated to be true. There is no reason to accept that thesis as part of a general theory of truth, and good reason to reject its specific application to propositions about legal rights.

2. THE RIGHTS THESIS

A. Principles and policies

Theories of adjudication have become more sophisticated, but the most popular theories still put judging in the shade of legislation. The main outlines of this story are familiar. Judges should apply the law that other institutions have made; they should not make new law. That is the ideal, but for different reasons it cannot be realized fully in practice. Statutes and common law rules are often vague and must be interpreted before they can be applied to novel cases. Some cases, moreover, raise issues so novel that they cannot be decided even by stretching or reinterpreting existing rules. So judges must sometimes make new law, either covertly or explicitly. But when they do, they should act as deputy to the appropriate legislature, enacting the law that they suppose the legislature would enact if seized of the problem.

That is perfectly familiar, but there is buried in this common story a further level of subordination not always noticed. When judges make law, so the expectation runs, they will act not only as deputy to the legislature but as a deputy legislature. They will make law in response to evidence and arguments of the same character as would move the superior institution if it were acting on its own. This is a deeper level of subordination, because it makes any understanding of what judges do in hard cases parasitic on a prior understanding of what legislators do all the time. This deeper subordination is thus conceptual as well as political.

In fact, however, judges neither should be nor are deputy legislators, and the familiar assumption, that when they go beyond political decisions already made by someone else they are legislating, is misleading. It misses the importance of a fundamental distinction within political theory, which I shall now introduce in a crude form. This is the distinction between arguments of principle on the one hand and arguments of policy on the other.[1]

Arguments of policy justify a political decision by showing that the decision advances or protects some collective goal of the community as a whole. The argument in favor of a subsidy for aircraft manufacturers, that the subsidy will protect national defense, is an argument of policy. Arguments of principle justify a political decision by showing that the decision respects or secures some individual or group right. The argument in favor of anti-discrimination statutes, that a minority has a right to equal respect and concern, is an argument of principle. These two

---

[1] I discussed the distinction between principles and policies in Chapter 2. The more elaborate formulation in this chapter is an improvement; among other virtues it prevents the collapse of the distinction under the (artificial) assumptions described in the earlier article.

sorts of argument do not exhaust political argument. Sometimes, for example, a political decision, like the decision to allow extra income tax exemptions for the blind, may be defended as an act of public generosity or virtue rather than on grounds of either policy or principle. But principle and policy are the major grounds of political justification.

The justification of a legislative program of any complexity will ordinarily require both sorts of argument. Even a program that is chiefly a matter of policy, like a subsidy program for important industries, may require strands of principle to justify its particular design. It may be, for example, that the program provides equal subsidies for manufacturers of different capabilities, on the assumption that weaker aircraft manufacturers have some right not to be driven out of business by government intervention, even though the industry would be more efficient without them. On the other hand, a program that depends chiefly on principle, like an antidiscrimination program, may reflect a sense that rights are not absolute and do not hold when the consequences for policy are very serious. The program may provide, for example, that fair employment practice rules do not apply when they might prove especially disruptive or dangerous. In the subsidy case we might say that the rights conferred are generated by policy and qualified by principle; in the antidiscrimination case they are generated by principle and qualified by policy.

It is plainly competent for the legislature to pursue arguments of policy and to adopt programs that are generated by such arguments. If courts are deputy legislatures, then it must be competent for them to do the same. Of course, unoriginal judicial decisions that merely enforce the clear terms of some plainly valid statute are always justified on arguments of principle, even if the statute itself was generated by policy. Suppose an aircraft manufacturer sues to recover the subsidy that the statute provides. He argues his right to the subsidy; his argument is an argument of principle. He does not argue that the national defense would be improved by subsidizing him; he might even concede that the statute was wrong on policy grounds when it was adopted, or that it should have been repealed, on policy grounds, long ago. His right to a subsidy no longer depends on any argument of policy because the statute made it a matter of principle.

But if the case at hand is a hard case, when no settled rule dictates a decision either way, then it might seem that a proper decision could be generated by either policy or principle. Consider, for example, the problem of the recent *Spartan Steel* case.[1] The defendant's employees had broken an electrical cable belonging to a power company that supplied power to the plaintiff, and the plaintiff's factory was shut down

[1] *Spartan Steel & Alloys Ltd. v. Martin & Co.*, [1973] 1 Q.B. 27.

while the cable was repaired. The court had to decide whether to allow the plaintiff recovery for economic loss following negligent damage to someone else's property. It might have proceeded to its decision by asking either whether a firm in the position of the plaintiff had a right to a recovery, which is a matter of principle, or whether it would be economically wise to distribute liability for accidents in the way the plaintiff suggested, which is a matter of policy.

If judges are deputy legislators, then the court should be prepared to follow the latter argument as well as the former, and decide in favor of the plaintiff if that argument recommends. That is, I suppose, what is meant by the popular idea that a court must be free to decide a novel case like *Spartan Steel* on policy grounds; and indeed Lord Denning described his own opinion in that case in just that way.[1] I do not suppose he meant to distinguish an argument of principle from an argument of policy in the technical way I have, but he in any event did not mean to rule out an argument of policy in that technical sense.

I propose, nevertheless, the thesis that judicial decisions in civil cases, even in hard cases like *Spartan Steel*, characteristically are and should be generated by principle not policy. That thesis plainly needs much elaboration, but we may notice that certain arguments of political theory and jurisprudence support the thesis even in its abstract form. These arguments are not decisive, but they are sufficiently powerful to suggest the importance of the thesis, and to justify the attention that will be needed for a more careful formulation.

B. Principles and democracy

The familiar story, that adjudication must be subordinated to legislation, is supported by two objections to judicial originality. The first argues that a community should be governed by men and women who are elected by and responsible to the majority. Since judges are, for the most part, not elected, and since they are not, in practice, responsible to the electorate in the way legislators are, it seems to compromise that proposition when judges make law. The second argues that if a judge makes new law and applies it retroactively in the case before him, then the losing party will be punished, not because he violated some duty he had, but rather a new duty created after the event.

These two arguments combine to support the traditional ideal that adjudication should be as unoriginal as possible. But they offer much more powerful objections to judicial decisions generated by policy than to those generated by principle. The first objection, that law should be made by elected and responsible officials, seems unexceptionable when

[1] *Ibid.* 36.

we think of law as policy; that is, as a compromise among individual goals and purposes in search of the welfare of the community as a whole. It is far from clear that interpersonal comparisons of utility or preference, through which such compromises might be made objectively, make sense even in theory; but in any case no proper calculus is available in practice. Policy decisions must therefore be made through the operation of some political process designed to produce an accurate expression of the different interests that should be taken into account. The political system of representative democracy may work only indifferently in this respect, but it works better than a system that allows nonelected judges, who have no mail bag or lobbyists or pressure groups, to compromise competing interests in their chambers.

The second objection is also persuasive against a decision generated by policy. We all agree that it would be wrong to sacrifice the rights of an innocent man in the name of some new duty created after the event; it does, therefore, seem wrong to take property from one individual and hand it to another in order just to improve overall economic efficiency. But that is the form of the policy argument that would be necessary to justify a decision in *Spartan Steel*. If the plaintiff had no right to the recovery and the defendant no duty to offer it, the court could be justified in taking the defendant's property for the plaintiff only in the interest of wise economic policy.

But suppose, on the other hand, that a judge successfully justifies a decision in a hard case, like *Spartan Steel*, on grounds not of policy but of principle. Suppose, that is, that he is able to show that the plaintiff has a *right* to recover its damages. The two arguments just described would offer much less of an objection to the decision. The first is less relevant when a court judges principle, because an argument of principle does not often rest on assumptions about the nature and intensity of the different demands and concerns distributed throughout the community. On the contrary, an argument of principle fixes on some interest presented by the proponent of the right it describes, an interest alleged to be of such a character as to make irrelevant the fine discriminations of any argument of policy that might oppose it. A judge who is insulated from the demands of the political majority whose interests the right would trump is, therefore, in a better position to evaluate the argument.

The second objection to judicial originality has no force against an argument of principle. If the plaintiff has a right against the defendant, then the defendant has a corresponding duty, and it is that duty, not some new duty created in court, that justifies the award against him. Even if the duty has not been imposed upon him by explicit prior legislation, there is, but for one difference, no more injustice in enforcing the duty than if it had been.

The difference is, of course, that if the duty had been created by statute the defendant would have been put on much more explicit notice of that duty, and might more reasonably have been expected to arrange his affairs so as to provide for its consequences. But an argument of principle makes us look upon the defendant's claim, that it is unjust to take him by surprise, in a new light. If the plaintiff does indeed have a right to a judicial decision in his favor, then he is entitled to rely upon that right. If it is obvious and uncontroversial that he has the right, the defendant is in no position to claim unfair surprise just because the right arose in some way other than by publication in a statute. If, on the other hand, the plaintiff's claim is doubtful, then the court must, to some extent, surprise one or another of the parties; and if the court decides that on balance the plaintiff's argument is stronger, then it will also decide that the plaintiff was, on balance, more justified in his expectations. The court may, of course, be mistaken in this conclusion; but that possibility is not a consequence of the originality of its argument, for there is no reason to suppose that a court hampered by the requirement that its decisions be unoriginal will make fewer mistakes of principle than a court that is not.

C. Jurisprudence

We have, therefore, in these political considerations, a strong reason to consider more carefully whether judicial arguments cannot be understood, even in hard cases, as arguments generated by principle. We have an additional reason in a familiar problem of jurisprudence. Lawyers believe that when judges make new law their decisions are constrained by legal traditions but are nevertheless personal and original. Novel decisions, it is said, reflect a judge's own political morality, but also reflect the morality that is embedded in the traditions of the common law, which might well be different. This is, of course, only law school rhetoric, but it nevertheless poses the problem of explaining how these different contributions to the decision of a hard case are to be identified and reconciled.

One popular solution relies on a spatial image; it says that the traditions of the common law contract the area of a judge's discretion to rely upon his personal morality, but do not entirely eliminate that area. But this answer is unsatisfactory on two grounds. First, it does not elucidate what is at best a provocative metaphor, which is that some morality is embedded in a mass of particular decisions other judges have reached in the past. Second, it suggests a plainly inadequate phenomenological account of the judicial decision. Judges do not decide hard cases in two stages, first checking to see where the institutional constraints end, and then setting the books aside to stride off on their own. The institutional constraints they sense are pervasive and endure to the decision itself. We therefore need an account of the interaction of personal and institutional morality that is less metaphorical and explains more successfully that pervasive interaction.

The rights thesis, that judicial decisions enforce existing political rights, suggests an explanation that is more successful on both counts. If the thesis holds, then institutional history acts not as a constraint on the political judgment of judges but as an ingredient of that judgment, because institutional history is part of the background that any plausible judgment about the rights of an individual must accommodate. Political rights are creatures of both history and morality : what an individual is entitled to have, in civil society, depends upon both the practice and the justice of its political institutions. So the supposed tension between judicial originality and institutional history is dissolved : judges must make fresh judgments about the rights of the parties who come before them, but these political rights reflect, rather than oppose, political decisions of the past. When a judge chooses between the rule established in precedent and some new rule thought to be fairer, he does not choose between history and justice. He rather makes a judgment that requires some compromise between considerations that ordinarily combine in any calculation of political right, but here compete.

The rights thesis therefore provides a more satisfactory explanation of how judges use precedent in hard cases than the explanation provided by any theory that gives a more prominent place to policy. Judges, like all political officials, are subject to the doctrine of political responsibility. This doctrine states, in its most general form, that political officials must make only such political decisions as they can justify within a political theory that also justifies the other decisions they propose to make. The doctrine seems innocuous in this general form; but it does, even in this form, condemn a style of political administration that might be called, following Rawls, intuitionistic.[1] It condemns the practice of making decisions that seem right in isolation, but cannot be brought within some comprehensive theory of general principles and policies that is consistent with other decisions also thought right. Suppose a Congressman votes to prohibit abortion, on the ground that human life in any form is sacred, but then votes to permit the parents of babies born deformed to withhold medical treatment that will keep such babies alive. He might say that he feels that there is some difference, but the principle of responsibility, strictly applied, will not allow him these two votes unless he can in corporate the difference within some general political theory he sincerely holds.

[1] See Chapter 10.

The doctrine demands, we might say, articulate consistency. But this demand is relatively weak when policies are in play. Policies are aggregative in their influence on political decisions and it need not be part of a responsible strategy for reaching a collective goal that individuals be treated alike. It does not follow from the doctrine of responsibility, therefore, that if the legislature awards a subsidy to one aircraft manufacturer one month it must award a subsidy to another manufacturer the next. In the case of principles, however, the doctrine insists on distributional consistency from one case to the next, because it does not allow for the idea of a strategy that may be better served by unequal distribution of the benefit in question. If an official, for example, believes that sexual liberty of some sort is a right of individuals, then he must protect that liberty in a way that distributes the benefit reasonably equally over the class of those whom he supposes to have the right. If he allows one couple to use contraceptives on the ground that this right would otherwise be invaded, then he must, so long as he does not recant that earlier decision, allow the next couple the same liberty. He cannot say that the first decision gave the community just the amount of sexual liberty it needed, so that no more is required at the time of the second.

Judicial decisions are political decisions, at least in the broad sense that attracts the doctrine of political responsibility. If the rights thesis holds, then the distinction just made would account, at least in a very general way, for the special concern that judges show for both precedents and hypothetical examples. An argument of principle can supply a justification for a particular decision, under the doctrine of responsibility, only if the principle cited can be shown to be consistent with earlier decisions not recanted, and with decisions that the institution is prepared to make in the hypothetical circumstances. That is hardly surprising, but the argument would not hold if judges based their decisions on arguments of policy. They would be free to say that some policy might be adequately served by serving it in the case at bar, providing, for example, just the right subsidy to some troubled industry, so that neither earlier decisions nor hypothetical future decisions need be understood as serving the same policy.

Consistency here, of course, means consistency in the application of the principle relied upon, not merely in the application of the particular rule announced in the name of that principle. If, for example, the principle that no one has the duty to make good remote or unexpected losses flowing from his negligence is relied upon to justify a decision for the defendant in *Spartan Steel*, then it must be shown that the rule laid down in other cases, which allows recovery for negligent misstatements, is consistent with that principle; not merely that the rule about negligent misstatement is a different rule from the rule in *Spartan Steel*.

D. *Three problems*

We therefore find, in these arguments of political theory and jurisprudence, some support for the rights thesis in its abstract form. Any further defense, however, must await a more precise statement. The thesis requires development in three directions. It relies, first, on a general distinction between individual rights and social goals, and that distinction must be stated with more clarity than is provided simply by examples. The distinction must be stated, moreover, so as to respond to the following problem. When politicians appeal to individual rights, they have in mind grand propositions about very abstract and fundamental interests, like the right to freedom or equality or respect. These grand rights do not seem apposite to the decision of hard cases at law, except, perhaps, constitutional law; and even when they are apposite they seem too abstract to have much argumentative power. If the rights thesis is to succeed, it must demonstrate how the general distinction between arguments of principle and policy can be maintained between arguments of the character and detail that do figure in legal argument. In Section 3 of this chapter I shall try to show that the distinction between abstract and concrete rights, suitably elaborated, is sufficient for that purpose.

The thesis provides, second, a theory of the role of precedent and institutional history in the decision of hard cases. I summarized that theory in the last section, but it must be expanded and illustrated before it can be tested against our experience of how judges actually decide cases. It must be expanded, moreover, with an eye to the following problem. No one thinks that the law as it stands is perfectly just. Suppose that some line of precedents is in fact unjust, because it refuses to enforce, as a legal right, some political right of the citizens. Even though a judge deciding some hard case disapproves of these precedents for that reason, the doctrine of articulate consistency nevertheless requires that he allow his argument to be affected by them. It might seem that his argument cannot be an argument of principle, that is, an argument designed to establish the political rights of the parties, because the argument is corrupted, through its attention to precedent, by a false opinion about what these rights are. If the thesis is to be defended, it must be shown why this first appearance is wrong. It is not enough to say that the argument may be an argument of principle because it establishes the legal, as distinguished from the political, rights of the litigants. The rights thesis supposes that the right to win a law suit is a genuine political right, and though that right is plainly different from other forms of political rights, like the right of all citizens to be treated as equals, just noticing that difference does not explain why the former right may be altered by misguided earlier decisions. It is necessary, in order to understand that feature of legal argument, to consider the special qualities of institutional rights in general, which I consider in Section 4, and the particular qualities of legal rights, as a species of institutional rights, which I consider in Section 5.

But the explanation I give of institutional and legal rights exposes a third and different problem for the rights thesis. This explanation makes plain that judges must sometimes make judgments of political morality in order to decide what the legal rights of litigants are. The thesis may therefore be thought open, on that ground, to the first challenge to judicial originality that I mentioned earlier. It might be said that the thesis is indefensible because it cheats the majority of its right to decide questions of political morality for itself. I shall consider that challenge in Section 6.

These, then, are three problems that any full statement of the rights thesis must face. If that full statement shows these objections to the thesis misconceived, then it will show the thesis to be less radical than it might first have seemed. The thesis presents, not some novel information about what judges do, but a new way of describing what we all know they do; and the virtues of this new description are not empirical but political and philosophical.

3. RIGHTS AND GOALS

A. *Types of rights*

Arguments of principle are arguments intended to establish an individual right; arguments of policy are arguments intended to establish a collective goal. Principles are propositions that describe rights; policies are propositions that describe goals. But what are rights and goals and what is the difference? It is hard to supply any definition that does not beg the question. It seems natural to say, for example, that freedom of speech is a right, not a goal, because citizens are entitled to that freedom as a matter of political morality, and that increased munitions manufacture is a goal, not a right, because it contributes to collective welfare, but no particular manufacturer is entitled to a government contract. This does not improve our understanding, however, because the concept of entitlement uses rather than explains the concept of a right.

In this chapter I shall distinguish rights from goals by fixing on the distributional character of claims about rights, and on the force of these claims, in political argument, against competing claims of a different distributional character. I shall make, that is, a formal distinction that does not attempt to show which rights men and women actually have, or indeed that they have any at all. It rather provides a guide for discovering which rights a particular political theory supposes men and women to have. The formal distinction does suggest, of course, an approach to the more fundamental question : it suggests that we discover what rights people actually have by looking for arguments that would justify claims having the appropriate distributional character. But the distinction does not itself supply any such arguments.

I begin with the idea of a political aim as a generic political justification. A political theory takes a certain state of affairs as a political aim if, for that theory, it counts in favor of any political decision that the decision is likely to advance, or to protect, that state of affairs, and counts against the decision that it will retard or endanger it. A political right is an individuated political aim. An individual has a right to some opportunity or resource or liberty if it counts in favor of a political decision that the decision is likely to advance or protect the state of affairs in which he enjoys the right, even when no other political aim is served and some political aim is disserved thereby, and counts against that decision that it will retard or endanger that state of affairs, even when some other political aim is thereby served.[1] A goal is a nonindividuated political aim, that is, a state of affairs whose specification does not in this way call for any particular opportunity or resource or liberty for particular individuals.

Collective goals encourage trade-offs of benefits and burdens within a community in order to produce some overall benefit for the community as a whole. Economic efficiency is a collective goal : it calls for such distribution of opportunities and liabilities as will produce the greatest aggregate economic benefit defined in some way. Some conception of equality may also be taken as a collective goal; a community may aim at a distribution such that maximum wealth is no more than double minimum wealth, or, under a different conception, so that no racial or ethnic group is much worse off than other groups. Of course, any collective goal will suggest a particular distribution, given particular facts. Economic efficiency as a goal will suggest that a particular industry be subsidized in some circumstances, but taxed punitively in others. Equality as a goal will suggest immediate and complete redistribution in some circumstances, but partial and discriminatory redistribution in others. In each case distributional principles are subordinate to some conception of aggregate collective good, so that offering less of some benefit to one man can be justified simply by showing that this will lead to a greater benefit overall.

Collective goals may, but need not, be absolute. The community may

---

[1] I count legal persons as individuals, so that corporations may have rights; a political theory that counts special groups, like racial groups, as having some corporate standing within the community may therefore speak of group rights.

pursue different goals at the same time, and it may compromise one goal
for the sake of another. It may, for example, pursue economic efficiency,
but also military strength. The suggested distribution will then be determined by the sum of the two policies, and this will increase the permuta-
tions and combinations of possible trade-offs. In any case, these permu-
tations and combinations will offer a number of competing strategies
for serving each goal and both goals in combination. Economic efficiency
may be well served by offering subsidies to all farmers, and to no
manufacturers, and better served by offering double the subsidy to
some farmers and none to others. There will be alternate strategies of
pursuing any set of collective goals, and, particularly as the number of
goals increases, it will be impossible to determine in a piecemeal or case-
by-case way the distribution that best serves any set of goals. Whether
it is good policy to give double subsidies to some farmers and none to
others will depend upon a great number of other political decisions that
have been or will be made in pursuit of very general strategies into which
this particular decision must fit.

Rights also may be absolute : a political theory which holds a right
to freedom of speech as absolute will recognize no reason for not securing
the liberty it requires for every individual; no reason, that is, short of
impossibility. Rights may also be less than absolute; one principle might
have to yield to another, or even to an urgent policy with which it competes on particular facts. We may define the weight of a right, assuming it
is not absolute, as its power to withstand such competition. It follows from
the definition of a right that it cannot be outweighed by all social goals.
We might, for simplicity, stipulate not to call any political aim a right
unless it has a certain threshold weight against collective goals in general;
unless, for example, it cannot be defeated by appeal to any of the
ordinary routine goals of political administration, but only by a goal of
special urgency. Suppose, for example, some man says he recognizes the
right of free speech, but adds that free speech must yield whenever its
exercise would inconvenience the public. He means, I take it, that he
recognizes the pervasive goal of collective welfare, and only such distribution of liberty of speech as that collective goal recommends in particular circumstances. His political position is exhausted by the collective
goal; the putative right adds nothing and there is no point to recognizing
it as a right at all.

These definitions and distinctions make plain that the character of a
political aim – its standing as a right or goal – depends upon its place
and function within a single political theory. The same phrase might
describe a right within one theory and a goal within another, or a right
that is absolute or powerful within one theory but relatively weak within
another. If a public official has anything like a coherent political

theory that he uses, even intuitively, to justify the particular decisions he reaches, then this theory will recognize a wide variety of different types of rights, arranged in some way that assigns rough relative weight to each.

Any adequate theory will distinguish, for example, between background rights, which are rights that provide a justification for political decisions by society in the abstract, and institutional rights, that provide a justification for a decision by some particular and specified political institution. Suppose that my political theory provides that every man has a right to the property of another if he needs it more. I might yet concede that he does not have a legislative right to the same effect; I might concede, that is, that he has no institutional right that the present legislature enact legislation that would violate the Constitution, as such a statute presumably would. I might also concede that he has no institutional right to a judicial decision condoning theft. Even if I did make these concessions, I could preserve my initial background claim by arguing that the people as a whole would be justified in amending the Constitution to abolish property, or perhaps in rebelling and overthrowing the present form of government entirely. I would claim that each man has a residual background right that would justify or require these acts, even though I concede that he does not have the right to specific institutional decisions as these institutions are now constituted.

Any adequate theory will also make use of a distinction between abstract and concrete rights, and therefore between abstract and concrete principles. This is a distinction of degree, but I shall discuss relatively clear examples at two poles of the scale it contemplates, and therefore treat it as a distinction in kind. An abstract right is a general political aim the statement of which does not indicate how that general aim is to be weighed or compromised in particular circumstances against other political aims. The grand rights of political rhetoric are in this way abstract. Politicians speak of a right to free speech or dignity or equality, with no suggestion that these rights are absolute, but with no attempt to suggest their impact on particular complex social situations.

Concrete rights, on the other hand, are political aims that are more precisely defined so as to express more definitely the weight they have against other political aims on particular occasions. Suppose I say, not simply that citizens have a right to free speech, but that a newspaper has a right to publish defense plans classified as secret provided this publication will not create an immediate physical danger to troops. My principle declares for a particular resolution of the conflict it acknowledges between the abstract right of free speech, on the one hand, and competing rights of soldiers to security or the urgent needs of defense on the other. Abstract rights in this way provide arguments for concrete rights, but the claim of a concrete right is more definitive than any claim of abstract right that supports it.[1] ✓

B. Principles and utility

The distinction between rights and goals does not deny a thesis that is part of popular moral anthropology. It may be entirely reasonable to think, as this thesis provides, that the principles the members of a particular community find persuasive will be causally determined by the collective goals of that community. If many people in a community believe that each individual has a right to some minimal concern on the part of others, then this fact may be explained, as a matter of cultural history, by the further fact that their collective welfare is advanced by that belief. If some novel arrangement of rights would serve their collective welfare better, then we should expect, according to this thesis, that in due time their moral convictions will alter in favor of that new arrangement.

I do not know how far this anthropological theory holds in our own society, or any society. It is certainly untestable in anything like the simple form in which I have put it, and I do not see why its claim, that rights are psychologically or culturally determined by goals, is a priori more plausible than the contrary claim. Perhaps men and women choose collective goals to accommodate some prior sense of individual rights, rather than delineating rights according to collective goals. In either case, however, there must be an important time lag, so that at any given time most people will recognize the conflict between rights and goals, at

---

[1] A complete political theory must also recognize two other distinctions that I use implicitly in this chapter. The first is the distinction between rights against the state and rights against fellow citizens. The former justify a political decision that requires some agency of the government to act; the latter justify a decision to coerce particular individuals. The right to minimum housing, if accepted at all, is accepted as a right against the state. The right to recover damages for a breach of contract, or to be saved from great danger at minimum risk of a rescuer, is a right against fellow citizens. The right to free speech is, ordinarily, both. It seems strange to define the rights that citizens have against one another as political rights at all; but we are now concerned with such rights only insofar as they justify political decisions of different sorts. The present distinction cuts across the distinction between background and institutional rights; the latter distinguishes among persons or institutions that must make a political decision, the former between persons or institutions whom that decision directs to act or forbear. Ordinary civil cases at law, which are the principal subject of this essay, involve rights against fellow citizens; but I also discuss certain issues of constitutional and criminal law and so touch on rights against the state as well.

The second distinction is between universal and special rights; that is, between rights that a political theory provides for all individuals in the community, with exceptions only for phenomena like incapacity or punishment, and rights it provides for only one section of the community, or possibly only one member. I shall assume, in this essay, that all political rights are universal.

least in particular cases, that the general distinction between these two kinds of political aims presupposes.

The distinction presupposes, that is, a further distinction between the force of a particular right within a political theory and the causal explanation of why the theory provides that right. This is a formal way of putting the point, and it is appropriate only when, as I am now supposing, we can identify a particular political theory and so distinguish the analytical question of what it provides from the historical question of how it came to provide it. The distinction is therefore obscured when we speak of the morality of a *community* without specifying which of the many different conceptions of a community morality we have in mind. Without some further specification we cannot construct even a vague or abstract political theory as the theory of the community at any particular time, and so we cannot make the distinction between reasons and force that is analytically necessary to understand the concepts of principle and policy. We are therefore prey to the argument that the anthropological thesis destroys the distinction between the two; we speak as if we had some coherent theory in mind, as the community's morality; but we deny that it distinguishes principle from policy on the basis of an argument that seems plausible just because we do not have any particular theory in mind. Once we do make plain what we intend by some reference to the morality of a community, and proceed to identify, even crudely, what we take the principles of that morality to be, the anthropological argument is tamed.

There are political theories, however, that unite rights and goals not causally but by making the force of a right contingent upon its power, as a right, to promote some collective goal. I have in mind various forms of the ethical theory called rule utilitarianism. One popular form of that theory, for example, holds that an act is right if the general acceptance of a rule requiring that act would improve the average welfare of members of the community.[1] A political theory might provide for a right to free speech, for example, on the hypothesis that the general acceptance of that right by courts and other political institutions would promote the highest average utility of the community in the long run.

But we may nevertheless distinguish institutional rights, at least, from collective goals within such a theory. If the theory provides that an official of a particular institution is justified in making a political decision, and not justified in refusing to make it, whenever that decision is necessary to protect the freedom to speak of any individual, without regard to the impact of the decision on collective goals, the theory pro-

---

[1] See Brandt, 'Toward a Credible Form of Utilitarianism', in H. Castenada and G. Nakhnikian (eds.), *Morality and the Language of Conduct* (1963) 107.

vides free speech as a right. It does not matter that the theory stipulates this right on the hypothesis that if all political institutions do enforce the right in that way an important collective goal will in fact be promoted. What is important is the commitment to a scheme of government that makes an appeal to the right decisive in particular cases.

So neither the anthropological thesis nor rule utilitarianism offers any objection to the distinction between arguments of principle and arguments of policy. I should mention, out of an abundance of caution, one further possible challenge to that distinction. Different arguments of principle and policy can often be made in support of the same political decision. Suppose that an official wishes to argue in favor of racial segregation in public places. He may offer the policy argument that mixing races causes more overall discomfort than satisfaction. Or he may offer an argument of principle appealing to the rights of those who might be killed or maimed in riots that desegregation would produce. It might be thought that the substitutibility of these arguments defeats the distinction between arguments of principle and policy, or in any case makes the distinction less useful, for the following reason. Suppose it is conceded that the right to equality between races is sufficiently strong that it must prevail over all but the most pressing argument of policy, and be compromised only as required by competing arguments of principle. That would be an empty concession if arguments of principle could always be found to substitute for an argument of policy that might otherwise be made.

But it is a fallacy to suppose that because some argument of principle can always be found to substitute for an argument of policy, it will be as cogent or as powerful as the appropriate argument of policy would have been. If some minority's claim to an antidiscrimination statute were itself based on policy, and could therefore be defeated by an appeal to overall general welfare or utility, then the argument that cites the majority's discomfort or annoyance might well be powerful enough. But if the claim cites a right to equality that must prevail unless matched by a competing argument of principle, the only such argument available may be, as here, simply too weak. Except in extraordinary cases, the danger to any particular man's life that flows from desegregation adequately managed and policed will be very small. We might therefore concede that the competing right to life offers some argument countervailing against the right to equality here, and yet maintain that that argument is of negligible weight; strong enough, perhaps to slow the pace of desegregation but not strong enough even to slow it very much.

C. Economics and principle

The rights thesis, in its descriptive aspect, holds that judicial decisions in hard cases are characteristically generated by principle not policy. Recent research into the connections between economic theory and the common law might be thought to suggest the contrary: that judges almost always decide on grounds of policy rather than principle. We must, however, be careful to distinguish between two propositions said to be established by that research. It is argued, first, that almost every rule developed by judges in such disparate fields as tort, contract and property can be shown to serve the collective goal of making resource allocation more efficient.[1] It is argued, second, that in certain cases judges explicitly base their decisions on economic policy.[2] Neither of these claims subverts the rights thesis.

The first claim makes no reference to the intentions of the judges who decided the cases establishing rules that improve economic efficiency. It does not suppose that these judges were aware of the economic value of their rules, or even that they would have acknowledged that value as an argument in favor of their decisions. The evidence, for the most part, suggests the contrary. The courts that nourished the unfortunate fellow-servant doctrine, for example, thought that the rule was required by fairness, not utility, and when the rule was abolished it was because the argument from fairness, not the argument from utility, was found wanting by a different generation of lawyers.[3]

If this first claim is sound, it might seem to some an important piece of evidence for the anthropological thesis described in the last section. They will think that it suggests that judges and lawyers, reflecting the general moral attitudes of their time, thought that corporations and individuals had just those rights that an explicit rule utilitarian would legislate to serve the general welfare. But the first claim might equally well suggest the contrary conclusion I mentioned, that our present ideas of general welfare reflect our ideas of individual right. Professor Posner, for example, argues for that claim by presupposing a particular conception of efficient resource allocation. He says that the value of some scarce resource to a particular individual is measured by the amount of money he is willing to pay for it, so that community welfare is maximized when each resource is in the hands of someone who would pay more than anyone else to have it.[4] But that is hardly a self-evident or neutral conception of value. It is congenial to a political theory that celebrates competition, but far less congenial to a more egalitarian theory, because it demotes the claims of the poor who are willing to spend less because they have less to spend. Posner's conception of value, therefore, seems

---

[1] See, e.g., R. Posner, *Economic Analysis of Law* (1972) 10-104.
[2] See, e.g., Coase, 'The Problem of Social Cost', 3 *J. Law & Econ.* 1, 19-28 (1960).
[3] See Posner, 'A Theory of Negligence', 1 *J. Legal Stud.* (1972) 29, 71.
[4] Posner, *Economic Analysis*, 4.

as much the consequence as the cause of a theory of individual rights. In any case, however, the anthropological thesis of the first claim offers no threat to the rights thesis. Even if we concede that a judge's theory of rights is determined by some instinctive sense of economic value, rather than the other way about, we may still argue that he relies on that theory, and not economic analysis, to justify decisions in hard cases.

The second claim we distinguished, however, may seem to present a more serious challenge. If judges explicitly refer to economic policy in some cases, then these cases cannot be understood simply as evidence for the anthropological thesis. Learned Hand's theory of negligence is the most familiar example of this explicit reference to economics. He said, roughly, that the test of whether the defendant's act was unreasonable and therefore actionable, is the economic test which asks whether the defendant could have avoided the accident at less cost to himself than the plaintiff was likely to suffer if the accident occurred, discounted by the improbability of the accident.[1] It may be said that this economic test provides an argument of policy rather than principle, because it makes the decision turn on whether the collective welfare would have been advanced more by allowing the accident to take place or by spending what was necessary to avoid it. If so, then cases in which some test like Hand's is explicitly used, however few they might be, would stand as counterexamples to the rights thesis.

But the assumption that an economic calculation of any sort must be an argument of policy overlooks the distinction between abstract and concrete rights. Abstract rights, like the right to speak on political matters, take no account of competing rights; concrete rights, on the other hand, reflect the impact of such competition. In certain kinds of cases the argument from competing abstract principles to a concrete right can be made in the language of economics. Consider the principle that each member of a community has a right that each other member treat him with the minimal respect due a fellow human being.[2] That is a very abstract principle : it demands some balance, in particular cases, between the interests of those to be protected and the liberty of those from whom the principle demands an unstated level of concern and respect. It is natural, particularly when economic vocabulary is in fashion, to define the proper balance by comparing the sum of the utilities of these

---

[1] *United States v. Carroll Towing Co.*, 159 F.2d 169, 173 (2d Cir. 1947). Coase, 22-3, gives other examples, mostly of nuisance cases interpreting the doctrine that a 'reasonable' interference with the plaintiff's use of his property is not a nuisance.

[2] A more elaborate argument of principle might provide a better justification for Hand's test than does this simple principle. I described a more elaborate argument in a set of Rosenthal Lectures delivered at Northwestern University Law School in March, 1975. The simple principle, however, provides a sufficiently good justification for the present point.

two parties under different conditions. If one man acts in a way that he can foresee will injure another so that the collective utility of the pair will be sharply reduced by his act, he does not show the requisite care and concern. If he can guard or insure against the injury much more cheaply or effectively than the other can, for example, then he does not show care and concern unless he takes these precautions or arranges that insurance.

That character of argument is by no means novel, though perhaps its economic dress is. Philosophers have for a long time debated hypothetical cases testing the level of concern that one member of a community owes to another. If one man is drowning, and another may save him at minimal risk to himself, for example, then the first has a moral right to be saved by the second. That proposition might easily be put in economic form : if the collective utility of the pair is very sharply improved by a rescue, then the drowning man has a right to that rescue and the rescuer a duty to make it. The parallel legal proposition may, of course, be much more complex than that. It may specify special circumstances in which the crucial question is not whether the collective utility of the pair will be sharply advanced, but only whether it will be marginally advanced. It might put the latter question, for example, when one man's positive act, as distinct from a failure to act, creates a risk of direct and foreseeable physical injury to the person or property of another. If the rights thesis is sound, of course, then no judge may appeal to that legal proposition unless he believes that the principle of minimal respect states an abstract legal right; but if he does, then he may cast his argument in economic form without thereby changing its character from principle to policy.

Since Hand's test, and the parallel argument about rescuing a drowning man, are methods of compromising competing rights, they consider only the welfare of those whose abstract rights are at stake. They do not provide room for costs or benefits to the community at large, except as these are reflected in the welfare of those whose rights are in question. We can easily imagine an argument that does not concede these restrictions. Suppose someone argued that the principle requiring rescue at minimal risk should be amended so as to make the decision turn, not on some function of the collective utilities of the victim and rescuer, but on marginal utility to the community as a whole, so that the rescuer must take into account not only the relative risks to himself and the victim, but the relative social importance of the two. It might follow that an insignificant man must risk his life to save a bank president, but that a bank president need not even tire himself to save a nobody. The argument is no longer an argument of principle, because it supposes the victim to have a right to nothing but his expectations under general utility. Hand's formula, and more sophisticated variations, are not arguments of that character; they do not subordinate an individual right to some collective goal, but provide a mechanism for compromising competing claims of abstract right.

Negligence cases are not the only cases in which judges compromise abstract rights in defining concrete ones. If a judge appeals to public safety or the scarcity of some vital resource, for example, as a ground for limiting some abstract right, then his appeal might be understood as an appeal to the competing rights of those whose security will be sacrificed, or whose just share of that resource will be threatened if the abstract right is made concrete. His argument is an argument of principle if it respects the distributional requirements of such arguments, and if it observes the restriction mentioned in the last section : that the weight of a competing principle may be less than the weight of the appropriate parallel policy. We find a different sort of example in the familiar argument that certain sorts of law suits should not be allowed because to do so would 'swamp' the courts with litigation. The court supposes that if it were to allow that type of suit it would lack the time to consider promptly enough other law suits aiming to vindicate rights that are, taken together, more important than the rights it therefore proposes to bar.

This is an appropriate point to notice a certain limitation of the rights thesis. It holds in standard civil cases, when the ruling assumption is that one of the parties has a right to win; but it holds only asymmetrically when that assumption cannot be made. The accused in a criminal case has a right to a decision in his favor if he is innocent, but the state has no parallel right to a conviction if he is guilty. The court may therefore find in favor of the accused, in some hard case testing rules of evidence, for example, on an argument of policy that does not suppose that the accused has any right to be acquitted. The Supreme Court in *Linkletter v. Walker*[1] said that its earlier decision in *Mapp v. Ohio*[2] was such a decision. The Court said it had changed the rules permitting the introduction of illegally obtained evidence, not because Miss Mapp had any right that such evidence not be used if otherwise admissible, but in order to deter policemen from collecting such evidence in the future. I do not mean that a constitutional decision on such grounds is proper, or even that the Court's later description of its earlier decision was accurate. I mean only to point out how the geometry of a criminal prosection, which does not set opposing rights in a case against one another, differs from the standard civil case in which the rights thesis holds symmetrically.

[1] 381 U.S. 618 (1965).
[2] 367 U.S. 643 (1961).

4. INSTITUTIONAL RIGHTS

The rights thesis provides that judges decide hard cases by confirming or denying concrete rights. But the concrete rights upon which judges rely must have two other characteristics. They must be institutional rather than background rights, and they must be legal rather than some other form of institutional rights. We cannot appreciate or test the thesis, therefore, without further elaboration of these distinctions.

Institutional rights may be found in institutions of very different character. A chess player has a 'chess' right to be awarded a point in a tournament if he checkmates an opponent. A citizen in a democracy has a legislative right to the enactment of statutes necessary to protect his free speech. In the case of chess, institutional rights are fixed by constitutive and regulative rules that belong distinctly to the game, or to a particular tournament. Chess is, in this sense, an autonomous institution; I mean that it is understood, among its participants, that no one may claim an institutional right by direct appeal to general morality. No one may argue, for example, that he has earned the right to be declared the winner by his general virtue. But legislation is only partly autonomous in that sense. There are special constitutive and regulative rules that define what a legislature is, and who belongs to it, and how it votes, and that it may not establish a religion. But these rules belonging distinctly to legislation are rarely sufficient to determine whether a citizen has an institutional right to have a certain statute enacted; they do not decide, for example, whether he has a right to minimum wage legislation. Citizens are expected to repair to general considerations of political morality when they argue for such rights.

The fact that some institutions are fully and others partly autonomous has the consequence mentioned earlier, that the institutional rights a political theory acknowledges may diverge from the background rights it provides. Institutional rights are nevertheless genuine rights. Even if we suppose that the poor have an abstract background right to money taken from the rich, it would be wrong, not merely unexpected, for the referees of a chess tournament to award the prize money to the poorest contestant rather than the contestant with the most points. It would provide no excuse to say that since tournament rights merely describe the conditions necessary for calling the tournament a chess tournament, the referee's act is justified so long as he does not use the word 'chess' when he hands out the award. The participants entered the tournament with the understanding that chess rules would apply; they have genuine rights to the enforcement of these rules and no others.

Institutional autonomy insulates an official's institutional duty from the greater part of background political morality. But how far does the force of this insulation extend? Even in the case of a fully insulated institution like chess some rules will require interpretation or elaboration before an official may enforce them in certain circumstances. Suppose some rule of a chess tournament provides that the referee shall declare a game forfeit if one player 'unreasonably' annoys the other in the course of play. The language of the rule does not define what counts as 'unreasonable' annoyance; it does not decide whether, for example, a player who continually smiles at his opponent in such a way as to unnerve him, as the Russian grandmaster Tal once smiled at Fischer, annoys him unreasonably.

The referee is not free to give effect to his background convictions in deciding this hard case. He might hold, as a matter of political theory, that individuals have a right to equal welfare without regard to intellectual abilities. It would nevertheless be wrong for him to rely upon that conviction in deciding difficult cases under the forfeiture rule. He could not say, for example, that annoying behavior is reasonable so long as it has the effect of reducing the importance of intellectual ability in deciding who will win the game. The participants, and the general community that is interested, will say that his duty is just the contrary. Since chess is an intellectual game, he must apply the forfeiture rule in such a way as to protect, rather than jeopardize, the role of intellect in the contest.

We have, then, in the case of the chess referee, an example of an official whose decisions about institutional rights are understood to be governed by institutional constraints even when the force of these constraints is not clear. We do not think that he is free to legislate interstitially within the 'open texture' of imprecise rules.[1] If one interpretation of the forfeiture rule will protect the character of the game, and another will not, then the participants have a right to the first interpretation. We may hope to find, in this relatively simple case, some general feature of institutional rights in hard cases that will bear on the decision of a judge in a hard case at law.

I said that the game of chess has a character that the referee's decisions must respect. What does that mean? How does a referee know that chess is an intellectual game rather than a game of chance or an exhibition of digital ballet? He may well start with what everyone knows. Every institution is placed by its participants in some very rough category of institution; it is taken to be a game rather than a religious ceremony or a form of exercise or a political process. It is, for that reason, definitional of chess that it is a game rather than an exercise in digital skill. These conventions, exhibited in attitudes and manners and in history, are decisive. If everyone takes chess to be a game of chance,

---

[1] See generally H. L. A. Hart, *The Concept of Law* (1961) 121-32.

so that they curse their luck and nothing else when a piece *en prise* happens to be taken, then chess is a game of chance, though a very bad one.

But these conventions will run out, and they may run out before the referee finds enough to decide the case of Tal's smile. It is important to see, however, that the conventions run out in a particular way. They are not incomplete, like a book whose last page is missing, but abstract, so that their full force can be captured in a concept that admits of different conceptions; that is, in a *contested* concept.[1] The referee must select one or another of these conceptions, not to supplement the convention but to enforce it. He must *construct* the game's character by putting to himself different sets of questions. Given that chess is an intellectual game, is it, like poker, intellectual in some sense that includes ability at psychological intimidation? Or is it, like mathematics, intellectual in some sense that does not include that ability? This first set of questions asks him to look more closely at the game, to determine whether its features support one rather than the other of these conceptions of intellect. But he must also ask a different set of questions. Given that chess is an intellectual game of some sort, what follows about reasonable behavior in a chess game? Is ability at psychological intimidation, or ability to resist such intimidation, really an intellectual quality? These questions ask him to look more closely at the concept of intellect itself.

The referee's calculations, if they are self-conscious, will oscillate between these two sets of questions, progressively narrowing the questions to be asked at the next stage. He might first identify, by reflecting on the concept, different conceptions of intellect. He might suppose at this first stage, for example, that physical grace of the sort achieved in ballet is one form of intelligence. But he must then test these different conceptions against the rules and practices of the game. That test will rule out any physical conception of intelligence. But it may not discriminate between a conception that includes or a conception that rejects psychological intimidation, because either of these conceptions would provide an account of the rules and practices that is not plainly superior, according to any general canons of explanation, to the account provided by the other. He must then ask himself which of these two accounts offers a deeper or more successful account of what intellect really is. His calculations, so conceived, oscillate between philosophy of mind and the facts of the institution whose character he must elucidate.

[1] See Gallie, 'Essentially Contested Concepts', 56 *Proceedings of the Aristotelian Society* (1965) 167, 167-8. See also Chapter 10.

This is, of course, only a fanciful reconstruction of a calculation that will never take place; any official's sense of the game will have developed over a career, and he will employ rather than expose that sense in his judgments. But the reconstruction enables us to see how the concept of the game's character is tailored to a special institutional problem. Once an autonomous institution is established, such that participants have institutional rights under distinct rules belonging to that institution, then hard cases may arise that must, in the nature of the case, be supposed to have an answer. If Tal does not have a right that the game be continued, it must be because the forfeiture rule, properly understood, justifies the referee's intervention; if it does, then Fischer has a right to win at once. It is not useful to speak of the referee's 'discretion' in such a case. If some weak sense of discretion is meant, then the remark is unhelpful; if some strong sense is meant, such that Tal no longer has a right to win, then this must be, again, because the rule properly understood destroys the right he would otherwise have.[1] Suppose we say that in such a case all the parties have a right to expect is that the referee will use his best judgment. That is, in a sense, perfectly true, because they can have no more, by way of the referee's judgment, than his best judgment. But they are nevertheless entitled to his best judgment about which behavior is, in the circumstances of the game, unreasonable; they are entitled, that is, to his best judgment about what their rights are. The proposition that there is some 'right' answer to that question does not mean that the rules of chess are exhaustive and unambiguous; rather it is a complex statement about the responsibilities of its officials and participants.

But if the decision in a hard case must be a decision about the rights of the parties, then an official's reason for that judgment must be the sort of reason that justifies recognizing or denying a right. He must bring to his decision a general theory of why, in the case of his institution, the rules create or destroy any rights at all, and he must show what decision that general theory requires in the hard case. In chess the general ground of institutional rights must be the tacit consent or understanding of the parties. They consent, in entering a chess tournament, to the enforcement of certain and only those rules, and it is hard to imagine any other general ground for supposing that they have any institutional rights. But if that is so, and if the decision in a hard case is a decision about which rights they actually have, then the argument for the decision must apply that general ground to the hard case.

The hard case puts, we might say, a question of political theory. It asks what it is fair to suppose that the players have done in consenting

---

[1] See Chapter 2.

to the forfeiture rule. The concept of a game's character is a conceptual device for framing that question. It is a contested concept that internalizes the general justification of the institution so as to make it available for discriminations within the institution itself. It supposes that a player consents not simply to a set of rules, but to an enterprise that may be said to have a character of its own; so that when the question is put – To what did he consent in consenting to that? – the answer may study the enterprise as a whole and not just the rules.

5. LEGAL RIGHTS

A. *Legislation*

Legal argument, in hard cases, turns on contested concepts whose nature and function are very much like the concept of the character of a game. These include several of the substantive concepts through which the law is stated, like the concepts of a contract and of property. But they also include two concepts of much greater relevance to the present argument. The first is the idea of the 'intention' or 'purpose' of a particular statute or statutory clause. This concept provides a bridge between the political justification of the general idea that statutes create rights and those hard cases that ask what rights a particular statute has created. The second is the concept of principles that 'underlie' or are 'embedded in' the positive rules of law. This concept provides a bridge between the political justification of the doctrine that like cases should be decided alike and those hard cases in which it is unclear what that general doctrine requires. These concepts together define legal rights as a function, though a very special function, of political rights. If a judge accepts the settled practices of his legal system – if he accepts, that is, the autonomy provided by its distinct constitutive and regulative rules – then he must, according to the doctrine of political responsibility, accept some general political theory that justifies these practices. The concepts of legislative purpose and common law principles are devices for applying that general political theory to controversial issues about legal rights.

We might therefore do well to consider how a philosophical judge might develop, in appropriate cases, theories of what legislative purpose and legal principles require. We shall find that he would construct these theories in the same manner as a philosophical referee would construct the character of a game. I have invented, for this purpose, a lawyer of superhuman skill, learning, patience and acumen, whom I shall call Hercules. I suppose that Hercules is a judge in some representative American jurisdiction. I assume that he accepts the main uncontroversial constitutive and regulative rules of the law in his jurisdiction. He accepts, that is, that statutes have the general power to create and extinguish legal rights, and that judges have the general duty to follow earlier decisions of their court or higher courts whose rationale, as lawyers say, extends to the case at bar.

1. The constitution. Suppose there is a written constitution in Hercules' jurisdiction which provides that no law shall be valid if it establishes a religion. The legislature passes a law purporting to grant free busing to children in parochial schools. Does the grant establish a religion?[1] The words of the constitutional provision might support either view. Hercules must nevertheless decide whether the child who appears before him has a right to her bus ride.

He might begin by asking why the constitution has any power at all to create or destroy rights. If citizens have a background right to salvation through an established church, as many believe they do, then this must be an important right. Why does the fact that a group of men voted otherwise several centuries ago prevent this background right from being made a legal right as well? His answer must take some form such as this. The constitution sets out a general political scheme that is sufficiently just to be taken as settled for reasons of fairness. Citizens take the benefit of living in a society whose institutions are arranged and governed in accordance with that scheme, and they must take the burdens as well, at least until a new scheme is put into force either by discrete amendment or general revolution. But Hercules must then ask just what scheme of principles has been settled. He must construct, that is, a constitutional theory; since he is Hercules we may suppose that he can develop a full political theory that justifies the constitution as a whole. It must be a scheme that fits the particular rules of this constitution, of course. It cannot include a powerful background right to an established church. But more than one fully specified theory may fit the specific provision about religion sufficiently well. One theory might provide, for example, that it is wrong for the government to enact any legislation that will cause great social tension or disorder; so that since the establishment of a church will have that effect, it is wrong to empower the legislature to establish one. Another theory will provide a background right to religious liberty, and therefore argue that an established church is wrong, not because it will be socially disruptive, but because it violates that background right. In that case Hercules must turn to the remaining constitutional rules and settled practices under these rules to see which of these two theories provides a smoother fit with the constitutional scheme as a whole.

But the theory that is superior under this test will nevertheless be in-

[1] See *Everson v. Board of Educ.*, 330 U.S. 1 (1947).

sufficiently concrete to decide some cases. Suppose Hercules decides that the establishment provision is justified by a right to religious liberty rather than any goal of social order. It remains to ask what, more precisely, religious liberty is. Does a right to religious liberty include the right not to have one's taxes used for any purpose that helps a religion to survive? Or simply not to have one's taxes used to benefit one religion at the expense of another? If the former, then the free transportation legislation violates that right, but if the latter it does not. The institutional structure of rules and practice may not be sufficiently detailed to rule out either of these two conceptions of religious liberty, or to make one a plainly superior justification of that structure. At some point in his career Hercules must therefore consider the question not just as an issue of fit between a theory and the rules of the institution, but as an issue of political philosophy as well. He must decide which conception is a more satisfactory elaboration of the general idea of religious liberty. He must decide that question because he cannot otherwise carry far enough the project he began. He cannot answer in sufficient detail the question of what political scheme the constitution establishes.

So Hercules is driven, by this project, to a process of reasoning that is much like the process of the self-conscious chess referee. He must develop a theory of the constitution, in the shape of a complex set of principles and policies that justify that scheme of government, just as the chess referee is driven to develop a theory about the character of his game. He must develop that theory by referring alternately to political philosophy and institutional detail. He must generate possible theories justifying different aspects of the scheme and test the theories against the broader institution. When the discriminating power of that test is exhausted, he must elaborate the contested concepts that the successful theory employs.

2. *Statutes.* A statute in Hercules' jurisdiction provides that it is a federal crime for someone knowingly to transport in interstate commerce 'any person who shall have been unlawfully seized, confined, inveigled, decoyed, kidnapped, abducted, or carried away by any means whatsoever. . . .' Hercules is asked to decide whether this statute makes a federal criminal of a man who persuaded a young girl that it was her religious duty to run away with him, in violation of a court order, to consummate what he called a celestial marriage.[1] The statute had been passed after a famous kidnapping case, in order to enable federal authorities to join in the pursuit of kidnappers. But its words are sufficiently broad to apply to this case, and there is nothing in the legislative

---

[1] See *Chatwin v. United States,* 326 U.S. 455 (1946).

record or accompanying committee reports that says they do not.

Do they apply? Hercules might himself despise celestial marriage, or abhor the corruption of minors, or celebrate the obedience of children to their parents. The groom nevertheless has a right to his liberty, unless the statute properly understood deprives him of that right; it is inconsistent with any plausible theory of the constitution that judges have the power retroactively to make conduct criminal. Does the statute deprive him of that right? Hercules must begin by asking why any statute has the power to alter legal rights. He will find the answer in his constitutional theory: this might provide, for example, that a democratically elected legislature is the appropriate body to make collective decisions about the conduct that shall be criminal. But that same constitutional theory will impose on the legislature certain responsibilities: it will impose not only constraints reflecting individual rights, but also some general duty to pursue collective goals defining the public welfare. That fact provides a useful test for Hercules in this hard case. He might ask which interpretation more satisfactorily ties the language the legislature used to its constitutional responsibilities. That is, like the referee's question about the character of a game. It calls for the construction, not of some hypothesis about the mental state of particular legislators, but of a special political theory that justifies this statute, in the light of the legislature's more general responsibilities, better than any alternative theory.[1]

Which arguments of principle and policy might properly have persuaded the legislature to enact just that statute? It should not have pursued a policy designed to replace state criminal enforcement by federal enforcement whenever constitutionally possible. That would represent an unnecessary interference with the principle of federalism

---

[1] One previous example of the use of policy in statutory interpretations illustrates this form of constitution. In *Charles River Bridge v. Warren Bridge*, 24 Mass. (7 Pick.) 344 (1830), aff'd, 36 U.S. (11 Pet.) 420 (1837), the court had to decide whether a charter to construct a bridge across the Charles River was to be taken to be exclusive, so that no further charters could be granted. Justice Morton of the Supreme Judicial Court held that the grant was not to be taken as exclusive, and argued, in support of that interpretation, that:

[I]f consequences so inconsistent with the improvement and prosperity of the state result from the liberal and extended construction of the charters which have been granted, we ought, if the terms used will admit of it, rather to adopt a more limited and restricted one, than to impute such improvidence to the legislature.

. . . .

. . [Construing the grant as exclusive] would amount substantially to a covenant, that during the plaintiffs' charter an important portion of our commonwealth, as to facilities for travel and transportation, should remain *in statu quo*. I am on the whole irresistibly brought to the conclusion, that this construction is neither consonant with sound reason, with judicial authorities, with the course of legislation, nor with the principles of our free institutions.

Ibid. 460.

that must be part of Hercules' constitutional theory. It might, however, responsibly have followed a policy of selecting for federal enforcement all crimes with such an interstate character that state enforcement was hampered. Or it could responsibly have selected just specially dangerous or widespread crimes of that character. Which of these two responsible policies offers a better justification of the statute actually drafted? If the penalties provided by the statute are large, and therefore appropriate to the latter but not the former policy, the latter policy must be preferred. Which of the different interpretations of the statute permitted by the language serves that policy better? Plainly a decision that inveiglement of the sort presented by the case is not made a federal crime by the statute.

I have described a simple and perhaps unrepresentative problem of statutory interpretation, because I cannot now develop a theory of statutory interpretation in any detail. I want only to suggest how the general claim, that calculations judges make about the purposes of statutes are calculations about political rights, might be defended. There are, however, two points that must be noticed about even this simple example. It would be inaccurate, first, to say that Hercules supplemented what the legislature did in enacting the statute, or that he tried to determine what it would have done if it had been aware of the problem presented by the case. The act of a legislature is not, as these descriptions suggest, an event whose force we can in some way measure so as to say it has run out at a particular point; it is rather an event whose content is contested in the way in which the content of an agreement to play a game is contested. Hercules constructs his political theory as an argument about what the legislature has, on this occasion, done. The contrary argument, that it did not actually do what he said, is not a realistic piece of common sense, but a competitive claim about the true content of that contested event.

Second, it is important to notice how great a role the canonical terms of the actual statute play in the process described. They provide a limit to what must otherwise be, in the nature of the case, unlimited. The political theory Hercules developed to interpret the statute, which featured a policy of providing federal enforcement for dangerous crimes, would justify a great many decisions that the legislature did not, on any interpretation of the language, actually make. It would justify, for example, a statute making it a federal crime for a murderer to leave the state of his crime. The legislature has no general duty to follow out the lines of any particular policy, and it would plainly be wrong for Hercules to suppose that the legislature had in some sense enacted that further statute. The words of the statute they did enact enables this process of interpretation to operate without absurdity; it permits Hercules to say

E

that the legislature pushed some policy to the limits of the language it used, without also supposing that it pushed that policy to some indeterminate further point.

B. *The common law*

1. Precedent. One day lawyers will present a hard case to Hercules that does not turn upon any statute; they will argue whether earlier common law decisions of Hercules' court, properly understood, provide some party with a right to a decision in his favor. *Spartan Steel* was such a case. The plaintiff did not argue that any statute provided it a right to recover its economic damages; it pointed instead to certain earlier judicial decisions that awarded recovery for other sorts of damage, and argued that the principle behind these cases required a decision for it as well.

Hercules must begin by asking why arguments of that form are ever, even in principle, sound. He will find that he has available no quick or obvious answer. When he asked himself the parallel question about legislation he found, in general democratic theory, a ready reply. But the details of the practices of precedent he must now justify resist any comparably simple theory.

He might, however, be tempted by this answer. Judges, when they decide particular cases at common law, lay down general rules that are intended to benefit the community in some way. Other judges, deciding later cases, must therefore enforce these rules so that the benefit may be achieved. If this account of the matter were a sufficient justification of the practices of precedent, then Hercules could decide these hard common law cases as if earlier decisions were statutes, using the techniques he worked out for statutory interpretation. But he will encounter fatal difficulties if he pursues that theory very far. It will repay us to consider why, in some detail, because the errors in the theory will be guides to a more successful theory.

Statutory interpretation, as we just noticed, depends upon the availability of a canonical form of words, however vague or unspecific, that set limits to the political decisions that the statute may be taken to have made. Hercules will discover that many of the opinions that litigants cite as precedents do not contain any special propositions taken to be a canonical form of the rule that the case lays down. It is true that it was part of Anglo-American judicial style, during the last part of the nineteenth century and the first part of this century, to attempt to compose such canonical statements, so that one could thereafter refer, for example, to the rule in *Rylands v. Fletcher*.[1] But even in this period, lawyers and

---

[1] [1866] L.R. 1 Ex. 265, *aff'd,* (1868) L.R. 3 H.L. 330.

textbook writers disagreed about which parts of famous opinions should be taken to have that character. Today, in any case, even important opinions rarely attempt that legislative sort of draftsmanship. They cite reasons, in the form of precedents and principles, to justify a decision, but it is the decision, not some new and stated rule of law, that these precedents and principles are taken to justify. Sometimes a judge will acknowledge openly that it lies to later cases to determine the full effect of the case he has decided.

Of course, Hercules might well decide that when he does find, in an earlier case, a canonical form of words, he will use his techniques of statutory interpretation to decide whether the rule composed of these words embraces a novel case.[1] He might well acknowledge what could be called an enactment force of precedent. He will nevertheless find that when a precedent does have enactment force, its influence on later cases is not taken to be limited to that force. Judges and lawyers do not think that the force of precedents is exhausted, as a statute would be, by the linguistic limits of some particular phrase. If *Spartan Steel* were a New York case, counsel for the plaintiff would suppose that Cardozo's earlier decision in *MacPherson v. Buick*,[2] in which a woman recovered damages for injuries from a negligently manufactured automobile, counted in favor of his client's right to recover, in spite of the fact that the earlier decision contained no language that could plausibly be interpreted to enact that right. He would urge that the earlier decision exerts a gravitational force on later decisions even when these later decisions lie outside its particular orbit.

This gravitational force is part of the practice Hercules' general theory of precedent must capture. In this important respect, judicial practice differs from the practice of officials in other institutions. In chess, officials conform to established rules in a way that assumes full institutional autonomy. They exercise originality only to the extent required by the fact that an occasional rule, like the rule about forfeiture, demands that originality. Each decision of a chess referee, therefore, can be said to be directly required and justified by an established rule of chess, even though some of these decisions must be based on an interpretation, rather than on simply the plain and unavoidable meaning, of that rule.

---

[1] But since Hercules will be led to accept the rights thesis, see pp. 115-16 *infra*, his 'interpretation' of judicial enactments will be different from his interpretation of statutes in one important respect. When he interprets statutes he fixes to some statutory language, as we saw, arguments of principle or policy that provide the best justification of that language in the light of the legislature's responsibilities. His argument remains an argument of principle; he uses policy to determine what rights the legislature has already created. But when he 'interprets' judicial enactments he will fix to the relevant language only arguments of principle, because the rights thesis argues that only such arguments acquit the responsibility of the 'enacting' court.

[2] *MacPherson v. Buick Motor Co.*, 217 N.Y. 382, 111 N.E. 1050 (1916).

Some legal philosophers write about common law adjudication as if it were in this way like chess, except that legal rules are much more likely than chess rules to require interpretation. That is the spirit, for example, of Professor Hart's argument that hard cases arise only because legal rules have what he calls 'open texture'.[1] In fact, judges often disagree not simply about how some rule or principle should be interpreted, but whether the rule or principle one judges cites should be acknowledged to be a rule or principle at all. In some cases both the majority and the dissenting opinions recognize the same earlier cases as relevant, but disagree about what rule or principle these precedents should be understood to have established. In adjudication, unlike chess, the argument *for* a particular rule may be more important than the argument *from* that rule to the particular case; and while the chess referee who decides a case by appeal to a rule no one has ever heard of before is likely to be dismissed or certified, the judge who does so is likely to be celebrated in law school lectures.

Nevertheless, judges seem agreed that earlier decisions do contribute to the formulation of new and controversial rules in some way other than by interpretation; they are agreed that earlier decisions have gravitational force even when they disagree about what that force is. The legislator may very often concern himself only with issues of background morality or policy in deciding how to cast his vote on some issue. He need not show that his vote is consistent with the votes of his colleagues in the legislature, or with those of past legislatures. But the judge very rarely assumes that character of independence. He will always try to connect the justification he provides for an original decision with decisions that other judges or officials have taken in the past.

In fact, when good judges try to explain in some general way how they work, they search for figures of speech to describe the constraints they feel even when they suppose that they are making new law, constraints that would not be appropriate if they were legislators. They say, for example, that they find new rules immanent in the law as a whole, or that they are enforcing an internal logic of the law through some method that belongs more to philosophy than to politics, or that they are the agents through which the law works itself pure, or that the law has some life of its own even though this belongs to experience rather than to logic. Hercules must not rest content with these famous metaphors and personifications, but he must also not be content with any description of the judicial process that ignores their appeal to the best lawyers.

The gravitational force of precedent cannot be captured by any theory that takes the full force of precedent to be its enactment force as a piece of legislation. But the inadequacy of that approach suggests a superior

[1] H. L. A. Hart, *The Concept of Law*, 121-32.

theory. The gravitational force of a precedent may be explained by appeal, not to the wisdom of enforcing enactments, but to the fairness of treating like cases alike. A precedent is the report of an earlier political decision; the very fact of that decision, as a piece of political history, provides some reason for deciding other cases in a similar way in the future. This general explanation of the gravitational force of precedent accounts for the feature that defeated the enactment theory, which is that the force of a precedent escapes the language of its opinion. If the government of a community has forced the manufacturer of defective motor cars to pay damages to a woman who was injured because of the defect, then that historical fact must offer some reason, at least, why the same government should require a contractor who has caused economic damage through the defective work of his employees to make good that loss. We may test the weight of that reason, not by asking whether the language of the earlier decision, suitably interpreted, requires the contractor to pay damages, but by asking the different question whether it is fair for the government, having intervened in the way it did in the first case, to refuse its aid in the second.

Hercules will conclude that this doctrine of fairness offers the only adequate account of the full practice of precedent. He will draw certain further conclusions about his own responsibilities when deciding hard cases. The most important of these is that he must limit the gravitational force of earlier decisions to the extension of the arguments of principle necessary to justify those decisions. If an earlier decision were taken to be entirely justified by some argument of policy, it would have no gravitational force. Its value as a precedent would be limited to its enactment force, that is, to further cases captured by some particular words of the opinion. The distributional force of a collective goal, as we noticed earlier, is a matter of contingent fact and general legislative strategy. If the government intervened on behalf of Mrs MacPherson, not because she had any right to its intervention, but only because wise strategy suggested that means of pursuing some collective goal like economic efficiency, there can be no effective argument of fairness that it therefore ought to intervene for the plaintiff in *Spartan Steel*.

We must remind ourselves, in order to see why this is so, of the slight demands we make upon legislatures in the name of consistency when their decisions are generated by arguments of policy.[1] Suppose the legisla-

---

[1] In *Williamson v. Lee Optical Co.*, 348 U.S. 483 (1955), Justice Douglas suggested that legislation generated by policy need not be uniform or consistent:
> The problem of legislative classification is a perennial one, admitting of no doctrinaire definition. Evils in the same field may be of different dimensions and proportions, requiring different remedies. Or so the legislature may think. Or the reform may take one step at a time, addressing itself to the phase of the problem which seems most acute to the legislative mind. The legislature

ture wishes to stimulate the economy and might do so, with roughly the same efficiency, either by subsidizing housing or by increasing direct government spending for new roads. Road construction companies have no right that the legislature choose road construction; if it does, then home construction firms have no right, on any principle of consistency, that the legislature subsidize housing as well. The legislature may decide that the road construction program has stimulated the economy just enough, and that no further programs are needed. It may decide this even if it now concedes that subsidized housing would have been the more efficient decision in the first place. Or it might concede even that more stimulation of the economy is needed, but decide that it wishes to wait for more evidence – perhaps evidence about the success of the road program – to see whether subsidies provide an effective stimulation. It might even say that it does not now wish to commit more of its time and energy to economic policy. There is, perhaps, some limit to the arbitrariness of the distinctions the legislature may make in its pursuit of collective goals. Even if it is efficient to build all shipyards in southern California, it might be thought unfair, as well as politically unwise, to do so. But these weak requirements, which prohibit grossly unfair distributions, are plainly compatible with providing sizeable incremental benefits to one group that are withheld from others.

There can be, therefore, no general argument of fairness that a government which serves a collective goal in one way on one occasion must serve it that way, or even serve the same goal, whenever a parallel opportunity arises. I do not mean simply that the government may change its mind, and regret either the goal or the means of its earlier decision. I mean that a responsible government may serve different goals in a piecemeal and occasional fashion, so that even though it does not regret, but continues to enforce, one rule designed to serve a particular goal, it may reject other rules that would serve that same goal just as well. It might legislate the rule that manufacturers are responsible for damages flowing from defects in their cars, for example, and yet properly refuse to legislate the same rule for manufacturers of washing machines, let alone contractors who cause economic damage like the damage of

---

may select one phase of one field and apply a remedy there, neglecting the others. The prohibition of the Equal Protection Clause goes no further than the invidious discrimination.
Ibid. 489 (citations omitted).

Of course the point of the argument here, that the demands of consistency are different in the cases of principle and policy, is of great importance in understanding the recent history of the equal protection clause. It is the point behind attempts to distinguish 'old' from 'new' equal protection, or to establish 'suspect' classifications, and it provides a more accurate and intelligible distinction than these attempts have furnished.

Spartan Steel. Government must, of course, be rational and fair; it must make decisions that overall serve a justifiable mix of collective goals and nevertheless respect whatever rights citizens have. But that general requirement would not support anything like the gravitational force that the judicial decision in favour of Mrs MacPherson was in fact taken to have.

So Hercules, when he defines the gravitational force of a particular precedent, must take into account only the arguments of principle that justify that precedent. If the decision in favour of Mrs MacPherson supposes that she has a right to damages, and not simply that a rule in her favor supports some collective goal, then the argument of fairness, on which the practice of precedent relies, takes hold. It does not follow, of course, that anyone injured in any way by the negligence of another must have the same concrete right to recover that she has. It may be that competing rights require a compromise in the later case that they did not require in hers. But it might well follow that the plaintiff in the later case has the same abstract right, and if that is so then some special argument citing the competing rights will be required to show that a contrary decision in the later case would be fair.

2. *The seamless web.* Hercules' first conclusion, that the gravitational force of a precedent is defined by the arguments of principle that support the precedent, suggests a second. Since judicial practice in his community assumes that earlier cases have a *general* gravitational force, then he can justify that judicial practice only by supposing that the rights thesis holds in his community. It is never taken to be a satisfactory argument against the gravitational force of some precedent that the goal that precedent served has now been served sufficiently, or that the courts would now be better occupied in serving some other goal that has been relatively neglected, possibly returning to the goal the precedent served on some other occasion. The practices of precedent do not suppose that the *rationales* that recommend judicial decisions can be served piecemeal in that way. If it is acknowledged that a particular precedent is justified for a particular reason; if that reason would also recommend a particular result in the case at bar; if the earlier decision has not been recanted or in some other way taken as a matter of institutional regret; then that decision must be reached in the later case.

Hercules must suppose that it is understood in his community, though perhaps not explicitly recognized, that judicial decisions must be taken to be justified by arguments of principle rather than arguments of policy. He now sees that the familiar concept used by judges to explain their reasoning from precedent, the concept of certain principles that underlie or are embedded in the common law, is itself only a metaphorical statement of the rights thesis. He may henceforth use that concept in his decisions of hard common law cases. It provides a general test for deciding such cases that is like the chess referee's concept of the character of a game, and like his own concept of a legislative purpose. It provides a question – What set of principles best justifies the precedents? – that builds a bridge between the general justification of the practice of precedent, which is fairness, and his own decision about what that general justification requires in some particular hard case.

Hercules must now develop his concept of principles that underlie the common law by assigning to each of the relevant precedents some scheme of principle that justifies the decision of that precedent. He will now discover a further important difference between this concept and the concept of statutory purpose that he used in statutory interpretation. In the case of statutes, he found it necessary to choose some theory about the purpose of the particular statute in question, looking to other acts of the legislature only insofar as these might help to select between theories that fit the statute about equally well. But if the gravitational force of precedent rests on the idea that fairness requires the consistent enforcement of rights, then Hercules must discover principles that fit, not only the particular precedent to which some litigant directs his attention, but all other judicial decisions within his general jurisdiction and, indeed, statutes as well, so far as these must be seen to be generated by principle rather than policy. He does not satisfy his duty to show that his decision is consistent with established principles, and therefore fair, if the principles he cites as established are themselves inconsistent with other decisions that his court also proposes to uphold.

Suppose, for example, that he can justify Cardozo's decision in favor of Mrs MacPherson by citing some abstract principle of equality, which argues that whenever an accident occurs then the richest of the various persons whose acts might have contributed to the accident must bear the loss. He nevertheless cannot show that that principle has been respected in other accident cases, or, even if he could, that it has been respected in other branches of the law, like contract, in which it would also have great impact if it were recognized at all. If he decides against a future accident plaintiff who is richer than the defendant, by appealing to this alleged right of equality, that plaintiff may properly complain that the decision is just as inconsistent with the government's behavior in other cases as if *MacPherson* itself had been ignored. The law may not be a seamless web; but the plaintiff is entitled to ask Hercules to treat it as if it were.

You will now see why I called our judge Hercules. He must construct a scheme of abstract and concrete principles that provides a coherent justification for all common law precedents and, so far as these are to be justified on principle, constitutional and statutory provisions as well. We may grasp the magnitude of this enterprise by distinguishing, within the vast material of legal decisions that Hercules must justify, a vertical and a horizontal ordering. The vertical ordering is provided by distinguishing layers of authority; that is, layers at which official decisions might be taken to be controlling over decisions made at lower levels. In the United States the rough character of the vertical ordering is apparent. The constitutional structure occupies the highest level, the decisions of the Supreme Court and perhaps other courts interpreting that structure the next, enactments of the various legislatures the next and decisions of the various courts developing the common law different levels below that. Hercules must arrange justification of principle at each of these levels so that the justification is consistent with principles taken to provide the justification of higher levels. The horizontal ordering simply requires that the principles taken to justify a decision at one level must also be consistent with the justification offered for other decisions at that level.

Suppose Hercules, taking advantage of his unusual skills, proposed to work out this entire scheme in advance, so that he would be ready to confront litigants with an entire theory of law should this be necessary to justify any particular decision. He would begin, deferring to vertical ordering, by setting out and refining the constitutional theory he has already used. That constitutional theory would be more or less different from the theory that a different judge would develop, because a constitutional theory requires judgments about complex issues of institutional fit, as well as judgments about political and moral philosophy, and Hercules' judgments will inevitably differ from those other judges would make. These differences at a high level of vertical ordering will exercise considerable force on the scheme each judge would propose at lower levels. Hercules might think, for example, that certain substantive constitutional constraints on legislative power are best justified by postulating an abstract right to privacy against the state, because he believes that such a right is a consequence of the even more abstract right to liberty that the constitution guarantees. If so, he would regard the failure of the law of tort to recognize a parallel abstract right to privacy against fellow citizens, in some concrete form, as an inconsistency. If another judge did not share his beliefs about the connection between privacy and liberty, and so did not accept his constitutional interpretation as persuasive, that judge would also disagree about the proper development of tort.

So the impact of Hercules' own judgments will be pervasive, even though some of these will be controversial. But they will not enter his calculations in such a way that different parts of the theory he constructs can be attributed to his independent convictions rather than to the body of law that he must justify. He will not follow those classical theories of adjudication I mentioned earlier, which suppose that a judge follows statutes or precedent until the clear direction of these runs out, after which he is free to strike out on his own. His theory is rather a theory about what the statute or the precedent itself requires, and though he will, of course, reflect his own intellectual and philosophical convictions in making that judgment, that is a very different matter from supposing that those convictions have some independent force in his argument just because they are his.[1]

3. Mistakes. I shall not now try to develop, in further detail, Hercules' theory of law. I shall mention, however, two problems he will face. He must decide, first, how much weight he must give, in constructing a scheme of justification for a set of precedents, to the arguments that the judges who decided these cases attached to their decisions. He will not always find in these opinions any proposition precise enough to serve as a statute he might then interpret. But the opinions will almost always contain argument, in the form of propositions that the judge takes to recommend his decision. Hercules will decide to assign these only an initial or prima facie place in his scheme of justification. The purpose of that scheme is to satisfy the requirement that the government must extend to all, the rights it supposes some to have. The fact that one officer of the government offers a certain principle as the ground of his decision, may be taken to establish prima facie that the government does rely that far upon that principle.

But the main force of the underlying argument of fairness is forward-looking, not backward-looking. The gravitational force of Mrs Mac-Pherson's case depends not simply on the fact that she recovered for her Buick, but also on the fact that the government proposes to allow others in just her position to recover in the future. If the courts proposed to overrule the decision, no substantial argument of fairness, fixing on the actual decision in the case, survives in favor of the plaintiff in *Spartan Steel*. If, therefore, a principle other than the principle Cardozo cited can be found to justify *MacPherson*, and if this other principle also justifies a great deal of precedent that Cardozo's does not, or if it provides a smoother fit with arguments taken to justify decisions of a higher rank in vertical order, then this new principle is a more satisfactory basis for further decisions. Of course, this argument for not copying Cardozo's principle is unnecessary if the new principle is more abstract, and if Cardozo's principle can be seen as only a concrete form of that more abstract principle. In that case Hercules incorporates, rather than rejects, Cardozo's account of his decision. Cardozo, in fact, used the opinion in the earlier case of *Thomas v. Winchester*,[2] on which case he relied,

---

[1] See below, pp. 123-30.   [2] 6 N.Y. 397 (1852).

in just that fashion. It may be, however, that the new principle strikes out on a different line, so that it justifies a precedent or a series of precedents on grounds very different from what their opinions propose. Brandeis and Warren's famous argument about the right to privacy[1] is a dramatic illustration : they argued that this right was not unknown to the law but was, on the contrary, demonstrated by a wide variety of decisions, in spite of the fact that the judges who decided these cases mentioned no such right. It may be that their argument, so conceived, was unsuccessful, and that Hercules in their place, would have reached a different result. Hercules' theory nevertheless shows why their argument, sometimes taken to be a kind of brilliant fraud, was at least sound in its ambition.

Hercules must also face a different and greater problem. If the history of his court is at all complex, he will find, in practice, that the requirement of total consistency he has accepted will prove too strong, unless he develops it further to include the idea that he may, in applying this requirement, disregard some part of institutional history as a mistake. For he will be unable, even with his superb imagination, to find any set of principles that reconciles all standing statutes and precedents. This is hardly surprising : the legislators and judges of the past did not all have Hercules' ability or insight, nor were they men and women who were all of the same mind and opinion. Of course, any set of statutes and decisions can be explained historically, or psychologically, or sociologically, but consistency requires justification, not explanation, and the justification must be plausible and not sham. If the justification he constructs makes distinctions that are arbitrary and deploys principles that are unappealing, then it cannot count as a justification at all.

Suppose the law of negligence and accidents in Hercules' jurisdiction has developed in the following simplified and imaginary way. It begins with specific common law decisions recognizing a right to damages for bodily injury caused by very dangerous instruments that are defectively manufactured. These cases are then reinterpreted in some landmark decision, as they were in *MacPherson*, as justified by the very abstract right of each person to the reasonable care of others whose actions might injure his person or property. This principle is then both broadened and pinched in different ways. The courts, for example, decide that no concrete right lies against an accountant who has been negligent in the preparation of financial statements. They also decide that the right cannot be waived in certain cases; for example, in a standard form contract of automobile purchase. The legislature adds a statute providing that in certain cases of industrial accident, recovery will be allowed unless the

---

[1] Warren & Brandeis, 'The Right of Privacy', 4 *Harv. L. Rev.* (1890) 193.

defendant affirmatively establishes that the plaintiff was entirely to blame. But it also provides that in other cases, for example in airplane accidents, recovery will be limited to a stipulated amount, which might be much less than the actual loss; and it later adds that the guest in an automobile cannot sue his host even if the host drives negligently and the guest is injured. Suppose now, against this background, that Hercules is called upon to decide *Spartan Steel.*

Can he find a coherent set of principles that justifies this history in the way fairness requires? He might try the proposition that individuals have no right to recover for damages unless inflicted intentionally. He would argue that they are allowed to recover damages in negligence only for policy reasons, not in recognition of any abstract right to such damages, and he would cite the statutes limiting liability to protect airlines and insurance companies, and the cases excluding liability against accountants, as evidence that recovery is denied when policy argues the other way. But he must concede that this analysis of institutional history is incompatible with the common law decisions, particularly the landmark decision recognizing a general right to recovery in negligence. He cannot say, compatibly with the rest of his theory, that these decisions may themselves be justified on policy grounds, if he holds, by virtue of the rights thesis, that courts may extend liability only in response to arguments of principle and not policy. So he must set these decisions aside as mistakes.

He might try another strategy. He might propose some principle according to which individuals have rights to damages in just the circumstances of the particular cases that decided they did, but have no general right to such damages. He might concede, for example, a legal principle granting a right to recover for damages incurred within an automobile owned by the plaintiff, but deny a principle that would extend to other damage. But though he could in this way tailor his justification of institutional history to fit that history exactly, he would realize that this justification rests on distinctions that are arbitrary. He can find no room in his political theory for a distinction that concedes an abstract right if someone is injured driving his own automobile but denies it if he is a guest or if he is injured in an airplane. He has provided a set of arguments that cannot stand as a coherent justification of anything.

He might therefore concede that he can make no sense of institutional history except by supposing some general abstract right to recover for negligence: but he might argue that it is a relatively weak right and so will yield to policy considerations of relatively minor force. He will cite the limiting statutes and cases in support of his view that the right is a weak one. But he will then face a difficulty if, though the statute limiting liability in airplane accidents has never been repealed, the airlines have become sufficiently secure, and the mechanisms of insurance available to airlines so efficient and inexpensive, that a failure to repeal the statute can only be justified by taking the abstract right to be so weak that relatively thin arguments of policy are sufficient to defeat it. If Hercules takes the right to be that weak then he cannot justify the various common law decisions that support the right, as a concrete right, against arguments of policy much stronger than the airlines are now able to press. So he must choose either to take the failure to repeal the airline accident limitation statute, or the common law decisions that value the right much higher, as mistakes.

In any case, therefore, Hercules must expand his theory to include the idea that a justification of institutional history may display some part of that history as mistaken. But he cannot make impudent use of this device, because if he were free to take any incompatible piece of institutional history as a mistake, with no further consequences for his general theory, then the requirement of consistency would be no genuine requirement at all. He must develop some theory of institutional mistakes, and this theory of mistakes must have two parts. It must show the consequences for further arguments of taking some institutional event to be mistaken; and it must limit the number and character of the events than can be disposed of in that way.

He will construct the first part of this theory of mistakes by means of two sets of distinctions. He will first distinguish between the specific authority of any institutional event, which is its power as an institutional act to effect just the specific institutional consequences it describes, and its gravitational force. If he classifies some event as a mistake, then he does not deny its specific authority but he does deny its gravitational force, and he cannot consistently appeal to that force in other arguments. He will also distinguish between embedded and corrigible mistakes; embedded mistakes are those whose specific authority is fixed so that it survives their loss of gravitational force; corrigible mistakes are those whose specific authority depends on gravitational force in such a way that it cannot survive this loss.

The constitutional level of his theory will determine which mistakes are embedded. His theory of legislative supremacy, for example, will insure that any statutes he treats as mistakes will lose their gravitational force but not their specific authority. If he denies the gravitational force of the aircraft liability limitation statute, the statute is not thereby repealed; the mistake is embedded so that the specific authority survives. He must continue to respect the limitations the statute imposes upon liability, but he will not use it to argue in some other case for a weaker right. If he accepts some strict doctrine of precedent, and designates some judicial decision, like the decision denying a right in negligence against an accountant, a mistake, then the strict doctrine may preserve the specific authority of that decision, which might be limited to its enactment force, but the decision will lose its gravitational force; it will become in Justice Frankfurter's phrase, a piece of legal flotsam or jetsam. It will not be necessary to decide which.

That is fairly straightforward, but Hercules must take more pains with the second part of his theory of mistakes. He is required, by the justification he has fixed to the general practice of precedent, to compose a more detailed justification, in the form of a scheme of principle, for the entire body of statutes and common law decisions. But a justification that designates part of what is to be justified as mistaken is prima facie weaker than one that does not. The second part of his theory of mistakes must show that it is nevertheless a stronger justification than any alternative that does not recognize any mistakes, or that recognizes a different set of mistakes. That demonstration cannot be a deduction from simple rules of theory construction, but if Hercules bears in mind the connection he earlier established between precedent and fairness, this connection will suggest two guidelines for his theory of mistakes. In the first place, fairness fixes on institutional history, not just as history but as a political program that the government proposed to continue into the future; it seizes, that is, on forward-looking, not the backward-looking implications of precedent. If Hercules discovers that some previous decision, whether a statute or a judicial decision, is now widely regretted within the pertinent branch of the profession, that fact in itself distinguishes that decision as vulnerable. He must remember, second, that the argument from fairness that demands consistency is not the only argument from fairness to which government in general, or judges in particular, must respond. If he believes, quite apart from any argument of consistency, that a particular statute or decision was wrong because unfair, within the community's own concept of fairness, then that belief is sufficient to distinguish the decision, and make it vulnerable. Of course, he must apply the guidelines with a sense of the vertical structure of his overall justification, so that decisions at a lower level are more vulnerable than decisions at a higher.

Hercules will therefore apply at least two maxims in the second part of his theory of mistakes. If he can show, by arguments of history or by appeal to some sense of the legal community, that a particular principle, though it once had sufficient appeal to persuade a legislature or court to a legal decision, has now so little force that it is unlikely to generate any further such decisions, then the argument from fairness that supports that principle is undercut. If he can show by arguments of political morality that such a principle, apart from its popularity, is unjust, then the argument from fairness that supports that principle is overridden. Hercules will be delighted to find that these discriminations are familiar in the practice of other judges. The jurisprudential importance of his career does not lie in the novelty, but just in the familiarity, of the theory of hard cases that he has now created.

6. POLITICAL OBJECTIONS

The rights thesis has two aspects. Its descriptive aspect explains the present structure of the institution of adjudication. Its normative aspect offers a political justification for that structure. The story of Hercules shows how familiar judicial practice might have developed from a general acceptance of the thesis. This at once clarifies the thesis by showing its implications in some detail, and offers powerful, if special, argument for its descriptive aspect. But the story also provides a further political argument in favour of its normative aspect. Hercules began his calculations with the intention, not simply to replicate what other judges do, but to enforce the genuine institutional rights of those who came to his court. If he is able to reach decisions that satisfy our sense of justice, then that argues in favor of the political value of the thesis.

It may now be said, however, by way of rebuttal, that certain features of Hercules' story count against the normative aspect of the thesis. In the introductory part of this chapter, I mentioned a familiar objection to judicial originality: this is the argument from democracy that elected legislators have superior qualifications to make political decisions. I said that this argument is weak in the case of decisions of principle, but Hercules' story may give rise to fresh doubts on that score. The story makes plain that many of Hercules' decisions about legal rights depend upon judgments of political theory that might be made differently by different judges or by the public at large. It does not matter, to this objection, that the decision is one of principle rather than policy. It matters only that the decision is one of political conviction about which reasonable men disagree. If Hercules decides cases on the basis of such judgments, then he decides on the basis of his own convictions and preferences, which seems unfair, contrary to democracy, and offensive to the rule of law.

That is the general form of the objection I shall consider in this final section. It must first be clarified in one important respect. The objection charges Hercules with relying upon his own convictions in matters of political morality. That charge is ambiguous, because there are two ways in which an official might rely upon his own opinions in making such a decision. One of these, in a judge, is offensive, but the other is inevitable. Sometimes an official offers, as a reason for his decision, the fact that some person or group holds a particular belief or opinion. A legislator might offer, as a reason for voting for an anti-abortion statute, the fact that his constituents believe that abortion is wrong. That is a form of appeal to authority: the official who makes that appeal does not himself warrant the substance of the belief to which he appeals, nor does he count the soundness of the belief as part of his argument. We might imagine a judge appealing, in just this way, to the fact that he *himself* has a particular political preference. He might be a philosophical skeptic in matters of political morality. He might say that one man's opinion in such matters is worth no more than another's because neither has any objective standing, but that, since he himself happens to favor abortion, he will hold anti-abortion statutes unconstitutional.

That judge relies upon the naked fact that he holds a particular political view as itself a justification for his decision. But a judge may rely upon his own belief in the different sense of relying upon the truth or soundness of that belief. Suppose he believes, for example, that the due process clause of the Constitution, as a matter of law, makes invalid any constraint of a fundamental liberty, and that anti-abortion statutes constrain a fundamental liberty. He might rely upon the soundness of those convictions, not the fact that he, as opposed to others, happens to hold them. A judge need not rely upon the soundness of any *particular* belief in this way. Suppose the majority of his colleagues, or the editors of a prominent law journal, or the majority of the community voting in some referendum, holds a contrary view about abortion. He may decide that it is his duty to defer to their judgment of what the Constitution requires, in spite of the fact that their view is, as he thinks, unsound. But in that case he relies upon the soundness of his own conviction that his institutional duty is to defer to the judgment of others in this matter. He must, that is, rely upon the substance of his own judgment at some point, in order to make any judgment at all.

Hercules does not rely upon his own convictions in the first of these two ways. He does not count the fact that he himself happens to favor a particular conception of religious liberty, for example, as providing an argument in favor of a decision that advances that conception. If the objection we are considering is pertinent, therefore, it must be an objection to his relying upon his own convictions in the second way. But in that case the objection cannot be a blanket objection to his relying upon any of his convictions, because he must, inevitably, rely on some. It is rather an objection to his relying on the soundness of certain of his own convictions; it argues that he ought to defer to others in certain judgments even though their judgments are, as he thinks, wrong.

It is difficult, however, to see *which* of his judgments the objection supposes he should remand to others. We would not have any such problem if Hercules had accepted, rather than rejected, a familiar theory of adjudication. Classical jurisprudence supposes, as I said earlier, that judges decide cases in two steps: they find the limit of what the explicit law requires, and they then exercise an independent discretion to legislate on issues which the law does not reach. In the recent abortion cases,[1] according to this theory, the Supreme Court justices first determined that the language of the due process clause and of prior Supreme Court decisions did not dictate a decision either way. They then set aside the Constitution and the cases to decide whether, in their opinion, it is fundamentally unfair for a state to outlaw abortion in the first trimester.

Let us imagine another judge, called Herbert, who accepts this theory of adjudication and proposes to follow it in his decisions. Herbert might believe both that women have a background right to abort fetuses they carry, and that the majority of citizens think otherwise. The present objection argues that he must resolve that conflict in favor of democracy, so that, when he exercises his discretion to decide the abortion cases, he must decide in favor of the prohibitive statutes. Herbert might agree, in which case we should say that he has set aside his morality in favor of the people's morality. That is, in fact, a slightly misleading way to put the point. His own morality made the fact that the people held a particular view decisive; it did not withdraw in favor of the substance of that view. On the other hand, Herbert might disagree. He might believe that background rights in general, or this right in particular, must prevail against popular opinion even in the legislature, so that he has a duty, when exercising a legislative discretion, to declare the statutes unconstitutional. In that case, the present objection argues that he is mistaken, because he insufficiently weighs the principle of democracy in his political theory.

In any case, however, these arguments that seem tailor-made for Herbert are puzzling as arguments against Hercules. Hercules does not first find the limits of law and then deploy his own political convictions to supplement what the law requires. He uses his own judgment to determine what legal rights the parties before him have, and when that judgment is made nothing remains to submit to either his own or the public's convictions. The difference is not simply a difference in ways of describing the same thing: we saw in Section 4 that a judgment of institutional right, like the chess referee's judgment about the forfeiture rule, is very different from an independent judgment of political morality made in the interstices provided by the open texture of rules.

Herbert did not consider whether to consult popular morality until he had fixed the legal rights of the parties. But when Hercules fixes legal rights he has already taken the community's moral traditions into

[1] *Roe v. Wade*, 410 U.S. 113 (1973); *Doe v. Bolton*, 410 U.S. 179 (1973).

account, at least as these are captured in the whole institutional record that it is his office to interpret. Suppose two coherent justifications can be given for earlier Supreme Court decisions enforcing the due process clause. One justification contains some principle of extreme liberality that cannot be reconciled with the criminal law of most of the states, but the other contains no such principle. Hercules cannot seize upon the former justification as license for deciding the abortion cases in favor of abortion, even if he is himself an extreme liberal. His own political convictions, which favor the more liberal justification of the earlier cases, must fall, because they are inconsistent with the popular traditions that have shaped the criminal law that his justification must also explain.

Of course, Hercules' techniques may sometimes require a decision that opposes popular morality on some issue. Suppose no justification of the earlier constitutional cases can be given that does not contain a liberal principle sufficiently strong to require a decision in favor of abortion. Hercules must then reach that decision, no matter how strongly popular morality condemns abortion. He does not, in this case, enforce his own convictions against the community's. He rather judges that the community's morality is inconsistent on this issue : its constitutional morality, which is the justification that must be given for its constitution as interpreted by its judges, condemns its discrete judgment on the particular issue of abortion. Such conflicts are familiar within individual morality; if we wish to use the concept of a community morality in political theory, we must acknowledge conflicts within that morality as well. There is no question, of course, as to how such a conflict must be resolved. Individuals have a right to the consistent enforcement of the principles upon which their institutions rely. It is this institutional right, as defined by the community's constitutional morality, that Hercules must defend against any inconsistent opinion however popular.

These hypothetical cases show that the objection designed for Herbert is poorly cast as an objection against Hercules. Hercules' theory of adjudication at no point provides for any choice between his own political convictions and those he takes to be the political convictions of the community at large. On the contrary, his theory identifies a particular conception of community morality as decisive of legal issues; that conception holds that community morality is the political morality presupposed by the laws and institutions of the community. He must, of course, rely on his own judgment as to what the principles of that morality are, but this form of reliance is the second form we distinguished, which at some level is inevitable.

It is perfectly true that in some cases Hercules' decision about the content of this community morality, and thus his decision about legal rights, will be controversial. This will be so whenever institutional history must be justified by appeal to some contested political concept, like fairness or liberality or equality, but it is not sufficiently detailed so that it can be justified by only one among different conceptions of that concept. I offered, earlier, Hercules' decision of the free busing case as an example of such a decision; we may now take a more topical example. Suppose the earlier due process cases can be justified only by supposing some important right to human dignity, but do not themselves force a decision one way or the other on the issue of whether dignity requires complete control over the use of one's uterus. If Hercules sits in the abortion cases, he must decide that issue and must employ his own understanding of dignity to do so.

It would be silly to deny that this is a political decision, or that different judges, from different subcultures, would make it differently. Even so, it is nevertheless a very different decision from the decision whether women have, all things considered, a background right to abort their fetuses. Hercules might think dignity an unimportant concept; if he were to attend a new constitutional convention he might vote to repeal the due process clause, or at least to amend it so as to remove any idea of dignity from its scope. He is nevertheless able to decide whether that concept, properly understood, embraces the case of abortion. He is in the shoes of the chess referee who hates meritocracy, but is nevertheless able to consider whether intelligence includes psychological intimidation.

It is, of course, necessary that Hercules have some understanding of the concept of dignity, even if he denigrates that concept; and he will gain that understanding by noticing how the concept is used by those to whom it is important. If the concept figures in the justification of a series of constitutional decisions, then it must be a concept that is prominent in the political rhetoric and debates of the time. Hercules will collect his sense of the concept from its life in these contexts. He will do the best he can to understand the appeal of the idea to those to whom it does appeal. He will devise, so far as he can, a conception that explains that appeal to them.

This is a process that can usefully be seen as occupying two stages. Hercules will notice, simply as a matter of understanding his language, which are the clear, settled cases in which the concept holds. He will notice, for example, that if one man is thought to treat another as his servant, though he is not in fact that man's employer, then he will be thought to have invaded his dignity. He will next try to put himself, so far as he can, within the more general scheme of beliefs and attitudes of those who value the concept, to look at these clear cases through their eyes. Suppose, for example, that they believe in some Aristotelian doctrine of the urgency of self-fulfillment or they take self-reliance to be a very great virtue. Hercules must construct some general theory of the concept that explains why those who hold that belief, or accept that virtue, will also prize dignity; if his theory also explains why he, who does not accept the belief or the virtue, does not prize dignity, then the theory will be all the more successful for that feature.

Hercules will then use his theory of dignity to answer questions that institutional history leaves open. His theory of dignity may connect dignity with independence, so that someone's dignity is comprised whenever he is forced, against his will, to devote an important part of his activity to the concerns of others. In that case, he may well endorse the claim that women have a constitutional liberty of abortion, as an aspect of their conceded constitutional right to dignity.

That is how Hercules might interpret a concept he does not value, to reach a decision that, as a matter of background morality, he would reject. It is very unlikely, however, that Hercules will often find himself in that position; he is likely to value most of the concepts that figure in the justification of the institutions of his own community. In that case his analysis of these concepts will not display the same self-conscious air of sociological inquiry. He will begin within, rather than outside, the scheme of values that approves the concept, and he will be able to put to himself, rather than to some hypothetical self, questions about the deep morality that gives the concept value. The sharp distinction between background and institutional morality will fade, not because institutional morality is displaced by personal convictions, but because personal convictions have become the most reliable guide he has to institutional morality.

It does not follow, of course, that Hercules will even then reach exactly the same conclusions that any other judge would reach about disputed cases of the concept in question. On the contrary, he will then become like any reflective member of the community willing to debate about what fairness or equality or liberty requires on some occasion. But we now see that it is wrong to suppose that reflective citizens, in such debates, are simply setting their personal convictions against the convictions of others. They too are contesting different conceptions of a concept they suppose they hold in common; they are debating which of different theories of that concept best explains the settled or clear cases that fix the concept. That character of their debate is obscured by the fact that they do value the concepts they contest, and therefore reason intuitively or introspectively rather than in the more sociological mode that an outsider might use; but, so long as they put their claims as claims about concepts held in common, these claims will have the same structure as the outsider's. We may summarize these important points this way: the community's morality, on these issues at least, is not some sum or combination or function of the competing claims of its members; it is rather what each of the competing claims claims to be. When Hercules relies upon his own conception of dignity, in the second sense of reliance we distinguished, he is still relying on his own sense of what the community's morality provides.

It is plain, therefore, that the present objection must be recast if it is to be a weapon against Hercules. But it cannot be recast to fit Hercules better without losing its appeal. Suppose we say that Hercules must defer, not to his own judgment of the institutional morality of his community, but to the judgment of most members of that community about what that is. There are two apparent objections to tht recommendation. It is unclear, in the first place, how he could discover what that popular judgment is. It does not follow from the fact that the man in the street disapproves of abortion, or supports legislation making it criminal, that he has considered whether the concept of dignity presupposed by the Constitution, consistently applied, supports his political position. That is a sophisticated question requiring some dialectical skill, and though that skill may be displayed by the ordinary man when he self-consciously defends his position, it is not to be taken for granted that his political preferences, expressed casually or in the ballot, have been subjected to that form of examination.

But even if Hercules is satisfied that the ordinary man has decided that dignity does not require the right to abortion, the question remains why Hercules should take the ordinary man's opinion on that issue as decisive. Suppose Hercules thinks that the ordinary man is wrong; that he is wrong, that is, in his philosophical opinions about what the community's concepts require. If Herbert were in that position, he would have good reason to defer to the ordinary man's judgments. Herbert thinks that when the positive rules of law are vague or indeterminate, the litigants have no institutional right at all, so that any decision he might reach is a piece of fresh legislation. Since nothing he decides will cheat the parties of what they have a right to have at his hands, the argument is plausible, at least, that when he legislates he should regard himself as the agent of the majority. But Hercules cannot take that view of the matter. He knows that the question he must decide is the question of the parties' institutional rights. He knows that if he decides wrongly, as he would do if he followed the ordinary man's lead, he cheats the parties of what they are entitled to have. Neither Hercules nor Herbert would submit an ordinary legal question to popular opinion; since Hercules thinks that parties have rights in hard cases as well as in easy ones, he will not submit to popular opinion in hard cases either.

Of course, any judge's judgment about the rights of parties in hard cases may be wrong, and the objection may try, in one final effort, to capitalize on that fact. It might concede, *arguendo,* that Hercules' technique is appropriate to Hercules, who by hypothesis has great moral insight. But it would deny that the same technique is appropriate for judges generally, who do not. We must be careful, however, in assessing this challenge, to consider the alternatives. It is a matter of injustice when judges make mistakes about legal rights, whether these mistakes are in favor of the plaintiff or defendant. The objection points out that they will sometimes make such mistakes, because they are fallible and in any event disagree. But of course, though we, as social critics, know that mistakes will be made, we do not know when because we are not Hercules either. We must commend techniques of adjudication that might be expected to reduce the number of mistakes overall based on some judgment of the relative capacities of men and women who might occupy different roles.

Hercules' technique encourages a judge to make his own judgments about institutional rights. The argument from judicial fallibility might be thought to suggest two alternatives. The first argues that since judges are fallible they should make no effort at all to determine the institutional rights of the parties before them, but should decide hard cases only on grounds of policy, or not at all. But that is perverse; it argues that because judges will often, by misadventure, produce unjust decisions they should make no effort to produce just ones. The second alternative argues that since judges are fallible they should submit questions of institutional right raised by hard cases to someone else. But to whom? There is no reason to credit any other particular group with better facilities of moral argument; or, if there is, then it is the process of selecting judges, not the techniques of judging that they are asked to use, that must be changed. So this form of skepticism does not in itself argue against Hercules' technique of adjudication, though of course it serves as a useful reminder to any judge that he might well be wrong in his political judgments, and that he should therefore decide hard cases with humility.

5

Constitutional Cases

1.

When Richard Nixon was running for President he promised that he would appoint to the Supreme Court men who represented his own legal philosophy, that is, who were what he called 'strict constructionists'. The nominations he subsequently made and talked about, however, did not all illuminate that legal philosophy; jurisprudence played little part in the nation's evaluation of Haynesworth and Carswell, let alone those almost nominated, Hershell Friday and Mildred Lilly. But the President presented his successful choices, Lewis Powell and William Rehnquist, as examples of his theory of law, and took the occasion to expand on that theory for a national television audience. These men, he said, would enforce the law as it is, and not 'twist or bend' it to suit their own personal convictions, as Nixon accused the Warren Court of doing.

Nixon claimed that his opposition to the Warren Court's desegregation decisions, and to other decisions it took, were not based simply on a personal or political distaste for the results. He argued that the decisions violated the standards of adjudication that the Court should follow. The Court was usurping, in his views, powers that rightly belong to other institutions, including the legislatures of the various states whose school systems the Court sought to reform. He was, of course, not alone in this view. It has for some time been part of general conservative attitudes that the Supreme Court has exceeded its rightful authority. Nixon, Ford and many Congressmen and representatives have canvassed ways to limit the Court's authority by legislation. Nixon, for example, asked for a Congressional statute that would have purported to reverse important decisions, including the decision in *Swan v. Charlotte-Mecklenburg Board of Education* which gave federal courts wide powers to use busing orders as a remedy for certain forms of *de facto* segregation, and Senator Jackson and others have for some time campaigned for a constitutional amendment to the same point.

I shall not be concerned with the correctness of any of the Court's controversial decisions, nor with the wisdom of these various attempts, so far unsuccessful, to check its powers by some form of legislation or amendment. I am concerned rather with the philosophy of constitutional adjudication that the politicians who oppose the Court suppose that they hold. I shall argue that there is in fact no coherent philosophy to which such politicians may consistently appeal. I shall also try to show how the general theory of adjudication I described and defended in Chapter 4 supports the constitutional philosophy, if not the particular decisions, of the Warren Court.

Nixon is no longer president, and his crimes were so grave that no one is likely to worry very much any more about the details of his own legal philosophy. Nevertheless in what follows I shall use the name 'Nixon' to refer, not to Nixon, but to any politician holding the set of attitudes about the Supreme Court that he made explicit in his political campaigns. There was, fortunately, only one real Nixon, but there are, in the special sense in which I use the name, many Nixons.

What can be the basis of this composite Nixon's opposition to the controversial decisions of the Warren Court? He cannot object to these decisions simply because they went beyond prior law, or say that the Supreme Court must never change its mind. Indeed the Nixon Court itself seems intent on limiting the liberal decisions of the Warren Court, like *Miranda*. The Constitution's guarantee of 'equal protection of the laws', it is true, does not in plain words determine that 'separate but equal' school facilities are unconstitutional, or that segregation was so unjust that heroic measures are required to undo its effects. But neither does it provide that as a matter of constitutional law the Court would be wrong to reach these conclusions. It leaves these issues to the Court's judgment, and the Court would have made law just as much if it had, for example, refused to hold the North Carolina statute unconstitutional. It would have made law by establishing, as a matter of precedent, that the equal protection clause does not reach that far.

So we must search further to find a theoretical basis for Nixon's position. It may be silly, of course, to suppose that Nixon has a jurisprudence. He might simply have strung together catch phrases of conservative rhetoric, or he might be recording a distaste for any judicial decision that seems to extend the rights of individuals against constituted authority. But Nixon is, after all, a lawyer, and in any event his conservative views are supported by a great many lawyers and some very distinguished legal scholars. It is therefore important to see how far this conservative position can be defended as a matter of principle and not simply of prejudice.

2.

The constitutional theory on which our government rests is not a simple majoritarian theory. The Constitution, and particularly the Bill of Rights, is designed to protect individual citizens and groups against certain decisions that a majority of citizens might want to make, even when that majority acts in what it takes to be the general or common interest. Some of these constitutional restraints take the form of fairly precise rules, like the rule that requires a jury trial in federal criminal proceedings or, perhaps, the rule that forbids the national Congress to abridge freedom of speech. But other constraints take the form of what are often called 'vague' standards, for example, the provision that the government shall not deny men due process of law, or equal protection of the laws.

This interference with democratic practice requires a justification. The draftsmen of the Constitution assumed that these restraints could be justified by appeal to moral rights which individuals possess against the majority, and which the constitutional provisions, both 'vague' and precise, might be said to recognize and protect.

The 'vague' standards were chosen deliberately, by the men who drafted and adopted them, in place of the more specific and limited rules that they might have enacted. But their decision to use the language they did has caused a great deal of legal and political controversy, because even reasonable men of good will differ when they try to elaborate, for example, the moral rights that the due process clause or the equal protection clause brings into the law. They also differ when they try to apply these rights, however defined, to complex matters of political administration, like the educational practices that were the subject of the segregation cases.

The practice has developed of referring to a 'strict' and a 'liberal' side to these controversies, so that the Supreme Court might be said to have taken the 'liberal' side in the segregation cases and its critics the 'strict' side. Nixon has this distinction in mind when he calls himself a 'strict constructionist'. But the distinction is in fact confusing, because it runs together two different issues that must be separated. Any case that arises under the 'vague' constitutional guarantees can be seen as posing two questions : (1) Which decision is required by strict, that is to say faithful, adherence to the text of the Constitution or to the intention of those who adopted that text ? (2) Which decision is required by a political philosophy that takes a strict, that is to say narrow, view of the moral rights that individuals have against society? Once these questions are distinguished, it is plain that they may have different answers. The text of the First Amendment, for example, says that Congress shall make *no* law abridging the freedom of speech, but a narrow view of individual rights would permit many such laws, ranging from libel and obscenity laws to the Smith Act.

In the case of the 'vague' provisions, however, like the due process and equal protection clauses, lawyers have run the two questions together because they have relied, largely without recognizing it, on a theory of meaning that might be put this way : If the framers of the Constitution used vague language, as they did when they condemned violations of 'due process of law', then what they 'said' or 'meant' is limited to the instances of official action that they had in mind as violations, or, at least, to those instances that they would have thought were violations if they had had them in mind. If those who were responsible for adding the due process clause to the Constitution believed that it was fundamentally unjust to provide separate education for different races, or had detailed views about justice that entailed that conclusion, then the segregation decisions might be defended as an application of the principle they had laid down. Otherwise they could not be defended in this way, but instead would show that the judges had substituted their own ideas of justice for those the constitutional drafters meant to lay down.

This theory makes a strict interpretation of the text yield a narrow view of constitutional rights, because it limits such rights to those recognized by a limited group of people at a fixed date of history. It forces those who favor a more liberal set of rights to concede that they are departing from strict legal authority, a departure they must then seek to justify by appealing only to the desirability of the results they reach.

But the theory of meaning on which this argument depends is far too crude; it ignores a distinction that philosophers have made but lawyers have not yet appreciated. Suppose I tell my children simply that I expect them not to treat others unfairly. I no doubt have in mind examples of the conduct I mean to discourage, but I would not accept that my 'meaning' was limited to these examples, for two reasons. First I would expect my children to apply my instructions to situations I had not and could not have thought about. Second, I stand ready to admit that some particular act I had thought was fair when I spoke was in fact unfair, or vice versa, if one of my children is able to convince me of that later; in that case I should want to say that my instructions covered the case he cited, not that I had changed my instructions. I might say that I meant the family to be guided by the *concept* of fairness, not by any specific *conception* of fairness I might have had in mind.

This is a crucial distinction which it is worth pausing to explore. Suppose a group believes in common that acts may suffer from a special moral defect which they call unfairness, and which consists in a wrongful division of benefits and burdens, or a wrongful attribution of praise or blame. Suppose also that they agree on a great number of standard cases of unfairness and use these as benchmarks against which to test other, more controversial cases. In that case, the group has a concept of unfairness, and its members may appeal to that concept in moral instruction or argument. But members of that group may nevertheless differ over a large number of these controversial cases, in a way that suggests that each either has or acts on a different theory of *why* the standard cases are acts of unfairness. They may differ, that is, on which more fundamental principles must be relied upon to show that a particular division or attribution is unfair. In that case, the members have different conceptions of fairness.

If so, then members of this community who give instructions or set standards in the name of fairness may be doing two different things. First they may be appealing to the concept of fairness, simply by instructing others to act fairly; in this case they charge those whom they instruct with the responsibility of developing and applying their own conception of fairness as controversial cases arise. That is not the same thing, of course, as granting them a discretion to act as they like; it sets a standard which they must try – and may fail – to meet, because it assumes that one conception is superior to another. The man who appeals to the concept in this way may have his own conception, as I did when I told my children to act fairly; but he holds this conception only as his own theory of how the standard he set must be met, so that when he changes his theory he has not changed that standard.

On the other hand, the members may be laying down a particular conception of fairness; I would have done this, for example, if I had listed my wishes with respect to controversial examples or if, even less likely, I had specified some controversial and explicit theory of fairness, as if I had said to decide hard cases by applying the utilitarian ethics of Jeremy Bentham. The difference is a difference not just in the *detail* of the instructions given but in the *kind* of instructions given. When I appeal to the concept of fairness I appeal to what fairness means, and I give my views on that issue no special standing. When I lay down a conception of fairness, I lay down what I mean by fairness, and my view is therefore the heart of the matter. When I appeal to fairness I pose a moral issue; when I lay down my conception of fairness I try to answer it.

Once this distinction is made it seems obvious that we must take what I have been calling 'vague' constitutional clauses as representing appeals to the concepts they employ, like legality, equality, and cruelty. The Supreme Court may soon decide, for example, whether capital punishment is 'cruel' within the meaning of the constitutional clause that prohibits 'cruel and unusual punishment'. It would be a mistake for the Court to be much influenced by the fact that when the clause was adopted capital punishment was standard and unquestioned. That would be decisive if the framers of the clause had meant to lay down a particular conception of cruelty, because it would show that the conception did not extend so far.

But it is not decisive of the different question the Court now faces, which is this : Can the Court, responding to the framers' appeal to the concept of cruelty, now defend a conception that does not make death cruel?

Those who ignore the distinction between concepts and conceptions, but who believe that the Court ought to make a fresh determination of whether the death penalty is cruel, are forced to argue in a vulnerable way. They say that ideas of cruelty change over time, and that the Court must be free to reject out-of-date conceptions; this suggests that the Court must change what the Constitution enacted. But in fact the Court can enforce what the Constitution says only by making up its own mind about what is cruel, just as my children, in my example, can do what I said only by making up their own minds about what is fair. If those who enacted the broad clauses had meant to lay down particular conceptions, they would have found the sort of language conventionally used to do this, that is, they would have offered particular theories of the concepts in question.

Indeed the very practice of calling these clauses 'vague', in which I have joined, can now be seen to involve a mistake. The clauses are vague only if we take them to be botched or incomplete or schematic attempts to lay down particular conceptions. If we take them as appeals to moral concepts they could not be made more precise by being more detailed.[1]

The confusion I mentioned between the two senses of 'strict' construction' is therefore very misleading indeed. If courts try to be faithful to the text of the Constitution, they will for that very reason be forced to decide between competing conceptions of political morality. So it is wrong to attack the Warren Court, for example, on the ground that it failed to treat the Constitution as a binding text. On the contrary, if we wish to treat fidelity to that text as an overriding requirement of constitutional interpretation, then it is the conservative critics of the Warren Court who are at fault, because their philosophy ignores the direction to face issues of moral principle that the logic of the text demands.

I put the matter in a guarded way because we may *not* want to accept fidelity to the spirit of the text as an overriding principle of constitutional adjudication. It may be more important for courts to decide constitutional cases in a manner that respects the judgments of other institutions of government, for example. Or it may be more important for courts to protect established legal doctrines, so that citizens

---

[1] It is less misleading to say that the broad clauses of the Constitution 'delegate' power to the Court to enforce its own conceptions of political morality. But even this is inaccurate if it suggests that the Court need not justify its conception by arguments showing the connections between its conception and standard cases, as described in the text. If the Court finds that the death penalty is cruel, it must do so on the basis of some principles or groups of principles that unite the death penalty with the thumbscrew and the rack.

and the government can have confidence that the courts will hold to what they have said before. But it is crucial to recognize that these other policies compete with the principle that the Constitution is the fundamental and imperative source of constitutional law. They are not, as the 'strict constructionists' suppose, simply consequences of that principle.

3.

Once the matter is put in this light, moreover, we are able to assess these competing claims of policy, free from the confusion imposed by the popular notion of 'strict construction'. For this purpose I want now to compare and contrast two very general philosophies of how the courts should decide difficult or controversial constitutional issues. I shall call these two philosophies by the names they are given in the legal literature – the programs of 'judicial activism' and 'judicial restraint' – though it will be plain that these names are in certain ways misleading.

The program of judicial activism holds that courts should accept the directions of the so-called vague constitutional provisions in the spirit I described, in spite of competing reasons of the sort I mentioned. They should work out principles of legality, equality, and the rest, revise these principles from time to time in the light of what seems to the Court fresh moral insight, and judge the acts of Congress, the states, and the President accordingly. (This puts the program in its strongest form; in fact its supporters generally qualify it in ways I shall ignore for the present.)

The program of judicial restraint, on the contrary, argues that courts should allow the decisions of other branches of government to stand, even when they offend the judges' own sense of the principles required by the broad constitutional doctrines, except when these decisions are so offensive to political morality that they would violate the provisions on any plausible interpretation, or, perhaps, when a contrary decision is required by clear precedent. (Again, this put the program in a stark form; those who profess the policy qualify it in different ways.)

The Supreme Court followed the policy of activism rather than restraint in cases like the segregation cases because the words of the equal protection clause left it open whether the various educational practices of the states concerned should be taken to violate the Constitution, no clear precedent held that they did, and reasonable men might differ on the moral issues involved. If the Court had followed the program of judicial restraint, it would therefore have held in favor of the North Carolina statute in *Swann*, not against it. But the program of restraint would not always act to provide decisions that would please political conservatives. In the early days of the New Deal, as critics of the Warren Court are quick to point out, it was the liberals who objected to Court decisions that struck down acts of Congress in the name of the due process clause.

It may seem, therefore, that if Nixon has a legal theory it depends crucially on some theory of judicial restraint. We must now, however, notice a distinction between two forms of judicial restraint, for there are two different, and indeed incompatible, grounds on which that policy might be based.

The first is a theory of political *skepticism* that might be described in this way. The policy of judicial activism presupposes a certain objectivity of moral principle; in particular it presupposes that citizens do have certain moral rights against the state, like a moral right to equality of public education or to fair treatment by the police. Only if such moral rights exist in some sense can activism be justified as a program based on something beyond the judge's personal preferences. The skeptical theory attacks activism at its roots; it argues that in fact individuals have no such moral rights against the state. They have only such *legal* rights as the Constitution grants them, and these are limited to the plain and uncontroversial violations of public morality that the framers must have had actually in mind, or that have since been established in a line of precedent.

The alternative ground of a program of restraint is a theory of judicial *deference*. Contrary to the skeptical theory, this assumes that citizens do have moral rights against the state beyond what the law expressly grants them, but it points out that the character and strength of these rights are debatable and argues that political institutions other than courts are responsible for deciding which rights are to be recognized.

This is an important distinction, even though the literature of constitutional law does not draw it with any clarity. The skeptical theory and the theory of deference differ dramatically in the kind of justification they assume, and in their implications for the more general moral theories of the men who profess to hold them. These theories are so different that most American politicians can consistently accept the second, but not the first.

A skeptic takes the view, as I have said, that men have no moral rights against the state and only such legal rights as the law expressly provides. But what does this mean, and what sort of argument might the skeptic make for his view? There is, of course, a very lively dispute in moral philosophy about the nature and standing of moral rights, and considerable disagreement about what they are, if they are anything at all. I shall rely, in trying to answer these questions, on a low-keyed theory of moral rights against the state which I develop in Chapter 7. Under that theory, a man has a moral right against the state if for some reason the state would do wrong to treat him in a certain way, even though it would be in the general interest to do so. So a black child has a moral right to an equal education, for example, if it is wrong for the state not to provide that education, even if the community as a whole suffers thereby.

I want to say a word about the virtues of this way of looking at moral rights against the state. A great many lawyers are wary of talking about moral rights, even though they find it easy to talk about what is right or wrong for government to do, because they suppose that rights, if they exist at all, are spooky sorts of things that men and women have in much the same way as they have non-spooky things like tonsils. But the sense of rights I propose to use does not make ontological assumptions of that sort : it simply shows a claim of right to be a special, in the sense of a restricted, sort of judgment about what is right or wrong for governments to do.

Moreover, this way of looking at rights avoids some of the notorious puzzles associated with the concept. It allows us to say, with no sense of strangeness, that rights may vary in strength and character from case to case, and from point to point in history. If we think of rights as things, these metamorphoses seem strange, but we are used to the idea that moral judgments about what it is right or wrong to do are complex and are affected by considerations that are relative and that change.

The skeptic who wants to argue against the very possibility of rights against the state of this sort has a difficult brief. He must rely, I think, on one of three general positions : (a) He might display a more pervasive moral skepticism, which holds that even to speak of an act being morally right or wrong makes no sense. If no act is morally wrong, then the government of North Carolina cannot be wrong to refuse to bus school children. (b) He might hold a stark form of utilitarianism, which assumes that the only reason we ever have for regarding an act as right or wrong is its impact on the general interest. Under that theory, to say that busing may be morally required even though it does not benefit the community generally would be inconsistent. (c) He might accept some form of totalitarian theory, which merges the interests of the individual in the good of the general community, and so denies that the two can conflict.

Very few American politicians would be able to accept any of these three grounds. Nixon, for example, could not, because he presents himself as a moral fundamentalist who knows in his heart that pornography is wicked and that some of the people of South Vietnam have rights of self-determination in the name of which they and we may properly kill many others.

I do not want to suggest, however, that no one would in fact argue for judicial restraint on grounds of skepticism; on the contrary, some of the best known advocates of restraint have pitched their arguments entirely on skeptical grounds. In 1957, for example, the great judge Learned Hand delivered the Oliver Wendell Holmes lectures at Harvard. Hand was a student of Santayana and a disciple of Holmes, and skepticism in morals was his only religion. He argued for judicial restraint, and said that the Supreme Court had done wrong to declare school segregation illegal in the *Brown* case. It is wrong to suppose, he said, that claims about moral rights express anything more than the speakers' preferences. If the Supreme Court justifies its decisions by making such claims, rather than by relying on positive law, it is usurping the place of the legislature, for the job of the legislature, representing the majority, is to decide whose preferences shall govern.

This simple appeal to democracy is successful if one accepts the skeptical premise. Of course, if men have no rights against the majority, if political decision is simply a matter of whose preferences shall prevail, then democracy does provide a good reason for leaving that decision to more democratic institutions than courts, even when these institutions make choices that the judges themselves hate. But a very different, and much more vulnerable, argument from democracy is needed to support judicial restraint if it is based not on skepticism but on deference, as I shall try to show.

4.

If Nixon holds a coherent constitutional theory, it is a theory of restraint based not on skepticism but on deference. He believes that courts ought not to decide controversial issues of political morality because they ought to leave such decisions to other departments of government. If we ascribe this policy to Nixon, we can make sense of his charge that the Warren Court 'twisted and bent' the law. He would mean that they twisted and bent the principle of judicial deference, which is an understatement, because he would be more accurate if he said that they ignored it. But are there any good reasons for holding this policy of deference? If the policy is in fact unsound, then Nixon's jurisprudence is undermined, and he ought to be dissuaded from urging further Supreme Court appointments, or encouraging Congress to oppose the Court, in its name.

There is one very popular argument in favor of the policy of deference, which might be called the argument from democracy. It is at least debatable, according to this argument, whether a sound conception of equality forbids segregated education or requires measures like busing to break it down. Who ought to decide these debatable issues of moral and political theory? Should it be a majority of a court in Washington, whose members are appointed for life and are not politically responsible to the public whose lives will be affected by the decision? Or should it be the elected and responsible state or national legislators? A democrat, so this argument supposes, can accept only the second answer.

But the argument from democracy is weaker than it might first appear. The argument assumes, for one thing, that state legislatures are in fact responsible to the people in the way that democratic theory assumes. But in all the states, though in different degrees and for different reasons, that is not the case. In some states it is very far from the case. I want to pass that point, however, because it does not so much undermine the argument from democracy as call for more democracy, and that is a different matter. I want to fix attention on the issue of whether the appeal to democracy in this respect is even right in principle.

The argument assumes that in a democracy all unsettled issues, including issues of moral and political principle, must be resolved only by institutions that are politically responsible in the way that courts are not. Why should we accept that view of democracy? To say that that is what democracy means does no good, because it is wrong to suppose that the word, as a word, has anything like so precise a meaning. Even if it did, we should then have to rephrase our question to ask why we should have democracy, if we assume that is what it means. Nor is it better to say that that view of democracy is established in the American Constitution, or so entrenched in our political tradition that we are committed to it. We cannot argue that the Constitution, which provides no rule limiting judicial review to clear cases, establishes a theory of democracy that excludes wider review, nor can we say that our courts have in fact consistently accepted such a restriction. The burden of Nixon's argument is that they have.

So the argument from democracy is not an argument to which we are committed either by our words or our past. We must accept it, if at all, on the strength of its own logic. In order to examine the arguments more closely, however, we must make a further distinction. The argument as I have set it out might be continued in two different ways: one might argue that judicial deference is required because democratic institutions, like legislatures, are in fact likely to make *sounder* decisions than courts about the underlying issues that constitutional cases raise, that is, about the nature of an individual's moral rights against the state.

Or one might argue that it is for some reason *fairer* that a democratic institution rather than a court should decide such issues, even though there is no reason to believe that the institution will reach a sounder decision. The distinction between these two arguments would make no sense to a skeptic, who would not admit that someone could do a better

F

or worse job at identifying moral rights against the state, any more than someone could do a better or worse job of identifying ghosts. But a lawyer who believes in judicial deference rather than skepticism must acknowledge the distinction, though he can argue both sides if he wishes.

I shall start with the second argument, that legislatures and other democratic institutions have some special title to make constitutional decisions, apart from their ability to make better decisions. One might say that the nature of this title is obvious, because it is always fairer to allow a majority to decide any issue than a minority. But that, as has often been pointed out, ignores the fact that decisions about rights against the majority are not issues that in fairness ought to be left to the majority. Constitutionalism – the theory that the majority must be restrained to protect individual rights – may be a good or bad political theory, but the United States has adopted that theory, and to make the majority judge in its own cause seems inconsistent and unjust. So principles of fairness seem to speak against, not for, the argument from democracy.

Chief Justice Marshall recognized this in his decision in *Marbury v. Madison*, the famous case in which the Supreme Court first claimed the power to review legislative decisions against constitutional standards. He argued that since the Constitution provides that the Constitution shall be the supreme law of the land, the courts in general, and the Supreme Court in the end, must have power to declare statutes void that offend that Constitution. Many legal scholars regard his argument as a *non sequitur*, because, they say, although constitutional constraints are part of the law, the courts, rather than the legislature itself, have not necessarily been given authority to decide whether in particular cases that law has been violated.[1] But the argument is not a *non sequitur* if we take the principle that no man should be judge in his own cause to be so fundamental a part of the idea of legality that Marshall would have been entitled to disregard it only if the Constitution had expressly denied judicial review.

Some might object that it is simple-minded to say that a policy of

---

[1] I distinguish this objection to Marshall's argument from the different objection, not here relevant, that the Constitution should be interpreted to impose a legal *duty* on Congress not, for example, to pass laws abridging freedom of speech, but it should not be interpreted to detract from the legal *power* of Congress to make such a law valid if it breaks its duty. In this view, Congress is in the legal position of a thief who has a legal duty not to sell stolen goods, but retains legal power to make a valid transfer if he does. This interpretation has little to recommend it since Congress, unlike the thief, cannot be disciplined except by denying validity to its wrongful acts, at least in a way that will offer protection to the individuals the Constitution is designed to protect.

deference leaves the majority to judge its own cause. Political decisions are made, in the United States, not by one stable majority but by many different political institutions each representing a different constituency which itself changes its composition over time. The decision of one branch of government may well be reviewed by another branch that is also politically responsible, but to a larger or different constituency. The acts of the Arizona police which the Court held unconstitutional in *Miranda*, for example, were in fact subject to review by various executive boards and municipal and state legislatures of Arizona, as well as by the national Congress. It would be naïve to suppose that all of these political institutions are dedicated to the same policies and interests, so it is wrong to suppose that if the Court had not intervened the Arizona police would have been free to judge themselves.

But this objection is itself too glib, because it ignores the special character of disputes about individual moral rights as distinct from other kinds of political disputes. Different institutions do have different constituencies when, for example, labor or trade or welfare issues are involved, and the nation often divides sectionally on such issues. But this is not generally the case when individual constitutional rights, like the rights of accused criminals, are at issue. It has been typical of these disputes that the interests of those in political control of the various institutions of the government have been both homogeneous and hostile. Indeed that is why political theorists have conceived of constitutional rights as rights against the 'state' or the 'majority' as such, rather than against any particular body or branch of government.

The early segregation cases are perhaps exceptions to that generality, for one might argue that the only people who wanted *de jure* segregation were white Southerners. But the fact remains that the national Congress had not in fact checked segregation, either because it believed it did not have the legal power to do so or because it did not want to; in either case the example hardly argues that the political process provides an effective check on even local violations of the rights of politically ineffective minorities. In the dispute over busing, moreover, the white majority mindful of its own interests has proved to be both national and powerful. And of course decisions of the national government, like executive decisions to wage war or congressional attempts to define proper police policy, as in the Crime Control Act of 1968, are subject to no review if not court review.

It does seem fair to say, therefore, that the argument from democracy asks that those in political power be invited to be the sole judge of their own decisions, to see whether they have the right to do what they have decided they want to do. That is not a final proof that a policy of judicial activism is superior to a program of deference. Judicial activism involves risks of tyranny; certainly in the stark and simple form I set out. It might even be shown that these risks override the unfairness of asking the majority to be judge in its own cause. But the point does undermine the argument that the majority, in fairness, must be allowed to decide the limits of its own power.

We must therefore turn to the other continuation of the argument from democracy, which holds that democratic institutions, like legislatures, are likely to reach *sounder* results about the moral rights of individuals than would courts. In 1969 the late Professor Alexander Bickel of the Yale Law School delivered his Holmes Lectures at Harvard and argued for the program of judicial restraint in a novel and ingenious way. He allowed himself to suppose, for purposes of argument, that the Warren Court's program of activism could be justified if in fact it produced desirable results.[1] He appeared, therefore, to be testing the policy of activism on its own grounds, because he took activism to be precisely the claim that the courts have the moral right to improve the future, whatever legal theory may say. Learned Hand and other opponents of activism had challenged that claim. Bickel accepted it, as least provisionally, but he argued that activism fails its own test.

The future that the Warren Court sought has already begun not to work, Bickel said. The philosophy of racial integration it adopted was too crude, for example, and has already been rejected by the more imaginative leaders of the black community. Its thesis of simple and radical equality has proved unworkable in many other ways as well; its simple formula of one-man-one-vote for passing on the fairness of election districting, for instance, has produced neither sense nor fairness.

Why should a radical Court that aims at improving society fail even on its own terms? Bickel has this answer: Courts, including the Supreme Court, must decide blocks of cases on principle, rather than responding in a piecemeal way to a shifting set of political pressures. They must do so not simply because their institutional morality requires it, but because their institutional structure provides no means by which they might gauge political forces even if they wanted to. But government by principle is an inefficient and in the long run fatal form of government, no matter how able and honest the statesmen who try to administer it. For there is a limit to the complexity that any principle can contain and remain a recognizable principle, and this limit falls short of the complexity of social organization.

The Supreme Court's reapportionment decisions, in Bickel's view,

---

[1] Professor Bickel also argued, with his usual very great skill, that many of the Warren Court's major decisions could not even be justified on conventional grounds, that is, by the arguments the Court advanced in its opinions. His criticism of these opinions is often persuasive, but the Court's failures of craftsmanship do not affect the argument I consider in the text. (His Holmes lectures were amplified in his book *The Supreme Court and the Idea of Progress,* 1970.)

were not mistaken just because the Court chose the wrong principle. One-man-one-vote is too simple, but the Court could not have found a better, more sophisticated principle that would have served as a successful test for election districting across the country, or across the years, because successful districting depends upon accommodation with thousands of facts of political life, and can be reached, if at all, only by the chaotic and unprincipled development of history. Judicial activism cannot work as well as government by the more-or-less democratic institutions, not because democracy is required by principle, but, on the contrary, because democracy works without principle, forming institutions and compromises as a river forms a bed on its way to the sea.

What are we to make of Bickel's argument? His account of recent history can be, and has been, challenged. It is by no means plain, certainly not yet, that racial integration will fail as a long-term strategy; and he is wrong if he thinks that black Americans, of whom more still belong to the NAACP than to more militant organizations, have rejected it. No doubt the nation's sense of how to deal with the curse of racism swings back and forth as the complexity and size of the problem become more apparent, but Bickel may have written at a high point of one arc of the pendulum.

He is also wrong to judge the Supreme Court's effect on history as if the Court were the only institution at work, or to suppose that if the Court's goal has not been achieved the country is worse off than if it had not tried. Since 1954, when the Court laid down the principle that equality before the law requires integrated education, we have not had, except for a few years of the Johnson Administration, a national executive willing to accept that principle as an imperative. For the past several years we have had a national executive that seems determined to undermine it. Nor do we have much basis for supposing that the racial situation in America would now be more satisfactory, on balance, if the Court had not intervened, in 1954 and later, in the way that it did.

But there is a very different, and for my purpose much more important, objection to take to Bickel's theory. His theory is novel because it appears to concede an issue of principle to judicial activism, namely, that the Court is entitled to intervene if its intervention produces socially desirable results. But the concession is an illusion, because his sense of what is socially desirable is inconsistent with the presupposition of activism that individuals have moral rights against the state. In fact, Bickel's argument cannot succeed, even if we grant his facts and his view of history, except on a basis of a skepticism about rights as profound as Learned Hand's.

I presented Bickel's theory as an example of one form of the argument from democracy, the argument that since men disagree about rights, it is safer to leave the final decision about rights to the political process, safer in the sense that the results are likely to be sounder. Bickel suggests a reason why the political process is safer. He argues that the endurance of a political settlement about rights is some evidence of the political morality of that settlement. He argues that this evidence is better than the sorts of argument from principle that judges might deploy if the decision were left to them.

There is a weak version of this claim, which cannot be part of Bickel's argument. This version argues that no political principle establishing rights can be sound, whatever abstract arguments might be made in its favor, unless it meets the test of social acceptance in the long run; so that, for example, the Supreme Court cannot be right in its views about the rights of black children, or criminal suspects, or atheists, if the community in the end will not be persuaded to recognize these rights.

This weak version may seem plausible for different reasons. It will appeal, for instance, to those who believe both in the fact and in the strength of the ordinary man's moral sense, and in his willingness to entertain appeals to that sense. But it does not argue for judicial restraint except in the very long run. On the contrary, it supposes what lawyers are fond of calling a dialogue between the judges and the nation, in which the Supreme Court is to present and defend its reflective view of what the citizen's rights are, much as the Warren Court tried to do, in the hope that the people will in the end agree.

We must turn, therefore, to the strong version of the claim. This argues that the organic political process will secure the genuine rights of men more certainly if it is not hindered by the artificial and rationalistic intrusion of the courts. On this view, the rights of blacks, suspects, and atheists will emerge through the process of political institutions responding to political pressures in the normal way. If a claim of right cannot succeed in this way, then for that reason it is, or in any event it is likely to be, an improper claim of right. But this bizarre proposition is only a disguised form of the skeptical point that there are in fact no rights against the state.

Perhaps, as Burke and his modern followers argue, a society will produce the institutions that best suit it only by evolution and never by radical reform. But rights against the state are claims that, if accepted, require society to settle for institutions that may not suit it so comfortably. The nerve of a claim of right, even on the demythologized analysis of rights I am using, is that an individual is entitled to protection against the majority even at the cost of the general interest. Of course the comfort of the majority will require some accommodation for minorities but only to the extent necessary to preserve order; and that is usually an accommodation that falls short of recognizing their rights.

Indeed the suggestion that rights can be demonstrated by a process of history rather than by an appeal to principle shows either a confusion or no real concern about what rights are. A claim of right presupposes a moral argument and can be established in no other way. Bickel paints the judicial activists (and even some of the heroes of judicial restraint, like Brandeis and Frankfurter, who had their lapses) as eighteenth-century philosophers who appeal to principle because they hold the optimistic view that a blueprint may be cut for progress. But this picture confuses two grounds for the appeal to principle and reform, and two senses of progress.

It is one thing to appeal to moral principle in the silly faith that ethics as well as economics moves by an invisible hand, so that individual rights and the general good will coalesce, and law based on principle will move the nation to a frictionless utopia where everyone is better off than he was before. Bickel attacks that vision by his appeal to history, and by his other arguments against government by principle. But it is quite another matter to appeal to principle *as* principle, to show, for example, that it is unjust to force black children to take their public education in black schools, even if a great many people *will* be worse off if the state adopt the measures needed to prevent this.

This is a different version of progress. It is moral progress, and though history may show how difficult it is to decide where moral progress lies, and how difficult to persuade others once one has decided, it cannot follow from this that those who govern us have no responsibility to face that decision or to attempt that persuasion.

5.

This has been a complex argument, and I want to summarize it. Our constitutional system rests on a particular moral theory, namely, that men have moral rights against the state. The difficult clauses of the Bill of Rights, like the due process and equal protection clauses, must be understood as appealing to moral concepts rather than laying down particular conceptions; therefore a court that undertakes the burden of applying these clauses fully as law must be an activist court, in the sense that it must be prepared to frame and answer questions of political morality.

It may be necessary to compromise that activist posture to some extent, either for practical reasons or for competing reasons of principle. But Nixon's public statements about the Supreme Court suggest that the activist policy must be abandoned altogether, and not merely compromised, for powerful reasons of principle. If we try to state these reasons of principle, we find that they are inconsistent with the assumption of a constitutional system, either because they leave the majority to judge its own cause, or because they rest on a skepticism about moral rights that neither Nixon nor most American politicians can consistently embrace.

So Nixon's jurisprudence is a pretense and no genuine theory at all. It cannot be supported by arguments he can accept, let alone by arguments he has advanced. Nixon abused his legal credentials by endorsing an incoherent philosophy of law and by calling into question the good faith of other lawyers because they do not accept what he cannot defend.

The academic debate about the Supreme Court's power of judicial review must, however, have contributed to Nixon's confusion. The failure to draw the distinctions I have described, between appealing to a concept and laying down a conception, and between skepticism and deference, has posed a false choice between judicial activism as the program of moral crusade and judicial restraint as the program of legality. Why has a sophisticated and learned profession posed a complex issue in this simple and misleading way?

The issue at the heart of the academic debate might be put this way. If we give the decisions of principle that the Constitution requires to the judges, instead of to the people, we act in the spirit of legality, so far as our institutions permit. But we run a risk that the judges may make the wrong decisions. Every lawyer thinks that the Supreme Court has gone wrong, even violently wrong, at some point in its career. If he does not hate the conservative decisions of the early 1930s, which threatened to block the New Deal, he is likely to hate the liberal decisions of the last decade.

We must not exaggerate the danger. Truly unpopular decisions will be eroded because public compliances will be grudging, as it has been in the case of public school prayers, and because old judges will die or retire and be replaced by new judges appointed because they agree with a President who has been elected by the people. The decisions against the New Deal did not stand, and the more daring decisions of recent years are now at the mercy of the Nixon Court. Nor does the danger of wrong decisions lie entirely on the side of excess; the failure of the Court to act in the McCarthy period, epitomized by its shameful decision upholding the legality of the Smith Act in the *Dennis* case, may be thought to have done more harm to the nation than did the Court's conservative bias in the early Roosevelt period.

Still, we ought to design our institutions to reduce the risk of error, so far as this is possible. But the academic debate has so far failed to produce an adequate account of where error lies. For the activists, the segregation decisions were right because they advanced a social goal they think desirable, or they were wrong because they advanced a social goal they dislike. For the advocates of restraint they were wrong, whether they approve or disapprove that social goal, because they violated the principle that the Court is not entitled to impose its own view of the social good on the nation.

Neither of these tests forces lawyers to face the special sort of moral issue I described earlier, the issue of what moral rights an individual has against the state. The activists rest their case, when they argue it at all, on the assumption either that their social goals are self-evidently good or that they will in the long run work for the benefit of everybody; this optimism exposes them to Bickel's argument that this is not necessarily so. Those who want restraint argue that some principle of legality protects constitutional lawyers from facing any moral issues at all.

Constitutional law can make no genuine advance until it isolates the problem of rights against the state and makes that problem part of its own agenda. That argues for a fusion of constitutional law and moral theory, a connection that, incredibly, has yet to take place. It is perfectly understandable that lawyers dread contamination with moral philosophy, and particularly with those philosophers who talk about rights, because the spooky overtones of that concept threaten the graveyard of reason. But better philosophy is now available than the lawyers may remember. Professor Rawls of Harvard, for example, has published an abstract and complex book about justice which no constitutional lawyer will be able to ignore.[1] There is no need for lawyers to play a passive role in the development of a theory of moral rights against the state, however, any more than they have been passive in the development of legal sociology and legal economics. They must recognize that law is no more independent from philosophy than it is from these other disciplines.

[1] *A Theory of Justice*, 1972. See Chapter 6.

6

Justice and Rights

I trust that it is not necessary to describe John Rawls's famous idea of the original position in any great detail.[1] It imagines a group of men and women who come together to form a social contract. Thus far it resembles the imaginary congresses of the classical social contract theories. The original position differs, however, from these theories in its description of the parties. They are men and women with ordinary tastes, talents, ambitions, and convictions, but each is temporarily ignorant of these features of his own personality, and must agree upon a contract before his self-awareness returns.

Rawls tries to show that if these men and women are rational, and act only in their own self-interest, they will choose his two principles of justice. These provide, roughly, that every person must have the largest political liberty compatible with a like liberty for all, and that inequalities in power, wealth, income, and other resources must not exist except in so far as they work to the absolute benefit of the worst-off members of society. Many of Rawls's critics disagree that men and women in the original position would inevitably choose these two principles. The principles are conservative, and the critics believe they would be chosen only by men who were conservative by temperament, and not by men who were natural gamblers. I do not think this criticism is well-taken, but in this essay, at least, I mean to ignore the point. I am interested in a different issue.

Suppose that the critics are wrong, and that men and women in the original position would in fact choose Rawls's two principles as being in their own best interest. Rawls seems to think that that fact would provide an argument in favor of these two principles as a standard of justice against which to test actual political institutions. But it is not immediately plain why this should be so.

If a group contracted in advance that disputes amongst them would be settled in a particular way, the fact of that contract would be a powerful argument that such disputes should be settled in that way

[1] John Rawls, *A Theory of Justice*, 1972.

when they do arise. The contract would be an argument in itself, independent of the force of the reasons that might have led different people to enter the contract. Ordinarily, for example, each of the parties supposes that a contract he signs is in his own interest; but if someone has made a mistake in calculating his self-interest, the fact that he did contract is a strong reason for the fairness of holding him nevertheless to the bargain.

Rawls does not suppose that any group ever entered into a social contract of the sort he describes. He argues only that if a group of rational men did find themselves in the predicament of the original position, they would contract for the two principles. His contract is hypothetical, and hypothetical contracts do not supply an independent argument for the fairness of enforcing their terms. A hypothetical contract is not simply a pale form of an actual contract; it is no contract at all.

If, for example, I am playing a game, it may be that I would have agreed to any number of ground rules if I had been asked in advance of play. It does not follow that these rules may be enforced against me if I have not, in fact, agreed to them. There must be reasons, of course, why I would have agreed if asked in advance, and these may also be reasons why it is fair to enforce these rules against me even if I have not agreed. But my hypothetical agreement does not count as a reason, independent of these other reasons, for enforcing the rules against me, as my actual agreement would have.

Suppose that you and I are playing poker and we find, in the middle of a hand, that the deck is one card short. You suggest that we throw the hand in, but I refuse because I know I am going to win and I want the money in the pot. You might say that I would certainly have agreed to that procedure had the possibility of the deck being short been raised in advance. But your point is not that I am somehow committed to throwing the hand in by an agreement I never made. Rather you use the device of a hypothetical agreement to make a point that might have been made without that device, which is that the solution recommended is so obviously fair and sensible that only someone with an immediate contrary interest could disagree. Your main argument is that your solution is fair and sensible, and the fact that I would have chosen it myself adds nothing of substance to that argument. If I am able to meet the main argument nothing remains, rising out of your claim that I would have agreed, to be answered or excused.

In some circumstances, moreover, the fact that I would have agreed does not even suggest an independent argument of this character. Everything depends on your reasons for supposing that I would have agreed. Suppose you say that I would have agreed, if you had brought up the point and insisted on your solution, because I very much wanted to play and would have given in rather than miss my chance. I might concede that I would have agreed for that reason, and then add that I am lucky that you did not raise the point. The fact that I would have agreed if you had insisted neither adds nor suggests any argument why I should agree now. The point is not that it would have been unfair of you to insist on your proposal as a condition of playing; indeed, it would not have been. If you had held out for your proposal, and I had agreed, I could not say that my agreement was in any way nullified or called into question because of duress. But if I had not in fact agreed, the fact that I would have in itself means nothing.

I do not mean that it is never relevant, in deciding whether an act affecting someone is fair, that he would have consented if asked. If a doctor finds a man unconscious and bleeding, for example, it might be important for him to ask whether the man would consent to a transfusion if he were conscious. If there is every reason to think that he would, that fact is important in justifying the transfusion if the patient later, perhaps because he has undergone a religious conversion, condemns the doctor for having proceeded. But this sort of case is beside the present point, because the patient's hypothetical agreement shows that his will was inclined towards the decision at the time and in the circumstances that the decision was taken. He has lost nothing by not being consulted at the appropriate time, because he would have consented if he had been. The original position argument is very different. If we take it to argue for the fairness of applying the two principles we must take it to argue that because a man would have consented to certain principles if asked in advance, it is fair to apply those principles to him later, under different circumstances, when he does not consent.

But that is a bad argument. Suppose I did not know the value of my painting on Monday; if you had offered me $100 for it then I would have accepted. On Tuesday I discovered it was valuable. You cannot argue that it would be fair for the courts to make me sell it to you for $100 on Wednesday. It may be my good fortune that you did not ask me on Monday, but that does not justify coercion against me later.

We must therefore treat the argument from the original position as we treat your argument in the poker game; it must be a device for calling attention to some independent argument for the fairness of the two principles – an argument that does not rest on the false premise that a hypothetical contract has some pale binding force. What other argument is available? One might say that the original position shows that the two principles are in the best interests of every member of any political community, and that it is fair to govern in accordance with them for that reason. It is true that if the two principles could be shown to be in everyone's interest, that would be a sound argument for their fairness, but it is hard to see how the original position can be used to show that they are.

We must be careful to distinguish two senses in which something might be said to be in my interest. It is in my *antecedent* interest to make a bet on a horse that, all things considered, offers the best odds, even if, in the event, the horse loses. It is in my *actual* interest to bet on the horse that wins, even if the bet was, at the time I made it, a silly one. If the original position furnishes an argument that it is in everyone's interest to accept the two principles over other possible bases for a constitution, it must be an argument that uses the idea of antecedent and not actual interest. It is not in the actual best interests of everyone to choose the two principles, because when the veil of ignorance is lifted some will discover that they would have been better off if some other principle, like the principle of average utility, had been chosen.

A judgment of antecedent interest depends upon the circumstances under which the judgment is made, and, in particular, upon the knowledge available to the man making the judgment. It might be in my antecedent interest to bet on a certain horse at given odds before the starting gun, but not, at least at the same odds, after he has stumbled on the first turn. The fact, therefore, that a particular choice is in my interest at a particular time, under conditions of great uncertainty, is not a good argument for the fairness of enforcing that choice against me later under conditions of much greater knowledge. But that is what, on this interpretation, the original position argument suggests, because it seeks to justify the contemporary use of the two principles on the supposition that, under conditions very different from present conditions, it would be in the antecedent interest of everyone to agree to them. If I have bought a ticket on a longshot it might be in my antecedent interest, before the race, to sell the ticket to you for twice what I paid; it does not follow that it is fair for you to take it from me for that sum when the longshot is about to win.

Someone might now say that I have misunderstood the point of the special conditions of uncertainty in the original position. The parties are made ignorant of their special resources and talents to prevent them from bargaining for principles that are inherently unfair because they favor some collection of resources and talents over others. If the man in the original position does not know his special interests, he cannot negotiate to favor them. In that case, it might be said, the uncertainty of the original position does not vitiate the argument from antecedent interest as I have suggested, but only limits the range within which self-interest might operate. The argument shows that the two principles are in everyone's interest once obviously unfair principles are removed from consideration by the device of uncertainty. Since the only additional knowledge contemporary men and women have over men and women in the original position is knowledge that they ought not to rely upon in choosing principles of justice, their antecedent interest is, so far as it is relevant, the same, and if that is so the original position argument does offer a good argument for applying the two principles to contemporary politics.

But surely this confuses the argument that Rawls makes with a different argument that he might have made. Suppose his men and women had full knowledge of their own talents and tastes, but had to reach agreement under conditions that ruled out, simply by stipulation, obviously unfair principles like those providing special advantage for named individuals. If Rawls could show that, once such obviously unfair principles had been set aside, it would be in the interest of everyone to settle for his two principles, that would indeed count as an argument for the two principles. My point – that the antecedent self-interest of men in the original position is different from that of contemporary men – would no longer hold because both groups of men would then have the same knowledge about themselves, and be subject to the same moral restrictions against choosing obviously unfair principles.

Rawls's actual argument is quite different, however. The ignorance in which his men must choose affects their calculations of self-interest, and cannot be described merely as setting boundaries within which these calculations must be applied. Rawls supposes, for example, that his men would inevitably choose conservative principles because this would be the only rational choice, in their ignorance, for self-interested men to make. But some actual men, aware of their own talents, might well prefer less conservative principles that would allow them to take advantage of the resources they know they have. Someone who considers the original position an argument for the conservative principles, therefore, is faced with this choice. If less conservative principles, like principles that favor named individuals, are to be ruled out as obviously unfair, then the argument for the conservative principles is complete at the outset, on grounds of obvious fairness alone. In that case neither the original position nor any considerations of self-interest it is meant to demonstrate play any role in the argument. But if less conservative principles cannot be ruled out in advance as obviously unfair, then imposing ignorance on Rawls's men, so that they prefer the more conservative principles, cannot be explained simply as ruling out obviously unfair choices. And since this affects the antecedent self-interest of these men, the argument that the original position demonstrates the antecedent self-interest of actual men must therefore fail. This same dilemma can, of course, be constructed for each feature of the two principles.

I recognize that the argument thus far seems to ignore a distinctive feature of Rawls's methodology, which he describes as the technique of seeking a 'reflective equilibrium' between our ordinary, unreflective moral beliefs and some theoretical structure that might unify and justify these ordinary beliefs.[1] It might now be said that the idea of an original position plays a part in this reflective equilibrium, which we will miss if we insist, as I have, on trying to find a more direct, one-way argument from the original position to the two principles of justice.

The technique of equilibrium does play an important role in Rawls's argument, and it is worth describing that technique briefly here. The technique assumes that Rawls's readers have a sense, which we draw upon in our daily life, that certain particular political arrangements or decisions, like conventional trials, are just and others, like slavery, are unjust. It assumes, moreover, that we are each able to arrange these immediate intuitions or convictions in an order that designates some of them as more certain than others. Most people, for example, think that it is more plainly unjust for the state to execute innocent citizens of its own than to kill innocent foreign civilians in war. They might be prepared to abandon their position on foreign civilians in war, on the basis of some argument, but would be much more reluctant to abandon their view on executing innocent countrymen.

It is the task of moral philosophy, according to the technique of equilibrium, to provide a structure of principles that supports these immediate convictions about which we are more or less secure, with two goals in mind. First, this structure of principles must explain the convictions by showing the underlying assumptions they reflect; second it must provide guidance in those cases about which we have either no convictions or weak or contradictory convictions. If we are unsure, for example, whether economic institutions that allow great disparity of wealth are unjust, we may turn to the principles that explain our confident convictions, and then apply these principles to that difficult issue.

But the process is not simply one of finding principles that accommodate our more-or-less settled judgments. These principles must support, and not merely account for, our judgments, and this means that the principles must have independent appeal to our moral sense. It might be, for example, that a cluster of familiar moral convictions could be shown to serve an undeserving policy – perhaps, that the

[1] pp. 48 ff.

standard judgments we make without reflection serve the purpose of maintaining one particular class in political power. But this discovery would not vouch for the principle of class egoism; on the contrary, it would discredit our ordinary judgments, unless some other principle of a more respectable sort could be found that also fits our intuitions, in which case it would be this principle and not the class-interest principle that our intuitions would recommend.

It might be that no coherent set of principles could be found that has independent appeal and that supports the full set of our immediate convictions; indeed it would be surprising if this were not often the case. If that does happen, we must compromise, giving way on both sides. We might relax, though we could not abandon, our initial sense of what might be an acceptable principle. We might come to accept, for example, after further reflection, some principle that seemed to us initially unattractive, perhaps the principle that men should sometimes be made to be free. We might accept this principle if we were satisfied that no less harsh principle could support the set of political convictions we were especially reluctant to abandon. On the other hand, we must also be ready to modify or adjust, or even to give up entirely, immediate convictions that cannot be accommodated by any principle that meets our relaxed standards; in adjusting these immediate convictions we will use our initial sense of which seem to us more and which less certain, though in principle no immediate conviction can be taken as immune from reinspection or abandonment if that should prove necessary. We can expect to proceed back and forth between our immediate judgments and the structure of explanatory principles in this way, tinkering first with one side and then the other, until we arrive at what Rawls calls the state of reflective equilibrium in which we are satisfied, or as much satisfied as we can reasonably expect.

It may well be that, at least for most of us, our ordinary political judgments stand in this relation of reflective equilibrium with Rawls's two principles of justice, or, at least, that they could be made to do so through the process of adjustment just described. It is nevertheless unclear how the idea of the original position fits into this structure or, indeed, why it has any role to play at all. The original position is not among the ordinary political convictions that we find we have, and that we turn to reflective equilibrium to justify. If it has any role, it must be in the process of justification, because it takes its place in the body of theory we construct to bring our convictions into balance. But if the two principles of justice are themselves in reflective equilibrium with our convictions, it is unclear why we need the original position to supplement the two principles on the theoretical side of the balance. What can the idea contribute to a harmony already established?

We should consider the following answer. It is one of the cond[...]
we impose on a theoretical principle, before we allow it to figure
justification of our convictions, that the people the principle w[...]
govern would have accepted that principle, at least under certain
conditions, if they had been asked, or at least that the principle can be
shown to be in the antecedent interest of every such person. If this is so,
then the original position plays an essential part in the process of justification through equilibrium. It is used to show that the two principles
conform to this established standard of acceptability for political principles. At the same time, the fact that the two principles, which do
conform to that standard, justify our ordinary convictions in reflective
equilibrium reinforces our faith in the standard and encourages us to
apply it to other issues of political or moral philosophy.

This answer does not advance the case that the original position
furnishes an argument for the two principles, however; it merely
restates the ideas we have already considered and rejected. It is certainly
not part of our established political traditions or ordinary moral understanding that principles are acceptable only if they would be chosen
by men in the particular predicament of the original position. It is, of
course, part of these traditions that principles are fair if they have in
fact been chosen by those whom they govern, or if they can at least be
shown to be in their antecedent common interest. But we have already
seen that the original position device cannot be used to support either
of these arguments in favor of applying the two principles to contemporary politics. If the original position is to play any role in a structure
of principles and convictions in reflective equilibrium, it must be by
virtue of assumptions we have not yet identified.

It is time to reconsider an earlier assumption. So far I have been
treating the original position construction as if it were either the foundation of Rawls's argument or an ingredient in a reflective equilibrium
established between our political intuitions and his two princples of
justice. But, in fact, Rawls does not treat the original position that way.
He describes the construction in these words :

> I have emphasized that this original position is purely hypotheti-
> cal. It is natural to ask why, if this agreement is never actually
> entered into, we should take any interest in these principles, moral
> or otherwise. The answer is that the conditions embodied in the
> description of the original position are ones that we do in fact
> accept. Or if we do not, then perhaps we can be persuaded to do
> so by philosophical reflection. Each aspect of the contractual situa-
> tion can be given supporting grounds. . . . On the other hand,
> this conception is also an intuitive notion that suggests its own

elaboration, so that led on by it we are drawn to define more
clearly the standpoint from which we can best interpret moral
relationships. We need a conception that enables us to envision
our objective from afar : the intuitive notion of the original position is to do this for us.[1]

This description is taken from Rawls's first statement of the original
position. It is recalled and repeated in the very last paragraph of the
book.[2] It is plainly of capital importance, and it suggests that the original
position, far from being the foundation of his argument, or an expository
device for the technique of equilibrium, is one of the major substantive
products of the theory as a whole. Its importance is reflected in another
crucial passage. Rawls describes his moral theory as a type of psychology.
He wants to characterize the structure of our (or, at least, one person's)
capacity to make moral judgments of a certain sort, that is, judgments
about justice. He thinks that the conditions embodied in the original
position are the fundamental 'principles governing our moral powers,
or, more specifically, our sense of justice'.[3] The original position is therefore a schematic representation of a particular mental process of at least
some, and perhaps most, human beings, just as depth grammar, he
suggests, is a schematic presentation of a different mental capacity.

All this suggests that the original position is an intermediate conclusion, a halfway point in a deeper theory that provides philosophical
arguments for its conditions. In the next part of this essay I shall try
to describe at least the main outlines of this deeper theory. I shall distinguish three features of the surface argument of the book – the technique
of equilibrium, the social contract, and the original position itself –
and try to discern which of various familiar philosophical principles or
positions these represent.

First, however, I must say a further word about Rawls's exciting, if
imprecise, idea that the principles of this deeper theory are constitutive
of our moral capacity. That idea can be understood on different levels
of profundity. It may mean, at its least profound, that the principles
that support the original position as a device for reasoning about justice
are so widely shared and so little questioned within a particular community, for whom the book is meant, that the community could not
abandon these principles without fundamentally changing its patterns
of reasoning and arguing about political morality. It may mean, at its
most profound, that these principles are innate categories of morality
common to all men, imprinted in their neural structure, so that man

[1] pp. 21-2.
[2] p. 587.
[3] p. 51.

could not deny these principles short of abandoning the power to reason about morality at all.

I shall be guided, in what follows, by the less profound interpretation, though what I shall say, I think, is consistent with the more profound. I shall assume, then, that there is a group of men and women who find, on reading Rawls, that the original position does strike them as a proper 'intuitive notion' from which to think about problems of justice, and who would find it persuasive, if it could be demonstrated that the parties to the original position would in fact contract for the two principles he describes. I suppose, on the basis of experience and the literature, that this group contains a very large number of those who think about justice at all, and I find that I am a member myself. I want to discover the hidden assumptions that bend the inclinations of this group that way, and I shall do so by repeating the question with which I began. Why does Rawls's argument support his claim that his two principles are principles of justice? My answer is complex and it will take us, at times, far from his text, but not, I think, from its spirit.

2.

A. Equilibrium

I shall start by considering the philosophical basis of the technique of equilibrium I just described. I must spend several pages in this way, but it is important to understand what substantive features of Rawls's deep theory are required by his method. This technique presupposes, as I said, a familiar fact about our moral lives. We all entertain beliefs about justice that we hold because they seem right, not because we have deduced or inferred them from other beliefs. We may believe in this way, for example, that slavery is unjust, and that the standard sort of trial is fair.

These different sorts of beliefs are, according to some philosophers, direct perceptions of some independent and objective moral facts. In the view of other philosophers they are simply subjective preferences, not unlike ordinary tastes, but dressed up in the language of justice to indicate how important they seem to us. In any event, when we argue with ourselves or each other about justice we use these accustomed beliefs – which we call 'intuitions' or 'convictions' – in roughly the way Rawls's equilibrium technique suggests. We test general theories about justice against our own institutions, and we try to confound those who disagree with us by showing how their own intuitions embarrass their own theories.

Suppose we try to justify this process by setting out a philosophical position about the connection between moral theory and moral intuition. The technique of equilibrium supposes what might be called a 'coherence' theory of morality.[1] But we have a choice between two general models that define coherence and explain why it is required, and the choice between these is significant and consequential for our moral philosophy. I shall describe these two models, and then argue that the equilibrium technique makes sense on one but not the other.

I call the first a 'natural' model. It presupposes a philosophical position that can be summarized in this way. Theories of justice, like Rawls's two principles, describe an objective moral reality; they are not, that is, created by men or societies but are rather discovered by them, as they discover laws of physics. The main instrument of this discovery is a moral faculty possessed by at least some men, which produces concrete intuitions of political morality in particular situations, like the intuition that slavery is wrong. These intuitions are clues to the nature and existence of more abstract and fundamental moral principles, as physical observations are clues to the existence and nature of fundamental physical laws. Moral reasoning or philosophy is a process of reconstructing the fundamental principles by assembling concrete judgments in the right order, as a natural historian reconstructs the shape of the whole animal from the fragments of its bones that he has found.

The second model is quite different. It treats intuitions of justice not as clues to the existence of independent principles, but rather as stipulated features of a general theory to be constructed, as if a sculptor set himself to carve the animal that best fits a pile of bones he happened to find together. This 'constructive' model does not assume, as the natural model does, that principles of justice have some fixed, objective existence, so that descriptions of these principles must be true or false in some standard way. It does not assume that the animal it matches to the bones actually exists. It makes the different, and in some ways more complex, assumption that men and women have a responsibility to fit the particular judgments on which they act into a coherent program of action, or, at least, that officials who exercise power over other men have that sort of responsibility.

This second, constructive, model is not unfamiliar to lawyers. It is analogous to one model of common law adjudication. Suppose a judge is faced with a novel claim – for example, a claim for damages based on a legal right to privacy that courts have not heretofore recognized.[2] He

[1] See Feinberg, 'Justice, Fairness and Rationality', 81 *Yale L. J.* 1004, 1018-21 (1972).
[2] I have here in mind the famous argument of Brandeis and Warren. See Brandeis & Warren, 'The Right to Privacy', 4 *Harv. L. Rev.* 193 (1890), which is a paradigm of argument in the constructive model. See Chapter 4, pp. 118-19.

must examine such precedents as seem in any way relevant to see whether any principles that are, as we might say, 'instinct' in these precedents bear upon the claimed right to privacy. We might treat this judge as being in the position of a man arguing from moral intuitions to a general moral theory. The particular precedents are analogous to intuitions; the judge tries to reach an accommodation between these precedents and a set of principles that might justify them and also justify further decisions that go beyond them. He does not suppose, however, that the precedents are glimpses into a moral reality, and therefore clues to objective principles he ends by declaring. He does not believe that the principles are 'instinct' in the precedents in that sense. Instead, in the spirit of the constructive model, he accepts these precedents as specifications for a principle that he must construct, out of a sense of responsibility for consistency with what has gone before.

I want to underline the important difference between the two models. Suppose that an official holds, with reasonable conviction, some intuition that cannot be reconciled with his other intuitions by any set of principles he can now fashion. He may think, for example, that it is unjust to punish an attempted murder as severely as a successful one, and yet be unable to reconcile that position with his sense that a man's guilt is properly assessed by considering only what he intended, and not what actually happened. Or he may think that a particular minority race, as such, is entitled to special protection, and be unable to reconcile that view with his view that distinctions based on race are inherently unfair to individuals. When an official is in this position the two models give him different advice.

The natural model supports a policy of following the troublesome intuition, and submerging the apparent contradiction, in the faith that a more sophisticated set of principles, which reconciles that intuition does in fact exist though it has not been discovered. The official, according to this model, is in the position of the astronomer who has clear observational data that he is as yet unable to reconcile in any coherent account, for example, of the origin of the solar system. He continues to accept and employ his observational data, placing his faith in the idea that some reconciling explanation does exist though it has not been, and for all he knows may never be, discovered by men.

The natural model supports this policy because it is based on a philosophical position that encourages the analogy between moral intuitions and observational data. It makes perfect sense, on that assumption, to suppose that direct observations, made through a moral faculty, have outstripped the explanatory powers of those who observe. It also makes sense to suppose that some correct explanation, in the shape of principles of morality, does in fact exist in spite of this failure; if the direct observations are sound, some explanation must exist for why matters are as they have been observed to be in the moral universe, just as some explanation must exist for why matters are as they have been observed to be in the physical universe.

The constructive model, however, does not support the policy of submerging apparent inconsistency in the faith that reconciling principles must exist. On the contrary, it demands that decisions taken in the name of justice must never outstrip an official's ability to account for these decisions in a theory of justice, even when such a theory must compromise some of his intuitions. It demands that we act on principle rather than on faith. Its engine is a doctrine of responsibility that requires men to integrate their intuitions and subordinate some of these, when necessary, to that responsibility. It presupposes that articulated consistency, decisions in accordance with a program that can be made public and followed until changed, is essential to any conception of justice. An official in the position I describe, guided by this model, must give up his apparently inconsistent position; he must do so even if he hopes one day, by further reflection, to devise better principles that will allow all his initial convictions to stand as principles.[1]

The constructive model does not presuppose skepticism or relativism. On the contrary, it assumes that the men and women who reason within the model will each hold sincerely the convictions they bring to it, and that this sincerity will extend to criticizing as unjust political acts or systems that offend the most profound of these. The model does not deny, any more than it affirms, the objective standing of any of these convictions; it is therefore consistent with, though as a model of reasoning it does not require, the moral ontology that the natural model presupposes.

It does not require that ontology because its requirements are independent of it. The natural model insists on consistency with conviction, on the assumption that moral intuitions are accurate observations; the requirement of consistency follows from that assumption. The constructive model insists on consistency with conviction as an independent requirement, flowing not from the assumption that these convictions are accurate reports, but from the different assumption that it is unfair for officials to act except on the basis of a general public theory that will constrain them to consistency, provide a public standard for testing or debating or predicting what they do, and not allow appeals to

[1] The famous debate between Professor Wechsler, 'Toward Neutral Principles in Constitutional Law', 73 *Hart. L. Rev.* 1 (1959), and his critics may be illuminated by this distinction. Wechsler proposes a constructive model for constitutional adjudication, while those who favor a more tentative or intuitive approach to constitutional law are following the natural model.

unique intuitions that might mask prejudice or self-interest in particular cases. The constructive model requires coherence, then, for independent reasons of political morality; it takes convictions held with the requisite sincerity as given, and seeks to impose conditions on the acts that these intuitions might be said to warrant. If the constructive model is to constitute morality, in either of the senses I have distinguished these independent reasons of political morality are at the heart of our political theories.

The two models, therefore, represent different standpoints from which theories of justice might be developed. The natural model, we might say, looks at intuitions from the personal standpoint of the individual who holds them, and who takes them to be discrete observations of moral reality. The constructive model looks at these intuitions from a more public standpoint; it is a model that someone might propose for the governance of a community each of whose members has strong convictions that differ, though not too greatly, from the convictions of others.

The constructive model is appealing, from this public standpoint, for an additional reason. It is well suited to group consideration of problems of justice, that is, to developing a theory that can be said to be the theory of a community rather than of particular individuals, and this is an enterprise that is important, for example, in adjudication. The range of initial convictions to be assessed can be expanded or contracted to accommodate the intuitions of a larger or smaller group, either by including all convictions held by any members, or by excluding those not held by all, as the particular calculation might warrant. This process would be self-destructive on the natural model, because every individual would believe that either false observations were being taken into account or accurate observations disregarded, and hence that the inference to objective morality was invalid. But on the constructive model that objection would be unavailable; the model, so applied, would be appropriate to identify the program of justice that best accommodates the community's common convictions, for example, with no claim to a description of an objective moral universe.

Which of these two models, then, better supports the technique of equilibrium? Some commentators seem to have assumed that the technique commits Rawls to the natural model.[1] But the alliance between that model and the equilibrium technique turns out to be only superficial; when we probe deeper we find that they are incompatible. In

[1] See e.g., Hare, 'Rawls' Theory of Justice – 1', 23 *Philosophical Quarterly* 144 (1973).

the first place, the natural model cannot explain one distinctive feature of the technique. It explains why our theory of justice must fit our intuitions about justice, but it does not explain why we are justified in amending these intuitions to make the fit more secure.

Rawls's notion of equilibrium, as I said earlier, is a two-way process; we move back and forth between adjustments to theory and adjustments to conviction until the best fit possible is achieved. If my settled convictions can otherwise be captured by, for example, a straightforward utilitarian theory of justice, that may be a reason, within the technique, for discarding my intuition that slavery would be wrong even if it advanced utility. But on the natural model this would be nothing short of cooking the evidence, as if a naturalist rubbed out the footprints that embarrassed his efforts to describe the animal that left them, or the astronomer just set aside the observations that his theory could not accommodate.

We must be careful not to lose this point in false sophistication about science. It is common to say – Rawls himself draws the comparison[1] – that scientists also adjust their evidence to achieve a smooth set of explanatory principles. But if this is true at all, their procedures are very different from those recommended by the technique of equilibrium. Consider, to take a familiar example, optical illusions or hallucinations. It is perfectly true that the scientist who sees water in the sand does not say that the pond was really there until he arrived at it, so that physics must be revised to provide for disappearing water; on the contrary, he uses the apparent disappearing as evidence of an illusion, that is, as evidence that, contrary to his observation, there was never any water there at all.

The scientists, of course, cannot leave the matter at that. He cannot dismiss mirages unless he supplements the laws of physics with laws of optics that explain them. It may be that he has, in some sense, a choice amongst competing sets of explanations of all his observations taken together. He may have a choice, for example, between either treating mirages as physical objects of a special sort and then amending the laws of physics to allow for disappearing objects of this sort, or treating mirages as optical illusions and then developing laws of optics to explain such illusions. He has a choice in the sense that his experience does not absolutely force either of these explanations upon him; the former is a possible choice, though it would require wholesale revision of both physics and common sense to carry it off.

This is, I take it, what is meant by philosophers like Quine who suppose that our concepts and our theories face our experience as a whole,

---

[1] Rawls draws attention to the distinction, p. 49.

so that we might react to recalcitrant or surprising experience by making different revisions at different places in our theoretical structures if we wish.[1] Regardless of whether this is an accurate picture of scientific reasoning, it is not a picture of the procedure of equilibrium, because this procedure argues not simply that alternative structures of principle are available to explain the same phenomena, but that some of the phenomena, in the form of moral convictions, may simply be ignored the better to serve some particular theory.

It is true that Rawls sometimes describes the procedure in a more innocent way. He suggests that if our tentative theories of justice do not fit some particular intuition, this should act as a warning light requiring us to reflect on whether the conviction is really one we hold.[2] If my convictions otherwise support a principle of utility, but I feel that slavery would be unjust even if utility were improved, I might think about slavery again, in a calmer way, and this time my intuitions might be different and consistent with that principle. In this case, the initial inconsistency is used as an occasion for reconsidering the intuition, but not as a reason for abandoning it.

Still, this need not happen. I might continue to receive the former intuition, no matter how firmly I steeled myself against it. In that case the procedure nevertheless authorizes me to set it aside if that is required to achieve the harmony of equilibrium. But if I do, I am not offering an alternative account of the evidence, but simply disregarding it. Someone else, whose intuitions are different, may say that mine are distorted, perhaps because of some childhood experience, or because I am insufficiently imaginative to think of hypothetical cases in which slavery might actually improve utility. He may say, that is, that my sensibilties are defective here, so that my intuitions are not genuine perceptions of moral reality, and may be set aside like the flawed reports of a color-blind man.

But I cannot accept that about myself, as an explanation for my own troublesome convictions, so long as I hold these convictions and they seem to me sound, indistinguishable in their moral quality from my other convictions. I am in a different position from the color-blind man who need only come to understand that others' perceptions differ from his. If I believe that my intuitions are a direct report from some moral reality, I cannot accept that one particular intuition is false until I come to feel or sense that it is false. The bare fact that others disagree, if they do, may be an occasion for consulting my intuitions again, but if my convictions remain the same, the fact that others may explain them in

[1] W. V. Quine, 'Two Dogmas of Empiricism', in *From a Logical Point of View* 20 (2d ed. rev. 1964).
[2] p. 48.

a different way cannot be a reason for my abandoning them, instead of retaining them in the faith that a reconciliation of these with my other convictions does in fact exist.

Thus, the natural model does not offer a satisfactory explanation of the two-way feature of equilibrium. Even if it did, however, it would leave other features of that technique unexplained; it would leave unexplained, for example, the fact that the results of the technique, at least in Rawls's hands, are necessarily and profoundly practical. Rawlsian men and women in the original position seek to find principles that they and their successors will find it easy to understand and publicize and observe; principles otherwise appealing are to be rejected or adjusted because they are too complex or are otherwise impractical in this sense. But principles of justice selected in this spirit are compromises with infirmity, and are contingent in the sense that they will change as the general condition and education of people change. This seems inconsistent with the spirit, at least, of the natural model, according to which principles of justice are timeless features of some independent moral reality, to which imperfect men and women must attempt to conform at best they can.

The equilibrium technique, moreover, is designed to produce principles that are relative in at least two ways. First, it is designed to select the best theory of justice from a list of alternative theories that must not only be finite, but short enough to make comparisons among them feasible. This limitation is an important one; it leads Rawls himself to say that he has no doubt that an initial list of possible theories expanded well beyond the list he considers would contain a better theory of justice than his own two principles.[1] Second, it yields results that are relative to the area of initial agreement among those who jointly conduct the speculative experiments it recommends. It is designed, as Rawls says, to reconcile men who disagree by fixing on what is common ground among them.[2] The test concededly will yield different results for different groups, and for the same group at different times, as the common ground of confident intuition shifts.

If the equilibrium technique were used within the natural model, the authority of its conclusions would be seriously compromised by both forms of relativism. If the equilibrium argument for Rawls's two principles, for example, shows only that a better case can be made for them than for any other principles on a restricted short list, and if Rawls himself is confident that further study would produce a better theory, then we have very little reason to suppose that these two principles are

[1] p. 581.
[2] pp. 580-1.

an accurate description of moral reality. It is hard to see, on the natural model, why they then should have any authority at all.

Indeed, the argument provides no very good ground for supposing even that the two principles are a better description of moral reality than other theories on the short list. Suppose we are asked to choose, among five theories of justice, the theory that best unites our convictions in reflective equilibrium, and we pick, from among these, the fifth. Let us assume that there is some sixth theory that we would have chosen had it appeared on the list. This sixth theory might be closer to, for example, the first on our original list than to the fifth, at least in the following sense: over a long term, a society following the first might reach more of the decisions that a society following the sixth would reach than would a society following the fifth.

Suppose, for example, that our original list included, as available theories of justice, classical utilitarianism and Rawls's two principles, but did not include average utilitarianism. We might have rejected classical utilitarianism on the ground that the production of pleasure for its own sake, unrelated to any increase in the welfare of particular human beings or other animals, makes little sense, and then chosen Rawls's two principles as the best of the theories left. We might nevertheless have chosen average utilitarianism as superior to the two principles, if it had been on the list, because average utilitarianism does not suppose that just any increase in the total quantity of pleasure is good. But classical utilitarianism, which we rejected, might be closer to average utilitarianism, which we would have chosen if we could have, than are the two principles which we did choose. It might be closer, in the sense described, because it would dictate more of the particular decisions that average utilitarianism would require, and thus be a better description of ultimate moral reality, than would the two principles. Of course, average utilitarianism might itself be rejected in a still larger list, and the choice we should then make might indicate that another member of the original list was better than either classical utilitarianism or the two principles.

The second sort of relativism would be equally damaging on the natural model, for reasons I have already explained. If the technique of equilibrium is used by a single person, and the intuitions allowed to count are just his and all of his, then the results may be authoritative for him. Others, whose intuitions differ, will not be able to accept his conclusions, at least in full, but he may do so himself. If, however, the technique is used in a more public way, for example, by fixing on what is common amongst the intuitions of a group, then the results will be those that no one can accept as authoritative, just as no one could accept as authoritative a scientific result reached by disregarding what he believed to be evidence at least as pertinent as the evidence used.

So the natural model turns out to be poor support for the equilibrium technique. None of the difficulties just mentioned count, however, if we assume the technique to be in the service of the constructive model. It is, within that model, a reason for rejecting even a powerful conviction that it cannot be reconciled with other convictions by a plausible and coherent set of principles; the conviction is rejected not as a false report, but simply as ineligible within a program that meets the demands of the model. Nor does either respect in which the technique is relative embarrass the constructive model. It is not an embarrassment that some theory not considered might have been deemed superior if it had been considered. The model requires officials or citizens to proceed on the best program they can now fashion, for reasons of consistency that do not presuppose, as the natural model does, that the theory chosen is in any final sense true. It does not undermine a particular theory that a different group, or a different society, with different culture and experience, would produce a different one. It may call into question whether any group is entitled to treat its moral intuitions as in any sense objective or transcendental, but not that a particular society, which does treat particular convictions in that way, is therefore required to follow them in a principled way.

I shall assume, therefore, at least tentatively, that Rawls's methodology presupposes the constructive model of reasoning from particular convictions to general theories of justice, and I shall use that assumption in my attempt to show the further postulates of moral theory that lie behind his theory of justice.

B. The Contract

I come, then, to the second of the three features of Rawls's methodology that I want to discuss, which is the use he makes of the old idea of a social contract. I distinguish, as does Rawls, the general idea that an imaginary contract is an appropriate device for reasoning about justice, from the more specific features of the original position, which count as a particular application of that general idea. Rawls thinks that all theories that can be seen to rest on a hypothetical social contract of some sort are related and are distinguished as a class from theories that cannot; he supposes, for example, that average utilitarianism, which can be seen as the product of a social contract on a particular interpretation, is more closely related to his own theory than either is to classical utilitarianism, which cannot be seen as the product of a contract on any interpretation.[1] In the next section I shall consider the theoretical basis

---

[1] Chapter 30.

of the original position. In this section I want to consider the basis of the more general idea of the contract itself.

Rawls says that the contract is a powerful argument for his principles because it embodies philosophical principles that we accept, or would accept if we thought about them. We want to find out what these principles are, and we may put our problem this way. The two principles comprise a theory of justice that is built up from the hypothesis of a contract. But the contract cannot sensibly be taken as the fundamental premise or postulate of that theory, for the reasons I described in the first part of this article. It must be seen as a kind of halfway point in a larger argument, as itself the product of a deeper political theory that argues for the two principles *through* rather than *from* the contract. We must therefore try to identify the features of a deeper theory that would recommend the device of a contract as the engine for a theory of justice, rather than the other theoretical devices Rawls mentions, like the device of the impartial spectator.[1]

We shall find the answer, I think, if we attend to and refine the familiar distinction philosophers make between two types of moral theories, which they call teleological theories and deontological theories.[2] I shall argue that any deeper theory that would justify Rawls's use of the contract must be a particular form of deontological theory, a theory that takes the idea of rights so seriously as to make them fundamental in political morality. I shall try to show how such a theory would be distinguished, as a type, from other types of political theories, and why only such a theory could give the contract the role and prominence Rawls does.

I must begin this argument, however, by explaining how I shall use some familiar terms. (1) I shall say that some state of affairs is a *goal* within a particular political theory if it counts in favor of a political act, within that theory, that the act will advance or preserve that state of affairs, and counts against an act that it will retard or threaten it. Goals may be relatively specific, like full employment or respect for authority, or relatively abstract, like improving the general welfare, advancing the power of a particular nation, or creating a utopian society according to a particular concept of human goodness or of the good life. (2) I shall say that an individual has a *right* to a particular political act, within a political theory, if the failure to provide that act, when he calls for it, would be unjustified within that theory even if the goals of the theory would, on the balance, be disserviced by that act. The strength of a particular right, within a particular theory, is a function of the degree of disservice to the goals of the theory, beyond a mere

[1] p. 144 ff.
[2] Rawls defines these terms at pp. 24-5 and 30.

disservice on the whole, that is necessary to justify refusing an act called for under the right. In the popular political theory apparently prevailing in the United States, for example, individuals have rights to free public speech on political matters and to a certain minimum standard of living, but neither right is absolute and the former is much stronger than the latter. (3) I shall say that an individual has a *duty* to act in a particular way, within a political theory, if a political decision constraining such act is justified within that theory notwithstanding that no goal of the system would be served by that decision. A theory may provide, for example, that individuals have a duty to worship God, even though it does not stipulate any goal served by requiring them to do so.[1]

The three concepts I have described work in different ways, but they all serve to justify or to condemn, at least pro tanto, particular political decisions. In each case, the justification provided by citing a goal, a right, or a duty is in principle complete, in the sense that nothing need be added to make the justification effective, if it is not undermined by some competing considerations. But, though such a justification is in this sense complete, it need not, within the theory, be ultimate. It remains open to ask why the particular goal, right, or duty is itself justified, and the theory may provide an answer by deploying a *more basic* goal, right, or duty that is served by accepting this less basic goal, right, or duty as a complete justification in particular cases.

A particular goal, for example, might be justified as contributing to a more basic goal; thus, full employment might be justified as contributing to greater average welfare. Or a goal might be justified as serving a more basic right or duty; a theory might argue, for example, that improving the gross national product, which is a goal, is necessary to enable the state to respect the rights of individuals to a decent minimum standard of living, or that improving the efficiency of the police process is necessary to enforce various individual duties not to sin. On the other hand, rights and duties may be justified on the ground that, by acting as a complete justification on particular occasions, they in fact serve more fundamental goals; the duty of individuals to drive carefully may be justified, for example, as serving the more basic goal of improving the general welfare. This form of justification does not, of course, suggest that the less basic right or duty itself justifies political decisions only when these decisions, considered one by one, advance the more basic goal. The point is rather the familiar one of rule utilitarianism, that treating the right or duty as a complete justification in particular cases,

---

[1] I do not count, as goals, the goal of respecting rights or enforcing duties. In this and other apparent ways my use of the terms I define is narrower than ordinary language permits.

without reference to the more basic goal, will in fact advance the goal in the long run.

So goals can be justified by other goals or by rights or duties, and rights or duties can be justified by goals. Rights and duties can also be justified, of course, by other, more fundamental duties or rights. Your duty to respect my privacy, for example, may be justified by my right to privacy. I do not mean merely that rights and duties may be correlated, as opposite sides of the same coin. That may be so when, for example, a right and the corresponding duty are justified as serving a more fundamental goal, as when your right to property and my corresponding duty not to trespass are together justified by the more fundamental goal of socially efficient land use. In many cases, however, corresponding rights and duties are not correlative, but one is derivative from the other, and it makes a difference which is derivative from which. There is a difference between the idea that you have a duty not to lie to me because I have a right not to be lied to, and the idea that I have a right that you not lie to me because you have a duty not to tell lies. In the first case I justify a duty by calling attention to a right; if I intend any further justification it is the right that I must justify, and I cannot do so by calling attention to the duty. In the second case it is the other way around. The difference is important because, as I shall shortly try to show, a theory that takes rights as fundamental is a theory of a different character from one that takes duties as fundamental.

Political theories will differ from one another, therefore, not simply in the particular goals, rights, and duties each sets out, but also in the way each connects the goals, rights, and duties it employs. In a well-formed theory some consistent set of these, internally ranked or weighted, will be taken as fundamental or ultimate within the theory. It seems reasonable to suppose that any particular theory will give ultimate pride of place to just one of these concepts; it will take some overriding goal, or some set of fundamental rights, or some set of transcendent duties, as fundamental, and show other goals, rights, and duties as subordinate and derivative.[1]

We may therefore make a tentative initial classification of the political theories we might produce, on the constructive model, as deep theories that might contain a contract as an intermediate device. Such a theory might be *goal-based*, in which case it would take some goal, like improving the general welfare, as fundamental; it might be *right-based*, taking some right, like the right of all men to the greatest possible overall liberty, as fundamental; or it might be *duty-based*, taking some duty, like the duty to obey God's will as set forth in the Ten Commandments,

---

[1] But an 'intuitionist' theory, as Rawls uses that term, need not. See p. 34.

as fundamental. It is easy to find examples of pure, or nearly pure, cases of each of these types of theory. Utilitarianism is, as my example suggested, a goal-based theory; Kant's categorical imperatives compose a duty-based theory; and Tom Paine's theory of revolution is right-based.

Theories within each of these types are likely to share certain very general characteristics. The types may be contrasted, for example, by comparing the attitudes they display towards individual choice and conduct. Goal-based theories are concerned with the welfare of any particular individual only in so far as this contributes to some state of affairs stipulated as good quite apart from his choice of that state of affairs. This is plainly true of totalitarian goal-based theories, like fascism, that take the interest of a political organization as fundamental. It is also true of the various forms of utilitarianism, because, though they count up the impact of political decisions on distinct individuals, and are in this way concerned with individual welfare, they merge these impacts into overall totals or averages and take the improvement of these totals or averages as desirable quite apart from the decision of any individual that it is. It is also true of perfectionist theories, like Aristotle's, that impose upon individuals an ideal of excellence and take the goal of politics to be the culture of such excellence.

Right-based and duty-based theories, on the other hand, place the individual at the center, and take his decision or conduct as of fundamental importance. But the two types put the individual in a different light. Duty-based theories are concerned with the moral quality of his acts, because they suppose that it is wrong, without more, for an individual to fail to meet certain standards of behavior. Kant thought that it was wrong to tell a lie no matter how beneficial the consequences, not because having this practice promoted some goal, but just because it was wrong. Right-based theories are, in contrast, concerned with the independence rather than the conformity of individual action. They presuppose and protect the value of individual thought and choice. Both types of theory make use of the idea of moral rules, codes of conduct to be followed, on individual occasions, without consulting self-interest. Duty-based theories treat such codes of conduct as of the essence, whether set by society to the individual or by the individual to himself. The man at their center is the man who must conform to such a code, or be punished or corrupted if he does not. Right-based theories, however, treat codes of conduct as instrumental, perhaps necessary to protect the rights of others, but having no essential value in themselves. The man at their center is the man who benefits from others' compliance, not the man who leads the life of virtue by complying himself.

We should, therefore, expect that the different types of theories would be associated with different metaphysical or political temperaments, and that one or another would be dominant in certain sorts of political economy. Goal-based theories, for example, seem especially compatible with homogeneous societies, or those at least temporarily united by an urgent, overriding goal, like self-defense or economic expansion. We should also expect that these differences between types of theory would find echoes in the legal systems of the communities they dominate. We should expect, for example, that a lawyer would approach the question of punishing moral offenses through the criminal law in a different way if his inchoate theory of justice were goal-, right- or duty-based. If his theory were goal-based he would consider the full effect of enforcing morality upon his overriding goal. If this goal were utilitarian, for example, he would entertain, though he might in the end reject, Lord Devlin's arguments that the secondary effects of punishing immorality may be beneficial.[1] If his theory were duty-based, on the other hand, he would see the point of the argument, commonly called retributive, that since immorality is wrong the state must punish it even if it harms no one. If his theory were right-based, however, he would reject the retributive argument, and judge the utilitarian argument against the background of his own assumption that individual rights must be served even at some cost to the general welfare.

All this is, of course, superficial and trivial as ideological sociology. My point is only to suggest that these differences in the character of a political theory are important quite apart from the details of position that might distinguish one theory from another of the same character. It is for this reason that the social contract is so important a feature of Rawls's methodology. It signals that his deep theory is a right-based theory, rather than a theory of either of the other two types.

The social contract provides every potential party with a veto : unless he agrees, no contract is formed. The importance, and even the existence, of this veto is obscured in the particular interpretation of the contract that constitutes the original position. Since no one knows anything about himself that would distinguish him from anyone else, he cannot rationally pursue any interest that is different. In these circumstances nothing turns on each man having a veto, or, indeed, on there being more than one potential party to the contract in the first place. But the original position is only one interpretation of the contract, and in any other interpretation in which the parties do have some knowledge with which to distinguish their situation or ambitions from those of others, the veto that the contract gives each party becomes crucial. The force of the veto each individual has depends, of course, upon his knowledge, that is to say, the particular interpretation of the contract we in the end

---

[1] See Chapter 10.

G

choose. But the fact that individuals should have any veto at all is in itself remarkable.

It can have no place in a purely goal-based theory, for example. I do not mean that the parties to a social contract could not settle on a particular social goal and make that goal henceforth the test of the justice of political decisions. I mean that no goal-based theory could make a contract the proper device for deciding upon a principle of justice in the first place; that is, the deep theory we are trying to find could not itself be goal-based.

The reason is straightforward. Suppose some particular overriding goal, like the goal of improving the average welfare in a community, or increasing the power and authority of a state, or creating a utopia according to a particular conception of the good, is taken as fundamental within a political theory. If any such goal is fundamental, then it authorizes such distribution of resources, rights, benefits, and burdens within the community as will best advance that goal, and condemns any other. The contract device, however, which supposes each individual to pursue his own interest and gives each a veto on the collective decision, applies a very different test to determine the optimum distribution. It is designed to produce the distribution that each individual deems in his own best interest, given his knowledge under whatever interpretation of the contract is specified, or at least to come as close to that distribution as he thinks he is likely to get. The contract, therefore, offers a very different test of optimum distribution than a direct application of the fundamental goal would dictate. There is no reason to suppose that a system of individual vetoes will produce a good solution to a problem in which the fairness of a distribution, considered apart from the contribution of the distribution to an overall goal, is meant to count for nothing.

It might be, of course, that a contract would produce the result that some fundamental goal dictates. Some critics, in fact, think that men in the original position, Rawls's most favored interpretation of the contract, would choose a theory of justice based on principles of average utility, that is, just the principles that a deep theory stipulating the fundamental goal of average utility would produce.[1] But if this is so, it is either because of coincidence or because the interpretation of the contract has been chosen to produce this result; in either case the contract is supererogatory, because the final result is determined by the fundamental goal and the contract device adds nothing.

One counterargument is available. Suppose it appears that the fundamental goal will in fact be served only if the state is governed in accord-

[1] John Mackie presented a forceful form of this argument to an Oxford seminar in the fall of 1972.

ance with principles that all men will see to be, in some sense, in their own interest. If the fundamental goal is the aggrandizement of the state, for example, it may be that this goal can be reached only if the population does not see that the government acts for this goal, but instead supposes that it acts according to principles shown to be in their individual interests through a contract device; only if they believe this will they work in the state's interest at all. We cannot ignore this devious, if unlikely, argument, but it does not support the use that Rawls makes of the contract. The argument depends upon a deception, like Sidgewick's famous argument that utilitarianism can best be served by keeping the public ignorant of that theory.[1] A theory that includes such a deception is ineligible on the constructivist model we are pursuing, because our aim, on that model, is to develop a theory that unites our convictions and can serve as a program for public action; publicity is as much a requirement of our deep theory as of the conception of justice that Rawls develops within it.

So a goal-based deep theory cannot support the contract, except as a useless and confusing appendage. Neither can a duty-based deep theory, for much the same reasons. A theory that takes some duty or duties to be fundamental offers no ground to suppose that just institutions are those seen to be in everyone's self-interest under some description. I do not deny, again, that the parties to the contract may decide to impose certain duties upon themselves and their successors, just as they may decide to adopt certain goals, in the exercise of their judgment of their own self-interest. Rawls describes the duties they would impose upon themselves under his most favored interpretation, the original position, and calls these natural duties.[2] But this is very different from supposing that the deep theory, which makes this decision decisive of what these duties are, can itself be duty-based.

It is possible to argue, of course, as many philosophers have, that a man's self-interest lies in doing his duty under the moral law, either because God will punish him otherwise, or because fulfilling his role in the natural order is his most satisfying activity, or, as Kant thought, because only in following rules he could consistently wish universal can he be free. But that says a man's duties define his self-interest, and not the other way round. It is an argument not for deciding upon a man's particular duties by letting him consult his own interest, but rather for his setting aside any calculations of self-interest except calculations of duty. It could not, therefore, support the role of a Rawlsian contract in a duty-based deep theory.

[1] H. Sidgewick, *The Methods of Ethics* 489 ff. (7th ed. 1907).
[2] Chapter 19.

It is true that if a contract were a feature of a duty-based deep theory, an interpretation of the contract could be chosen that would dissolve the apparent conflict between self-interest and duty. It might be a feature of the contract situation, for example, that all parties accepted the idea just mentioned, that their self-interest lay in ascertaining and doing their duty. This contract would produce principles that accurately described their duties, at least if we add the supposition that they are proficient, for some reason, in discovering what their duties are. But then, once again, we have made the contract supererogatory, a march up the hill and then back down again. We would have done better simply to work out principles of justice from the duties the deep theory takes as fundamental.

The contract does, however, make sense in a right-based deep theory. Indeed, it seems a natural development of such a theory. The basic idea of a right-based theory is that distinct individuals have interests that they are entitled to protect if they so wish. It seems natural, in developing such a theory, to try to identify the institutions an individual would veto in the exercise of whatever rights are taken as fundamental. The contract is an excellent device for this purpose, for at least two reasons. First, it allows us to distinguish between a veto in the exercise of these rights and a veto for the sake of some interest that is not so protected, a distinction we can make by adopting an interpretation of the contract that reflects our sense of what these rights are. Second, it enforces the requirements of the constructive model of argument. The parties to the contract face a practical problem; they must devise a constitution from the options available to them, rather than postponing their decision to a day of later moral insight, and they must devise a program that is both practical and public in the sense I have described.

It seems fair to assume, then, that the deep theory behind the original position must be a right-based theory of some sort. There is another way to put the point, which I have avoided until now. It must be a theory that is based on the concepts of rights that are *natural,* in the sense that they are not the product of any legislation, or convention, or hypothetical contract. I have avoided that phrase because it has, for many people, disqualifying metaphysical associations. They think that natural rights are supposed to be spectral attributes worn by primitive men like amulets, which they carry into civilization to ward off tyranny. Mr. Justice Black, for example, thought it was a sufficient refutation of a judicial philosophy he disliked simply to point out that it seemed to rely on this preposterous notion.[1]

But on the constructive model, at least, the assumption of natural

---

[1] *Griswold v. Connecticut,* 381 U.S. 479, 507 (1964) (dissenting opinion).

rights is not a metaphysically ambitious one. It requires no more than the hypothesis that the best political program, within the sense of that model, is one that takes the protection of certain individual choices as fundamental, and not properly subordinated to any goal or duty or combination of these. This requires no ontology more dubious or controversial than any contrary choice of fundamental concepts would be and, in particular, no more than the hypothesis of a fundamental goal that underlies the various popular utilitarian theories would require. Nor is it disturbing that a Rawlsian deep theory makes these rights natural rather than legal or conventional. Plainly, any right-based theory must presume rights that are not simply the product of deliberate legislation or explicit social custom, but are independent grounds for judging legislation and custom. On the constructive model, the assumption that rights are in this sense natural is simply one assumption to be made and examined for its power to unite and explain our political convictions, one basic programmatic decision to submit to this test of coherence and experience.

C. The original position

I said that the use of a social contract, in the way that Rawls uses it, presupposes a deep theory that assumes natural rights. I want now to describe, in somewhat more detail, how the device of a contract applies that assumption. It capitalizes on the idea, mentioned earlier, that some political arrangements might be said to be in the antecedent interest of every individual even though they are not, in the event, in his actual interest.

Everyone whose consent is necessary to a contract has a veto over the terms of that contract, but the worth of that veto, to him, is limited by the fact that his judgment must be one of antecedent rather than actual self-interest. He must commit himself, and so abandon his veto, at a time when his knowledge is sufficient only to allow him to estimate the best odds, not to be certain of his bet. So the contract situation is in one way structurally like the situation in which an individual with specific political rights confronts political decisions that may disadvantage him. He has a limited, political right to veto these, a veto limited by the scope of the rights he has. The contract can be used as a model for the political situation by shaping the degree or character of a party's ignorance in the contractual situation so that this ignorance has the same force on his decision as the limited nature of his rights would have in the political situation.

This shaping of ignorance to suit the limited character of political rights is most efficiently done simply by narrowing the individual goals that the parties to the contract know they wish to pursue. If we take Hobbes's deep theory, for example, to propose that men have a fundamental natural right to life, so that it is wrong to take their lives, even for social goals otherwise proper, we should expect a contract situation of the sort he describes. Hobbes's men and women, in Rawls's phrase, have lexically ordered security of life over all other individual goals; the same situation would result if they were simply ignorant of any other goals they might have and unable to speculate about the chances that they have any particular one or set of these.

The ignorance of the parties in the original position might thus be seen as a kind of limiting case of the ignorance that can be found, in the form of a distorted or eccentric ranking of interests, in classical contract theories and that is natural to the contract device. The original position is a limiting case because Rawls's men are not simply ignorant of interests beyond a chosen few; they are ignorant of all the interests they have. It would be wrong to suppose that this makes them incapable of any judgments of self-interest. But the judgments they make must nevertheless be very abstract; they must allow for any combination of interests, without the benefit of any supposition that some of these are more likely than others.

The basic right of Rawls's deep theory, therefore, cannot be a right to any particular individual goal, like a right to security of life, or a right to lead a life according to a particular conception of the good. Such rights to individual goals may be produced by the deep theory, as rights that men in the original position would stipulate as being in their best interest. But the original position cannot itself be justified on the assumption of such a right, because the parties to the contract do not know that they have any such interest or rank it lexically ahead of others.

So the basic right of Rawls's deep theory must be an abstract right, that is, not a right to any particular individual goal. There are two candidates, within the familiar concepts of political theory, for this role. The first is the right to liberty, and it may strike many readers as both plausible and comforting to assume that Rawls's entire structure is based on the assumption of a fundamental natural right to liberty – plausible because the two principles that compose his theory of justice give liberty an important and dominant place, and comforting because the argument attempting to justify that place seems uncharacteristically incomplete.[1]

Nevertheless, the right to liberty cannot be taken as the fundamental right in Rawls's deep theory. Suppose we define general liberty as the

[1] See Hart, 'Rawls on Liberty and Its Priority', 40 *U. Chi. L. Rev.* 534 (1973).

overall minimum possible constraints, imposed by government or by other men, on what a man might want to do.[1] We must then distinguish this general liberty from particular liberties, that is, freedom from such constraints on particular acts thought specially important, like participation in politics. The parties to the original position certainly have, and know that they have, an interest in general liberty, because general liberty will, *pro tanto*, improve their power to achieve any particular goals they later discover themselves to have. But the qualification is important, because they have no way of knowing that general liberty will in fact improve this power overall, and every reason to suspect that it will not. They know that they might have other interests, beyond general liberty, that can be protected only by political constraints on acts of others.

So if Rawlsian men must be supposed to have a right to liberty of some sort, which the contract situation is shaped to embody, it must be a right to particular liberties. Rawls does name a list of basic liberties, and it is these that his men do choose to protect through their lexically ordered first principle of justice.[2] But Rawls plainly casts this principle as the product of the contract rather than as a condition of it. He argues that the parties to the original position would select these basic liberties to protect the basic goods they decide to value, like self-respect, rather than taking these liberties as goals in themselves. Of course they might, in fact, value the activities protected as basic liberties for their own sake, rather than as means to some other goal or interest. But they certainly do not know that they do.

The second familiar concept of political theory is even more abstract than liberty. This is equality, and in one way Rawlsian men and women cannot choose other than to protect it. The state of ignorance in the original position is so shaped that the antecedent interest of everyone must lie, as I said, in the same solution. The right of each man to be treated equally without regard to his person or character or tastes is enforced by the fact that no one else can secure a better position by virtue of being different in any such respect. In other contract situations, when ignorance is less complete, individuals who share the same goal may nevertheless have different antecedent interests. Even if two men value life above everything else, for example, the antecedent interest of the weaker might call for a state monopoly of force rather than some provision for private vengeance, but the antecedent interest of the stronger might not. Even if two men value political participation above all else, the knowledge that one's views are likely to be more unorthodox or unpopular than those of the other will suggest that his antecedent

[1] Cf. Rawls's definition of liberty at p. 202.
[2] p. 61.

interest calls for different arrangements. In the original position no such discrimination of antecedent interests can be made.

It is true that, in two respects, the principles of justice that Rawls thinks men and women would choose in the original position may be said to fall short of an egalitarian ideal. First, they subordinate equality in material resources, when this is necessary, to liberty of political activity, by making the demands of the first principle prior to those of the second. Second, they do not take account of relative deprivation, because they justify any inequality when those worse off are better off than they would be, in absolute terms, without that inequality.

Rawls makes plain that these inequalities are required, not by some competing notion of liberty or some overriding goal, but by a more basic sense of equality itself. He accepts a distinction between what he calls two conceptions of equality:

> Some writers have distinguished between equality as it is invoked in connection with the distribution of certain goods, some of which will almost certainly give higher status or prestige to those who are more favored, and equality as it applies to the respect which is owed to persons irrespective of their social position. Equality of the first kind is defined by the second principle of justice . . . . But equality of the second kind is fundamental.[1]

We may describe a right to equality of the second kind, which Rawls says is fundamental, in this way. We might say that individuals have a right to equal concern and respect in the design and administration of the political institutions that govern them. This is a highly abstract right. Someone might argue, for example, that it is satisfied by political arrangements that provide equal opportunity for office and position on the basis of merit. Someone else might argue, to the contrary, that it is satisfied only by a system that guarantees absolute equality of income and status, without regard to merit. A third man might argue that equal concern and respect is provided by that system, whatever it is, that improves the average welfare of all citizens counting the welfare of each on the same scale. A fourth might argue, in the name of this fundamental equality, for the priority of liberty, and for the other apparent inequalities of Rawls's two principles.

The right to equal concern and respect, then, is more abstract than the standard conceptions of equality that distinguish different political theories. It permits arguments that this more basic right requires one or another of these conceptions as a derivative right or goal.

[1] p. 511.

The original portion may now be seen as a device for testing these competing arguments. It supposes, reasonably, that political arrangements that do not display equal concern and respect are those that are established and administered by powerful men and women who, whether they recognize it or not, have more concern and respect for members of a particular class, or people with particular talents or ideals, than they have for others. It relies on this supposition in shaping the ignorance of the parties to the contract. Men who do not know to which class they belong cannot design institutions, consciously or unconsciously, to favor their own class. Men who have no idea of their own conception of the good cannot act to favor those who hold one ideal over those who hold another. The original position is well designed to enforce the abstract right to equal concern and respect, which must be understood to be the fundamental concept of Rawls's deep theory.

If this is right, then Rawls must not use the original position to argue for this right in the same way that he uses it, for example, to argue for the rights to basic liberties embodied in the first principle. The text confirms that he does not. It is true that he once says that equality of respect is 'defined' by the first principle of justice.[1] But he does not mean, and in any case he does not argue, that the parties choose to be respected equally in order to advance some more basic right or goal. On the contrary, the right to equal respect is not, on his account, a product of the contract, but a condition of admission to the original position. This right, he says, is 'owed to human beings as moral persons', and follows from the moral personality that distinguishes humans from animals. It is possessed by all men who can give justice, and only such men can contract.[2] This is one right, therefore, that does not emerge from the contract, but is assumed, as the fundamental right must be, in its design.

Rawls is well aware that his argument for equality stands on a different footing from his argument for the other rights within his theory:

> Now of course none of this is literally argument. I have not set out the premises from which this conclusion follows, as I have tried to do, albeit not very rigorously, with the choice of conceptions of justice in the original position. Nor have I tried to prove that the characterization of the parties must be used as the basis of equality. Rather this interpretation seems to be the natural completion of justice as fairness.[3]

[1] *Id.*
[2] Chapter 77.
[3] p. 509.

It is the 'natural completion', that is to say, of the theory as a whole. It completes the theory by providing the fundamental assumption that charges the original position, and makes it an 'intuitive notion' for developing and testing theories of justice.

We may therefore say that justice as fairness rests on the assumption of a natural right of all men and women to equality of concern and respect, a right they possess not by virtue of birth or characteristic or merit or excellence but simply as human beings with the capacity to make plans and give justice. Many readers will not be surprised by this conclusion, and it is, as I have said, reasonably clear from the text. It is an important conclusion, nevertheless, because some forms of criticism of the theory, already standard, ignore it. I shall close this long essay with one example.

One form of criticism has been expressed to me by many colleagues and students, particularly lawyers. They point out that the particular political institutions and arrangements that Rawls says men in the original position would choose are merely idealized forms of those now in force in the United States. They are the institutions, that is, of liberal constitutional democracy. The critics conclude that the fundamental assumptions of Rawls's theory must, therefore, be the assumptions of classical liberalism, however they define these, and that the original position, which appears to animate the theory, must somehow be an embodiment of these assumptions. Justice as fairness therefore seems to them, in its entirety, a particularly subtle rationalization of the political status quo, which may safely be disregarded by those who want to offer a more radical critique of the liberal tradition.

If I am right, this point of view is foolish, and those who take it lose an opportunity, rare for them, to submit their own political views to some form of philosophical examination. Rawls's most basic assumption is not that men have a right to certain liberties that Locke or Mill thought important, but that they have a right to equal respect and concern in the design of political institutions. This assumption may be contested in many ways. It will be denied by those who believe that some goal, like utility or the triumph of a class or the flowering of some conception of how men should live, is more fundamental than any individual right, including the right to equality. But it cannot be denied in the name of any more radical concept of equality, because none exists.

Rawls does argue that this fundamental right to equality requires a liberal constitution, and supports an idealized form of present economic and social structures. He argues, for example, that men in the original position would protect the basic liberties in the interest of their right to equality, once a certain level of material comfort has been reached, because they would understand that a threat to self-respect, which the basic liberties protect, is then the most serious threat to equal respect. He also argues that these men would accept the second principle in preference to material equality because they would understand that sacrifice out of envy for another is a form of subordination to him. These arguments may, of course, be wrong. I have certainly said nothing in their defense here. But the critics of liberalism now have the responsibility to show that they are wrong. They cannot say that Rawls's basic assumptions and attitudes are too far from their own to allow a confrontation.

7

Taking Rights Seriously

The language of rights now dominates political debate in the United States. Does the Government respect the moral and political rights of its citizens? Or does the Government's foreign policy, or its race policy, fly in the face of these rights? Do the minorities whose rights have been violated have the right to violate the law in return? Or does the silent majority itself have rights, including the right that those who break the law be punished? It is not surprising that these questions are now prominent. The concept of rights, and particularly the concept of rights against the Government, has its most natural use when a political society is divided, and appeals to co-operation or a common goal are pointless.

The debate does not include the issue of whether citizens have *some* moral rights against their Government. It seems accepted on all sides that they do. Conventional lawyers and politicians take it as a point of pride that our legal system recognizes, for example, individual rights of free speech, equality, and due process. They base their claim that our law deserves respect, at least in part, on that fact, for they would not claim that totalitarian systems deserve the same loyalty.

Some philosophers, of course, reject the idea that citizens have rights apart from what the law happens to give them. Bentham thought that the idea of moral rights was 'nonsense on stilts'. But that view has never been part of our orthodox political theory, and politicians of both parties appeal to the rights of the people to justify a great part of what they want to do. I shall not be concerned, in this essay, to defend the thesis that citizens have moral rights against their governments; I want instead to explore the implications of that thesis for those, including the present United States Government, who profess to accept it.

It is much in dispute, of course, what *particular* rights citizens have. Does the acknowledged right to free speech, for example, include the right to participate in nuisance demonstrations? In practice the Government will have the last word on what an individual's rights are, because its police will do what its officials and courts say. But that does not mean that the Government's view is necessarily the correct view; anyone who thinks it does must believe that men and women have only such moral rights as Government chooses to grant, which means that they have no moral rights at all.

All this is sometimes obscured in the United States by the constitutional system. The American Constitution provides a set of individual *legal* rights in the First Amendment, and in the due process, equal protection, and similar clauses. Under present legal practice the Supreme Court has the power to declare an act of Congress or of a state legislature void if the Court finds that the act offends these provisions. This practice has led some commentators to suppose that individual moral rights are fully protected by this system, but that is hardly so, nor could it be so.

The Constitution fuses legal and moral issues, by making the validity of a law depend on the answer to complex moral problems, like the problem of whether a particular statute respects the inherent equality of all men. This fusion has important consequences for the debates about civil disobedience; I have described these elsewhere[1] and I shall refer to them later. But it leaves open two prominent questions. It does not tell us whether the Constitution, even properly interpreted, recognizes all the moral rights that citizens have, and it does not tell us whether, as many suppose, citizens would have a duty to obey the law even if it did invade their moral rights.

Both questions become crucial when some minority claims moral rights which the law denies, like the right to run its local school system, and which lawyers agree are not protected by the Constitution. The second question becomes crucial when, as now, the majority is sufficiently aroused so that Constitutional amendments to eliminate rights, like the right against self-incrimination, are seriously proposed. It is also crucial in nations, like the United Kingdom, that have no constitution of a comparable nature.

Even if the Constitution were perfect, of course, and the majority left it alone, it would not follow that the Supreme Court could guarantee the individual rights of citizens. A Supreme Court decision is still a legal decision, and it must take into account precedent and institutional considerations like relations between the Court and Congress, as well as morality. And no judicial decision is necessarily the right decision. Judges stand for different positions on controversial issues of law and morals and, as the fights over Nixon's Supreme Court nominations showed, a President is entitled to appoint judges of his own persuasion, provided that they are honest and capable.

[1] See Chapter 8.

So, though the constitutional system adds something to the protection of moral rights against the Government, it falls far short of guaranteeing these rights, or even establishing what they are. It means that, on some occasions, a department other than the legislature has the last word on these issues, which can hardly satisfy someone who thinks such a department profoundly wrong.

It is of course inevitable that some department of government will have the final say on what law will be enforced. When men disagree about moral rights, there will be no way for either side to prove its case, and some decision must stand if there is not to be anarchy. But that piece of orthodox wisdom must be the beginning and not the end of a philosophy of legislation and enforcement. If we cannot insist that the Government reach the right answers about the rights of its citizens, we can insist at least that it try. We can insist that it take rights seriously, follow a coherent theory of what these rights are, and act consistently with its own professions. I shall try to show what that means, and how it bears on the present political debates.

2. RIGHTS AND THE RIGHT TO BREAK THE LAW

I shall start with the most violently argued issue. Does an American ever have the moral right to break a law? Suppose someone admits a law is valid; does he therefore have a duty to obey it? Those who try to give an answer seem to fall into two camps. The conservatives, as I shall call them, seem to disapprove of any act of disobedience; they appear satisfied when such acts are prosecuted, and disappointed when convictions are reversed. The other group, the liberals, are much more sympathetic to at least some cases of disobedience; they sometimes disapprove of prosecutions and celebrate acquittals. If we look beyond these emotional reactions, however, and pay attention to the arguments the two parties use, we discover an astounding fact. Both groups give essentially the same answer to the question of principle that supposedly divides them.

The answer that both parties give is this. In a democracy, or at least a democracy that in principle respects individual rights, each citizen has a general moral duty to obey all the laws, even though he would like some of them changed. He owes that duty to his fellow citizens, who obey laws that they do not like, to his benefit. But this general duty cannot be an absolute duty, because even a society that is in principle just may produce unjust laws and policies, and a man has duties other than his duties to the State. A man must honour his duties to his God and to his conscience, and if these conflict with his duty to the State, then he is entitled, in the end, to do what he judges to be right. If he decides that he must break the law, however, then he must submit to the judgment and punishment that the State imposes, in recognition of the fact that his duty to his fellow citizens was overwhelmed but not extinguished by his religious or moral obligation.

Of course this common answer can be elaborated in very different ways. Some would describe the duty to the State as fundamental, and picture the dissenter as a religious or moral fanatic. Others would describe the duty to the State in grudging terms, and picture those who oppose it as moral heroes. But these are differences in tone, and the position I described represents, I think, the view of most of those who find themselves arguing either for or against civil disobedience in particular cases.

I do not claim that it is everyone's view. There must be some who put the duty to the State so high that they do not grant that it can ever be overcome. There are certainly some who would deny that a man ever has a moral duty to obey the law, at least in the United States today. But these two extreme positions are the slender tails of a bell curve, and all those who fall in between hold the orthodox position I described – that men have a duty to obey the law but have the right to follow their consciences when it conflicts with that duty.

But if that is so, then we have a paradox in the fact that men who give the same answer to a question of principle should seem to disagree so much, and to divide so fiercely, in particular cases. The paradox goes even deeper, for each party, in at least some cases, takes a position that seems flatly inconsistent with the theoretical position they both accept. This position was tested, for example, when someone evaded the draft on grounds of conscience, or encouraged others to commit this crime. Conservatives argued that such men must be prosecuted, even though they are sincere. Why must they be prosecuted? Because society cannot tolerate the decline in respect for the law that their act constitutes and encourages. They must be prosecuted, in short, to discourage them and others like them from doing what they have done.

But there seems to be a monstrous contradiction here. If a man has a right to do what his conscience tells him he must, then how can the State be justified in discouraging him from doing it? Is it not wicked for a state to forbid and punish what it acknowledges that men have a right to do?

Moreover, it is not just conservatives who argue that those who break the law out of moral conviction should be prosecuted. The liberal is notoriously opposed to allowing racist school officials to go slow on desegregation, even though he acknowledges that these school officials think they have a moral right to do what the law forbids. The liberal does not often argue, it is true, that the desegregation laws must be enforced to encourage general respect for law. He argues instead that the desegregation laws must be enforced because they are right. But his position also seems inconsistent: can it be right to prosecute men for doing what their conscience requires, when we acknowledge their right to follow their conscience?

We are therefore left with two puzzles. How can two parties to an issue of principle, each of which thinks it is in profound disagreement with the other, embrace the same position on that issue? How can it be that each side urges solutions to particular problems which seem flatly to contradict the position of principle that both accept? One possible answer is that some or all of those who accept the common position are hypocrites, paying lip service to rights of conscience which in fact they do not grant.

There is some plausibility in this charge. A sort of hypocrisy must have been involved when public officials who claim to respect conscience denied Muhammad Ali the right to box in their states. If Ali, in spite of his religious scruples, had joined the Army, he would have been allowed to box even though, on the principles these officials say they honour, he would have been a worse human being for having done so. But there are few cases that seem so straightforward as this one, and even here the officials did not seem to recognize the contradiction between their acts and their principles. So we must search for some explanation beyond the truth that men often do not mean what they say.

The deeper explanation lies in a set of confusions that often embarrass arguments about rights. These confusions have clouded all the issues I mentioned at the outset and have crippled attempts to develop a coherent theory of how a government that respects rights must behave.

In order to explain this, I must call attention to the fact, familiar to philosophers, but often ignored in political debate, that the word 'right' has different force in different contexts. In most cases when we say that someone has 'right' to do something, we imply that it would be wrong to interfere with his doing it, or at least that some special grounds are needed for justifying any interference. I use this strong sense of right when I say that you have the right to spend your money gambling, if you wish, though you ought to spend it in a more worthwhile way. I mean that it would be wrong for anyone to interfere with you even though you propose to spend your money in a way that I think is wrong.

There is a clear difference between saying that someone has a right to do something in this sense and saying that it is the 'right' thing for him to do, or that he does no 'wrong' in doing it. Someone may have the right to do something that is the wrong thing for him to do, as might be the case with gambling. Conversely, something may be the right thing for him to do and yet he may have no right to do it, in the sense that it would not be wrong for someone to interfere with his trying. If our army captures an enemy soldier, we might say that the right thing for him to do is to try to escape, but it would not follow that it is wrong for us to try to stop him. We might admire him for trying to escape, and perhaps even think less of him if he did not. But there is no suggestion here that it is wrong of us to stand in his way; on the contrary, if we think our cause is just, we think it right for us to do all we can to stop him.

Ordinarily this distinction, between the issues of whether a man has a right to do something and whether it is the right thing for him to do, causes no trouble. But sometimes it does, because sometimes we say that a man has a right to do something when we mean only to deny that it is the wrong thing for him to do. Thus we say that the captured soldier has a 'right' to try to escape when we mean, not that we do wrong to stop him, but that he has no duty not to make the attempt. We use 'right' this way when we speak of someone having the 'right' to act on his own principles, or the 'right' to follow his own conscience. We mean that he does no wrong to proceed on his honest convictions, even though we disagree with these convictions, and even though, for policy or other reasons, we must force him to act contrary to them.

Suppose a man believes that welfare payments to the poor are profoundly wrong, because they sap enterprise, and so declares his full income-tax each year but declines to pay half of it. We might say that he has a right to refuse to pay, if he wishes, but that the Government has a right to proceed against him for the full tax, and to fine or jail him for late payment if that is necessary to keep the collection system working efficiently. We do not take this line in most cases; we do not say that the ordinary thief has a right to steal, if he wishes, so long as he pays the penalty. We say a man has the right to break the law, even though the State has a right to punish him, only when we think that, because of his convictions, he does no wrong in doing so.[1]

These distinctions enable us to see an ambiguity in the orthodox question : Does a man ever have a right to break the law? Does that question mean to ask whether he ever has a right to break the law in the strong sense, so that the Government would do wrong to stop him, by arresting and prosecuting him? Or does it mean to ask whether he ever does the

---

[1] It is not surprising that we sometimes use the concept of having a right to say that others must not interfere with an act and sometimes to say that the act is not the wrong thing to do. Often, when someone has *no* right to do something, like attacking another man physically, it is true *both* that it is the wrong thing to do and that others are entitled to stop it, by demand, if not by force. It is therefore natural to say that someone has a right when we mean to deny *either* of these consequences, as well as when we mean to deny both.

right thing to break the law, so that we should all respect him even though the Government should jail him?

If we take the orthodox position to be an answer to the first – and most important – question, then the paradoxes I described arise. But if we take it as an answer to the second, they do not. Conservatives and liberals do agree that sometimes a man does not do the wrong thing to break a law, when his conscience so requires. They disagree, when they do, over the different issue of what the State's response should be. Both parties do think that sometimes the State should prosecute. But this is not inconsistent with the proposition that the man prosecuted did the right thing in breaking the law.

The paradoxes seem genuine because the two questions are not usually distinguished, and the orthodox position is presented as a general solution to the problem of civil disobedience. But once the distinction is made, it is apparent that the position has been so widely accepted only because, when it is applied, it is treated as an answer to the second question but not the first. The crucial distinction is obscured by the troublesome idea of a right to conscience; this idea has been at the centre of most recent discussions of political obligation, but it is a red herring drawing us away from the crucial political questions. The state of a man's conscience may be decisive, or central, when the issue is whether he does something morally wrong in breaking the law; but it need not be decisive or even central when the issue is whether he has a right, in the strong sense of that term, to do so. A man does not have the right, in that sense, to do whatever his conscience demands, but he may have the right, in that sense, to do something even though his conscience does not demand it.

If that is true, then there has been almost no serious attempt to answer the questions that almost everyone means to ask. We can make a fresh start by stating these questions more clearly. Does an American ever have the right, in a strong sense, to do something which is against the law? If so, when? In order to answer these questions put in that way, we must try to become clearer about the implications of the idea, mentioned earlier, that citizens have at least some rights against their government.

I said that in the United States citizens are supposed to have certain fundamental rights against their Government, certain moral rights made into legal rights by the Constitution. If this idea is significant, and worth bragging about, then these rights must be rights in the strong sense I just described. The claim that citizens have a right to free speech must imply that it would be wrong for the Government to stop them from speaking, even when the Government believes that what they will say will cause more harm than good. The claim cannot mean, on the prisoner-of-war analogy, only that citizens do no wrong in speaking their minds, though the Government reserves the right to prevent them from doing so.

This is a crucial point, and I want to labour it. Of course a responsible government must be ready to justify anything it does, particularly when it limits the liberty of its citizens. But normally it is a sufficient justification, even for an act that limits liberty, that the act is calculated to increase what the philosophers call general utility – that it is calculated to produce more over-all benefit than harm. So, though the New York City government needs a justification for forbidding motorists to drive up Lexington Avenue, it is sufficient justification if the proper officials believe, on sound evidence, that the gain to the many will outweigh the inconvenience to the few. When individual citizens are said to have rights against the Government, however, like the right of free speech, that must mean that this sort of justification is not enough. Otherwise the claim would not argue that individuals have special protection against the law when their rights are in play, and that is just the point of the claim.

Not all legal rights, or even Constitutional rights, represent moral rights against the Government. I now have the legal right to drive either way on Fifty-seventh Street, but the Government would do no wrong to make that street one-way if it thought it in the general interest to do so. I have a Constitutional right to vote for a congressman every two years, but the national and state governments would do no wrong if, following the amendment procedure, they made a congressman's term four years instead of two, again on the basis of a judgment that this would be for the general good.

But those Constitutional rights that we call fundamental like the right of free speech, are supposed to represent rights against the Government in the strong sense; that is the point of the boast that our legal system respects the fundamental rights of the citizen. If citizens have a moral right of free speech, then governments would do wrong to repeal the First Amendment that guarantees it, even if they were persuaded that the majority would be better off if speech were curtailed.

I must not overstate the point. Someone who claims that citizens have a right against the Government need not go so far as to say that the State is *never* justified in overriding that right. He might say, for example, that although citizens have a right to free speech, the Government may override that right when necessary to protect the rights of others, or to prevent a catastrophe, or even to obtain a clear and major public benefit (though if he acknowledged this last as a possible justification he would be treating the right in question as not among the most important or fundamental). What he cannot do is to say that the Government is justified in overriding a right on the minimal grounds that would be sufficient if no such right existed. He cannot say that the Government is entitled to act on no more than a judgment that its act is likely to produce, overall, a benefit to the community. That admission would make his claim of a right pointless, and would show him to be using some sense of 'right' other than the strong sense necessary to give his claim the political importance it is normally taken to have.

But then the answers to our two questions about disobedience seem plain, if unorthodox. In our society a man does sometimes have the right, in the strong sense, to disobey a law. He has that right whenever that law wrongly invades his rights against the Government. If he has a moral right to free speech, that is, then he has a moral right to break any law that the Government, by virtue of his right, had no right to adopt. The right to disobey the law is not a separate right, having something to do with conscience, additional to other rights against the Government. It is simply a feature of these rights against the Government, and it cannot be denied in principle without denying that any such rights exist.

These answers seem obvious once we take rights against the Government to be rights in the strong sense I described. If I have a right to speak my mind on political issues, then the Government does wrong to make it illegal for me to do so, even if it thinks this is in the general interest. If, nevertheless, the Government does make my act illegal, then it does a further wrong to enforce that law against me. My right against the Government means that it is wrong for the Government to stop me from speaking; the Government cannot make it right to stop me just by taking the first step.

This does not, of course, tell us exactly what rights men do have against the Government. It does not tell us whether the right of free speech includes the right of demonstration. But it does mean that passing a law cannot affect such rights as men do have, and that is of crucial importance, because it dictates the attitude that an individual is entitled to take toward his personal decision when civil disobedience is in question.

Both conservatives and liberals suppose that in a society which is generally decent everyone has a duty to obey the law, whatever it is. That is the source of the 'general duty' clause in the orthodox position, and though liberals believe that this duty can sometimes be 'overridden', even they suppose, as the orthodox position maintains, that the duty of obedience remains in some submerged form, so that a man does well to accept punishment in recognition of that duty. But this general duty is almost incoherent in a society that recognizes rights. If a man believes he has a right to demonstrate, then he must believe that it would be wrong for the Government to stop him, with or without benefit of a law.

If he is entitled to believe that, then it is silly to speak of a duty to obey the law as such, or of a duty to accept the punishment that the State has no right to give.

Conservatives will object to the short work I have made of their point. They will argue that even if the Government was wrong to adopt some law, like a law limiting speech, there are independent reasons why the Government is justified in enforcing the law once adopted. When the law forbids demonstration, then, so they argue, some principle more important than the individual's right to speak is brought into play, namely the principle of respect for law. If a law, even a bad law, is left unenforced, then respect for law is weakened, and society as a whole suffers. So an individual loses his moral right to speak when speech is made criminal, and the Government must, for the common good and for the general benefit, enforce the law against him.

But this argument, though popular, is plausible only if we forget what it means to say that an individual has a right against the State. It is far from plain that civil disobedience lowers respect for law, but even if we suppose that it does, this fact is irrelevant. The prospect of utilitarian gains cannot justify preventing a man from doing what he has a right to do, and the supposed gains in respect for law are simply utilitarian gains. There would be no point in the boast that we respect individual rights unless that involved some sacrifice, and the sacrifice in question must be that we give up whatever marginal benefits our country would receive from overriding these rights when they prove inconvenient. So the general benefit cannot be a good ground for abridging rights, even when the benefit in question is a heightened respect for law.

But perhaps I do wrong to assume that the argument about respect for law is only an appeal to general utility. I said that a state may be justified in overriding or limiting rights on other grounds, and we must ask, before rejecting the conservative position, whether any of these apply. The most important – and least well understood – of these other grounds invokes the notion of *competing rights* that would be jeopardized if the right in question were not limited. Citizens have personal rights to the State's protection as well as personal rights to be free from the State's interference, and it may be necessary for the Government to choose between these two sorts of rights. The law of defamation, for example, limits the personal right of any man to say what he thinks, because it requires him to have good grounds for what he says. But this law is justified, even for those who think that it does invade a personal right, by the fact that it protects the right of others not to have their reputations ruined by a careless statement.

The individual rights that our society acknowledges often conflict in this way, and when they do it is the job of government to discriminate.

If the Government makes the right choice, and protects the more important at the cost of the less, then it has not weakened or cheapened the notion of a right; on the contrary it would have done so had it failed to protect the more important of the two. So we must acknowledge that the Government has a reason for limiting rights if it plausibly believes that a competing right is more important.

May the conservative seize on this fact? He might argue that I did wrong to characterize his argument as one that appeals to the general benefit, because it appeals instead to competing rights, namely the moral right of the majority to have its laws enforced, or the right of society to maintain the degree of order and security it wishes. These are the rights, he would say, that must be weighed against the individual's right to do what the wrongful law prohibits.

But this new argument is confused, because it depends on yet another ambiguity in the language of rights. It is true that we speak of the 'right' of society to do what it wants, but this cannot be a 'competing right' of the sort that may justify the invasion of a right against the Government. The existence of rights against the Government would be jeopardized if the Government were able to defeat such a right by appealing to the right of a democratic majority to work its will. A right against the Government must be a right to do something even when the majority thinks it would be wrong to do it, and even when the majority would be worse off for having it done. If we now say that society has a right to do whatever is in the general benefit, or the right to preserve whatever sort of environment the majority wishes to live in, and we mean that these are the sort of rights that provide justification for overruling any rights against the Government that may conflict, then we have annihilated the latter rights.

In order to save them, we must recognize as competing rights only the rights of other members of the society as individuals. We must distinguish the 'rights' of the majority as such, which cannot count as a justification for overruling individual rights, and the personal rights of members of a majority, which might well count. The test we must use is this. Someone has a competing right to protection, which must be weighed against an individual right to act, if that person would be entitled to demand that protection from his government on his own title, as an individual, without regard to whether a majority of his fellow citizens joined in the demand.

It cannot be true, on this test, that anyone has a right to have all the laws of the nation enforced. He has a right to have enforced only those criminal laws, for example, that he would have a right to have enacted if they were not already law. The laws against personal assault may well fall into that class. If the physically vulnerable members of the community – those who need police protection against personal violence – were only a small minority, it would still seem plausible to say that they were entitled to that protection. But the laws that provide a certain level of quiet in public places, or that authorize and finance a foreign war, cannot be thought to rest on individual rights. The timid lady on the streets of Chicago is not entitled to just the degree of quiet that now obtains, nor is she entitled to have boys drafted to fight in wars she approves. There are laws – perhaps desirable laws – that provide these advantages for her, but the justification for these laws, if they can be justified at all, is the common desire of a large majority, not her personal right. If, therefore, these laws do abridge someone else's moral right to protest, or his right to personal security, she cannot urge a competing right to justify the abridgement. She has no personal right to have such laws passed, and she has no competing right to have them enforced either.

So the conservative cannot advance his argument much on the ground of competing rights, but he may want to use another ground. A government, he may argue, may be justified in abridging the personal rights of its citizens in an emergency, or when a very great loss may be prevented, or perhaps, when some major benefit can clearly be secured. If the nation is at war, a policy of censorship may be justified even though it invades the right to say what one thinks on matters of political controversy. But the emergency must be genuine. There must be what Oliver Wendell Holmes described as a clear and present danger, and the danger must be one of magnitude.

Can the conservative argue that when any law is passed, even a wrongful law, this sort of justification is available for enforcing it? His argument might be something of this sort. If the Government once acknowledges that it may be wrong – that the legislature might have adopted, the executive approved, and the courts left standing, a law that in fact abridges important rights – then this admission will lead not simply to a marginal decline in respect for law, but to a crisis of order. Citizens may decide to obey only those laws they personally approve, and that is anarchy. So the Government must insist that whatever a citizen's rights may be before a law is passed and upheld by the courts, his rights thereafter are determined by that law.

But this argument ignores the primitive distinction between what may happen and what will happen. If we allow speculation to support the justification of emergency or decisive benefit, then, again, we have annihilated rights. We must, as Learned Hand said, discount the gravity of the evil threatened by the likelihood of reaching that evil. I know of no genuine evidence to the effect that tolerating some civil disobedience, out of respect for the moral position of its authors, will increase such disobedience, let alone crime in general. The case that it will must be based on vague assumptions about the contagion of ordinary crimes, assumptions that are themselves unproved, and that are in any event largely irrelevant. It seems at least as plausible to argue that tolerance will increase respect for officials and for the bulk of the laws they promulgate, or at least retard the rate of growing disrespect.

If the issue were simply the question whether the community would be marginally better off under strict law enforcement, then the Government would have to decide on the evidence we have, and it might not be unreasonable to decide, on balance, that it would. But since rights are at stake, the issue is the very different one of whether tolerance would destroy the community or threaten it with great harm, and it seems to me simply mindless to suppose that the evidence makes that probable or even conceivable.

The argument from emergency is confused in another way as well. It assumes that the Government must take the position either that a man never has the right to break the law, or that he always does. I said that any society that claims to recognize rights at all must abandon the notion of a general duty to obey the law that holds in all cases. This is important, because it shows that there are no short cuts to meeting a citizen's claim to right. If a citizen argues that he has a moral right not to serve in the Army, or to protest in a way he finds effective, then an official who wants to answer him, and not simply bludgeon him into obedience, must respond to the particular point he makes, and cannot point to the draft law or a Supreme Court decision as having even special, let alone decisive, weight. Sometimes an official who considers the citizen's moral arguments in good faith will be persuaded that the citizen's claim is plausible, or even right. It does not follow, however, that he will always be persuaded or that he always should be.

I must emphasize that all these propositions concern the strong sense of right, and they therefore leave open important questions about the right thing to do. If a man believes he has the right to break the law, he must then ask whether he does the right thing to exercise that right. He must remember that reasonable men can differ about whether he has a right against the Government, and therefore the right to break the law, that he thinks he has; and therefore that reasonable men can oppose him in good faith. He must take into account the various consequences his acts will have, whether they involve violence, and such other considerations as the context makes relevant; he must not go beyond the rights he can in good faith claim, to acts that violate the rights of others.

On the other hand, if some official, like a prosecutor, believes that the citizen does *not* have the right to break the law, then *he* must ask whether he does the right thing to enforce it. In Chapter 8 I argue that certain features of our legal system, and in particular the fusion of legal and moral issues in our Constitution, mean that citizens often do the right thing in exercising what they take to be moral rights to break the law, and that prosecutors often do the right thing in failing to prosecute them for it. I will not anticipate those arguments here; instead I want to ask whether the requirement that Government take its citizens' rights seriously has anything to do with the crucial question of what these rights are.

3. CONTROVERSIAL RIGHTS

The argument so far has been hypothetical: if a man has a particular moral right against the Government, that right survives contrary legislation or adjudication. But this does not tell us what rights he has, and it is notorious that reasonable men disagree about that. There is wide agreement on certain clearcut cases; almost everyone who believes in rights at all would admit, for example, that a man has a moral right to speak his mind in a non-provocative way on matters of political concern, and that this is an important right that the State must go to great pains to protect. But there is great controversy as to the limits of such paradigm rights, and the so-called 'anti-riot' law involved in the famous Chicago Seven trial of the last decade is a case in point.

The defendants were accused of conspiring to cross state lines with the intention of causing a riot. This charge is vague – perhaps unconstitutionally vague – but the law apparently defines as criminal emotional speeches which argue that violence is justified in order to secure political equality. Does the right of free speech protect this sort of speech? That, of course, is a legal issue, because it invokes the free-speech clause of the First Amendment of the Constitution. But it is also a moral issue, because, as I said, we must treat the First Amendment as an attempt to protect a moral right. It is part of the job of governing to 'define' moral rights through statutes and judicial decisions, that is, to declare officially the extent that moral rights will be taken to have in law. Congress faced this task in voting on the anti-riot bill, and the Supreme Court has faced it in countless cases. How should the different departments of government go about defining moral rights?

They should begin with a sense that whatever they decide might be wrong. History and their descendants may judge that they acted unjustly when they thought they were right. If they take their duty seriously, they must try to limit their mistakes, and they must therefore try to discover where the dangers of mistake lie.

They might choose one of two very different models for this purpose. The first model recommends striking a balance between the rights of the individual and the demands of society at large. If the Government *infringes* on a moral right (for example, by defining the right of free speech more narrowly than justice requires), then it has done the individual a wrong. On the other hand, if the Government *inflates* a right (by defining it more broadly than justice requires) then it cheats society of some general benefit, like safe streets, that there is no reason it should not have. So a mistake on one side is as serious as a mistake on the other. The course of government is to steer to the middle, to balance the general good and personal rights, giving to each its due.

When the Government, or any of its branches, defines a right, it must bear in mind, according to the first model, the social cost of different proposals and make the necessary adjustments. It must not grant the same freedom to noisy demonstrations as it grants to calm political discussion, for example, because the former causes much more trouble than the latter. Once it decides how much of a right to recognize, it must enforce its decision to the full. That means permitting an individual to act within his rights, as the Government has defined them, but not beyond, so that if anyone breaks the law, even on grounds of conscience, he must be punished. No doubt any government will make mistakes, and will regret decisions once taken. That is inevitable. But this middle policy will ensure that errors on one side will balance out errors on the other over the long run.

The first model, described in this way, has great plausibility, and most laymen and lawyers, I think, would respond to it warmly. The metaphor of balancing the public interest against personal claims is established in our political and judicial rhetoric, and this metaphor gives the model both familiarity and appeal. Nevertheless, the first model is a false one, certainly in the case of rights generally regarded as important, and the metaphor is the heart of its error.

The institution of rights against the Government is not a gift of God, or an ancient ritual, or a national sport. It is a complex and troublesome practice that makes the Government's job of securing the general benefit more difficult and more expensive, and it would be a frivolous and wrongful practice unless it served some point. Anyone who professes to take rights seriously, and who praises our Government for respecting them, must have some sense of what that point is. He must accept, at the minimum, one or both of two important ideas. The first is the vague but powerful idea of human dignity. This idea, associated with Kant, but defended by philosophers of different schools, supposes that there are ways of treating a man that are inconsistent with recognizing him as a full member of the human community, and holds that such treatment is profoundly unjust.

The second is the more familiar idea of political equality. This supposes that the weaker members of a political community are entitled to the same concern and respect of their government as the more powerful members have secured for themselves, so that if some men have freedom of decision whatever the effect on the general good, then all men must have the same freedom. I do not want to defend or elaborate these ideas here, but only to insist that anyone who claims that citizens have rights must accept ideas very close to these.[1]

It makes sense to say that a man has a fundamental right against the Government, in the strong sense, like free speech, if that right is necessary to protect his dignity, or his standing as equally entitled to concern and respect, or some other personal value of like consequence. It does not make sense otherwise.

So if rights make sense at all, then the invasion of a relatively important right must be a very serious matter. It means treating a man as less than a man, or as less worthy of concern than other men. The institution of rights rests on the conviction that this is a grave injustice, and that it is worth paying the incremental cost in social policy or efficiency that is necessary to prevent it. But then it must be wrong to say that inflating rights is as serious as invading them. If the Government errs on the side of the individual, then it simply pays a little more in social efficiency than it has to pay; it pays a little more, that is, of the same coin that it has already decided must be spent. But if it errs against the individual it inflicts an insult upon him that, on its own reckoning, it is worth a great deal of that coin to avoid.

So the first model is indefensible. It rests, in fact, on a mistake I discussed earlier, namely the confusion of society's rights with the rights of members of society. 'Balancing' is appropriate when the Government must choose between competing claims of right – between the Southerner's claim to freedom of association, for example, and the black man's claim to an equal education. Then the Government can do nothing but estimate the merits of the competing claims, and act on its estimate. The first model assumes that the 'right' of the majority is a competing right that must be balanced in this way; but that, as I argued before, is a confusion that threatens to destroy the concept of individual rights. It is worth noticing that the community rejects the first model in that area

---

[1] He need not consider these ideas to be axiomatic. He may, that is, have reasons for insisting that dignity or equality are important values, and these reasons may be utilitarian. He may believe, for example, that the general good will be advanced, *in the long run*, only if we treat indignity or inequality as very great injustices, and never allow our *opinions* about the general good to justify them. I do not know of any good arguments for or against this sort of 'institutional' utilitarianism, but it is consistent with my point, because it argues that we must treat violations of dignity and equality as special moral crimes, beyond the reach of ordinary utilitarian justification.

where the stakes for the individual are highest, the criminal process. We say that it is better that a great many guilty men go free than that one innocent man be punished, and that homily rests on the choice of the second model for government.

The second model treats abridging a right as much more serious than inflating one, and its recommendations follow from that judgment. It stipulates that once a right is recognized in clear-cut cases, then the Government should act to cut off that right only when some compelling reason is presented, some reason that is consistent with the suppositions on which the original right must be based. It cannot be an argument for curtailing a right, once granted, simply that society would pay a further price for extending it. There must be something special about that further cost, or there must be some other feature of the case, that makes it sensible to say that although great social cost is warranted to protect the original right, this particular cost is not necessary. Otherwise, the Government's failure to extend the right will show that its recognition of the right in the original case is a sham, a promise that it intends to keep only until that becomes inconvenient.

How can we show that a particular cost is not worth paying without taking back the initial recognition of a right? I can think of only three sorts of grounds that can consistently be used to limit the definition of a particular right. First, the Government might show that the values protected by the original right are not really at stake in the marginal case, or are at stake only in some attenuated form. Second, it might show that if the right is defined to include the marginal case, then some competing right, in the strong sense I described earlier, would be abridged. Third, it might show that if the right were so defined, then the cost to society would not be simply incremental, but would be of a degree far beyond the cost paid to grant the original right, a degree great enough to justify whatever assault on dignity or equality might be involved.

It is fairly easy to apply these grounds to one group of problems the Supreme Court faced, imbedded in constitutional issues. The draft law provided an exemption for conscientious objectors, but this exemption, as interpreted by the draft boards, has been limited to those who object to *all* wars on *religious* grounds. If we suppose that the exemption is justified on the ground that an individual has a moral right not to kill in violation of his own principles, then the question is raised whether it is proper to exclude those whose morality is not based on religion, or whose morality is sufficiently complex to distinguish among wars. The Court held, as a matter of Constitutional law, that the draft boards were wrong to exclude the former, but competent to exclude the latter.

None of the three grounds I listed can justify either of these exclusions as a matter of political morality. The invasion of personality in forcing men to kill when they believe killing immoral is just as great when these beliefs are based on secular grounds, or take account of the fact that wars differ in morally relevant ways, and there is no pertinent difference in competing rights or in national emergency. There are differences among the cases, of course, but they are insufficient to justify the distinction. A government that is secular on principle cannot prefer a religious to a non-religious morality as such. There are utilitarian arguments in favour of limiting the exception to religious or universal grounds – an exemption so limited may be less expensive to administer, and may allow easier discrimination between sincere and insincere applicants. But these utilitarian reasons are irrelevant, because they cannot count as grounds for limiting a right.

What about the anti-riot law, as applied in the Chicago trial? Does the law represent an improper limitation of the right to free speech, supposedly protected by the First Amendment? If we were to apply the first model for government to this issue, the argument for the anti-riot law would look strong. But if we set aside talk of balancing as inappropriate, and turn to the proper grounds for limiting a right, then the argument becomes a great deal weaker. The original right of free speech must suppose that it is an assault on human personality to stop a man from expressing what he honestly believes, particularly on issues affecting how he is governed. Surely the assault is greater, and not less, when he is stopped from expressing those principles of political morality that he holds most passionately, in the face of what he takes to be outrageous violations of these principles.

It may be said that the anti-riot law leaves him free to express these principles in a non-provocative way. But that misses the point of the connection between expression and dignity. A man cannot express himself freely when he cannot match his rhetoric to his outrage, or when he must trim his sails to protect values he counts as nothing next to those he is trying to vindicate. It is true that some political dissenters speak in ways that shock the majority, but it is arrogant for the majority to suppose that the orthodox methods of expression are the proper ways to speak, for this is a denial of equal concern and respect. If the point of the right is to protect the dignity of dissenters, then we must make judgments about appropriate speech with the personalities of the dissenters in mind, not the personality of the 'silent' majority for whom the anti-riot law is no restraint at all.

So the argument fails, that the personal values protected by the original right are less at stake in this marginal case. We must consider whether competing rights, or some grave threat to society, nevertheless justify the anti-riot law. We can consider these two grounds together, because the only plausible competing rights are rights to be free from violence, and violence is the only plausible threat to society that the context provides.

I have no right to burn your house, or stone you or your car, or swing a bicycle chain against your skull, even if I find these to be natural means of expression. But the defendants in the Chicago trial were not accused of direct violence; the argument runs that the acts of speech they planned made it likely that others would do acts of violence, either in support of or out of hostility to what they said. Does this provide a justification?

The question would be different if we could say with any confidence how much and what sort of violence the anti-riot law might be expected to prevent. Will it save two lives a year, or two hundred, or two thousand? Two thousand dollars of property, or two hundred thousand, or two million? No one can say, not simply because prediction is next to impossible, but because we have no firm understanding of the process by which demonstration disintegrates into riot, and in particular of the part played by inflammatory speech, as distinct from poverty, police brutality, blood lust, and all the rest of human and economic failure. The Government must try, of course, to reduce the violent waste of lives and property, but it must recognize that any attempt to locate and remove a cause of riot, short of a reorganization of society, must be an exercise in speculation, trial, and error. It must make its decisions under conditions of high uncertainty, and the institution of rights, taken seriously, limits its freedom to experiment under such conditions.

It forces the Government to bear in mind that preventing a man from speaking or demonstrating offers him a certain and profound insult, in return for a speculative benefit that may in any event be achieved in other if more expensive ways. When lawyers say that rights may be limited to protect other rights, or to prevent catastrophe, they have in mind cases in which cause and effect are relatively clear, like the familiar example of a man falsely crying 'Fire!' in a crowded theater.

But the Chicago story shows how obscure the causal connections can become. Were the speeches of Hoffman or Rubin necessary conditions of the riot? Or had thousands of people come to Chicago for the purposes of rioting anyway, as the Government also argues? Were they in any case sufficient conditions? Or could the police have contained the violence if they had not been so busy contributing to it, as the staff of the President's Commission on Violence said they were?

These are not easy questions, but if rights mean anything, then the Government cannot simply assume answers that justify its conduct. If a man has a right to speak, if the reasons that support that right extend to provocative political speech, and if the effects of such speech on violence are unclear, then the Government is not entitled to make its first attack on that problem by denying that right. It may be that abridging the right to speak is the least expensive course, or the least damaging to police morale, or the most popular politically. But these are utilitarian arguments in favor of starting one place rather than another, and such arguments are ruled out by the concept of rights.

This point may be obscured by the popular belief that political activists look forward to violence and 'ask for trouble' in what they say. They can hardly complain, in the general view, if they are taken to be the authors of the violence they expect, and treated accordingly. But this repeats the confusion I tried to explain earlier between having a right and doing the right thing. The speaker's motives may be relevant in deciding whether he does the right thing in speaking passionately about issues that may inflame or enrage the audience. But if he has a right to speak, because the danger in allowing him to speak is speculative, his motives cannot count as independent evidence in the argument that justifies stopping him.

But what of the individual rights of those who will be destroyed by a riot, of the passer-by who will be killed by a sniper's bullet or the shop-keeper who will be ruined by looting? To put the issue in this way, as a question of competing rights, suggests a principle that would undercut the effect of uncertainty. Shall we say that some rights to protection are so important that the Government is justified in doing all it can to maintain them? Shall we therefore say that the Government may abridge the rights of others to act when their acts might simply increase the risk, by however slight or speculative a margin, that some person's right to life or property will be violated?

Some such principle is relied on by those who oppose the Supreme Court's recent liberal rulings on police procedure. These rulings increase the chance that a guilty man will go free, and therefore marginally increase the risk that any particular member of the community will be murdered, raped, or robbed. Some critics believe that the Court's decisions must therefore be wrong.

But no society that purports to recognize a variety of rights, on the ground that a man's dignity or equality may be invaded in a variety of ways, can accept such a principle. If forcing a man to testify against himself, or forbidding him to speak, does the damage that the rights against self-incrimination and the right of free speech assume, then it would be contemptuous for the State to tell a man that he must suffer this damage against the possibility that other men's risk of loss may be marginally reduced. If rights make sense, then the degrees of their importance cannot be so different that some count not at all when others are mentioned.

Of course the Government may discriminate and may stop a man from exercising his right to speak when there is a clear and substantial risk that his speech will do great damage to the person or property of others, and no other means of preventing this are at hand, as in the case of the man shouting 'Fire!' in a theater. But we must reject the suggested principle that the Government can simply ignore rights to speak when life and property are in question. So long as the impact of speech on these other rights remains speculative and marginal, it must look elsewhere for levers to pull.

4. WHY TAKE RIGHTS SERIOUSLY?

I said at the beginning of this essay that I wanted to show what a government must do that professes to recognize individual rights. It must dispense with the claim that citizens never have a right to break its law, and it must not define citizens' rights so that these are cut off for supposed reasons of the general good. Any Government's harsh treatment of civil disobedience, or campaign against vocal protest, may therefore be thought to count against its sincerity.

One might well ask, however, whether it is wise to take rights all that seriously after all. America's genius, at least in her own legend, lies in not taking any abstract doctrine to its logical extreme. It may be time to ignore abstractions, and concentrate instead on giving the majority of our citizens a new sense of their Government's concern for their welfare, and of their title to rule.

That, in any event, is what former Vice-President Agnew seemed to believe. In a policy statement on the issue of 'weirdos' and social misfits, he said that the liberals' concern for individual rights was a headwind blowing in the face of the ship of state. That is a poor metaphor, but the philosophical point it expresses is very well taken. He recognized, as many liberals do not, that the majority cannot travel as fast or as far as it would like if it recognizes the rights of individuals to do what, in the majority's terms, is the wrong thing to do.

Spiro Agnew supposed that rights are divisive, and that national unity and a new respect for law may be developed by taking them more skeptically. But he is wrong. America will continue to be divided by its social and foreign policy, and if the economy grows weaker again the divisions will become more bitter. If we want our laws and our legal institutions to provide the ground rules within which these issues will be contested then these ground rules must not be the conqueror's law that the dominant class imposes on the weaker, as Marx supposed the law of a capitalist society must be. The bulk of the law – that part which defines and implements social, economic, and foreign policy – cannot be neutral. It must state, in its greatest part, the majority's view of the common good. The institution of rights is therefore crucial, because it represents the majority's promise to the minorities that their dignity and equality will be respected. When the divisions among the groups are most violent, then this gesture, if law is to work, must be most sincere.

The institution requires an act of faith on the part of the minorities, because the scope of their rights will be controversial whenever they are important, and because the officers of the majority will act on their own notions of what these rights really are. Of course these officials will disagree with many of the claims that a minority makes. That makes it all the more important that they take their decisions gravely. They must show that they understand what rights are, and they must not cheat on the full implications of the doctrine. The Government will not re-establish respect for law without giving the law some claim to respect. It cannot do that if it neglects the one feature that distinguishes law from ordered brutality. If the Government does not take rights seriously, then it does not take law seriously either.

H

8

Civil Disobedience

How should the government deal with those who disobey the draft laws out of conscience? Many people think the answer is obvious: The government must prosecute the dissenters, and if they are convicted it must punish them. Some people reach this conclusion easily, because they hold the mindless view that conscientious disobedience is the same as lawlessness. They think that the dissenters are anarchists who must be punished before their corruption spreads. Many lawyers and intellectuals come to the same conclusion, however, on what looks like a more sophisticated argument. They recognize that disobedience to law may be *morally* justified, but they insist that it cannot be *legally* justified, and they think that it follows from this truism that the law must be enforced. Erwin Griswold, once Solicitor General of the United States, and before that Dean of the Harvard Law School, appears to have adopted this view. '[It] is of the essence of law,' he said, 'that it is equally applied to all, that it binds all alike, irrespective of personal motive. For this reason, one who contemplates civil disobedience out of moral conviction should not be surprised and must not be bitter if a criminal conviction ensues. And he must accept the fact that organized society cannot endure on any other basis.'

The New York Times applauded that statement. A thousand faculty members of several universities had signed a *Times* advertisement calling on the Justice Department to quash the indictments of the Rev. William Sloane Coffin, Dr. Benjamin Spock, Marcus Raskin, Mitchell Goodman, and Michael Ferber, for conspiring to counsel various draft offenses. The *Times* said that the request to quash the indictments 'confused moral rights with legal responsibilties'.

But the argument that, because the government believes a man has committed a crime, it must prosecute him is much weaker than it seems. Society 'cannot endure' if it tolerates all disobedience; it does not follow, however, nor is there evidence, that it will collapse if it tolerates some. In the United States prosecutors have discretion whether to enforce criminal laws in particular cases. A prosecutor may properly decide not to press charges if the lawbreaker is young, or inexperienced, or the sole support of a family, or is repentant, or turns state's evidence, or if the law is unpopular or unworkable or generally disobeyed, or if the courts are clogged with more important cases, or for dozens of other reasons. This discretion is not license – we expect prosecutors to have good reasons for exercising it – but there are, at least *prima facie*, some good reasons for not prosecuting those who disobey the draft laws out of conscience. One is the obvious reason that they act out of better motives than those who break the law out of greed or a desire to subvert government. If motive can count in distinguishing between thieves, then why not in distinguishing between draft offenders? Another is the practical reason that our society suffers a loss if it punishes a group that includes – as the group of draft dissenters does – some of its most loyal and law-respecting citizens. Jailing such men solidifies their alienation from society, and alienates many like them who are deterred by the threat. If practical consequences like these argued for not enforcing prohibition, why do they not argue for tolerating offenses of conscience?

Those who think that conscientious draft offenders should always be punished must show that these are not good reasons for exercising discretion, or they must find contrary reasons that outweigh them. What arguments might they produce? There are practical reasons for enforcing draft laws, and I shall consider some of these later. But Dean Griswold and those who agree with him seem to rely on a fundamental moral argument that it would be unfair, not merely impractical, to let the dissenters go unpunished. They think it would be unfair, I gather, because society could not function if everyone disobeyed laws he disapproved of or found disadvantageous. If the government tolerates those few who will not 'play the game', it allows them to secure the benefits of everyone else's deference to law, without shouldering the burdens, such as the burden of the draft.

This argument is a serious one. It cannot be answered simply by saying that the dissenters would allow everyone else the privilege of disobeying a law he believed immoral. In fact, few draft dissenters would accept a changed society in which sincere segregationists were free to break civil rights laws they hated. The majority want no such change, in any event, because they think that society would be worse off for it; until they are shown this is wrong, they will expect their officials to punish anyone who assumes a privilege which they, for the general benefit, do not assume.

There is, however, a flaw in the argument. The reasoning contains a hidden assumption that makes it almost entirely irrelevant to the draft cases, and indeed to any serious case of civil disobedience in the United States. The argument assumes that the dissenters know that they are breaking a valid law, and that the privilege they assert is the privilege to do that. Of course, almost everyone who discusses civil disobedience recognizes that in America a law may be invalid because it is unconstitutional. But the critics handle this complexity by arguing on separate hypotheses: If the law is invalid, then no crime is committed, and society may not punish. If the law is valid, then a crime has been committed, and society must punish. This reasoning hides the crucial fact that the validity of the law may be doubtful. The officials and judges may believe that the law is valid, the dissenters may disagree, and both sides may have plausible arguments for their positions. If so, then the issues are different from what they would be if the law were clearly valid or clearly invalid, and the argument of fairness, designed for these alternatives, is irrelevant.

Doubtful law is by no means special or exotic in cases of civil disobedience. On the contrary. In the United States, at least, almost any law which a significant number of people would be tempted to disobey on moral grounds would be doubtful – if not clearly invalid – on constitutional grounds as well. The constitution makes our conventional political morality relevant to the question of validity; any statute that appears to compromise that morality raises constitutional questions, and if the compromise is serious, the constitutional doubts are serious also.

The connection between moral and legal issues was especially clear in the draft cases of the last decade. Dissent was based at the time on the following moral objections: (a) The United States is using immoral weapons and tactics in Vietnam. (b) The war has never been endorsed by deliberate, considered, and open vote of the peoples' representatives. (c) The United States has no interest at stake in Vietnam remotely strong enough to justify forcing a segment of its citizens to risk death there. (d) If an army is to be raised to fight that war, it is immoral to raise it by a draft that defers or exempts college students, and thus discriminates against the economically underprivileged. (e) The draft exempts those who object to all wars on religious grounds, but not those who object to particular wars on moral grounds; there is no relevant difference between these positions, and so the draft, by making the distinction, implies that the second group is less worthy of the nation's respect than the first. (f) The law that makes it a crime to counsel draft resistance stifles those who oppose the war, because it is morally impossible to argue that the war is profoundly immoral, without encouraging and assisting those who refuse to fight it.

Lawyers will recognize that these moral positions, if we accept them, provide the basis for the following constitutional arguments: (a) The constitution makes treaties part of the law of the land, and the United States is a party to international conventions and covenants that make illegal the acts of war the dissenters charged the nation with committing. (b) The constitution provides that Congress must declare war; the legal issue of whether our action in Vietnam was a 'war' and whether the Tonkin Bay Resolution was a 'declaration' is the heart of the moral issue of whether the government had made a deliberate and open decision. (c) Both the due process clause of the Fifth and Fourteenth Amendments and equal protection clause of the Fourteenth Amendment condemn special burdens placed on a selected class of citizens when the burden or the classification is not reasonable; the burden is unreasonable when it patently does not serve the public interest, or when it is vastly disproportionate to the interest served. If our military action in Vietnam was frivolous or perverse, as the dissenters claimed, then the burden we placed on men of draft age was unreasonable and unconstitutional. (d) In any event, the discrimination in favor of college students denied to the poor the equal protection of the law that is guaranteed by the constitution. (e) If there is no pertinent difference between religious objection to all wars and moral objection to some wars, then the classification the draft made was arbitrary and unreasonable, and unconstitutional on that ground. The 'establishment of religion' clause of the First Amendment forbids governmental pressure in favor of organized religion; if the draft's distinction coerced men in this direction, it was invalid on that count also. (f) The First Amendment also condemns invasions of freedom of speech. If the draft law's prohibition on counseling did inhibit expression of a range of views on the war, it abridged free speech.

The principal counterargument, supporting the view that the courts ought not to have held the draft unconstitutional, also involves moral issues. Under the so-called 'political question' doctrine, the courts deny their own jurisdiction to pass on matters – such as foreign or military policy – whose resolution is best assigned to other branches of the government. The Boston court trying the Coffin, Spock case declared, on the basis of this doctrine, that it would not hear arguments about the legality of the war. But the Supreme Court has shown itself (in the reapportionment cases, for example) reluctant to refuse jurisdiction when it believed that the gravest issues of political morality were at stake and that no remedy was available through the political process. If the dissenters were right, and the war and the draft were state crimes of profound injustice to a group of citizens, then the argument that the courts should have refused jurisdiction is considerably weakened.

We cannot conclude from these arguments that the draft (or any part of it) was unconstitutional. When the Supreme Court was called upon to rule on the question, it rejected some of them, and refused to consider the others on grounds that they were political. The majority of lawyers agreed with this result. But the arguments of unconstitutionality were at least plausible, and a reasonable and competent lawyer might well think that they present a stronger case, on balance, than the counterarguments. If he does, he will consider that the draft was not constitutional, and there will be no way of proving that he is wrong.

Therefore we cannot assume, in judging what should have been done with the draft dissenters, that they were asserting a privilege to disobey valid laws. We cannot decide that fairness demanded their punishment until we try to answer further questions: What should a citizen do when the law is unclear, and when he thinks it allows what others think it does not? I do not mean to ask, of course, what it is *legally* proper for him to do, or what his *legal* rights are – that would be begging the question, because it depends upon whether he is right or they are right. I mean to ask what his proper course is as a citizen, what, in other words, we would consider to be 'playing the game'. That is a crucial question, because it cannot be unfair not to punish him if he is acting as, given his opinions, we think he should.[1]

There is no obvious answer on which most citizens would readily agree, and that is itself significant. If we examine our legal institutions and practices, however, we shall discover some relevant underlying principles and policies. I shall set out three possible answers to the question, and then try to show which of these best fits our practices and expectations. The three possibilities I want to consider are these:

(1) If the law is doubtful, and it is therefore unclear whether it permits someone to do what he wants, he should assume the worst, and act on the assumption that it does not. He should obey the executive authorities who command him, even though he thinks they are wrong, while using the political process, if he can, to change the law.

(2) If the law is doubtful, he may follow his own judgment, that is, he may do what he wants if he believes that the case that the law permits this is stronger than the case that it does not. But he may follow his own judgment only until an authoritative institution, like a court, decides the other way in a case involving him or someone else. Once an institutional decision has been reached, he must abide by that decision, even though he thinks that it was wrong. (There are, in theory, many subdivisions of this second possibility. We may say that the individual's choice is foreclosed by the contrary decision of any court, including the lowest court in the system if the case is not appealed. Or we may require

[1] I do not mean to imply that the government should always punish a man who deliberately breaks a law he knows is valid. There may be reasons of fairness or practicality, like those I listed in the third paragraph, for not prosecuting such men. But cases like the draft cases present special arguments for tolerance; I want to concentrate on these arguments and therefore have isolated these cases.

a decision of some particular court or institution. I shall discuss this second possibility in its most liberal form, namely that the individual may properly follow his own judgment until a contrary decision of the highest court competent to pass on the issue, which, in the case of the draft, was the United States Supreme Court.)

(3) If the law is doubtful, he may follow his own judgment, even after a contrary decision by the highest competent court. Of course, he must take the contrary decision of any court into account in making his judgment of what the law requires. Otherwise the judgment would not be an honest or reasonable one, because the doctrine of precedent, which is an established part of our legal system, has the effect of allowing the decision of the courts to *change* the law. Suppose, for example, that a taxpayer believes that he is not required to pay tax on certain forms of income. If the Supreme Court decides to the contrary, he should, taking into account the practice of according great weight to the decisions of the Supreme Court on tax matters, decide that the Court's decision has itself tipped the balance, and that the law now requires him to pay the tax.

Someone might think that this qualification erases the difference between the third and the second models, but it does not. The doctrine of precedent gives different weights to the decisions of different courts, and greatest weight to the decisions of the Supreme Court, but it does not make the decisions of any court conclusive. Sometimes, even after a contrary Supreme Court decision, an individual may still reasonably believe that the law is on his side; such cases are rare, but they are most likely to occur in disputes over constitutional law when civil disobedience is involved. The Court has shown itself more likely to overrule its past decisions if these have limited important personal or political rights, and it is just these decisions that a dissenter might want to challenge.

We cannot assume, in other words, that the Constitution is always what the Supreme Court says it is. Oliver Wendell Holmes, for example, did not follow such a rule in his famous dissent in the *Gitlow* case. A few years before, in *Abrams*, he had lost his battle to persuade the court that the First Amendment protected an anarchist who had been urging general strikes against the government. A similar issue was presented in *Gitlow*, and Holmes once again dissented. 'It is true,' he said, 'that in my opinion this criterion was departed from [in *Abrams*] but the convictions that I expressed in that case are too deep for it to be possible for me as yet to believe that it . . . settled the law.' Holmes voted for acquitting Gitlow, on the ground that what Gitlow had done was no crime, even though the Supreme Court had recently held that it was.

Here then are three possible models for the behavior of dissenters who disagree with the executive authorities when the law is doubtful. Which of them best fits our legal and social practices?

I think it plain that we do not follow the first of these models, that is, that we do not expect citizens to assume the worst. If no court has decided the issue, and a man thinks, on balance, that the law is on his side, most of our lawyers and critics think it perfectly proper for him to follow his own judgment. Even when many disapprove of what he does – such as peddling pornography – they do not think he must desist just because the legality of his conduct is subject to doubt.

It is worth pausing a moment to consider what society would lose if it did follow the first model or, to put the matter the other way, what society gains when people follow their own judgment in cases like this. When the law is uncertain, in the sense that lawyers can reasonably disagree on what a court ought to decide, the reason usually is that different legal principles and policies have collided, and it is unclear how best to accommodate these conflicting principles and policies.

Our practice, in which different parties are encouraged to pursue their own understanding, provides a means of testing relevant hypotheses. If the question is whether a particular rule would have certain undesirable consequences, or whether these consequences would have limited or broad ramifications, then, before the issue is decided, it is useful to know what does in fact take place when some people proceed on that rule. (Much anti-trust and business regulation law has developed through this kind of testing.) If the question is whether and to what degree a particular solution would offend principles of justice or fair play deeply respected by the community, it is useful, again, to experiment by testing the community's response. The extent of community indifference to anti-contraception laws, for example, would never have become established had not some organizations deliberately flouted those laws.

If the first model were followed, we would lose the advantages of these tests. The law would suffer, particularly if this model were applied to constitutional issues. When the validity of a criminal statute is in doubt, the statute will almost always strike some people as being unfair or unjust, because it will infringe some principle of liberty or justice or fairness which they take to be built into the Constitution. If our practice were that whenever a law is doubtful on these grounds, one must act as if it were valid, then the chief vehicle we have for challenging the law on moral grounds would be lost, and over time the law we obeyed would certainly become less fair and just, and the liberty of our citizens would certainly be diminished.

We would lose almost as much if we used a variation of the first model, that a citizen must assume the worst unless he can anticipate that the courts will agree with his view of the law. If everyone deferred to his guess of what the courts would do, society and its law would be poorer. Our assumption in rejecting the first model was that the record a citizen makes in following his own judgment, together with the arguments he makes supporting that judgment when he has the opportunity, are helpful in creating the best judicial decision possible. This remains true even when, at the time the citizen acts, the odds are against his success in court. We must remember, too, that the value of the citizen's example is not exhausted once the decision has been made. Our practices require that the decision be criticized, by the legal profession and the law schools, and the record of dissent may be invaluable here.

Of course a man must consider what the courts will do when he decides whether it would be *prudent* to follow his own judgment. He may have to face jail, bankruptcy, or opprobrium if he does. But it is essential that we separate the calculation of prudence from the question of what, as a good citizen, he may properly do. We are investigating how society ought to treat him when its courts believe that he judged wrong; therefore we must ask what he is justified in doing when his judgment differs from others. We beg the question if we assume that what he may properly do depends on his guess as to how society will treat him.

We must also reject the second model, that if the law is unclear a citizen may properly follow his own judgment until the highest court has ruled that he is wrong. This fails to take into account the fact that any court, including the Supreme Court, may overrule itself. In 1940 the Court decided that a West Virginia law requiring students to salute the Flag was constitutional. In 1943 it reversed itself, and decided that such a statute was unconstitutional after all. What was the duty as citizens, of those people who in 1941 and 1942 objected to saluting the Flag on grounds of conscience, and thought that the Court's 1940 decision was wrong? We can hardly say that their duty was to follow the first decision. They believed that saluting the Flag was unconscionable, and they believed, reasonably, that no valid law required them to do so. The Supreme Court later decided that in this they were right. The Court did not simply hold that after the second decision failing to salute would not be a crime; it held (as in a case like this it almost always would) that it was no crime after the first decision either.

Some will say that the flag-salute dissenters should have obeyed the Court's first decision, while they worked in the legislatures to have the law repealed, and tried in the courts to find some way to challenge the law again without actually violating it. That would be, perhaps, a plausible recommendation if conscience were not involved, because it would then be arguable that the gain in orderly procedure was worth the personal sacrifice of patience. But conscience was involved, and if the dissenters had obeyed the law while biding their time, they would have suffered the irreparable injury of having done what their conscience forbade them to do. It is one thing to say that an individual must sometimes violate his conscience when he knows that the law commands him to do it. It is quite another to say that he must violate his conscience even when he reasonably believes that the law does not require it, because it would inconvenience his fellow citizens if he took the most direct, and perhaps the only, method of attempting to show that he is right and they are wrong.

Since a court may overrule itself, the same reasons we listed for rejecting the first model count against the second as well. If we did not have the pressure of dissent, we would not have a dramatic statement of the degree to which a court decision against the dissenter is felt to be wrong, a demonstration that is surely pertinent to the question of whether it was right. We would increase the chance of being governed by rules that offend the principles we claim to serve.

These considerations force us, I think, from the second model, but some will want to substitute a variation of it. They will argue that once the Supreme Court has decided that a criminal law is valid, then citizens have a duty to abide by that decision until they have a reasonable belief, not merely that the decision is a bad law, but that the Supreme Court is likely to overrule it. Under this view the West Virginia dissenters who refused to salute the Flag in 1942 were acting properly, because they might reasonably have anticipated that the Court would change its mind. But once the Court held laws like the draft laws constitutional, it would be improper to continue to challenge these laws, because there would be no great likelihood that the Court would soon change its mind. This suggestion must also be rejected, however. For once we say that a citizen may properly follow his own judgment of the law, in spite of his judgment that the courts will probably find against him, there is no plausible reason why he should act differently because a contrary decision is already on the books.

Thus the third model, or something close to it, seems to be the fairest statement of a man's social duty in our community. A citizen's allegiance is to the law, not to any particular person's view of what the law is, and he does not behave unfairly so long as he proceeds on his own considered and reasonable view of what the law requires. Let me repeat (because it is crucial) that this is not the same as saying that an individual may disregard what the courts have said. The doctrine of precedent lies near the core of our legal system, and no one can make a reasonable effort to follow the law unless he grants the courts the general power to alter it by their decisions. But if the issue is one touching fundamental personal or political rights, and it is arguable that the Supreme Court has made a mistake, a man is within his social rights in refusing to accept that decision as conclusive.

One large question remains before we can apply these observations to the problems of draft resistance. I have been talking about the case of a man who believes that the law is not what other people think, or what the courts have held. This description may fit some of those who disobey the draft laws out of conscience, but it does not fit most of them. Most of the dissenters are not lawyers or political philosophers; they believe that the laws on the books are immoral, and inconsistent with their country's legal ideals, but they have not considered the question of whether they may be invalid as well. Of what relevance to their situation, then, is the proposition that one may properly follow one's own view of the law?

To answer this, I shall have to return to the point I made earlier. The Constitution, through the due process clause, the equal protection clause, the First Amendment, and the other provisions I mentioned, injects an extraordinary amount of our political morality into the issue of whether a law is valid. The statement that most draft dissenters are unaware that the law is invalid therefore needs qualification. They hold beliefs that, if true, strongly support the view that the law is on their side; the fact that they have not reached that further conclusion can be traced, in at least most cases, to their lack of legal sophistication. If we believe that when the law is doubtful people who follow their own judgment of the law may be acting properly, it would seem wrong not to extend that view to those dissenters whose judgments come to the same thing. No part of the case that I made for the third model would entitle us to distinguish them from their more knowledgeable colleagues.

We can draw several tentative conclusions from the argument so far: When the law is uncertain, in the sense that a plausible case can be made on both sides, then a citizen who follows his own judgment is not behaving unfairly. Our practices permit and encourage him to follow his own judgment in such cases. For that reason, our government has a special responsibility to try to protect him, and soften his predicament, whenever it can do so without great damage to other policies. It does not follow that the government can guarantee him immunity – it cannot adopt the rule that it will prosecute no one who acts out of conscience, or convict no one who reasonably disagrees with the courts. That would paralyze the government's ability to carry out its policies; it would, moreover, throw away the most important benefit of following the third model. If the state never prosecuted, then the courts could not act on the experience and the arguments the dissent has generated. But it does follow that when the practical reasons for prosecuting are relatively weak in a particular case, or can be met in other ways, the path of fairness lies in tolerance. The popular view that the law is the law and must always be enforced refuses to distinguish the man who acts on his own judgment of a doubtful law, and thus behaves as our practices provide, from the common criminal. I know of no reason, short of moral blindness, for not drawing a distinction in principle between the two cases.

I anticipate a philosophical objection to these conclusions: that I am treating law as a 'brooding omnipresence in the sky'. I have spoken of people making judgments about what the law requires, even in cases in which the law is unclear and undemonstrable. I have spoken of cases in which a man might think that the law requires one thing, even though the Supreme Court has said that it requires another, and even when it was not likely that the Supreme Court would soon change its mind. I will therefore be charged with the view that there is always a 'right answer' to a legal problem to be found in natural law or locked up in some transcendental strongbox.

The strongbox theory of law is, of course, nonsense. When I say that people hold views on the law when the law is doubtful, and that these views are not merely predictions of what the courts will hold, I intend no such metaphysics. I mean only to summarize as accurately as I can many of the practices that are part of our legal process.

Lawyers and judges make statements of legal right and duty, even when they know these are not demonstrable, and support them with arguments even when they know that these arguments will not appeal to everyone. They make these arguments to one another, in the professional journals, in the classrooms, and in the courts. They respond to these arguments, when others make them, by judging them good or bad or mediocre. In so doing they assume that some arguments for a given doubtful position are better than others. They also assume that the case on one side of a doubtful proposition may be stronger than the case on the other, which is what I take a claim of law in a doubtful case to mean. They distinguish, without too much difficulty, these arguments from predictions of what the courts will decide.

These practices are poorly represented by the theory that judgments of law on doubtful issues are nonsense, or are merely predictions of what the courts will do. Those who hold such theories cannot deny the fact of these practices; perhaps these theorists mean that the practices are not sensible, because they are based on suppositions that do not hold, or for some other reason. But this makes their objection mysterious, because they never specify what they take the purposes underlying these practices to be; and unless these goals are specified, one cannot decide whether the practices are sensible. I understand these underlying purposes to be those I described earlier: the development and testing of the law through experimentation by citizens and through the adversary process.

Our legal system pursues these goals by inviting citizens to decide the strengths and weaknesses of legal arguments for themselves, or through their own counsel, and to act on these judgments, although that permission is qualified by the limited threat that they may suffer if the courts do not agree. Success in this strategy depends on whether there is sufficient agreement within the community on what counts as good or bad argument, so that, although different people will reach different judgments, these differences will be neither so profound nor so frequent as to make the system unworkable, or dangerous for those who act by their own lights. I believe there is sufficient agreement on the criteria of the argument to avoid these traps, although one of the main tasks of legal philosophy is to exhibit and clarify these criteria. In any event, the practices I have described have not yet been shown to be misguided; they therefore must count in determining whether it is just and fair to be lenient to those who break what others think is the law.

I have said that the government has a special responsibility to those who act on a reasonable judgment that a law is invalid. It should make accommodation for them as far as possible, when this is consistent with other policies. It may be difficult to decide what the government ought to do, in the name of that responsibility, in particular cases. The decision will be a matter of balance, and flat rules will not help. Still, some principles can be set out.

I shall start with the prosecutor's decision whether to press charges. He must balance both his responsibility to be lenient and the risk that convictions will rend the society, against the damage to the law's policy that may follow if he leaves the dissenters alone. In making his calculation he must consider not only the extent to which others will be harmed, but also how the law evaluates that harm; and he must therefore make the following distinction. Every rule of law is supported, and presumably justified, by a set of policies it is supposed to advance and principles it is supposed to respect. Some rules (the laws prohibiting murder and theft, for example) are supported by the proposition that the individuals protected have a moral right to be free from the harm proscribed. Other rules (the more technical anti-trust rules, for example) are not supported by any supposition of an underlying right; their support comes chiefly from the alleged utility of the economic and social policies they promote. These may be supplemented with moral principles (like the view that it is a harsh business practice to undercut a weak competitor's prices) but these fall short of recognizing a moral right against the harm in question.

The point of the distinction here is this: if a particular rule of law represents an official decision that individuals have a moral right to be free from some harm, then that is a powerful argument against tolerating violations that inflict those injuries. Laws protecting people from personal injury or the destruction of their property, for example, do represent that sort of decision, and this is a very strong argument against tolerating civil disobedience that involves violence.

It may be controversial, of course, whether a law does rest on the assumption of a moral right. The question is whether it is reasonable to suppose, from the background and administration of the law, that its authors recognized such a right. There are cases, in addition to rules against violence, where it is plain that they did; the civil rights laws are examples. Many sincere and ardent segregationists believe that the civil rights laws and decisions are unconstitutional, because they compromise principles of local government and of freedom of association. This is an arguable, though not a persuasive, view. But these laws and decisions clearly embody the view that Negroes, as individuals, have a right not to be segregated. They do not rest simply on the judgment that other national policies are best pursued by preventing racial segregation. If we take no action against the man who blocks the school house door, therefore, we violate the moral rights, confirmed by law, of the schoolgirl he blocks. The responsibility of leniency cannot go this far.

The schoolgirl's position is different, however, from that of the draftee who may be called up sooner or given a more dangerous post if draft offenders are not punished. The draft laws, taken as a whole and with an eye to their administration, cannot be said to reflect the judgment that a man has a moral right to be drafted only after certain other men or groups have been called. The draft classifications, and the order-of-call within classifications, are arranged for social and administrative convenience. They also reflect considerations of fairness, like the proposition that a mother who has lost one of two sons in war ought not to be made to risk losing the other. But they presuppose no fixed rights. The draft boards are given considerable discretion in the classification process, and the army, of course, has almost complete discretion in assigning dangerous posts. If the prosecutor tolerates draft offenders, he makes small shifts in the law's calculations of fairness and utility. These may cause disadvantage to others in the pool of draftees but that is a different matter from contradicting their moral rights.

This difference between segregation and the draft is not an accident of how the laws happen to have been written. It would run counter to a century of practice to suppose that citizens have moral rights with respect to the order in which they are called to serve; the lottery system of selection, for example, would be abhorrent under that supposition. If our history had been different, and if the community had recognized such a moral right, it seems fair to suppose that some of the draft dissenters, at least, would have modified their acts so as to try to respect these rights.

So it is wrong to analyze draft cases in the same way as cases of violence or civil rights cases, as many critics do when considering whether tolerance is justified. I do not mean that fairness to others is irrelevant in draft cases; it must be taken into account, and balanced against fairness to dissenters and the long-term benefit to society. But it does not play the commanding role here that it does when rights are at stake.

Where, then, does the balance of fairness and utility lie in the case of those who counseled draft resistance? If these men had encouraged violence or otherwise trespassed on the rights of others, then there would have been a strong case for prosecution. But in the absence of such actions, the balance of fairness and utility seems to me to lie the other way, and I therefore think that the decision to prosecute Coffin, Spock, Raskin, Goodman, and Ferber was wrong. It might have been argued that if those who counsel draft resistance are free from prosecution, the number who resist induction will increase; but not, I think, much beyond the number of those who would resist in any event.

If this is wrong, and there is much greater resistance, then a sense of this residual discontent is of importance to policy makers, and it ought not to have been hidden under a ban on speech. Conscience is deeply involved – it is hard to believe that many who counseled resistance did so on any other grounds. The case is strong that the laws making counseling a crime are unconstitutional; even those who do not find the case persuasive will admit that its arguments have substance. The harm to potential draftees, both those who may have been persuaded to resist and those who may have been called earlier because others have been persuaded, was remote and speculative.

The cases of men who refused induction when drafted are more complicated. The crucial question is whether a failure to prosecute will lead to wholesale refusals to serve. It may not – there were social pressures, including the threat of career disadvantages, that would have forced many young Americans to serve if drafted, even if they knew they would not go to jail if they refused. If the number would not much have increased, then the State should have left the dissenters alone, and I see no great harm in delaying any prosecution until the effect of that policy became clearer. If the number of those who refuse induction turned out to be large, this would argue for prosecution. But it would also make the problem academic, because if there had been sufficient dissent to bring us to that pass, it would have been most difficult to pursue the war in any event, except under a near-totalitarian regime.

There may seem to be a paradox in these conclusions. I argued earlier that when the law is unclear citizens have the right to follow their own judgment, partly on the grounds that this practice helps to shape issues for adjudication; now I propose a course that eliminates or postpones adjudication. But the contradiction is only apparent. It does not follow from the fact that our practice facilitates adjudication, and renders it more useful in developing the law, that a trial should follow whenever citizens do act by their own lights. The question arises in each case whether the issues are ripe for adjudication, and whether adjudication would settle these issues in a manner that would decrease the chance of, or remove the grounds for, further dissent.

In the draft cases, the answer to both these questions was negative: there was much ambivalence about the war, and uncertainty and ignorance about the scope of the moral issues involved in the draft. It was far from the best time for a court to pass on these issues, and tolerating dissent for a time was one way of allowing the debate to continue until it produced something clearer. Moreover, it was plain that an adjudication of the constitutional issues would not settle the law. Those who had doubts whether the draft was constitutional had the same doubts even after the Supreme Court said that it was. This is one of those cases, touching fundamental rights, in which our practices of precedent encourage such doubts.

Even if the prosecutor does not act, however, the underlying problem will be only temporarily relieved. So long as the law appears to make acts of dissent criminal, a man of conscience will face danger. What can Congress, which shares the responsibility of leniency, do to lessen this danger?

Congress can review the laws in question to see how much accommodation can be given the dissenters. Every program a legislature adopts is a mixture of policies and restraining principles. We accept loss of efficiency in crime detection and urban renewal, for example, so that we can respect the rights of accused criminals and compensate property owners for their damages. Congress may properly defer to its responsibility toward the dissenters by adjusting or compromising other policies. The relevant questions are these: What means can be found for allowing the greatest possible tolerance of conscientious dissent while minimizing its impact on policy? How strong is the government's responsibility for leniency in this case – how deeply is conscience involved, and how strong is the case that the law is invalid after all? How important is the policy in question – is interference with that policy too great a price to pay? These questions are no doubt too simple, but they suggest the heart of the choices that must be made.

For the same reasons that those who counseled resistance should not have been prosecuted, I think that the law that makes this a crime should be repealed. The case is strong that this law abridges free speech. It certainly coerces conscience, and it probably serves no beneficial effect. If counseling would persuade only a few to resist who otherwise would not, the value of the restraint is small; if counseling would persuade many, that is an important political fact that should be known.

The issues are more complex, again, in the case of draft resistance itself. Those who believed that the war in Vietnam was itself a grotesque blunder would have favored any change in the law that made peace more likely. But if we take the position of those who think the war was necessary, then we must admit that a policy that continued the draft but wholly exempted dissenters would have been unwise. Two less drastic alternatives should have been considered, however: a volunteer army, and an expanded conscientious objector category that included those who found the war immoral. There is much to be said against both proposals, but once the requirement of respect for dissent is recognized, the balance of principle may be tipped in their favor.

So the case for not prosecuting conscientious draft offenders, and for changing the laws in their favor, was a strong one. It would have been unrealistic to expect this policy to prevail, however, for political pressures opposed it.

We must consider, therefore, what the courts could and should have done. A court might, of course, have upheld the arguments that the draft laws were in some way unconstitutional, in general or as applied to the defendants in the case at hand. Or it might acquit the defendants because the facts necessary for conviction are not proved. I shall not argue the constitutional issues, or the facts of any particular case. I want instead to suggest that a court ought not to convict, at least in some circumstances, even if it sustains the statutes and finds the facts as charged. The Supreme Court had not ruled on the chief arguments that the draft was unconstitutional, nor had it held that these arguments raised political questions that are not within its jurisdiction, when several of the draft cases arose. There are strong reasons why a Court should acquit in these circumstances even if it does then sustain the draft. It ought to acquit on the ground that before its decision the validity of the draft was doubtful, and it is unfair to punish men for disobeying a doubtful law.

There would be precedent for a decision along these lines. The Court has several times reversed criminal convictions, on due process grounds, because the law in question was too vague. (It has overturned convictions, for example, under laws that made it a crime to charge 'unreasonable prices' or to be a member of a 'gang'.) Conviction under a vague criminal law offends the moral and political ideals of due process in two ways. First, it places a citizen in the unfair position of either acting at his peril or accepting a more stringent restriction on his life than the legislature may have authorized: As I argued earlier, it is not acceptable, as a model of social behavior, that in such cases he ought to assume the worst. Second, it gives power to the prosecutor and the courts to make criminal law, by opting for one or the other possible interpretations after the event. This would be a delegation of authority by the legislature that is inconsistent with our scheme of separation of powers.

Conviction under a criminal law whose terms are not vague, but whose constitutional validity is doubtful, offends due process in the first of these ways. It forces a citizen to assume the worst, or act at his peril. It offends due process in something like the second way as well. Most citizens would be deterred by a doubtful statute if they were to risk jail by violating it. Congress, and not the courts, would then be the effective voice in deciding the constitutionality of criminal enactments, and this also violates the separation of powers.

If acts of dissent continue to occur after the Supreme Court has ruled that the laws are valid, or that the political question doctrine applies, then acquittal on the grounds I have described is no longer appropriate. The Court's decision will not have finally settled the law, for the reasons given earlier, but the Court will have done all that can be done to settle it. The courts may still exercise their sentencing discretion, however, and impose minimal or suspended sentences as a mark of respect for the dissenters' position.

Some lawyers will be shocked by my general conclusion that we have a responsibility toward those who disobey the draft laws out of conscience, and that we may be required not to prosecute them, but rather to change our laws or adjust our sentencing procedures to accommodate them. The simple Draconian propositions, that crime must be punished, and that he who misjudges the law must take the consequences, have an extraordinary hold on the professional as well as the popular imagination. But the rule of law is more complex and more intelligent than that and it is important that it survive.

9

Reverse Discrimination

I.

In 1945 a black man named Sweatt applied to the University of Texas Law School, but was refused admission because state law provided that only whites could attend. The Supreme Court declared that this law violated Sweatt's rights under the Fourteenth Amendment to the United States Constitution, which provides that no state shall deny any man the equal protection of its laws.[1] In 1971 a Jew named DeFunis applied to the University of Washington Law School; he was rejected although his test scores and college grades were such that he would have been admitted if he had been a black or a Filipino or a Chicano or an American Indian. DeFunis asked the Supreme Court to declare that the Washington practice, which required less exacting standards of minority groups, violated his rights under the Fourteenth Amendment.[2]

The Washington Law School's admissions procedures were complex. Applications were divided into two groups. The majority – those not from the designated minority groups – were first screened so as to eliminate all applicants whose predicted average, which is a function of college grades and aptitude test scores, fell below a certain level. Majority applicants who survived this initial cut were then placed in categories that received progressively more careful consideration. Minority-group applications, on the other hand, were not screened; each received the most careful consideration by a special committee consisting of a black professor of law and a white professor who had taught in programs to aid black law students. Most of the minority applicants who were accepted in the year in which DeFunis was rejected had predicted averages below the cutoff level, and the law school conceded that any minority applicant with his average would certainly have been accepted.

The *DeFunis* case split those political action groups that have tradi-

---

[1] *Sweatt v. Painter*, 339 U.S. 629, 70 S. Ct. 848.
[2] *DeFunis v. Odegaard*, 94 S. Ct. 1704 (1974).

tionally supported liberal causes. The B'nai Brith Anti-Defamation League and the AFL-CIO, for example, filed briefs as *amici curiae* in support of DeFunis' claim, while the American Hebrew Women's Council, the UAW, and the UMWA filed briefs against it.

These splits among old allies demonstrate both the practical and the philosophical importance of the case. In the past liberals held, within one set of attitudes, three propositions: that racial classification is an evil in itself; that every person has a right to an educational opportunity commensurate with his abilities; and that affirmative state action is proper to remedy the serious inequalities of American society. In the last decade, however, the opinion has grown that these three liberal propositions are in fact not compatible, because the most effective programs of state action are those that give a competitive advantage to minority racial groups.

That opinion has, of course, been challenged. Some educators argue that benign quotas are ineffective, even self-defeating, because preferential treatment will reinforce the sense of inferiority that many blacks already have. Others make a more general objection. They argue that any racial discrimination, even for the purpose of benefiting minorities, will in fact harm those minorities, because prejudice is fostered whenever racial distinctions are tolerated for any purpose whatever. But these are complex and controversial empirical judgments, and it is far too early, as wise critics concede, to decide whether preferential treatment does more harm or good. Nor is it the business of judges, particularly in constitutional cases, to overthrow decisions of other officials because the judges disagree about the efficiency of social policies. This empirical criticism is therefore reinforced by the moral argument that even if reverse discrimination does benefit minorities and does reduce prejudice in the long run, it is nevertheless wrong because distinctions of race are inherently unjust. They are unjust because they violate the rights of individual members of groups not so favored, who may thereby lose a place as DeFunis did.

DeFunis presented this moral argument, in the form of a constitutional claim, to the courts. The Supreme Court did not, in the end, decide whether the argument was good or bad. DeFunis had been admitted to the law school after one lower court had decided in his favor, and the law school said that he would be allowed to graduate however the case was finally decided. The Court therefore held that the case was moot and dismissed the appeal on that ground. But Mr. Justice Douglas disagreed with this neutral disposition of the case; he wrote a dissenting opinion in which he argued that the Court should have upheld DeFunis's claim on the merits. Many universities and colleges have taken Justice Douglas's opinion as handwriting on the wall, and have changed their practices in anticipation of a later Court decision in which his opinion prevails. In fact, his opinion pointed out that law schools might achieve much the same result by a more sophisticated policy than Washington used. A school might stipulate, for example, that applicants from all races and groups would be considered together, but that the aptitude tests of certain minority applicants would be graded differently, or given less weight in overall predicted average, because experience had shown that standard examinations were for different reasons a poorer test of the actual ability of these applicants. But if this technique is used deliberately to achieve the same result, it is devious, and it remains to ask why the candid program used by the University of Washington was either unjust or unconstitutional.

2.

DeFunis plainly has no constitutional right that the state provide him a legal education of a certain quality. His rights would not be violated if his state did not have a law school at all, or if it had a law school with so few places that he could not win one on intellectual merit. Nor does to have a right to insist that intelligence be the exclusive test of admission. Law schools do rely heavily on intellectual tests for admission. That seems proper, however, not because applicants have a right to be judged in that way, but because it is reasonable to think that the community as a whole is better off if its lawyers are intelligent. That is, intellectual standards are justified, not because they reward the clever, but because they seem to serve a useful social policy.

Law schools sometimes serve that policy better, moreover, by supplementing intelligence tests with other sorts of standards : they sometimes prefer industrious applicants, for example, to those who are brighter but lazier. They also serve special policies for which intelligence is not relevant. The Washington Law School, for example, gave special preference not only to the minority applicants but also to veterans who had been at the school before entering the military, and neither DeFunis nor any of the briefs submitted in his behalf complained of that preference.

DeFunis does not have an absolute right to a law school place, nor does he have a right that only intelligence be used as a standard for admission. He says he nevertheless has a right that race *not* be used as a standard, no matter how well a racial classification might work to promote the general welfare or to reduce social and economic inequality. He does not claim, however, that he has this right as a distinct and independent political right that is specifically protected by the Constitution, as is his right to freedom of speech and religion. The Constitution does not condemn racial classification directly, as it does condemn censorship or the establishment of a state religion. DeFunis claims that his right that race not be used as a criterion of admission follows from the more abstract right of equality that is protected by the Fourteenth Amendment, which provides that no state shall deny to any person the equal protection of the law.

But the legal arguments made on both sides show that neither the text of the Constitution nor the prior decisions of the Supreme Court decisively settle the question whether, as a matter of law, the Equal Protection Clause makes all racial classifications unconstitutional. The Clause makes the concept of equality a test of legislation, but it does not stipulate any particular conception of that concept.[1] Those who wrote the Clause intended to attack certain consequences of slavery and racial prejudice, but it is unlikely that they intended to outlaw all racial classifications, or that they expected such a prohibition to be the result of what they wrote. They outlawed whatever policies would violate equality, but left it to others to decide, from time to time, what that means. There cannot be a good legal argument in favor of DeFunis, therefore, unless there is a good moral argument that all racial classifications, even those that make society as a whole more equal, are inherently offensive to an individual's right to equal protection for himself.

There is nothing paradoxical, of course, in the idea that an individual's right to equal protection may sometimes conflict with an otherwise desirable social policy, including the policy of making the community more equal overall. Suppose a law school were to charge a few middle-class students, selected by lot, double tuition in order to increase the scholarship fund for poor students. It would be serving a desirable policy – equality of opportunity – by means that violated the right of the students selected by lot to be treated equally with other students who could also afford the increased fees. It is, in fact, part of the importance of DeFunis's case that it forces us to acknowledge the distinction between equality as a policy and equality as a right, a distinction that political theory has virtually ignored. He argues that the Washington Law School violated his individual right to equality for the sake of a policy of greater equality overall, in the same way that double tuition for arbitrarily chosen students would violate their rights for the same purpose.

We must therefore concentrate our attention on that claim. We must try to define the central concept on which it turns, which is the concept of an individual right to equality made a constitutional right by the Equal Protection Clause. What rights to equality do citizens have as

[1] See Chapter 5.

individuals which might defeat programs aimed at important economic and social policies, including the social policy of improving equality overall?

There are two different sorts of rights they may be said to have. The first is the right to *equal treatment*, which is the right to an equal distribution of some opportunity or resource or burden. Every citizen, for example, has a right to an equal vote in a democracy; that is the nerve of the Supreme Court's decision that one person must have one vote even if a different and more complex arrangement would better secure the collective welfare. The second is the right to *treatment as an equal*, which is the right, not to receive the same distribution of some burden or benefit, but to be treated with the same respect and concern as anyone else. If I have two children, and one is dying from a disease that is making the other uncomfortable, I do not show equal concern if I flip a coin to decide which should have the remaining dose of a drug. This example shows that the right to treatment as an equal is fundamental, and the right to equal treatment, derivative. In some circumstances the right to treatment as an equal will entail a right to equal treatment, but not, by any means, in all circumstances.

DeFunis does not have a right to equal treatment in the assignment of law school places; he does not have a right to a place just because others are given places. Individuals may have a right to equal treatment in elementary education, because someone who is denied elementary education is unlikely to lead a useful life. But legal education is not so vital that everyone has an equal right to it.

DeFunis does have the second sort of right – a right to treatment as an equal in the decision as to which admissions standards should be used. That is, he has a right that his interests be treated as fully and sympathetically as the interests of any others when the law school decides whether to count race as a pertinent criterion for admission. But we must be careful not to overstate what that means.

Suppose an applicant complains that his right to be treated as an equal is violated by tests that place the less intelligent candidates at a disadvantage against the more intelligent. A law school might properly reply in the following way. Any standard will place certain candidates at a disadvantage as against others, but an admission policy may nevertheless be justified if it seems reasonable to expect that the overall gain to the community exceeds the overall loss, and if no other policy that does not provide a comparable disadvantage would produce even roughly the same gain. An individual's right to be treated as an equal means that his potential loss must be treated as a matter of concern, but that loss may nevertheless be outweighed by the gain to the community as a whole. If it is, then the less intelligent applicant cannot claim that he is cheated of his right to be treated as an equal just because he suffers a disadvantage others do not.

Washington may make the same reply to DeFunis. Any admissions policy must put some applicants at a disadvantage, and a policy of preference for minority applicants can reasonably be supposed to benefit the community as a whole, even when the loss to candidates such as DeFunis is taken into account. If there are more black lawyers, they will help to provide better legal services to the black community, and so reduce social tensions. It might well improve the quality of legal education for all students, moreover, to have a greater number of blacks as classroom discussants of social problems. Further, if blacks are seen as successful law students, then other blacks who do meet the usual intellectual standards might be encouraged to apply, and that, in turn, would raise the intellectual quality of the bar. In any case, preferential admissions of blacks should decrease the difference in wealth and power that now exists between different racial groups, and so make the community more equal overall. It is, as I said, controversial whether a preferential admissions program will in fact promote these various policies, but it cannot be said to be implausible that it will. The disadvantage to applicants such as DeFunis is, on that hypothesis, a cost that must be paid for a greater gain; it is in that way like the disadvantage to less intelligent students that is the cost of ordinary admissions policies.[1]

We now see the difference between DeFunis's case and the case we imagined, in which a law school charged students selected at random higher fees. The special disadvantage to these students was not necessary to achieve the gain in scholarship funds, because the same gain would have been achieved by a more equal distribution of the cost amongst all the students who could afford it. That is not true of DeFunis. He did suffer from the Washington policy more than those majority applicants who were accepted. But that discrimination was not arbitrary; it was a consequence of the meritocratic standards he approves. DeFunis's argu-

---

[1] I shall argue later in this Chapter that there are circumstances in which a policy violates someone's right to be treated as an equal in spite of the fact that the social gains from that policy may be said to outweigh the losses. These circumstances arise when the gains that outweigh the losses include the satisfaction of prejudices and other sorts of preferences that it is improper for officials or institutions to take into account at all. But the hypothetical social gains described in this paragraph do not include gains of that character. Of course, if DeFunis had some other right, beyond the right to be treated as an equal, which the Washington policy violated, then the fact that the policy might achieve an overall social gain would not justify the violation (See Chapter 6). If the Washington admissions procedure included a religious test that violated his right to religious freedom, for example, it would offer no excuse that using such a test might make the community more cohesive. But DeFunis does not rely on any distinct right beyond his right to equality protected by the Equal Protection Clause.

ment therefore fails. The Equal Protection Clause gives constitutional standing to the right to be treated as an equal, but he cannot find, in that right, any support for his claim that the clause makes all racial classifications illegal.

3.

If we dismiss DeFunis's claim in this straightforward way, however, we are left with this puzzle. How can so many able lawyers, who supported his claim both in morality and law, have made that mistake? These lawyers all agree that intelligence is a proper criterion for admission to law schools. They do not suppose that anyone's constitutional right to be treated as an equal is compromised by that criterion. Why do they deny that race, in the circumstances of this decade, may also be a proper criterion?

They fear, perhaps, that racial criteria will be misused; that such criteria will serve as an excuse for prejudice against the minorities that are not favored, such as Jews. But that cannot explain their opposition. Any criteria may be misused, and in any case they think that racial criteria are wrong in principle and not simply open to abuse.

Why? The answer lies in their belief that, in theory as well as in practice, *DeFunis* and *Sweatt* must stand or fall together. They believe that it is illogical for liberals to condemn Texas for raising a color barrier against Sweatt, and then applaud Washington for raising a color barrier against DeFunis. The difference between these two cases, they suppose, must be only the subjective preference of liberals for certain minorities now in fashion. If there is something wrong with racial classifications, then it must be something that is wrong with racial classifications as such, not just classifications that work against those groups currently in favor. That is the inarticulate premise behind the slogan, relied on by defendants of DeFunis, that the Constitution is color blind. That slogan means, of course, just the opposite of what it says : it means that the Constitution is so sensitive to color that it makes any institutional racial classification invalid as a matter of law.

It is of the greatest importance, therefore, to test the assumption that Sweatt and DeFunis must stand or fall together. If that assumption is sound, then the straightforward argument against DeFunis must be fallacious after all, for no argument could convince us that segregation of the sort practiced against Sweatt is justifiable or constitutional.[1]

---

[1] In the actual *Sweatt* decision, the Supreme Court applied the old rule which held that segregation was constitutionally permitted if facilities were provided for blacks that were 'separate but equal'. Texas had provided a separate law school for blacks, but the Court held that that school was by no means the equal of the white

Superficially, moreover, the arguments against DeFunis do indeed seem available against Sweatt, because we can construct an argument that Texas might have used to show that segregation benefits the collective welfare, so that the special disadvantage to blacks is a cost that must be paid to achieve an overall gain.

Suppose the Texas admissions committee, though composed of men and women who themselves held no prejudices, decided that the Texas economy demanded more white lawyers than they could educate, but could find no use for black lawyers at all. That might have been, after all, a realistic assessment of the commercial market for lawyers in Texas just after World War II. Corporate law firms needed lawyers to serve booming business but could not afford to hire black lawyers, however skillful, because the firms' practices would be destroyed if they did. It was no doubt true that the black community in Texas had great need of skillful lawyers, and would have preferred to use black lawyers if these were available. But the committee might well have thought that the commercial needs of the state as a whole outweighed that special need.

Or suppose the committee judged, no doubt accurately, that alumni gifts to the law school would fall off drastically if it admitted a black student. The committee might deplore that fact, but nevertheless believe that the consequent collective damage would be greater than the damage to black candidates excluded by the racial restriction.

It may be said that these hypothetical arguments are disingenuous, because any policy of excluding blacks would in fact be supported by a prejudice against blacks as such, and arguments of the sort just described would be rationalization only. But if these arguments are, in fact, sound, then they might be accepted by men who do not have the prejudices the objection assumes. It therefore does not follow from the fact that the admissions officers were prejudiced, if they were, that they would have rejected these arguments if they had not been.

In any case, arguments such as those I describe were in fact used by officials who might have been free from prejudice against those they excluded. Many decades ago, as the late Professor Bickel reminds us in his brief for the B'nai Brith, President Lowell of Harvard University argued in favor of a quota limiting the number of Jews who might be accepted by his university. He said that if Jews were accepted in numbers larger than their proportion of the population, as they certainly would have been if intelligence were the only test, then Harvard would no

---

school. *Sweatt* was decided before the famous *Brown* case in which the Court finally rejected the 'separate but equal' rule, and there is no doubt that an all-white law school would be unconstitutional today, even if an all-black law school were provided that was, in a material sense, the equal of that provided for whites.

longer be able to provide to the world men of the qualities and temperament it aimed to produce, men, that is, who were more well-rounded and less exclusively intellectual than Jews tended to be, and who, therefore, were better and more likely leaders of other men, both in and out of government. It was no doubt true, when Lowell spoke, that Jews were less likely to occupy important places in government or at the heads of large public companies. If Harvard wished to serve the general welfare by improving the intellectual qualities of the nation's leaders, it was rational not to allow its classes to be filled up with Jews. The men who reached that conclusion might well prefer the company of Jews to that of the Wasps who were more likely to become senators. Lowell suggested he did, though perhaps the responsibilities of his office prevented him from frequently indulging his preference.

It might now be said, however, that discrimination against blacks, even when it does serve some plausible policy, is nevertheless unjustified because it is invidious and insulting. The briefs opposing DeFunis make just that argument to distinguish his claim from Sweatt's. Because blacks were the victims of slavery and legal segregation, they say, any discrimination that excludes blacks will be taken as insulting by them, whatever arguments of general welfare might be made in its support. But it is not true, as a general matter, that any social policy is unjust if those whom it puts at a disadvantage feel insulted. Admission to law school by intelligence is not unjust because those who are less intelligent feel insulted by their exclusion. Everything depends upon whether the feeling of insult is produced by some more objective feature that would disqualify the policy even if the insult were not felt. If segregation does improve the general welfare, even when the disadvantage to blacks is fully taken into account, and if no other reason can be found why segregation is nevertheless unjustified, then the insult blacks feel, while understandable, must be based on misperception.

It would be wrong, in any case, to assume that men in the position of DeFunis will not take *their* exclusion to be insulting. They are very likely to think of themselves, not as members of some other minority, such as Jews or Poles or Italians, whom comfortable and successful liberals are willing to sacrifice in order to delay more violent social change. If we wish to distinguish *DeFunis* from *Sweatt* on some argument that uses the concept of an insult, we must show that the treatment of the one, but not the other, is in fact unjust.

4.

So these familiar arguments that might distinguish the two cases are unconvincing. That seems to confirm the view that Sweatt and DeFunis must be treated alike, and therefore that racial classification must be outlawed altogether. But fortunately a more successful ground of distinction can be found to support our initial sense that the cases are in fact very different. This distinction does not rely, as these unconvincing arguments do, on features peculiar to issues of race or segregation, or even on features peculiar to issues of educational opportunity. It relies instead on further analysis of the idea, which was central to my argument against DeFunis, that in certain circumstances a policy which puts many individuals at a disadvantage is nevertheless justified because it makes the community as a whole better off.

Any institution which uses that idea to justify a discriminatory policy faces a series of theoretical and practical difficulties. There are, in the first place, two distinct senses in which a community may be said to be better off as a whole, in spite of the fact that certain of its members are worse off, and any justification must specify which sense is meant. It may be better off in a *utilitarian* sense, that is, because the average or collective level of welfare in the community is improved even though the welfare of some individuals falls. Or it may be better off in an *ideal* sense, that is, because it is more just, or in some other way closer to an ideal society, whether or not average welfare is improved. The University of Washington might use either utilitarian or ideal arguments to justify its racial classification. It might argue, for example, that increasing the number of black lawyers reduces racial tensions, which improves the welfare of almost everyone in the community. That is a utilitarian argument. Or it might argue that, whatever effect minority preference will have on average welfare, it will make the community more equal and therefore more just. That is an ideal, not a utilitarian, argument.

The University of Texas, on the other hand, cannot make an ideal argument for segregation. It cannot claim that segregation makes the community more just whether it improves the average welfare or not. The arguments it makes to defend segregation must therefore all be utilitarian arguments. The arguments I invented, like the argument that white lawyers could do more than black lawyers to improve commercial efficiency in Texas, are utilitarian, since commercial efficiency makes the community better off only if it improves average welfare.

Utilitarian arguments encounter a special difficulty that ideal arguments do not. What is meant by average or collective welfare? How can the welfare of an individual be measured, even in principle, and how can gains in the welfare of different individuals be added and then compared with losses, so as to justify the claim that gains outweigh losses overall? The utilitarian argument that segregation improves average welfare presupposes that such calculations can be made. But how?

Jeremy Bentham, who believed that only utilitarian arguments could justify political decisions, gave the following answer. He said that the effect of a policy on an individual's welfare could be determined by discovering the amount of pleasure or pain the policy brought him, and that effect of the policy on the collective welfare could be calculated by adding together all the pleasure and subtracting all of the pain it brought to everyone. But, as Bentham's critics insisted, it is doubtful whether there exists a simple psychological state of pleasure common to all those who benefit from a policy or of pain common to all those who lose by it; in any case it would be impossible to identify, measure, and add the different pleasures and pains felt by vast numbers of people.

Philosophers and economists who find utilitarian arguments attractive, but who reject Bentham's psychological utilitarianism, propose a different concept of individual and overall welfare. They suppose that whenever an institution or an official must decide upon a policy, the members of the community will each prefer the consequences of one decision to the consequences of others. DeFunis, for example, prefers the consequences of the standard admissions policy to the policy of minority preference Washington used, while the blacks in some urban ghetto might each prefer the consequences of the latter policy to the former. If it can be discovered what each individual prefers, and how intensely, then it might be shown that a particular policy would satisfy on balance more preferences, taking into account their intensity, than alternative policies. On this concept of welfare, a policy makes the community better off in a utilitarian sense if it satisfies the collection of preferences better than alternative policies would, even though it dissatisfies the preferences of some.[1]

Of course, a law school does not have available any means of making accurate judgments about the preferences of all those whom its admissions policies will affect. It may nevertheless make judgments which, though speculative, cannot be dismissed as implausible. It is, for example, plausible to think that in post-War Texas, the preferences of the people were overall in favor of the consequences of segregation in law schools, even if the intensity of the competing preference for integration, and not simply the number of those holding that preference, is taken into account. The officials of the Texas law school might have relied upon voting behavior, newspaper editorials, and simply their own sense of

[1] Many economists and philosophers challenge the intelligibility of preference utilitarianism as well as psychological utilitarianism. They argue that there is no way, even in principle, to calculate and compare the intensity of individual preferences. Since I wish to establish a different failing in certain utilitarian arguments, I assume, for purposes of this essay, that at least rough and speculative calculations about overall community preferences can be made.

their community in reaching that decision. Though they might have been wrong, we cannot now say, even with the benefit of hindsight, that they were.

So even if Bentham's psychological utilitarianism is rejected, law schools may appeal to preference utilitarianism to provide at least a rough and speculative justification for admissions policies that put some classes of applicants at a disadvantage. But once it is made clear that these utilitarian arguments are based on judgments about the actual preferences of members of the community, a fresh and much more serious difficulty emerges.

The utilitarian argument, that a policy is justified if it satisfies more preferences overall, seems at first sight to be an egalitarian argument. It seems to observe strict impartiality. If the community has only enough medicine to treat some of those who are sick, the argument seems to recommend that those who are sickest be treated first. If the community can afford a swimming pool or a new theater, but not both, and more people want the pool, then it recommends that the community build the pool, unless those who want the theater can show that their preferences are so much more intense that they have more weight in spite of the numbers. One sick man is not to be preferred to another because he is worthier of official concern; the tastes of the theater audience are not to be preferred because they are more admirable. In Bentham's phrase, each man is to count as one and no man is to count as more than one.

These simple examples suggest that the utilitarian argument not only respects, but embodies, the right of each citizen to be treated as the equal of any other. The chance that each individual's preferences have to succeed, in the competition for social policy, will depend upon how important his preference is to him, and how many others share it, compared to the intensity and number of competing preferences. His chance will not be affected by the esteem or contempt of either officials or fellow citizens, and he will therefore not be subservient or beholden to them.

But if we examine the range of preferences that individuals in fact have, we shall see that the apparent egalitarian character of a utilitarian argument is often deceptive. Preference utilitarianism asks officials to attempt to satisfy people's preferences so far as this is possible. But the preferences of an individual for the consequences of a particular policy may be seen to reflect, on further analysis, either a *personal* preference for his own enjoyment of some goods or opportunities, or an *external* preference for the assignment of goods and opportunities to others, or both. A white law school candidate might have a personal preference for the consequences of segregation, for example, because the policy improves his own chances of success, or an external preference for those consequences because he has contempt for blacks and disapproves social situations in which the races mix.

The distinction between personal and external preferences is of great importance for this reason. If a utilitarian argument counts external preferences along with personal preferences, then the egalitarian character of that argument is corrupted, because the chance that anyone's preferences have to succeed will then depend, not only on the demands that the personal preferences of others make on scarce resources, but on the respect or affection they have for him or for his way of life. If external preferences tip the balance, then the fact that a policy makes the community better off in a utilitarian sense would *not* provide a justification compatible with the right of those it disadvantages to be treated as equals.

This corruption of utilitarianism is plain when some people have external preferences because they hold political theories that are themselves contrary to utilitarianism. Suppose many citizens, who are not themselves sick, are racists in political theory, and therefore prefer that scarce medicine be given to a white man who needs it rather than a black man who needs it more. If utilitarianism counts these political preferences at face value, then it will be, from the standpoint of personal preferences, self-defeating, because the distribution of medicine will then not be, from that standpoint, utilitarian at all. In any case, self-defeating or not, the distribution will not be egalitarian in the sense defined. Blacks will suffer, to a degree that depends upon the strength of the racist preference, from the fact that others think them less worthy of respect and concern.

There is a similar corruption when the external preferences that are counted are altruistic or moralistic. Suppose many citizens, who themselves do not swim, prefer the pool to the theater because they approve of sports and admire athletes, or because they think that the theater is immoral and ought to be repressed. If the altruistic preferences are counted, so as to reinforce the personal preferences of swimmers, the result will be a form of double counting : each swimmer will have the benefit not only of his own preference, but also of the preference of someone else who takes pleasure in his success. If the moralistic preferences are counted, the effect will be the same : actors and audiences will suffer because their preferences are held in lower respect by citizens whose personal preferences are not themselves engaged.

In these examples, external preferences are independent of personal preferences. But of course political, altruistic, and moralistic preferences are often not independent, but grafted on to the personal preferences they reinforce. If I am white and sick, I may also hold a racist political theory. If I want a swimming pool for my own enjoyment I may also be altruistic in favor of my fellow athlete, or I may also think that the theater is immoral. The consequences of counting these external preferences will be as grave for equality as if they were independent of personal preference, because those against whom the external preferences run might be unable or unwilling to develop reciprocal external preferences that would right the balance.

External preferences therefore present a great difficulty for utilitarianism. That theory owes much of its popularity to the assumption that it embodies the right of citizens to be treated as equals. But if external preferences are counted in overall preferences, then this asssumption is jeopardized. That is, in itself, an important and neglected point in political theory; it bears, for example, on the liberal thesis, first made prominent by Mill, that the government has no right to enforce popular morality by law. It is often said that this liberal thesis is inconsistent with utilitarianism, because if the preferences of the majority that homosexuality should be repressed, for example, are sufficiently strong, utilitarianism must give way to their wishes. But the preference against homosexuality is an external preference, and the present argument provides a general reason why utilitarians should not count external preferences of any form. If utilitarianism is suitably reconstituted so as to count only personal preferences, then the liberal thesis is a consequence, not an enemy, of that theory.

It is not always possible, however, to reconstitute a utilitarian argument so as to count only personal preferences. Sometimes personal and external preferences are so inextricably tied together, and so mutually dependent, that no practical test for measuring preferences will be able to discriminate the personal and external elements in any individual's overall preference. That is especially true when preferences are affected by prejudice. Consider, for example, the associational preference of a white law student for white classmates. This may be said to be a personal preference for an association with one kind of colleague rather than another. But it is a personal preference that is parasitic upon external preferences : except in very rare cases a white student prefers the company of other whites because he has racist, social, and political convictions, or because he has contempt for blacks as a group. If these associational preferences are counted in a utilitarian argument used to justify segregation, then the egalitarian character of the argument is destroyed just as if the underlying external preferences were counted directly. Blacks would be denied their right to be treated as equals because the chance that their preferences would prevail in the design of admissions policy would be crippled by the low esteem in which others hold them. In any community in which prejudice against a particular minority is strong, then the personal preferences upon which a utilitarian argument must fix will be saturated with that prejudice; it follows that in such a community no utilitarian argument purporting to justify a disadvantage to that minority can be fair.[1]

This final difficulty is therefore fatal to Texas' utilitarian arguments in favor of segregation. The preferences that might support any such argument are either distinctly external, like the preferences of the community at large for racial separation, or are inextricably combined with and dependent upon external preferences, like the associational preferences of white students for white classmates and white lawyers for white colleagues. These external preferences are so widespread that they must corrupt any such argument. Texas' claim, that segregation makes the community better off in a utilitarian sense, is therefore incompatible with Sweatt's right to treatment as an equal guaranteed by the Equal Protection Clause.

It does not matter, to this conclusion, whether external preferences figure in the justification of a fundamental policy or in the justification of derivative policies designed to advance a more fundamental policy. Suppose Texas justifies segregation by pointing to the apparently neutral economic policy of increasing community wealth, which satisfies the personal preferences of everyone for better homes, food, and recreation. If the argument that segregation will improve community wealth depends upon the fact of external preference; if the argument notices, for example, that because of prejudice industry will run more efficiently if factories are segregated; then the argument has the consequence that the black man's personal preferences are defeated by what others think of him. Utilitarian arguments that justify a disadvantage to members of a race against whom prejudice runs will always be unfair arguments, unless it can be shown that the same disadvantage would have been justified in the absence of the prejudice. If the prejudice is widespread and pervasive, as in fact it is in the case of blacks, that can never be shown. The preferences on which any economic argument justifying

---

[1] The argument of this paragraph is powerful, but it is not, in itself, sufficient to disqualify all utilitarian arguments that produce substantial disadvantages to minorities who suffer from prejudice. Suppose the government decides, on a utilitarian argument, to allow unemployment to increase because the loss to those who lose their jobs is outweighed by the gain to those who would otherwise suffer from inflation. The burden of this policy will fall disproportionately on blacks, who will be fired first because prejudice runs against them. But though prejudice in this way affects the consequences of the policy of unemployment, it does not figure, even indirectly, in the utilitarian argument that supports that policy. (It figures, if at all, as a utilitarian argument against it.) We cannot say, therefore, that the special damage blacks suffer from a high unemployment policy is unjust for the reasons described in this essay. It may well be unjust for other reasons; if John Rawls is right, for example, it is unjust because the policy improves the condition of the majority at the expense of those already worse off.

I

segregation must be based will be so intertwined with prejudice that they cannot be disentangled to the degree necessary to make any such contrary-to-fact hypothesis plausible.

We now have an explanation that shows why any form of segregation that disadvantages blacks is, in the United States, an automatic insult to them, and why such segregation offends their right to be treated as equals. The argument confirms our sense that utilitarian arguments purporting to justify segregation are not simply wrong in detail but misplaced in principle. This objection to utilitarian arguments is not, however, limited to race or even prejudice. There are other cases in which counting external preferences would offend the rights of citizens to be treated as equals and it is worth briefly noticing these, if only to protect the argument against the charge that it is constructed ad hoc for the racial case. I might have a moralistic preference against professional women, or an altruistic preference for virtuous men. It would be unfair for any law school to count preferences like these in deciding whom to admit to law schools; unfair because these preferences, like racial prejudices, make the success of the personal preferences of an applicant depend on the esteem and approval, rather than on the competing personal preferences, of others.

The same objection does not hold, however, against a utilitarian argument used to justify admission based on intelligence. That policy need not rely, directly or indirectly, on any community sense that intelligent lawyers are intrinsically more worthy of respect. It relies instead upon the law school's own judgment, right or wrong, that intelligent lawyers are more effective in satisfying personal preferences of others, such as the preference for wealth or winning law suits. It is true that law firms and clients prefer the services of intelligent lawyers; that fact might make us suspicious of any utilitarian argument that is said not to depend upon that preference, just as we are suspicious of any argument justifying segregation that is said not to depend upon prejudice. But the widespread preference for intelligent lawyers is, by and large, not parasitic on external preferences: law firms and clients prefer intelligent lawyers because they also hold the opinion that such lawyers will be more effective in serving their personal preferences. Instrumental preferences, of that character, do not themselves figure in utilitarian arguments, though a law school may accept, on its own responsibility, the instrumental hypothesis upon which such preferences depend.[1]

[1] No doubt the preference that some men and women have for intellectual companions is parasitic on external preferences; they value these companions not as a means to anything else, but because they think that intelligent people are better, and more worthy of honor, than others. If such preferences were sufficiently strong and

5.

We therefore have the distinctions in hand necessary to distinguish *DeFunis* from *Sweatt*. The arguments for an admissions program that discriminates against blacks are all utilitarian arguments, and they are all utilitarian arguments that rely upon external preferences in such a way as to offend the constitutional right of blacks to be treated as equals. The arguments for an admissions program that discriminates in favor of blacks are both utilitarian and ideal. Some of the utilitarian arguments do rely, at least indirectly, on external preferences, such as the preference of certain blacks for lawyers of their own race; but the utilitarian arguments that do not rely on such preferences are strong and may be sufficient. The ideal arguments do not rely upon preferences at all, but on the independent argument that a more equal society is a better society even if its citizens prefer inequality. That argument does not deny anyone's right to be treated as an equal himself.

We are therefore left, in *DeFunis*, with the simple and straightforward argument with which we began. Racial criteria are not necessarily the right standards for deciding which applicants should be accepted by law schools. But neither are intellectual criteria, nor indeed, any other set of criteria. The fairness – and constitutionality – of any admissions program must be tested in the same way. It is justified if it serves a proper policy that respects the right of all members of the community to be treated as equals, but not otherwise. The criteria used by schools that refused to consider blacks failed that test, but the criteria used by the Washington University Law School do not.

We are all rightly suspicious of racial classifications. They have been used to deny, rather than to respect, the right of equality, and we are all conscious of the consequent injustice. But if we misunderstand the nature of that injustice because we do not make the simple distinctions that are necessary to understand it, then we are in danger of more injustice still. It may be that preferential admissions programs will not, in fact, make a more equal society, because they may not have the effects their advocates believe they will. That strategic question should be at the center of debate about these programs. But we must not corrupt the debate by supposing that these programs are unfair even if they do work. We must take care not to use the Equal Protection Clause to cheat ourselves of equality.

---

pervasive we might reach the same conclusion here that we reached about segregation: that no utilitarian argument purporting to justify discrimination against less intelligent men and women could be trusted to be fair. But there is no reason to assume that the United States is that intellectualistic; certainly no reason to think that it is intellectualistic to the degree that it is racist.

10

Liberty and Moralism

No doubt most Americans and Englishmen think that homosexuality, prostitution, and the publication of pornography are immoral. What part should this fact play in the decision whether to make them criminal? This is a tangled question, full of issues with roots in philosophical and sociological controversy. It is a question lawyers must face, however, and recent and controversial events – publication of the Wolfenden Report in England,[1] followed by a public debate on prostitution and homosexuality, and a series of obscenity decisions in the United States Supreme Court[2] – press it upon us.

Several positions are available, each with its own set of difficulties. Shall we say that public condemnation is sufficient, in and of itself, to justify making an act a crime? This seems inconsistent with our traditions of individual liberty, and our knowledge that the morals of even the largest mob cannot come warranted for truth. If public condemnation is not sufficient, what more is needed? Must there be some demonstration of present harm to particular persons directly affected by the practice in question? Or is it sufficient to show some effect on social customs and institutions which alters the social environment, and thus affects all members of society indirectly? If the latter, must it also be demonstrated that these social changes threaten long-term harm of some standard sort, like an increase in crime or a decrease in productivity? Or would it be enough to show that the vast bulk of the present community would deplore the change? If so, does the requirement of harm add much to the bare requirement of public condemnation?

In 1958 Lord Devlin delivered the second Maccabaean Lecture to the British Academy. He called his lecture 'The Enforcement of Morals', and devoted it to these issues of principle.[3] His conclusions he summarized in these remarks about the practice of homosexuality: 'We should ask

---

[1] *Report of the Committee on Homosexual Offences and Prostitution*, Cmd. no. 247 (1957).

[2] *Memoirs v. Massachusetts (Fanny Hill)*, 383 U.S. 413 (1966), *Ginzburg v. United States*, 383 463 U.S. (1966), *Mishkin v. New York*, 383 U.S. 502 (1966).

[3] Devlin, *The Enforcement of Morals* (1959). Reprinted in Devlin, *The Enforcement of Morals* (1965). [The latter is hereinafter cited as Devlin.]

ourselves in the first instance whether, looking at it calmly and dis-
passionately, we regard it as a vice so abominable that its mere presence
is an offence. If that is the genuine feeling of the society in which we
live, I do not see how society can be denied the right to eradicate it.'[1]

The lecture, and in particular this hypothetical position on punishing
homosexuals, provoked a tide of rebuttal that spilled over from academic
journals into the radio and the almost-popular press.[2] Lord Devlin has
since republished the Maccabaean Lecture, together with six further
essays developing and defending the views there expressed, a preface to
the whole, and some important new footnotes to the original lecture.[3]

American lawyers ought to attend to Lord Devlin's arguments. His
conclusions will not be popular, although the swaggering insensitivity
some of his critics found disappears with careful reading. Popular or
not, we have no right to disregard them until we are satisfied that his
arguments can be met. One of these arguments – the second of the two
I shall discuss – has the considerable merit of focusing our attention on
the connection between democratic theory and the enforcement of
morals. It provokes us to consider, more closely than we have, the crucial
concept upon which this connection depends – the concept of a public
morality.

LORD DEVLIN'S DISENCHANTMENT

The preface to the new book contains a revealing account of how Lord
Devlin came to his controversial opinions. When he was invited to
prepare his Maccabaean Lecture the celebrated Wolfenden Committee
had recently published its recommendation that homosexual practices in
private between consenting adults no longer be criminal. He had read
with complete approval the Committee's expression of the proper division
between crime and sin:

> In this field, its [the law's] function, as we see it, is to preserve
> public order and decency, to protect the citizen from what is offen-
> sive or injurious, and to provide sufficient safeguards against
> exploitation and corruption of others . . . . It is not, in our view,
> the function of the law to intervene in the private lives of citizens,
> or to seek to enforce any particular pattern of behaviour, further
> than is necessary to carry out the purposes which we have out-
> lined . . . .

[1] Devlin 17. This position was carefully stated as hypothetical. Apparently Lord
Devlin does not now think that the condition is met, because he has publically urged
modification of the laws on homosexuality since the book's publication.

[2] Lord Devlin includes references to these comments in a bibliography. Devlin xiii.

[3] Devlin.

[T]here must remain a realm of private morality and immorality which is, in brief and crude terms, not the law's business.[1]

Lord Devlin believed that these ideals, which he recognized as derived from the teachings of Jeremy Bentham and John Stuart Mill, were unquestionable. He decided to devote his lecture to a painstaking consideration of what further changes, beyond the changes in the crime of homosexuality that the Committee recommended, would be necessary to make the criminal law of England conform to them. But study, in his words, 'destroyed instead of confirming the simple faith in which I had begun my task'[2] and he ended in the conviction that these ideals were not only questionable, but wrong.

The fact of his disenchantment is clear, but the extent of his disenchantment is not. He seems sometimes to be arguing the exact converse of the Committee's position, namely that society has a right to punish conduct of which its members strongly disapprove, even though that conduct has no effects which can be deemed injurious to others, on the ground that the state has a role to play as moral tutor and the criminal law is its proper tutorial technique. Those readers who take this to be his position are puzzled by the fact that distinguished philosophers and lawyers have concerned themselves to reply, for this seems a position that can safely be regarded as eccentric. In fact he is arguing not this position, but positions which are more complex and neither so eccentric nor so flatly at odds with the Wolfenden ideals. They are nowhere summarized in any crisp form (indeed the statement on homosexuality I have already quoted is as good a summary as he gives) but must be taken from the intricate arguments he develops.

There are two chief arguments. The first is set out in structured form in the Maccabaean Lecture. It argues from society's right to protect its own existence. The second, a quite different and much more important argument, develops in disjointed form through various essays. It argues from the majority's right to follow its own moral convictions in defending its social environment from change it opposes. I shall consider these two arguments in turn, but the second at greater length.

THE FIRST ARGUMENT: SOCIETY'S RIGHT TO PROTECT ITSELF

The first argument – and the argument which has received by far the major part of the critics' attention – is this:[3]

---

[1] *Report of the Committee on Homosexual Offences and Prostitution*, 9-10, 24.
[2] Devlin vii.
[3] It is developed chiefly in Devlin 7-25.

(1) In a modern society there are a variety of moral principles which some men adopt for their own guidance and do not attempt to impose upon others. There are also moral standards which the majority places beyond toleration and imposes upon those who dissent. For us, the dictates of particular religion are an example of the former class, and the practice of monogamy an example of the latter. A society cannot survive unless some standards are of the second class, because some moral conformity is essential to its life. Every society has a right to preserve its own existence, and therefore the right to insist on some such conformity.

(2) If society has such a right, then it has the right to use the institutions and sanctions of its criminal law to enforce the right – '[S]ociety may use the law to preserve morality in the same way it uses it to safeguard anything else if it is essential to its existence.'[1] Just as society may use its law to prevent treason, it may use it to prevent a corruption of that conformity which ties it together.

(3) But society's right to punish immorality by law should not necessarily be exercised against every sort and on every occasion of immorality – we must recognize the impact and the importance of some restraining principles. There are several of these, but the most important is that there 'must be toleration of the maximum individual freedom that is consistent with the integrity of society.'[2] These restraining principles, taken together, require that we exercise caution in concluding that a practice is considered profoundly immoral. The law should stay its hand if it detects any uneasiness or half-heartedness or latent toleration in society's condemnation of the practice. But none of these restraining principles apply, and hence society is free to enforce its rights, when public feeling is high, enduring and relentless, when, in Lord Devlin's phrase, it rises to 'intolerance, indignation and disgust'.[3] Hence the summary conclusion about homosexuality : if it is genuinely regarded as an abominable vice, society's right to eradicate it cannot be denied.

We must guard against a possible, indeed tempting, misconception of this argument. It does not depend upon any assumption that when the vast bulk of a community thinks a practice is immoral they are likely right. What Lord Devlin thinks is at stake, when our public morality is challenged, is the very survival of society, and he believes that society is entitled to preserve itself without vouching for the morality that holds it together.

[1] *Ibid.* 11.
[2] *Ibid.* 16.
[3] *Ibid.* 17.

Is this argument sound? Professor H. L. A. Hart, responding to its appearance at the heart of the Maccabaean lecture,[1] thought that it rested upon a confused conception of what a society is. If one holds anything like a conventional notion of a society, he said, it is absurd to suggest that every practice the society views as profoundly immoral and disgusting threatens its survival. This is as silly as arguing that society's existence is threatened by the death of one of its members or the birth of another, and Lord Devlin, he reminds us, offers nothing by way of evidence to support any such claim. But if one adopts an artificial definition of a society, such that a society consists of that particular complex of moral ideas and attitudes which its members happen to hold at a particular moment in time, it is intolerable that each such moral status quo should have the right to preserve its precarious existence by force. So, Professor Hart argued, Lord Devlin's argument fails whether a conventional or an artificial sense of 'society' is taken.

Lord Devlin replies to Professor Hart in a new and lengthy footnote. After summarizing Hart's criticism he comments, 'I do not assert that *any* deviation from a society's shared morality threatens its existence any more than I assert that *any* subversive activity threatens its existence. I assert that they are both activities which are capable in their nature of threatening the existence of society so that neither can be put beyond the law.'[2] This reply exposes a serious flaw in the architecture of the argument.

It tells us that we must understand the second step of the argument – the crucial claim that society has a right to enforce its public morality by law – as limited to a denial of the proposition that society never has such a right. Lord Devlin apparently understood the Wolfenden Report's statement of a 'realm of private morality . . . not the law's business' to assert a fixed jurisdictional barrier placing private sexual practices forever beyond the law's scrutiny. His arguments, the new footnote tells us, are designed to show merely that no such constitutional barrier should be raised, because it is possible that the challenge to established morality might be so profound that the very existence of a conformity in morals, and hence of the society itself, would be threatened.[3]

We might well remain unconvinced, even of this limited point. We

[1] H. L. A. Hart, *Law, Liberty and Morality* 51 (1963).

[2] Devlin 13.

[3] This reading had great support in the text even without the new footnote: 'I think, therefore, that it is not possible to set theoretical limits to the power of the State to legislate against immorality. It is not possible to settle in advance exceptions to the general rule or to define inflexibly areas of morality into which the law is in no circumstances to be allowed to enter.' (Devlin 12-13).

The arguments presented bear out this construction. They are of the *reductio ad absurdum* variety, exploiting the possibility that what is immoral can in theory become might believe that the danger which any unpopular practice can present to the existence of society is so small that it would be wise policy, a prudent protection of individual liberty from transient hysteria, to raise just this sort of constitutional barrier and forbid periodic reassessment of the risk.

But if we were persuaded to forego this constitutional barrier we would expect the third step in the argument to answer the inevitable next question: Granted that a challenge to deep-seated and genuine public morality may conceivably threaten society's existence, and so must be placed above the threshold of the law's concern, how shall we know when the danger is sufficiently clear and present to justify not merely scrutiny but action? What more is needed beyond the fact of passionate public disapproval to show that we are in the presence of an actual threat?

The rhetoric of the third step makes it seem responsive to this question – there is much talk of 'freedom' and 'toleration' and even 'balancing'. But the argument is not responsive, for freedom, toleration and balancing turn out to be appropriate only when the public outrage diagnosed at the second step is shown to be overstated, when the fever, that is, turns out to be feigned. When the fever is confirmed, when the intolerance, indignation and disgust are genuine, the principle that calls for 'the maximum individual freedom consistent with the integrity of society' no longer applies. But this means that nothing more than passionate public disapproval is necessary after all.

In short, the argument involves an intellectual sleight of hand. At the second step, public outrage is presented as a threshold criterion, merely placing the practice in a category which the law is not forbidden to regulate. But offstage, somewhere in the transition to the third step, this threshold criterion becomes itself a dispositive affirmative reason for action, so that when it is clearly met the law may proceed without more. The power of this manoeuvre is proved by the passage on homosexuality.

---

subversive of society. 'But suppose a quarter or a half of the population got drunk every night, what sort of society would it be? You cannot set a theoretical limit to the number of people who can get drunk before society is entitled to legislate against drunkenness. The same may be said of gambling.' (*Ibid.* 14.)

Each example argues that no jurisdictional limit may be drawn, not that every drunk or every act of gambling threatens society. There is no suggestion that society is entitled actually to make drunkenness or gambling crimes if the practice in fact falls below the level of danger. Indeed Lord Devlin quotes the Royal Commission on Betting, Lotteries, and Gaming to support his example on gambling: 'If we were convinced that whatever the degree of gambling this effect [on the character of the gambler as a member of society] must be harmful we should be inclined to think that it was the duty of the state to restrict gambling to the greatest extent practicable.' (Cmd. no. 8190 at para. 159 (1951), quoted in Devlin 14). The implication is that society may scrutinize and be ready to regulate, but should not actually do so until the threat in fact exists.

Lord Devlin concludes that if our society hates homosexuality enough it is justified in outlawing it, and forcing human beings to choose between the miseries of frustration and persecution, because of the danger the practice presents to society's existence. He manages this conclusion without offering evidence that homosexuality presents any danger at all to society's existence, beyond the naked claim that all 'deviations from a society's shared morality . . . are capable in their nature of threatening the existence of society' and so 'cannot be put beyond the law'.[1]

THE SECOND ARGUMENT: SOCIETY'S RIGHT TO FOLLOW ITS OWN LIGHTS

We are therefore justified in setting aside the first argument and turning to the second. My reconstruction includes making a great deal explicit which I believe implicit, and so involves some risk of distortion, but I take the second argument to be this:[2]

(1) If those who have homosexual desires freely indulged them, our social environment would change. What the changes would be cannot be calculated with any precision, but it is plausible to suppose, for example, that the position of the family, as the assumed and natural institution around which the educational, economic and recreational arrangements of men center, would be undermined, and the further ramifications of that would be great. We are too sophisticated to suppose that the effects of an increase in homosexuality would be confined to those who participate in the practice alone, just as we are too sophisticated to suppose that prices and wages affect only those who negotiate them. The environment in which we and our children must live is determined, among other things, by patterns and relationships formed privately by others than ourselves.

(2) This in itself does not give society the right to prohibit homosexual practices. We cannot conserve every custom we like by jailing those who do not want to preserve it. But it means that our legislators must inevitably decide some moral issues. They must decide whether the institutions which seem threatened are sufficiently valuable to protect at the cost of human freedom. And they must decide whether the practices which threaten that institution are immoral, for if they are then the freedom of an individual to pursue them counts for less. We do not need so strong a justification, in terms of the social importance of the institutions being protected, if we are confident that no one has a moral right

---

[1] Devlin 13, n.l.
[2] Most of the argument appears in Devlin chs. 5, 6 and 7. See also an article published after the book: 'Law and Morality', 1 *Manitoba* L.S.J. 243 (1964/65).

to do what we want to prohibit. We need less of a case, that is, to abridge someone's freedom to lie, cheat or drive recklessly, than his freedom to choose his own jobs or to price his own goods. This does not claim that immorality is sufficient to make conduct criminal; it argues, rather, that on occasion it is necessary.

(3) But how shall a legislator decide whether homosexual acts are immoral? Science can give no answer, and a legislator can no longer properly turn to organized religion. If it happens, however, that the vast bulk of the community is agreed upon an answer, even though a small minority of educated men may dissent, the legislator has a duty to act on the consensus. He has such a duty for two closely connected reasons : (a) In the last analysis the decision must rest on some article of moral faith, and in a democracy this sort of issue, above all others, must be settled in accordance with democratic principles. (b) It is, after all, the community which acts when the threats and sanctions of the criminal law are brought to bear. The community must take the moral responsibility, and it must therefore act on its own lights – that is, on the moral faith of its members.

This, as I understand it, is Lord Devlin's second argument. It is complex, and almost every component invites analysis and challenge. Some readers will dissent from its central assumption, that a change in social institutions is the sort of harm a society is entitled to protect itself against. Others who do not take this strong position (perhaps because they approve of laws which are designed to protect economic institutions) will nevertheless feel that society is not entitled to act, however immoral the practice, unless the threatened harm to an institution is demonstrable and imminent rather than speculative. Still others will challenge the thesis that the morality or immorality of an act ought even to count in determining whether to make it criminal (though they would no doubt admit that it does count under present practice), and others still will argue that even in a democracy legislators have the duty to decide moral questions for themselves, and must not refer such issues to the community at large. I do not propose to argue now for or against any of these positions. I want instead to consider whether Lord Devlin's conclusions are valid on his own terms, or the assumption, that is, that society does have a right to protect its central and valued social institutions against conduct which the vast bulk of its members disapproves on moral principle.

I shall argue that his conclusions are not valid, even on these terms, because he misunderstands what it is to disapprove on moral principle. I might say a cautionary word about the argument I shall present. It will consist in part of reminders that certain types of moral language (terms like 'prejudice' and 'moral position', for example) have standard uses in moral argument. My purpose is not to settle issues of political morality by the fiat of a dictionary, but to exhibit what I believe to be mistakes in Lord Devlin's moral sociology. I shall try to show that our conventional moral practices are more complex and more structured than he takes them to be, and that he consequently misunderstands what it means to say that the criminal law should be drawn from public morality. This is a popular and appealing thesis, and it lies near the core not only of Lord Devlin's, but of many other, theories about law and morals. It is crucial that its implications be understood.

THE CONCEPT OF A MORAL POSITION

We might start with the fact that terms like 'moral position' and 'moral conviction' function in our conventional morality as terms of justification and criticism, as well as of description. It is true that we sometimes speak of a group's 'morals', or 'morality', or 'moral beliefs', or 'moral positions' or 'moral convictions', in what might be called an anthropological sense, meaning to refer to whatever attitudes the group displays about the propriety of human conduct, qualities or goals. We say, in this sense, that the morality of Nazi Germany was based on prejudice, or was irrational. But we also use some of these terms, particularly 'moral position' and 'moral conviction', in a discriminatory sense, to contrast the positions they describe with prejudices, rationalizations, matters of personal aversion or taste, arbitrary stands, and the like. One use – perhaps the most characteristic use – of this discriminatory sense is to offer a limited but important sort of justification for an act, when the moral issues surrounding that act are unclear or in dispute.

Suppose I tell you that I propose to vote against a man running for a public office of trust because I know him to be a homosexual and because I believe that homosexuality is profoundly immoral. If you disagree that homosexuality is immoral, you may accuse me of being about to cast my vote unfairly, acting on prejudice or out of a personal repugnance which is irrelevant to the moral issue. I might then try to convert you to my position on homosexuality, but if I fail in this I shall still want to convince you of what you and I will both take to be a separate point – that my vote was based upon *a* moral position, in the discriminatory sense, even though one which differs from yours. I shall want to persuade you of this, because if I do I am entitled to expect that you will alter your opinion of me and of what I am about to do. Your judgment of my character will be different – you might still think me eccentric (or puritanical or unsophisticated) but these are types of character and not faults of character. Your judgment of my act will also be different, in this respect. You will admit that so long as I hold my moral position, I have a moral right to vote against the homosexual, because I have a right (indeed a duty) to vote my own convictions. You would not admit such a right (or duty) if you were still persuaded that I was acting out of a prejudice or a personal taste.

I am entitled to expect that your opinion will change in these ways, because these distinctions are a part of the conventional morality you and I share, and which forms the background for our discussion. They enforce the difference between positions we must respect, although we think them wrong, and positions we need not respect because they offend some ground rule of moral reasoning. A great deal of debate about moral issues (in real life, although not in philosophy texts) consists of arguments that some position falls on one or the other side of this crucial line.

It is this feature of conventional morality that animates Lord Devlin's argument that society has the right to follow its own lights. We must therefore examine that discriminatory concept of a moral position more closely, and we can do so by pursuing our imaginary conversation. What must I do to convince you that my position is a moral position?

(a) I must produce some reasons for it. This is not to say that I have to articulate a moral principle I am following or a general moral theory to which I subscribe. Very few people can do either, and the ability to hold a moral position is not limited to those who can. My reason need not be a principle or theory at all. It must only point out some aspect or feature of homosexuality which moves me to regard it as immoral: the fact that the Bible forbids it, for example, or that one who practices homosexuality becomes unfit for marriage and parenthood. Of course, any such reason would presuppose my acceptance of some general principle or theory, but I need not be able to state what it is, or realize that I am relying upon it.

Not every reason I might give will do, however. Some will be excluded by general criteria stipulating sorts of reasons which do not count. We might take note of four of the most important such criteria:

(i) If I tell you that homosexuals are morally inferior because they do not have heterosexual desires, and so are not 'real men', you would reject that reason as showing one type of prejudice. Prejudices, in general, are postures of judgment that take into account considerations our conventions exclude. In a structured context, like a trial or a contest, the ground rules exclude all but certain considerations, and a prejudice is a basis of judgment which violates these rules. Our conventions stipulate some ground rules of moral judgment which obtain even apart from such special contexts, the most important of which is that a man must not be held morally inferior on the basis of some physical, racial or other characteristic he cannot help having. Thus a man whose moral judgments about Jews, or Negroes, or Southerners, or women, or effeminate men are based on his belief that any member of these classes automatically deserves less respect, without regard to anything he himself has done, is said to be prejudiced against that group.

(ii) If I base my view about homosexuals on a personal emotional reaction ('they make me sick') you would reject that reason as well. We distinguish moral positions from emotional reactions, not because moral positions are supposed to be unemotional or dispassionate – quite the reverse is true – but because the moral position is supposed to justify the emotional reaction, and not vice versa. If a man is unable to produce such reasons, we do not deny the fact of his emotional involvement, which may have important social or political consequences, but we do not take this involvement as demonstrating his moral conviction. Indeed, it is just this sort of position – a severe emotional reaction to a practice or a situation for which one cannot account – that we tend to describe, in lay terms, as a phobia or an obsession.

(iii) If I base my position on a proposition of fact ('homosexual acts are physically debilitating') which is not only false, but is so implausible that it challenges the minimal standards of evidence and argument I generally accept and impose upon others, then you would regard my belief, even though sincere, as a form of rationalization, and disqualify my reason on that ground. (Rationalization is a complex concept, and also includes, as we shall see, the production of reasons which suggest general theories I do not accept.)

(iv) If I can argue for my own position only by citing the beliefs of others ('everyone knows homosexuality is a sin') you will conclude that I am parroting and not relying on a moral conviction of my own. With the possible (though complex) exception of a deity, there is no moral authority to which I can appeal and so automatically make my position a moral one. I must have my own reasons, though of course I may have been taught these reasons by others.

No doubt many readers will disagree with these thumbnail sketches of prejudice, mere emotional reaction, rationalization and parroting. Some may have their own theories of what these are. I want to emphasize now only that these are distinct concepts, whatever the details of the differences might be, and that they have a role in deciding whether to treat another's position as a moral conviction. They are not merely epithets to be pasted on positions we strongly dislike.

(b) Suppose I do produce a reason which is not disqualified on one of these (or on similar) grounds. That reason will presuppose some general moral principle or theory, even though I may not be able to state that principle or theory, and do not have it in mind when I speak. If I offer, as my reason, the fact that the Bible forbids homosexual acts, or that homosexual acts make it less likely that the actor will marry and raise children, I suggest that I accept the theory my reason presupposes, and you will not be satisfied that my position is a moral one if you believe that I do not. It may be a question of my sincerity – do I in fact believe that the injunctions of the Bible are morally binding as such, or that all men have a duty to procreate? Sincerity is not, however, the only issue, for consistency is also in point. I may believe that I accept one of these general positions, and be wrong, because my other beliefs, and my own conduct on other occasions, may be inconsistent with it. I may reject certain Biblical injunctions, or I may hold that men have a right to remain bachelors if they please or use contraceptives all their lives.

Of course, my general moral positions may have qualifications and exceptions. The difference between an exception and an inconsistency is that the former can be supported by reasons which presuppose other moral positions I can properly claim to hold. Suppose I condemn all homosexuals on Biblical authority, but not all fornicators. What reason can I offer for the distinction? If I can produce none which supports it, I cannot claim to accept the general position about Biblical authority. If I do produce a reason which seems to support the distinction, the same sorts of question may be asked about that reason as were asked about my original reply. What general position does the reason for my exception presuppose? Can I sincerely claim to accept that further general position? Suppose my reason, for example, is that fornication is now very common, and has been sanctioned by custom. Do I really believe that what is immoral becomes moral when it becomes popular? If not, and if I can produce no other reason for the distinction, I cannot claim to accept the general position that what the Bible condemns is immoral. Of course, I may be persuaded, when this is pointed out, to change my views on fornication. But you would be alert to the question of whether this is a genuine change of heart, or only a performance for the sake of the argument.

In principle there is no limit to these ramifications of my original claim, though of course, no actual argument is likely to pursue very many of them.

(c) But do I really have to have a reason to make my position a matter of moral conviction? Most men think that acts which cause unnecessary suffering, or break a serious promise with no excuse, are immoral, and yet they could give no reason for these beliefs. They feel that no reason is necessary, because they take it as axiomatic or self-evident that these are immoral acts. It seems contrary to common sense to deny that a position held in this way can be a moral position.

Yet there is an important difference between believing that one's position is self-evident and just not having a reason for one's position. The former presupposes a positive belief that no further reason is necessary, that the immorality of the act in question does not depend upon its social effects, or its effects on the character of the actor, or its proscription by a deity, or anything else, but follows from the nature of the act itself. The claim that a particular position is axiomatic, in other words, does supply a reason of a special sort, namely that the act is immoral in and of itself, and this special reason, like the others we considered, may be inconsistent with more general theories I hold.

The moral arguments we make presuppose not only moral principles, but also more abstract positions about moral reasoning. In particular, they presuppose positions about what kinds of acts can be immoral in and of themselves. When I criticize your moral opinions, or attempt to justify my own disregard of traditional moral rules I think are silly, I will likely proceed by denying that the act in question has any of the several features that can make an act immoral – that it involves no breach of an undertaking or duty, for example, harms no one including the actor, is not proscribed by any organized religion, and is not illegal. I proceed in this way because I assume that the ultimate grounds of immorality are limited to some such small set of very general standards. I may assert this assumption directly or it may emerge from the pattern of my argument. In either event, I will enforce it by calling positions which can claim no support from any of these ultimate standards *arbitrary*, as I should certainly do if you said that photography was immoral, for instance, or swimming. Even if I cannot articulate this underlying assumption, I shall still apply it, and since the ultimate criteria I recognize are among the most abstract of my moral standards, they will not vary much from those my neighbors recognize and apply. Although many who despise homosexuals are unable to say why, few would claim affirmatively that one needs no reason, for this would make their position, on their own standards, an arbitrary one.

(d) This anatomy of our argument could be continued, but it is already long enough to justify some conclusions. If the issue between us is whether my views on homosexuality amount to a moral position, and hence whether I am entitled to vote against a homosexual on that ground, I cannot settle the issue simply by reporting my feelings. You will want to consider the reasons I can produce to support my belief, and whether my other views and behavior are consistent with the theories these reasons presuppose. You will have, of course, to apply your own understanding, which may differ in detail from mine, of what a prejudice or a rationalization is, for example, and of when one view is inconsistent with another. You and I may end in disagreement over whether my position is a moral one, partly because of such differences in understanding, and partly because one is less likely to recognize these illegitimate grounds in himself than in others.

We must avoid the skeptical fallacy of passing from these facts to the conclusion that there is no such thing as a prejudice or a rationalization or an inconsistency, or that these terms mean merely that the one who uses them strongly dislikes the positions he describes this way. That would be like arguing that because different people have different understandings of what jealousy is, and can in good faith disagree about whether one of them is jealous, there is no such thing as jealousy, and one who says another is jealous merely means he dislikes him very much.

LORD DEVLIN'S MORALITY

We may now return to Lord Devlin's second argument. He argues that when legislators must decide a moral issue (as by his hypothesis they must when a practice threatens a valued social arrangement), they must follow any consensus of moral position which the community at large has reached, because this is required by the democratic principle, and because a community is entitled to follow its own lights. The argument would have some plausibility if Lord Devlin meant, in speaking of the moral consensus of the community, those positions which are moral positions in the discriminatory sense we have been exploring.

But he means nothing of the sort. His definition of a moral position shows he is using it in what I called the anthropological sense. The ordinary man whose opinion we must enforce, he says, '. . . is not expected to reason about anything and his judgment may be largely a matter of feeling.'[1] 'If the reasonable man believes,' he adds, 'that a practice is immoral and believes also – no matter whether the belief is right or wrong, so be it that it is honest and dispassionate – that no right-minded member of his society could think otherwise, then for the purpose of the law it is immoral.'[2] Elsewhere he quotes with approval Dean Rostow's attribution to him of the view that 'the common morality of a society at any time is a blend of custom and conviction, of reason

[1] Devlin 15.
[2] *Ibid.* 22-3.

and feeling, of experience and prejudice.'[1] His sense of what a moral conviction is emerges most clearly of all from the famous remark about homosexuals. If the ordinary man regards homosexuality 'as a vice so abominable that its mere presence is an offence',[2] this demonstrates for him that the ordinary man's feelings about homosexuals are a matter of moral conviction.[3]

His conclusions fail because they depend upon using 'moral position' in this anthropological sense. Even if it is true that most men think homosexuality an abominable vice and cannot tolerate its presence, it remains possible that this common opinion is a compound of prejudice (resting on the assumption that homosexuals are morally inferior creatures because they are effeminate), rationalization (based on assumptions of fact so unsupported that they challenge the community's own standards of rationality), and personal aversion (representing no conviction but merely blind hate rising from unacknowledged self-suspicion). It remains possible that the ordinary man could produce no reason for his view, but would simply parrot his neighbor who in turn parrots him, or that he would produce a reason which presupposes a general moral position he could not sincerely or consistently claim to hold. If so, the principles of democracy we follow do not call for the enforcement of the consensus, for the belief that prejudices, personal aversions and rationalizations do not justify restricting another's freedom itself occupies a critical and fundamental position in our popular morality. Nor would the bulk of the community then be entitled to follow its own lights, for the community does not extend that privilege to one who acts on the basis of prejudice, rationalization, or personal aversion. Indeed, the distinction between these and moral convictions, in the discriminatory sense, exists largely to mark off the former as the sort of positions one is not entitled to pursue.

A conscientious legislator who is told a moral consensus exists must test the credentials of that consensus. He cannot, of course, examine

---

[1] Rostow, 'The Enforcement of Morals', 1960 *Camb. L.J.* 174, 197; reprinted in E. V. Rostow, *The Sovereign Prerogative* 45, 78 (1962). Quoted in Devlin 95.

[2] *Ibid.* 17.

[3] In the preface (*Ibid.* viii) Lord Devlin acknowledges that the language of the original lecture might have placed 'too much emphasis on feeling and too little on reason', and he states that the legislator is entitled to disregard 'irrational' beliefs. He gives as an example of the latter the belief that homosexuality causes earthquakes, and asserts that the exclusion of irrationality 'is usually an easy and comparatively unimportant process'. I think it fair to conclude that this is all Lord Devlin would allow him to exclude. If I am wrong, and Lord Devlin would ask him to exclude prejudices, personal aversions, arbitrary stands and the rest as well, he should have said so, and attempted to work some of these distinctions out. If he had, his conclusions would have been different and would no doubt have met with a different reaction.

the beliefs or behavior of individual citizens; he cannot hold hearings on the Clapham omnibus. That is not the point.

The claim that a moral consensus exists is not itself based on a poll. It is based on an appeal to the legislator's sense of how his community reacts to some disfavored practice. But this same sense includes an awareness of the grounds on which that reaction is generally supported. If there has been a public debate involving the editorial columns, speeches of his colleagues, the testimony of interested groups, and his own correspondence, these will sharpen his awareness of what arguments and positions are in the field. He must sift these arguments and positions, trying to determine which are prejudices or rationalizations, which presuppose general principles or theories vast parts of the population could not be supposed to accept, and so on. It may be that when he has finished this process of reflection he will find that the claim of a moral consensus has not been made out. In the case of homosexuality, I expect, it would not be, and that is what makes Lord Devlin's undiscriminating hypothetical so serious a misstatement. What is shocking and wrong is not his idea that the community's morality counts, but his idea of what counts as the community's morality.

Of course the legislator must apply these tests for himself. If he shares the popular views he is less likely to find them wanting, though if he is self-critical the exercise may convert him. His answer, in any event, will depend upon his own understanding of what our shared morality requires. That is inevitable, for whatever criteria we urge him to apply, he can apply them only as he understands them.

A legislator who proceeds in this way, who refuses to take popular indignation, intolerance and disgust as the moral conviction of his community, is not guilty of moral elitism. He is not simply setting his own educated views against those of a vast public which rejects them. He is doing his best to enforce a distinct, and fundamentally important, part of his community's morality, a consensus more essential to society's existence in the form we know it than the opinion Lord Devlin bids him follow.

No legislator can afford to ignore the public's outrage. It is a fact he must reckon with. It will set the boundaries of what is politically feasible, and it will determine his strategies of persuasion and enforcement within these boundaries. But we must not confuse strategy with justice, nor facts of political life with principles of political morality. Lord Devlin understands these distinctions, but his arguments will appeal most, I am afraid, to those who do not.

POSTSCRIPT ON PORNOGRAPHY

I have been discussing homosexuality because that is Lord Devlin's example. I should like to say a word about pornography, if only because it was, at the time of Britain's concern over Lord Devlin's theories, more in the American legal headlines than homosexuality. The Supreme Court had just decided three important cases: *Ginzburg, Mishkin* and *Fanny Hill*.[1] In two of these, convictions (and jail sentences) for the distribution of pornography were upheld, and in the third, while the Court reversed a state ban on an allegedly obscene novel, three justices dissented.

Two of the cases involved review of state procedures for constitutionality, and the third the interpretation and application of a federal statute. The Court therefore had to pass on the constitutional question of how far a state or the nation may legally restrict the publication of erotic literature, and on questions of statutory construction. But each decision nevertheless raised issues of political principle of the sort we have been considering.

A majority of the Court adhered to the constitutional test laid down some years ago by *Roth*.[2] Under that test, a book was obscene and as such not protected by the first amendment, if: '(a) the dominant theme of the material taken as a whole appeals to a prurient interest in sex; (b) the material is patently offensive because it affronts contemporary community standards relating to the description or representation of sexual matters; and (c) the material is utterly without redeeming social value.'[3] We might put the question of political principle this way: What gives the federal government, or any state, the moral right to prohibit the publication of books which are obscene under the *Roth* test?

Justice Brennan's opinion in *Mishkin* floated one answer: erotic literature, he said, incites some readers to crime. If this is true, if in a significant number of such cases the same readers would not have been incited to the same crime by other stimuli, and if the problem cannot effectively be handled in other ways, this might give society a warrant to ban these books. But these are at least speculative hypotheses, and in any event they are not pertinent to a case like *Ginzburg*, in which the Court based its decision not on the obscene character of the publications themselves, but on the fact that they were presented to the public as salacious rather than enlightening. Can any other justification be given for the prohibition of obscene books?

An argument like Lord Devlin's second argument can be constructed, and many of those who feel society is entitled to ban pornography are

---

[1] Above, n. 2.
[2] *Roth v. United States*, 354 U.S. 476 (1957).
[3] *Memoirs v. Massachusetts (Fanny Hill)*, 383 U.S. 413, 418 (1966).

in fact moved by some such argument. It might take this form :

(1) If we permit obscene books freely to be sold, to be delivered as it were with the morning milk, the whole tone of the community will eventually change. That which is now thought filthy and vulgar in speech and dress, and in public behavior, will become acceptable. A public which could enjoy pornography legally would soon settle for nothing very much tamer, and all forms of popular culture would inevitably move closer to the salacious. We have seen these forces at work already – the same relaxations in our legal attitudes which enabled books like *Tropic of Cancer* to be published have already had an effect on what we find in movies and magazines, on beaches and on the city streets. Perhaps we must pay that price for what many critics plausibly consider works of art, but we need not pay what would be a far greater price for trash – mass-manufactured for profit only.

(2) It is not a sufficient answer to say that social practices will not change unless the majority willingly participates in the change. Social corruption works through media and forces quite beyond the control of the mass of the people, indeed quite beyond the control of any conscious design at all. Of course, pornography attracts while it repels, and at some point in the deterioration of community standards the majority will not object to further deterioration, but that is a mark of the corruption's success, not proof that there has been no corruption. It is precisely that possibility which makes it imperative that we enforce our standards while we still have them. This is an example – it is not the only one – of our wishing the law to protect us from ourselves.

(3) Banning pornography abridges the freedom of authors, publishers and would-be readers. But if what they want to do is immoral, we are entitled to protect ourselves at that cost. Thus we are presented with a moral issue; does one have a moral right to publish or to read 'hard-core' pornography which can claim no value or virtue beyond its erotic effect? This moral issue should not be solved by fiat, nor by self-appointed ethical tutors, but by submission to the public. The public at present believes that hard-core pornography is immoral, that those who produce it are panderers, and that the protection of the community's sexual and related mores is sufficiently important to justify restricting their freedom.

But surely it is crucial to this argument, whatever else one might think of it, that the consensus described in the last sentence be a consensus of moral conviction. If it should turn out that the ordinary man's dislike of pornographers is a matter of taste, or an arbitrary stand, the argument would fail because these are not satisfactory reasons for abridging freedom.

It will strike many readers as paradoxical even to raise the question whether the average man's views on pornography are moral convictions. For most people the heart of morality is a sexual code, and if the ordinary man's views on fornication, adultery, sadism, exhibitionism and the other staples of pornography are not moral positions, it is hard to imagine any beliefs he is likely to have that are. But writing and reading about these adventures is not the same as performing in them, and one may be able to give reasons for condemning the practices (that they cause pain, or are sacrilegious, or insulting, or cause public annoyance) which do not extend to producing or savoring fantasies about them.

Those who claim a consensus of moral conviction on pornography must provide evidence that this exists. They must provide moral reasons or arguments which the average member of society might sincerely and consistently advance in the manner we have been describing. Perhaps this can be done, but it is no substitute simply to report that the ordinary man – within or without the jury box – turns his thumb down on the whole business.

Liberty and Liberalism

John Stuart Mill's famous essay *On Liberty* has on the whole served conservatives better than liberals. From Fitzjames Stephen to Wilmore Kendall and Lord Devlin, critics of liberalism have been pleased to cite the essay as the most cogent philosophical defense of that theory, and then, by noticing the defects in its argument, argue that liberalism is flawed. In *Liberty and Liberalism: The Case of John Stuart Mill*, Miss Gertrude Himmelfarb uses the essay in the same way, but with this difference. She does not attack Mill's arguments, but argues *ad hominem* against Mill himself. She says that he himself condemns, in his other writings, the philosophical premises upon which *On Liberty* is built. Friedrich Hayek made the same point years ago, and Miss Himmelfarb touched upon it in her 1962 edition of Mill's essays. Now she documents her case in great detail.

If, as she believes, *On Liberty* runs against the grain of everything Mill wrote before or after it, then it is necessary to explain why he took such time and care, in that essay, to refute himself. She finds the answer in his long association with Harriet Taylor, who had become his wife when *On Liberty* was written, though she died before it was published. Mill dedicated *On Liberty* to her in extravagant terms; he said that her ideas inspired the essay, and that she was an active collaborator in the long process of revising and polishing it. Miss Himmelfarb argues that this was understatement; that Miss Taylor was so much the dominant partner in the enterprise that she was able to drive him to unnatural intellectual positions. She also thinks that Miss Taylor's outrage, which provoked the essay, was generated by the legal and social subjugation of women in Victorian England, a topic hardly mentioned in the essay, but of great concern to Miss Taylor.

But her only argument in favor of the hypothesis that Miss Taylor took over Mill's mind is that no other explanation of the inconsistency in his thought can be found. There is no direct evidence, either internal or external to the essay. Miss Himmelfarb claims that the lack of internal evidence only shows how intimate the collaboration was, and explains the absence of external evidence by noticing that the Mills lived in isolation from all friends while the essay was being written. If there is in fact no genuine inconsistency between *On Liberty* and Mill's other work, then no evidence remains for Miss Himmelfarb's interesting speculation.

Her argument for the supposed inconsistency is this. Mill discussed liberty not only in the famous essay but in many books and papers, including his autobiography, his early essay 'The Spirit of the Age', his famous essay on Coleridge, and his major work on utilitarianism. In these other works, he argues in favor of both complexity and historicism in political theory. He condemns Bentham, the founder of utilitarianism, for reducing social psychology and political theory to simple axioms. He deploys a pessimistic theory of human nature, emphasizes the value of cultural and historical constraints on egotism, and insists on the role of the state in educating its citizens away from individual appetite and toward social conscience.

But *On Liberty*, in Miss Himmelfarb's view, contradicts each of these propositions. It begins by asserting:

> one very simple principle, as entitled to govern absolutely the dealings of society with the individual in the way of compulsion and control. . . . That principle is, that the sole end for which mankind are warranted, individually or collectively, in interfering with the liberty of action of any of their number, is self-protection. That the only purpose for which power can be rightfully exercised over any member of a civilized community, against his will, is to prevent harm to others. His own good, either physical or moral, is not a sufficient warrant.

She condemns, first, the absolute character of this assertion: Mill is false to his own sophistication, she says, when he asserts that 'one very simple principle' can 'govern absolutely' the complex connections between society and individual. She then characterizes this simple principle as an 'extreme' claim for liberty in defiance of Mill's more characteristic claims for tradition and education. *On Liberty*, she says, encouraged individuals to 'prize and cultivate their personal desires, impulses, inclinations, and wills, to see these as the source of all good, the force behind individual and social well-being'; it supported a philosophy 'which recognized no higher, no more worthy subject than the individual, which made the individual the repository of wisdom and virtue, and which made the freedom of the individual the sole aim of social policy.' It did all this in the face of Mill's own philosophy, developed in other essays, that individuals achieve virtue and excellence through concern for others rather than attention to themselves.

Miss Himmelfarb's argument begins with a blunder from which it does not recover. It confuses the force of a principle with its range. Bentham's theories of human nature and utility, which Mill thought too simple, were absolute in their range. Bentham thought that every human act and decision was motivated by some calculation of pleasures and pains, and thought that every political decision should be made on that same calculation, that is, to maximize the net product of simple pleasure over pain for the community as a whole.

But Mill's principle is of very limited range. It speaks only to those relatively rare occasions when a government is asked to prohibit some act on the sole ground that the act is dangerous to the actor, like driving a motorcycle without a helmet. Or on the ground that it is offensive to community standards of morality, like practicing homosexuality or publishing or reading pornography. Such decisions form a very small part of the business of any responsible government. The principle says nothing about how the government shall distribute scarce resources like income or security or power, or even how it shall decide when to limit liberty for the sake of some other value. It does not counsel government, for example, to respect the liberty of conscience of draft resisters at the cost of military efficiency, or the liberty of protest at the cost of property damage, or the liberty of a land user at the cost of the nuisance he causes.

The more limited the range of a principle, the more plausibly it may be said to be absolute. Even the most sophisticated philosophers might believe, for example, that it is always wrong for the government gratuitously to insult one class of its citizens. Mill thought his principle was also sufficiently limited to be absolute, and though he may have been wrong in this he can hardly be said to be simple-minded or fanatical because he thought so.

Miss Himmelfarb's confusion between the range and force of Mill's principle is responsible for the curious argument of the last part of her book. In recent years, she says, liberals have carried that principle to its logical extreme, with results that show that they have not yet learned that 'absolute liberty may corrupt absolutely' and that 'A populace that cannot respect principles of prudence and moderation is bound to behave so imprudently and immoderately as to violate every other principle, including the principle of liberty.' But her own account hardly suggests any connection between Mill and any social disorder. She says, for example, that the radical 'counterculture' celebrates spontaneity, and she therefore claims it as Mill's creature. But she concedes that the language of this 'counterculture' emphasizes community more than individuality. She might have added that its proponents have held liberalism in general, and Mill in particular, in special contempt, and have much preferred such writers as Marcuse, whose hostility to *On Liberty* they find congenial.

Her other evidence of social corruption is limited to familiar examples of sexual explicitness. It is true that laws punishing homosexuals have been relaxed, that *Deep Throat* was shown uncut in some cities, and that there are more naked bathers on the beach than there used to be. But these are not threats to any principle of justice. The genuine damage we have suffered to liberty, like Harvard's refusal and Yale's inability to allow Professor Shockley to speak, suggest not too much attention to Mill but too little.

Miss Himmelfarb believes that these changes in sexual mores are previews or symptoms of a more general social anarchy and lawlessness. She thinks that Mill introduced a new and consuming *idea* of liberty; that his own distinction, between decisions affecting oneself and decisions affecting others, was simply an arbitrary and illogical line he drew to contain this corrosive idea; that since this line cannot hold, the idea must soon expand into violence and anarchy, into the absolute corruption that absolute liberty guarantees. Only her sense that Mill's principle has this inner logic and inevitable consequence, that its inherent range as well as its force must be absolute, can explain the rhetoric of the last third of her book.

But her argument, whatever its other defects, betrays a huge misunderstanding of *On Liberty*; it confuses two concepts of liberty and assigns the wrong one to Mill's essay. It does not distinguish between the idea of liberty as license, that is, the degree to which a person is free from social or legal constraint to do what he might wish to do, and liberty as independence, that is, the status of a person as independent and equal rather than subservient. These two ideas are of course closely related. If a person is much cramped by legal and social constraints, then that is strong evidence, at least, that he is in a politically inferior position to some group that uses its power over him to impose those constraints. But the two ideas are nevertheless different in very important ways.

Liberty as license is an indiscriminate concept because it does not distinguish among forms of behavior. Every prescriptive law diminishes a citizen's liberty as license : good laws, like laws prohibiting murder, diminish this liberty in the same way, and possibly to a greater degree, as bad laws, like laws prohibiting political speech. The question raised by any such law is not whether it attacks liberty, which it does, but whether the attack is justified by some competing value, like equality or safety or public amenity. If a social philosopher places a very high value on liberty as license, he may be understood as arguing for a lower relative value for these competing values. If he defends freedom of speech, for example, by some general argument in favor of license, then his argument also supports, at least *pro tanto*, freedom to form monopolies or smash storefront windows.

But liberty as independence is not an indiscriminate concept in that way. It may well be, for example, that laws against murder or monopoly do not threaten, but are necessary to protect, the political independence of citizens generally. If a social philosopher places a high value on liberty as independence he is not necessarily denigrating values like safety or amenity, even in a relative way. If he argues for freedom of speech, for example, on some general argument in favor of independence and equality, he does not automatically argue in favor of greater license when these other values are not at stake.

Miss Himmelfarb's argument, that the inner logic of Mill's principle threatens anarchy, assumes that the principle promotes liberty as license. In fact it promotes the more complex idea of liberty as independence. Bentham and Mill's father, John Mill, thought that political independence would be sufficiently secured by wide distribution of the right to vote and other political liberties: that is, by democracy. Mill saw independence as a further dimension of equality; he argued that an individual's independence is threatened, not simply by a political process that denies him equal voice, but by political decisions that deny him equal respect. Laws that recognize and protect common interests, like laws against violence and monopoly, offer no insult to any class or individual; but laws that constrain one man, on the sole ground that he is incompetent to decide what is right for himself, are profoundly insulting to him. They make him intellectually and morally subservient to the conformists who form the majority, and deny him the independence to which he is entitled. Mill insisted on the political importance of these moral concepts of dignity, personality, and insult. It was these complex ideas, not the simpler idea of license, that he tried to make available for political theory, and to use as the basic vocabulary of liberalism.

This distinction between acts that are self-regarding and those that are other-regarding was not an arbitrary compromise between the claims of license and other values. It was intended to define political independence, because it marked the line between regulation that connoted equal respect and regulation that denied it. That explains why he had such difficulty making the distinction, and why he drew it in different ways on different occasions. He conceded what his critics have always labored: that any act, no matter how personal, may have important effects on others. He acknowledged, for example, that if a man drinks himself sick, this act will cause pain to well-meaning men and women who will grieve at the waste of human life. The decision to drink is nevertheless self-regarding, not because these consequences are not real or socially important, but because they work, as Mill says, *through* the personality of the actor. We could not suppose that society has a right to be free from sympathy or regret without supposing that it has a right to decide what sort of personality its members shall have, and it is this right that Mill thought incompatible with freedom.

Once these two concepts of liberty are distinguished then Miss Himmelfarb's argument, that Mill contradicts *On Liberty* in other essays, collapses. She quotes, for example, this passage from one of his early papers :

> Liberty in its original sense, means freedom from restraint. In this sense, every law, and every rule of morals, is contrary to liberty. A despot, who is entirely emancipated from both, is the only person whose freedom of action is complete. A measure of government, therefore, is not necessarily bad, because it is contrary to liberty; and to blame it for that reason leads to confusion of ideas.

The 'original' sense of liberty the youthful Mill had in mind was, of course, liberty as license, and nothing here contradicts *On Liberty*, either in letter or in spirit. She also cites passages from the essay on Coleridge in which Mill includes, as among the functions of education in a good society, 'To train the human being in the habit, and thence the power, of subordinating his personal impulses and aims, to what were considered the ends of society. . . .' But educating men to accept the aims of society is educating them to accept constraints on license in order to respect the interests of others, not to subordinate their own personality when these interests are not in play.

She cites Mill's approval, in the same essay, of the feeling of nationality, that is, of a common public philosophy, and she suggests that that sort of nationality is opposed to the individuality of *On Liberty*. But she fails to mention Mill's immediate proviso that 'the only shape in which [that] feeling is likely to exist hereafter' is as a common respect for 'principles of individual freedom and social equality, as realized in institutions which as yet exist nowhere, or exist only in a rudimentary state.' Nor does she mention that in the Coleridge essay he described education and nationality not as compromises with the *philosophe's* goals of liberty but as conditions under which that goal might be achieved, as conditions necessary, that is, for 'vigor and manliness of character' to be preserved. Each essay Miss Himmelfarb mentions confirms rather than contradicts the point of *On Liberty*, that independence of personality must be distinguished from license and anarchy, and established as a special and distinct condition of a just society.

If she had understood this she would not have repeated the silly proposition that true liberals must respect economic as well as intellectual liberty, nor would she have taxed Mill, who was a socialist, with inconsistency in that respect as well. Economic license and intellectual liberty must stand on the same footing only if liberty means license; they are plainly distinguishable, and at some point inconsistent, if liberty means independence.

The Supreme Court confused these two ideas, decades ago, when it decided, temporarily, that if the Constitution protects liberty at all it must protect the liberty of an employer to hire workers on such terms as he wishes. Conservatives confuse these ideas when they use 'permissiveness' to describe both sexual independence and political violence and to suggest that these differ only in degree. Radicals confuse these ideas when they identify liberalism with capitalism, and therefore suppose that individual rights are responsible for social injustice. Mill's collected works are not the source of that sort of confusion, but its antidote.

12

What Rights Do We Have?

Do we have a right to liberty?[1] Thomas Jefferson thought so, and since his day the right to liberty has received more play than the competing rights he mentioned to life and the pursuit of happiness. Liberty gave its name to the most influential political movement of the last century, and many of those who now despise liberals do so on the ground that they are not sufficiently libertarian. Of course, almost everyone concedes that the right to liberty is not the only political right, and that therefore claims to freedom must be limited, for example, by restraints that protect the security or property of others. Nevertheless the consensus in favor of some right to liberty is a vast one, though it is, as I shall argue in this chapter, misguided.

The right to liberty is popular all over this political spectrum. The rhetoric of liberty fuels every radical movement from international wars of liberation to campaigns for sexual freedom and women's liberation. But liberty has been even more prominent in conservative service. Even the mild social reorganizations of the anti-trust and unionization movements, and of the early New Deal, were opposed on the grounds that they infringed the right to liberty, and just now efforts to achieve some racial justice in America through techniques like the busing of black and white schoolchildren, and social justice in Britain through constraints in private education are bitterly opposed on that ground.

It has become common, indeed, to describe the great social issues of domestic politics, and in particular the racial issue, as presenting a conflict between the demands of liberty and equality. It may be, it is said, that the poor and the black and the uneducated and the unskilled have an abstract right to equality, but the prosperous and the whites and the educated and the able have a right to liberty as well and any efforts at social reorganization in aid of the first set of rights must reckon with and respect the second. Everyone except extremists recognizes, therefore, the need to compromise between equality and liberty. Every

[1] I use 'liberty' in this essay in the sense Isaiah Berlin called 'negative'.

piece of important social legislation, from tax policy to integration plans, is shaped by the supposed tension between these two goals.

I have this supposed conflict between equality and liberty in mind when I ask whether we have a *right* to liberty, as Jefferson and everyone else has supposed. That is a crucial question. If freedom to choose one's schools, or employees, or neighborhood is simply something that we all want, like air conditioning or lobsters, then we are not entitled to hang on to these freedoms in the face of what we concede to be the rights of others to an equal share of respect and resources. But if we can say, not simply that we want these freedoms, but that we are ourselves entitled to them, then we have established at least a basis for demanding a compromise.

There is now a movement, for example, in favor of a proposed amendment to the constitution of the United States that would guarantee every school child the legal right to attend a 'neighborhood school' and thus outlaw busing. The suggestion, that neighborhood schools somehow rank with jury trials as constitutional values, would seem silly but for the sense many Americans have that forcing school children into buses is somehow as much an interference with the fundamental right to liberty as segregated schooling was an insult to equality. But that seems to me absurd; indeed it seems to me absurd to suppose that men and women have any general right to liberty at all, at least as liberty has traditionally been conceived by its champions.

I have in mind the traditional definition of liberty as the absence of constraints placed by a government upon what a man might do if he wants to. Isaiah Berlin, in the most famous modern essay on liberty, put the matter this way: 'The sense of freedom, in which I use this term, entails not simply the absence of frustration but the absence of obstacles to possible choices and activities – absence of obstructions on roads along which a man can decide to walk.' This conception of liberty as license is neutral amongst the various activities a man might pursue, the various roads he might wish to walk. It diminishes a man's liberty when we prevent him from talking or making love as he wishes, but it also diminishes his liberty when we prevent him from murdering or defaming others. These latter constraints may be justifiable, but only because they are compromises necessary to protect the liberty or security of others, and not because they do not, in themselves, infringe the independent value of liberty. Bentham said that any law whatsoever is an 'infraction' of liberty, and though some such infractions might be necessary, it is obscurantist to pretend that they are not infractions after all. In this neutral, all embracing sense of liberty as license, liberty and equality are plainly in competition. Laws are needed to protect equality, and laws are inevitably compromises of liberty.

Liberals like Berlin are content with this neutral sense of liberty, because it seems to encourage clear thinking. It allows us to identify just what is lost, though perhaps unavoidably, when men accept constraints on their actions for some other goal or value. It would be an intolerable muddle, on this view, to use the concept of liberty or freedom in such a way that we counted a loss of freedom only when men were prevented from doing something that we thought they ought to do. It would allow totalitarian governments to masquerade as liberal, simply by arguing that they prevent men from doing only what is wrong. Worse, it would obscure the most distinctive point of the liberal tradition, which is that interfering with a man's free choice to do what he might want to do is in and of itself an insult to humanity, a wrong that may be justified but can never be wiped away by competing considerations. For a true liberal, any constraint upon freedom is something that a decent government must regret, and keep to the minimum necessary to accommodate the other rights of its constituents.

In spite of this tradition, however, the neutral sense of liberty seems to me to have caused more confusion than it has cured, particularly when it is joined to the popular and inspiring idea that men and women have a right to liberty. For we can maintain that idea only by so watering down the idea of a right that the right to liberty is something hardly worth having at all.

The term 'right' is used in politics and philosophy in many different senses, some of which I have tried to disentangle elsewhere.[1] In order sensibly to ask whether we have a right to liberty in the neutral sense, we must fix on some one meaning of 'right'. It would not be difficult to find a sense of that term in which we could say with some confidence that men have a right to liberty. We might say, for example, that someone has a right to liberty if it is in his interest to have liberty, that is, if he either wants it or if it would be good for him to have it. In this sense, I would be prepared to concede that citizens have a right to liberty. But in this sense I would also have to concede that they have a right, at least generally, to vanilla ice cream. My concession about liberty, moreover, would have very little value in political debate. I should want to claim, for example, that people have a right to equality in a much stronger sense, that they do not simply want equality but that they are entitled to it, and I would therefore not recognize the claim that some men and women want liberty as requiring any compromise in the efforts that I believe are necessary to give other men and women the equality to which they are entitled.

If the right to liberty is to play the role cut out for it in political

[1] See Chapter 7.

debate, therefore, it must be a right in a much stronger sense. In Chapter 7 I defined a strong sense of right that seems to me to capture the claims men mean to make when they appeal to political and moral rights. I do not propose to repeat my analysis here, but only to summarize it in this way. A successful claim of right, in the strong sense I described, has this consequence. If someone has a right to something, then it is wrong for the government to deny it to him even though it would be in the general interest to do so. This sense of a right (which might be called the anti-utilitarian concept of a right) seems to me very close to the sense of right principally used in political and legal writing and argument in recent years. It marks the distinctive concept of an individual right against the State which is the heart, for example, of constitutional theory in the United States.

I do not think that the right to liberty would come to very much, or have much power in political argument, if it relied on any sense of the right any weaker than that. If we settle on this concept of a right, however, then it seems plain that there exists no general right to liberty as such. I have no political right to drive up Lexington Avenue. If the government chooses to make Lexington Avenue one-way down town, it is a sufficient justification that this would be in the general interest, and it would be ridiculous for me to argue that for some reason it would nevertheless be wrong. The vast bulk of the laws which diminish my liberty are justified on utilitarian grounds, as being in the general interest or for the general welfare; if, as Bentham supposes, each of these laws diminishes my liberty, they nevertheless do not take away from me any thing that I have a right to have. It will not do, in the one-way street case, to say that although I have a right to drive up Lexington Avenue, nevertheless the government for special reasons is justified in overriding that right. That seems silly because the government needs no special justification – but only *a* justification – for this sort of legislation. So I can have a political right to liberty, such that every act of constraint diminishes or infringes that right, only in such a weak sense of right that the so called right to liberty is not competitive with strong rights, like the right to equality, at all. In any strong sense of right, which would be competitive with the right to equality, there exists no general right to liberty at all.

It may now be said that I have misunderstood the claim that there is a right to liberty. It does not mean to argue, it will be said, that there is a right to all liberty, but simply to important or basic liberties. Every law is, as Bentham said, an infraction of liberty, but we have a right to be protected against only fundamental or serious infractions. If the constraint on liberty is serious or severe enough, then it is indeed true that the government is not entitled to impose that constraint simply because

K

that would be in the general interest; the government is not entitled to constrain liberty of speech, for example, whenever it thinks that would improve the general welfare. So there is, after all, a general right to liberty as such, provided that that right is restricted to important liberties or serious deprivations. This qualification does not affect the political arguments I described earlier, it will be said, because the rights to liberty that stand in the way of full equality are rights to basic liberties like, for example, the right to attend a school of one's choice.

But this qualification raises an issue of great importance for liberal theory, which those who argue for a right to liberty do not face. What does it mean to say that the right to liberty is limited to basic liberties, or that it offers protection only against serious infractions of liberty? That claim might be spelled out in two different ways, with very different theoretical and practical consequences. Let us suppose two cases in which government constrains a citizen from doing what he might want to do: the government prevents him from speaking his mind on political issues; from driving his car uptown on Lexington Avenue. What is the connection between these two cases, and the difference between them, such that though they are both cases in which a citizen is constrained and deprived of liberty, his right to liberty is infringed only in the first, and not in the second?

On the first of the two theories we might consider, the citizen is deprived of the same commodity, namely liberty, in both cases, but the difference is that in the first case the amount of that commodity taken away from him is, for some reason, either greater in amount or greater in its impact than in the second. But that seems bizarre. It is very difficult to think of liberty as a commodity. If we do try to give liberty some operational sense, such that we can measure the relative diminution of liberty occasioned by different sorts of laws or constraints, then the result is unlikely to match our intuitive sense of what are basic liberties and what are not. Suppose, for example, we measure a diminution in liberty by calculating the extent of frustration that it induces. We shall then have to face the fact that laws against theft, and even traffic laws, impose constraints that are felt more keenly by most men than constraints on political speech would be. We might take a different tack, and measure the degree of loss of liberty by the impact that a particular constraint has on future choices. But we should then have to admit that the ordinary criminal code reduces choice for most men more than laws which forbid fringe political activity. So the first theory – that the difference between cases covered and those not covered by our supposed right to liberty is a matter of degree – must fail.

The second theory argues that the difference between the two cases has to do, not with the degree of liberty involved, but with the special character of the liberty involved in the case covered by the right. On this theory, the offense involved in a law that limits free speech is of a different character, and not just different in degree, from a law that prevents a man from driving up Lexington Avenue. That sounds plausible, though as we shall see it is not easy to state what this difference in character comes to, or why it argues for a right in some cases though not in others. My present point, however, is that if the distinction between basic liberties and other liberties is defended in this way, then the notion of a general right to liberty as such has been entirely abandoned. If we have a right to basic liberties not because they are cases in which the commodity of liberty is somehow especially at stake, but because an assault on basic liberties injures us or demeans us in some way that goes beyond its impact on liberty, then what we have a right to is not liberty at all, but to the values or interests or standing that this particular constraint defeats.

This is not simply a question of terminology. The idea of a right to liberty is a misconceived concept that does a dis-service to political thought in at least two ways. First, the idea creates a false sense of a necessary conflict between liberty and other values when social regulation, like the busing program, is proposed. Second, the idea provides too easy an answer to the question of why we regard certain kinds of restraints, like the restraint on free speech or the exercise of religion, as especially unjust. The idea of a right to liberty allows us to say that these constraints are unjust because they have a special impact on liberty as such. Once we recognize that this answer is spurious, then we shall have to face the difficult question of what is indeed at stake in these cases.

I should like to turn at once to that question. If there is no general right to liberty, then why do citizens in a democracy have rights to any specific kind of liberty, like freedom of speech or religion or political activity? It is no answer to say that if individuals have these rights, then the community will be better off in the long run as a whole. This idea – that individual rights may lead to overall utility – may or may not be true, but it is irrelevant to the defence of rights as such, because when we say that someone has a right to speak his mind freely, in the relevant political sense, we mean that he is entitled to do so even if this would not be in the general interest. If we want to defend individual rights in the sense in which we claim them, then we must try to discover something beyond utility that argues for these rights.

I mentioned one possibility earlier. We might be able to make out a case that individuals suffer some special damage when the traditional rights are invaded. On this argument, there is something about the liberty to speak out on political issues such that if that liberty is denied the individual suffers a special kind of damage which makes it wrong to inflict that damage upon him even though the community as a whole would benefit. This line of argument will appeal to those who themselves would feel special deprivation at the loss of their political and civil liberties, but it is nevertheless a difficult argument to pursue for two reasons.

First, there are a great many men and women and they undoubtedly form the majority even in democracies like Britain and the United States, who do not exercise political liberties that they have, and who would not count the loss of these liberties as especially grievous. Second, we lack a psychological theory which would justify and explain the idea that the loss of civil liberties, or any particular liberties, involves inevitable or even likely psychological damage. On the contrary, there is now a lively tradition in psychology, led by psychologists like Ronald Laing, who argue that a good deal of mental instability in modern societies may be traced to the demand for too much liberty rather than too little. In their account, the need to choose, which follows from liberty, is an unnecessary source of destructive tension. These theories are not necessarily persuasive, but until we can be confident that they are wrong, we cannot assume that psychology demonstrates the opposite, however appealing that might be on political grounds.

If we want to argue for a right to certain liberties, therefore, we must find another ground. We must argue on grounds of political morality that it is wrong to deprive individuals of these liberties, for some reason, apart from direct psychological damage, in spite of the fact that the common interest would be served by doing so. I put the matter this vaguely because there is no reason to assume, in advance, that only one kind of reason would support that moral position. It might be that a just society would recognize a variety of individual rights, some grounded on very different sorts of moral considerations from others. In what remains of this chapter I shall try to describe only one possible ground for rights. It does not follow that men and women in civil society have only the rights that the argument I shall make would support; but it does follow that they have at least these rights, and that is important enough.

2. THE RIGHT TO LIBERTIES

The central concept of my argument will be the concept not of liberty but of equality. I presume that we all accept the following postulates of political morality. Government must treat those whom it governs with concern, that is, as human beings who are capable of suffering and frustration, and with respect, that is, as human beings who are capable of forming and acting on intelligent conceptions of how their lives should be lived. Government must not only treat people with concern and respect, but with equal concern and respect. It must not distribute goods or opportunities unequally on the ground that some citizens are entitled to more because they are worthy of more concern. It must not constrain liberty on the ground that one citizen's conception of the good life of one group is nobler or superior to another's. These postulates, taken together, state what might be called the liberal conception of equality; but it is a conception of equality, not of liberty as license, that they state.

The sovereign question of political theory, within a state supposed to be governed by the liberal conception of equality, is the question of what inequalities in goods, opportunities and liberties are permitted in such a state, and why. The beginning of an answer lies in the following distinction. Citizens governed by the liberal conception of equality each have a right to equal concern and respect. But there are two different rights that might be comprehended by that abstract right. The first is the right to equal treatment, that is, to the same distribution of goods or opportunities as anyone else has or is given. The Supreme Court, in the Reapportionment Cases, held that citizens have a right to equal treatment in the distribution of voting power; it held that one man must be given one vote in spite of the fact that a different distribution of votes might in fact work for the general benefit. The second is the right to treatment as an equal. This is the right, not to an equal distribution of some good or opportunity, but the right to equal concern and respect in the political decision about how these goods and opportunities are to be distributed. Suppose the question is raised whether an economic policy that injures long-term bondholders is in the general interest. Those who will be injured have a right that their prospective loss be taken into account in deciding whether the general interest is served by the policy. They may not simply be ignored in that calculation. But when their interest is taken into account it may nevertheless be outweighed by the interests of others who will gain from the policy, and in that case their right to equal concern and respect, so defined, would provide no objection. In the case of economic policy, therefore, we might wish to say that those who will be injured if inflation is permitted have a right to treatment as equals in the decision whether that policy would serve the general interest, but no right to equal treatment that would outlaw the policy even if it passed that test.

I propose that the right to treatment as an equal must be taken to be fundamental under the liberal conception of equality, and that the more restrictive right to equal treatment holds only in those special circumstances in which, for some special reason, it follows from the more fundamental right, as perhaps it does in the special circumstance of the Reapportionment Cases. I also propose that individual rights to distinct liberties must be recognized only when the fundamental right to treatment as an equal can be shown to require these rights. If this is correct, then the right to distinct liberties does not conflict with any supposed competing right to equality, but on the contrary follows from a conception of equality conceded to be more fundamental.

I must now show, however, how the familiar rights to distinct liberties – those established, for example, in the United States constitution – might be thought to be required by that fundamental conception of equality. I shall try to do this, for present purposes, only by providing a skeleton of the more elaborate argument that would have to be made to defend any particular liberty on this basis, and then show why it would be plausible to expect that the more familiar political and civil liberties would be supported by such an argument if it were in fact made.

A government that respects the liberal conception of equality may properly constrain liberty only on certain very limited types of justification. I shall adopt, for purposes of making this point, the following crude typology of political justifications. There are, first, arguments of principle, which support a particular constraint on liberty on the argument that the constraint is required to protect the distinct right of some individual who will be injured by the exercise of the liberty. There are, second, arguments of policy, which support constraints on the different ground that such constraints are required to reach some overall political goal, that is, to realize some state of affairs in which the community as a whole, and not just certain individuals, are better off by virtue of the constraint. Arguments of policy might be further subdivided in this way. Utilitarian arguments of policy argue that the community as a whole will be better off because (to put the point roughly) more of its citizens will have more of what they want overall, even though some of them will have less. Ideal arguments of policy, on the other hand, argue that the community will be better off, not because more of its members will have more of what they want, but because the community will be in some way closer to an ideal community, whether its members desire the improvement in question or not.

The liberal conception of equality sharply limits the extent to which ideal arguments of policy may be used to justify any constraint on liberty. Such arguments cannot be used if the idea in question is itself controversial within the community. Constraints cannot be defended, for example, directly on the ground that they contribute to a culturally sophisticated community, whether the community wants the sophistication or not, because that argument would violate the canon of the liberal conception of equality that prohibits a government from relying on the claim that certain forms of life are inherently more valuable than others.

Utilitarian arguments of policy, however, would seem secure from that objection. They do not suppose that any form of life is inherently more valuable than any other, but instead base their claim, that constraints on liberty are necessary to advance some collective goal of the community, just on the fact that that goal happens to be desired more widely or more deeply than any other. Utilitarian arguments of policy, therefore, seem not to oppose but on the contrary to embody the fundamental right of equal concern and respect, because they treat the wishes of each member of the community on a par with the wishes of any other, with no bonus or discount reflecting the view that that member is more or less worthy of concern, or his views more or less worthy of respect, than any other.

This appearance of egalitarianism has, I think, been the principal source of the great appeal that utilitarianism has had, as a general political philosophy, over the last century. In Chapter 9, however, I pointed out that the egalitarian character of a utilitarian argument is often an illusion. I will not repeat, but only summarize, my argument here.

Utilitarian arguments fix on the fact that a particular constraint on liberty will make more people happier, or satisfy more of their preferences, depending upon whether psychological or preference utilitarianism is in play. But people's overall preference for one policy rather than another may be seen to include, on further analysis, both preferences that are *personal*, because they state a preference for the assignment of one set of goods or opportunities to him and preferences that are *external*, because they state a preference for one assignment of goods or opportunities to others. But a utilitarian argument that assigns critical weight to the external preferences of members of the community will not be egalitarian in the sense under consideration. It will not respect the right of everyone to be treated with equal concern and respect.

Suppose, for example, that a number of individuals in the community holds racist rather than utilitarian political theories. They believe, not that each man is to count for one and no one for more than one in the distribution of goods, but rather that a black man is to count for less and a white man therefore to count for more than one. That is an external preference, but it is nevertheless a genuine preference for one policy rather than another, the satisfaction of which will bring pleasure. Nevertheless if this preference or pleasure is given the normal weight in a utilitarian calculation, and blacks suffer accordingly, then their own assignment of goods and opportunities will depend, not simply on the competition among personal preferences that abstract statements of utilitarianism suggest, but precisely on the fact that they are thought less worthy of concern and respect than others are.

Suppose, to take a different case, that many members of the community disapprove on moral grounds of homosexuality, or contraception, or pornography, or expressions of adherence to the Communist party. They prefer not only that they themselves do not indulge in these activities, but that no one else does so either, and they believe that a community that permits rather than prohibits these acts is inherently a worse community. These are external preferences, but, once again, they are no less genuine, nor less a source of pleasure when satisfied and displeasure when ignored, than purely personal preferences. Once again, however, if these external preferences are counted, so as to justify a constraint on liberty, then those constrained suffer, not simply because their personal preferences have lost in a competition for scarce resources with the personal preferences of others, but precisely because their conception of a proper or desirable form of life is despised by others.

These arguments justify the following important conclusion. If utilitarian arguments of policy are to be used to justify constraints on liberty, then care must be taken to insure that the utilitarian calculations on which the argument is based fix only on personal and ignore external preferences. That is an important conclusion for political theory because it shows, for example, why the arguments of John Stuart Mill in *On Liberty* are not counter-utilitarian but, on the contrary, arguments in service of the only defensible form of utilitarianism.

Important as that conclusion is at the level of political philosophy, however, it is in itself of limited practical significance, because it will be impossible to devise political procedures that will accurately discriminate between personal and external preferences. Representative democracy is widely thought to be the institutional structure most suited, in a complex and diverse society, to the identification and achievement of utilitarian policies. It works imperfectly at this, for the familiar reason that majoritarianism cannot sufficiently take acount of the intensity, as distinct from the number, of particular preferences, and because techniques of political persuasion, backed by money, may corrupt the accuracy with which votes represent the genuine preferences of those who have voted. Nevertheless democracy seems to enforce utilitarianism more satisfactorily, in spite of these imperfections, than any alternative general political scheme would.

But democracy cannot discriminate, within the overall preferences imperfectly revealed by voting, distinct personal and external components, so as to provide a method for enforcing the former while ignoring the latter. An actual vote in an election or referendum must be taken to represent an overall preference rather than some component of the preference that a skilful cross-examination of the individual voter, if time and expense permitted, would reveal. Personal and external preferences are sometimes so inextricably combined, moreover, that the discrimination is psychologically as well as institutionally impossible. That will be true, for example, in the case of the associational preferences that many people have for members of one race, or people of one talent or quality, rather than another, for this is a personal preference so parasitic upon external preferences that it is impossible to say, even as a matter of introspection, what personal preferences would remain if the underlying external preference were removed. It is also true of certain self-denying preferences that many individuals have; that is preferences for less of a certain good on the assumption, or rather proviso, that other people will have more. That is also a preference, however noble, that is parasitic upon external preferences, in the shape of political and moral theories, and they may no more be counted in a defensible utilitarian argument than less attractive preferences rooted in prejudice rather than altruism.

I wish now to propose the following general theory of rights. The concept of an individual political right, in the strong anti-utilitarian sense I distinguished earlier, is a response to the philosophical defects of a utilitarianism that counts external preferences and the practical imposibility of a utilitarianism that does not. It allows us to enjoy the institutions of political democracy, which enforce overall or unrefined utilitarianism, and yet protect the fundamental right of citizens to equal concern and respect by prohibiting decisions that seem, antecedently, likely to have been reached by virtue of the external components of the preferences democracy reveals.

It should be plain how this theory of rights might be used to support the idea, which is the subject of this chapter, that we have distinct rights to certain liberties like the liberty of free expression and of free choice in personal and sexual relations. It might be shown that any utilitarian constraint on these liberties must be based on overall preferences in the community that we know, from our general knowledge of society, are likely to contain large components of external preferences, in the shape of political or moral theories, which the political process cannot discriminate and eliminate. It is not, as I said, my present purpose to frame the arguments that would have to be made to defend particular rights to liberty in this way, but only to show the general character such arguments might have.

I do wish, however, to mention one alleged right that might be called into question by my general argument, which is the supposed individual right to the free use of property. In chapter 11 I complained about the argument, popular in certain quarters, that it is inconsistent for liberals to defend a liberty of speech, for example, and not also concede a parallel right of some sort of property and its use. There might be force in that argument if the claim, that we have a right of free speech, depended on the more general proposition that we have a right to something called liberty as such. But that general idea is untenable and incoherent; there is no such thing as any general right to liberty. The argument for any given specific liberty may therefore be entirely independent of the argument for any other, and there is no antecedent inconsistency or even implausibility in contending for one while disputing the other.

What can be said, on the general theory of rights I offer, for any particular right of property? What can be said, for example, in favor of the right to liberty of contract sustained by the Supreme Court in the famous *Lochner* case, and later regretted, not only by the court, but by liberals generally? I cannot think of any argument that a political decision to limit such a right, in the way in which minimum wage laws limited it, is antecedently likely to give effect to external preferences, and in that way offend the right of those whose liberty is curtailed to equal concern and respect. If, as I think, no such argument can be made out, then the alleged right does not exist; in any case there can be no inconsistency in denying that it exists while warmly defending a right to other liberties.

13

Can Rights be Controversial?

1.

In this final chapter I must defend the arguments of the book against a pervasive and, if successful, destructive objection. My arguments suppose that there is often a single right answer to complex questions of law and political morality. The objection replies that there is sometimes no single right answer, but only answers.

An attractive attitude supports this objection. It is a mixture of tolerance and common sense, expressed in judgments like these. When men and women disagree about whether the right of free speech extends to abusive language, or whether capital punishment is cruel and unusual within the meaning of the constitution, or whether a group of inconclusive precedents establishes a right to recover for merely economic damage in tort, then it is both silly and arrogant to pretend that there is somehow, latent in the controversy, a single right answer. It is wiser and more realistic to concede that though some answers may be plainly wrong, and some arguments plainly bad, there is nevertheless a set of answers and arguments that must be acknowledged to be, from any objective or neutral standpoint, equally good.

If so, then the choice of one of these is just that : a choice rather than a decision forced by reason. If a prosecution is required to decide whether protesters have a moral right to protest, or whether economic damage is recoverable in tort, then all the public is entitled to expect is that his choice will be made honestly and in a cool moment, free from bias or passion or zeal. It is not entitled to any particular decision, because that supposes that there is a single right answer to the question he must decide.

This book does not respect these modest sentiments. In Chapters 2 and 3, for example, I oppose the popular theory that judges have discretion to decide hard cases. I concede that principles of law are sometimes so well balanced that those favoring a decision for the plaintiff will seem stronger, taken together, to some lawyers but weaker to others. I argue that even so it makes perfect sense for each party to claim that it is entitled to win, and therefore each to deny that the judge has a discretion to find for the other. In Chapter 4 I describe a process of decision that gives content to that claim; but I do not claim (indeed I deny) that that process of decision will always yield the same decision in the hands of different judges. Nevertheless I insist that the process, even in hard cases, can sensibly be said to be aimed at discovering, rather than inventing, the rights of the parties concerned, and that the political justification of the process depends upon the soundness of that characterization.

So the no-right-answer thesis is hostile to the rights thesis I defend. The former is supported by the attractive attitude I described. Is it also supported by argument? We may distinguish two kinds of arguments that might be made. The first of these is practical. It concedes, arguendo, that there may be in principle one right answer to a controversial issue at law. But it insists that it is useless to say that the parties have a right to that answer, or that a judge has a duty to find it, since no one can be sure what the right answer is. Suppose I bet you that *Lear* is a better play than *Endgame*. Even if we are objectivists in aesthetics, and believe that there is, in principle, a right answer to the question, this is nevertheless a silly bet, because it can never be settled to the satisfaction of the losing party. It would be pointless to settle the bet by calling in a third party as umpire. He can offer no more than a third personal opinion, and the fact of that opinion would not (at least should not) convince either of us that he was wrong. So it is with a judge in a hard law suit. Even if there is, in principle, one best theory of law, and so one right answer to a hard case, that right answer is locked in legal philosopher's heaven, inaccessible to laymen, lawyers and judges alike. Each can have only his own opinion, and the opinion of the judge comes no more warranted for truth than the opinion of anyone else.

This practical argument of the 'no right answer' thesis is easily met. It argues that it is pointless to demand that a judge seek to find the right answer, even if there is one, because his answer is no more likely to be right than anyone else's, and because there is no way to prove that his is the right answer even if it is. We must be careful to distinguish the following three questions. (a) Do reasonable hard lawyers ever disagree whether a litigant in a hard case has a right to win, even after all the facts, including facts of institutional history, are agreed? (b) Is it possible that a litigant may have a right to win a hard case even though reasonable lawyers do disagree after all the facts are agreed? (c) Is it sensible or fair for the state to enforce the decision of a particular group of judges in a hard case, even though a different group, equally reasonable and competent, would have reached a different decision?

What logical relations should hold among positive answers to these three questions? The practical argument assumes that a positive answer to the first excludes a positive answer to the third, even given a positive answer to the second. But that is plainly wrong. It is clear that a positive answer to the second is necessary to a positive answer to the third. If the litigants in a hard case can have no right to a particular decision, it is both pointless and unfair to let the case between them be decided by a controversial (or for that matter uncontroversial) decision about the rights they have. It is also clear that a positive answer to the second is not in itself sufficient for a positive answer to the third. It is necessary also to be satisfied that, though the decision of any particular group of judges is fallible, and may never be proved right to the satisfaction of all other lawyers, it is nevertheless better to let that decision stand than to assign the decision to some other institution, or to ask judges to decide on grounds of policy, or in some other way; that does not require their best judgment about the rights of the parties. But of course one might be satisfied of that in some way other than by answering the first question 'no'. There are many reasons (perfectly practical reasons among them) for asking judges to decide hard cases on their best judgment about rights even when that judgment cannot be demonstrated to be true to the satisfaction of all, and may in fact be false.

The practical argument assumes that the answer to the first question is decisive of the third. Let it once be conceded that rights may be controversial; the argument takes hold and insists that controversial rights can have no place in adjudication. But that is simplistic. The third question is comparative. Suppose (which may be contested) that a 'yes' answer to the first question counts against a 'yes' answer to the third. We would be happier with the rights thesis if there were no hard cases. It does not follow that we must reject the rights thesis if hard cases are inevitable. Everything depends on the alternatives. In Chapter 4 I described those alternatives and found them unappealing; none of them was more practical or more dependable than the rights thesis, and they were all a good deal less fair.

The second form of argument we must consider, which is theoretical rather than practical, is more powerful. It argues that the second of the three questions we distinguished must have a negative answer. If it is inherently controversial whether some party has a particular legal or political right, then, according to this argument, it cannot be true that he has this right.

I shall consider, in the balance of this chapter, whether that argument holds for legal rights. I want first to notice, however, how thoroughly the theoretical argument condemns ordinary practice, not only in law, but in a large variety of other enterprises as well. Historians and scientists, for example, suppose that what they say can be true even though it cannot be, in the way the theoretical argument requires, proved to be true. They have arguments to back their judgments, and they make and change opinion through these arguments. But these are not arguments that hang by chains of logic from uncontroversial premises. In Chapter 4 I described the position of a chess referee called upon to apply the rule that players must not annoy each other unreasonably. I said that a referee in that position would have to make a judgment about the character of the game of chess, and that reasonable referees might well disagree about the exact characterization that some particular issue might require. Suppose two referees do disagree: one judges (to recall the example of that chapter) that chess is a game of intelligence in a sense that excludes psychological intimidation and the other disagrees. The theoretical argument holds that neither opinion can be true; that there can be no answer to the question, but only answers, each of which must be as sound as the other. But of course the two referees who debate cannot look upon their argument that way, because that analysis leaves each with a theory about nothing. Each knows that the other disagrees, and that there is no common test that can adjudicate their dispute so as to dissolve the disagreement. But each nevertheless thinks his answer is a superior answer to the question that divides them: if he does not think that, then what does he think?

It adds nothing to say that each knows that his judgment represents a choice rather than a decision forced upon him by reason. His choice is a choice of (what seems to him) the best characterization; it is a choice forced upon him by his judgment just as surely as when the case is controversial, and others disagree, as when it is easy and they do not. Nor is it useful to stress that the choice is just *his* judgment, as if that somehow modified the character of the judgment he makes; indeed the last sentence might be changed by deleting the phrase in parentheses without changing either its sense or its truth. The referees might accept, as a sound piece of common sense, that there is no 'right answer' to their question. But if they take that proposition as a negative answer to the second, and not simply the first, of the three questions I distinguished, then their common sense makes no sense of what they do when they act as professionals and not as philosophers.

It does not follow, of course, that the 'no right answer' thesis is wrong. If some philosophical theory compels us to concede that a proposition cannot be true unless there is some agreed test through which its truth might be demonstrated, then so much the worse for ordinary experience, including ordinary legal experience. But happily the shoe is on the other foot. The theoretical argument is not so compelling that we must reject ordinary experience in its place. On the contrary it is unclear what the 'no right answer' thesis, as interpreted by the theoretical argument, even means.

2.

Suppose the judges of a particular jurisdiction met in convention and determined each to follow the rights thesis, and otherwise to decide cases as Hercules did in Chapter 4. They therefore agree to act as participants in an enterprise which stipulates certain truth conditions for propositions of law, like the proposition that capital punishment is not in itself cruel and unusual punishment, or that those who suffer merely economic damage from negligence may recover in tort. A proposition of law may be asserted as true if it is more consistent with the theory of law that best justifies settled law than the contrary proposition of law. It may be denied as false if it is less consistent with that theory of law than the contrary. Suppose that this enterprise proceeds with the ordinary success of modern legal systems. Judges often agree about the truth values of propositions of law, and when they disagree they understand the arguments of their opponents sufficiently well to be able to locate the level of disagreement, and to rank these arguments in rough order of plausibility.

Suppose now that a philosopher visits the next convention of these judges and tells them that they have made a very serious mistake. They seem to think that there is a right answer to a difficult question of law, whereas in fact there is no right answer but only answers. They are wrong to think that in hard cases any particular proposition of law may be true, so that its contrary is false. It may be (the philosopher adds) that there is some political value in propagating the myth that there is a right answer, and that they therefore have no discretion in deciding hard cases. But the judges must concede (at least among themselves) that the idea is indeed a myth.

Why should the judges be persuaded by what this philosopher says? His arguments are compromised, for a start, by the following consideration. Suppose the judges persuade the philosopher to attend law school for the standard period of three years, and then himself to take up a position on the bench for a period of several years thereafter. He will find that he himself will be able to form judgments of the sort he believes rest on mistake. He will find that one theory of law seems to him to provide a better justification of settled law than competetive theories. He will be able to provide reasons for that belief, even though he knows that others will not find these reasons conclusive. How can he say that, according to arguments he finds persuasive, economic damage may be recovered in tort, and yet deny that such a proposition can be true? How can he have reasons for his belief, and yet deny that anyone can have reasons for such a belief?

Suppose the philosopher says that though he has such beliefs he has these only because he has been trained in law and therefore joined an enterprise whose members have been seduced by their training into a myth. He denies that an independent observer, not himself a participant in the enterprise, would be able to decide that one participant's theories and judgments were superior to another's, at least in controversial cases. But what could he mean, here, by the idea of an independent observer? If he means someone who has had no legal training, then it is neither surprising nor relevant that such an observer would be incompetent to form opinions about what the participants do. If he means, on the other hand, someone who has had the requisite training, but has not been invited to sit as a judge, then it is wholly unclear why that lack of authority should affect that persons's capacity to form the judgments he would form if he had it.

So the philosopher's own capacities will embarrass him. He will have, moreover, a further, though related, problem. He wants to argue that neither of the parties in a hard case has a right to a decision in his favor. He will say, for example, that the plaintiff in *Spartan Steel*[1] does not have a right to recover for its economic damage, and also that the defendant does not have a right to be free from liability for that damage. He thinks that the proposition that a company in the position of the defendant is liable for economic damage is not true, though neither is the proposition that the defendant is not liable. Neither proposition is false (because that would make the other true) but neither is true. That is, presumably, the consequence of the no right answer thesis for the truth values of propositions.

Now none of this will necessarily seem strange or outrageous to the judges of the enterprise. Each of these judgments about the truth value of propositions of law is one that a judge might sensibly make, under certain conditions, *within the ground rules of the enterprise.* Suppose a judge thinks that the case for a theory of the relevant law that makes the defendant liable for economic damage is exactly as strong as the case for a theory that frees him from that liability. The rules of the enterprise, as so far described, acknowledge that situation as a theoretical possibility; and if that possibility is realized, then judges cannot, under these rules, assert either proposition as true or deny it as false. In any particular hard case, therefore, a judge may sensibly make, for that case, the same judgment as the philosopher seems to make for all hard cases.

[1] See Chapter 7.

The judgment that neither of these contrary propositions is true we may call the 'tie' judgment. We may now notice the following features of tie judgments, as judgments within the judge's enterprise. (a) The tie judgment is a judgment of the same character as the judgment that one or the other of these contrary propositions is true and the other false. We may conceive of a hard case as presenting, for each judge, a scale of confidence running from a left-hand point at which the judge is confident that the proposition favoring the plaintiff is true, through points at which he believes that proposition is true, but with progressively less confidence, to a right-hand side with points representing progressively more confidence that the proposition favouring the defendant is true. Then the tie point is the single point at the center of this scale. In a hard case judges may hold one of three views. Some may think that the case should be located at some point to the left of the center, others may think it should be located at some point to the right of center, and some may think that it should be located at the very center itself. But the tie judgment is a positive judgment of the same character as the other two. It is competitive with these, and makes exactly the same epistemological or ontological presuppositions (whatever these might be). We may say that the third judgment is a 'no right answer' judgment if we take that to mean simply that neither of the other two available answers is right; but the third judgment is a judgment that itself claims to be *the* right answer.

(b) Suppose a judge in the enterprise says (I) 'Neither the proposition that the defendant is liable (p) nor the proposition that he is not liable (- p) is true.' That does not mean the same thing as (II) 'I cannot see any difference in the case for (p) or (- p).' A judge who is in the position described by (II) can do no better, if he must decide while in that position, than to assert (I). It may even be that, for him, (II) counts as evidence of (I). But that is not the same thing as saying that (I) and (II) are identical. 'It seems to me that the case for the plaintiff is the stronger' is not the same as 'The case for the plaintiff is the stronger', even in the mouth of the same judge; so, and in the same way, is (II) different from (I). Suppose a judge says both (I) and (II) but later is persuaded, by a fellow judge, that in fact the case for the plaintiff is stronger than the case for the defendant. He will then say that, at the time of his earlier statements, (I) was false, but not, of course, (II).

I stress the difference between (I) and (II) to reinforce the point just made, that the so-called 'no right answer' answer, as a judgment within the enterprise, is a judgment of the same character, and is equally fallible, as either of the other available answers. It is not a residuary answer, or an answer in default, that is automatically true whenever no persuasive argument is available for any other answer, or whenever good arguments are available for both other answers. The judge who asserts (I) is making a leap from his own analysis to a conclusion that reports more than the fact of that analysis, just as a judge who finds for the plaintiff is making a leap from the fact of his own arguments to the conclusion that they are right.

We can imagine an enterprise in which the difference between (I) and (II) is less clear-cut. Suppose the management of a horse racing track purchases less than the most precise equipment for photo finishes. It might lay down a track rule that if a photograph taken by this equipment is so indistinct that it cannot be clearly established which horse won, then they shall be deemed to have tied, in spite of the fact that superior equipment might well have shown a winner. In that case, the proposition that the machine cannot distinguish a winner and the proposition that there is no winner come to the same thing. But that is not the enterprise the judges have established. Nothing in the rules of the enterprise provides that what strikes a particular judge or a particular group of judges as a tie is therefore a tie.

(c) The judgment, by a particular judge, that a case is a tie, and therefore offers 'no right answer' within the enterprise, is very likely to be controversial. We can speak, nevertheless, about the antecedent probability that the enterprise will produce many or few cases that are in fact ties. Suppose the legal system in which the judges operate is a primitive legal system : there are very few judicial precedents or statutes, and a very rudimentary constitution. It is probable, in advance of any particular judicial term, both that the judges will judge that several cases in that term are ties, and that in fact several cases will be ties. Since there is very little settled law, more than one theory of law, critically different for the result in a hard case, will often offer equally good justifications for the settled law, and will seem to offer equally good justifications to many judges.

But suppose, on the other hand, that the legal system these judges administer is very advanced, and is thick with constitutional rules and practices, and dense with precedents and statutes. The antecedent probability of a tie is very much lower; indeed it might well be so low as to justify a further ground rule of the enterprise which instructs judges to eliminate ties from the range of answers they might give. That instruction does not deny the theoretical possibility of a tie, but it does suppose that, given the complexity of the legal materials at hand, judges will, if they think long and hard enough, come to think that one side or the other has, all things considered and marginally, the better of the case. This further instruction will be rational if the antecedent probability of error in a judicial decision seems to be greater than the antecedent probability that some case will indeed be, in fact, a tie, and if there are advantages of finality or other political advantages to be gained by denying the possibility of tie cases at law. Of course, the instruction will be not rational but silly if the legal system is not sufficiently complex to justify that calculation of antecedent probabilities.

We may now return to the philosopher's claim that the judges are making a profound mistake by assuming that there can be a right answer in a hard case. If we take his claim to be a claim within the enterprise, such as a judge himself might make, then the claim is almost certainly false. It comes to this: the tie judgment is necessarily the right judgment in every single controversial case, that is, in every case in which one answer cannot be proved in a way that can only be challenged by the irrational. Now (unless the special instruction to ignore ties is part of the enterprise) every judge will concede that some hard cases may in fact be ties, but no judge will suppose that they all are ties. The philosopher, to support his claim against their opinion, would have to produce arguments affirmatively establishing that all hard cases will lie at the exact center of the scale we imagined, and that claim is so implausible that it can be set aside at once.

If the enterprise has adopted the special instruction just mentioned, then the philosopher's claim might be taken in a more modest way. He might oppose the rationality or reasonableness of that instruction, by arguing that the antecedent probability of a genuine tie is sufficiently great that it is silly to instruct judges to ignore that possibility. His claim then must be amended: he does not argue that there is no right answer in any hard case, but only that it is irrational to stipulate that there must be a right answer in every hard case. This more modest claim, which is a recommendation that the enterprise be amended so as to allow for ties, will deserve consideration, though the judges might do well to reject that recommendation if their system is sufficiently complex.

So if we take the philosopher's claim to be a claim made within the enterprise, in either of these two versions, then it is not a claim that need trouble the judges very long, for it is a claim that presupposes, rather than challenges, the fundamental soundness of their enterprise. The philosopher might object that his claim must not be construed as a claim within the enterprise; it must not be construed as a claim that the judges, faithful to the enterprise, may themselves make. It is rather a profound attack on the very rationality of the enterprise, and must be understood as such. But we must now face this crucial question. Is there any way to take the philosopher's claim *other than* as a claim within the judge's enterprise? How can we understand it as an external criticism of that entire enterprise?

There are two possibilities that seem open. We might take the philosopher's claim as a claim made from within a different judicial enterprise, which stipulates different truth conditions for propositions of law. Or we may take it as a claim external to all such enterprises, as a claim about facts of the real world which judges, whatever truth conditions they might choose for their propositions, must in the end respect. But neither of these two possibilities will serve the philosopher's purpose at all.

(1) We might easily imagine a legal enterprise in which the philosopher's judgment, that there is never a right answer in a hard case, is perfectly sound. Suppose a group of judges decided to observe the following rules. A proposition of law may be asserted as true if that proposition may be derived from settled law, on facts agreed or stipulated, simply by deduction. A proposition of law may be denied as false if its contrary may be derived from settled law, on facts agreed or stipulated, simply by deduction. Under these rules, in any hard case, neither the proposition of law favoring the plaintiff nor the proposition favoring the defendant may be asserted as true, and neither may be denied as false. There will be, in any hard case, no right answer in that sense.

But the enterprise conducted by the judges we imagine is plainly not that enterprise. So the philosopher's claim, however sound in some other enterprise, is irrelevant to this one. The philosopher may now say that *his* enterprise, just described, is the legal enterprise actually in force in, for example, Britain and the United States, and that the judges' enterprise I described is simply imaginary. In Chapter 4 I argued that the legal systems in force in those countries (and no doubt elsewhere) are actually very like the enterprise I have imagined here. If so, then the philosopher can hardly claim that his enterprise is more faithful to reality. But suppose I was wrong, and that his enterprise is more like those actually in play. The theoretical argument for the no right answer thesis was supposed to show that, in principle, there could be no single right answer to a hard case. But it now argues only that, as a matter of fact, familiar legal systems recognize truth conditions for propositions of law that do not permit a right answer in a hard case. That would be a much more modest claim, even if it were true, which it is not.

(2) Suppose the philosopher claims that he is speaking, not from within some alternate enterprise with different ground rules of assertion and denial, but about the real world. His argument is that there can be no right answer in fact to a hard case at law, so that if any legal enterprise adopts rules which presuppose that there can be, that enterprise is based on a myth. He reports, not a different enterprise, but objective facts that any enterprise must face if it is to be realistic.

But what is this objective reality? It must contain rights and duties, including legal rights and duties, as objective facts, independent of the structure or content of conventional systems. That idea is familiar in the theories of natural lawyers, but it is a surprising toy to find in the hands of the philosopher who argues, in the name of common sense, that there can be no right answer in a hard case. After all, if rights and duties are part of some objective and independent world, then why should we not suppose that someone can have a right even when no one else thinks he does, or when no one can prove he does?

So it is dangerous for our philosopher to claim that he speaks of objective legal reality whose truth conditions are independent of human convention. It is also dangerous in a different way. It threatens to make his most basic claim incomprehensible. He argues that (p) (The defendant is liable for economic damage) and (– p) (The defendant is not liable for economic damage) may neither be true though neither is false. How can we make sense of this? If liability is a matter of objective fact, independent of enterprises like those we have been describing, and if a proposition asserting a right of recovery (like (p)) is not true, it must be false.

We can *only* make sense of the philosopher's claim if we take it to report the special truth conditions of an enterprise. His claim would be sound, as I just conceded, in an enterprise having truth conditions which permitted an assertion or denial of a proposition only in an easy case. Then, in a hard case, a proposition of law could neither be asserted as true nor denied as false. Its falsity would not follow from the failure of its truth. In the enterprise our judges established (but without the special instruction forbidding ties) that condition remains a theoretical possibility, though the probability that it will actually occur, in a very developed legal system, is small. If the special instruction is added, then the rules forbid by fiat the combination of a failure to assert and a failure to deny, relying on a prediction that the failure to allow that combination will not, for the reasons I described, inhibit the operation of the enterprise. But without *some* special truth conditions, which enable us to resist the inference that if a proposition is not true then it is false, the no right answer thesis cannot be maintained at all.

I have made this same argument, but at much greater length, elsewhere, and those interested in the general question of whether there is aways a right answer to a question of law should pursue that longer argument.[1] I should mention, however, one possible objection to this portion of my argument not foreseen in that discussion. This appeals, in a general way, to an argument which is familiar among philosophers of language, namely that propositions about non-existent entities are neither

---

[1] 'No Right Answer', in *Law, Morality and Society: Essays in Honour of H. L. A. Hart*, London 1977.

true nor false. There is a tradition which argues that the proposition that the present King of France is bald is neither true nor false (though there is also a tradition which argues that this proposition, properly understood, is simply false). The proposition about the King of France does not seem to be a proposition which can only be understood within some special enterprise like those we have considered and yet (according to one view) it is neither true nor false. So (I have heard it argued) propositions of law, not meant as propositions within special enterprises, may also be neither true nor false.

But the comparison between propositions of law in hard cases and propositions about non-existent entities is plainly worthless. The latter pose problems only because it is understood that the subject of the proposition does not exist, and the proposition assumes rather than asserts its existence. Controversial propositions of law either assert or deny the existence of a legal right or some other legal relation. The controversy is precisely over whether that assertion or denial is correct. If we once assume that a right to recover for economic damage does not exist, then the proposition that the plaintiff in such a case has a right to recover is not problematical. It is simply false. The comparable proposition is the proposition that there is now a King of France. No one supposes that that proposition is neither true nor false. It is either (as most of us think) false, or (as some extreme supporters of the Comte de Paris believe) true.

3.

What shall we then say, finally, about the general objection which has been the subject of this chapter? It is no longer so clear that either common sense or realism supports the objection that there can be no right answer, but only a range of acceptable answers, in a hard case. The practical argument for that claim is misconceived. The theoretical argument is contradicted by the capacities of those who make the argument, and it cannot even be stated, or so it seems, in a way that does not dissolve its claims into the very background it seeks to challenge. Surely it *cannot* be that in a genuinely hard case one side is simply right and the other simply wrong. But why not? It may be that the supposition that one side may be right and the other wrong is cemented into our habits of thought at a level so deep that we cannot coherently deny that supposition, no matter how skeptical or hard-headed we wish to be in such matters. That would explain our difficulty in stating the theoretical argument in a coherent way. The 'myth' that there is one right answer in a hard case is both recalcitrant and successful. Its recalcitrance and success count as arguments that it is no myth.

Index